HANDBOOK
ON THE
PENTATEUCH

HANDBOOK ON THE PENTATEUCH

Genesis

Exodus

Leviticus

Numbers

Deuteronomy

SECOND EDITION

Victor P. Hamilton

Baker Academic

a division of Baker Publishing Group
Grand Rapids, Michigan

© 1982, 2005 by Victor P. Hamilton

Published by Baker Academic
a division of Baker Publishing Group
P.O. Box 6287, Grand Rapids, MI 49516-6287
www.bakeracademic.com

Paperback edition published 2015
ISBN 978-0-8010-9773-7

Printed in the United States of America

The Library of Congress has cataloged the hardcover edition as follows:
Hamilton, Victor P.
    Handbook on the Pentateuch : Genesis, Exodus, Leviticus, Numbers, Deuter-
onomy / Victor P. Hamilton.—2nd ed.
      p.   cm.
    Includes bibliographical references and indexes.
    ISBN 10: 0-8010-2716-0 (hardcover)
    ISBN 978-0-8010-2716-1 (hardcover)
    1. Bible. O.T. Pentateuch—Criticism, interpretation, etc. I. Title.
BS1225.52.H36 2005
222′.107—dc22
                                                           2005009478

In keeping with biblical principles of creation stewardship, Baker Publishing Group advocates the responsible use of our natural resources. As a member of the Green Press Initiative, our company uses recycled paper when possible. The text paper of this book is composed in part of post-consumer waste.

19   20   21   7   6   5   4

To my wife, Shirley

Contents

Part 4 Numbers

Part 5 Deuteronomy

Abbreviations

AB	Anchor Bible
ABR	*Australian Biblical Review*
ACCS	Ancient Christian Commentary on Scripture
AnBib	Analecta biblica
AOAT	Alter Orient und Altes Testament
AOTC	Abingdon Old Testament Commentaries
ASTI	*Annual of the Swedish Theological Institute*
AThR	*Anglican Theological Review*
AUSS	*Andrews University Seminary Studies*
BA	*Biblical Archaeologist*
BAR	*Biblical Archaeology Review*
BASOR	*Bulletin of the American Schools of Oriental Research*
BBR	*Bulletin for Biblical Research*
BETL	Bibliotheca ephemeridum theologicarum louvaniensium
Bib	*Biblica*
BibInt	*Biblical Interpretation*
BIS	Biblical Interpretation Series
BJRL	*Bulletin of the John Rylands University Library*
BJS	Brown Judaic Studies
BN	*Biblische Notizen*
BRes	*Biblical Research*
BRev	*Biblical Review*
BSac	*Bibliotheca sacra*
BT	*The Bible Translator*
BTB	*Biblical Theology Bulletin*
BZ	*Biblische Zeitschrift*

BZAW	Beihefte zur Zeitschrift für die alttestamentliche Wissenschaft
CBC	Cambridge Bible Commentary
CBQ	*Catholic Biblical Quarterly*
CT	*Christianity Today*
CTJ	*Calvin Theological Journal*
CurBS	Currents in Research: Biblical Studies
EncJud	*Encyclopaedia Judaica*
ERT	*Evangelical Review of Theology*
ETL	*Ephemerides theologicae lovanienses*
EvQ	*The Evangelical Quarterly*
ExpT	*Expository Times*
FOTL	Forms of Old Testament Literature
HBT	*Horizons in Biblical Theology*
HS	*Hebrew Studies*
HSM	Harvard Semitic Monographs
HTR	*Harvard Theological Review*
HUCA	*Hebrew Union College Annual*
IDB	*Interpreter's Dictionary of the Bible Supplement.* Edited by G. A. Buttrick. 4 vols. Nashville, 1962
IDBSup	*Interpreter's Dictionary of the Bible: Supplementary Volume.* Edited by K. Crim. Nashville, 1976
IEJ	*Israel Exploration Journal*
ILR	*Israel Law Review*
Int	*Interpretation*
IRT	Issues in Religion and Theology
ITC	International Theological Commentary
ITQ	*Irish Theological Quarterly*
JAAR	*Journal of the American Academy of Religion*
JANES	*Journal of the Ancient Near Eastern Society*
JAOS	*Journal of the American Oriental Society*
JB	Jerusalem Bible
JBL	*Journal of Biblical Literature*
JBQ	*Jewish Bible Quarterly*
JES	*Journal of Ecumenical Studies*
JETS	*Journal of the Evangelical Theological Society*
JJS	*Journal of Jewish Studies*
JNES	*Journal of Near Eastern Studies*
JNSL	*Journal of Northwest Semitic Languages*
JQR	*Jewish Quarterly Review*
JSOT	*Journal for the Study of the Old Testament*
JSOTSup	Journal for the Study of the Old Testament: Supplement Series
JTS	*Journal of Theological Studies*
KJV	King James Version

LTQ	*Lexington Theological Quarterly*
MSU	Mitteilungen des Septuaginta-Unternehmens
NAC	New American Commentary
NASB	New American Standard Bible
NCBC	New Century Bible Commentary
NEB	New English Bible
NIBCOT	New International Biblical Commentary on the Old Testament
NICOT	New International Commentary on the Old Testament
NIV	New International Version
NJPS	New Jewish Publication Society translation
NKJV	New King James Version
NRSV	New Revised Standard Version
NTS	*New Testament Studies*
OBT	Overtures to Biblical Theology
OTG	Old Testament Guides
OTL	Old Testament Library
OTS	Old Testament Studies
OtSt	*Oudtestamentische Studiën*
PEQ	*Palestine Exploration Quarterly*
PTMS	Pittsburgh Theological Monograph Series
RB	*Revue Biblique*
RelSRev	*Religious Studies Review*
RestQ	*Restoration Quarterly*
RevExp	*Review and Expositor*
RSV	Revised Standard Version
SAC	Studies in Antiquity and Christianity
SBLDS	Society of Biblical Literature Dissertation Series
SBLSP	*Society of Biblical Literature Seminar Papers*
SBLSymS	Society of Biblical Literature Symposium Series
SBT	Studies in Biblical Theology
SBTS	Sources for Biblical and Theological Study
SemeiaSt	Semeia Studies
SJCA	Studies in Judaism and Christianity in Antiquity
SJLA	Studies in Judaism in Late Antiquity
SJT	*Scottish Journal of Theology*
SR	*Studies in Religion*
ST	*Studia Theologica*
TBT	*The Bible Today*
TDOT	*Theological Dictionary of the Old Testament*. Edited by G. J. Botterweck and H. Ringgren. Translated by J. T. Willis, G. W. Bromiley, and D. E. Green. 8 vols. Grand Rapids, 1974–
ThTo	*Theology Today*
TOTC	Tyndale Old Testament Commentaries

TynB	*Tyndale Bulletin*
UF	*Ugarit-Forschungen*
USQR	*Union Seminary Quarterly Review*
VT	*Vetus Testamentum*
VTSup	Supplements to Vetus Testamentum
WBC	Word Biblical Commentary
WBComp	Westminster Bible Companion
WTJ	*Westminster Theological Journal*
ZAW	*Zeitschrift für die alttestamentliche Wissenschaft*
ZPEB	*Zondervan Pictorial Encyclopedia of the Bible.* Edited by M. C. Tenney. 5 vols. Grand Rapids, 1975

Preface to the Second Edition

In 1982 Baker Book House kindly published the first edition of my *Handbook on the Pentateuch*. Since then the book has been used as a text in Pentateuch classes both at the undergraduate and graduate levels and in educational institutions throughout North America and around the world. It has been translated into Russian and is being translated into Korean. Although the book has gone through some twenty printings and its wide use and usefulness are not waning, Baker and I both agreed that it was time to produce a new edition.

I have, as is standard with new editions, updated the bibliographies. More importantly, however, I have rewritten many sections, substantially adding to or revising what I wrote back in the early 1980s. What the reader will encounter is my own developed and developing thoughts on passages within the Pentateuch, informed and enriched greatly by interaction with scholarly colleagues in the Old Testament part of the biblical academy.

I express my appreciation to Brian Bolger and his colleagues at Baker Academic for their immense help in seeing this second edition through to publication.

Also, I thank Leigh C. Andersen of the Society of Biblical Literature for permission to reproduce the chart of Bernhard Anderson that appears on p. 72. Similarly, I thank Father Peter Brook, SJ, of the Biblical Institute Press, for permission to reprint a chart by Anson Rainey that first appeared in *Biblica*. In this second edition it appears on pp. 356–57.

Once again my wife, Shirley, has taken on an invaluable role. In addition to her assistance in helping to produce the new edition, she constantly helped me with her encouragement, wisdom, and insight.

Finally, all praise goes to our Lord for the privilege of studying and teaching his word in the classroom and in the church. May the thoughts of my mind and the words of my pen be acceptable in the sight of the One who is my Rock and my Redeemer.

Preface to the First Edition

Few sections of the Old Testament have been treated as thoroughly by scholars as has the Pentateuch. A glance at any bibliographical reference volume covering biblical research will reveal immediately the vast amount of material produced in any given year on this portion of Scripture. Perhaps it is more accurate to say that Genesis and Exodus have been studied most copiously, with studies in Deuteronomy running a close second. Articles, monographs, and commentaries on Leviticus and Numbers, by contrast, lag far behind in terms of volume.

In spite of all this research there have been few studies of recent vintage that have tried to put all of the Pentateuch into a one-volume commentary. That is my purpose in the pages that follow. More specifically, I have tried to produce a book that may function as a text in English Bible classes at both the undergraduate and seminary levels.

At no point are my explorations of the biblical text exhaustive. To assist the student who desires to go beyond the reflections in this book, I have placed a bibliography at the end of each chapter. Two guidelines have controlled my selections. First, the entries in these bibliographies are limited mostly to studies that have appeared in the last ten years. Most of them will document more than adequately all previous research in that particular area. Second, I have limited my choices almost exclusively to studies that have appeared in English. The academic journals on the Continent and the European presses are constantly producing much that is valuable in biblical research, but few undergraduate students will be able to pursue and read technical articles in French, German, Italian, Spanish, and Swedish.

Readers will note immediately that I have omitted areas of possible analysis in which they might have great interest. For example, I have not addressed the question of creation versus evolution in my discussion of the opening chapters of Genesis. This exercise I prefer to leave to the scientist rather than to the biblical scholar.

I have not discussed some areas of historical import, such as the historicity of the patriarchs or the date of the exodus. It appears to me that the ground has been well covered here by both the critics and the traditionalists. For that same reason I have not devoted one major section of my manuscript to the question of the "origins" of the Pentateuch. Instead I have limited myself to a study, here and there, of some passages in the Pentateuch that are often cited as parade examples of multiple sources within the books of Moses.

As I wrote this book, I had in mind the student not only as a scholar of God's Word, but also as a proclaimer of God's Word. Therefore I have attempted to write something that is as usable in the pastor's study as it is in the classroom, something that is as devotional as it is scholarly.

I am indebted to a host of biblical scholars from whose wells I have drawn much. Especially I would like to express my appreciation to Professors Brevard Childs and Jacob Milgrom, whose studies in Exodus, and Leviticus and Numbers, respectively, have made a profound impact on my comprehension of the biblical text. Dr. Dennis Kinlaw, formerly my mentor in Old Testament studies at Asbury Theological Seminary, and Dr. Robert Traina, Professor of English Bible at Asbury Theological Seminary, have made decisive contributions to my thought in historical and inductive Bible study.

I would like to express my appreciation to Professor John Hayes, editor of the *Journal of Biblical Literature,* and Professor Bernhard Anderson for their permission to reproduce a chart by Dr. Anderson from *JBL* 97 (1978): 38 that appears in ch. 2. I am indebted also to Father Albert Vanhoye, SJ, editor of *Biblica,* for his permission to reproduce portions of a chart by Dr. Anson Rainey from *Bib* 51 (1970): 492–93 that appear in ch. 18.

It is a pleasure for me to thank the Committee on Faculty Research and Development of Asbury College for a work leave and a financial grant, both of which contributed greatly to the implementation of this study.

Finally, I wish to acknowledge the indispensable role that my wife, Shirley, has assumed for the last several years, for really we have worked together. In addition to providing constant encouragement and stimulation, she has typed the entire manuscript and has offered many invaluable suggestions.

PART ONE

Genesis

1

Creation and the Fall

GENESIS 1–3

There are numerous ways in which the first book of the Bible may be outlined. Perhaps the simplest is:

I. Primeval history (chs. 1–11)
   A. The creation (chs. 1–2)
   B. The fall (chs. 3–11)
      1. The cause (ch. 3)
      2. The effects (chs. 4–11)
II. Patriarchal history (chs. 12–50)
   A. Abraham (chs. 12–25)
   B. Jacob (chs. 26–36)
   C. Joseph (chs. 37–50)

This outline accurately reflects the content of Genesis but fails to suggest any relationship between the parts or any progression in emphases. It is preferable to allow Genesis to outline itself and follow the units suggested by the text. These units are readily discernible.

I. The story of creation (1:1–2:3)
II. The generations of the heavens and the earth (2:4–4:26)

III. The generations of Adam (5:1–6:8)
IV. The generations of Noah (6:9–9:29)
V. The generations of the sons of Noah (10:1–11:9)
VI. The generations of Shem (11:10–26)
VII. The generations of Terah (11:27–25:11)
VIII. The generations of Ishmael (25:12–18)
IX. The generations of Isaac (25:19–35:29)
X. The generations of Esau (36:1–37:1)
XI. The generations of Jacob (37:2–50:26)

Thus Genesis is composed of an introductory section, followed by ten more sections, each introduced with the phrase "these are the generations of" (*tôlĕdôt*). Structurally, then, Genesis divides itself not into two sections (one on primeval history, constituting about a fourth of the book; one on patriarchal history, constituting about three-fourths of the book), but rather into two quite unequal sections: 1:1–2:3 (an introduction) and 2:4–50:26 (composed of ten subsections). And yet the primeval/patriarchal divisions cannot be totally laid aside, for one observes that the first five uses of the *tôlĕdôt* formula appear throughout 2–11, and the remaining five appear throughout 12–50 (or to be more exact, in the outline above, II–VI = 2:4–11:26; VII–XI = 11:27–50:26). Although there is no "these are the generations of Abraham," his appearance at the end of VI (see 11:26) and his dominant role in VII make him a bridge figure between primeval and patriarchal history, between the origins of the nations of the earth and the origins of the chosen nation.

The movement in each of the last ten sections is from source to stream, from cause to result, from progenitor to progeny. That movement is described either through subsequent narrative after the superscription (II, IV, VII, IX, XI) or a genealogy that follows the superscription (III, V, VI, VIII, X).

The result created by this introduction-superscription-sequel pattern in Genesis is that of a unified composition, neatly arranged by the author (or the narrator or editor). Furthermore, the testimony of the text is to emphasize movement, a plan, something in progress and motion. What is in motion is nothing less than the initial stages of a divine plan, a plan that has its roots in creation. From the earth, Adam will come forward. From Adam, Abraham and his progeny will emerge. Eventually, out of Abraham, Jesus Christ will emerge. In the words of VanGemeren (1988: 70), "The *toledot* formula provides a redemptive-historical way of looking at the past as a series of interrelated events."

Creation (1–2)

The first thing that strikes the reader of the Bible is the brevity (just two chapters) with which the story of the creation of the world and humankind is told. The arithmetic of Genesis is surprising. Only two chapters are devoted to the subject of creation, and one to the entrance of sin into the human race. By contrast, thirteen chapters are given to Abraham, ten to Jacob, and twelve to Joseph (who was neither a patriarch nor the son through whom the covenantal promises were perpetuated). We face, then, the phenomenon of twelve chapters for Joseph, and two for the theme of creation. Can one person be, as it were, six times more important than the world?

Nevertheless, our understanding of the Bible surely would be impoverished—rather, jeopardized—without these first two chapters. What are they about? A skeletal outline of the contents of 1:1–2:3 is helpful, as shown in figure 1.

Figure 1

Day	Day
1 light	**4** luminaries (sun, moon, stars)
2 heavens	**5** fish, birds
3 earth, edible vegetation	**6** land animals, man
Day 7 the Sabbath	

It is obvious that the first six days fall into two groups of three. Each day in the second column is an extension of its counterpart in the first column. The days in the first column are about the creation (or preparation) of environment or habitat. The days in the second column are about the creation of those phenomena that inhabit that environment. Thus, on day one, God created light in general or light-bearers; on day four, specific kinds of light appear. On day two, God made the firmament separating waters above from waters below; on day five, God made creatures of sky and water. On day three, God first created the earth and then vegetation; on day six, God first made the creatures of land and then humankind. The climax to creation is the seventh day, the day of rest for God. The preceding days he called good. This one alone he "sanctified" (the only occurrence in Genesis of the important Hebrew root q-d-š, apart from the reference to Tamar, Judah's daughter-in-law, as a "shrine prostitute" [38:21, 22 NIV]).

In addition to this horizontal literary arrangement, one can observe a fundamental literary pattern throughout all of Genesis 1. Using the language of Claus Westermann (1974: 7), we note this pattern:

1. announcement: "and God said"
2. command: "let there be/let it be gathered/let it bring forth"
3. report: "and it was so"
4. evaluation: "and God saw that it was good"
5. temporal framework: "and there was evening and there was morning"

An alternative pattern is:

1. introduction: "and God said"
2. creative word: "let there be"
3. fulfillment of the word: "and there was/and it was so"
4. description of the act in question: "and God separated/and God made/and God set/so God created"
5. name-giving or blessing: "and he called/blessed"
6. divine commendation: "and it was good"
7. concluding formula: "there was evening and morning"

The Relationship of 1:1–2:3 (or 4a) to 2:4 (or 4b)–25

Genesis 2:4–25 often has been described as a second creation story, although less so among biblical scholars today. Furthermore, it is suggested that not only is this a second story about creation, but also it comes from a different source than that of Gen. 1:1–2:3. Scholars who embrace the documentary hypothesis believe that the first creation story is the work of an anonymous Priestly editor or editors (P) around the time of the Babylonian exile (sixth century) or immediately thereafter. These scholars believe that the second creation story comes from a much earlier writer, usually designated as the Yahwist (J), an anonymous writer or writers from Jerusalem in the time of David and Solomon (the tenth century). Often, therefore, a scholar who subscribes to this hypothesis deals with the texts in their perceived chronological order of production, discussing 2:4–25 before 1:1–2:3.

There are several reasons for making this distinction. First, there is the different and, at points, contradictory account of the sequence of the orders of creation: the first sequence is vegetation, birds and fish, animals, man and woman; the second sequence is man, vegetation, animals, woman. Second, in the first sequence the exclusive name for the deity is "God" (*Elohim*), but in the second sequence it is "Lord God" (*Yahweh Elohim*). Third, in the first sequence God creates primarily by speaking: "and God said, 'Let there be,' and it was"—that is, creation by fiat. In the second sequence the emphasis is on God as potter or artisan: "the Lord God formed man of dust" (2:7 RSV); "out of the ground the Lord God formed every beast of the field" (2:19 KJV); "and the rib . . . he made into a woman" (2:22 RSV). Fourth, in the first sequence the emphasis is on cosmogony: whence this world? In the second sequence the emphasis is on anthropology: whence humankind? Fifth, some interpreters draw a distinction between the poetic features of 1:1–2:3, with its use of stanzas and repetitions, and the narrative prose presentation of creation in 2:4–25.

Thus, the contention is that Genesis presents two originally independent creation stories, about five hundred years apart in origin. This phenomenon of "doublets" we will encounter again in the discussion of the flood story, where the unanimous opinion of literary and source critics is that originally there were two independent accounts of the deluge, again J and P, but with one distinct difference: the redactor (or redactors) of these opening chapters *juxtaposed* the two creation stories but *spliced* the two flood stories. As far as I know, attempts to provide a reason for this redactive distinction have not proved satisfactory.

In regard to the creation narrative, is it necessary to posit two mutually exclusive, antithetical accounts? Could 2:4–25 be a continuation of rather than a break in the creation story, "a close-up after the panorama of Genesis 1" (Ryken 1974: 37), or even simply an extended commentary on the sixth day of creation? The order of events in ch. 1 is chronological; the order of events in ch. 2 is logical and topical, from humankind to its environment. It is unnecessary to posit conflicting accounts about when God created human creatures of both sexes (in 1:1–2:3, at the same time; in 2:4–25, first the male and then later the female). As Barr (1998b) has argued, it is quite possible that in Gen. 1:26 God says, "Let us make a man in our image," and that is followed by "male and [subsequently] female he made them" in 1:27. This seems to be the reading that Paul follows in 1 Cor. 11:7 when he distinguishes between man being the image and glory of God and woman being the glory of man: "A man ought not to cover his head, since he is the image and glory of God; but the woman is the glory of man" (NIV). Most of the information in 2:4–25 is an amplification of 1:26–29. Chapter 1 is concerned with the world, while ch. 2 is concerned with a garden; one is cosmic, the other localized. God's relationship to the world is in his capacity as *Elohim,* while his relationship to a couple in a garden is in his capacity as *Yahweh Elohim;* the first suggests his majesty and transcendence, the second his intimacy and involvement with his creation. Exactly why we must not posit a unity in Genesis 1–2 escapes me.

Theological Themes in Genesis 1–2

What the Themes Teach about God

The most obvious observation is the emphasis in these two chapters on the truth of God's oneness. Instead of encountering a host of deities, the reader meets the one God. Unlike pagan gods, God has no spouse or consort. What is the significance of this? Can this be the Bible's way of saying that God's self-fulfillment requires nothing and no one outside of himself? Indeed, all the resources for self-fulfillment are within him. Everything else in the created order is, on its own, unfulfilled and must look elsewhere for fulfillment. It is God's oneness that alone makes sense of words such as "*uni*verse" or "*uni*versality."

A second truth affirmed by these chapters is that there is a line of distinction between God as creator and humankind as creature that is never effaced. Tracing Mesopotamian chronologies back to their furthest point, as is done in, for example, the Sumerian King List (a document produced by Sumerian scribes shortly after 2000 B.C. that lists the names of rulers from the advent of kingship onward), one discovers that the remote ancestors are divine beings. The distinction between divine and human has been erased. Genesis 1–2 traces the human race back as far as possible and still finds Adam/man. Then comes the gulf. Through Hosea the Lord says succinctly, "I am God, and not man" (Hos. 11:9 NIV), and it is said in a context of hope not haughtiness. If Israel's salvation is in humankind, there is despair. If salvation is in God, there is hope.

A third truth is that God is plural in his nature. Genesis 1:26 says, "Let *us* make man in *our* image, after *our* likeness" (RSV). From an exegetical viewpoint, it cannot be said that this refers to the Trinity. At least six interpretations have been placed on the words "let us" here. One of these is the mythological interpretation. One god, perhaps the chief god, speaks to the other deities and informs them of his intentions or solicits their advice and help in some project, in this case, the creation of humankind as a whole. The contention is that the writer of Genesis 1 failed to expurgate completely the mythological motifs that he was borrowing. Another interpretation is that God is speaking to the creation, the earth. Earth then becomes a partner with God in the creation of humankind and a constituent part of humankind's composite nature, balancing the divine inbreathing. A third possibility is that God is speaking to the angels, the heavenly court, and thus human beings bear certain resemblances to both God and the angels. This view implies that in the creation of humankind God had assistance from his angels. The fourth interpretation is that this is a plural of majesty—that is, God speaks of himself and with himself in the plural (cf. Gen. 11:7, "Come, let *us* go down" [NIV]; Isa. 6:8, "Whom shall I send, and who will go for *us?"* [NIV]). The very name of God in ch. 1, *Elohim*, is plural, the suffix *-im* indicating masculine plural nouns. A fifth possibility is that the expression can be described as a plural of self-deliberation, as in the English usage, for example, "Let's see, what should I do?" Where we clearly have this, however, the language tends to be first-person singular rather than first-person plural (e.g., "Shall I hide from Abraham what I am about to do?" [Gen. 18:17 NIV]). Sixth, and most plausible to me, is the explanation that sees in the "us" a plural of fullness or plurality within the Godhead. Perhaps God is addressing his Spirit (already mentioned in 1:2). That God is triune is a fact that awaits the preachment of the New Testament revelation.

A fourth truth is that God is moral and holy. To Adam, God said both "you may eat" and "you may not eat." One of the books most frequently referred to in this area is *The Idea of the Holy,* by the German Protestant theologian and historian of religion Rudolph Otto. Otto's book was first published in 1917 and translated into English in 1923. The essential theme of the book is an emphasis on the "holy" as the distinguishing feature of religious experience. To use Otto's phrase, the "holy" is *mysterium tremendum et fascinosum*—that is, that which elicits in the worshiper both fear and fascination, "lashed with terror, leashed with longing," to use the phrase of the poet Francis Thompson.

Important for Otto is his contention that the moral and the ethical are not identical with the holy. What Otto does not address is the fact that God's holiness gives the basis to his moral demands. The purpose of the Decalogue is to show Israel how to live with a holy God. Even in paradise there is the institution of law.

A fifth truth emphasized in these two chapters is God's sovereignty and majesty. Effortlessly he speaks the created order into existence, shaping it as a potter produces a masterpiece from clay. At no point does God encounter antagonism or resistance in his work of creation.

Two illustrations will suffice. One is the way in which the emergence of the sun, moon, and stars is delineated. The order of narration in Genesis is interesting: sun, moon, stars. In the *Enuma Elish* (Creation Epic) the order is stars, sun, and moon. Here, the stars are not created, but are understood to be independent realities; there is a divine aura about them. Another point of interest about the sun and moon in the Genesis account, given the adulation of these luminaries in the ancient world, is that they are simply called "the greater light" and "the lesser light." Furthermore, the stars are treated with the matter-of-fact observation, almost an afterthought, "he made the stars too." A final point is that the function of the sun and moon is explicitly spelled out to emphasize their position as servants, given their orders and duty by God.

A second illustration of divine sovereignty is the lack of any reference to God's confrontation with celestial monsters or opponents, a theme that is prevalent in the *Enuma Elish*. The closest that Genesis 1 or 2 comes is the reference to the "sea monsters" (1:21). What is of interest is the use of the Hebrew word *bārā'*, occurring in 1:1, 21 and three times in 1:27 in connection with the creation of humans to describe their origin. God "created" them. Whenever this verb is used in the Old Testament, God is always the subject. And the verb is never followed by the accusative of material, unlike, for example, the verbs in "[he] formed man of dust" (2:7 RSV) and "the rib . . . he made into a woman" (2:22 NRSV). Although it probably goes too far to say that this use of *bārā'* explicitly teaches *creatio ex nihilo*, it does indeed lean in that direction. We should also note that Genesis 1 uses another verb for God's creating, the verb "make" (1:7, 16 [2x], 25, 26). The verb *'āśâ*, unlike *bārā'*, often has a human subject. There is something unique about God's creating (conveyed by *bārā'*), but there is also something similar between God's making and humans' making (conveyed by the verb *'āśâ*).

It has long been suggested that the reference in Gen. 1:2 to "the deep" (*tĕhôm*) is a veiled allusion to Tiamat of Babylonian fame. Even if that is the case, one would be hard pressed to see any obvious mythic allusions in the use of *tĕhôm* by the Genesis author. Absolutely no idea of the "deep" as the enemy of God emerges from the text. Rather, the "deep" is an inanimate part of the created order. In addition, very strong linguistic arguments militate against the equation of Tiamat and *tĕhôm*.

And yet there are references in Scripture to God doing battle with the monster. For example, Isa. 51:9 speaks of God cutting Rahab into pieces and piercing the dragon, and Ps. 74:13–14 says that God has broken the heads of the dragons in the waters and crushed the heads of Leviathan. Indeed, Isa. 27:1; 51:9; Ps. 74:13 use the same Hebrew word for "dragon" or "sea monster" as does Gen. 1:21. But the dragon of Isaiah and of the psalm is an adversary of God. The dragon of Gen. 1:21 is created by God and called "good."

What may be said about these references, outside of Genesis, to monstrous antagonists of God? First, the allusions to Leviathan, Rahab, and the dragons would have to have been intelligible to the hearers of these words in order for them to grasp the forcefulness of the speaker's point. After all, would the psalmist's "You crushed the heads of Leviathan" mean anything if the mythical Leviathan was unknown to the audience? We can surmise, therefore, that the people of God were familiar with the mythological literature of their neighbors.

Second, the language and motifs of mythology find their clearest expression not in the opening chapters of Genesis, where one might expect them, but rather in prophetic literature and the Psalter. More importantly, the context in which these "battles" take place is redemption, not creation. For example, cutting Rahab into pieces and piercing the dragon (Isa. 51:9) are parallel with God's parting of the Red Sea "for the redeemed to pass over" (Isa. 51:10). Similarly, crushing the heads of Leviathan and breaking the heads of the dragons (Ps. 74:13–14) appear in a psalm of lamentation in which the author prays for deliverance from his enemies; the deliverer is God, who is "working salvation in the midst of the earth" (Ps. 74:12 RSV).

The biblical writers deliberately use these mythical allusions not in the setting of creation, but in the context of redemption. There is no evil inherent in the world that God has made. Where is evil conquered? In creation? No! Rather, evil and chaos and disruption are conquered within time, in the redemption of God's people.

The climax of creation is the Sabbath (Gen. 2:1–3). This episode likewise may be seen as an extension of the implicit emphasis on divine sovereignty and majesty. God's rest on this day is not to renew his strength after combat with turbulent forces of evil. The day's purpose is to provide rest for God after a week's work of creation. Rest supersedes the act of creation. There is silence before creation, before God speaks. After creation there is silence again. This silence God has sanctified (Gen. 2:3).

What the Themes Teach about Humankind

The pattern of creation mostly by fiat in Genesis 1 is broken by the observation that God's act of creation of humankind is preceded by a collaborative statement and a statement of divine intention (1:26a).

Specifically, we are told that God created humans in his own "image" and "likeness." This is the only place in the Old Testament where these two nouns appear in connection with one another, and one immediately asks about their relationship. Are they interchangeable, an example of the pervasive penchant for listing synonyms in biblical Hebrew? Two observations may support this. In 1:26, referring to God's decision to create, both words are used. But in 1:27, which deals with the actual work of creation, only "image" is used. In 5:1, "he made him in the likeness of God" (NIV), the Hebrew word for "likeness" is translated in the Septuagint not by the usual *homoiōsis*, but by *eikōn*, normally the Greek equivalent for the Hebrew word for "image."

A second possibility is that the word "likeness" modifies the word "image." The function of "likeness" then would be to limit the meaning of "image." Such qualification, it is suggested, helps to avoid the implication that human beings are a precise copy of God. Some credence may be lent to this view by the fact that "likeness" appears in the Old Testament twenty-four times, and fourteen of these are in chs. 1 and 10 of Ezekiel. In these passages the prophet is careful never to say that he saw God or his entourage, but only the likeness of God.

A third suggestion is the reverse of the second one. Thus, "likeness" does not soften the concept about "image," but rather amplifies it. The human being is not simply an image of God, but a likeness-image. That is, more than simply representative, human beings are representational of the invisible God.

Whatever the best explanation may be on this technical matter, it is plain to see that humankind is set apart from the rest of creation and indeed is placed on a pedestal. Unlike the views of pagan accounts that we will examine, in Genesis humankind neither is created as an afterthought nor is consigned to drudge as a substitute for recalcitrant deities. Manual labor is a God-given privilege, not a sentence or a penalty.

Genesis 1 also affirms that humankind was created to "subdue" and "have dominion" over the earth and over living creatures of the sea, land, and air. Some scholars have suggested, in light of the wording of 1:26, that it is precisely humankind's domination of the world that constitutes the image of God (although the relation is more a consequence than a definition).

But what does it mean to subdue and have dominion over? The latter verb is used twenty-four times in the Old Testament, normally to denote human relationships: a master over a hired servant (Lev. 25:43); chief officers over laborers (1 Kings 5:16); a king over his subjects (Ps. 72:8); the rule of one nation over another (Lev. 26:17). Several of these passages (e.g., Lev. 25:43; Ezek. 34:4) suggest that dominion is to be exercised with care and responsibility. Nothing destructive or exploitative is permissible. Presumably the same nuance is present in Gen. 1:28. The same verb applied to humankind in 1:28 is applied to the sun and moon in 1:16—"to rule," respectively, the day and the night—and certainly no concept of indiscriminate or manipulative action is included there. It is not incidental that in Genesis 1 both humans and animals are vegetarians, each being given access to one element of vegetation (1:29–30).

It is remarkable that a large section of the creation story is given over to a separate and distinct account of the creation of woman. By implication Eve is referred to in the "them" and "female" of 1:26–29, with the specific mention found in 2:18–25. Such a separate narration of woman's creation is without parallel in ancient Near Eastern literature.

The long-overdue emphasis on women's rights has, in our time, stimulated many scholars to restudy the opening chapters of Genesis for essential clues on the identity of woman and for principles determining male-female relationships. Such a study reveals, as examples, the following. First, both man and woman are made in the image of God (if one reads the creation of the male and the female in 1:27 as synchronous rather than sequential). Sexual identification is irrelevant, certainly not a qualifying factor. Thus the command to rule and have dominion is directed to both male and female. Second, the origins of both man and woman are similar: both owe their existence to raw material—dirt and rib. Neither is actively involved in the creation of the other. Third, woman is described as a "helper fit" for Adam. What Eve is (2:19), the animals are not (2:20). Interestingly, the writer describes Eve with a word that preponderantly is applied to God elsewhere in the Old Testament. The "helper" par excellence is God. The helper who is invoked for assistance normally is stronger than the one who stands in need. Fourth, upon first seeing Eve, Adam says, "This at last is bone of my bones and flesh of my flesh" (v. 23a RSV). Similar words appear in Gen. 29:14; Judg. 9:2; 2 Sam. 5:1; 19:12–13, where a case could be made for the fact that the phrase "your bone and your flesh" is an affirmation not simply of kinship but of loyalty. Thus the phrase would be the equivalent of our modern commitment "in sickness and in health." That is, circumstances will not dictate or determine a relationship previously agreed to by both parties, and certainly adverse circumstances will not undermine it.

The follow-up to this also bears examination. A man is "to leave" his father and mother and "cleave" to his wife (2:24). The verb "to leave" may also be translated "forsake" with God as object (as in Jer. 1:16), meaning to terminate a loyalty. The second Hebrew verb, "to cleave," may also describe one's covenantal commitment to God (as in Deut. 10:20; 11:22). The marriage relationship is then an oath, a covenant, never an arbitrary relationship of convenience.

A fifth observation about male-female relationships is that quite clearly Genesis sets subordination of the woman to the man not in the context of creation, but in the context of the fall (see 3:16).

I have already suggested that according to Genesis 1 and 2 human beings are unique, set apart from everything else God created. They alone bear God's image, and they alone subdue. But the same passage of Scripture that underlines the uniqueness of humankind (Gen. 1:26–31) also modifies that uniqueness (Gen. 2:15–17). Human beings are not autonomous, but live under a divine law. There are boundaries, much as there are for the people Israel, whom God puts in their garden, Canaan. As long as one lives in ways that honor God, one remains in the garden/Canaan. But defiance of the boundaries set by God means expulsion from the garden/Canaan.

The man is placed in a garden, "put" there (Gen. 2:8) by God himself. The location of the garden is not easy to fix, but it is to be found "in the east" (Gen. 2:8), a Hebrew word that could also be translated "long ago." The presence of the Tigris and Euphrates (Gen. 2:14) suggests Mesopotamia. If that is the case, then the first sin (Genesis 3) and the last sin of primeval history (Genesis 11) both had their setting in Mesopotamia. Additionally, Eden, if placed outside the limits of Palestine, is a further illustration of the international and universal emphases within Genesis 1–2. Sailhamer (1995) is one of the few commentators on Genesis who does not place the garden of Eden in Mesopotamia, but rather equates the garden with the land that God later promised to Abraham and to his progeny.

In the garden the man has a dual responsibility: till the soil (Gen. 2:15) and abstain from eating of "the tree of the knowledge of good and evil" (Gen. 2:17 NIV). The penalty for transgressing these commands is death, which in this instance could mean mortality, but not necessarily so. If death equals mortality, then it explains why later in the narrative God prohibits further access by Adam and Eve to the tree of life (Gen. 3:22). But this interpretation can be challenged. A close reading of 3:22 suggests another possibility. In what is God's only unfinished sentence in the Bible (Humphreys 2001: 49), he says, "And now, lest he reach out his hand and take also from the tree of life and eat and live forever. . . ." God expels the man from the garden not because of what he has done, but because of what he might do if allowed to remain: eat from the tree of life and become immortal. This suggests that humankind was already mortal. Other understandings of "die" in "on the day you eat of it you shall die" must be proposed. I suggest that "die" means the loss of a relationship of intimacy with God, replaced by alienation from God. Something in the man and the woman dies that makes impossible the continuation of a vibrant walk with God.

No small amount of debate has centered on the meaning of "the knowledge of good and evil." What does this phrase imply? Can "evil" be inside the garden too? Does the "knowledge of good and evil" designate either omniscience or sexual awakening? Those are the two interpretations most commonly offered by scholars. But there are problems with both, especially the latter, in light of Gen. 3:22. Passages in which the phrase or a similar one occurs may or may not help us determine its meaning in Genesis 2–3. In Deut. 1:39 Moses refers to the second and younger generation of Israelites as "your children who do not yet know good from bad/evil" (NIV); that is, they cannot be responsible for their actions because they lack the moral judgment that one expects of those who have reached the point of accountability. In a similar fashion (i.e., speaking of a very young person) Isa. 7:15 speaks of the promised child who "will eat curds and honey by the time he knows enough to reject the wrong/the bad and choose the right/the good." In 2 Sam. 14:17 the wise woman praises David as one "like an angel of God in discerning good and evil" (NIV). So, what is the meaning of the phrase in Genesis 2–3? If we allow the context, rather than possible parallel passages, to

determine the meaning, then the interpretation must fit with the emphases of Genesis 3, which is about prohibition, enticement, disobedience,
falling away, and death of some kind. One might then suggest that "the
knowledge of good and evil" is moral autonomy. In deciding for themselves what is good and proper and what is not, the couple are making
themselves the final moral authority for their lives (in a diabolical way
becoming their own god) and "stepping out of the position of creaturely
dependence and trust in the creator" (Moberly 1992: 24).

Perhaps we should limit ourselves to the observation that in Eden
God placed limits on human freedom. As we will see shortly, Genesis
3–11 points out that the act of sin often consists of precisely this: over-
stepping divinely imposed limits.

The First Verse of the Bible

At least two problems form around Gen. 1:1: how should the verse be
translated, and what is its relationship to 1:2 and 1:3–31? First, how
should the verse be translated? Two possibilities exist. One is to treat v. 1
as a dependent, temporal clause. The translation then could be, "When
God began to create the heaven and the earth . . ." or "In the beginning,
when God made heaven and earth. . . ." In modern times this translation is as old as Moffatt's translation (1922), and it is reflected in more
recent translations such as the New Jewish Publication Society version,
the New English Bible, the translation of Genesis by E. A. Speiser in the
Anchor Bible commentaries, and the New Revised Standard Version.
Possible support for this rendering appears in 2:4b, which begins with
"When the Lord God made the earth and the heavens" (NIV), followed
by a description of desolation (2:5–6) and then God's first creative action (2:7).

The more traditional translation renders Gen. 1:1 as an independent
clause: "In the beginning God created the heavens and the earth." This
is reflected in the KJV, RSV, NASB, NIV, and JB.

If the first possibility is followed, taking 1:1 as a dependent clause,
then the additional facts are that v. 2 is a parenthetical comment, set off
by hyphens from what precedes and follows, and that the main clause
appears in v. 3, "And God said. . . ." The result is an unusually long,
rambling sentence, which is not unheard of per se but is quite out of
place in this chapter, laced as it is with a string of staccato sentences.

As far as the biblical evidence itself is concerned, the problem of
translation originates with the first word of the Bible, *běrēʾšît* (KJV, RSV:
"in the beginning"; NEB, NJPS: "when").

In biblical Hebrew nouns are classified, in terms of syntax, as being in
either the construct state or the absolute state. For example, in the phrase

"word of the Lord," "word" is in the construct state because it is dependent upon the next word, "the Lord." It cannot stand by itself and make any sense. A word in the construct state normally does not take a definite article, although an article may be placed in a translation for sense and smoothness. Conversely, "Lord," in the absolute state, is independent and stands alone. The question is this: is *běrē'šît* in the absolute or the construct state? If it is absolute, then Gen. 1:1 is an independent clause; if it is construct, then the verse is a dependent clause.

Although this is no relief for the reader, it must be pointed out that grammatically *běrē'šît* can be defined, as it stands, as being in either the absolute or the construct case. The preference should be given, however, to the absolute case. At least, this is how all the ancient versions understood it. Those opting for the temporal interpretation of the verse point out, in protest, that if this were the case, one would expect a reading *barē'šît*. The difference in Hebrew between *běrē'šît* and *barē'šît* is that the latter includes the definite article, "in *the* beginning." The objection is not fatal, however. The counterargument for the traditional translation is the observation that time designations in adverbial expressions, especially when the reference is to remote time, do not need the article, seldom use the article, and occur in the absolute state.

Gerhard von Rad (1972: 48), in his celebrated commentary on Genesis, maintains that "syntactically perhaps both translations are possible, but not theologically." Brevard Childs (1962: 41) contends that "to read verse 1 as a temporal clause does not take seriously enough the struggle which is evidenced in this chapter." Keeping in mind the pagan emphasis on creation out of eternal and preexistent matter (e.g., Tiamat's corpse), and the emphasis on confrontation, struggle, and manipulation as antecedents to creation, one cannot miss the fact that the Scripture writer in this opening declaration is repudiating that very concept.

Further confirmation of this is found in the verb employed by the writer in 1:1, *bārā'*. It is used again in 1:21, 27 (3x); 2:3; 5:1–2 (3x); 6:7, and elsewhere in the Bible. Two things may be said about this verb. First, the subject of *bārā'* is never anyone but God. Therefore, such activity is exclusively divine. Second, whenever this verb is used, its direct object is always the product created, never the materials used as the means in creation. To quote von Rad (1972: 49) again, "It is correct to say that the verb *bārā'* 'create' contains the idea both of complete effortlessness and *creatio ex nihilo*, since it is never connected with any statement of the material. The hidden grandeur of this statement is that God is Lord of the world." Childs (1962: 41) observes, "The omission of the accusative of material along with the simultaneous emphasis on the uniqueness of God's action could hardly be brought into a smooth harmony with the fact of a preexistent chaos. World reality is a result of creation, not a reshaping of existing matter."

All of this brings us to the second major problem, the relationship of 1:1 to what immediately follows, especially v. 2. At least three major views have been propounded. These are summarized in table 1.

The first view has been called the "gap" or "restitution" theory. An alternate version of this approach is to suggest two distinct creations (without any "gap" or "restitution" emphasis). Verse 1 describes creation out of nothing, the unformed product of which appears in v. 2, and vv. 3–31 describe God's subsequent creation of the formed world.

Table 1

Verse	Theory 1	Theory 2	Theory 3
1	original creation	original creation	superscription, or summary statement, of everything developed in the following verses. The words "the heavens/the sky and the earth/land" may be a biblical rhetorical device known as merismus, a means of expressing totality through the use of antonyms (e.g., "I've been through thick and thin" or "I've looked up and down for the paper"). The statement then affirms that all that is owes its existence to God.
2	gap, indeterminable in terms of length—"the earth *had become* without form and void" (due to Satan's expulsion from heaven?)	condition of the earth at its inception: formless and void; dark; the Spirit of God moved over the waters	situation before creation, the preprimeval period. Almost cryptically, the words "without form and void, darkness, deep" and "waters" stand alone and without explanation or commentary. F. Derek Kidner (1967: 44) correctly captures the contrast: "The sombre terms of 2a throw into relief the mounting glory of the seven days." To assume, however, that these terms are reflective of a chaos, outside of God's creation and antagonistic to his divine plan, finds no justification in the text.
3–31	God's second act of creation, or the divine act of re-creation	gradual order and symmetry were imposed on the formless cosmos, the movement being from imperfection to perfection, incompletion to completion	sequential narration of creation

Nonbiblical Creation Stories

Every ancient civilization produced its own corpus of mythical literature in which the general topic was either the origins and behavior of the gods (properly called myths) or the exploits of ancient heroes (properly called legends). In the myths the actors exclusively are the gods. In the legends the actors primarily are people, but the gods also assume major roles in the stories.

Of course, not every piece of ancient literature has survived or has been excavated by archaeologists. It is, for example, a moot question whether there was a strong emphasis on creation theology among the Canaanites. That question arises from the fact that no specific creation story has yet been discovered in the literature from Ras Shamra. Ras Shamra, located on the eastern shore of the Mediterranean, is the modern Arabic name for ancient Ugarit. From 1929 to the present, large amounts of Canaanite texts, to say nothing of texts in other languages, have been discovered there. The general subject of these texts is either economic or political concerns, but a good number of the texts also have had a religious dimension, either myths (Baal and Anat versus Mot or Yamm) or legends (Daniel and King Keret).

It does not need to be debated whether these myths and legends, those produced both inside and outside of Canaan, were known to God's people Israel. I have already argued that references in the Old Testament to Rahab, Leviathan, and the dragon presuppose an intelligent awareness on the part of the worshipers of Yahweh of the traditions surrounding these suprahuman beings. Furthermore, one section of the Gilgamesh Epic, a Mesopotamian deluge story, has been discovered at the Israelite city of Megiddo.

What do these stories contribute to our knowledge and understanding of the Old Testament? Why should we study them, apart from any information that they may add to our awareness of ancient religions and cultures?

Obviously, one does not need an extensive or even a superficial knowledge of mythology to understand the message of Genesis 1–2. And yet I am persuaded that the implications of the creation story of Genesis emerge most dramatically when it is compared with the creation literature of, for example, Mesopotamia (be that literature Sumerian, Assyrian, or Babylonian). For it is in the comparison of literature having an identical general theme that the distinctiveness of the biblical faith and message appears.

We need to remember that Genesis 1–2 was not produced by the nation called Israel, in the sense that these chapters are the mature reflections of some individual (or individuals) on the questions of origins. Rather, this material is the result of divine revelation, truth that human beings could not know unless it was revealed to them from above.

A study of mythology helps the believer to see how ancient people tried to answer ultimate questions about life and reality without the light of revelation having dawned upon them. Interestingly, the answers provided to those questions by ancient people are not all that different from the answers provided by modern but unredeemed people.

In the study that follows I limit myself to material from Mesopotamia, the *Enuma Elish* (the first two words in the poem, which may be translated as "when on high"), and pertinent sections of the Atrahasis Epic.

There are several reasons for limiting my study to compositions from that part of the world. First, the stories that I will discuss are among the most remarkably preserved specimens of ancient literature. They are relatively free from problems of translation and from large gaps in the text. Often there are multiple copies, as later generations copied the story out for themselves.

Second, it is precisely these stories from Mesopotamia that are thought by many scholars to provide the source of the biblical material in Genesis 1–2 and 6–9. The scriptural stories, according to this theory, are adaptations of pagan myth with appropriate editorial revisions and deletions. I will respond specifically to this in my discussion of the flood episode.

Third, we know that Abraham came from Ur of the Chaldeans. It is more than likely that the stories that I am about to discuss were part of his upbringing. If nothing else, a knowledge of these particular myths and legends will help us to understand something of the world out of which God called Abraham. The shift was nothing short of radical. That shift was as much theological and philosophical as it was geographical.

The *Enuma Elish*

As I have noted, there are two stories from Mesopotamia in which creation is a prominent theme. Since its publication in the nineteenth century, the better-known one is the *Enuma Elish*. Two critical questions, apart from interpretation, are open to debate in any discussion of the *Enuma Elish*. One is the date of composition, and the other is the degree to which the epic is typical of Mesopotamian (a period covering some three to four thousand years) belief about creation. Is it normative or is it exceptional? Concerning date, two opinions exist. Although no extant copies of the epic are earlier than the first millennium B.C., cuneiform specialists such as E. A. Speiser and T. Jacobsen believe, on the basis of internal evidence, that the epic was first produced in the Old Babylonian period, meaning the early part of the second millennium B.C. (Speiser), or sometime during the middle of the latter half of the second millennium B.C. (Jacobsen). On the other hand, another cuneiform specialist, W. G. Lambert, thinks that the story is not earlier than 1100 B.C. He also states that the *Enuma Elish* is not typical of Sumerian or Babylonian cosmology, but rather is a sectarian and aberrant account. The Assyrians in the first millennium apparently did not find it aberrant, and so did not hesitate to borrow the epic from the Babylonians, making only such changes as necessary for the story to fit its new milieu (e.g., the hero is no longer Marduk, but the Assyrian god Ashur).

What of the contents of the story? Before the creation of anything there were two divine beings, Apsu, the male divine personification of fresh waters, and Tiamat, the female divine personification of marine waters. Through their mingling (or mating) a second generation is produced, Lahmu and Lahamu, both perhaps to be associated with the silt produced by these waters. Then comes a third generation, Anshar and Kishar, the horizon. And from them comes Anu the god of heaven, and from him Ea (Enki).

The senior deity Apsu is, however, unable to sleep because these younger deities are making too much noise. Over the protests of Tiamat his wife, but at the prompting of Mummu his servant, Apsu plans to remedy the problem by killing these boisterous gods. But before he can implement his plan, Ea places a magic spell on Apsu and then kills him.

Aroused and indignant over her husband's unfortunate end and spurred on by some sympathetic supporters, Tiamat vows to carry out Apsu's plan of deicide. She takes as her second husband Kingu.

At this point the major character of the story, Marduk the son of Ea, emerges. He is charged with the responsibility of leading and defending those marked for execution by Tiamat, a challenge that he accepts with the qualification that if he is successful, the gods will make him their head. After being suckled by goddesses, he is ready for battle (theomachy).

Marduk swiftly eliminates Tiamat and captures Kingu and the rest of the entourage. Marduk then splits Tiamat in two, making heaven from one half of her cadaver, and the earth from the other half. The imprisoned gods he subsequently charges with the responsibility of building him a permanent home, Babylon.

Further reflection and an outburst of protest by the employed gods lead Marduk to relieve the gods of this manual work by a second creation, the creation of humankind. He does this by having Kingu killed and using his blood to create humankind. The story concludes with a royal banquet at which Marduk formally receives permanent kingship, and finally the listing of his fifty names, each of which extols Marduk.

The Atrahasis Epic

The second account to be considered is the Atrahasis Epic, dating originally to no later than 1700 B.C., from which the earliest surviving copies come. Though dealing eventually and more extensively with the flood, I will limit myself here to those parts dealing with creation. The epic begins with a description of the world as it was before humankind was created. The three supreme gods had partitioned the universe among themselves. Anu rules over heaven, Enlil over earth, and Enki over all bodies of water. The focus in the epic is on the earth, the overseeing of which is a mixed blessing, more to be endured than enjoyed. Specifically, Enlil is in charge of the gods whose primary job is to dig the Tigris and Euphrates rivers. But as is true also in many modern labor disputes, the employees refuse to work, and they rebel against Enlil to the point where even Enlil is alarmed by the violence of these mutineers, even though they are his own children. Observing how intransigent his children are, Enlil starts to weep and threatens to tender his resignation and retire to heaven to live with Anu.

The arbiter is Enki. He is sympathetic to the complaints of the hard-pressed, overworked gods. His suggestion is to create humankind and thus free the gods from their toil. At Enki's suggestion the gods kill one of their own, We-ila (the perpetrator of the rebellion?). From his blood and flesh, along with clay, humankind is created, with the help of the birth goddess Nintu(r)/Mami. In appreciation the gods confer on her the honorific title Mistress of all the gods. In all, seven males and seven females are created.

The Epics Compared

There are, of course, other creation accounts in cuneiform literature. I have outlined the two that best parallel the Old Testament. The following observations may be made.

First, the primary function of the *Enuma Elish* is not to describe the creation of the world or the creation of humankind. At best, that is a subplot. Its primary purpose is theogonic—that is, to explain the origin of the gods, and especially Marduk. How did a relatively minor deity (Marduk) climb from virtual obscurity to become the chief god of Babylon? In that sense the story is an etiology of Babylon's patron god.

Second, the epic was composed with religious functions in mind. Evidence indicates that the *Enuma Elish* was recited in Babylon annually at the Akitu festival, the beginning of the new year. Tiamat was associated with the forces of chaos, Marduk with the forces of order. As in the myth Marduk triumphed over Tiamat, so for the coming year the ritual recitation of the text, it was hoped, would go a long way toward guaranteeing the victory of order over chaos in the unpredictable world of nature. The idea is that the right words in the right places at the right times implement the most desirable results. We ought to observe Lambert's cautious note, however, that too much has been made of the cultic reading of the epic, and that nothing in the content of the story unequivocally implies a specific cultic function.

Third, both stories are set within the framework of a polytheistic system. According to the *Enuma Elish*, in the beginning there were two gods, Apsu and Tiamat. Marduk, the creator god, is a sixth-generation god. See figure 2.

Figure 2

Apsu and Tiamat
|
Lahmu and Lahamu
|
Anshar and Kishar
|
Anu
|
Ea (Enki/Nudimmud)
|
Marduk

The Babylonians' portrayal of their gods is interesting. Both epics serve as a window into their concept of gods—origin, character, and destiny. Creation is told in terms of procreation. In the beginning there were two, not one. Through the "mingling" of these partners a part of the created order appears. (In Sumerian there is one word for "water" and "semen.") Anu, the numinous power in the sky and thus the source of rain, has as his spouse Ki, the earth. Through impregnating her, Anu produces vegetation (and a host of demons and gods). Thus the gods are products of sexual activity, and they are subject by their nature to sexual needs. Pagans could see no future for their world and for their gods apart from a sexual relationship.

The needs, characters, and destinies of the gods are not markedly different from those of humans. Apsu is annoyed because he is deprived of sleep. He is also tossed betwixt and between listening to Tiamat, his spouse, who urges against the plan for execution, and Mummu, his vizier and counselor, who urges its implementation. Faced with mutually exclusive advice, Apsu opts for Mummu's directive over that of his consort. The god, unable to act independently, is swayed by his counselor.

Apsu, although divine, is subject to magic, and he is successfully immobilized by Ea's spell and subsequently killed. If myth is the poetic expression of pagan religion, magic is its practical expression, and it can be called on in situations of god against human, human against god, or god against god. The reason for this is the concept in paganism of a realm transcending even the powers of the deities, a realm to which they may be subservient. Israeli scholar Yehezkel Kaufmann called this area the "metadivine." In this sense no god is sovereign and without limitations, not even Apsu.

Gods can be killed and can attempt to kill simply out of impulsive anger or for self-serving reasons. The attempt to murder may be motivated by revenge (e.g., Tiamat).

Fourth, in the *Enuma Elish* heaven and earth are not spoken into existence by the creative word of one majestic god, but are formed from the corpse of a slain god, Tiamat. The created order is thus divine, more a "thou" than an "it."

Fifth, both in the *Enuma Elish* and the Atrahasis Epic humankind is created to relieve the gods of the necessity of manual labor, a chore that the gods soon complained about and felt was beneath their dignity. In the *Enuma Elish* humankind is created from the blood of a rebellious god, Kingu; in the Atrahasis Epic it is from the blood of We-ila (mixed with clay). In no sense can the creation of humankind be termed climactic, nor is there any unique dignity conferred on human beings. The human being is created as servant, not as king. Perhaps it goes too far to see a Mesopotamian doctrine of original sin in these accounts, but may not the episodes serve as an etiology to account for humankind's proclivity to evil? Having been made that way, humankind is therefore the product of an inscrutable determinism.

The Fall (3)

Chapter 3 of Genesis raises tantalizing questions in the mind of the reader, but for these questions an answer is not supplied. For example, no detailed account is given of the serpent at this point. Certainly he is not called Satan. If he is indeed a cosmic antagonist to God, once in the angelic host but now expelled, Genesis 3 does not pause to tell us that. To be sure, the New Testament unequivocally refers to "that ancient serpent, who is called the Devil and Satan, the deceiver of the whole world" (Rev. 12:9 NRSV; cf. 20:2).

The Serpent

There is uncertainty about the etymological origin of the Hebrew word for "serpent." The Hebrew word is *nāḥāš*. Is it to be related to the Hebrew *něḥōšet,* "copper, bronze," suggestive perhaps of something luminous ("an angel of light")? Indeed, in the wilderness Moses made a bronze serpent (Num. 21:9), only to have it demolished centuries later by Hezekiah when the image became a fetish and an object of worship (2 Kings 18:4). Or is the word for "serpent" to be related to the Hebrew verb *nāḥaš,* "to practice divination"?

We should note that information in the Old Testament about Satan, and indeed for the whole world of demonology, is at a precious premium. And for good reason. It is as unlikely that the Old Testament will address itself to this issue at any length as it is that it will address itself in depth to an explication of the Trinity. When one remembers that Israel was surrounded by nations whose religious ideas about supernatural forces included a belief not only in gods but also in hosts of demons, it is easy to see why the Old Testament rarely mentions demonology.

In fact, the word *śāṭan* is employed in a number of ways (but never in Genesis 3). It refers, surprisingly, to the angel of the Lord, who may be an "adversary" (Num. 22:22, 32); to a person who functions as an "adversary" (1 Sam. 29:4; 2 Sam. 19:22; 1 Kings 5:4; 11:14, 23, 25; Ps. 109:6); to Satan, opponent of God and intruder into the angelic host (Job). In this last category the word occurs eighteen times (fourteen of them in Job 1–2). What is interesting is that in all but one of these eighteen occurrences (the exception is 1 Chron. 21:1) *śāṭan* has the definite article attached, "the satan." This indicates that "the satan" is a title, not a personal name. Satan is not *who* he is, but *what* he is. He does not merit a name, and in antiquity, not to have a name was to be reduced to virtual nonexistence.

All that the chapter says, then, about this serpent is that he or it was one of the wild creatures that the Lord God had made. That is, the serpent was a created being, neither eternal nor divine. Also, the serpent was unlike any other animal, "subtle/crafty." This in itself is not pejorative. The same word is used in Proverbs eight times (12:16, 23; 13:16; 14:8, 15, 18; 22:3; 27:12), and translates there as "the prudent [person]," who is contrasted with the "fool" in the first four of these references, and with the "simple" or "naïve" in the remaining four—thus, it suggests a good and commendable quality. It is no wonder that Jesus instructed his disciples to be as wise as serpents (Matt. 10:16).

On the other hand, the word is translated as the "crafty" whom God loathes in Job, another Old Testament wisdom book (Job 5:12; 15:5), the opposite in tone of the passages in Proverbs. Similarly, the feminine counterpart to this word translates as "prudence" in Proverbs (e.g., 1:4), but by contrast in Exod. 21:14 it means "treachery," or scheming in murder.

It should also be pointed out that the Hebrew word for "subtle" used in Gen. 3:1, *ʿārûm*, sounds very much like the word for "naked" in the last verse of ch. 2—*ʿărûmmîm*. No great theological conclusion should be gleaned from that. However, the use in consecutive verses of two words that are written alike and sound alike but mean two different things is an indication of the author's use of key words to link the narratives. In this case chs. 2 and 3 of Genesis are nicely linked.

The Temptation

If Genesis 3 is unconcerned with amplification about the identity of the serpent, it is equally unconcerned with answering another question that intrigues the modern reader: why did the serpent tempt the woman and not the man, or both at the same time?

It seems fair to assume that the narrator does not intend to have the reader suppose that Adam and Eve are in two different places when the dialogue is in progress. The "you shall not eat" of vv. 1, 3, the "you shall die" of v. 3, and the "you shall not die" of v. 4 are plural verbs. Adam and Eve are the subjects. Also, the KJV rendering of 3:6b is quite clear: "and [she] gave also to her husband with her." This is to be preferred over the RSV's "and she also gave some to her husband." The NRSV blends both: "she also gave some to her husband, who was with her."

Answers to the question of why it was Eve who was tempted are legion. At one extreme is the view that the temptation aimed initially at the woman is reflective of women as the weaker sex, the one more inclined to engage in fanciful speculation. Thus, the respected scholar Gerhard von Rad (1972: 90) hastens to generalize that it is women more than men who have "shown an inclination for obscure astrological cults" (biblically, is von Rad referring to texts such as Ezek. 8:14?). At the other end of the spectrum are moderate feminists, such as Phyllis Trible (1978: 110), who suggest that in the story as presented Eve is the more challenging of the two. She is theologian-philosopher, aggressive rationalist, and God's defense attorney all rolled into one. If the serpent can make her capitulate, then her silent, uninvolved mate will follow suit.

The apostle Paul states, "Adam was not the one deceived; it was the woman who was deceived and became a sinner" (1 Tim. 2:14 NIV). And in that emphasis Paul correctly lists the chronology of the trespass: first Eve, then Adam. She leads, he assents. But the apostle does not raise the issue of why Eve was tempted first.

The prohibition against eating from the tree of the knowledge of good and evil was directed to the man (2:16–17). Nowhere are we clearly informed about how Eve learned of the prohibition. Presumably she learned of it from her husband, as her dialogue with the serpent (3:1–3) makes it obvious that she knows the prohibition well.

Possibly, then, the serpent chose Eve because she received the command from God only through an intermediary, her husband. One who had received God's command directly would be less likely to acquiesce. (As an example of this in another context, note who yielded to the temptation to idolatry and built the golden calf: not Moses, God's spokesman, but the people and Aaron, who received God's word through Moses.)

It is perhaps something of a surprise that the snake and Eve are able to converse at all without an interpreter. This observation is not made tongue-in-cheek. Granted that there are parallels in ancient literature, such as the Egyptian shipwrecked sailor who, being the sole survivor of a wreck at sea and then cast upon an island, finds himself engrossed in conversation with the island's lone occupant, a snake. But is the ability of the woman and the animal to converse simply mythological window dressing? Might our modern ability to communicate with pets be a remnant of a situation that once indeed did exist? Sin caused a rupture of Adam's relationship to God, to Eve, and to the ground. May we include also his relationship to the animal world? How interesting it is that animals are accountable for their actions and behavior (Gen. 9:5). The postdiluvian covenant is made with animals too (Gen. 9:9), not just humankind. Isaiah sees ahead to the messianic age, in which the wolf will become lamblike or the lamb will become wolflike (metaphors for the nations of the world?).

If all of this is incidental, some elements in the text are quite clear and present themselves to the reader with forcefulness and precision. To use J. R. W. Stott's (1965: 741) outline, we find here:

1. a permission to eat from every tree in the garden
2. a prohibition not to eat from one tree
3. a penalty for disobedience

How does the serpent attempt to undercut all of this? What is the essential intent of the temptation, and how far is it paradigmatic for the rest of the Bible, whenever the actions of the evil one are delineated?

The intent of the temptation is twofold. First, the temptation raises questions in Eve's mind about the integrity of God. Her mental image of God is attacked. God is portrayed more as fiend than friend. The method is to twist and misquote God's words in regard to the prohibition: you shall not eat *of any tree* of the garden. How cruel and vicious of God! The serpent implied, "You may observe them with the eye, work among them with the hands, but not partake of them with the mouth." In this context we might change the title of J. B. Phillips's interesting book from

Your God Is Too Small to *Your God Is Too Mean*. Stott's observation (1965: 743) is perceptive: "God's provision for Adam and Eve was perfect. They lacked nothing in the Garden of Eden. God knew that their happiness lay in enjoying what he had permitted and abstaining from what he had prohibited. His permission and his prohibition both issued from his sheer goodness and love." This is what the serpent must distort.

Second, the temptation encourages Eve to declare autonomy, quite apart from any guidance God may have given, which is to be considered absurd and irrelevant. "You will not die; . . . when you eat of it your eyes will be opened, and you will be like God, knowing good and evil" (vv. 4–5 NRSV).

Von Rad (1972: 89) summarizes correctly what these words mean: "The serpent holds out . . . the independence that enables a man to de- cide for himself what will help him or hinder him. . . . God had provided what was good for man, and had given him complete security. But now man will go beyond this to decide for himself." The temptation, then, is for humankind to overstep its limits. The difference between Adam and Eve in the garden and Jesus in the wilderness is that the former acquiesced to temptation. For Jesus, obedience to the Father's will was paramount.

What is next after Adam and Eve cross their Rubicon? Shame (v. 7), guile (vv. 8–11), and the search for a scapegoat (vv. 12–13). Then God speaks, not in the dialogue of vv. 8–13, but in a monologue: first to the serpent (vv. 14–15), then to the woman (v. 16), climactically and more extensively to the man (vv. 17–19).

It is, I believe, incorrect to see in these words of God to Adam and Eve primarily a punitive message, as if God is speaking only prescriptively, laying down the law, rather than descriptively: pain in pregnancy, dis- ruption in the family, minimal returns for manual labor. The writer is not picturing God as a petulant deity, sulking, determined to teach these rascals a lesson that they will not soon forget. Like a surgeon who cuts with a scalpel only in order to heal, God initiates a means of redemp- tion to reclaim the prodigals. His plan? To place at the respective point of highest self-fulfillment in the life of a woman and man problems of suffering, misery, and frustration. These "sentences" are not prescribed impositions from a volatile deity. Rather, they are gifts of love, strewn in the pathway of human beings, to bring them back to God. One may recall that C. S. Lewis, while reflecting on the ills and problems in the world, came to the conclusion that his reasons for not believing in God were actually much better reasons for believing in God, and thus was begun Lewis's pilgrimage into faith and his being "surprised by joy."

Commentators, in trying to salvage at least a ray of light from this chapter, usually have focused on either v. 21, "the Lord God made for them garments of skin, and clothed them," or v. 15, sometimes called the *prot(o)evangelium*, literally, "the first good news." It is tempting to see atonement in v. 21, or at least to contrast God's covering with that made by human hands (v. 7). And if this is not atonement, at least it is preservation, a gauge of God's concern and compassion. Note that God's act of grace (providing a covering for the delinquent couple) precedes their expulsion from the garden, just as in ch. 4 God's gracious provision of a protecting mark for Cain precedes his departure from God's presence.

The First Word of Promise

Genesis 3:15 traditionally has been viewed by Christians as the first word of promise—in a prophetic sense—of deliverance from sin. The provision of a covering for Adam and Eve is immediate atonement. By contrast, v. 15 places atonement in an eschatological context. Its concern is the future, not the present.

Not all commentators, however, endorse the christological interpretation of Gen. 3:15. On the contrary, many biblical scholars eschew any messianic message in the verse. For example, Westermann (1974: 100) attempts to crush under his own exegetical feet all who support the time-honored interpretation, beginning with Luther. For him, such an analysis fails to respect the original meaning of the verse and reads into the text something alien from the author's intention. For reasons that I will delineate, I find it impossible to follow Westermann and others like him.

The Hebrew verb for "bruise" or "crush" is *šûp*. Outside of Gen. 3:15 it is found only in Job 9:17, "he crushes me with a tempest" (NRSV), and Ps. 139:11, "let only darkness cover me" (RSV). The serpent will crush the heel of the woman's seed (a temporary and healable injury), but the seed of the woman will crush the head of the serpent (a fatal injury).

The older versions of the Old Testament have interesting translations of this verb. The Septuagint translates both occurrences with a verb meaning "to watch, guard (lie in wait for?)." The Vulgate translates the actions of the woman's seed ("*she* will . . .") with a verb meaning "to crush," and the actions of the serpent and his seed with a verb meaning "to lie in wait for."

In the New Testament this verse does not appear anywhere except in Paul's comment that "the God of peace will soon crush Satan under your feet" (Rom. 16:20 NIV). And it is clear in this text that Paul is speaking not of Christ's feet, but of the feet of those to whom he is writing ("your feet"), the believers at Rome, and by extension, all of Christ's followers. Key words and phrases are, however, highlighted elsewhere. In the Old

Testament, clustering around David, are the promises of God that David is but the start of something new, something that God will perpetuate through David's "seed" (2 Sam. 7:12; Ps. 89:4, 29, 36). Anyone who tries to oppose David and/or his seed, God will "crush" (Ps. 89:23, but not the same verb as in Gen. 3:15). In a prayer for the king (Ps. 72:9), the one petition asks that the king's enemies might "lick the dust" (NIV). This is analogous to the king's enemies viewed as the king's "footstool" (Ps. 110:1 NRSV). Jesus, the seed of David (Rom. 1:3), and one "born of a woman" (Gal. 4:4 NRSV), "must reign until he has put all his enemies under his feet" (1 Cor. 15:25 NIV).

There are at least three phenomena in Gen. 3:15 that all too often have been ignored by commentators. And it is precisely the glossing over of these that has resulted in downplaying the messianic import of the verse. First, this is the only place in the Old Testament that the Hebrew word for "seed" or "descendant" occurs with a third-person, feminine, pronominal suffix—"her seed." The uniqueness of the construction becomes even more apparent in the Septuagint, with its reference to the woman's sperm ("her *sperma*")! (Where is the man, the father?)

In the Old Testament descent is virtually always through the male. The son is the seed of his father rather than of his mother. Exceptions are rare, as in the cases of Hagar's seed (Gen. 16:10) and Rebekah's seed (Gen. 24:60), but both references, by context, clearly point to individuals, not an individual. (Eve later will refer to Seth as her "other seed" [Gen. 4:25].)

Second, the Septuagint translation of the "he" in "he shall crush/bruise your head" is the masculine form of the pronoun, whose antecedent is the word "seed," which is neuter in gender, not masculine. Of the more than one hundred uses of the pronoun "he" in the Greek translation of Genesis, this is the only instance where the "he" does not agree in gender with its antecedent where literal translation is involved. That is to say, the translators could easily have used "it" instead of "he," as Greek has three genders, unlike Hebrew, which has only masculine and feminine. The Septuagint, then, emphasizes the "he-ness" of the woman's seed, not the seed's "it-ness" or "they-ness" in some collective sense (Kaiser 1978: 36–37).

Third, the first part of the verse boldly proclaims that this future confrontation is not an accident of history, an event that catches God unawares. He is actually the producer of this warfare: "I will put enmity between you and the woman" (RSV). It is an event that is as foreordained as the incarnation of Jesus. Interestingly, the passage anticipates not the crushing of the head of the serpent's seed, but the crushing of the head of the serpent himself: "he shall crush your head."

For these reasons I believe that any reflection on Gen. 3:15 that fails to underscore the messianic emphasis of the verse is guilty of a serious exegetical error. There is no doubt that the ultimate significance failed to occur to Eve. Did she think that Cain was that promised seed (Gen. 4:1), or maybe Seth (4:25)? Then again, who would care to suggest that Abraham saw the long-range significance of the promise that he was to receive in Genesis 12, a promise that would take at least four hundred years for its implementation, or two millennia for its full implementation? All this is not to say that Gen. 3:15 points to Jesus, and only to Jesus, and leaves out everybody between Eve and Christ when it speaks of "her seed." The redemptive line of Eve's seed begins with Seth and climaxes with the Messiah. Alexander (1995: 31) correctly observes that Gen. 3:15 "anticipates the creation of a royal line through which the terrible consequences of the disobedience of the man and the woman in the Garden of Eden will be reversed."

Thus far I have suggested that in Genesis 3, at least in the second half, God's concern is redemption. This concern is manifest in the provision of a covering, the promise of a seed of the woman, and the pronouncement of words of judgment that are redemptive and not vindictive in purpose.

Expulsion from the Garden

Is another evidence of this emphasis on redemption to be found in the expulsion of the man from the garden, to which reentry is blocked by cherubim and flaming sword (3:22–24)? Parents are aware that if they have in their home a particularly delinquent youth, say, for example, a son in his late teens or early twenties, perhaps the healthiest thing they can do for that young man, however difficult it may be, is to expel him from the home. Something as simple as a shift in geography in itself can be a motivation for change. Why should we want to abandon our sins if we can retain them and still have the presence of God as well?

So the man is sent out of the garden. But to do what? The answer is provided in 3:23b: "to till the ground from which he was taken" (NRSV). We read in 2:5b that "there was no man to till the ground" (RSV), and in 2:15 we are informed that the Lord put the man in the garden of Eden precisely to fill that void: "to till it and keep it" (NRSV). Thus, we are confronted by a man who is indeed expelled from God's presence, but who is not barred from continuing the vocation for which he was created. He is still a tiller of the soil, but a soil that now is cursed.

Just prior to the announcement of the expulsion Adam had named his wife "Eve," a word connected with the Hebrew word for "life" or "living" (3:20). In the context, however, almost every event narrated points to death. Relationships with God, spouse, and soil are fractured. Nevertheless, here is life. Westermann (1974: 104) comments, "Despite man's disobedience and punishment, the blessing given with the act of creation remains intact . . . man who is now far from God is always man blessed by God."

It is interesting that the characters in Genesis 3 are not mentioned again, with the exception of the genealogical reference to Adam in 1 Chron. 1:1, until the New Testament, first in the Lukan genealogy of Jesus (Luke 3:38), then in some of the Pauline Epistles (e.g., Rom. 5:12–21; 1 Cor. 15:22). One might expect the expulsion from the garden to be a paradigm that the prophets would use to drive home their point about the consequences of disobedience, as they did, for example, with the episode about Sodom and Gomorrah. But it was left untouched.

The verses from Paul are, of course, the linchpin in what is commonly called the doctrine of original sin. Both the Old and New Testaments affirm the doctrine (Gen. 6:5; 1 Kings 8:46; Ps. 51:5; Rom. 5:19; Eph. 2:3), but they do not explain it in terms of theological origins. Anyone who is prone to dismiss the idea as medieval, negative, or absurd should recall a comment made by G. K. Chesterton in his biography of St. Francis of Assisi: "There is a bias in man and Christianity was the discovery of how to correct the bias. . . . It is profoundly true to say that the glad good news brought by the Gospel was the news of original sin" (*St. Francis of Assisi* [Garden City, N.Y.: Image Books, 1957], 28). Bad news may be good news!

Commentaries and Major Studies on the Pentateuch

Alexander, T. Desmond. 1995. *From Paradise to Promised Land: An Introduction to the Main Themes of the Pentateuch.* Carlisle: Paternoster.

Bailey, L. R. 1981. *The Pentateuch.* Nashville: Abingdon.

Baker, D., and T. Desmond Alexander, eds. 2002. *Dictionary of the Old Testament: Pentateuch.* Downers Grove, Ill.: InterVarsity Press.

Blenkinsopp, J. 1992. *The Pentateuch: An Introduction to the First Five Books of the Bible.* New York: Doubleday.

Brueggemann, W., and Hans W. Wolff. 1974. *The Vitality of Old Testament Traditions.* Atlanta: John Knox.

Campbell, A. F., and M. A. O'Brien. 1993. *Sources of the Pentateuch: Texts, Introductions, Annotations.* Minneapolis: Fortress.

Cassuto, U. 1961. *The Documentary Hypothesis and the Composition of the Pentateuch.* Trans. I. Abrahams. Jerusalem: Magnes.

Christensen, D. L., and M. Narucki. 1989. "The Mosaic Authorship of the Pentateuch." *JETS* 32:465–71.

Clines, D. J. A. 1978. *The Theme of the Pentateuch.* 2nd ed., 1997. JSOTSup 10. Sheffield: JSOT Press.

Emerton, J. A., ed. 1990. *Studies in the Pentateuch.* VTSup 41. Leiden and New York: Brill.

Fox, E. 1995. *The Five Books of Moses.* 5 vols. The Schocken Bible. New York: Schocken.

Fretheim, T. E. 1996. *The Pentateuch.* Nashville: Abingdon.

Friedman, R. E. 2001. *Commentary on the Torah with a New English Translation and the Hebrew Text.* San Francisco: HarperSanFrancisco.

Gooder, P. 2002. *The Pentateuch: A Story of Beginnings.* Biblical Studies Series. New York: Continuum.

Guinan, M. 1990. *The Pentateuch.* Collegeville, Minn.: Liturgical Press.

Hallo, W. W. 1991. *The Book of the People.* BJS 225. Atlanta: Scholars Press.

Kugel, J. L. 1998. *Traditions of the Bible as It Was at the Start of the Common Era.* Cambridge, Mass.: Harvard University Press.

Laffey, A. L. 1998. *The Pentateuch: A Liberation-Critical Reading.* Minneapolis: Fortress.

Livingston, G. H. 1974. *The Pentateuch in Its Cultural Environment.* 2nd ed., 1987. Grand Rapids: Baker.

Lohfink, N. 1994. *Theology of the Pentateuch: Themes of the Priestly Narrative and Deuteronomy.* Trans. Linda M. Maloney. Minneapolis: Fortress.

Mann, T. W. 1988. *The Book of the Torah: The Narrative Integrity of the Pentateuch.* Atlanta: John Knox.

McDermott, J. J. 2002. *Reading the Pentateuch: A Historical Introduction.* New York: Paulist Press.

McEvenue, S. E. 1990. *Interpreting the Pentateuch.* Collegeville, Minn.: Liturgical Press.

Montgomery, R. M. 1971. *An Introduction to Source Analysis of the Pentateuch.* Nashville: Abingdon.

Mullen, E. Theodore, Jr. 1997. *Ethnic Myths and Pentateuchal Foundations: A New Approach to the Formation of the Pentateuch.* SemeiaSt. Atlanta: Scholars Press.

Murphy, R. E. 1996. *Responses to 101 Questions on the Biblical Torah: Reflections on the Pentateuch.* New York: Paulist Press.

Nicholson, E. W. 1998. *The Pentateuch in the Twentieth Century: The Legacy of Julius Wellhausen.* Oxford: Clarendon; New York: Oxford University Press.

Noth, M. 1972. *A History of Pentateuchal Traditions.* Trans. B. W. Anderson. Englewood Cliffs, N.J.: Prentice-Hall. Repr., Atlanta: Scholars Press, 1981.

Plaut, W. Gunther. 1981. *The Torah: A Modern Commentary.* New York: Union of American Hebrew Congregations.

Rendtorff, R. 1990. *The Problem of the Process of Transmission in the Pentateuch.* Trans. J. Scullion. JSOTSup 89. Sheffield: JSOT Press.

Rofé, A. 1999. *Introduction to the Composition of the Pentateuch.* Trans. H. N. Bock. Biblical Seminar 58. Sheffield: Sheffield Academic Press.

Rogerson, J. W., ed. 1996. *The Pentateuch*. Biblical Seminar 39. Sheffield: Sheffield Academic Press.

Sailhamer, J. H. 1992. *The Pentateuch as Narrative: A Biblical-Theological Commentary*. Library of Biblical Interpretation. Grand Rapids: Zondervan.

VanGemeren, W. 1988. *The Progress of Redemption: The Story of Salvation from Creation to the New Jerusalem*. Grand Rapids: Baker. Pp. 39–179.

Van Seters, J. 1999. *The Pentateuch: A Social-Science Commentary*. Trajectories 1. Sheffield: Sheffield Academic Press.

Walton, J. H., and V. H. Matthews. 1997. *The IVP Bible Background Commentary: Genesis-Deuteronomy*. Downers Grove, Ill.: InterVarsity Press.

Watts, J. W. 1999. *Reading Law: The Rhetorical Shaping of the Pentateuch*. Biblical Seminar 59. Sheffield: Sheffield Academic Press.

———, ed. 2001. *Persia and Torah. The Theory of the Imperial Authorization of the Pentateuch*. SBLSymS 17. Atlanta: Society of Biblical Literature.

Whybray, R. N. 1987. *The Making of the Pentateuch: A Methodological Study*. JSOTSup 53. Sheffield: Sheffield Academic Press.

———. 1996. *Introduction to the Pentateuch*. Grand Rapids: Eerdmans.

Wolf, H. 1990. *An Introduction to the Old Testament Pentateuch*. Chicago: Moody.

Wynn-Williams, D. J. 1997. *The State of the Pentateuch: A Comparison of the Approaches of M. Noth and E. Blum*. BZAW 249. Berlin: de Gruyter.

Genesis Commentaries and Major Studies

Aalders, G. C. 1981. *Genesis*. Trans. W. Heynen. 2 vols. Bible Student's Commentary. Grand Rapids: Zondervan.

Alter, R. 1996. *Genesis: Translation and Commentary*. New York: Norton.

Armstrong, K. 1996. *In the Beginning: A New Interpretation of Genesis*. New York: Knopf.

Arnold, B. T. 1998. *Encountering the Book of Genesis*. Encountering Biblical Studies. Grand Rapids: Baker.

Boice, J. M. 1982–1987. *Genesis: An Expositional Commentary*. 3 vols. Grand Rapids: Zondervan.

Brenner, A., ed. 1993. *A Feminist Companion to Genesis*. The Feminist Companion to the Bible 2. Sheffield: JSOT Press.

Brodie, T. L. 2001. *Genesis as Dialogue: A Literary, Historical, and Theological Commentary*. New York: Oxford University Press.

Brueggemann, W. 1982. *Genesis*. Interpretation. Atlanta: John Knox.

Carr, D. M. 1996. *Reading the Fractures of Genesis: Historical and Literary Approaches*. Louisville: Westminster John Knox.

Coats, G. W. 1983. *Genesis, with an Introduction to Old Testament Literature*. FOTL 1. Grand Rapids: Eerdmans.

Cotter, D. W. 2003. *Genesis*. Berit Olam. Collegeville, Minn.: Liturgical Press.

Davies, P. R., and D. J. A. Clines, eds. 1998. *The World of Genesis: Persons, Places, Perspectives.* JSOTSup 257. Sheffield: Sheffield Academic Press.

Fleming, D. 2003. "History in Genesis." *WTJ* 65:251–62.

Fokkelman, J. P. 1975. *Narrative Art in Genesis: Specimens of Stylistic and Structural Analysis.* Assen: Van Gorcum.

Fox, E. 1983. *In the Beginning: A New English Rendition of the Book of Genesis.* New York: Schocken.

Fretheim, T. E. 1994. "Genesis." In *The New Interpreter's Bible.* Vol. 1. Ed. L. E. Keck et al. Nashville: Abingdon. Pp. 319–674.

Garrett, D. 1991. *Rethinking Genesis: The Sources and Authorship of the First Book of the Pentateuch.* Grand Rapids: Baker.

Gunkel, H. 1997 [German, 1910]. *Genesis.* Trans. M. E. Biddle. Macon, Ga.: Mercer University Press.

Gunn, D., and D. Fewell. 1993. *Gender, Power and Promise: The Subject of the Bible's First Story.* Nashville: Abingdon.

Hamilton, V. P. 1990–1995. *The Book of Genesis.* 2 vols. NICOT. Grand Rapids: Eerdmans.

Hartley, J. 2000. *Genesis.* NIBCOT 1. Peabody, Mass.: Hendrickson.

Hess, R. S., G. J. Wenham, and P. E. Satterthwaite. 1994. *He Swore an Oath: Biblical Themes from Genesis 12–50.* 2nd ed. Grand Rapids: Baker.

Humphreys, W. L. 2001. *The Character of God in the Book of Genesis.* Louisville: Westminster John Knox.

Janzen, J. G. 1993. *Abraham and All the Families of the Earth: A Commentary on the Book of Genesis 12–50.* ITC. Grand Rapids: Eerdmans.

Jeansonne, S. 1990. *The Women of Genesis.* Minneapolis: Fortress.

Kidner, D. 1967. *Genesis: An Introduction and Commentary.* TOTC. Downers Grove, Ill.: InterVarsity Press.

Lipton, D. 1999. *Revisions of the Night: Politics and Promise in the Patriarchal Dreams of Genesis.* JSOTSup 288. Sheffield: Sheffield Academic Press.

Millard, A. R., and D. J. Wiseman, eds. 1980. *Essays on the Patriarchal Narratives.* Winona Lake, Ind.: Eisenbrauns.

Moberly, R. W. L. 1992. *Genesis 12–50.* OTG. Sheffield: JSOT Press.

Moyers, Bill, et al. 1996. *Genesis: A Living Conversation.* Ed. B. S. Flowers. New York: Doubleday.

Oden, Thomas C., gen. ed. 2001. *Genesis 1–11.* Ed. A. Louth and M. Conti. ACCS 1. Downers Grove, Ill.: InterVarsity Press.

———. 2002. *Genesis 12–50.* Ed. M. Sheridan. ACCS 2. Downers Grove, Ill.: Inter-Varsity Press.

Rad, G. von. 1972. *Genesis.* Trans. J. H. Marks. Rev. ed. OTL. Philadelphia: Westminster.

Radday, Y., and H. Shore. 1985. *Genesis: An Authorship Study.* AnBib 103. Rome: Biblical Institute Press.

Rashkow, I. 1993. *The Phallacy of Genesis: A Feminist-Psychological Approach.* Louisville: Westminster.

Rendsburg, G. 1986. *The Redaction of Genesis*. Winona Lake, Ind.: Eisenbrauns.

Roop, E. F. 1987. *Genesis*. Scottdale, Pa.: Herald.

Rosenberg, D., ed. 1996. *Genesis, As It Is Written: Contemporary Writers on Our First Stories*. San Francisco: HarperSanFrancisco.

Ross, A. P. 1988. *Creation and Blessing: A Guide to the Study and Exposition of Genesis*. Grand Rapids: Baker.

Sailhamer, J. H. 1990. "Genesis." In *The Expositor's Bible Commentary*. Vol. 2. Ed. F. E. Gaebelein. Grand Rapids: Zondervan. Pp. 1–284.

Saltzman, S. 1996. *A Small Glimmer of Light: Reflections on the Book of Genesis*. Hoboken, N.J.: Ktav.

Sarna, N. 1966. *Understanding Genesis*. Heritage of Biblical Israel 1. New York: McGraw-Hill.

———. 1989. *Genesis: The Traditional Hebrew Text with the New JPS Translation*. JPS Torah Commentary. Philadelphia: The Jewish Publication Society.

Schaeffer, F. 1972. *Genesis in Space and Time: The Flow of Biblical History*. Downers Grove, Ill.: InterVarsity Press.

Scullion, J. J. 1992. *Genesis: A Commentary for Students, Teachers and Preachers*. OTS 6. Collegeville, Minn.: Liturgical Press.

Speiser, E. A. 1964. *Genesis*. AB 1. New York: Doubleday.

Steinberg, N. 1993. *Kinship and Marriage in Genesis: A Household Economics Perspective*. Minneapolis: Fortress.

Steinmetz, D. 1991. *Kinship, Conflict and Continuity in Genesis*. Louisville: Westminster John Knox.

Stigers, H. G. 1976. *A Commentary on Genesis*. Zondervan Commentary Series. Grand Rapids: Zondervan.

Thomas, W. H. Griffith. 1958 [1907]. *Genesis: A Devotional Commentary*. Grand Rapids: Eerdmans.

Thompson, T. L. 1987. *The Origin Tradition of Ancient Israel*. Vol. 1, *The Literary Formation of Genesis and Exodus 1–23*. JSOTSup 55. Sheffield: JSOT Press.

Towner, W. S. 2001. *Genesis*. WBComp. Louisville: Westminster John Knox.

Turner, L. A. 1990. *Announcement of Plots in Genesis*. JSOTSup 96. Sheffield: Sheffield Academic Press.

———. 2000. *Genesis*. Readings: A New Biblical Commentary. Sheffield: Sheffield Academic Press.

Vawter, B. 1977. *On Genesis: A New Reading*. New York: Doubleday.

Vos, H. F. 1982. *Genesis*. Chicago: Moody.

Waltke, B. K., and C. Fredericks. 2001. *Genesis: A Commentary*. Grand Rapids: Zondervan.

Walton, J. 2001. *Genesis*. NIV Application Commentary. Grand Rapids: Zondervan.

Wenham, G. 1987–1994. *Genesis*. 2 vols. WBC 1, 2. Dallas: Word.

Wénin, A., ed. 2001. *Studies in the Book of Genesis: Literary, Redaction and Historical*. BETL 155. Leuven: Leuven University Press.

Westermann, C. 1984–1986. *Genesis*. Trans. J. J. Scullion. 3 vols. Minneapolis: Augsburg.

———. 1987. *Genesis: A Practical Commentary*. Trans. D. E. Green. Grand Rapids: Eerdmans.

Wevers, J. 1974. *Genesis*. Septuaginta: Vetus Testamentum Graecum. Göttingen: Vandenhoeck & Ruprecht.

Wheedbee, J. William. 1998. *The Bible and the Comic Vision*. Cambridge: Cambridge University Press. Pp. 15–126.

White, H. C. 1991. *Narration and Discourse in the Book of Genesis*. Cambridge: Cambridge University Press.

Williams, W. G. 2000. *Genesis*. A Bible Commentary in the Wesleyan Tradition. Indianapolis: Wesleyan Publishing House.

Williamson, P. R. 2000. *Abraham, Israel and the Nations: The Patriarchal Promise and Its Covenantal Development in Genesis*. JSOTSup 35. Sheffield: Sheffield Academic Press.

Genesis 1–11

Anderson, B. W. 1977. "From Analysis to Synthesis: The Interpretation of Genesis 1–11." *JBL* 97:23–39.

Clines, D. J. A. 1976. "Themes in Genesis 1–11." *CBQ* 38:483–507.

Coats, G. W. 1975. "Power and Obedience in the Primeval History." *Int* 29:227–39.

Fretheim, T. E. 1969. *Creation, Fall and Flood*. Minneapolis: Augsburg.

Hendel, R. S. 1998. *The Text of Genesis 1–11: Textual Studies and Critical Edition*. Oxford: Clarendon.

Hess, R. S. 1993. *Studies in the Personal Names of Genesis 1–11*. AOAT 234. Neukirchen-Vluyn: Neukirchener Verlag.

Hess, R. S., and D. T. Tsumura. 1994. *"I Studied Inscriptions from before the Flood": Ancient Near Eastern, Literary, and Linguistic Approaches to Genesis 1–11*. Sources for Biblical and Theological Studies 4. Winona Lake, Ind.: Eisenbrauns.

Kikawada, I., and A. Quinn. 1985. *Before Abraham Was: The Unity of Genesis 1–11*. Nashville: Abingdon.

Krasovec, J. 1994. "Punishment and Mercy in the Primeval History (Genesis 1–11)." *ETL* 70:5–33.

Mathews, K. A. 1996. *Genesis 1–11:26*. NAC 1A. Nashville: Broadman & Holman.

Miller, P. D., Jr. 1978. *Genesis 1–11: Studies in Structure and Theme*. JSOTSup 8. Sheffield: University of Sheffield Department of Biblical Studies.

Oden, R. A. 1981. "Divine Aspirations in Atrahasis and in Genesis 1–11." *ZAW* 93:197–216.

Sailhamer, J. 2000. "Creation, Genesis 1–11, and the Canon." *BBR* 10:89–106.

Scullion, J. J. 1974. "New Thinking on Creation and Sin in Genesis i–xi." *ABR* 22:1–10.

Smith, G. 1988. "Structure and Purpose of Genesis 1–11." *JETS* 20:307–19.

Weeks, N. 1978. "The Hermeneutical Problem of Genesis 1–11." *Themelios* 4:12–19.

Wolde, E. van. 1994. *Words Become Worlds: Semantic Studies of Genesis 1–11*. BIS 6. Leiden: Brill.

———. 1998. "Facing the Earth: Primaeval History in a New Perspective." In *The World of Genesis: Persons, Places, Perspectives*. Ed. P. R. Davies and D. J. A. Clines. JSOTSup 257. Sheffield: Sheffield Academic Press. Pp. 22–47.

Genesis 1–3

Anderson, B. W. 1977. "A Stylistic Study of the Priestly Creation Story." In *Canon and Authority*. Ed. G. W. Coats and B. O. Long. Philadelphia: Fortress. Pp. 148–62.

———, ed. 1984. *Creation in the Old Testament*. IRT 6. Philadelphia: Fortress.

Anderson, G. A. 1999. "Is Eve the Problem?" In *Theological Exegesis: Essays in Honor of Brevard S. Childs*. Ed. C. Seitz and K. Greene-McCreight. Grand Rapids: Eerdmans. Pp. 96–123.

Bailey, J. 1970. "Initiation and the Primal Women in Gilgamesh and Genesis 2–3." *JBL* 89:137–50.

Barr, James. 1968. "The Image of God in the Book of Genesis—A Study of Terminology." *BJRL* 51:11–26.

———. 1972. "Man and Nature—The Ecological Controversy and the Old Testament." *BJRL* 55:9–32.

———. 1993a. *The Garden of Eden and the Hope of Immortality*. Minneapolis: Fortress.

———. 1993b. *Biblical Faith and Natural Theology*. Oxford: Clarendon.

———. 1998a. "Was Everything That God Created Really Good? A Question on the First Verse of the Bible." In *God in the Fray: A Tribute to Walter Brueggemann*. Ed. T. Linafet and T. K. Beal. Minneapolis: Fortress. Pp. 55–65.

———. 1998b. "Adam: Single Man or All Humanity?" In *Hesed ve-emet: Studies in Honor of Ernest S. Frerichs*. Ed. J. Magness and S. Gitin. BJS 320. Atlanta: Scholars Press.

Beattie, D. R. G. 1980–1981. "What Is Genesis 2–3 About?" *ExpT* 92:8–10.

Bechtel, L. M. 1995. "Genesis 2:4b–3:24: A Myth about Human Maturation." *JSOT* 67:3–26.

Bird, P. A. 1981. "'Male and Female He Created Them': Gen. 1:27b in the Context of the Priestly Account of Creation." *HTR* 74:129–59.

Blenkinsopp, J. 1976. "The Structure of P." *Bib* 38:275–92.

Brichto, H. C. 1998. *The Names of God: Poetic Readings in Biblical Beginnings*. Oxford: Clarendon.

Brueggemann, W. 1970. "Of the Same Flesh and Bone (GN2, 23a)." *CBQ* 32:532–42.

———. 1972. "From Dust to Kingship." *ZAW* 84:1–18.

Carlson, G. I. 1973. "The Two Creation Accounts in Schematic Contrast." *TBT* 66:1192–94.

Childs, B. S. 1962a. *Myth and Reality in the Old Testament.* SBT 27. London: SCM Press.

———. 1962b. "Adam." *IDB* 1:42–44.

———. 1962c. "Eden." *IDB* 2:22–23.

———. 1962d. "Eve." *IDB* 2:181–82.

———. 1962e. "Tree of Knowledge, Tree of Life." *IDB* 4:695–97.

Clark, W. M. 1969. "A Legal Background to the Yahwist's Use of Good and Evil." *JBL* 88:266–78.

Clines, D. J. A. 1968. "The Image of God in Man." *TynB* 19:53–103.

———. 1990. *What Does Eve Do to Help? And Other Readerly Questions to the Old Testament.* JSOTSup 94. Sheffield: Sheffield Academic Press.

Collins, J. 1997. "A Syntactical Note (Genesis 3:15): Is the Woman's Seed Singular or Plural?" *TynB* 48:139–48.

Dumbrell, W. J. 2002. "Genesis 2:1–17: A Foreshadowing of the New Creation." In *Biblical Theology: Retrospect and Prospect.* Ed. S. J. Hafemann. Downers Grove, Ill.: InterVarsity Press. Pp. 53–65.

Ellington, J. 1979. "Man and Adam in Genesis 1–5." *BT* 30:201–5.

Firmage, E. 1999. "Genesis 1 and the Priestly Agenda." *JSOT* 82:97–114.

Foh, S. T. 1975. "What Is the Woman's Desire?" *WTJ* 37:376–83.

Hasel, G. F. 1971. "Recent Translations of Gen 1,1." *BT* 22:154–68.

———. 1972. "The Significance of the Cosmology in Genesis 1 in Relation to Ancient Near Eastern Parallels." *AUSS* 10:1–20.

———. 1974. "The Polemic Nature of the Genesis Cosmology," *EvQ* 46:81–102.

———. 1975. "The Meaning of 'Let Us' in Gn 1:26." *AUSS* 13:58–66.

Hauser, A. J. 1980. "Linguistic and Thematic Links between Genesis 4:1–16 and Genesis 2–3." *JETS* 23:297–305.

———. 1982. "Genesis 2–3: The Theme of Intimacy and Alienation." In *Art and Meaning: Rhetoric in Biblical Literature.* Ed. D. J. A. Clines et al. JSOTSup 19. Sheffield: JSOT Press. Pp. 20–36.

Hess, R. S. 1992–1993. "The Roles of the Woman and Man in Genesis 3." *Themelios* 3:15–19.

Higgins, J. M. 1976. "The Myth of Eve: The Temptress." *JAAR* 44:639–47.

Hoffmeier, J. K. 1983. "Some Thoughts on Genesis 1–2 and Egyptian Cosmology." *JANES* 15:34–49.

Hyers, C. 1984. *The Meaning of Creation.* Atlanta: John Knox.

Jobling, D. 1978. "A Structural Analysis of Genesis 2:4b–3:24." *SBL Abstracts* 1:61–69.

Joines, K. R. 1974. *Serpent Symbolism in the Old Testament.* Haddonfield, N.J.: Haddonfield House.

Kaiser, W. C. 1975. "The Serpent in Genesis 3." *ZAW* 87:1–11.

———. 1978. *Toward an Old Testament Theology.* Grand Rapids: Zondervan.

Kikawada, I. M. 1972. "Two Notes on Eve." *JBL* 91:33–37.

Kimelman, R. 1996. "The Seduction of Eve and the Exegetical Politics of Gender." *BibInt* 4:1–39.

Levenson, J. D. 1988. *Creation and the Persistence of Evil.* San Francisco: Harper & Row.

Martin, R. A. 1965. "The Earliest Messianic Interpretation of Genesis 3:15." *JBL* 84:425–27.

Mendenhall, G. E. 1974. "The Shady Side of Wisdom: The Date and Purpose of Genesis 3." In *A Light unto My Path: Old Testament Studies in Honor of Jacob H. Myers.* Ed. H. N. Bream et al. Gettysburg Theological Studies 4. Philadelphia: Temple University Press. Pp. 319–34.

Middleton, J. R. 2004. "Created in the Image of a Violent God? The Ethical Problem of the Conquest of Chaos in Biblical Creation Texts." *Int* 58:341–55.

Miller, J. M. 1972. "In the 'Image' and 'Likeness' of God." *JBL* 91:289–304.

Moberly, R. W. L. 1988. "Did the Serpent Get It Right?" *JTS* 39:1–27. Repr., in *From Eden to Golgotha: Essays in Biblical Theology.* South Florida Studies in the History of Judaism 52. Atlanta: Scholars Press, 1992. Pp. 1–27.

Moran, W. L. 1970. "The Creation of Man in Atrahasis I, 192–248." *BASOR* 200:48–56.

Naidoff, B. 1978. "A Man to Work the Soil: A New Interpretation of Genesis 2–3." *JSOT* 5:2–14.

Nielsen, E. 1972. "Creation and the Fall of Man: A Cross-Disciplinary Investigation." *HUCA* 43:1–22.

Nixon, R. 1994. "Images of the Creator in Genesis 1 and 2." *Theology* 97:188–97.

Phipps, W. E. 1976. "Adam's Rib: Bone of Contention." *Theology Today* 33:263–73.

Pinnock, C. H. 1989. "Climbing Out of a Swamp: The Evangelical Struggle to Understand the Creation Texts." *Int* 43:143–55.

Provan, I. 2001. "Creation and Holistic Ministry: A Study of Genesis 1:1–2:3." *ERT* 25:292–303.

Ramsey, G. W. 1988. "Is Name-Giving an Act of Domination in Genesis 2:23 and Elsewhere?" *CBQ* 50:24–35.

Ruger, H. P. 1976. "On Some Versions of Genesis 3:15, Ancient and Modern." *BT* 27:105–10.

Ryken, L. 1974. *The Literature of the Bible.* Grand Rapids: Zondervan. Pp. 33–42.

Sailhamer, J. 1996. *Genesis Unbound: A Provocative New Look at the Creation Account.* Sisters, Ore.: Multnomah.

Sawyer, J. 1974. "The Meaning of 'In the Image of Elohim,' in Genesis I–X." *JTS* 25:418–26.

Shea, W. H. 1977. "Adam in Ancient Mesopotamian Traditions." *AUSS* 15:27–41.

Sterchi, D. A. 1996. "Does Genesis 1 Provide a Chronological Sequence?" *JETS* 39:529–36.

Stitzinger, M. F. 1981. "Genesis 1–3 and the Male/Female Relationship." *Grace Theological Journal* 2:23–44.

Stott, J. R. W. 1965. "The Subtlety of Satan." *CT* 9:740–44.

Stratton, B. J. 1995. *Out of Eden: Reading, Rhetoric, and Ideology in Genesis 2–3.* JSOTSup 208. Sheffield: Sheffield Academic Press.

Thompson, P. 1971. "The Yahwist Creation Story." *VT* 21:197–208.

Toews, B. G. 2002. "Genesis 1–4: The Genesis of Old Testament Instruction." In *Biblical Theology: Retrospect and Prospect.* Ed. S. J. Hafemann. Downers Grove, Ill.: InterVarsity Press. Pp. 38–52.

Trible, P. 1972. "Eve and Adam: Genesis 2–3 Reread." *Andover Newton Quarterly* 14:251–58.

———. 1978. *God and the Rhetoric of Sexuality.* OBT. Philadelphia: Fortress.

Vogels, W. 1996. "The Power Struggle between Man and Woman (Gen 3, 16b)." *Bib* 77:197–209.

———. 1998. "Like One of Us, Knowing *tob* and *raᶜ* (Gen. 3:22)." *Semeia* 81:145–57.

Walsh, J. T. 1977. "Genesis 2:4b–3:24: A Synchronic Approach." *JBL* 96:161–77.

Waltke, B. 1975. "The Creation Account in Genesis 1:1–3." *BSac* 132:25–36, 136–44, 216–28, 327–42.

Weinfeld, M. 1981. "Sabbath, Temple, and the Enthronement of the Lord: The Problem of the Sitz-im-Leben of Genesis 1:1–2:3." In *Mélanges bibliques et orientaux en l'honneur de M. Henri Cazelles.* Ed. A. Caquot and M. Delcor. AOAT 212. Kevelaer: Butzon & Bercker; Neukirchen-Vluyn: Neukirchener Verlag. Pp. 501–12.

Westermann, C. 1974. *Creation.* Trans. J. J. Scullion. Philadelphia: Fortress.

Wifall, W. 1974a. "The Breath of His Nostrils: Gen. 2:7b." *CBQ* 36:237–40.

———. 1974b. "Genesis 3:15—A Protoevangelium?" *CBQ* 36:361–65.

Williams, A. J. 1977. "The Relationship of Genesis 3:20 to the Serpent." *ZAW* 89:357–74.

Williams, J. G. 1981. "Genesis 3." *Int* 35:274–79.

Wolde, E. van. 1998. "The Creation of Coherence [Genesis 1–3]." *Semeia* 81:159–74.

Woudstra, M. H. 1971. "Recent Translations of Genesis 3:15." *CTJ* 6:194–203.

Wright, D. P. 1996. "Holiness, Sex, and Death in the Garden of Eden." *Bib* 77:305–29.

Wyatt, N. 1981. "Interpreting the Creation and Fall Story in Genesis 1–2." *ZAW* 93:10–21.

2

The Sequence after Creation and the Fall

GENESIS 4–11

Genesis 3 sets in motion a series of events that have their roots in the activities in Eden. In ch. 3 the man and the woman sin and thereby violate a vertical relationship: communion with God. In chs. 4–11 people violate a horizontal relationship: fellowship with others. The movement, then, is from cause to effect. What all these malignant activities have in common (Genesis 3–11) is a demonstration of the human desire to be like God. Having once overstepped the limits imposed by God, humankind subsequently surrenders its standards. The results are:

1. fratricide engendered by jealousy—4:8, Cain kills Abel
2. polygamy and retaliation—4:23–24, Lamech
3. titanic lust—6:1–4, sons of God and daughters of men
4. corruption and violence in the earth—6:5, 11–12
5. incest (?)—9:20–27, the curse on Canaan
6. a city with a tower to the heavens—11:1–9, Babel

Undoubtedly the spread of sin is described in these chapters, as these six events testify. In the description of ch. 3, however, we observed a mixture of sin and grace, a divine word of both judgment and promise.

I suggest that the same dual emphases continue throughout chs. 4–11. We will see in operation both sin and judgment and grace and promise. Neither the sin of individuals (Cain, Lamech, and Ham) nor of groups (sons of God and daughters of men, the whole earth, and the builders of the city and the tower) eclipses completely the mercy and sovereignty of God. Here too, where sin abounds, grace much more abounds.

Fratricide (4:8)

Obviously, there is no break between chs. 3 and 4 of Genesis. The narrative is to be read as a continuous whole. This continuity is emphasized by the repetition in both chapters of key vocabulary: for example, "and they knew that they were naked" (3:7 NRSV) and "Now Adam knew Eve his wife" (4:1 KJV); "your desire shall be for your husband" (3:16 NRSV) and "sin is crouching at the door; its desire is for you" (4:7 RSV); "and he shall rule over you" (3:16 RSV) and "but you must master it" (4:7 NRSV [the same Hebrew verb as "rule" in 3:16]); "he drove out the man" (3:24 NRSV) and "today you have driven me away from the soil" (4:14 NRSV); "and at the east of the garden of Eden he placed the cherubim" (3:24 NRSV) and "then Cain . . . dwelt in the land of Nod, east of Eden" (4:16 RSV).

Interestingly, but not without later parallel, history's first recorded crime of inhumanity has its context in an act of worship. Two brothers, apparently acting spontaneously, bring to the Lord an offering. Cain offers part of his agricultural produce. Abel, the second-born, presents one of the firstlings of his flock. From here on the story is well known. God accepts the offering of Abel but rejects that of Cain. Unable to graciously accept God's decision on the matter, Cain gives way to sulking and anger, and eventually he kills his own brother.

The intriguing question is why the Lord accepted the offering of Abel but refused that of Cain. Was it because Abel's offering involved a blood sacrifice? But the Old Testament allows for nonblood sacrifices when such sacrifices are not primarily expiatory (Leviticus 2; and Lev. 5:11–13 even allows the substitution of fine flour for doves or pigeons for a sin offering in certain circumstances). Even the Hebrew word for Cain's "offering" is the same as for the "cereal offering" of Leviticus 2.

Did Abel present his best, while Cain offered only what was conveniently available? Is the difference one of attitude in that Abel offered his by faith (Heb. 11:4)? Was Cain's offering rejected because it was not matched by an inner righteousness (1 John 3:12; Jude 11)? Perhaps this idea is hinted at in God's question to Cain, "If you do well, will you not be accepted?" (Gen. 4:7 NRSV). Several times, especially in prophetic literature, we are informed that God's reason for rejecting a sacrifice or an offering was that religious ritual had become a substitute for obedience and holy living.

Can we move backward from the prophets to the incident in Genesis 4 and assume the same inconsistency in the life of Cain that the prophets saw in the lives of their contemporaries? In light of God's question to Cain in Gen. 4:7, I am inclined to say yes, but one cannot be dogmatic here. Is the Bible perhaps not as wise in its reservations as it is in its revelations?

There is another possible explanation of why God rejected Cain's offering, and the advantage of this approach is that it unites chs. 3 and 4. (It is common among interpreters to suggest that originally the story of Cain and Abel was separate from the story of Adam and Eve, and the two later were joined only by a fictional genealogy—for why is Cain afraid that whoever finds him will kill him [4:14], and where did his wife [4:17] come from, if at the time he and his parents were the only living humans on the planet?) As Herion (1995) and Spina (1992) have observed, the context of chs. 2 and 3 suggests that God rejected Cain's offering because Cain offered a gift from the very ground that God had just cursed (3:17). If it is wrong to offer to God what costs the offerer nothing (2 Sam. 24:24), it is also wrong to offer to God that which bears the consequences of God's curse.

After his sin Cain has the opportunity to talk with God. The dialogue swiftly degenerates into sarcasm on Cain's part. He answers God's question "Where is Abel your brother?" with a question of his own: "Am I my brother's keeper?" (Gen. 4:9 RSV).

The answer to Cain's question is an emphatic no. God never meant for Cain, or anybody, to be his brother's keeper. "To keep" means "to control, to regulate and rule"—"the Lord God took the man and put him in the garden . . . to . . . keep it" (Gen. 2:15 NRSV). Zoos, bees, and prisons have keepers. Here activities must be regulated and supervised. Not without reason is God consistently called in Scripture "Israel's keeper." That is his role, for he is their Lord. Cain indeed was called to love and respect his brother, but never was he called to keep his brother.

As with Adam and Eve, the punishment for Cain is banishment or exile from the presence of the Lord (4:16). But again as with Adam and Eve, there is a manifestation of mercy just prior to the manifestation of judgment. Before Adam and Eve are expelled (3:22–24), they are provided with clothing (3:21). Before Cain is expelled (4:16), God places a mark (on his forehead?) to spare him from becoming the victim of someone's vengeance (4:15). As David J. A. Clines (1978: 63) has noted, "God's grace . . . is not only revealed in and after the judgment, but even *before* the execution of judgment."

We cannot be sure of the nature of Cain's mark. As a mark that grants protection, it finds parallels with (1) the blood on the houses that grants protection to the occupants from danger on the first Passover in Egypt (Exod. 12:13); (2) the mark on the foreheads of those who grieve and lament over Jerusalem's collapse and God's departure from it (Ezek. 9:4); and (3) the seal on the forehead of the 144,000 faithful (Rev. 7:3). In light of the fact that one of the very first things that Cain does when he departs is build a city (4:17), Sailhamer (1990: 62) suggests that Cain's mark might be the city he built. As such, Cain's city would be the first "city of refuge" (cf. Num. 35:9–15; Deut. 4:41–43; 19:1–10; Josh. 20:1–9). These are asylum cities where someone who commits homicide can be protected from blood vengeance until a trial can determine whether the killing was accidental or deliberate. Cain's homicide seems, however, to be an intentional act. This is seen plainly in the text, particularly in one Hebrew expression: Cain "rose up against" (*qûm ʾel*) his brother (4:8 NRSV). Deuteronomy 19:11 (right after the "cities of refuge" section [19:1–10]) turns to the matter of intentional murder. It describes the actions of such criminals with these words: "If out of hate someone assaults [*qûm ʿāl*, lit., 'rises up against'] and kills a neighbor"—the exact expression used with Cain, except for the insignificant change of the preposition after the verb.

Polygamy and Retaliation (4:23–24)

For the first but not the last time God's pattern of one man for one woman and one woman for one man breaks down. No particular verse in the Old Testament prohibits polygamy, but the crucial point is that there is hardly any polygamist whose life is not extremely complicated and bruised. Witness Abraham with Hagar and Sarah, or Jacob with Leah and Rachel, or the fiascoes in the lives of David and Solomon.

Added to Lamech's violation of the marriage pattern is his unchecked penchant for revenge and violence. He glories in macabre statistics (4:23–24).

It is something of a paradox that the descendants of Cain emerge as the heralds of culture and industry (4:21–22), specifically, farming and herding (Jabal), music (Jubal), and metallurgy (Tubal-cain). All are sons of Lamech.

Yet none of these novelties, however noble they may be, restrains humankind's diabolical tendencies. The announcement of this cultural history comes between the account of Lamech's polygamy and his spiteful song of revenge. Secular culture, then, is advanced by the line of

Cain, but it is through the line of Seth (4:25–5:32) that God's plan of redemption will move.

Nothing is said about the life span of the descendants of Cain (4:17–22), but for each of the descendants of Seth (5:1–32) a life span is given, and in each case one that is spectacularly long. It is not wide of the mark, I believe, to interpret both the notation of life span and the longevity of those life spans as a reflection of God's unique blessing on the seed of Seth, as opposed to the seed of Cain. To be sure, none of them escaped death, with the exception of Enoch (5:24), for the possibility of "living forever" ceased with the announcement in Gen. 3:22—if, in fact, it ever existed. Still, the sons of Seth were "being fruitful, multiplying, and filling the earth." Not only does the notice about life span distinguish the line of Seth from that of Cain, but so also does the constant inclusion of the refrain "and he had other sons and daughters" for the representative Sethites.

The tenth individual in the Sethite genealogy is Noah. His name is connected here with the verb "bring relief or comfort" (5:29). This word is the same Hebrew verb, but in a different form, used in Gen. 6:6–7 to express God's regret and repentance in regard to the creation and behavior of humankind. Father Lamech predicts—the source of his foreknowledge is not revealed—that his son Noah "shall bring relief from our work and from the toil of our hands because of the ground which the LORD hath cursed" (5:29 KJV).

The language in this verse is reminiscent of language in Gen. 3:17: "cursed is the ground [in 5:29, too] because of you; in toil [the same word as the 'toil' of 5:29] you shall eat of it" (NRSV). The curse placed in Adam's time is now to be lifted, or significantly diminished, in the tenth generation. Genesis 3:17 gives way to Gen. 5:29. A new day is dawning.

The "Sons of God" and the "Daughters of Men" (6:1–4)

Few passages in Scripture have appeared so enigmatic to the interpreter as Gen. 6:1–4. The thorniest problem is the identification of the "sons of God" and "daughters of men." Again we note that the Scriptures introduce these two groups without fanfare or explanation. No commentary on their origin or specific identification is offered.

Three possibilities for the identification of the villains and victims in the story enjoy popularity among the commentators. First, a number of both modern and ancient exegetes see in the "sons of God" a reference to the descendants of Seth, and in the "daughters of men" a reference to the descendants of Cain. The particular sin is an unfortunate inter-

mingling in marriage between the godly Sethite line and the ungodly
Cainite line.

The immediate advantage of this explanation is that it takes cogni-
zance of the material in the immediately preceding chapters, especially
chs. 4 and 5, in which the line of Cain is contrasted with the line of
Seth. Furthermore, there are some explicit parallels in the activities of
Sethites and Cainites and the two groups mentioned in Gen. 6:1–4. For
example, the sudden mention of "daughters of men" (6:2) possibly finds
its antecedent in the daughters of the various Sethites, the only other
reference so far in Scripture to daughters (5:4, 7, 10, 13, 16, 19, 22, 26,
30). Another example of parallelism might be found in the sons of God
"taking wives" for themselves (6:2), and the Cainite Lamech, who "took
two wives" (4:19).

Pursuing these parallels, however, one quickly observes that they
equate the sons of God with the Cainites (the Cainite Lamech took wives
for himself, as did the sons of God for themselves), and the daughters of
men with the Sethites—the reverse of a time-honored explanation (see
Eslinger 1979: 65–73). The objection has been made that this theory
is untenable because it must posit one meaning for "man" in 6:1 (humankind in general) and another, restricted meaning for "man" in 6:2
(either Sethites or Cainites). In response I note that it is possible for one
word to assume several distinctive meanings within one chapter. I cite
as an example 2 Samuel 7—the institution of the Davidic covenant—in
which "house" has four different nuances. "House" designates a temple
in vv. 5, 6, 7, 13; a palace in vv. 1, 2; a dynasty in vv. 11, 16, 19, 25, 26,
27, 29; and reputation or status in v. 18.

A second interpretation of the narrative suggests that the sons of God
are ancient dynastic rulers, and the daughters of men are their royal
harems, as inviting to the rulers as was the forbidden fruit to Eve (see
Kline 1962; 1978). This interpretation moves the identification from
Cainites and Sethites to something more ambiguous: a group of regal
individuals whose existence has not yet been mentioned in the opening chapters of Scripture. Presumably, if the sons of God are heads of
state, the narrative then would refer to a limited number of individuals. And yet God's penalty is aimed at humankind. We then would be
faced with the imbalance between sin in limited places—but in high
places—and judgment that will reach almost cosmic proportions. This
is not impossible, however. Witness the seventy thousand who died in
Israel because of the sin of their monarch David at the taking of the
census (2 Sam. 24:15, 17).

A third interpretation suggests that the sons of God are angels. The
expression "sons of God" is indeed a name for the angelic host in Job
1:6; 2:1; 38:7; Ps. 29:1; 89:6. The sin then is cohabitation between super-

natural and natural beings. Some support for this may be found in Jude 6 and 7 (perhaps also 1 Pet. 3:19–20; 2 Pet. 2:4). If the function of Jude 7 is to compare the immorality and unnatural lust of Sodom and Gomorrah with similar behavior of the angels mentioned in Jude 6, then much credence is lent to this interpretation. On the other hand, if the purpose of Jude 6 and 7 is to provide two illustrations of divine judgment on different forms of sin at the angelic level and the human level, then these two verses have no bearing on Gen. 6:1–4.

Moreover, the reference in Genesis does not appear to be to rape or the indulgence of unbridled lust, but to marriage: "and they took to wife such of them as they chose" (RSV). The sin is not sexual violation, but the establishment of an illicit marital relationship in which the two partners cannot possibly become one flesh. And Jesus reminds us that angels do not marry (Mark 12:25).

It has been suggested that the most serious flaw in this explanation is that the perpetrators of the crime are nonhuman beings, but the recipients of judgment are human beings: "My spirit shall not abide in mortals forever, for they are flesh; their days shall be one hundred twenty years" (NRSV). Although the explanation that the passage refers to angels or divine beings may have some attendant problems, the preceding criticism is not all that forceful. For if we are prepared to decipher an inconsistency and non sequitur here, what will we do with the next few verses in Genesis 6: "The wickedness of humankind was great. . . . The Lord was sorry that he had made humankind. . . . 'I will blot out human beings . . . people and beasts and creeping things and birds of the air'" (6:5–7)? The criminals are human beings. The victims are both humans and animals.

Can we detect here, however faint, a voice of grace? I suggest that we can hear that voice, and the clue is to be found in 6:3: "but their days shall be a hundred and twenty years." Once again the interpretation of this part of v. 3 is anything but unanimous. There are two possibilities. The 120 years refers either to the diminished life span that God will now impose on humankind or to a period of grace (preceding the flood) in which God's hand of judgment will be restrained.

Either way, it appears to me that the notation suggests grace. If the reference is to the former—a shorter life span—then it is obvious that this enforcement is not immediate but long-range. Noah, introduced before this episode, lives for 950 years. Abraham's father, Terah, lives for 205 years, and Abraham himself lives for 175 years. In the Book of Genesis only Joseph fails to surpass the 120-year maximum. God had told Adam that if he ate the forbidden fruit, he would die. He ate, but he did not die immediately.

On the other hand, if the reference is to a period of respite in which God voluntarily restrains himself—an interpretation that I find quite natural—then again grace is easy to discern. A parallel to that exercise of self-restraint on the part of God is Jonah's message to Nineveh: "Yet forty days, and Nineveh shall be overthrown!" (Jon. 3:4 RSV). The best parallel is in the New Testament, 2 Thessalonians 2. Before the coming of Jesus Christ will be the coming of "the man of lawlessness." The withdrawal of the restraint on this "son of perdition" will release him from his confinement. Until now, however, he is being held in check. Thus the opportunity to receive and offer grace is available.

The Flood (6:5, 11–12)

Paramount in this whole section is the description of the flood. Two well-preserved extrabiblical accounts of an ancient flood are from Mesopotamia: the Gilgamesh Epic and the Atrahasis Epic. Several English translations of these epics, and of other ancient Near Eastern texts, are available in sources such as (1) J. B. Pritchard, ed., *Ancient Near Eastern Texts Relating to the Old Testament* (3rd ed., with supplement; Princeton, N.J.: Princeton University Press, 1969); (2) W. Beyerlin, ed., *Near Eastern Texts Relating to the Old Testament* (Philadelphia: Westminster, 1978); (3) John Walton, *Ancient Israelite Literature in Its Cultural Context: A Survey of Parallels between Biblical and Ancient Near Eastern Texts* (Grand Rapids: Zondervan, 1990); (4) Victor H. Matthews and D. C. Benjamin, *Old Testament Parallels: Laws and Stories from the Ancient Near East* (2nd ed.; New York: Paulist Press, 1997); (5) W. W. Hallo and K. Lawson Younger, eds., *The Context of Scripture: Monumental Inscriptions from the Biblical World* (3 vols.; Leiden: Brill, 1997–2002); (6) B. T. Arnold and B. E. Beyer, *Readings from the Ancient Near East: Primary Sources for Old Testament Study* (Grand Rapids: Baker, 2001).

The Gilgamesh Epic

Named after Gilgamesh, king of Uruk (Erech in Gen. 10:10) around 2600 B.C., this epic dates to approximately 1600 B.C., according to Thorkild Jacobsen. Gilgamesh is a tyrannical and brutal king, causing deep resentments among his subjects. In order to topple him the people solicit one of their gods to create an antagonist. The one formed is named Enkidu. He is "humanized" or "civilized" only after a week-long spirited orgy with a prostitute. A fight follows between Enkidu and Gilgamesh. It produces neither a victor nor a victim. Rather, the combatants become colleagues, battling all sorts of celestial, maleficent monsters. In the process the mortal Gilgamesh is proposed to by none other than the stunning goddess Ishtar, but he spurns her, primarily because of her poor record in marital fidelity!

Because of effrontery to Ishtar, Enkidu dies, setting off a pathological fear of death in Gilgamesh's own life. His mind is at least clear enough to recall that one of his ancestors, Utnapishtim, had bypassed death and gained immortality. If Gilgamesh can find Utnapishtim, maybe he can learn the secret and save his own life. A tortuous trip through the various parts of the underworld follows. At last he meets Utnapishtim. And this is the story that Utnapishtim tells Gilgamesh.

One day the god Ea tells Utnapishtim that Enlil was preparing to destroy humankind with a flood. Utnapishtim, if he is wise, should build a boat, upon which he is to take members of his family, cattle, some valuables, and professional sailors. The storm begins, and it continues for seven days and nights, only to have Utnapishtim's boat snag on a mountaintop. After the abating of the waters, he leaves his boat and worships his gods. Subsequently it comes to Enlil's attention that two mortals have escaped drowning. To finish his job of ridding the earth of humankind, he confers immortality on Utnapishtim and his wife.

But Utnapishtim's experience is unique and thus produces further chagrin for Gilgamesh. After additional frustrating experiences, Gilgamesh returns to his home of Uruk, resigned to reality. Denied personal immortality, he will at least live on in the minds of his people through impressive Uruk, which he has built. Immortality thus is the work of his hands.

The Atrahasis Epic

I have already traced the Atrahasis Epic through the account of creation. After their creation, humans multiply so swiftly and make so much noise that Enlil has insomnia. He plans to reduce the population with a plague. Suddenly Atrahasis is introduced, who, with the guidance of his god Enki, manages to have the plague averted.

The problem is rectified, but after twelve hundred years the land is "bellowing like a bull." Enlil's plan this time is a drought, and once more Atrahasis intercedes and has the drought brought to a speedy end by placating the offended deity. Then the cycle starts a third time, and the punishment this time is a renewal of the drought.

Exasperated that this does not work either, Enlil orders a flood. What follows is much like the Gilgamesh Epic, except that the hero is Atrahasis, not Gilgamesh. On Enki's advice Atrahasis builds a boat to weather the storm, destined to last seven days and nights. So devastating was the storm and so thorough was the annihilation of humanity that even the gods had serious questions about the sagacity of Enlil's plan.

After disembarking, Atrahasis, like Utnapishtim, offers a sacrifice to the gods for his preservation, and none too soon, for they have been without food for the duration of the flood. Their source of food, the food sacrifices of mortals, has been dissipated.

Permanent countermeasures are then invoked that will put a ceiling on the ever-increasing world population. The plan is birth control: the creation of some permanently barren women, the creation of a demon whose function is to "snatch the baby away from the lap of her who bore it," and the creation of several categories of priestesses for whom childbearing is prohibited.

The Epics Compared

A comparison of the Gilgamesh Epic and the Atrahasis Epic with Genesis 6–9 clearly shows similarities in details regarding the catastrophic flood. Does this mean, however, that the Hebrews borrowed and then edited the story from Mesopotamian literature, with only the names changed to protect the innocent? Could not stories be shared by the Bible and surrounding cultures because they are both based on a historical event? Both Scripture and Mesopotamian literature mention a flood because there indeed was a flood.

If so, it is just as interesting, if not more so, to contrast as to compare how two different traditions handled the same material, the same event. Such a contrast reveals crucial differences in mentality and worldview. One of the benefits to the believer who reads mythology is insight into how ancient people answered ultimate questions about life without the light of revelation.

For example, the Gilgamesh Epic is virtually silent about a motive for the flood. The only pertinent line is "That city was ancient, [as were] the gods within it / When their heart led the great gods to produce the flood." After the flood Ea remonstrates with Enlil: "Thou wisest of gods, thou hero, How couldst thou, unreasoning, bring on the deluge? On the sinner impose his sin, on the transgressor impose his transgression!" (11:179–181). In the Atrahasis Epic it is the noise of the multitudes that triggers Enlil's anger and vengeance. And most cuneiform specialists are convinced that the words used for noise indicate simply that, not moral turbulence.

Enlil, then, acts out of anger, selfishness, and capriciousness. His judgment is totally punitive; for the masses this judgment certainly is not therapeutic. But can one of the pantheon impose a catastrophe on humankind because of the sins of the latter? After all, the gods themselves fall short of being pure.

Also, it is equally difficult to discern a reason why one mortal is saved. In the Gilgamesh Epic it is Ea who warns Utnapishtim of Enlil's scheme, and in the other it is the divine Enki who informs Atrahasis. Again the closest that the literature comes to a saving of one who is righteous is in the Sumerian account of the deluge. There, the one saved from drowning is Ziusudra, a pious, reverent king, although even here the nexus between his character and his salvation is not underscored.

Furthermore, the dimensions of the ship built by the heroes are strange: "equal shall be her width and her length"—that is, cubic, as later lines in the epic confirm. Along with his family and animals, the hero takes aboard professional sailors. It is human skill and ingenuity that will keep this ship afloat. In addition, Utnapishtim takes aboard copious amounts of silver and gold, a little nest egg with which to start over if indeed he ever emerges from this nightmare alive.

Finally, both pagan stories lack a clear didactic function. What are they trying to say, and what is the significance of their theme? Does either story intricately involve the reader? The concern of the Gilgamesh Epic is more with Gilgamesh than with Utnapishtim, and more with the former's epic wanderings than the latter's escape from drowning. One might conceivably extract from the story this principle: be satisfied with what you have and where you are, and do not try to overstep your limits (Genesis 3?). Precious little, however, in the dialogue of the text firmly establishes this.

The ending of the Atrahasis Epic is even more dour. Having failed three times, Enlil delivers an ultimatum: close the wombs, let any births be stillbirths, impose celibacy. Obviously, this is not a note designed to engender respect in mortals for their gods—fear and suspicion, perhaps, but not love and trust.

The Epics Contrasted with the Genesis Account

Something of the uniqueness of the biblical account can be demonstrated by pursuing the aforementioned four points of contrast into the deluge story in Genesis.

Genesis affirms that the impetus for the flood comes from the sin of humankind. Enough of this has been indicated in the narratives of chs. 3–5 and the first four verses of ch. 6. To this will be added: "the wickedness of humankind was great in the earth, . . . every inclination of the thoughts of their hearts was only evil continually" (6:5 NRSV); "now the earth was corrupt . . . filled with violence" (6:11 NRSV); "all flesh had corrupted their way upon the earth" (6:12 RSV).

Although it cannot be reflected in English translation, in the Hebrew text the "corrupt" of vv. 11 and 12 (2x) is built from the same Hebrew root as the "I will destroy" of v. 13b. Is this one way by which God destroys? Rather than interrupt and impede, he allows the evil started by humankind to run to its inevitable conclusion. Note, for example, "The iniquity of the Amorites is not yet complete" (Gen. 15:16 NRSV). Similarly, the apostle Paul, in speaking of the expression of God's wrath against sin, uses the expression "God gave them up" (Rom. 2:24, 26, 28), surely more passive than active, more gentle than raging.

Yet, lest we draw the conclusion that God is simply an unmoved spectator of this morass, we must note that God himself suffers emotional pain: God was "grieved" (Gen. 6:6). How interesting that the Hebrew word here for "pain" in the phrase "and his heart was filled with pain" (NIV) is from the same root as the word for the "pain" that Eve will experience in childbirth (3:16) and that the man will confront in his working and attempting to make productive the soil (3:17). Humankind's pain has become God's pain! Of course, the pain of the man and the woman is quite physical and an unfortunate consequence of their own misbehavior. God's pain is the pain of disappointment over the misconduct of humankind. It is significant that God's first response in Genesis 6 to pervasive sinfulness in his creation is not rage or indignation, but brokenness.

Noah is not spared on the basis of capriciousness or favoritism. On the contrary, he "was a righteous man, blameless . . . Noah walked with God" (6:9 NRSV; cf. 7:1). Character, either way, does determine destiny.

To be more precise, Noah is told to build not a boat, but an ark (6:14), more a chest than a ship. Its dimensions (approximately 450 ft. x 75 ft. x 45 ft.), far from being nonsensical, are quite worthy of a seagoing vessel. No sailors accompany Noah aboard, nor is there reference to any type of navigational equipment (unless one counts the window in the ceiling through which to see the stars, or the birds as the mariner's homing pigeons). Salvation will be from God alone. No material possessions are to be packed away either. Noah is no more entitled to this than was Achan.

Far from being a hair-raising but irrelevant story sung around campfires in generations to come, the deluge story relates profoundly to successive generations. First of all there is a retraction by God of the curse placed on the ground (8:21; cf. 3:17), evidenced by the story of Noah's vineyard, in itself a verification of the abrogation of the curse (9:20–29). Connecting 8:21 with 6:5, Gerhard von Rad (1972: 123) observes, "v. 21 is one of the most remarkable theological statements in the Old Testament: it shows the pointed and concentrated way in which the Yahwist can express himself at decisive points. The same condition which in the prologue [6:5] is the basis for God's judgment in the epilogue reveals God's grace and providence. The contrast between God's punishing anger and his supporting grace . . . is here presented . . . as an adjustment by God towards man's sinfulness."

This promise is then followed by the institution of a covenant with Noah in ch. 9. What God had once said to Adam (1:28), he now says to Noah (9:1). Thus, there is a second start, a second chance for humankind, albeit with qualifications (9:2–6).

What this covenant does is establish not uniqueness, but precedence. Noah is the first in a series of persons with whom God is making this commitment. What is unrepeatable is the flood (9:11). This covenant is God's responsibility at the point of maintenance. Note that the rainbow in the sky is for God's benefit (9:12–17). God almighty writes himself a memo! Such is the extension of this story into the lives of its readers.

Two Flood Stories?

I have had previous occasion to draw attention to the documentary hypothesis of source critics in dealing with the creation account. Genesis 6–9 is an example thought to substantiate once and for all the validity of this approach. A surface reading of Genesis 6–9, say the source critics, demonstrates palpably that these four chapters are not a homogeneous work. Several observations are culled to buttress this idea.

The first category includes blatant inconsistencies. One of these is the number of animals that go aboard. According to 6:19–20; 7:9, 15 (all from P), the number is set at two of every kind, male and female. But 7:2 (J) says that Noah is to take with him "seven pairs" of clean animals, one pair of unclean animals, the male and his mate ("man" and "woman" are the words used here, as in 2:23).

A second example is the mention of conflicting durations for the flood. One section establishes the length as forty days and nights (7:4, 12, 17; 8:6 [all from J]). Another tradition has the flood lasting 150 days (7:24 [P]).

Another example is the nature of the flood. Was it rain from above (7:4, 12 [J]), or was it a bursting open of the subterranean waters (7:11 [P])?

The second category that the source critics cite is a distinctive shift in the use of the divine name. They list these examples:

a. 6:5: "the Lord saw"; also 6:6–8
b. 6:9: "Noah walked with God"; also 6:11, 12, 13, 22
a. 7:1: "the Lord said to Noah"; also 7:5

b. 7:9: "as God had commanded"; also 7:16a
a. 7:16b: "the Lord shut him in"
b. 8:1: "but God remembered Noah . . . God made a wind"; also 8:15
a. 8:20: "Noah built an altar to the Lord"; also 8:21
b. 9:1: "God blessed Noah"; also 9:6, 8, 12, 16, 17

A third category is that the account points to two different conclusions: (1) Noah's offering, God's inhaling of its pleasant odor, and the lifting of the curse on the ground (8:20–22 [J]); (2) God's blessings to Noah and the institution of the Noahic covenant (9:1–18 [P]).

The fourth category is that the account features two distinctive styles and modes of expression. For instance, God is at one time pictured very much in human terms—he repents, is grieved, inhales a sacrificial odor, has second thoughts; at another point in the story he is pictured as the completely otherworldly, all-powerful supernatural force standing over the world.

The conclusion drawn from all this is that originally there were two flood stories, one traceable to a writer or writers in approximately the tenth or early ninth centuries B.C. (the Yahwist), the other produced about four hundred years later (the Priestly account, ca. 550–450 B.C.). Subsequently the two stories were spliced together by an editor or editors. In the text as we have it, Genesis 6–9 can be divided this way:

6:5–8	J	7:12	J	8:3b–5	P
6:9–22	P	7:13–16a	P	8:6–12	J
7:1–5	J	7:16b–17	J	8:13a	P
7:6	P	7:18–21	P	8:13b	J
7:7–8	J	7:22–23	J	8:14–19	P
7:9	P	7:24–8:2a	P	8:20–22	J
7:10	J	8:2b–8:3a	J	9:1–17	P
7:11	P				

Not a few voices of protest have been raised against this division of the flood story, and for that matter the entire Pentateuch, into originally separate sources. The works of modern scholars such as Umberto Cassuto, Cyrus Gordon, and Kenneth Kitchen take the theory to task on several grounds. For Cassuto, such fragmentation of the pericope fails to do justice to the literary structure of the text. Heterogeneity raises more problems than it solves. For Gordon and Kitchen, source division is suspect on the grounds that similar phenomena exist in the ancient literature of the Mediterranean world, but to draw from this a multiple-source theory is ludicrous.

We may make the following observations, particularly concerning the flood section of Genesis.

First, some of the supposedly telltale evidences of confluence in the text may not be all that evident. Are "two pair" and "seven" mutually exclusive? Why cannot the "two" of 6:19–20 and 7:9, 15 be the standard number of animals (a male and female for breeding—even the unclean animals are preserved!) taken into the ark? "Seven" would apply only to sacrificial animals—that is, animals in a category by themselves. Is this solution any less probable than applying "two" to J and "seven" to P? Again, does the text indicate an inconsistency in the duration of the flood, forty versus 150 days? Was not the actual downpour forty days and nights, followed by five months (150 days) of rising water until the water level peaked?

Second, Scandinavian scholar Eduard Nielsen has called into question, on the basis of the principles of oral tradition, the splitting of the flood account. To illustrate, Nielsen points out that 7:9 is, on the multiple-source theory, from P. The reason? The name "God" occurs in this verse, a sure sign of P: "two and two . . . went into the ark with Noah, as God had commanded" (NRSV). But just a few verses later (7:15, ascribed by all critics also to P) exactly the same thing is said, "They went into the ark with Noah, two and two" (NRSV). Duplication in the same document! Anyone who is ready to explain v. 15 as an editorial insertion should first recall Nielsen's (1954: 98) rejoinder: "It is reassuring and sometimes necessary to have a Redactor up one's sleeve."

Third, on the basis of an examination of the grammatical structure of the text, Francis Andersen (1974: 124–26) is able to isolate and identify units that have been scissored by the source critics. Thus, grammatically, 7:6–17 is a unit with a distinct and clearly identifiable structure; yet the documentary hypothesis wants this section to seesaw from P to J and back at least seven times. As Andersen remarks, "If the documentary hypothesis is valid, some editor has put together scraps of parallel versions of the same story with scissors and paste, and yet has achieved a result which, from the point of view of discourse grammar, looks as if it has been made out of whole cloth."

Fourth, scholars such as B. W. Anderson and G. J. Wenham are convinced that in treating the text of the flood in Scripture we must go beyond the analytical probing (dissect the whole to recover the original parts), beyond the diachronic probing (how did the parts converge to form the whole?), to the synchronic dimensions of the text (what is observable about the final form of the text?). Thus, in scrutinizing the flood narrative, Anderson produces the overall interesting design shown in figure 3.

Figure 3

1. Violence in God's creation, 6:11–12
2. First divine address: resolution to destroy, 6:13–22
3. Second divine address: command to enter the ark, 7:1–10
4. Beginning of the flood, 7:11–16
5. The rising flood waters, 7:17–24

    God's Remembrance of Noah

6. The flood waters recede, 8:1–5
7. Drying of the earth, 8:6–14
8. Third divine address: command to leave the ark, 8:15–19
9. God's resolution to preserve order, 8:20–22
10. Fourth divine address: blessings and covenant, 9:1–17

From B. W. Anderson, "From Analysis to Synthesis: The Interpretation of Genesis 1–11," *JBL* 97 (1978): 38. Used by permission.

Anderson is not attempting to use this chart in any way to establish Genesis 6–9 as a unified work. It certainly does not rule out originally independent stories. But does not this smoothness in the account raise the possibility that Genesis 6–9 is from one source? After producing his own palistrophe on these chapters, Wenham (1978: 347–48) states, "The documentary hypothesis may yet be defended if one is prepared to posit a most ingenious and thorough redactor who blended J and P into a marvellous and coherent unity." But is that the more likely explanation? It is, to be sure, a possible explanation. But if we believe that Genesis 6–9 is the result of the editing of J and P together into the flood story, we surely cannot think that the redactor's work was poorly done and insensitive to blatant contradictions arising from such combining of sources. To do so would be to make the compiler into a postmodernist! And yet this is precisely what many a Genesis commentator has done. As Halpern (1995: 17) has suggested, to treat Genesis 6–9 as an arbitrary, irrational work of redaction is historically untenable in that it suggests that the editors of the Pentateuch were mentally inferior to modern philologians. It is also morally untenable "because the failure of the modern analyst to arrive at a hypothesis securing the dignity of the ancient writer is not evidence of a defect in the ancient editor."

The Curse on Canaan (9:20–27)

At least two problems are present here: the nature of the crime committed by Ham against his father, and why Noah placed a curse upon Ham's son Canaan, and not upon Ham himself.

It is true that the drunkenness of Noah is not made the focal point of any exhortation, even though the actions of Ham presumably would not have taken place if his father had been sober. When one recalls, however, that the two explicit incidents of drunkenness recorded in Genesis—here and Gen. 19:30–38—became occasions for the obnoxious, then perhaps the scenarios that follow each incident are sufficient commentary on overindulgence. (One might also compare Laban's giving to Jacob Leah instead of Rachel in Gen. 29:23. The text does not state how the father-in-law managed this deceit, but more than likely Jacob was so drunk by this time in the wedding celebration as to be unable to distinguish one sister from another. Notice that when he finally wakes up, he says to Laban: "What is this you have done to me?" [Gen. 29:25 NIV]. Compare that with "When Noah awoke from his wine and knew what his youngest son had done to him . . ." [Gen. 9:24 NRSV].)

Ham's sin is described in v. 22: "[he] saw the nakedness of his father" (NRSV). Is Ham's sin simply the accidental viewing of his naked father, which subsequently he related to his brothers? The text implies more, for upon awakening, Noah "knew what his youngest son *had done* to him." How he knew it was his youngest son we are not told.

The suggestion has been made (see Basset 1971) that Ham's sin was incest. While Noah was asleep, Ham had intercourse with his mother, and a child, Canaan, was produced by this incestuous relationship. This explains why Noah's curse is on Canaan. There are two other clarion instances in Genesis of incest: Reuben with his father's concubine (Gen. 35:22; 49:3–4), and Lot with his daughters, from which relationship sons are born (Gen. 19:30–38).

Support for this interpretation may be found in sections of the Pentateuch that deal with forbidden sexual relations. Leviticus 18 and 20 repeatedly use the phrase "you shall not uncover the nakedness of . . ." in dealing with cases of possible incest, and the relationship is always heterosexual, never homosexual. Thus, to uncover the nakedness of one's father is to have sexual intercourse with one's mother. The verb that is used consistently in these legal sections is "uncover" (see Gen. 9:21 for Noah, who was "uncovered" before the trespass), except for Lev. 20:17, which speaks of "seeing" the nakedness of one's sister.

Plausible as it is, this interpretation has three problems. First, the story in Genesis presupposes the birth of Canaan *before* the episode, not as a result of the episode, unless one is prepared to say that the reference to Canaan in 9:18 is an explanatory gloss by the narrator of Genesis that is without chronological significance. That is possible.

Second, taken at face value, the story suggests that Noah was made aware shortly after he recovered from his hangover of what Ham had done to him, and immediately he pronounced the curse on the grandson. The incest theory would necessitate Noah learning of his wife's pregnancy, the birth of Canaan nine months later, and the imprecation then put on Canaan.

The third weakness in this theory is that it fails to provide a rationale for the actions of Ham's two brothers, Shem and Japheth. What is involved in their "walking backward and covering the nakedness of their father"? And should we see any parallel between Shem and Japheth covering their father's nakedness with some kind of garment here and God covering Adam and Eve's nakedness with some kind of garment in 3:21? By explaining Ham's action as a case of incest, this can only mean that the brothers refrained from imitating their younger brother's folly.

The second major problem—why the grandson is cursed—also avoids a watertight solution. I have already mentioned one possibility in the preceding paragraphs: Canaan is the offspring of an incestuous relationship.

One can easily say (see von Rad 1972: 135) that the words "Ham, the father of" in vv. 18, 22 are later insertions by a redactor. This nicely eliminates the problem, but it does so by way of subjective deletion of parts of the text. It was Canaan who saw his (grand)father's nakedness, and thus it is he who is cursed.

Perhaps the curse is placed on Canaan because he is the youngest son of Ham (10:6), as Ham is the youngest son of Noah (9:24). We have already seen instances in our study of Genesis in which the innocent suffer because of the guilty: the ground is cursed because of Adam and Eve's sin; if the sons of God are angels, then it is humankind that is punished for the sin of the angels; most animals and birds are drowned in the flood because of the sins of humankind.

This is the only negative event in Genesis 3–11 in which God does not say a word. Or as an extension of that, this is the first time in Scripture that one person places a curse on another person. God has placed a curse, but now so does Noah.

In that word of Noah there is in addition to the curse a word of blessing. What have thus far been divine prerogatives are now assumed by a mortal. Noah's announcements must have as much validity and carry as much force as similar announcements made by God. By what logic could one understand blessings and curses in God's mouth as actual decisions but then limit the same words in Noah's mouth to simple wishes?

Noah's first word is to Shem: "Blessed be the LORD, the God of Shem" (RSV, alternate translation). Of special interest here is that for the first time in the Bible God is called the God of a particular individual, or the larger group that emerges from that individual. For a parallel to "the God of Shem" we will have to wait until we meet Abraham's servant speaking of "the God of my master Abraham" (Gen. 24:12, 42, 48).

Crucial to the interpretation of v. 27—"God enlarge Japheth, and let *him* dwell in the tents of Shem" (RSV)—is the identification of "him." Is the subject Japheth or God? Is Noah's prophecy one in which Japheth will dwell in the tents of Shem—that is, the gathering of Gentiles into the fold of God's people? Or is Noah's prophecy one in which God himself will dwell in the tents of Shem? The majority of ancient commentators identify "him" as God, while most contemporary writers opt for Japheth (but with little agreement on precisely what the phrase means).

Walter Kaiser (1978: 82) has argued, convincingly to my mind, for the translation "But he [God] will dwell in the tents of Shem." The prophecy may then be taken as a further narrowing of the family line through which God's plan of redemption and word of promise are transmitted. Ultimately, this family will produce Abraham.

The Tower at Babel (11:1–9)

Several of the incidents in Genesis 4–11 are bracketed by similar genealogical notes. The account of the sons of God and daughters of men (6:1–8) is preceded and followed by a note about Noah's three sons (5:32; 6:9–10). The flood account is surrounded by the same reference to Noah's progeny (6:9–10; 9:18–19). The tower of Babel incident has as its forerunner and follow-up the genealogy of Shem (10:21–31; 11:10–32).

There has been a strong emphasis on the east in these opening chapters of Genesis. The garden of Eden is in the east (2:8). At the east of the garden of Eden God placed the cherubim to block reentry to the garden (3:24). Cain dwells in the land of Nod, east of Eden (4:16). Several of Shem's descendants lived "in . . . the hill country of the east" (10:30 NRSV). This story about the tower opens with the migration of people from the east (11:2) to the plain of Shinar. Once again the geographical milieu of our story is placed outside of the land of Palestine.

The sin of the people does not lie in the desire to build a city, which is a neutral, amoral act. It is the motivation behind this undertaking that is most prominent: "Come, let us build *ourselves* a city, and a tower with *its top in the heavens,* and *let us make a name for ourselves*" (Gen. 11:4 NRSV). This is the pagan concept of immortality. Long after the demise of the artist, the sculptor, the poet, the musician, the architect, and the author, their memory will be perpetuated by their productions. Immortality is based on an achievement. One lives on in perpetuity because of his or her skills.

God does not embrace that idea, however. The narrative reports that the antics of these builders goaded God into action. Their titanic project grinds to a halt when God "confuses the language" and disperses those who insisted on becoming more sedentary. Babel (v. 9), "the gate of God," had instead become "Babbleville."

Miller (1978: 27–36) emphasizes that throughout Genesis 3–11 there is a correspondence between the nature of each sin and the nature of the judgment on that sin. For example, the serpent, who seduced Eve into eating what she was not supposed to eat, will have to eat dust for the remainder of its life. Cain, by vocation a farmer, for whom being settled is essential, now becomes a fugitive and a wanderer, thus ending his farming days. In the tower incident in 11:1–9 God's punishment is directed at both the instrument of sin that made the building project possible, the one language, and at the intention of that sin, to avoid being scattered over the earth. Throughout Genesis 3–11 God's response to sin and disobedience is never arbitrary. He never reaches blindly into his "bag" of judgment possibilities and randomly draws one out. The similarities between crime and punishment highlight the nature of the trespass and the nature of divine justice at work.

The narrative begins by saying that the earth had "one language and few words." Does this imply that up until this time the earth had been linguistically uniform? Hardly so! In the "table of nations" in the preceding chapter we are told not once but three times (vv. 5, 20, 31) that the sons of Japheth, Ham, and Shem were divided "by their families, their languages, their lands, and their nations."

One can see a conflict between these two chapters, as do proponents of the documentary hypothesis. In that system there are two explanations for the scattering of humankind: the P source (ch. 10), in which the scattering is a sign of blessing; and the J source (ch. 11), in which the scattering is a sign of divine dissatisfaction, a penalty.

It is also possible to explain the juxtaposition of these two chapters by suggesting that two different linguistic aspects are in view here. Chapter 10 refers to individual dialects or languages. By contrast the "one language" of ch. 11 refers to a lingua franca, an international language that makes cooperation and interchange possible among people of different languages.

The point of ch. 11, then, as argued by Cyrus Gordon (*Before Columbus: Links between the Old World and Ancient America* [New York: Crown, 1971], 107, 165–66), would be not that God divided one language into many languages, but that he made incomprehensible the one common language that was understandable to everyone engaged in the building program.

A third suggestion has been offered by Clines (1978: 68–69): "If the material of ch. 10 had followed the Babel story, the whole Table of Nations would have to be read under the sign of judgment; where it stands it functions as the fulfillment of the divine command of 9:1." This last interpretation has the advantage, in my estimation, as it provides another example of a constant element that we have seen in Genesis 3–11: the voice of God in both judgment and redemption, wrath and mercy. In all things God is working for good, annoyed by the stupidity of some, but swayed from his plan by none. It is possible that if a general statement of the creation of human life (1:26–30) is followed immediately by a more specific account of the creation of that human life (2:4–5), then we may have the same here: a general account of the origins of languages (10:1–32) followed immediately by a more specific account of the origins of that phenomenon (11:1–9).

Genesis 4–11

Andersen, F. 1974. *The Sentence in Biblical Hebrew.* The Hague: Mouton.

Anderson, B. W. 1978. "From Analysis to Synthesis: The Interpretation of Genesis 1–11." *JBL* 97:23–39.

Barnard, A. N. 1971. "Was Noah a Righteous Man? Studies in Texts: Genesis 6, 8." *Theology* 74:311–14.

Barr, J. 2003. "Reflections on the Covenant with Noah." In *Covenant as Context: Essays in Honour of E. W. Nicholson.* Ed. A. D. H. Mayes and R. B. Salters. Oxford: Oxford University Press. Pp. 11–22.

Basset, F. W. 1971. "Noah's Nakedness and the Curse of Canaan: A Case of Incest?" *VT* 21:232–37.

Brueggemann, W. 1968. "David and His Theologian." *CBQ* 30:156–81.

———. 1971. "Kingship and Chaos (A Study in Tenth Century Theology)." *CBQ* 33:317–32.

Bryan, D. T. 1987. "A Reevaluation of Genesis 4 and 5 in the Light of Recent Studies in Genealogical Fluidity." *ZAW* 99:180–88.

Cassuto, U. 1973. "The Episode of the Sons of God and the Daughters of Men (Genesis vi:1–4)." In *Biblical and Oriental Studies.* Trans. I. Abrahams. 2 vols. Jerusalem: Magnes. Vol. 1, pp. 17–28.

Christensen, D. 1986. "Janus Parallelism in Genesis 6:3." *HS* 27:20–24.

Clark, W. M. 1971. "The Flood and the Structure of the Pre-patriarchal History." *ZAW* 83:184–211.

Clines, D. J. A. 1972–1973. "Noah's Flood. I: The Theology of the Flood Narrative." *Faith and Thought* 100:128–42.

———. 1978. *The Theme of the Pentateuch.* 2nd ed., 1997. JSOTSup 10. Sheffield: JSOT Press.

———. 1979. "The Significance of the 'Sons of God' Episode (Genesis 6:1–4) in the Context of the 'Primeval History' (Genesis 1–11)." *JSOT* 13:33–46.

Cohen, H. H. 1974. *The Drunkenness of Noah.* Judaic Studies 4. University, Ala.: University of Alabama Press.

Cohen, N. 1996. *Noah's Flood: The Genesis Story in Western Thought.* New Haven: Yale University Press.

DeWitt, D. S. 1979. "The Historical Background of Genesis 11:1–9: Babel or Ur?" *JETS* 22:15–26.

Eslinger, L. 1979. "A Contextual Identification of the *bene ha'elohim* and *benoth ha'adam* in Genesis 6:1–4." *JSOT* 13:65–73.

Fewell, D. 2001. "Building Babel." In *Postmodern Interpretations of the Bible: A Reader.* Ed. A. K. M. Adam. St. Louis: Chalice. Pp.1–15.

Fisher, E. 1970. "Gilgamesh and Genesis: The Flood Story in Context." *CBQ* 32: 392–403.

Forrest, R. W. E. 1994. "Paradise Lost Again: Violence and Obedience in the Flood Narrative." *JSOT* 62:3–18.

Frymer-Kensky, T. 1974. "What the Babylonian Flood Stories Can and Cannot Teach Us about the Genesis Flood." *BAR* 4 (4):32–41.

———. 1977. "The Atrahasis Epic and Its Significance for Our Understanding of Genesis 1–9." *BA* 40:147–55.

Gruber, M. I. 1978. "The Tragedy of Cain and Abel: A Case of Depression." *JQR* 69:89–97.

———. 1980. "Was Cain Angry or Depressed?" *BAR* 6 (4):35–36.

Halpern, B. 1995. "What They Don't Know Won't Hurt Them: Genesis 6–9." In *Fortunate the Eyes That See: Essays in Honor of David Noel Freedman on His Seventieth Birthday.* Ed. A. B. Beck et al. Grand Rapids: Eerdmans. Pp. 16–34.

Harland, P. J. 1998. "Vertical or Horizontal: The Sin of Babel." *VT* 48:515–33.

Harrison, R. K. 1994. "From Adam to Noah: A Reconsideration of the Antediluvian Patriarchs' Ages [Gen 5, 3–32]." *JETS* 37:161–68.

Hartmann, T. C. 1972. "Some Thoughts on the Sumerian King List and Genesis 5 and 11b." *JBL* 91:25–32.

Hasel, G. F. 1978. "The Genealogies of Genesis 5 and 11 and Their Alleged Babylonian Background." *AUSS* 16:361–74.

Hendel, R. S. 1987. "Of Demigods and the Deluge: Toward an Interpretation of Genesis 6:1–4." *JBL* 106:13–26.

Herion, G. A. 1995. "Why God Rejected Cain's Offering: The Obvious Answer." In *Fortunate the Eyes That See: Essays in Honor of David Noel Freedman on His Seventieth Birthday.* Ed. A. B. Beck et al. Grand Rapids: Eerdmans. Pp. 52–65.

Kaiser, W. C. 1978. *Toward an Old Testament Theology.* Grand Rapids: Zondervan.

Kessler, M. 1974. "Rhetorical Criticism of Genesis 7." In *Rhetorical Criticism: Essays in Honor of James Muilenburg.* Ed. J. J. Jackson and M. Kessler. PTMS 1. Pittsburgh: Pickwick. Pp. 18–32.

Kline, M. 1962. "Divine Kingship and Genesis 6:1–4." *WTJ* 24:187–204.

———. 1978. "Oracular Origin of the State." In *Biblical and Near Eastern Studies.* Ed. G. Tuttle. Grand Rapids: Eerdmans. Pp. 132–41.

Lambert, W. G., and A. R. Millard. 1969. *Atra-hasis: The Babylonian Story of the Flood.* Oxford: Clarendon.

Landy, F. 1998. "Flood and Fludd." In *Biblical Studies/Cultural Studies: The Third Sheffield Colloquium*. Ed. J. C. Exum and S. Moore. JSOTSup 266. Sheffield: Sheffield Academic Press. Pp. 117–58.

Larsson, G. 2000. "Remarks concerning the Noah-Flood Complex." *ZAW* 112:75–77.

Laurin, R. B. 1978. "The Tower of Babel Revisited." In *Biblical and Near Eastern Studies*. Festschrift for W. S. LaSor. Ed. G. Tuttle. Grand Rapids: Eerdmans. Pp. 142–45.

Levin, S. 1979. "The More Savory Offering: A Key to the Problem of Genesis 4:3–5." *JBL* 98:85.

Lewis, J. P. 1994. "The Offering of Abel (Gen. 4:4): A History of Interpretation." *JETS* 37:481–96.

Longacre, R. 1976. "The Discourse Structure of the Flood Narrative." In *SBLSP 1976*. Ed. G. W. MacRae. Missoula, Mont.: Scholars Press. Pp. 235–62.

Merrill, E. 1997. "The Peoples of the Old Testament according to Genesis 10." *BSac* 154:3–22.

Miller, J. M. 1974. "The Descendants of Cain: Notes on Genesis 4." *ZAW* 86:164–74.

Miller, P. D., Jr. 1978. *Genesis 1–11: Studies in Structure and Theme*. JSOTSup 8. Sheffield: University of Sheffield Department of Biblical Studies.

Moberly, R. W. L. 2000. "Why Did Noah Send Out a Raven?" *VT* 50:345–56.

Nielsen, E. 1954. *Oral Tradition: A Modern Problem in the Old Testament Introduction*. SBT 11. Chicago: Allenson.

Obed, B. 1986. "The Table of Nations (Genesis 10)—A Socio-Cultural Approach." *ZAW* 98:14–31.

Paul, M. J. 1996. "Genesis 4:17–24: A Case-Study in Eisegesis." *TynB* 47:143–62.

Petersen, D. L. 1976. "The Yahwist on the Flood." *VT* 26:438–46.

———. 1979. "Genesis 6:1–4, Yahweh and the Organization of the Cosmos." *JSOT* 13:47–64.

Rad, G. von. 1972. *Genesis*. Trans. J. H. Marks. Rev. ed. OTL. Philadelphia: Westminster.

Riemann, P. 1970. "Am I My Brother's Keeper?" *Int* 24:482–91.

Robertson, O. Palmer. 1998. "Current Critical Questions concerning the 'Curse of Ham' (Gen. 9:20–27)." *JETS* 41:177–88.

Ross, A. P. 1980a. "The Curse of Canaan." *BSac* 137:223–40.

———. 1980b. "The Table of Nations in Genesis 10—Its Structure." *BSac* 137:340–53.

Sasson, J. 1975. "Word Play in Gen 6:8–9." *CBQ* 37:165–66.

———. 1980. "The 'Tower of Babel' as a Clue to the Redactional Structuring of Primeval History [Gen. 1–11:9]." In *The Bible World: Essays in Honor of Cyrus H. Gordon*. Ed. G. Rendsburg et al. New York: Ktav. Pp. 211–19.

Spina, F. 1992. "The 'Ground' for Cain's Rejection: ʾadamah in the Context of Gen 1–11." *ZAW* 104:319–32.

Steinmetz, D. 1994. "Vineyard, Farm and Garden: The Drunkenness of Noah in the Context of Primeval History." *JBL* 113:193–207.

Tigay, J. H., ed. 1985. *The Gilgamesh Epic: Empirical Models for Biblical Criticism.* Philadelphia: University of Pennsylvania Press.

Turner, L. A. 1993. "The Rainbow as the Sign of the Covenant in Genesis ix: 11–13." *VT* 43:119–24.

VanGemeren, W. 1981. "The Sons of God in Genesis 6:1–4 (An Example of Evangelical Demythologization?)." *WTJ* 43:320–48.

Vervenne, M. 1995. "What Shall We Do with the Drunken Sailor? Critical Re-examination of Genesis 9:20–27." *JSOT* 68:33–55.

Waltke, B. 1986. "Cain and His Offering." *WTJ* 48:363–72.

Wenham, G. J. 1978. "The Coherence of the Flood Narrative." *VT* 28:336–48.

Wickham, L. R. 1974. "The Sons of God and the Daughters of Men: Gen vi 2 in Early Christian Exegesis." *OtSt* 19:135–47.

Wifall, W. 1975. "Genesis 6:1–4—A Royal Davidic Myth?" *BTB* 5:294–301.

3

Abraham

Only two chapters are devoted in the opening book of the Bible to the story of creation, and the narration of the fall of humankind from sinlessness into sin is limited to one. Yet the story of Abraham covers thirteen chapters in Genesis, as well as parts of two other chapters. Is there a clue here about the essential purpose of Scripture? Its primary function is not to address itself to philosophical, metaphysical questions that engage, properly, the modern mind. If pressed for a definition of God, or how one can know that God works in history, an ancient Hebrew would give an answer something like one given by jazz artist Louis Armstrong, who, when asked to define jazz, replied, "Man, if you have to ask, you'll never know."

The Old Testament is more theological than it is philosophical. How do God and humans ever reach an agreement and become compatible? The answers are in Leviticus and in a substantial part of Exodus. How does God encourage a person amidst the most forbidding circumstances? Look to Joseph's story. How does God call one person out of anonymity and use that life to challenge and change the world? Consider Abraham's life.

Still, we do not find, in the technical sense, a biography of Abraham in Genesis. We are unable to trace his life in detail. However, certain events of his life are highlighted, and a particular section of his life is emphasized. Table 2 shows this. We have no information about Abraham for the first seventy-five years of his life, and only minimal information about the last seventy-five years of his life. The crucial twenty-five years are those from Abraham's seventy-fifth to one hundredth years.

Table 2

Scripture	Age of Abraham	Event
12:4	75	Abraham departs from Haran
16:3	85	Abraham living in Canaan ten years
16:16	86	birth of Ishmael
17:1	99	the covenant
21:5	100	birth of Isaac
23:1	137	death of Sarah
25:7	175	death of Abraham

From Adam through Noah's progeny (1–11) models of faithlessness have easily outnumbered models of obedience. Abraham is set in contrast to these unpromising individuals. One cannot miss, for example, the contrast between "let us make a name for ourselves" (11:4 NRSV) and "I will make your name great" (12:2 NIV). Human machinations contrast with divine initiative, self-promotion with passively receiving God's promises.

The transition from prepatriarchal to patriarchal history is marked by the opening words of Genesis 12. Hans W. Wolff (1974: 47) correctly categorizes the grammatical parts of the passage:

1. an imperative: "Go!" (12:1)
2. five imperfect verbs, with God as subject: "I will make . . . I will bless . . . I will make great . . . I will bless . . . I will curse."
3. one perfect verb: "by you all the families of the earth [Genesis 10–11?] shall be blessed" or "shall bless themselves." (It is interesting that a promise for the future is put in the perfect. Is one's future ahead or behind? Does one walk into or back into the future?)

Within these three verses the word "bless(ing)," as verb or noun, appears five times. Wolff (1974: 54) contrasts this fivefold use of "bless(ing)" with the fivefold use of "curse" in Genesis 1–11:

1. 3:14: "cursed are you above the cattle"
2. 3:17: "cursed is the ground because of you"
3. 4:11: "you are cursed from the ground"
4. 5:29: "the ground which the Lord has cursed"
5. 9:25: "cursed be Canaan"
   (8:21 uses a different Hebrew verb than do these five)

One might also be inclined to link the blessings of Gen. 12:1–3 on God's lips with a similar number of blessings in Genesis 1–11: "and God blessed them" (1:22 RSV); "and God blessed them" (1:28 RSV); "so God blessed the seventh day" (2:3 NRSV); "male and female . . . he blessed them" (5:2 NRSV); "and God blessed Noah" (9:1 RSV). Source critics, however, would not allow the equation because, they maintain, Gen. 12:1–3 is from J, and these five are from P.

What events then follow in Abraham's life?

1. Abraham travels to Egypt with Sarah because of famine (12:10–20)
2. Back from Egypt, Abraham and Lot must parcel the land between themselves (13:1–18)
3. Abraham rescues Lot from his captors (14:1–17, 21–24), and in the process he confronts Melchizedek (14:18–20)
4. God makes the covenant with Abraham (15), a covenant that is later sealed with circumcision (17); Ishmael is born (16)
5. God judges Sodom and Gomorrah (18–19)
6. Abraham, away from home, again tries unsuccessfully to deceive a king by identifying Sarah as his sister (20)
7. Isaac is born and subsequently offered (21–22)
8. Sarah dies (23)
9. Abraham sends his servant back home to obtain a wife for Isaac (24) (Note that the longest chapter in Genesis deals with the subject of marriage.)
10. Abraham dies (25:1–11)

The Theme of Promise

Our knowledge about Abraham is limited to what we find in Scripture. As is true of the majority of biblical personalities, there are no extra-biblical references to him in any extant literature from the patriarchal age. There are individuals who had (approximately) the same name—for example, at ancient Ebla—a fact that bears witness to the antiquity of the tradition. But none of these persons is the biblical Abraham.

One reference to the patriarch Abraham—or Moses, for that matter—in a cuneiform or hieroglyphic text would be sufficient to squelch much of the speculation that has swirled around these early characters. The absence of such a reference, however, has unleashed the imagination of much of modern scholarship in the search for the "historical Abraham." Even those scholars who have, based on archaeological discoveries, underscored the authentic cultural background of the patriarchal traditions would not admit that here we have an illustration of pure history. Even for them, historical reporting in its sterling sense does not emerge until the "objective" account of David and his family in the "Succession Narrative" (2 Samuel 9–20; 1 Kings 1–2).

In addition, those critics who have expressed a conservative historical judgment on the patriarchs would also, by and large, affirm that the stories—mixtures of fact and legend or saga—are products of Israel and Judah from the period of the monarchy's establishment down to the return from exile (1000–500 B.C.). As such, all the narratives about the patriarchs were part of a long oral tradition, and subsequently they underwent a process of collection, revision, and editing in which many of the stories were far removed from their original context and purpose. Compatible with this emphasis is the suggestion that some of the patriarchal stories are sheer inventions of a later age, stories that were artificially set in an earlier period.

This approach obviously minimizes or ignores the crucial role given to the patriarchs in Genesis: to be the initial channels through which God's promises for the future are launched. In the words of Geerhardus Vos (1948: 67), "If according to the Bible they [the patriarchs] are real actors in the drama of redemption, the actual beginning of the people of God . . . then the denial of their historicity makes them useless." Instead, they become either murky figures from an ancient and undecipherable past or parabolic characters (e.g., more like the prodigal son in Jesus' parable than John the Baptist) from which any generation may extract timeless truths to be applied to its age.

The significant part played by the patriarchs in redemptive history is made most prominent in Genesis by the constant emphasis on divine promise. Everything starts with Abraham, Isaac, and Jacob, but nothing ends with them. All three individuals are means to an end that reaches well beyond their lifetimes. They are catalysts and not conclusions. Thus, we read the accounts of Abraham in Genesis not primarily to gain a perspective on daily life in the second millennium B.C., but to become informed of the promises of God for the future. Ultimately, our interest is prophetic, not historical.

As we will observe, the life of Abraham appears as an interesting amalgamation of faith and folly, movements forward and movements backward. At most points the reader will have no problem in applauding the Abraham of faith. But several incidents will reveal the absence of faith.

What is it that puts both the positive and the negative events in perspective? Gerhard von Rad (1962: 1:167) has answered that question: "The whole has nevertheless a scaffolding supporting and connecting it, the so-called promise to the patriarchs. At least it can be said that this whole variegated mosaic of stories is given cohesion of subject-matter . . . by means of the constantly recurring divine promise." Brevard Childs (1979: 151) similarly suggests that the promises provide "the constant element in the midst of all the changing situations of this very chequered history."

Moreover, these promises are absolute and not conditional. This emphasis shifts the promises away from the idea of a reward (something earned) to the idea of a gift (something unsolicited). We can see this point made rather strongly in 12:1–3, the very first instance of a promise to Abraham (a promise of both blessing and increase). First there is the divine imperative, "Go!" (v. 1). Then comes the divine promise, "I will" (vv. 2–3). Then follows the human response, "so Abraham went" (v. 4). The entire intent of the passage would have been changed radically had v. 4 preceded vv. 2–3. If it had, then the promises could only be read as a result of Abraham's obedience. The divine word then would have been reduced from an initiating word to a responding word.

Precisely the same structure is found in 13:14–18, the second reference to promise: the divine imperative, "Lift up" (v. 14); the divine promise, "I will" (vv. 15–17); the human response, "so Abram moved his tent" (v. 18). The third reference to promise, in 15:1–6, demonstrates the same: the divine imperative, "Look" (v. 5a); the divine promise, "so shall your descendants be" (v. 5b); the human response, "and he believed the Lord" (v. 6).

This is not to say that Abraham is absolved of all responsibility. He is "to walk before God and be blameless" (17:1). He must "keep the covenant" (17:9). He is to do "righteousness and justice; so that the LORD may bring to Abraham what he has promised him" (18:19 RSV). A causal nexus between obedience and fulfillment is suggested by "*because* you have done this . . . I will indeed bless you . . . *because* you have obeyed my voice" (22:15–18 NRSV). The same nuance is present in 26:4–5: "I will multiply your descendants . . . *because* Abraham obeyed my voice" (RSV). This last passage, however, promises multiplication of Isaac's descendants because of Abraham's, not Isaac's, obedience!

My point is not that human responsibility is obliterated. After all, even in a unilateral covenant there must be some reciprocity. What if Abraham had not gone out as the Lord told him? What if he had not

believed? What if he had chosen consistently not to walk before God
and be blameless? What if he had chosen to refuse to offer Isaac? These
options must have been open to Abraham unless we are prepared to say
that for him, as the chosen of the Lord (18:19), God's grace was irresistible. My point is that human responsibility is repeatedly subordinated
to God's word of promise.

The first stipulation, in terms of conduct, is placed on Abraham (17:1)
only after he has already been, on numerous occasions, the recipient
of a promissory word (12:1–3, 7; 13:14–17; 15:1–6, 7–21). In terms of
chronology, God's first word of promise was spoken to Abraham in his
seventy-fifth year (12:4). God's first word to Abraham in terms of con-
ditionality is in Abraham's ninety-ninth year (17:1), almost a quarter
of a century later.

The promises of God to the patriarchs cover the following areas:
the birth of a son; the increase of descendants; land; divine presence;
blessing. Some of these may occur by themselves ("Sarah your wife
shall have a son" [18:10 RSV]; "to your descendants I will give this land"
[12:7 RSV]), but normally they occur in clusters. To illustrate, 22:15–18
includes a promise of blessing ("I indeed will bless you" [RSV]); a promise of the increase of descendants ("I will multiply your descendants
as the stars of heaven" [RSV]); a promise of land ("your descendants
shall possess the gate of their enemies" [RSV]); and a second promise
of blessing ("and by your descendants shall all the nations of the earth
bless themselves" [RSV]).

More promises are made to Abraham than to either his son or grandson. In listing the promise of descendants, David J. A. Clines (1978: 32–33)
cites nineteen passages from Genesis. Thirteen of them are directed to
Abraham, while there is only one to Hagar (21:18), two to Isaac (26:4,
24), and three to Jacob (28:14; 35:11; 46:3). Clines lists thirteen passages
from Genesis about the promise of land. Nine of these are addressed to
Abraham, one to Isaac (26:3), and three to Jacob (28:13, 15 [also 48:4];
35:12; 46:4).

In connection with the promise of land we note variations even in
how the promise is given. In 12:7 God will give the land "to your descendants." In 13:15 God will give the land "to you and to your descendants."
In 13:17 God will give the land "to you." Even the tense "I will give" in
these verses may shift to "I give" (in 15:18, literally, "I have given").

Abraham, of course, never possessed the land as did the Israelites
under Joshua. His "possession" is limited to staking out the land—"Arise,
walk through the length and breadth of the land" (RSV)—that his seed
one day will occupy. At least that is how we see it in retrospect. There
is no indication in any early text that Abraham himself saw it that way.
Ostensibly, he was anticipating a more immediate fulfillment of the prom-

ise when it was first announced to him in 12:7. Only a divine indication of a four-hundred-year hiatus (15:12–16) put to rest any questions that Abraham may have entertained. On several occasions he does ask God, "Where is my heir?" But never does he ask God, "Where is my land?" For him, living in tents was fully satisfying (Heb. 11:9–10).

It is obvious that most of the promises that God gave to Abraham, and to Isaac and Jacob, could not be fulfilled during the lifetime of the patriarch. This certainly is true for the two promises that appear most frequently, that of a vast number of descendants and that of the gift of land. God begins with Abraham a process whose climax is in the distant future.

But what about Abraham? He has a son, or two, but not a myriad of descendants. He has a tent and wealth, but no land, except for the purchase of a tiny bit of property on which to bury his wife (Genesis 23). And during the last seventy-five years of his life how many families of the earth are blessed in him?

One rich blessing Abraham has. True, he does not have, in terms of personal realization, all the promises of God, but he does have the God of all the promises. God himself is Abraham's shield and reward (15:1). The giver, not the gifts, is Abraham's highest reward and his consuming obsession. Not without reason, therefore, is Abraham referred to three times in the Bible as "the friend of God" (2 Chron. 20:7; Isa. 41:8; James 2:23). Worth consulting on this phrase is the study by M. Goshen-Gottstein (1987), particularly his interpretation of why the Septuagint renders the Hebrew active participle (Abraham is one who loves God) as passive (Abraham is one who is loved by God). They enjoyed each other's company.

Abraham, Man without Faith

Through all the experiences recorded in Genesis 12–25 Abraham emerges as an individual of great obedience and trust. His pilgrimage begins (Genesis 12, "go") and climaxes (Genesis 22, "offer Isaac") at the point of being tested by God. In between he appears as the paragon of patience, promised an heir at the age of seventy-five, and willing to wait a quarter of a century before he first gets the chance to change diapers. Like the Suffering Servant whom Isaiah describes (53:12), Abraham makes intercession for the transgressor (in Gen. 18:16–33 he pleads to God for Sodom). Although he does not condone them, he at least tolerates the quirks of his will-o'-the-wisp nephew Lot.

However, all is not perfect. Looming large in Abraham's story are some questionable activities on the part of this hero. In this way Abraham becomes the prototype for Jacob, Moses, and David, a curious mixture of the sacred and the profane, the lofty and the languid.

Abraham is weak enough to use his wife, Sarah, to save his own life. Caught in a threatening situation, he persuades Sarah to identify herself to the Egyptians as his sister, not his wife (12:10–20). One may explain the tactics of Abraham by appealing, as does commentator E. A. Speiser, to Hurrian documents (a territory where Abraham spent a part of his life [11:31c]) in which marriage is followed by adoption. The woman becomes first wife, then sister, to cement the relationship, and such a reading, of course, "saves" Abraham's reputation. He is giving Sarah higher status in hopes that the Egyptians will treat her more considerately.

One would be hard pressed to read that into the narrative. Moreover, Abraham's culpability is enforced by the fact that he is silent throughout the whole episode. He is only listener, not conversationalist. And we must note Sarah's silence too. She is the first of a number of women in Scripture whom some man is prepared to sacrifice to other men, and the sacrifice usually involves sex (Lot's daughters [Gen. 19:6–8]; the Levite's concubine and the owner's daughter [Judg. 19:23–24]). When Sarah is "taken" (Gen. 12:15), Abraham does nothing. When he hears that his nephew Lot has been "taken" (14:14), he immediately goes into action to retrieve him. To be sure, Abraham obtains wealth (12:16) for his sinister part in the episode, but not as an evidence of God's blessing. We have not yet gone beyond the "I will bless" of 12:3 to the "Lord had blessed" of 24:1.

Abraham stores away in his mind the strategy used on this occasion, perhaps to be used again if dire circumstances prevail. A second trip away from home provides such an opportunity (ch. 20). This time, among the neighboring Philistines, Sarah once again is prevailed upon to deceive the king and make herself vulnerable for her husband's sake, notwithstanding the fact that God has told Abraham that his covenant with Abraham is through Sarah (17:15–16; 18:10), and has announced that she will give birth to the promised Isaac (17:19). None of this deters Abraham from being prepared to relinquish Sarah.

Unlike the incident in ch. 12, where it appears, or is at least hinted, that Pharaoh and Sarah had a sexual relationship (12:15b), here adultery is averted before it can begin (20:4a, 6b). Once again Abraham is materially enriched (20:14–16), but primarily as a vindication for Sarah. His philosophy of ethics is unchanged: the end justifies the means. The end? Nothing must happen that will cast a cloud of uncertainty over God's promises (a great nation, seed). The means? If necessary, use Sarah as a pawn. But that is not God's view of Sarah. She is as important to God's plan as is Abraham. Abraham will do what he has to do to save Lot. God will do what he has to do to save Sarah.

Alas, like father, like son: Isaac resorts to the same subterfuge (ch. 26). Robert Polzin (1975: 93) draws attention to the way in which the innocent monarch in each instance was apprised of the woman's real identity. In 12:17 it is through plagues; in 20:3 it is through a dream; in 26:8 it is through the king's observing Isaac fondling Rebekah. One is the acting of God in history (the law?); the second is the revelation of God through visions and dreams (the prophets?); the third is through the use of one's eyes (the emphasis on wisdom?). There is an incredibly large bibliography on these incidents. The reader would do well to explore these studies for further reflections: Niditch (1987: 23–69); Biddle (1990); Ronning (1991); Rashkow (1992: 57–73); Hoffmeier (1992); Alexander (1992); Exum (1993); Eichler (1997).

It may well be that Abraham's rascality is prompted not simply by a desire to save himself. The larger issue is the promise that God had given earlier (blessing and descendants). First there is the famine in the land. Later Old Testament literature (e.g., Deut. 28:17–18, 22–24) saw famine as a manifestation of God's displeasure with disobedience. So the first question in Genesis 12 is: will Abraham survive the famine, and if so, how?

The second question in Genesis 12 is: will Abraham survive Egypt? Perhaps Abraham's own question is: will God's promises survive? For if there is no Abraham, there can be no subsequent great nation. If that is his thinking at this point, and thus the explanation for his attempted ruse, then Abraham becomes the standard-bearer for many other believers who felt that God needed a little assistance in extricating himself from a potentially damaging and embarrassing situation. In any case, Abraham's descent to Egypt, caused by a famine in Canaan, and his eventual departure from Egypt with wealth in hand foreshadow Israel's descent to Egypt, caused by a famine in Canaan, and its eventual departure from Egypt with wealth in hand (Exod. 12:33–36).

The story does indeed illustrate an immediate fulfillment of one part of God's earlier promise to Abraham: those who curse Abraham, God will curse. Taking another man's wife, even innocently, has catastrophic repercussions. This one part of the first promise of God to Abraham illustrates an important distinction between the covenant with Abraham and the covenant with Israel at Sinai. In the latter God's curse is directed at the Israelite who disobeys (see Deut. 27:15–26; 28:15–19); in the former God's curse is directed at the non-Israelite who attempts to damage God's covenant people.

Still, the reader of Abraham's odyssey to Egypt wonders where is Abraham's Nathan, with his "You are the man" (see 2 Sam. 12:7 NRSV), unless it is Pharaoh himself. Through deceit Abraham has become rich.

He exits Egypt with his coffers full, his wife tainted, and without any demonstrable tinge of remorse. To compound the issue, God apparently ignores Abraham's foolhardiness.

Does divine silence imply divine approval? I suggest that the silence is to be explained not as an insinuation of God's approbation of duplicity, but by the desired emphasis that the story wishes to make. That emphasis is not to comment on Abraham's behavior, however despicable it may be, but to use the story as a graphic illustration of divine providence. God's promise to Abraham cannot be voided even when the greatest threat to that promise is the bearer of the promise.

Not unlike Job, Abraham is both patient and impatient; once relaxing, then fretting; once passive, then manipulative. Still not quite sure that God is able to implement the promise, or at least frustrated because God is not on his timetable, Abraham is prepared to adopt his servant Eliezer as his heir (15:2–3). I recognize that such a contrivance finds analogy in the fifteenth-century B.C. cuneiform texts from Nuzi. In the event of childlessness a slave might be adopted as one's legal heir. But in the Abrahamic cycle the event becomes simply another illustration of God's testing of the venerable patriarch.

Similarly, Sarah's presentation of Hagar to Abraham as a surrogate (16:3) because of her own infertility finds precedent in cuneiform literature. If in the preceding episodes it was Abraham who initiated the scheme, with Sarah as the go-between, here it is Sarah herself who takes the initiative. Abraham, rather than protesting, acquiesces. The Eve-Adam mentality is not difficult to discern (16:2b). Unable to see the long-range implications of their action, Abraham offers no resistance. But we should observe that 16:3 reports that Sarah resorts to surrogacy only after she and her husband had been living in Canaan for ten years; that is, only after they have exhausted their attempts at the normal methods of reproduction do they turn to Hagar. And turning to Hagar, an Egyptian, for a solution to the infertility of a womb parallels other times in Genesis when an Abraham or a Jacob turns to a fertile Egypt as a solution to infertility in the land of Canaan (Duguid 1994). Possibly their mistake is seeing the promise of God not as a privilege, but as an obligation. Instead of saying, "We're going to have a baby!" they say, "We've got to have a baby!" And whenever one sees the fruit of God's promises as something to be achieved rather than received, all sorts of options present themselves.

What is the sequel? There is obvious divisiveness between Hagar and Sarah. Just as sin separated Adam from Eve, Cain from Abel, Noah from his (grand)son, it now drives a wedge between Hagar and Sarah. Hostility and mutual recrimination loom large, resulting in Hagar's fleeing her mistress's home precipitously, and pregnant at that. But in fleeing

Sarah, several unique things happen with Hagar. She is the first person in the Bible to whom "the angel of the Lord" appears (16:11a). She is the first woman in the Bible to whom God directly makes a promise (16:11b–12). She is the only person in the Old Testament to give God a new name (16:13). And lastly, her meeting with the angel "is the only encounter between God and a woman that results in a commemorative place name ['Beer Lahai Roi' (16:14)]" (Humphreys 2001: 105). More than a decade later the animosity has only intensified, not evaporated (21:9–14). This time Hagar leaves not on her own; she is summarily dismissed together with Ishmael.

This is another narrative seen by critics as a prima facie case for underlying sources. We are told that there are three sources behind the Hagar-Ishmael stories. The text breaks down as follows:

16:1	P	16:4–14	J
16:2	J	16:15–16	P
16:3	P	21:9–21	E

Fundamentally, say the critics, the two stories are in conflict and therefore cannot both be true in their facts. To illustrate, in ch. 16 Hagar is haughty and contemptuous toward Sarah; in ch. 21 she is more victim than villain. In 16:6 Abraham willingly turns Hagar over to Sarah and does not interfere. In 21:11, however, Abraham, far from being passive, finds his wife's reactions nauseating. He makes sure that Hagar has provisions, albeit meager given Abraham's wealth and abundant possessions, for physical sustenance for her trek into the wilderness (21:14).

But most palpable of all is the picture we get of Ishmael in ch. 21. By this time Ishmael must be, at a minimum, thirteen years old (17:25). He is born when Abraham is eighty-six (16:16), and Abraham is one hundred when Isaac is born (21:4), which means that Ishmael is fourteen or fifteen. Yet, along with bread and water, Abraham places on the shoulder of Hagar her teenage son (21:14)! Facing certain death in the desert, she "casts" the child under a bush (21:15), a child about to die of thirst. Is this a picture of a teenager or a helpless infant?

In defense of the unity of chs. 16 and 21 and of the consistency between the two I make the following points.

Does 21:14 support the idea that Abraham did indeed load Ishmael onto Hagar's shoulders? Literally, the verse says that Abraham "took bread and water and gave them over to Hagar, there upon her shoulder, and the child." Nothing in this translation demands that the child was carried on the mother's shoulder.

Anyone who is prepared to favor the translation "gave" as meaning "place" or "set" should recall that the same Hebrew word, *nātan*, also means "to deliver" in the sense of "commit, entrust," as in Exod. 22:7, 10. Could it be that Abraham is not "placing" the items on Hagar's shoulder but is "entrusting" Ishmael to Hagar's guardianship?

The translation "cast" in 21:15 is unfortunate (cf. NIV: "put"). Ishmael certainly is not being thrown to the ground, be he infant or adolescent. H. C. White (1975: 287, 302) observes that the Hebrew verb used here, *šālak*, almost always refers to the placing of a dead body into a grave, if the object of the verb is a person. "They took Absalom, and *threw* him into a great pit" (2 Sam. 18:17 RSV); "the man was *cast* into the grave of Elisha" (2 Kings 13:21 RSV); Ishmael "*cast* them [the bodies of the men he had slain] into a cistern" (Jer. 41:7 RSV). It may also apply to a person who is being placed in what presumably will be his or her grave (Gen. 37:20, 22, 24; Jer. 38:6). What sane mother would throw her feeble child like a ball under a tree?

Abraham, Man of Faith

Although momentarily sidetracked by the lapses described in the preceding section, it is to the credit of Abraham that he rises above these negative experiences. Such experiences were intrusions into and momentary interruptions of God's plan for his life. It may be more than incidental that almost all the individuals assembled by the author of Hebrews 11 to illustrate faith have somewhere in their life a fatal flaw, and sometimes more than one. Those who adamantly reject God's will for their life find that their decision is honored. But those who at least stumble and fall forward in the direction of God's will find a divine resource and promise from God. The mosaic of faith includes the following examples.

Genesis 12. How does God break into a person's life where there have been few or no John the Baptists to prepare the way? Abraham was cradled in a world of polytheism and idolatry. His father, Terah, appropriately traveled from Ur to Haran, for both were ancient centers for the worship of the moon god Sin. Genesis does not even record as directly and plainly as does Acts 7:2 that God appeared to Abraham when "he was in Mesopotamia, before he lived in Haran" (RSV) (unless one translates the "said" of Gen. 12:1 as "had said").

In a sense, then, God's voice comes to Abraham without warning. The patriarch is perceptive enough to recognize that voice the first time he hears it. Not only is he perceptive enough to hear, but also he is wise enough to obey: "So Abram went, as the LORD had told him" (12:4 NRSV). Abraham's adventure is made even more risky because he is merely pointed in the right direction by that voice, given only a minimum of directions and explanations: "Go . . . to the land I will show you" (12:1 NRSV). The direction is plain, but the destination is unknown.

Genesis 13. Abraham returns to Canaan not because the famine is past, but because he has worn out his welcome in Egypt (12:20). He receives from Pharaoh orders to return to the place from which he came. Does he learn any lesson from his mistake? Are there any indications of subsequent change in his life? Chapter 13 answers those questions affirmatively.

The focus in this chapter is on the strife that developed between Abraham's and Lot's herders. There is almost as much material about Lot in these narratives as there is about his uncle. The crucial chapters describing the covenant with Abraham (chs. 15 and 17) are framed by stories about Lot: his herders (ch. 13) and his capture (ch. 14) on one side, and his connection to Sodom and Gomorrah on the other (chs. 18 and 19). At no point does Lot emerge as a worthy and creditable person. More often than not he is an albatross around Abraham's neck. Lot's herders cannot "dwell" together with Abraham's (13:6), but each can safely dwell with the Canaanites and Perizzites (13:7). Getting along together within the family is more difficult than getting along with those outside the family.

In the contention that developed between their employees, Abraham might easily have solved the situation by asserting his authority over his nephew. After all, he was the elder, the head of the clan. Instead, he is content to let Lot choose which pasturage he desires for his cattle.

But what if Lot chooses the land that God is going to give to Abraham? Maybe Abraham needs to be more self-assertive, more insistent on his rights. The matter, however delicate, can be left in God's hands. No move by Lot can thwart the promise of God. Unfortunately, Abraham had not lived by that philosophy while he was in Egypt.

Genesis 14. In many ways the incident in Genesis 14 is the most unusual one recorded in Abraham's life. The first half of the chapter—a battle between four powerful kings from the east and five minor kings in the Dead Sea area—is not about Abraham at all. Only the capture of Lot brings Abraham into the narrative. In ch. 13 the emphasis had been on family strife. Here the emphasis is on international strife.

With characteristic brevity the chapter records Abraham's victory—with the help of 318 "servants"—over these four titanic kings. In theory, the odds were against Abraham with his miniscule army. But God had said to him, "Those who curse you I will curse." Will God keep that promise? Just as Sarah was "taken" (12:15) by Egyptians—with resulting plagues on the takers—now Lot is taken (14:12) by outsiders (although, to be sure, when Sarah is "taken," Abraham does nothing, but when Lot is "taken," he immediately launches a search-and-rescue mission).

The consequence for their action is just as devastating as it was for the Egyptians: a humiliating defeat ("and he routed them" [v. 15]) at the hands of a peanut-sized force of fighters.

Even Melchizedek, the king of Salem, gives this quick but accurate analysis of the incident: "Blessed be God . . . who has delivered your enemies into your hand" (v. 20 NRSV). It is not without interest that the Hebrew word for "deliver" used here (*miggēn*) is from the same root as "shield" (*māgēn*) of 15:1. This is another illustration of identical vocabulary used at key points to link individual stories within the larger unit.

From Melchizedek Abraham accepts a minimal gift, a meal, if it can even be called that (v. 18). But the offer of booty from the king of Sodom he refuses (vv. 21–24). God will supply all his needs, but not this way. Once all too eager to accept a purse from Pharaoh, Abraham has now learned to exercise restraint in accepting handouts. For now he is seeking grace, not graft.

Genesis 15, 17. These two chapters describe the actual institution and confirmation of the Abrahamic covenant. For good reason the promises of God to Abraham are more abundant in these two chapters than elsewhere. There is the promise of a son (15:4; 17:16, 19); the promise of descendants (15:5, 13, 16, 18; 17:2, 4–8, 19); the promise of land (15:7, 8, 16, 18–21; 17:8); the promise of blessing (17:16).

It would go too far to describe these two chapters as serious dialogue. Abraham's conversational role is limited to two questions (15:2, 8; and perhaps surprising is Abraham's blunt question in v. 8, just two verses after the affirmation of his faith in Yahweh in v. 6) and one exclamatory comment (17:18). By contrast, God speaks repeatedly: "the word of the LORD came to Abram in a vision" (15:1 NRSV); "and behold, the word of the LORD came to him" (15:4 RSV); "and [he] said . . . then he said to him" (15:5 RSV); "and he said to him" (15:7 RSV); "he said to him" (15:9 RSV); "then the LORD said to Abram" (15:13 RSV); "on that day the LORD made a covenant with Abram, saying" (15:18 RSV); "the LORD appeared to Abram, and said to him" (17:1 RSV); "and God said to him" (17:3 RSV); "and God said to Abraham" (17:9 RSV); "and God said to Abraham" (17:15 RSV); "God said" (17:19 RSV).

Abraham's response to these grand promises of God is summed up with this terse declaration: "And he believed [in] the LORD; and the LORD reckoned it to him as righteousness" (15:6 NRSV). God's responsibility is promise and performance; humankind's responsibility is belief. Von Rad (1972: 185) rightly observes, "Abraham's righteousness is not the result of any accomplishments. . . . Rather it is stated programmatically that belief alone has brought Abraham into a proper relationship to God."

This is not the only illustration of faith in Genesis, but it is the only place in Genesis where there is an explicit reference to faith. We do not read, in so many words, that Isaac, or Jacob, or Joseph believed in the Lord and that such belief was reckoned to them as righteousness. The promises given to Abraham are essentially repeated to Isaac and Jacob. The faith of Abraham is all that is accentuated. The emphasis, then, falls on God's faithfulness from generation to generation with his renewed promise, rather than upon each successive generation's appropriation of that promise in faith.

The remainder of ch. 15 is God's ceremonial ratification of this covenant. After Abraham arranges the animal remains in parallel columns, God himself passes between the two rows in fiery manifestation. The intent of the ritual could hardly be more daring. God is unilaterally obligating himself to Abraham and his seed to the degree that God places himself under a potential curse. Should this God of promise prove to be unreliable, then may his fate be dismemberment, as with these animals (on the significance of cutting animals in two as part of covenant ritual see Jer. 34:18).

It is impossible to know the age of Abraham in ch. 15. Between chs. 16 and 17 there are thirteen years (in 16:16 Abraham is eighty-six; in 17:1 he is ninety-nine). Thus, between Abraham's reception of the covenant and his own name change and circumcision there is a decade and a half.

The source critics are almost unanimous in their identification of the traditions behind these two chapters. Customarily, 15:1–6 is assigned to E, 15:7–21 to J principally because of the unit's exclusive use of "LORD/Yahweh," and 17:1–27 to P principally because of the unit's exclusive use of "God/Elohim." In fact, 17:1–27 is the first place in the Abraham story where "God/Elohim" occurs at all, apart from the abbreviated form of Elohim in compound names such as "El Elyon" (14:18–20) and "El-roi" (16:13). So, in the very chapter where Abram becomes Abraham (17:5), Yahweh becomes Elohim. Evangelical scholars typically have countered with the suggestion that the narrative in ch. 17 is not a duplicate of that in ch. 15, but rather is a reconfirmation by God to Abraham of his promises, especially on the heels of the less-than-happy results of Abraham's cohabitation with Hagar in ch. 16. This reassuring word, sequential to an Abrahamic debacle, recalls another reassuring, reconfirming word to Abraham (13:14–17) after another debacle (12:10–20). Abraham is still not even a father of the son of promise!

There is more here, however, than reconfirmation. Two new items enter the covenant promises in ch. 17. In the first place, Abram becomes Abraham. Only one verse, 17:5, is devoted to this shift. This new name universalizes Abraham's experience with God. He is to be "the father of a multitude of nations."

The second new item is the introduction of circumcision. This particularizes Abraham's experience with God. He is to be the father of the Jews. Six verses are devoted to this innovation (17:9–14), plus five more

(17:23–27) for Abraham's actual circumcision and that of Ishmael and the other males in Abraham's house.

This mark, indelibly cut into the flesh, now becomes a witness to identity with Yahweh and Yahweh's people. The connection of circumcision with the covenant is made clear by the emphasis on the body part involved. If circumcision's significance was merely the cutting or marking of some part of the human body, then something such as cutting one's hair or piercing one's nose or ear, or even branding a mark on one's hand or forehead, would have sufficed. Circumcision, however, "requires a cutting of the part of the body through which God's promise will be fulfilled" (Goldingay 2000: 9). That the female has no corresponding mark on her body is not to be understood as a reflection of a male chauvinist mentality, as if to suggest that Old Testament religion marginalizes women as covenantally insignificant other than for their wombs. On the contrary, now that two have become "one flesh" (2:24), a mark on only one is necessary.

Clearly, ch. 17 is occupied more with Abraham's circumcision than it is with his name change. Why is the institution of this rite delayed? Could Abraham's circumcision have been recorded in ch. 15 instead? I suggest that the chronological gap between the institution of the covenant and Abraham's circumcision is meant to put divine promise and human obligation in perspective. The latter is subordinated to the former. Circumcision surfaces only once again in Genesis (that of Isaac [21:4]), except for the debacle described in ch. 34. The covenant promises of God, by contrast, continue as a refrain through the rest of Genesis.

Genesis 18–19. Informed of God's intention to obliterate Sodom and Gomorrah because of the gravity of their sensual and social sins (Gen. 19:1–11; cf. Ezek. 16:49–50), Abraham becomes the intercessor for the transgressor. Rather than rejoicing in evil (cf. 1 Cor. 13:6), Abraham goes boldly to God to plead for mercy, and like the Suffering Servant of Isa. 53:12, he makes "intercession for the transgressors." Abraham does not urge Sodom to repent; rather, he appeals to God for mercy. And in doing so, his prayers parallel the prayers of other intercessors (Moses: Exod. 32:11–13, 31–34; 33:12–15; 34:9; Num. 12:11–13; 14:3–9; Deut. 9:16–29; Samuel: 1 Sam. 7:5–9; 12:19–25; Elijah: 1 Kings 17:17–23; Elisha: 2 Kings 4:33; 6:15–20; Amos: Amos 7:1–6; Job: Job 42:7–9). The prayer presupposes a belief and faith in a God who is merciful as well as just, compassionate as well as holy, tender as well as stern, a God who, to quote Pascal, "lends to His creatures the dignity of causality."

Genesis 20. Introduced in ch. 18 to Abraham the intercessor, the reader confronts the patriarch again in a similar role. Because of the prayers of Abraham, the Lord restores fertility to the wife and concubines of a pagan king, Abimelech (v. 17). Apparently, Abraham's act of duplicity perpetrated against Abimelech does not disqualify him from acting as prophetic intercessor. But is it not ironic that Abraham's prayers result in the opening of wombs in Philistine women, but still his own wife is unable to conceive?

Genesis 21–22. A quarter of a century of waiting concludes with the birth of Isaac. We have followed Abraham, chronologically, from septuagenarian (12:4) to centenarian (21:5). Despite setbacks, unwise moves, and frustrations, Abraham has never lost sight of the original promise that he received from God: "a great nation" (12:2). The incredible has become real.

But then the incredible resurfaces. Incredible that Sarah may yet need the services of an obstetrician? Yes. Incredible too, at least for Abraham (and maybe for the reader as well?), that God now will ask Abraham to offer Isaac, "your son, your only son Isaac, whom you love" (NRSV)? Yes.

We would like to know something about the time between Isaac's birth and his being offered. Was he a helpless child, an inquisitive adolescent, or a consenting adult? The Isaac of ch. 22 is referred to as a *na'ar* ("lad" [22:5, 12]), a Hebrew word that can describe a male from infancy (the baby Moses [Exod. 2:6]), to a teenager (seventeen-year-old Joseph [Gen. 37:2]), to men old enough to serve in such capacities as spies (Josh. 6:23). Indeed, the same word applied to Isaac in this chapter is applied also to the two servants whom the father and son took with them (22:3, 5). Isaac himself carries the wood for the fire (22:6; thus, as it were, "bearing his own cross" [cf. John 19:17]). He is able to ask intelligent questions (22:7).

In his *Antiquities of the Jews* (1.13) Josephus states that Isaac was twenty-five at this time. Although Josephus does not explain the source of his information, the figure perhaps refers to the minimum age for active military service at the close of the Second Temple period (five years more than the minimum twenty of Scripture [Num. 1:3, 45]). A midrash on Genesis (*Genesis Rabbah* 56:8) states that Isaac was thirty-seven on this occasion! This figure is based on Sarah's age of ninety at the birth of Isaac, and her death thirty-seven years later at the age of 127 (Gen. 23:1), precipitated by the false announcement of her son's death! In any event, the Isaac of this chapter is anything but a child.

In chs. 18–19 we met the loquacious Abraham, trying to make God reconsider, asking questions, demanding answers, becoming audacious. By contrast, here he is silent, passive, following divine directions. Or is he?

Concerning Abraham, George W. Coats comments (1973: 397), "He appears in superhuman, unemotional, somewhat unrealistic dress. He never objects to the unreasonable, slightly insane commandment to sacrifice his son, as the Abraham of Genesis 12 or Genesis 16 most certainly would have done. To the contrary, he seems to move about his grim task with silent resignation, as if he were an automaton." On the other hand, A. W. Tozer (1948: 25) remarks, "The sacred writer spares us a close-up of the agony that night on the slopes near Beersheba when the aged man had it out with his God, but respectful imagination may view in awe the bent form and convulsive wrestling alone under the stars. Possibly not again until a Greater than Abraham wrestled in the Garden of Gethsemane did such mortal pain visit a human soul."

J. D. Levenson (1994: 151–53) holds the pleading Abraham of Genesis 18 and the passive Abraham of Genesis 22 together in proper tension. He observes that these two presentations, almost adjacent to one another, "delimit a theology in which human judgment neither replaces the inscrutable God who commands [Genesis 22] nor becomes superfluous within the life lived in faithfulness to him [Genesis 18]. In this larger dialectical theology, both arguing with God and obeying him can be central spiritual acts, although when to do which remains necessarily unclear." Elsewhere Levenson (1998: 272) suggests that the difference between chs. 18 and 22 is one of context: "The context of Sodom and Gomorrah is *forensic*, whereas that of the aqedah is *sacrificial*. In a forensic context the death of an innocent person is an outrage; in a sacrificial context . . . the innocence of the human victim is no grounds for protest. Abraham raises his voice against God himself at the thought of an unjust *execution*. He is prepared to offer even his beloved son himself to the same God as a *sacrifice*. There is no contradiction in the text." Perhaps one might see a parallel between the behavior of Abraham and Jesus at this point, especially when Jesus is on the cross. Jesus too makes intercession for sinners (Luke 23:34), but he refuses to save himself from the cross, which the crowd urged him to do (Luke 23:35), and which he had the resources to do had he so chosen (Matt. 26:53). This option, however, he expressly refuses to exercise (John 12:27). In other words, both Abraham and Jesus used their unique relationship with God and the influential spiritual power that comes with that relationship to benefit others but not to benefit themselves, to make salvation possible for others but not to save themselves (Moberly 2000: 160).

Chapter 22 is introduced as a testing from God for Abraham. Certainly the patriarch's faith is being tested ("now I know that you fear God" [v. 12 NRSV]), but it is then only another in a series of divine testings at the point of faith, a faith that was challenged as early as ch. 12: "Go forth!"

Ultimately, the episode is more revealing about God than it is about Abraham. The climax is: "So Abraham called the name of that place The LORD will provide" (v. 14 RSV). The name draws attention to God, not Abraham. It is not "Abraham-has-performed," but "God-will-provide." Faith, then, ultimately is based on God's character and the reliability of his word.

Although Abraham will live a good while beyond this event, and although his life will cover two and a half chapters of Scripture yet to come, never again is there any dialogue between him and God. For the last time Abraham receives the promise of many descendants, the promise of land, and the promise of blessing to the nations in his seed (vv. 15–18).

Genesis 24. God will provide. Abraham discovered this at Moriah. God provided a ram. Will God now provide a wife for Isaac? The longest chapter in Genesis is devoted to answering this question. For Abraham, there is no doubt but that the answer to this question is an unqualified yes (v. 7). Inspired by his master's faith, the servant too places the search in God's hands (vv. 12–14 [on the servant see Teugels 1995]). Nothing of chance or coincidence is allowed to intrude. For this union God has "chosen/appointed" a wife (vv. 14, 44). Throughout this incident God is present in the speech of others rather than through his own speech. The narrator speaks of Yahweh (vv. 1, 21, 52), as do Abraham (vv. 3, 7, 40), the servant (vv. 12, 27, 35, 42, 48, 56), Laban (v. 31), and Laban and Bethuel (vv. 50–51). And although it is common and justified to look to the Joseph story in Genesis as a compelling illustration of divine providence in operation, the contribution of Genesis 24 to that teaching should not be overlooked. In its own way Genesis 24 is all about a "Jehovah-jireh" God. God provides an animal to take the place of Isaac although it is a ram (22:13 and see 15:9–10 for another ram) instead of the expected lamb (22:7–8). God provides Rebekah for Isaac. God provides first a sheep, and then a spouse, and both times Isaac is the beneficiary.

Abraham in the New Testament

Surprisingly, the New Testament nowhere explicitly connects Abraham's near-sacrifice of Isaac with the offering of Jesus. Perhaps the closest analogy is in Paul's words about how God "did not spare his own Son, but gave him up for us all" (Rom. 8:32 RSV).

What the New Testament, and especially Paul, does with Abraham is elevate him as the paragon of faith. Involved in a clash with proponents of works-righteousness, Paul refers to Abraham, a pre-Sinaitic (prelegal) model, and then bases his whole argument for justification by faith around his life.

Toward the end of Romans 3 Paul affirms that it is through faith, and faith alone, that one is justified (3:22, 27, 28, 30). Chapter 4 is then a test case of this thesis. Justification is not through works (4:1–8). Justification is not through circumcision (4:9–12). Justification is not through keeping the law (4:13–15). It is by faith (4:16–25). As proof, consider Abraham, who believed and was justified (apart from works, circumcision, and the law).

What is faith, though? How did it operate in Abraham's case? How is he illustrative of the principle? Paul proceeds to list nine characteristics of Abraham's faith (4:17–20).

1. It is theistic: "in the presence of God in whom he believed"—a God who gives life to the dead (resurrection) and calls into being things that do not exist (creation). This is precisely what God must do with the womb of Sarah and the loins of Abraham, both of which have lost their capacity to procreate. He must create or resurrect their life-producing power.
2. It is suprarational: "in hope he believed against hope." Faith is not against reason (i.e., irrational), but it does surpass reason. Behind the human realities of the situation are divine realities. If there is a God, he can do this. This God transcends human resources.
3. It is purposeful: "that he should become the father of many nations, as he had been told." Abraham's desire is not just a normal urge for a child, but to realize the implementation of God's plan for his life.
4. It is intelligent and realistic: "he did not weaken in faith when he considered his own body." Facts are faced, not avoided. But such facts never become dominating or intimidating.
5. It is unwavering: "no distrust made him waver." Abraham did not hold faith; faith held him.
6. It is well grounded: "concerning the promise of God." It is not faith in faith, or faith in feelings, but faith in God's promise.
7. It is strengthening: "he grew strong in his faith." Character was the by-product.
8. It is worshiping: "as he gave glory to God."
9. It is assuring: "fully convinced that God was able."

This is the kind of faith, then, that justified Abraham. It is interesting that in this mosaic of faith Paul nowhere draws specifically on the offering of Isaac. Instead, he concentrates on another major aspect of Abraham's life, his inability to father a child when both he and Sarah were well beyond child-generating years (see Gen. 18:12), although God had promised an innumerable seed. In a more limited way Paul presents a similar argument to that of Romans in Gal. 3:6–18.

The writer of Hebrews, on the other hand, gives more of an overview of Abraham's odyssey (11:8–22).

1. By faith Abraham *obeyed* (v. 8) when he was called, although the final destination of his journey remained unknown.
2. By faith he *sojourned* (v. 9), living in tents.
3. By faith he *offered* up Isaac (v. 17), convinced in advance of a resurrection for the son.

The writer of the Epistle of James (2:21–23) also uses Genesis 22 to buttress the observation that in offering Isaac, Abraham was justified by works. He was justified by a faith that works. Works as a *merit* for salvation? No. Works as a *mark* of salvation? Yes.

If we are somewhat surprised by Paul's omission in Romans and Galatians of any clear reference to Abraham's offering of Isaac as an example of faith, then we must be similarly surprised by the omission in Hebrews of any clear reference to Abraham's one great act of faith, recorded in Gen. 15:6. There is no "by faith he believed" in Hebrews 11.

There is good reason for the omissions by both authors. Paul uses Abraham's faith as an illustration of the necessity of faith in becoming a child of God. Hence, he focuses on Abraham's faith as it relates to the problems surrounding Isaac's birth.

The writer of Hebrews uses Abraham's faith as an illustration of faith in the daily walk of the child of God. Hence, he does not focus on one incident at the beginning of Abraham's pilgrimage, but chooses instead to give a kaleidoscopic view of Abraham's life, starting with God's first imperative to Abraham and concluding with God's last imperative to Abraham.

Genesis 11:26–25:11 (Abraham)

Aitken, K. T. 1984. "The Wooing of Rebekah: A Study in the Development of Tradition." *JSOT* 30:3–23.

Alexander, T. D. 1983. "Genesis 22 and the Covenant of Circumcision." *JSOT* 25:17–22.

———. 1985. "Lot's Hospitality: A Clue to His Righteousness." *JBL* 104:289–91.

———. 1990. "The Hagar Traditions in Genesis XVI and XXI." In *Studies in the Pentateuch*. Ed. J. A. Emerton. VTSup 41. Leiden: Brill. Pp. 131–48.

———. 1992. "Are the Wife/Sister Incidents of Genesis Literary Compositional Variants?" *VT* 42:145–53.

Andersen, F. I. 1995. "Genesis 14: An Enigma." In *Pomegranates and Golden Bells: Studies in Biblical, Jewish, and Near Eastern Ritual, Law, and Literature in Honor of Jacob Milgrom*. Ed. D. P. Wright, D. N. Freedman, and A. Hurvitz. Winona Lake, Ind.: Eisenbrauns. Pp. 497–508.

Andreasen, N.-E. 1980. "Genesis 14 in Its Near Eastern Context." In *Scripture in Context: Essays on the Comparative Method*. Ed. C. D. Evans, W. W. Hallo, and J. B. White. PTMS 34. Pittsburgh: Pickwick. Pp. 59–77.

Biddle, M. E. 1990. "The 'Endangered Ancestress' and Blessing for the Nations." *JBL* 109:599–611.

Blenkinsopp, J. 1982. "Abraham and the Righteous of Sodom." *JJS* 33:119–32.

Boehm, O. 2002. "The Binding of Isaac: An Inner-Biblical Polemic on the Question of 'Disobeying' a Manifestly Illegal Order." *VT* 52:1–12.

Bolin, T. M. 2004. "The Role of Exchange in Ancient Mediterranean Religion and Its Implications for Reading Genesis 18–19." *JSOT* 29:37–56.

Bray, J. S. 1993. "Genesis 23—A Priestly Paradigm for Burial." *JSOT* 60:69–73.

Brock, S. 1984. "Genesis 22: Where Was Sarah?" *ExpT* 96:14–17.

Bruckner, J. S. 2001. *Implied Law in the Abraham Narrative: A Literary and Theological Analysis.* JSOTSup 335. Sheffield: Sheffield Academic Press.

Brueggemann, W. 1982. "'Impossibility' and Epistemology in the Faith Tradition of Abraham and Sarah." *ZAW* 94:615–34.

Carroll, J. 1996. "The Story of Abraham." In *Genesis, As It Is Written: Contemporary Writers on Our First Stories.* Ed. D. Rosenberg. San Francisco: HarperSanFrancisco. Pp. 71–76.

Childs, B. 1979. *Introduction to the Old Testament as Scripture.* Philadelphia: Westminster.

Clines, D. J. A. 1978. *The Theme of the Pentateuch.* 2nd ed., 1997. JSOTSup 10. Sheffield: JSOT Press.

Coats, G. W. 1973. "Abraham's Sacrifice of Faith: A Form Critical Study of Genesis 22." *Int* 27:389–400.

———. 1985. "Lot: A Foil in the Abraham Saga." In *Understanding the Word: Essays in Honour of Bernhard W. Anderson.* Ed. J. T. Butler, E. W. Conrad, and B. Ollenburger. JSOTSup 37. Sheffield: JSOT Press. Pp. 113–32.

Davies, P. R., and B. D. Chilton. 1978. "The Aqedah: A Revised Tradition History." *CBQ* 40:514–46.

Dozeman, T. B. 1998. "The Wilderness and Salvation History in the Hagar Story." *JBL* 117:23–43.

Drey, P. R. 2002. "The Role of Hagar in Genesis 16." *AUSS* 40:179–95.

Duguid, I. M. 1994. "Hagar the Egyptian: A Note on the Allure of Egypt in the Abraham Cycle." *WTJ* 56:419–21.

Eichler, B. 1997. "On Reading Genesis 12:10–20." In *Tehillah le-Moshe: Biblical and Judaic Studies in Honor of Moshe Greenberg.* Ed. M. Cogan et al. Winona Lake, Ind.: Eisenbrauns. Pp. 23–38.

Emerton, J. A. 1971a. "The Riddle of Genesis XIV." *VT* 21:403–39.

———. 1971b. "Some False Clues in the Study of Genesis XIV." *VT* 21:24–27.

Exum, J. C. 1993. "Who's Afraid of the 'Endangered Ancestress'?" In *The New Literary Criticism and the Hebrew Bible.* Ed. J. C. Exum and D. J. A. Clines. JSOTSup 143. Sheffield: JSOT Press. Pp. 91–113. Repr., in *Fragmented Women: Feminist (Sub)versions of Biblical Narrative.* Valley Forge, Pa.: Trinity, 1993. Pp. 148–69.

Exum, J. C., and J. W. Whedbee. 1985. "Isaac, Samson, and Saul: Reflections on the Comic and Tragic Visions." *Semeia* 32:5–21.

Firestone, R. 1993. "Prophethood, Marriageable Consanguinity and Text: The Problem of Abraham and Sarah's Kinship Relationship and the Response of Jewish and Islamic Exegesis." *JQR* 83:331–47.

Fleishman, J. 2002. "On the Significance of a Name Change and Circumcision in Genesis 17." *JANES* 28:19–32.

Fox, M. V. 1974. "The Sign of the Covenant: Circumcision in the Light of the Priestly *ʾot* Etiologies." *RB* 81:557–96.

Freedman, R. D. 1976. "'Put Your Hand under My Thigh'—The Patriarchal Oath." *BAR* 2 (2):2–4, 42.

Fretheim, T. 1995. "God, Abraham and the Abuse of Isaac." *Word and World* 15:49–57.

Gillmayr-Bucher, S. 1998. "The Woman of Their Dreams: The Image of Rebekah in Genesis 24." In *The World of Genesis: Persons, Places, Perspectives.* Ed. P. R. Davies and D. J. A. Clines. JSOTSup 257. Sheffield: Sheffield Academic Press. Pp. 90–101.

Goldingay, J. 2000. "The Significance of Circumcision." *JSOT* 88:3–18.

Goshen-Gottstein, M. 1987. "Abraham—Lover or Beloved of God?" In *Love and Death in the Ancient Near East.* Ed. J. H. Marks and R. M. Good. Guilford, Conn.: Four Quarters. Pp. 101–4.

Gossai, H. 1995. "A Voice Crying in the Wilderness." In *Power and Marginality in the Abraham Narrative.* Lanham, Md.: University Press of America. Pp. 1–23.

———. 1997. "Divine Vulnerability and Human Marginality in the *Akedah:* Exploring a Tension." *HBT* 19:1–23.

Grayson, A. K., and J. Van Seters. 1975. "The Childless Wife in Assyria and the Stories of Genesis." *Orientalia* 44:485–86.

Greengus, S. 1975. "Sisterhood Adoption at Nuzi and the 'Wife-Sister' in Genesis." *HUCA* 46:5–31.

Gunn, D. M., and D. N. Fewell. 1993. *Narrative in the Hebrew Bible.* Oxford: Oxford University Press. Pp. 90–100.

Handy, L. K. 1997. "Biblical Bronze Age Memories: The Abraham Cycle as Usable Past." *BRes* 42:43–57.

Hartman, G. 1996. "The Story of Isaac's Sacrifice." In *Genesis, As It Is Written: Contemporary Writers on Our First Stories.* Ed. D. Rosenberg. San Francisco: HarperSanFrancisco. Pp. 139–50.

Hasel, G. F. 1981. "The Meaning of the Animal Rite in Genesis 15." *JSOT* 19:61–78.

Hayward, C. T. R. 1990. "The Sacrifice of Isaac and Jewish Polemic against Christianity." *CBQ* 52:292–306.

Helyer, L. R. 1983. "The Separation of Abram and Lot: Its Significance in the Patriarchal Narratives." *JSOT* 26:77–88.

———. 1995. "Abraham's Eight Crises: The Bumpy Road to Fulfilling God's Promise of an Heir." *BRev* 11 (5):20–27, 44.

Hendel, R. S. 2005. *Remembering Abraham: Culture, Memory, and History in the Hebrew Bible.* Oxford: Oxford University Press.

Hepner, G. 2003. "Abraham's Incestuous Marriage with Sarah: A Violation of the Holiness Code." *VT* 53:143–55.

Hoffmeier, J. 1992. "The Wives' Tale of Genesis 12, 20 and 26 and the Covenants at Beer-Sheba." *TynB* 43:81–99.

Humphreys, W. L. 1999. "Where's Sarah? Echoes of a Silent Voice in the *Akedah*." *Soundings* 82:491–512.

———. 2001. *The Character of God in the Book of Genesis.* Louisville: Westminster John Knox.

Janzen, J. G. 1991. "Hagar in Paul's Eyes and in the Eyes of Yahweh [Genesis 16]: A Study in Horizons." *HBT* 13:1–22.

Jensen, R. M. 1994. "The Offering of Isaac in Jewish and Christian Tradition: Image and Text." *BibInt* 2:85–110.

Kaminski, J. 2000. "Humor and the Theology of Hope: Isaac as a Humorous Figure." *Int* 54:363–75.

Kline, M. 1968. "Abram's Amen." *WTJ* 31:1–11.

Kunin, S. D. 1994. "The Death of Isaac: Structuralist Analyses of Genesis 22." *JSOT* 64:57–81.

Kuschel, K.-J. 1995. *Abraham: A Symbol of Hope for Jews, Christians and Muslims.* London: SCM Press.

Landy, F. 1988. "Narrative Techniques and Symbolic Transactions in the Akedah." In *Signs and Wonders: Biblical Texts in Literary Focus.* Ed. J. C. Exum. SemeiaSt. Atlanta: Scholars Press. Pp. 1–40.

Levenson, J. 1993. *The Death and Resurrection of the Beloved Son: The Transformation of Child Sacrifice in Judaism and Christianity.* New Haven: Yale University Press.

———. 1994. *Creation and the Persistence of Evil: The Jewish Drama of Divine Omnipotence.* 2nd ed. Princeton, N.J.: Princeton University Press.

———. 1998. "Abusing Abraham: Traditions, Religious Histories, and Modern Misinterpretations." *Judaism* 47:259–77.

Loewenstamm, S. E. 1971. "The Divine Grants of Land to the Patriarchs." *JAOS* 91:509–10.

Longenecker, R. 1977. "The 'Faith of Abraham' Theme in Paul, James and Hebrews: A Study in the Circumstantial Nature of New Testament Teaching." *JETS* 20:203–12.

Lundbom, J. R. 1983. "Abraham and David in the Theology of the Yahwist." In *The Word of the Lord Shall Go Forth.* Festschrift for D. N. Freedman. Ed. C. L. Myers and M. O'Connor. Winona Lake, Ind.: Eisenbrauns. Pp. 203–9.

MacDonald, N. 2004. "Listening to Abraham—Listening to Yhwh: Divine Justice and Mercy in Genesis 18:16–33." *CBQ* 66:25–43.

Margalit, O. 2000. "The Riddle of Genesis 14 and Melchizedek." *ZAW* 112:501–8.

Martin, T. W. 2003. "The Covenant of Circumcision (Genesis 17:9–14) and the Situational Antithesis in Galatians 3:28." *JBL* 122:111–25.

Matthews, V. H. 1992. "Hospitality and Hostility in Genesis 19 and Judges 19." *BTB* 22:3–11.

Mays, J. L. 2001–2. "'Now I Know': An Exposition of Genesis 22:1–19 and Matthew 26:36–46." *ThTo* 58:519–25.

Mazor, Y. 1986. "Genesis 22: The Ideological Rhetoric and the Psychological Composition." *Bib* 67:81–88.

McCarthy, D. J. 1976. "Three Covenants in Genesis." *CBQ* 26:179–89.

McEvenue, S. E. 1975. "A Comparison of Narrative Styles in the Hagar Stories." *Semeia* 3:64–77.

Miller, P. D. 1984. "Syntax and Theology in Gen XII 3a." *VT* 34:472–75.

Moberly, R. W. L. 1988. "The Earliest Commentary on the Akedah." *VT* 38:302–23. Repr., in *From Eden to Golgotha: Essays in Biblical Theology.* South Florida Studies in the History of Judaism 52. Atlanta: Scholars Press, 1992. Pp. 55–73.

———. 2000. *The Bible, Theology, and Faith: A Study of Abraham and Jesus.* Cambridge: Cambridge University Press.

Moltz, H. 2001. "God and Abraham in the Binding of Isaac." *JSOT* 96:59–69.

Muffs, Y. 1982. "Abraham the Noble Warrior: Patriarchal Politics and Laws of War in Ancient Israel." *JJS* 33:81–107.

Neff, R. 1970. "The Birth and Election of Isaac in the Priestly Tradition." *BRes* 15:5–18.

———. 1972. "The Annunciation in the Birth Narratives of Ishmael." *BRes* 17:51–60.

Niditch, S. 1982. "The 'Sodomite' Theme in Judges 19–20: Family, Community, and Social Disintegration." *CBQ* 44:365–78.

———. 1987. *Underdogs and Tricksters: A Prelude to Biblical Folklore.* New Voices in Biblical Studies. San Francisco: Harper & Row.

Nikaido, S. 2001. "Hagar and Ishmael as Literary Figures: An Intertextual Study." *VT* 51:219–42.

Noegel, S. B. 1998. "A Crux and a Taunt: Night-time Then Sunset in Genesis 15." In *The World of Genesis: Persons, Places, Perspectives.* Ed. P. R. Davies and D. J. A. Clines. JSOTSup 257. Sheffield: Sheffield Academic Press. Pp. 128–35.

O'Brien, M. A. 1990. "The Story of Abraham and the Debate over the Source Hypothesis." *ABR* 38:1–17.

Peck, W. 1976. "Murder, Timing, and the Ram in the Sacrifice of Isaac." *AThR* 58:24–43.

Phillips, G. A., and D. N. Fewell. 1997. "Drawn to Excess, or Reading beyond Betrothal [Gen 24; Jos 24]." *Semeia* 77:25–58.

Polzin, R. 1975. "The Ancestress of Israel in Danger." *Semeia* 3:81–98.

Pope, M. H. 1986. "Enigmatic Bible Passages: The Timing of the Snagging of the Ram, Genesis 22:13." *BA* 49:114–17.

Rad, G. von. 1962. *Old Testament Theology.* Trans. D. M. G. Stalker. 2 vols. New York: Harper & Row.

———. 1972. *Genesis.* Trans. J. H. Marks. Rev. ed. OTL. Philadelphia: Westminster.

Rashkow, I. 1992. "Intertextuality, Transference and Reader in/of Genesis 12 and 20." In *Reading between Texts: Intertextuality and the Hebrew Bible.* Ed. D. N. Fewell. Louisville: Westminster John Knox. Pp. 57–73.

Rendsburg, G. 1992. "Notes on Genesis XV." *VT* 42:266–72.

Ronning, J. 1991. "The Naming of Isaac: The Role of the Wife/Sister Episodes in the Redaction of Genesis." *WTJ* 53:1–27.

Rosen, N. 1996. "The Story of Sarah's Late Pregnancy." In *Genesis, As It Is Written: Contemporary Writers on Our First Stories.* Ed. D. Rosenberg. San Francisco: HarperSanFrancisco. Pp. 115–24.

Roth, W. M. W. 1972. "The Wooing of Rebekah: A Tradition-Critical Study of Genesis 24." *CBQ* 34:177–87.

Sarna, N. 1982. "Genesis 23: The Cave of Machpelah." *HS* 23:17–21.

Schwartz, J. 1995. "Ishmael at Play: On Exegesis and Jewish Society." *HUCA* 66:203–21.

Segal, L. 1996. "The Story of Sarah and Hagar." In *Genesis, As It Is Written: Contemporary Writers on Our First Stories.* Ed. D. Rosenberg. San Francisco: HarperSanFrancisco. Pp. 125–38.

Shanks, H. 1980. "Have Sodom and Gomorrah Been Found?" *BAR* 6 (5):26–36.

Sherwood, Y. 2004. "Binding—Unbinding: Divided Responses of Judaism, Christianity, and Islam to the 'Sacrifice' of Abraham's Beloved Son." *JAAR* 72:821–61.

Steinberg, N. 1984. "Gender Roles in the Rebekah Cycle." *USQR* 391:175–88.

Teugels, L. 1984. "'A Strong Woman, Who Can Find?' A Study of Characterization in Genesis 24, with Some Perspectives on the General Presentation of Isaac and Rebekah in the Genesis Narratives." *JSOT* 63:89–104.

———. 1995. "The Anonymous Matchmaker: An Enquiry into the Characterization of the Servant of Abraham in Genesis 24." *JSOT* 65:13–23.

Thompson, J. L. 1995. "Hagar: Test, Terror and Tradition." *Perspectives* 10:16–19.

———. 1997. "Hagar, Victim or Villain? Three Sixteenth Century Views." *CBQ* 59:213–33.

Thompson, T. L. 1974. *The Historicity of the Patriarchal Narratives: The Quest for the Historical Abraham.* BZAW 133. Berlin: de Gruyter.

Tonson, P. 2001. "Mercy without Covenant: A Literary Analysis of Genesis 19." *JSOT* 95:95–116.

Tozer, A. W. 1948. *The Pursuit of God.* Harrisburg, Pa.: Christian Publications.

Trible, P. 1984. "The Desolation of Rejection." In *Texts of Terror: Literary Feminist Readings of Biblical Narratives.* Philadelphia: Fortress. Pp. 9–35.

———. 1985. "The Other Woman: A Literary and Theological Study of the Hagar Narratives." In *Understanding the Word: Essays in Honour of Bernhard W. Anderson.* Ed. J. T. Butler, E. W. Conrad, and B. Ollenburger. JSOTSup 37. Sheffield: JSOT Press. Pp. 221–46.

———. 1991. "Genesis 22: The Sacrifice of Sarah." In *"Not in Heaven": Coherence and Complexity in Biblical Narrative.* Ed. J. Rosenblatt and J. Sitterson Jr. Bloomington: Indiana University Press. Pp. 170–91.

Turner, M. D. 1985. "Rebekah: Ancestor of Faith." *LTQ* 20:42–50.

Van Seters, J. 1975. *Abraham in History and Tradition.* New Haven: Yale University Press.

Vos, G. 1948. *Notes on Biblical Theology.* Grand Rapids: Eerdmans.

Walters, S. 1987. "Wood, Sand, and Stars: Structure and Theology in Genesis 22:1–19." *Toronto Journal of Theology* 3:301–30.

Wenham, G. J. 1982. "The Symbolism of the Animal Rite in Genesis 15: A Response to G. F. Hasel, *JSOT* 19 (1981): 61–78." *JSOT* 22:134–37.

———. 1995. "The Akedah: A Paradigm of Sacrifice." In *Pomegranates and Golden Bells: Studies in Biblical, Jewish, and Near Eastern Ritual, Law, and Literature in Honor of Jacob Milgrom*. Ed. D. P. Wright, D. N. Freedman, and A. Hurvitz. Winona Lake, Ind.: Eisenbrauns. Pp. 93–102.

Westbrook, R. 1991. "Purchase of the Cave of Machpelah." In *Property and the Family in Biblical Law*. JSOTSup 113. Sheffield: JSOT Press. Pp. 24–35.

White, H. C. 1973. "The Divine Oath in Genesis." *JBL* 92:165–79.

———. 1975. "The Initiation Legend of Ishmael." *ZAW* 87:267–305.

———. 1979. "The Initiation Legend of Isaac." *ZAW* 91:1–30.

Wiseman, D. J. 1977. "Abraham in History and Tradition." *BSac* 134:123–30, 228–37.

Wolff, H. W. 1974. "The Kerygma of the Yahwist." In *The Vitality of Old Testament Traditions*, by H. W. Wolff and W. Brueggemann. Atlanta: John Knox. Pp. 41–66.

4

Jacob

For twenty years Isaac and Rebekah lived together, but with no children. Married at the age of forty (25:20), Isaac does not father a child until he is sixty (25:26). Like her mother-in-law, Rebekah has had to endure an extended period of barrenness, but unlike her mother-in-law (30:3), she offers no substitute to Isaac.

Abraham's prayers result in the cessation of barrenness for other women (20:17), but not for his own wife. In the case of the third generation, Rachel's inability to conceive produces only friction, and sarcasm on Jacob's part (30:2). In contrast with both father Abraham and son Jacob, Isaac's prayer for his wife results in Rebekah's pregnancy (25:21).

The prayer was doubly answered. At least, Isaac and Rebekah got more than they bargained for—twins! In Abraham and Sarah's case the tension in the family begins with no children. In Isaac and Rebekah's case the tension in the family begins with more than one child. At the birth of Jacob and Esau, grandfather Abraham is 160 years old, and he still has fifteen years to live. But nowhere do the Scriptures hint of any meeting or relationship between the old patriarch and the grandchildren.

The three most important women in Genesis—Sarah, Rebekah, and Rachel—all experienced problems in producing children. A period of extended barrenness was a common frustration for all. This particular problem relates especially to God's promise to the patriarchs of many descendants. For how can God's promise be fulfilled when one encounters example after example of female sterility? Add to the problems created by an infertile womb the other exasperating situations described in Genesis, and the outlook for the implementation of God's promises becomes dim indeed.

Not one major character in this part of Scripture flies through history on "flowery beds of ease." Sometimes, of course, the problems are the direct result of an act of folly on the part of the patriarch. At other times, however, the problems are the result of situations over which the patriarchs have no control. This would include the barrenness of the wives and also the various famines that sent Abraham and Isaac scurrying hither and yon for food.

Such events merely happen. They are not punishments sent by God. But each of them does represent a "threat" to God's redemptive plan for humankind. A deceased and childless Abraham or an infertile Sarah is a sentence of death over that divine plan. Surely, these potentially disruptive circumstances serve as background material for illustrations of God's power to overcome obstacles and hurdles. And wherever the challenge is the greatest, God is there to enable the individual to weather the crisis.

In a stimulating study of Jacob's story Michael Fishbane (1975) examines chs. 25–36 of Genesis from the perspective of the symmetry of the whole. His conclusion is that there is a remarkable consistency in the arrangement of the narrative material in the story, even to the point that the story is framed by the genealogies of two individuals who are not a part of the chosen line (Ishmael's descendants [25:12–18] and Esau's descendants [36:1–43]). And surely the framing of the story of Jacob by two genealogies of nonelect people groups underscores the missional calling of those whom God has chosen to be his light-bearers. See the similar structuring of the Jacob narrative done by Walters (1997: 600).

This suggests that the most fruitful investigation of Jacob's history, in terms of theological analysis, is not to extract out of the whole the individual strands (if indeed such did ever exist) and then look for a J emphasis, an E emphasis, or P's genealogical, chronological framework and editorial insertions. One can become dizzy following the weaving back and forth of these sources in the text. To illustrate, in listing the different sources of Genesis 25–28, one encounters this mosaic (following scholarly consensus):

25:19–20	P	27:1–45	J	28:17–18	E
25:21–26a	J	27:46	P	28:19	J
25:26b	P	28:1–9	P	28:20–21a	E
25:27–34	J	28:10	J	28:21b	J
26:1–33	J	28:11–12	E	28:22	E
26:34–35	P	28:13–16	J		

Whether this account was originally composite and then edited or was originally a homogeneous work, we must deal with the unit as a whole as we have it in the text.

A broad overview of the Jacob cycle is provided in table 3.

Table 3

Reference	Description
25:19–28:9	need for transformation
28:10–32:21	preparation for transformation
32:22–32	transformation
33:1–36:40	results of transformation

Need for Transformation (25:19–28:9)

Genesis 25:19–26. Like the older Jacob, who will not let go of his divine assailant (32:26) until a blessing is forthcoming, the infant Jacob, after an *in utero* struggle, emerges into this life clasping his brother's heel. The Hebrew for "heel" is *ʿāqēb*, and the name "Jacob," *yaʿăqōb*, is a play on that word. The phrase "he had taken hold of Esau's heel" is not explained, but the implications seem clear. Obviously it is not a gesture of friendship, a hearty welcome extended to his twin brother. Even in infancy Jacob is a self-centered, self-oriented individual. The name is given to him proleptically (cf. "you are to name him Jesus, for he will save . . ." [Matt. 1:21 NRSV]), indicating a lifestyle ahead that is not commendable.

Genesis 25:27–34. Capitalizing on his brother's hunger, Jacob solicits from his brother the birthright in return for some food. A cup of broth or red pottage has become a bargaining tool. Esau is a skillful hunter, but Jacob is a skillful opportunist. Like the later Israelites who would have gladly surrendered their spiritual credentials (although in the wilderness) in return for three meals a day in Egypt (although it meant the forfeiture of freedom), Esau is glad to barter away his spiritual birthright to satisfy his gastronomic needs, a point not lost on the author of Hebrews: "See that no one is . . . godless like Esau, who for a single meal sold his inheritance rights as the oldest son" (Heb. 12:16 NIV). And Jacob is more than willing to oblige. An oath clinches the transaction (Gen. 25:33).

Genesis 27:1–45. To exploit one's own brother is bad enough, but to deliberately deceive one's own father, now senile and physically incapacitated, is to stoop even lower.

Rebekah is not much more of a saint than were Sarah and Eve. It is she who initiates the scheme of Jacob impersonating Esau. Jacob readily cooperates. Once the aggressive initiator, he is now a follower. Isaac, the deceiver in ch. 26, is about to become the deceived. It is unclear why Rebekah simply did not inform Isaac of the oracle she had received about their two sons in 25:23 rather than going to the great lengths she did in hatching this ruse, especially since 25:23 is the very first instance in the Bible of God responding to a woman who specifically sought God in prayer for clarification—"so she went to inquire of the Lord" (25:22c). Fear? Uncertainty about whether she would be believed or not? Fear that Isaac would discredit her? Her only way, she thinks, to guarantee that the prophecy will be fulfilled over Isaac's possible objections? Because her favorite is Jacob? Nor can we be certain whether she is acting from self-interest or whether she believes that in so acting and encouraging Jacob to act she is fulfilling God's plan. Even if her motive is something less noble than wanting to advance God's plan, Rebekah is not alone in Genesis, or the rest of Scripture, as an example of someone whose less-than-positive behavior ends up accomplishing precisely that. One thinks, for example, of Joseph's brothers selling him to Egypt-bound caravaneers. And it is significant that when Isaac first speaks to Jacob, knowing that he is Jacob (28:1–5), he upbraids neither his wife nor his son. Instead, he speaks only of the future that God has for Jacob. On the other hand, Rebekah's move to secure Jacob's future is similar to Sarah's move to secure Isaac's future. After Genesis 21 Sarah never sees Isaac again. After Genesis 27 Rebekah never sees Jacob again. In fact, neither mother appears as a character in Genesis after these respective chapters.

Furthermore, under the pretext of concern for maintaining purity in the line of descent, Rebekah reminds her husband of the compromising Esau (27:46). Wanting to avoid this at all costs, Isaac blesses Jacob and sends him on his way to find a wife in Paddan-aram (28:1–9).

The preceding chart on sources in chs. 25–28 shows that the critics assign 27:1–45 to J and 27:46–28:9 to P. The reason? The two episodes are irreconcilable. In J Jacob deceives his father, Esau discovers the intrigue, and Jacob flees home with a price placed on his head by Esau. In P Isaac blesses Jacob, there is no reference to deception, and Jacob's purpose for leaving is to obtain a wife. But my analysis of the passage shows this to be a misreading of the text. Far from being a contradiction to what precedes, 27:46–28:9 narrates a second scheme devised by Rebekah—this time to get Jacob away from Esau. Guile worked once. Why not again?

Preparation for Transformation (28:10–32:21)

Genesis 28:10–22. It is inaccurate to say that these episodes in Jacob's life are meant to put a premium on deceit. Ethically there is no question about the impropriety of Jacob's behavior. Here is a classic example of someone who arrogates the will of God. Was Jacob predestined to surpass his brother (25:23)? Yes. Does this give him the right to become manipulative, exploitative, and deceitful? A thousand times, no. The end does not justify the means.

The chapters about Abraham were introduced with God speaking to the patriarch: "now the Lord said to Abram" (12:1). By contrast, a number of episodes take place in Jacob's life before God enters the picture directly. All through the affair with Isaac, Esau, and Rebekah, God does not speak. Nor does God enter during the first part of Jacob's flight.

This changes at Bethel. For the first time God confronts Jacob directly, in a dream (a revelatory medium that God uses for the first time with anyone in the line of Abraham [with the possible exception of 15:12–16, where Abram is asleep, but the revelation is not called a dream], but one that God employed to get the attention of the Philistine king Abimelech [20:3]). We should also observe that this is the first time that Jacob is alone. On all previous occasions he is with someone else: he is with Esau in the womb (25:22); he is with Esau after the latter's hunting excursion (25:29); he is with his mother, Rebekah (17:6–17); he is disguised as Esau with his father, Isaac (27:18–29); he, as Jacob, is with his father (28:1–5). But on this occasion of solitude God steps into his life. Jacob's response upon waking is unusual but not unexpected: "and he was afraid" (28:17), afraid of God. He also is afraid of Laban (31:31) and Esau (32:7, 11).

What makes this response unusual is that it contrasts with that of Jacob's father and grandfather and even Lot, who, when confronted by God or angels, greeted them. On occasion, the angels might even be offered food and overnight lodging! The antecedent to Jacob's fear is Adam's "I heard the sound of you in the garden, and I was afraid" (3:10 NRSV). It is the fear spawned by a guilty conscience.

The divine presence is sufficient to score the point. At no juncture does God take Jacob to task. There are no lectures, no fulminations by God, no Nathan's "You are the man." On the contrary, Jacob found:

1. The gift of divine friendship: he was lonely and alone.
2. The grace of divine forgiveness: the guilt in his life is heavier than the stone on which his head rests.
3. The goal of a divine purpose: in vv. 13–15 he receives the same covenantal promises made to Abraham, and is thus a link in God's chain.

One must not overlook the context and circumstances of these promises. Humphreys (2001: 172) puts it well: "We must remember that God promises all this to a man in flight from the land of promise, a man in flight because he bilked his brother and deceived his father, a 'heel-grabber,' who now is on the run from the wrath of a brother out to kill him."

Commentators sometimes misconstrue Jacob's vow (28:20–22) as an attempt by Jacob to strike a bargain with God as he had done earlier with Esau ("If you do something for me, here is what I will do for you"). But for several reasons, that clearly is not the case. It misunderstands the role of vows in the Bible, the purpose of which surely is not to dictate to God on what terms one will serve him, a kind of *quid pro quo* discipleship. Again, the wording of a good bit of Jacob's vow simply picks up on what God has already promised Jacob. For example, God's "I am with you and will watch over you" resurfaces in Jacob's "If God will be with me and will watch over me." God does not strike deals, but he is not above being held accountable to the truthfulness of the word he has spoken.

Genesis 29–31. In this preparation for transformation God first has shown himself to Jacob. Now, God will hold up a mirror to Jacob. The method is to let Jacob spend the next twenty years living with a person whose character is much like his own: Laban.

At first Laban is the gracious host (29:13). He sounds almost like Adam when he first cast eyes on Eve, "Surely you are my bone and my flesh" (29:14 NRSV). He is a generous employer (29:15). He desires that his nephew/employee become his son-in-law (29:19).

But Jacob, a perpetrator of deceit, is about to become the victim of deceit at the hands of Laban. The irony is hard to miss. Jacob will see himself in Laban. The unsuspecting Jacob discovers, to his chagrin, that he has slept with Leah, not Rachel. Was the ruse possible because it was at night, or Leah was heavily veiled, or Jacob was too drunk to know or care who his bed partner was?

If the providence of God has intruded into the theophany at Bethel, similarly here out of chaos "God moves in a mysterious way his wonders

to perform." The third and fourth children mothered by Leah are Levi
and Judah (29:34–35). From Levi comes the line of priests. From Judah
comes one line of kings, and eventually Jesus. Two of the most significant institutions in the Old Testament have their origin in an unwanted
marriage, initiated only by duplicity! As Gerhard von Rad (1972: 291)
observes, "God's work descended deeply into the lowest worldliness and
there was hidden past recognition."

Jacob still has a way to go in his maturation. This can be observed
by contrasting how beautifully his two wives refer to God/LORD repeatedly on the birth of their children, as does the narrator, in contrast to
the one time that Jacob refers to God in chs. 29–30. Leah (29:32, 33,
35; 30:18, 20), Rachel (30:6, 23, 24), and the narrator (29:31; 30:17, 22)
speak movingly of God. He is a God who sees (29:32), hears (29:33), is
worthy of praise (29:35), rewards (30:18), vindicates (30:6), gives gifts
(30:20), remembers (30:22), removes disgrace (30:23). How different
this is from Jacob's one and only God-word while he is fathering twelve
children by four women. It is, in the phrasing of Fretheim (1994: 555),
"negative and in the form of an angry question": "Jacob became angry
with her [Rachel] and said, 'Am I in the place of God, who has kept you
from having children?'" (30:2 NIV).

That Jacob is still the supplanter, the trickster, is evidenced by the
narrative of 30:25–43. In an attempt to outwit Laban, he concocts a plan
to take a significant portion of Laban's flocks back with him to Canaan.
Jacob's animals will be those multicolored ones that he breeds from
Laban's monochromatic animals—a rarity indeed (at least Laban thinks
so!). Whether Jacob believed that the rods in the watering trough made
a difference (30:37–39), or whether the rods were just a decoy (Gabriel
1971), the plan is laced with deception.

To be sure, Jacob says to his wives, "God has taken away the livestock
of your father, and given them to me" (31:9 NRSV), an idea seconded by
the wives (31:16). He even lends credibility to his actions by appealing
to divine attestation (31:12).

But is Jacob making assumptions? Are the livestock a blessing from
God to Jacob *because* of Jacob or *in spite* of Jacob? Compare Abraham's
ill-gotten wealth from Pharaoh (12:16). Surely, God does not lend his
imprimatur to all the wily schemes of his children.

The narrative in 31:22–55 shows at least that Jacob and Rachel deserve each other! Laban outwits Jacob. Jacob outwits Laban. Rachel
outwits Laban by stealing the household gods (31:30, 34–35), resulting
in a confrontation between Jacob and Laban.

Is it possible here to read between the lines? Laban and Jacob reconcile, and Laban then goes home. But what about the gods upon which the
menstruating Rachel has been sitting? Presumably, Rachel confessed to

her husband after her father's departure. Can we see Jacob contentedly tolerating the presence of false gods in his entourage?

Genesis 32:1–21. Time does not always heal broken relationships. Often it intensifies them. Hurts die slowly. Although twenty years have passed, Esau still resents Jacob's bold moves—at least Jacob thinks so. To that end Jacob lays out another stratagem. Not yet convinced that his security is not in himself, but in God, the carnal Jacob goes into action.

First there is an advance mission (vv. 3–5), then a plan to avoid total obliteration by Esau (vv. 6–8), then a prayer of desperation with no expression of repentance, unless it is found in v. 10 (vv. 9–12), then an attempt to buy Esau's forgiveness (vv. 13–21). Does Jacob need to meet Esau or God? The next section will answer that question for us.

Transformation (32:22–32)

Twenty years earlier Jacob, alone then too, was confronted by God at Bethel. On the first occasion he was fleeing the land of promise; here, he is returning to that land of promise after an extended hiatus. In the blackness of night God and man met. Now it will happen again. Jacob is not the seeker, but the sought.

God, in the form of a "man," engages Jacob in a wrestling match, one that lasts through the night, almost until dawn (v. 24b). One is reminded of the nocturnal conversation between Jesus and Nicodemus (John 3), in which Jesus broke down systematically and thoroughly all of Nicodemus's defenses, verbally wrestled with Nicodemus, and went to the heart of the problem, which was Nicodemus's heart.

At least three distinguishing characteristics of Jacob surface here that separate him from the pre-Peniel Jacob:

1. A consciousness of weakness: "And Jacob's thigh was put out of joint as he wrestled with him" (v. 25b NRSV). The victor in his wrestlings with Esau, Isaac, and Laban, Jacob is now victim, not wrestling but clinging. Whether Jacob's affliction is temporary or permanent, he leaves this encounter with a physical reminder of who is to be in charge of Jacob's life. If the effects of the injury are temporary, then one may compare it with adult circumcision such as the second generation of Israelites experienced before they entered the Promised Land and Jericho (Joshua 5). Certainly that incision on the body was painful and necessitated a time for limping and recuperation and healing (Josh. 5:8).
2. A consuming hunger for God: "I will not let you go, unless you bless me" (v. 26b NRSV). The blessing of Isaac is meaningless un-

less accompanied by the blessing of God. Jacob obtained Isaac's blessing through duplicity, but he can obtain God's blessing only by honest and prayerful request. It is to Jacob's credit, however, that although he is injured (v. 25), he does not release his hold on the man (v. 26).

3. A confession of unworthiness: "'What is your name?' And he said, 'Jacob'" (v. 27 NRSV). His problem is his nature. (Cf. "And Jesus asked him, 'What is your name?' He replied, 'My name is Legion'" [Mark 5:9 NRSV].) The name "Jacob" is as much *what* he is as *who* he is.

This, then, is Jacob's response. What are the results?

1. A new name and character: "Your name shall no more be called Jacob, but Israel, for you have striven [Hebrew, *śrh*] with God [Hebrew, *ʾēl*] and with men and have prevailed" (v. 28 RSV). (One might parallel the objects of Jacob's striving with the statement "Jesus increased in . . . favor with God and man" [Luke 2:52 RSV].) Biblical Hebrew often uses some expression such as "shall no more be said" or "shall no more be called" to indicate some kind of a spiritual metamorphosis. See Gen. 17:5, and especially certain passages in Jeremiah where the phrase highlights moments of change, thanks to something God is doing (Jer. 3:16–17; 16:14–15; 19:6; 23:7–8; 31:29–30).
2. A new power: "you have prevailed" (v. 28b)
3. A new blessing: "and there he blessed him" (v. 29b)
4. A new testimony: "I have seen God face to face, and yet my life is preserved" (v. 30 NRSV). Jacob affirms the truth of a passage such as Exod. 33:20, in which God says, "No one may see me and live." The coming daylight is a danger not to God, but to Jacob. For that reason God says to Jacob, "Let me go, for it is daybreak."
5. A new day, a new start: "the sun rose upon him" (v. 31a)
6. A new reminder of his own weakness: "limping upon his thigh" (v. 31b). The name is changed, but the leg is not healed, at least not immediately.

Results of Transformation (33–36)

Genesis 33. Jacob's reconciliation with God must be followed by reconciliation with his brother. Note the difference between the pre-Peniel Jacob, who brings up the rear of his company ("Pass on before me" [32:16 RSV]), and the post-Peniel Jacob, who leads the procession to

Esau ("He himself went on before them" [33:3a RSV]). And not only is a new courage demonstrated, but also a new humility: "bowing himself to the ground seven times" (v. 3b NRSV). Then there is a new generosity: "Accept my present from my hand. . . . Please accept my gift" (vv. 10–11 NRSV). His motives in giving the gift to Esau are genuine. He no longer connives. We should also observe the transformation of some sort that Esau has experienced. The grudge-carrying, get-even Esau of ch. 27 has become the conciliatory Esau of ch. 33, and without any encounters with God to explain the change in attitude.

Genesis 34. This chapter records a vicious incident in the life of one of Jacob's children, Dinah, his only daughter. She is raped by Shechem, the son of Hamor. What will the "blessed" Jacob do now? Will he seek revenge? Will he attempt to take justice into his own hands (which is what the commandment "Thou shalt not kill" prohibits)?

We discover what Jacob's sons will do, at least two of them, Simeon and Levi. Through "deceit" (v. 13)—the same Hebrew word applied to Jacob in 27:35 and Laban in 29:25—Simeon and Levi lure the guilty parties to their death.

But what of Jacob? His first reaction to the news about Dinah is that he "held his peace" (v. 5). Was it because his peace held him? Upon learning of his sons' macabre war of revenge, he lashes out at Simeon and Levi (v. 30), reserving even harsher words for a later period (49:5–7). Their actions are unjustifiable. The end does not justify the means, although Jacob himself had once subscribed to such a philosophy. Some commentators have taken Jacob to task for his inaction. For them he is a do-nothing, indifferent, insensitive. If so, then the Jacob of ch. 34 hardly demonstrates "the results of transformation." On the other hand, Fewell and Gunn (1991: 198) point out that silence—that is, the ability to keep one's anger restrained in the face of terrible pain inflicted on oneself or on one's beloved—may be the most challenging and difficult response of all. Perhaps Jacob anticipates the prophet's Suffering Servant, who, when "oppressed and afflicted," opened not his mouth (Isa. 53:7).

Genesis 35. The false gods brought by Rachel from her father's household must be disposed of (vv. 2–4). The spiritual sensitivity of Jacob shows here. Their continued presence is incompatible with the worship of the one God.

For a second time Jacob comes to Bethel, where, more than twenty years earlier, God first met him (vv. 5–8). But now we see a Jacob who has gone from Bethel to El-Bethel, from the house of God to the God of the house of God (v. 7). God now is first; God's house is second.

To reaffirm the transaction at Peniel (ch. 32), God again informs Jacob that now he is Israel (vv. 9–10). Fishbane (1975: 28) comments correctly, "To be sure, Jacob had won the name of Israel earlier (32:29). But perhaps the narrative seeks to indicate that it is only *after* the resolution of his conflict with Esau (Genesis 33) that Jacob was, indeed, Israel."

The death of his wife, Rachel (vv. 16–21), the incest committed by his eldest son, Reuben (v. 22), and the death of his father, Isaac (vv. 27–29), do not overwhelm Jacob. The conclusion to the chapter is appropriate. Isaac is buried by "his sons Esau and Jacob." Alienation has been replaced by proximity.

Genesis 36. The "generations of Esau" (KJV) are introduced by a description of the final parting of Esau and Jacob. We began in ch. 28 with Jacob fleeing from Esau. Here it is Esau who leaves Jacob. Much like a parting earlier between Abraham and Lot (13:5–12), Esau and Jacob bid each other adieu, and go their separate ways amicably.

Genesis 25:11–36:42 (Jacob)

Anderson, B. W. 1969. "An Exposition of Genesis xxxii." *ABR* 17:21–26.

Bechtel, L. M. 1994. "What If Dinah Is Not Raped? (Genesis 34)." *JSOT* 62:19–36.

Brisman, L. 1990. *The Voice of Jacob: On the Composition of Genesis.* Indiana Studies in Biblical Literature. Bloomington: Indiana University Press.

Carr, D. 2000. "Untamable Text of an Untamable God: Genesis and Rethinking the Character of Scripture." *Int* 54:347–62.

Caspi, M. 1981. "The Story of the Rape of Dinah: The Narrator and the Reader." *HS* 26:25–45.

Coole, R. 1972. "The Meaning of the Name Israel." *HTR* 65:137–42.

Crusemann, F. 1994. "Dominion, Guilt, and Reconciliation: The Contribution of the Jacob Narrative in Genesis to Political Ethics." *Semeia* 66:67–77.

Curtis, E. M. 1987. "Structure, Style and Context as a Key to Interpreting Jacob's Encounter at Jabbok." *JETS* 30:129–37.

Diamond, J. A. 1984. "The Deception of Jacob: A New Perspective on an Ancient Solution to the Problem." *VT* 34:211–13.

Evans, C. D. 1986. "The Patriarch Jacob—An Innocent Man." *BRev* 2 (1):32–37.

Fewell, D. M., and D. M. Gunn. 1991. "Tipping the Balance: Sternberg's Reader and the Rape of Dinah." *JBL* 110:193–211.

Fishbane, M. 1975. "Composition and Structure in the Jacob Cycle (Genesis 25:19–35:22)." *JJS* 26:15–38. Repr., in *Text and Texture: Close Readings of Selected Biblical Texts.* New York: Schocken, 1979. Pp. 40–62.

Fleishman, J. 2004. "Shechem and Dinah—In the Light of Non-Biblical and Biblical Sources." *ZAW* 116:12–32.

Frankena, R. 1970. "Some Remarks on the Semitic Background of Chapters xxix–xxxi of the Book of Genesis." *OtSt* 17:53–64.

Fretheim, T. E. 1972. "The Jacob Traditions, Theology and Hermeneutic." *Int* 26:419–36.

———. 1994. "Genesis." In *The New Interpreter's Bible*. Vol. 1. Ed. L. E. Keck et al. Nashville: Abingdon. Pp. 319–674.

———. 2000. "Which Blessing Does Isaac Give Jacob?" In *Jews, Christians, and the Theology of the Hebrew Scriptures*. Ed. A. O. Bellis and J. S. Kaminsky. SBLSymS 8. Atlanta: Society of Biblical Literature. Pp. 279–91.

Frymer-Kensky, T. 2002. *Reading the Women of the Bible: A New Interpretation of Their Stories*. New York: Schocken. Pp. 5–23, 179–98.

Furman, N. 1989. "His Story versus Her Story: Male Genealogy and Female Strategy in the Jacob Cycle." *Semeia* 46:141–49.

Gabriel, M. L. 1971. "Biology." *EncJud* 4:1024–27.

Geller, S. A. 1990. "The Sack of Shechem: The Use of Typology in Biblical Covenant." *Prooftexts* 10:1–15. Repr. as "The Rape of Dinah: Sexuality and Transcendence," in *Sacred Enigmas: Literary Religion in the Hebrew Bible*. New York: Routledge, 1996. Pp. 142–56.

Gevirtz, S. 1981. "Simeon and Levi in 'the Blessing of Jacob' (Gen. 49:5–7)." *HUCA* 52:93–128.

Greenberg, M. 1962. "Another Look at Rachel's Theft of the Teraphim." *JBL* 81:239–48.

Hirsch, E. 1996. "The Story of Jacob's Wrestling with an Angel." In *Genesis, As It Is Written: Contemporary Writers on Our First Stories*. Ed. D. Rosenberg. San Francisco: HarperSanFrancisco. Pp. 179–88.

Holmgren, F. C. 1990. "Holding Your Own against God! Genesis 32:22–32 in the Context of Genesis 31–33." *Int* 44:5–17.

Houtman, C. 1977. "What Did Jacob See in His Dream at Bethel? Some Remarks on Genesis XXVIII 10–22." *VT* 27:337–51.

Humphreys, W. L. 2001. *The Character of God in the Book of Genesis*. Louisville: Westminster John Knox.

Knight, H. F. 1992. "Meeting Jacob at the Jabbok: Wrestling with a Text—A Midrash on Genesis 32:22–32." *JES* 29:451–60.

Lipton, D. 1999. *Revisions of the Night: Politics and Promise in the Patriarchal Dreams of Genesis*. JSOTSup 228. Sheffield: Sheffield Academic Press.

Malul, M. 1996. "ʿĀqēb 'Heel' and ʿĀqab 'to Supplant' and the Concept of Succession in the Jacob-Esau Narratives." *VT* 46:190–212.

Matthews, V. H. 1985. "Jacob the Trickster and Heir of the Covenant: A Literary Interpretation." *Perkins Religious Studies* 12:192–93.

McKay, H. A. 1987. "Jacob Makes It across the Jabbok: An Attempt to Solve the Success/Failure Ambivalence in Israel's Self-Consciousness." *JSOT* 38:3–13.

Miscall, P. D. 1978. "The Jacob and Joseph Stories as Analogies." *JSOT* 6:28–40.

Noble, P. 1996. "A 'Balanced' Reading of the Rape of Dinah: Some Exegetical and Methodological Observations." *BibInt* 4:173–204.

Oblath, M. 2001. "'To Sleep, Perchance to Dream': What Jacob Saw at Bethel." *JSOT* 95:117–26.

Parry, R. 2000. "Source Criticism and Genesis 34." *TynB* 51:121–38.

———. 2002. "Feminist Hermeneutics and Evangelical Concerns: The Rape of Dinah as a Case Study." *TynB* 53:1–28.

Peleg, Y. 2004. "Going Up and Down: A Key to Interpreting Jacob's Dream (Gen 28, 10–22)." *ZAW* 116:1–11.

Rad, G. von. 1972. *Genesis*. Trans. J. H. Marks. Rev. ed. OTL. Philadelphia: Westminster.

Rendsburg, G. 1984. "Notes on Genesis XXXV." *VT* 34:361–64.

Rosenblatt, N. H., and J. Horwitz. 1995. *Wrestling with Angels*. New York: Dell.

Ross, A. P. 1985. "Jacob's Vision: The Founding of Bethel." *BSac* 142:338–54.

Roth, M. W. 1977. "Structural Interpretations of 'Jacob at the Jabbok' (Genesis 32:22–32)." *BRes* 22:51–62.

Sapnier, G. K. 1992. "Rachel's Theft of the Teraphim: Her Struggle for Family Privacy." *VT* 42:404–12.

Scholz, S. 2000. *Rape Plots: A Feminist Cultural Study of Genesis 34*. New York: Lang.

Smith, S. M. 1990. "'Heel' and 'Thigh': The Concept of Sexuality in the Jacob-Esau Narratives." *VT* 40:464–73.

Spina, F. A. 1997. "The 'Face of God': Esau in Canonical Context." In *The Quest for Context and Meaning: Studies in Biblical Intertextuality in Honor of James A. Sanders*. Ed. C. Evans and S. Talmon. Leiden: Brill. Pp. 3–25.

Sternberg, M. 1987. *The Poetics of Biblical Narrative: Ideological Literature and the Drama of Reading*. Bloomington: Indiana University Press. Pp. 445–76.

———. 1992. "Biblical Poetics and Sexual Politics: From Reading to Counter-reading." *JBL* 111:463–88.

Van Seters, J. 1969. "Jacob's Marriages and Ancient Near Eastern Customs." *HTR* 62:377–95.

———. 1998. "Divine Encounter at Bethel (Gen 28, 10–22) in Recent Literary-Critical Study of Genesis." *ZAW* 110:503–13.

Walters, S. D. 1992. "Jacob Narrative." *ABD* 3:599–608.

5

Joseph

GENESIS 37–50

The story about Joseph opens ominously: "Now Israel loved Joseph more than any other of his children, because he was the son of his old age" (37:3 NRSV). It portends trouble as surely as did "Isaac loved Esau . . . but Rebekah loved Jacob" (25:28 NRSV). Perhaps "loved more than" should remind one of "was more subtle than" (3:1), also a harbinger of trouble ahead. The father supplies the son with a "coat of many colours" (KJV) or a "long robe with sleeves" (NRSV), according to 37:3. The brothers' reactions are envy and anger.

A Young Man with a Dream

To make matters worse, at least from the brothers' perspective, Joseph tells them about two of his dreams. In one the sheaves of his brothers bowed before his (37:5–7). In the second the luminaries bowed before him (37:9). How should we gauge Joseph's motives here? Does he, in the words of G. W. Coats (1976: 82), "dream grandiose dreams and freely flaunt them and their obvious significance to all members of the family"? Or, as W. L. Humphreys (2001: 206) has suggested, can we read

Joseph's dreams and his sharing of them as "somewhere on a scale that ranges from the psychological bravado of a spoiled seventeen-year-old teen to God-given signs of his family's future"?

Joseph's behavior is not unlike that of the youthful David, who is willing to take on Goliath (1 Sam. 17:26, 31) over the protestations of his older brothers and Saul. The dreams are from God. To the teenager Joseph the revelation means at least one thing: God has a plan for his life, and that plan includes some type of leadership. Here then is a teenager with a sense of destiny, divine destiny. He shares this fact out of enthusiasm, not out of brashness. "Here am I, Lord, send me." But the brothers cannot tolerate this.

This certainly is not the first time that Genesis draws attention to somebody's dream. Earlier dreams include Abraham's (15:12–16), Abimelech's (20:3), Jacob's (28:10–16), and Laban's (31:24). What distinguishes Joseph's dreams from these is that in all the other recorded dreams in Genesis God speaks clearly to the dreamer. In Joseph's two dreams, by contrast, God says nothing to Joseph. Joseph's two dreams, followed by his journey to Egypt, a trip that eventually results in the salvation of Israel (Gen. 45:5; 50:20), surely has a parallel in the dreams of the New Testament Joseph. He too heads to Egypt after two dreams (Matt. 1:20–21; 2:13) in less than ideal circumstances (Matt. 1:19–20), taking with him Mary and the child who "will save his people from their sins" (Matt. 1:21 NRSV).

Unsavory Experiences (37:9–36; 39–41)

Joseph has not yet seen everything in God's plan for his life. Some of it is about to appear.

Genesis 37. For the brothers, to dismiss Joseph as a fraud and ignore him is insufficient. He must be eliminated. After having second thoughts about killing their brother outright, they sell him to some traders going to Egypt. These latter are called within one verse (v. 28) both "Midianites" and "Ishmaelites." Along with other facts in the narrative, this phenomenon often is interpreted as an indication of two originally independent stories about Joseph, a J story ("Ishmaelite") and an E story ("Midianites"). That Judg. 8:22–24 expressly identifies the Midianites and the Ishmaelites as one and the same and that dual names for individuals and groups were common in antiquity are sufficient to undercut the credibility of this source division (on this phenomenon see Kidner 1967: 184–86; Kitchen 1966: 119, 123). One might suggest that "Ishmaelite" is an all-inclusive term for nomadic travelers in northern Arabia and southern Palestine, while "Midianite" is the more specific and ethnic term. When the brothers see these travelers from a distance, the travelers appear to be a group of Bedouin nomads (vv. 25, 26), "Ishmaelites." When this group is close enough to speak with Joseph's brothers, the text identifies them as "Midianites" (v. 28a) (see Longacre 1989: 31).

What, we may ask as we return to the narrative, are Joseph's thoughts through all this nightmare? Intended for a leadership role, he finds himself sold as a slave by his own brothers to total strangers traveling to a land about which he knows nothing! What about God's plan? How does this fit in?

Genesis 39. All goes well for a while. Joseph has security, a good job, and a respectable employer. But only for a while! In her husband's absence the wife of Potiphar propositions Joseph. It may be that this woman is simply a victim of boredom and her own unbridled lust. There may be another contributing factor, however. Potiphar is called Pharaoh's "official/officer." This is a perfectly good translation of the Hebrew word, but that word also is the word for "eunuch." Some ancient kings, for obvious reasons, insisted that their more powerful courtiers be eunuchs. Previously a victim of jealousy and anger, Joseph is about to become a victim of a vicious lie. For a crime of which he is totally innocent, Joseph will go to prison. But what about the dreams, and what about God's plan for his life?

Almost all commentators have observed the similarity between this story and the Egyptian "Tale of Two Brothers" from the thirteenth century B.C. An unmarried brother, Bata, lives with his older brother, Anubis, and his wife. In the husband's absence the wife attempts to seduce her brother-in-law: "Come, let's spend an hour sleeping [together]." Bata emphatically refuses and runs away "like a leopard." The wife's attempt to put the blame on Bata succeeds for a while. To save Bata from Anubis requires a miracle by Re, the sun god, who puts a body of water filled with crocodiles between the two. When Anubis discovers that his wife was the initiator, "he reached his house, and he killed his wife, and he threw her out to the dogs."

One of the major differences between the two stories is the fate of the seductive wife. We do not know what happens to Potiphar's wife. Nahum Sarna (1966: 216) suggests, "The reason for this disinterest is that our story was not intended for entertainment purposes and was not told for its own sake. The focus of attention is on Joseph's reaction." It may even be that Potiphar is suspicious of his wife's story, which could explain why Potiphar imprisons rather than executes Joseph.

Little does Joseph yet comprehend that even Potiphar's wife's malicious lie and his own subsequent imprisonment will be the means by which he will come to the attention of Pharaoh and eventually emerge

as the savior of the nation and of his own family. Had he remained in
Potiphar's house for the rest of his adult life, Joseph would never have
caught Pharaoh's interest, and he would never have become a person of
such influence in Egypt. Here is another instance in the Joseph narrative
of God working good from evil perpetrated by humans.

Interestingly, ch. 39 is the only chapter in 37–50, where the focus
is on Joseph (hence exclude ch. 38 and most of ch. 49), that speaks of
"Yahweh/LORD" (vv. 2, 3 [2x], 5 [2x], 21, 23 [NRSV, 2x]). And all eight [NIV,
seven] occurrences come from the narrator. In four of these eight the
narrator states that "the LORD was with Joseph" (vv. 2, 3, 21, 23). Just
as Joseph's presence makes a difference between death and survival
for Egypt, so Yahweh's presence makes a difference between death and
survival for Joseph.

Genesis 40. In prison Joseph befriends two of Pharaoh's employees
who have fallen out of favor with the king, the chief butler and the baker.
He also interprets their dreams for them. His one request for assistance
is directed to the butler: please tell Pharaoh that I am here unjustly and
want my release (vv. 14–15). However, "The chief butler did not remember Joseph, but forgot him" (v. 23 RSV). And for two more years (41:1)
Joseph remained incarcerated. Where is God in all of this?

Might there not be a "subtle serpent" around who will suggest to Joseph,
"Did not God say that your brothers will bow before you? Is this how your
God treats you in return for your obedience to him?" All the temptations
are there: to be angry, bitter, resentful, cynical, self-pitying.

Genesis 41. Pharaoh's dual dreams, unsettling to say the least, provide the opportunity for Joseph's release from prison. As in the case of
the dreams of the chief butler and the baker (40:8), Joseph is quick to
disclaim any innate gift for the interpretation of dreams (41:16).

After interpreting the dream, Joseph counsels Pharaoh to appoint
someone (is he hinting?) to oversee the stockpiling of food for the lean
years ahead. Forewarned is forearmed. Joseph is Pharaoh's choice (v. 41)
for this office.

We now have followed Joseph from the age of seventeen (37:2) to
the age of thirty (41:46). What began as something exhilarating for
Joseph turned into a nightmare that was to last thirteen years. But
light is now beginning to dawn. If Joseph had to endure thirteen years
of bewilderment, it was only half of what his great-grandfather had to
suffer through. Abraham received God's promise of a child at the age
of seventy-five, but he had to wait until he was one hundred before he
became the father of the child of promise.

The sense that Joseph's fortunes are about to change for the better emerges from his exogamous and fruitful marriage to the Egyptian Asenath (v. 45). From this marriage come two sons, whom Joseph

names Manasseh and Ephraim (vv. 51–52). The first son's name is a reminder that God is helping Joseph forget the hurts of his past—what some today might call "the healing of the memories," or in the words of Phil. 3:13, "forgetting what is behind." The second son's name is a reminder that God will make Joseph a fruitful servant even in a land of torment, uncertainty, and disappointment. Forgetfulness and fruitfulness are among God's choicest blessings to anybody enduring the likes of Joseph's odyssey.

In All Things God Works for Good (42–50)

The remaining chapters of Genesis describe the trips between Egypt and Canaan by Joseph's brothers in an attempt to procure grain. These trips climax in Joseph's self-disclosure to his brothers, reconciliation with them, and a final chance to be with his father. It has been at least twenty years since Joseph has seen his brothers: thirteen years in Egypt, followed by the seven good years. In ch. 37 he went to see his brothers. In ch. 42 his brothers come to see him.

What will Joseph's response be? Will he meet them with open arms? Will he let bygones be bygones? Joseph's greeting may surprise us. He first accuses his brothers of being spies, which they were not (42:9). Second, he puts them in prison, and he offers release only if one will return to Canaan and bring back the youngest brother (42:15–17). Third, Simeon is put in jail, while the other brothers return to fetch Benjamin. Meanwhile, Joseph loads their sacks with grain and also puts their money back inside the sacks. Not only spies, but thieves too (42:18–25)? Fourth, with Benjamin present, Joseph sends his brothers back to Canaan again, secretly putting his own valuable silver cup into Benjamin's sack (44:1–13). Judah begs Joseph to take him as a slave instead of Benjamin (44:14–34).

For a parallel to these machinations of Joseph, C. H. Gordon (1965: 113, 229) refers to the Middle Egyptian story called "The Complaints of the Eloquent Peasant." A peasant loses his donkeys to a rogue on the basis of a trumped-up charge of trespassing. The peasant complains eloquently to both Pharaoh and the man on whose property he allegedly trespassed. These two individuals listen carefully to the peasant and eventually decide in his favor, but all the time this is going on, they make sure that his wife and family are adequately provided for in terms of food and basic supplies.

In the context of the biblical story, however, how should the reader judge Joseph at this point? Is he ruthless, merciless? Is he toying with his brothers? Is Joseph acting in the same way that Jacob once did? Does he want to get even with his brothers and make them suffer? Will he play god with them (but see his claim in 42:18)? There have been weeping scenes before in Genesis (Esau's [27:38]; Jacob [29:11]; Esau and Jacob [33:4]). But Joseph weeps more often than everyone else put together in Genesis 12–50 (42:24; 43:30; 45:2, 14–15; 46:29; 50:1). That the text so often draws attention to Joseph's tears must be a way of informing the reader that Joseph is not being vindictive and that his motives, however mysterious, cannot be as sinister as they might appear.

We must admit that the language is rough and the tactics forceful (see 42:7). But may not such measures ultimately be redemptive? Joseph did speak to his brothers "roughly," but no more roughly than God spoke to Adam and Eve in Eden. And God's ultimate design in Eden is to restore these two. Rough words are redemptive words. R. Alter (1981: 140) refers to the necessary but "painful process by which the brothers come to accept responsibility for what they have done and are led to work out their guilt."

Joseph's refusal to accept adulation from his brothers, as the story concludes, is indicated by the words "Fear not, for am I in the place of God?" (50:19 RSV). B. Dahlberg (1976: 363), in attempting to link themes of the narrative about Joseph with similar ones in Genesis 1–11, contrasts this word of Joseph with the word of the serpent, "You will be like God" (3:5 NRSV). He also contrasts the words of Joseph, "You meant evil against me; but God meant it for good" (50:20 RSV), with the serpent's "knowing good and evil." Such comparisons illustrate the literary artistry that runs throughout this first book of the Bible. The Hebrew word behind the English "meant" in 50:20 may also be rendered "planned": "You 'planned' evil against me, but God 'planned' it for good." The same word in noun form appeared in 6:5: "The LORD saw . . . that every inclination of the thoughts of their hearts was only evil continually" (NRSV). Genesis begins and ends with those who plan evil. But the closest parallel to God planning something good for somebody is Jer. 29:11, again in the context of adversity—a promise to those in exile (and using the same Hebrew root for "plan" as in Gen. 6:5; 50:20)—"For I know the 'plans' I have for you . . . 'plans' to prosper you . . . 'plans' to give you hope and a future."

How does Joseph overcome the temptations that we noted? He simply related all his life experiences, good and bad alike, to the sovereign plan of God for his life. "God sent me before you to preserve life. . . . It was not you who sent me here, but God" (45:5–8 NRSV). Or again, "As for you, you meant evil against me; but God meant it for good" (50:20 RSV). Already the sentiment expressed much later in Rom. 8:28 has surfaced. We will see it again with Daniel (Dan. 6:10) and Paul (Phil. 1:12–14).

We may ask about what is "the life that is preserved" (45:5) or who are the "many people kept alive" (50:20) by Joseph's extended presence in Egypt. In one sense the reference is to the residents of Egypt. Had it not been for Joseph's wise counsel to prepare for the years of leanness, the Egyptians would have been decimated by the prolonged famine.

The text informed us that Joseph already has been the means of blessing on one Egyptian and his house (39:5). Is he now a means of blessing on all Egyptians and their houses? If so, then the providential sparing of these unbelievers becomes a graphic illustration of how God's word of promise to Abraham is fulfilled: "Those who bless you I will bless." We have already seen a dramatic fulfillment of "Those who curse you I will curse" in Genesis 12. The taking of a patriarch's wife into Pharaoh's harem becomes the occasion for an eruption of plagues in Pharaoh's house. Conversely, the taking of Abraham's great-grandson into the highest echelons of the Egyptian administration becomes the occasion for Egypt's salvation from a devastating crisis.

Primarily, the "preserved life" and the "many people" mentioned by Joseph to his brothers must refer to the descendants of Abraham. We have observed many instances in Genesis in which God's people have been threatened with extinction. And if the family that bears the covenant promise is annihilated, does this mean that all the promises of God evaporate into thin air?

In an exhibition of tangible, spiritual maturity Joseph sees himself and his experiences in Egypt as the divinely appointed means of perpetuating the promises of God for the people of God. The Joseph story is linked not only with Genesis 1–11 (Dahlberg 1976), but also more importantly with the theme of divine promise that begins with Abraham. The story also links Genesis with Exodus, as both this story and the opening chapters of Exodus highlight the same theme: potential threats to the divine promise.

There is no reservation, however, in Joseph's mind about whether the divine plan will succeed. About its implementation he is totally convinced. God will indeed "visit" Joseph's brothers (50:24–25) as God "visited" Sarah (21:1), and then he will bring them to the land of Abraham, Isaac, and Jacob.

The Joseph story is a powerful illustration of God's control over human history. In addition, it poignantly demonstrates that evil can beget more evil, but also that evil does not always produce more evil. From evil, good can come. But this needs some qualification. As Jacobs (2003: 335) remarks, "The hermeneutical significance of the [Joseph] story is not its claim about the universality of God's intervention in human affairs to bring good out of evil." Sometimes evil is transformed, sometimes not. Sometimes God intervenes unimaginably, sometimes not. Sometimes God provides a ram, sometimes not. What the Joseph story accomplishes is the hope, rather than a guarantee, that good may emerge from every evil.

Judah and Tamar (38)

Obviously, Genesis 38 interrupts the flow of Joseph's story. One can read chs. 37 and 39, avoiding ch. 38 entirely, without destroying the continuity of the story. Some commentators, such as Nahum Sarna (in his earlier Genesis commentary) and Eric Lowenthal, ignore the chapter altogether.

The chapter is about Judah, son of Jacob, brother of Joseph. He fathers, by a Canaanite woman, three sons: Er, Onan, and Shelah. Er, the oldest, marries Tamar. Er dies, leaving Tamar as a childless widow. It then becomes the responsibility of the second-oldest son, Onan, to father a child by his sister-in-law, thus preserving the name of the deceased firstborn (see Deut. 25:5–10 for the Mosaic legislation of the levirate marriage; *levir* is Latin for "brother-in-law"). Onan refuses by practicing a method of birth control, coitus interruptus (v. 9). For refusing to accept responsibility, Onan dies. Judah sends Tamar back to her own father, and promises to summon her when Shelah is old enough to have sexual intercourse with her.

The promise, however, is never honored. Taking matters into her own hands, Tamar dresses as a prostitute, eventually seduces her father-in-law, Judah, and bears twins by him. But how do we relate this to Joseph?

Donald Redford (1970: 17) comments, "The only reasonable explanation of the present order of the chapters must be chronological. Chapter 38 could not follow the Joseph Story, since Judah is then in Egypt for the rest of his life, while the setting of 38 is in Palestine. It could not precede the Joseph Story, for Judah is an old grandfather at the close of 38, while at the outset of the Joseph Story he is still a young man."

Apart from the chronological necessity, one cannot miss the vivid contrasts that this event presents with the Joseph story. In ch. 37 Jacob is deceived, in ch. 38 Judah is deceived, and in ch. 39 Potiphar is deceived, all by family members (sons, daughter-in-law, wife). In ch. 37 the bloodied coat of Joseph is the alleged evidence to Jacob of his son's death; in ch. 38 Tamar's possession of Judah's personal seal, cord, and staff is the evidence of the latter's culpability; in ch. 39 Potiphar's wife's clutching of Joseph's garment is the alleged evidence of his attempt to rape her. The adulterous Judah of ch. 38 contrasts with the faithful, uncompromising Joseph of ch. 39. Tamar is successful, but Potiphar's wife is not. All three chapters highlight part of someone's clothing: Joseph's robe (ch. 37); Tamar's widow's clothing and then her veil (ch. 38); Joseph's cloak (ch. 39). And interestingly, 37:32–33 and 38:25–26 use first the imperative of "recognize" (*nākar*) (Jacob's sons speaking to him about Joseph's bloodied coat [37:32]; Tamar speaking to Judah about the owner of the seal, cord, and staff that are in her possession [38:25]). And in the next verses in both cases (37:33; 38:26) we read: "Jacob 'recognized' it" and "Judah 'recognized' them." The first (ch. 37) is a lie-telling moment; the second (ch. 38) is a truth-telling moment.

Chapter 38 is in microcosm what chs. 37 and 39–50 are in macrocosm. God works his plan even in unsavory circumstances. Joseph survives hostility and becomes the physical salvation of his family. Zerah and Perez, twins in the messianic line (Matt. 1:3), have their origin in an incestuous relationship between father-in-law and daughter-in-law.

The significant role that Judah's daughter-in-law, Tamar, plays in preserving the "purity" of the line of Judah should not be overlooked. Judah, now that his three older brothers, Reuben, Simeon, and Levi, have defaulted, has assumed the role of the firstborn in Israel. But he has done something that Abraham did not want Isaac to do (24:3) and that Isaac did not want Jacob to do (28:1): he has married a Canaanite woman (38:2). Thus, his surviving son, Shelah, is of mixed parentage, of chosen and nonchosen seed, a fact that renders practically impossible the ongoing fulfillment of the promises of God to Abraham and Isaac. Judah's insemination of Tamar, assuming that she is not a Canaanite, allows for the promised line to continue through Judah and Tamar rather than through Judah and his Canaanite wife (see Sailhamer 1990: 232).

Both of the incidents in chs. 37 and 38 are heartaches for Jacob. In one, a son is mauled to death, so the father thinks; in the other, another son becomes an adulterer. In light of such experiences one can understand why Jacob later will say, "Few and evil have been the days of the years of my life" (47:9).

Genesis 37–50 (Joseph)

Ackerman, J. S. 1982. "Joseph, Judah, and Jacob." In *Literary Interpretations of Biblical Narratives*. Vol. 2. Ed. K. R. R. Gros Louis and J. S. Ackerman. Nashville: Abingdon. Pp. 85–113.

Alter, R. 1981. *The Art of Biblical Narrative*. New York: Basic Books. Pp. 3–12; 107–12; 137–40; 172–76.

Arbeitmann, Y. L. 2000. "Tamar's Name or Is It?" *ZAW* 112:341–55.

Battenfield, J. R. 1972. "A Consideration of the Identity of the Pharaoh of Genesis 47:11." *JETS* 25:77–85.

Bird, P. 1997. "The Harlot as Heroine: Narrative Art and Social Presuppositions in Three Old Testament Texts." In *Missing Persons and Mistaken Identities: Woman and Gender in Ancient Israel.* Ed. P. Bird. Minneapolis: Fortress. Pp. 197–218.

Brueggemann, W. 1983. "Genesis L 15–21: A Theological Exploration." In *Congress Volume, Salamanca 1983.* Ed. J. A. Emerton. VTSup 36. Leiden: Brill. Pp. 40–53.

Cassuto, U. 1973. "The Story of Tamar and Judah." In *Biblical and Oriental Studies.* Trans. I. Abrahams. 2 vols. Jerusalem: Magnes. Vol. 1, pp. 29–40.

Clifford, R. J. 2004. "Genesis 38: Its Contribution to the Jacob Story." *CBQ* 66:519–32.

Coats, G. W. 1972. "Widow's Rights: A Crux in the Structure of Gen. 38." *CBQ* 34:461–66.

———. 1973. "The Joseph Story and Ancient Wisdom: A Reappraisal." *CBQ* 35:285–97.

———. 1974. "Redactional Unity in Gen 37–50." *JBL* 93:15–21.

———. 1976. *From Canaan to Egypt: Structural and Theological Context for the Joseph Story.* Washington, D.C.: Catholic Biblical Association of America.

Curtis, E. M. 1990–1991. "Genesis 38: Its Context(s) and Function." *Criswell Theological Review* 5:247–57.

Dahlberg, B. 1976. "On Recognizing the Unity of Genesis." *Theology Digest* 24:360–67.

Emerton, J. A. 1975. "Some Problems in Genesis XXXVIII." *VT* 25:338–61.

———. 1976. "An Examination of a Recent Structuralist Interpretation of Genesis XXXVIII." *VT* 26:79–98.

Fox, M. V. 2001. "Wisdom in the Joseph Story." *VT* 51:26–41.

Fry, E. 1995. "How Was Joseph Taken to Egypt? (Genesis 37.12–36)." *BT* 46:445–48.

Fung, Yiu-Wing. 2000. *Victim and Victimizer: Joseph's Interpretation of His Destiny.* JSOTSup 308. Sheffield: Sheffield Academic Press.

Gevirtz, S. 1971. "The Reprimand of Reuben." *JNES* 30:87–98.

———. 1975. "Of Patriarchs and Puns: Joseph at the Fountain, Jacob at the Ford." *HUCA* 46:33–54.

Goldin, J. 1977. "The Youngest Son or Where Does Genesis 38 Belong?" *JBL* 96:27–44.

Gordon, C. H. 1965. *The Common Background of Greek and Hebrew Civilizations.* New York: Norton.

Greenstein, E. L. 1982. "An Equivocal Reading of the Sale of Joseph." In *Literary Interpretations of Biblical Narratives.* Vol. 2. Ed. K. R. R. Gros Louis and J. S. Ackerman. Nashville: Abingdon. Pp. 114–25.

Gunn, D. M., and D. N. Fewell. 1993. *Narrative in the Hebrew Bible.* Oxford: Oxford University Press. Pp. 34–45.

Heck, J. D. 1990. "A History of Interpretation of Genesis 49 and Deuteronomy 33." *BSac* 147:16–31.

Humphreys, W. L. 1988. *Joseph and His Family: A Literary Study.* Studies on Personalities of the Old Testament. Columbia: University of South Carolina Press.

———. 2001. *The Character of God in the Book of Genesis*. Louisville: Westminster John Knox.

Hurowitz, V. A. 1994. "Joseph's Enslavement of the Egyptians (Genesis 47:13–26) in Light of Famine Texts from Mesopotamia." *RB* 101:355–62.

Jacobs, M. R. 2003. "The Conceptual Dynamics of Good and Evil in the Joseph Story: An Exegetical and Hermeneutical Inquiry." *TynB* 27:309–38.

Kidner, D. 1967. *Genesis: An Introduction and Commentary*. TOTC. Downers Grove, Ill.: InterVarsity Press.

King, J. R. 1987. "The Joseph Story and Divine Politics: A Comparative Study of a Biographic Formula from the Ancient Near East." *JBL* 106:577–94.

Kitchen, K. A. 1962. "Joseph." *New Bible Dictionary*. Ed. J. D. Douglas. London: Inter-Varsity Fellowship. Pp. 656–60.

———. 1966. *Ancient Orient and Old Testament*. Chicago: Inter-Varsity Press.

Kugel, J. 1990. "The Case against Joseph." In *Lingering over Words: Studies in Ancient Near Eastern Literature in Honor of William L. Moran*. Ed. T. Abusch et al. Harvard Semitic Studies 37. Atlanta: Scholars Press. Pp. 271–87.

Lambe, A. J. 1999. "Judah's Development: The Pattern of Departure—Transition—Return." *JSOT* 83:53–68.

Longacre, R. E. 1989. *Joseph: A Story of Divine Providence: A Text Theoretical and Textlinguistic Analysis of Genesis 37 and 39–48*. 2nd ed., 2003. Winona Lake, Ind.: Eisenbrauns.

Lowenthal, E. I. 1973. *The Joseph Narrative in Genesis: An Interpretation*. New York: Ktav.

Matthew, V. H. 1995. "The Anthropology of Clothing in the Joseph Narrative." *JSOT* 65:25–36.

Matthewson, S. D. 1989. "An Exegetical Study of Genesis 38." *BSac* 146:373–92.

McKay, H. A. 1999. "Confronting Redundancy as Middle Manager and Wife: The Feisty Woman of Genesis 39." *Semeia* 87:215–31.

Niditch, S. 1979. "The Wrong Woman Righted: An Analysis of Genesis 38." *HTR* 72:143–49.

O'Brien, M. A. 1997. "The Contribution of Judah's Speech, Genesis 44:18–34, to the Characterization of Joseph." *CBQ* 59:429–47.

Pirson, R. 2002. *The Lord of the Dreams. A Semantic and Literary Analysis of Genesis 37–50*. JSOTSup 355. Sheffield: Sheffield Academic Press.

Prose, F. 1996. "The Story of Joseph in Egypt." In *Genesis, As It Is Written: Contemporary Writers on Our First Stories*. Ed. D. Rosenberg. San Francisco: HarperSanFrancisco. Pp. 189–202.

Rad, G. von. 1966. "The Joseph Narrative and Ancient Wisdom." In *The Problem of the Hexateuch and Other Essays*. Trans. E. W. Trueman Dicken. Edinburgh and London: Oliver & Boyd. Pp. 292–300.

Redford, D. B. 1970. *A Study of the Biblical Story of Joseph (Genesis 37–50)*. VTSup 20. Leiden: Brill.

Sailhamer, J. H. 1990. "Genesis." In *The Expositor's Bible Commentary*. Vol. 2. Ed. F. E. Gaebelein. Grand Rapids: Zondervan. Pp. 1–284.

Sarna, N. 1966. *Understanding Genesis.* Heritage of Biblical Israel 1. New York: McGraw-Hill.

Savage, M. 1980. "Literary Criticism and Biblical Studies: A Rhetorical Analysis of the Joseph Narrative." In *Scripture in Context: Essays on the Comparative Method.* Ed. C. D. Evans, W. W. Hallo, and J. B. White. PTMS 34. Pittsburgh: Pickwick. Pp. 79–100.

Schwartz, R. 1990. "Joseph's Bones and the Resurrection of the Text: Remembering in the Bible." In *The Book and the Text: The Bible and Literary Theory.* Ed. R. M. Schwartz. Oxford: Blackwell. Pp. 40–59.

Seebass, H. 1986. "The Joseph Story: Genesis 48 and the Canonical Process." *JSOT* 35:29–43.

Seybold, D. A. 1974. "Paradox and Symmetry in the Joseph Narrative." In *Literary Interpretations of Biblical Narratives.* Vol. 1. Ed. K. R. R. Gros Louis, J. S. Ackerman, and T. S. Warshaw. Nashville: Abingdon. Pp. 59–73.

Sternberg, M. 1990. *The Poetics of Biblical Narrative: Ideological Literature and the Drama of Reading.* Bloomington: Indiana University Press. Pp. 285–308, 394–402, 423–27.

White, H. C. 1985. "The Joseph Story: A Narrative Which 'Consumes' Its Content." *Semeia* 31:49–69.

Whybray, R. N. 1968. "The Joseph Story and Pentateuchal Criticism." *VT* 18:522–28.

Wildavsky, A. 1994. "Survival Must Not Be Gained through Sin: The Moral of the Joseph Stories Prefigured through Judah and Tamar." *RB* 101:355–62.

PART TWO

Exodus

6

The Emergence of Moses

EXODUS 1–6

It is possible to outline the Book of Exodus in one of the following three ways:

    I. Oppression (1:1–12:36)
    II. Liberation (12:37–15:21)
    III. Itineration (15:22–19:25)
    IV. Divine revelation (20:1–24:18)
    V. Divine veneration (25:1–40:38)

    I. In Egypt (1:1–15:21)
    II. To Sinai (15:22–19:2)
    III. At Sinai (19:3–40:38)

    I. God's Saving Act: Deliverance out of Distress (chs. 1–14)
       A. The distress (chs. 1–11)
       B. The deliverance (chs. 12–14)
    II. Man's Response in Praise (15:1–21)
    III. God's Action: Preservation (15:22–18:27)
       A. From thirst (15:22–27; 17:1–7)
       B. From hunger (ch. 16)

C. From despair (17:8–16; 18:1–27)
IV. Man's Response in Obedience (chs. 19–31)
V. Transgression and Renewal (chs. 32–40) (from Westermann 1967: 55–56)

In many ways the experiences of Moses in the first part of Exodus parallel the experiences of the Israelites in the latter portion of the book (Smith 1996: 38). Both flee from Egypt: Moses in ch. 2, Israel in ch. 12. Both come to a mountain where God speaks to them: Moses in ch. 3, Israel in ch. 19. God calls Moses into his service in chs. 3–4 and renews that call in ch. 6 after the unsavory experiences of ch. 5; God offers a covenant relationship to his people in chs. 19–24 and renews that covenant in ch. 34 after the horrific experiences of ch. 32.

Regardless of what language one uses in outlining Exodus, the basic divisions in the structure of the book are fairly clear. Unlike the Book of Genesis (the patriarchal section), which focuses on several human actors, Exodus highlights only one, Moses. Also unlike the Book of Genesis (again chs. 12–50), which spans a considerable period of time—at least four generations—Exodus 19–40 covers only about a year. The Israelites reached Sinai three months after their exit from Egypt (19:1). About eleven months later (Num. 10:11) the Israelites leave Sinai for Canaan. Thus Exodus, chronologically, follows the pattern in table 4.

As is true of the Genesis account about Abraham, the Exodus narrative is deliberately selective in describing Moses. The second chapter of Exodus deals with the first two-thirds of Moses' life. And even here only meager detail is recorded: he is born, put in a basket on a river, and reared by Pharaoh's daughter. Forty years later (Acts 7:23) he kills an Egyptian and is forced to live in exile in Midian. Four decades later, as an octogenarian (Acts 7:30; see also Exod. 7:7), Moses begins his ministry with the incident of the burning bush. George Mendenhall (1973: 20), using the incident of Moses slaying the Egyptian for insight into the question of the exercise of force, comments, "The great importance of this narrative for the origins of the religious ideology of ancient Israel is indicated by the fact that it is the only story preserved about Moses between infancy and his experience at the burning bush."

Table 4

Chapter	Duration	Reference
1	400 years	Gen. 15:13
2–15:21	80 years	Exod. 7:7; Acts 7:23, 30
15:22–19:2	3 months	Exod. 19:1
19:3–40:38	11 months	Num. 10:11

Moses as Infant and Refugee (1–2)

One cannot help but notice the difference between the end of Genesis and the first few verses in Exodus in terms of divine activity. With his life in jeopardy, Joseph bears witness to God's protection of his life. The story is as much about God as it is about Joseph.

Then follow the first seven verses of Exodus, a period covering no less than four hundred years. During this hiatus there is no explicit reference to the activity of God (apart from what is implied in Israel's preservation and population explosion in Egypt [1:7]). No great figure emerges on whom Scripture's spotlight will shine. These are four centuries over which the Scriptures pass in silence. The gulf is comparable to the period between Noah and Abraham. There are times when God is near (Isa. 55:6), and times when his presence is veiled.

Preservation by God

Still, we should not pass the first seven verses of Exodus too quickly. Note that Exod. 1:1 does not begin where Gen. 50:26 ended. Instead the narrative tape is rewound, and the reader of Exod. 1:1 is taken back to Gen. 46:8: "These are the names of the descendants of Israel, who came into Egypt" (RSV). Both genealogies introduce Jacob's sons as the "sons of Israel," not as the sons of Jacob. The covenant line is through the new covenant name given to Jacob at Peniel. Those who do multiply in Egypt are Israelites rather than Jacobites.

This four-hundred-year period is the time in which God's promises to the patriarchs continue toward fulfillment, especially the promise of numerous progeny. In Egypt, Israel was "fruitful and increased greatly; they multiplied and grew exceedingly strong" (Exod. 1:7 RSV). Not only is there a new king over Egypt who does not know Joseph, but also there now is a host of Israelites who do not know Joseph, at least as a contemporary.

The verbs used in these seven verses to describe Israel's growth in Egypt ("were fruitful, multiplied, became numerous, was filled with them") are simply the fulfillment of the promised blessings and mandates of God made to Adam (Gen. 1:28), Noah (Gen. 9:1, 7), Abraham (Gen. 13:16; 15:5; 17:2), and Jacob (Gen. 28:14; 46:3). In one sense, then, the reason that Pharaoh is on edge is because God is blessing his people. Wherever God's unique blessing is on his own, someone somewhere is sure to squirm or get riled. In Genesis 12–50 it was often infertility that posed a threat to the realization of God's promises. In the opening chapters of Exodus it is superfertility that poses a threat.

Like indigenous populations in countries today who are suspicious of growing minorities in their cities, the Egyptians began to fret over the presence of ever-increasing Israelites. To that end, the unnamed Pharaoh orders the institution of a plan to remedy the situation. To prevent both the escape of the Israelites and the possibility of them becoming fifth columnists in time of siege, Pharaoh has them perform excruciatingly difficult manual labor (1:8–14). The intent is to demoralize them, to impress on them their role of servitude, and to diminish as much as possible any likelihood of insurrection.

But the Egyptians discovered (as have, e.g., the Russians with Christian or Jewish believers in the former Soviet Union) that physical punishment only brings out the best in its religious minorities. Resiliency, not capitulation, is the result.

Subsequently, a second plan (1:16) and a third plan (1:22) are ordered by the Judophobic Pharaoh. The second stratagem is to kill at birth all Hebrew males. Commenting on this strange ultimatum, Moshe Greenberg (1969: 29) remarks that, if successful, "Israel would have been gradually reduced entirely to females. Insurrection would have been impossible, the people would have been dissolved, leaving to Egypt their women-power and reproductive capacity." Pharaoh believes that women are no threat to national security and his deified position of leadership. This time the malicious attempt at genocide is frustrated by the midwives. The fear of God is a deterrent sufficient to put restrictions on unquestioned obedience to the dictates of a superior. It is interesting that the Bible identifies these two midwives by name, Shiphrah and Puah, while it does not name the Pharaoh, or even Moses' parents in ch. 2 ("a man of the house of Levi married a Levite woman"). We cannot be certain if they are Hebrew or Egyptian midwives. The Hebrew text reads "Hebrew midwives," but the Greek text reads "midwives of the Hebrews." Their names appear to be good Hebrew names (just as the name "Moses" appears to be a good Egyptian name). That they "feared God" does not automatically decide the issue, for non-Israelites too were able to fear God (Gen. 20:11; 42:18 [Joseph speaking incognito to his brothers as an Egyptian]; Deut. 25:18). In any case, these two midwives parallel other women in these opening chapters of Exodus who are instrumental in preserving God's people when their lives are in serious danger. They join Moses' mother and sister, Pharaoh's daughter, and Moses' wife, Zipporah. The only difference is that the first five women save Israelites from the wrath of Pharaoh, who seeks to kill them, while the last one, Zipporah, saves Moses (or his son) from the wrath of Yahweh, who seeks to kill him.

Throughout this whole first chapter there is contrasted, by implication, the struggle between one king, who seeks to eliminate God's people through various pogroms, and another King, who is intent on preserving his people. A key word group throughout Exodus is "servant, service, serve," all from the Hebrew root ʿ-b-d, used to describe Israel. The related words occur almost one hundred times in Exodus, but most of these (sixty-seven out of ninety-four) occur in 1:1–15:21 (Leder 1999: 27). The opening few chapters of Exodus do not so much pursue the issue of slavery versus freedom as raise the question of "the identity and character of the master whom Israel must serve" (Isbell 1982: 45). Will Israel end up serving a god who is life-taking and oppressive, or a God who is life-giving and liberating? God wants to redeem his people from a service that is demonic to one that is delightful. And in describing the way that Yahweh goes about that, Exodus will "demythologize the Pharaoh's claim as divinely embodied ruler" (Weems 1992: 31).

If ch. 1 is devoted to a narration of God's saving his people as a whole, ch. 2 is devoted to a narration of God's saving one of his people, Moses. Both the group (ch. 1) and the individual (ch. 2) are in God's hands.

Significant Events in Moses' Life

Three things of long-range significance are to take place in Moses' life:

1. his birth and the conferment of his name (2:1–10)
2. his attempt to act as law enforcer, then peacemaker, the latter resulting in personal rebuff (2:11–15a)
3. his flight to Midian and his eventual marriage (2:15b–22)

Each of these events is a harbinger of Moses' career, although it will not begin for another eighty years.

Much as Joseph earlier had found himself in Pharaoh's employment, Moses is to find himself as adopted son of Pharaoh's daughter. The climax surrounding Moses' rescue from drowning is the name he receives, "Moses." Apart from the connection of "Moses" with the similar verbal element in Pharaonic names (Ah*mose*, Thut*mose*, Ra*mses*, borne by Egyptian kings in the Eighteenth and Nineteenth Dynasties [from the sixteenth to the twelfth centuries B.C.], in which -*ms* or -*mss* reflects the Egyptian verb *msy*, "to be born (of)," or the noun *ms*, "son, child of"), we are interested in the meaning attached to "Moses" by Scripture. The Bible (Exod. 2:10) connects "Moses" with the Hebrew verb *māšâ*, "to draw out." "Moses" is an active participle, in Hebrew *mōšeh*, of this verb; hence, the literal meaning of *mōšeh* is "one who draws out" or "a drawer out." This meaning of his name surfaces in Isa. 63:11: "They remembered the days of old, the one who drew out his people [*mōšeh ʿammô*]."

As with Jacob, Moses is not only *who* he is, but also *what* he is. His name is his mission. He is to "draw out" his people from Egypt and lead them to Canaan. Here, then, is an illustration of the premium placed on the name by Hebrews (but note the caution by Barr [1969: 20–21] that this principle is not absolute in the Old Testament).

The significance of Pharaoh's daughter's actions is brought out in the way that the verbs connected with her in ch. 2 are identical with the verbs connected with God in ch. 3. In ch. 2 she "goes down," "sees," and hears the baby "crying." In ch. 3 God "comes down" (v. 8), sees something (v. 7), and hears somebody "crying" (v. 9). She is moved by what she sees and hears. God is moved by what he sees and hears.

Although acting with good intentions (as Abraham had done with Sarah, also in Egypt), Moses takes the law into his own hands by murdering an Egyptian who was violently assaulting his kinsman (2:11–12). The man of God is following his natural instincts. We are interested here in observing Moses in the role of defender of the oppressed. Here Moses steps in between one Egyptian and one Hebrew; later, both antagonist and protagonist will be multiplied. The Hebrew verb behind what the Egyptian did to the Hebrew ("beating") in v. 11 is the same one used in v. 12 to describe what Moses did to the Egyptian ("killed"), *nākâ* (i.e., to administer a murderous beating). Later on Moses will do some more hard striking (again, *nākâ*): note 7:20, where Moses "struck" the Nile with his staff, and 17:5–6, where he "struck" the rock. But most importantly, what Moses did to one Egyptian, God will do to all Egyptians (3:20; 12:12).

That Moses is shunned by his own people (2:14) the next day "foreshadows the truculence and perverse ingratitude that Moses will experience from this people decades later" (Greenberg 1969: 45). It also anticipates a rejection by his own people of the One greater than Moses (Acts 7:35, 52), as suggested by Brevard Childs (1974: 34).

In the land of Midian (in Arabia) Moses again is propitiously placed in the role of arbitrator. Observing some shepherds who monopolize access to a well and thus make it difficult for seven women to draw their share of water, Moses comes to the rescue of these women (2:17). Once again Moses has championed and become the salvation of individuals who are unable to retaliate against the harassers.

Thus God prepares his vessel for his life vocation. To Abraham, God spoke a direct word. For Jacob, the divine word was announced to the mother. Joseph learned something of his future through dual dreams. Moses is plunged into the arena of experience. He is in the right place at the right time to do the right thing.

As Kunin (1996: 14) has observed, the parallels between Moses and Joseph are illuminating. Both are involved with Midianites: Joseph is taken to Egypt by them, while Moses lives among them for decades, and marries a Midianite. Joseph goes from slave to second-in-command in the nation, while Moses, in the opposite direction, goes from princess's son to slave. Joseph's actions lead Israel to Egypt, while Moses' actions lead Israel out of Egypt. Joseph saves Egypt from catastrophe, while Moses is involved with catastrophes that wreak havoc on Egypt.

Moses Meets God (3–5)

Pursuant to these experiences and prior to Moses' commissioning is the incident of the burning bush (3:1–6). The Hebrew word for "bush" (sěneh) appears in the Old Testament only here and in Deut. 33:16, where Moses sings of God as "one who dwelt/dwells in the (burning) bush." How appropriate it is that in Moses' last recorded words in Scripture (Deuteronomy 33) he speaks of, among other things, his first encounter with God at the incendiary bush! This Hebrew word sounds like and calls to mind "Sinai" (sny and snh). On two occasions God appears to Moses in fiery fashion, first at a snh (ch. 3), then at sny (ch. 19). God has a way of showing up at unexpected places such as bushes. It was at a bush that he appeared to Hagar (Gen. 21:15, using a different Hebrew word for "bush," śîaḥ), and it was at a bush that he first appeared to Moses. And speaking of God showing up at unexpected places, perhaps one might see a parallel between the angel of the Lord appearing in the middle of nowhere to a shepherding Moses to make an important announcement and the angels showing up to a group of shepherds in the middle of nowhere to make an important announcement (Luke 2:8–20).

Parallels in Moses' and Jacob's Experiences

So much of what is happening to Moses parallels experiences of Jacob.

Both are younger brothers who replace, in revelational significance, an older brother: Jacob over Esau, Moses over Aaron.

Unusual circumstances surround the birth, or the days immediately thereafter, of both. Jacob enters the world grasping the heel of his brother, while Moses, at three months of age, is set afloat in an ark.

Both manage to offend a brother: Jacob through exploitation, Moses through the usurpation of mediatorial power.

The result in both cases is a forced exile.

At some point in this exile God confronts the offender: Jacob through a dream, Moses through a burning bush.

At the human level the first response is fear. "And he [Jacob] was afraid" (Gen. 28:17 NRSV); "Moses hid his face, for he was afraid to look at God" (Exod. 3:6 NRSV).

In both men the fear is engendered by guilt. Both have acted outside of God's will: Jacob in taking advantage of Esau, Moses in killing the Egyptian.

In neither episode does God draw attention to the criminal behavior of the person. To the contrary, the word that both receive from God is positive and challenging (Gen. 28:13–15; Exod. 3:7–10).

On both occasions the initiative for confrontation is taken entirely by God. There is no indication in the text that either individual is aggressively seeking God. Jacob is a refugee, running from home. Moses is idling away his time and observing sheep nibbling the grass. God is the furthest thing from their thoughts. No other person is present.

In subsequent history the sites at which the theophanies occur become sacrosanct, Bethel and Sinai/Horeb.

Moses' theophany is preceded in the record by a marriage (Exod. 2:21); Jacob's is followed by a marriage (Gen. 29:28). The first scene for both eventual marriages is at a well (Gen. 29:2–10; Exod. 2:15b–27). Each marriage is consummated while the husband is in a strange land: Jacob in Paddan-aram, Moses in Midian.

In the lives of Jacob and Moses the first meeting with God is followed eventually by a second meeting. For Jacob, Bethel is followed by Peniel. Moses also needs a confirming word from God (Exod. 6:1–7:7). Note that between these experiences of divine visitation and revelation are interludes that are less than successful and spectacular. What Laban is to Jacob, Pharaoh is to Moses. Jacob is deceived, and he manages to escape his father-in-law only by a trick of his own. In Moses' case, Pharaoh taunts Moses and his God (5:2). Because Moses spoke to Pharaoh requesting release, the monarch responded by intensifying the workload of the Hebrews (5:4–18). As a result, Moses' own people turn against him (5:19–21), bringing him close to the point of complete despair (5:22–23).

First theophany	Jacob at Bethel (Gen. 28:10–22)	Moses in Midian (Exod. 3:1–6)
Interlude	Gen. 29:1–32:21	Exod. 3:7–5:22
Second theophany	Jacob at Peniel (Gen. 32:22–32)	Moses in Egypt (Exod. 6:1–7:7)

Moses Makes Excuses to God

Far from being nerved by his experience at the burning bush, Moses devises a series of excuses that he believes disqualify him as God's choice. Perhaps God has made a mistake in judgment! These excuses are:

Inadequacy (or self-belittlement): "Who am I that I should go to Pharaoh?" (3:11 NRSV)

Ignorance: "If I come to the people of Israel . . . and they ask me, 'What is his name?' what shall I say to them?" (3:13 RSV)

Incredibility: "But behold, they will not believe me or listen to my voice, for they will say, 'The LORD did not appear to you'" (4:1 RSV)

Inarticulateness: "Oh, my Lord, I am not eloquent . . . but I am slow of speech and of tongue" (4:10 RSV)

Insubordination: "Oh, my Lord, send, I pray, some other person" (4:13 RSV)

Childs (1974: 71) appropriately comments, "The progression of the dialogue is more visceral than rational."

It is, happily for Moses, a long-suffering God with whom he is conversing. God counters Moses' excuses at each point.

Inadequacy. The common denominator in Moses' various responses is that in all of them he is thinking in terms of his resources, not God's resources. To correct him, then, and to reply to the first excuse, God says, "I will be with you" (Exod. 3:12 NRSV). That is to say, for Moses the ultimate question is not "Who am I?" but "Whose am I?" (cf. the apostle Paul: "This very night there stood by me an angel of the God to whom I belong" [Acts 27:23]). D. E. Gowan, in a fascinating study of this formula ("I will be with you/the Lord was with him") in the Old Testament, points out that overwhelmingly it is used with people in, or about to assume, positions of leadership who face either grave danger or a task whose risk of failure is great. Accordingly, it was never intended as "an unconditional assurance of the security of the status quo . . . (or) as a platitude about general well-being" (Gowan 1994: 65). As a guarantee God provides a "sign" (3:12a). But to Moses' chagrin the sign will become evident only *after* Moses risks his life (3:12b). What he wants is a sign before, not after; not just the word of the Lord, but a tangible sign from the Lord.

Ignorance. Moses anticipates that he will be asked a question that he will be unable to answer satisfactorily. The thrust of Moses' concern is possibly his thought that the name of God has faded from the memory of the Hebrews, having been ensconced so long in Egypt, but more likely his concern is that he will be asked by his people to identify by name the God who sent him as a kind of a litmus test to validate his ministry to and among them. It is perhaps not an accident that Scripture never records an instance of anyone asking such a question. Nevertheless, God does not dismiss Moses' concern as illusory.

Out of God's response comes God's own name, Yahweh, or as it is often called, the Tetragrammaton (i.e., it is composed of four Hebrew letters: *y-h-w-h*). The number of biblical scholars who have addressed the matter of this name is legion. For beginners, we can take *y-h-w-h* as the third-person singular imperfect form of the verb *h-w/y-h*, "to be"—that is, "he is" or "he will be." The rendering in v. 14 of *'ehyeh 'ăšer 'ehyeh* usually is "I am who I am," although a few scholars (e.g., C. H. Gordon and C. Isbell) have suggested that this phrase is in the third person, not the first person, and thus should be read as "He is who He is."

But what is the significance of God's answer? Is it an evasion, an abasement of Moses, who has no more right to inquire about the holy name than did Jacob (Gen. 32:29) or Samson's mother (Judg. 13:6)? The point of v. 14b—"Say this to the people of Israel, 'I AM has sent me to you'" (RSV)—demonstrates that the answer is not an evasion. This is a sufficient and satisfying answer for Moses to give to the people if the issue is ever broached.

In Hebrew syntax, when the verb in the subordinate clause is the same as the verb in the principal clause, two possible translations present themselves. And that is what we encounter here: I AM WHO I AM (3:14). To illustrate, Exod. 4:13 reads, "Send whom thou wilt send" (KJV); that is, "Send somebody else, anybody except me." First Samuel 23:13 says, literally, "David and his men . . . arose and departed . . . and they went where they went"; that is, "They went wherever they could go" (RSV). In these latter two illustrations the speaker in the first and the writer in the second are deliberately general. Relating then this idiom to Exod. 3:14, Martin Noth (1962: 45) remarks, "That kind of indefiniteness is expressed which leaves open a large number of possibilities ('I am whatever I mean to be')."

The same idiom can convey not only indeterminacy but also intensity and actuality. For example, Exod. 33:19, "I will be gracious to whom I will be gracious, and will show mercy on whom I will show mercy" (RSV), suggests not indefiniteness but actuality. Likewise, Ezek. 12:25, "But I the LORD will speak the word which I will speak" (RSV), means that the Lord cannot be hushed or muted. A New Testament analogy would be Pilate's "What I have written I have written" (John 19:22 NRSV). The word is unchangeable and unerasable.

In this sense, then, "I AM WHO I AM" means "I am there (with you, wherever you are), I really am." Something of this nuance is suggested by the Septuagint's translation of the phrase as "I am the one who is." To return again to Hebrew syntax, the subject of the relative clause must be the same in number and gender as that of the principal clause. Thus, Exod. 20:2 literally reads, "I am the LORD your God, who *I* brought you out of the land of Egypt." In English syntax, of course, "who" alone would be the subject of the verb, but in Hebrew "who" is only a connecting word joining a principal clause and a subordinate clause. So then, an exact

English equivalent of "I AM WHO I AM" is "I am he who is." And because he is, he is present, even in the imbroglio in Egypt. That God reveals his name to Moses is an indication that one cannot have a meaningful relationship with someone whose name one does not know. But as Terence Fretheim (1991a: 65) points out, to know someone's name means that one can honor or dishonor that name. God is willing to take that chance, but not without raising a red flag. Hence, the God who reveals his name to Moses in Exodus 3 and 6 is careful to proscribe in Exodus 20 (v. 7) the wrongful use of that name.

Incredibility. Still haunted by the possibility of personal rejection, Moses suggests that his credibility will be attacked by his own people. The people of God are more of a thorn in the flesh than the enemies of God.

Three signs from God are granted to Moses as empirical evidence of his divine calling: a rod is changed into a snake, then back into a rod; a healthy hand becomes leprous, then is restored; a cup full of water from the Nile poured on the ground becomes blood (4:2–9). The first two, for Moses at least, would cause no little anxiety. George Knight (1976: 28) comments, "God must shake Moses out of his selfish rationalizings. Moses must learn that it is God who is calling him to do the absurdly difficult thing."

Inarticulateness. For someone to perform an unusual act is one thing. But what happens if the person also has to speak and is afraid of becoming tongue-tied or jumbling words? Would such verbal blundering wipe out any good effects that the signs might have on the audience?

It is interesting to observe that Stephen draws attention (Acts 7:22) to a Moses "instructed in all the wisdom of the Egyptians, and he was *mighty in his words* and deeds" (RSV). Either Stephen is deliberately using hyperbole or Moses is parading a false humility—that is, denying a gift that God indeed has given him. It may be, however, that Moses did indeed suffer from some kind of speech impediment (see Tigay 1978), which thus was a cause for concern at the beginning.

Insubordination. Moses' attempt to avoid his duty reaches its climax in his fifth objection: "Send some other person." God reluctantly cooperates with Moses' request, suggesting the appointment of Aaron as Moses' surrogate. Aaron's credentials? "He can speak well" (4:14). How well? At least well enough to solicit support and funds for the apostate act of building the golden calf (Exodus 32)!

Satisfied that God has at least provided him with an assistant, Moses returns to his father-in-law to bid him farewell (a little different from Jacob's departure from Laban!), and then he goes on to Egypt.

Next we read perhaps the strangest event narrated in the Book of Exodus. Before reaching his destination, Moses is met by the Lord, who seeks to kill him (Moses? Moses' [firstborn] son?). The passage bristles with problems. Why does the Lord seek to kill Moses just after commissioning him? In the phrase "the LORD . . . sought to kill him" (4:24 RSV), who is the referent of "him"? Is it Moses or one of his two sons, and if a son, which of the two? How does Zipporah, a pagan Midianite, know how to respond immediately to the crisis? In the phrase "and she touched his feet with it," whose feet are touched? Is it those of Moses, the son, or even the divine assailant (the NRSV freely supplies "Moses" for "his")? What does it mean when Zipporah says, "You are a bridegroom of blood" (KJV: "a bloody husband"), literally (and strangely), "You are a son-in-law/bridegroom of bloods"? As Frolov (1996: 520) has pointed out, the plural of "blood" with a noun standing in construct before it, and denoting an individual or group of people, "never implies anything but his/their evil deeds or intentions." Thus, Shimei curses David and calls him "a man of blood(s)" (2 Sam. 16:7–8). Psalm 55:23 speaks of "bloodthirsty men" (literally, "men of blood[s]"; see also Prov. 29:10). Second Samuel 21:1 refers to Saul's "blood-stained house" (literally, "house of blood[s]"). Ezekiel 22:2 refers to Jerusalem as a "city of bloodshed" (literally, "a city of blood[s]").

It is possible that the phrase "the LORD . . . sought to kill him" is an early way of stating that Moses became violently ill (for objections to this reading see Childs 1974: 103). Such wording would be analogous to "the LORD hardened his heart." Both sickness and an act of disobedience are subsumed under one ultimate cause, God. To attempt, however, to remove the stinger from this difficult phrase by understanding it as a reference to physical sickness, and nothing more, seems to be taking extreme liberty with language. Also, such an interpretation destroys the parallel with earlier "sought to/tried to" passages in Exodus where clearly that is not the meaning:

2:15: "Pharaoh *sought/tried* [*bāqaš*] to kill Moses"

5:19: "Go back to Egypt for all the men who *sought/tried/wanted* [*bāqaš*] to kill you are dead"

4:24: "the LORD met Moses/him and *sought/tried/was about to* [NIV] [*bāqaš*] kill him"

In other words, what Pharaoh set out to do to Moses in ch. 2, God sets out to do to Moses in ch. 4. And the only rationale for such divine rage must be either Moses' failure to be a fatherly priest/servant to his son by circumcising him or his persistent efforts to evade God's will for his life throughout chs. 3–4. If it is the former, then this is a classic case of a servant of God so caught up in the ministry to the congregants that he ignores his ministry to his own family. In the words of the last two lines of Song of Sol. 1:6, "[They] made me take care of the vineyards; my own vineyard I have neglected" (NIV).

Moses is assailed by the Lord, ostensibly for neglecting to circumcise one of his sons (Gershom, the older one?). Zipporah reacts spontaneously. She circumcises her son with a flint and then touches someone's feet (a euphemism for genitals?) with the foreskin. Because of the wife's alert behavior, Moses (or their son) is saved. Fretheim (1991a: 80) points out that Zipporah, in saving Moses (or their son) from the wrath of God, anticipates the later intercessory ministry of Moses (ch. 32), which saves Israel from the wrath of God. If Zipporah does not circumcise, then Moses (or their son) is dead. If Moses does not pray and plead for God's mercy, then Israel is dead, and God will start anew with Moses. Zipporah is like Rahab and Ruth: all three are Gentile women who display great wisdom and courage and are used by God to deliver and preserve his people.

The obvious fact stressed by the story is the importance of circumcision as a sign of the covenant. The rite is to be carried out not only when convenient. The worshiper is not consulted as to whether he considers this appropriate and relevant. Circumcision is a divine mandate. Ministry to one's family takes precedence over ministry to one's congregation. Of this incident C. H. Gordon (1965: 138) observes, "It is designed to warn the Hebrews of every generation: 'Don't fail to circumcise your sons! If Moses couldn't get away with it, how can you?'"

The narrative, however, serves as more than an object lesson to later generations. We have already seen that circumcision is the sign of God's special covenant with Abraham and his seed (Genesis 17). As the covenant mediator, Moses has to observe the covenant sign. Furthermore, Zipporah's circumcision of her son identifies both the son and Moses as being among the descendants of Abraham. God's covenant with Abraham includes Moses as a child of Abraham. Any attempt to draw rigid distinctions between the covenant with the patriarchs and the covenant at Sinai is defused by matching Moses' covenant obligations with those of Abraham.

Greenberg (1969: 111) connects the story thematically with Jacob's experience at Peniel. A divine assailant attacks an unsuspecting person under the cover of darkness. Jacob is anticipating reconciliation with Esau; Moses is returning to Egypt to be reunited with his fellow Hebrews and to face Pharaoh. The shedding of blood here, resulting in Moses' deliverance, presages Israel's deliverance from Egypt, but not without bloodshed too. The connections between this incident in Exodus 4 and Passover in Exodus 12 are especially interesting. Both take place at night (4:24; 12:8, 12, 29). In both circumcision plays a major role (4:25–26; 12:43–49). In both the verb "touch" (*nāgaʿ*) is used: in 4:25 Zipporah "touched" the feet of Moses or their son with the foreskin, while in 12:22 the people are to "touch" (NIV: "put") some of the blood on the top and sides of the doorframes of their houses. And most importantly, in both incidents the shedding of blood shields one from the wrath of God.

For this episode there are other parallel themes in Genesis and Exodus. For example, the Lord delivers, then commissions, then seeks to kill Moses. Similarly, the Lord delivers, then commissions, then seeks shortly thereafter to wipe out his people (Exod. 32:10). The judgment is provoked in both instances by a violation of the covenant. Zipporah's quick actions save Moses, and Moses' intercessory prayer saves the Israelites.

Just as shrewd action by Rachel saved Jacob from Laban, so alertness by Zipporah saves Moses from God. Knight (1976: 35) raises some interesting questions: "Did Zipporah . . . glimpse this idea about the Covenant more clearly than her husband? Did she believe that the union of a man and woman under God within the covenant reflected the significance of the divine covenant itself, and so had she come to believe that her husband had dishonoured both her and God? Had Zipporah intuitively glimpsed the great reality of revelation that there is no redemption . . . without the shedding of blood?"

At least for the immediate future Moses' life will not become one bit more pleasant. He has gone through a contentious dialogue with God (3:1–4:17), then found himself at the precipice of death (4:18–26). He has met God as debater, then God as holy aggressor. There is something of a momentary reprieve (4:27–31), as Moses is welcomed back, and together all of God's people join in a service of worship and praise.

But Pharaoh is obstinate. He is totally unsympathetic to the pleas of Moses (5:3). Pharaoh's words "I do not know the LORD" (5:2 NRSV) mean "I do not acknowledge his authority." His statement seems to be a combination of defiance and ignorance. An earlier Pharaoh did not "know" Joseph (1:8), and here is a Pharaoh who does not "know" Yahweh, just as the patriarchs are said in 6:3 not to "know" Yahweh as Yahweh.

To make matters worse, the workload of the Hebrews was unrealistically increased (5:4–18). Inevitably there is only deep resentment on the part of the Hebrews toward their alleged liberator (5:19–21). What a difference in reception! One day, adulation, and the next day, rejection. In response to another Liberator people would say one day, "Hosanna!" but the next day, "Crucify him!" Note the bluntness of Moses' words to God in vv. 22–23. In his anger and bewilderment he begins a tradition of truth telling in prayer, seen elsewhere in some psalms of lament (e.g., Psalm 73) and Jeremiah's "confessions" (Jer. 12:1–6; 15:16–18; 20:7).

Moses' Call Reconfirmed (6)

Just as Jacob received a confirmation of the events at Peniel (cf. Gen. 32:28 with 35:10), so Moses now is about to receive a confirmation of the events at the burning bush. To be sure, the old objections do not die easily (cf. Exod. 6:12, 30). In the first exchange of challenge and rejection Moses had emphasized his own inabilities. What troubles him here is that it is a much more formidable assignment to speak to Pharaoh than to his own people. On this latter assignment he had failed. How, then, can he possibly make his message register with Pharaoh? (Cf. Jer. 12:5: "If you have raced with men on foot, and they have wearied you, how will you compete with horses? And if in a safe land you fall down, how will you do in the jungle of the Jordan?" [RSV]) Moses is still far too focused on results.

In response God gives Moses seven encouraging "I wills" ringed by two "I am's." See table 5.

At least two critical matters occur in this chapter. One is Exod. 6:3: "I appeared to Abraham, to Isaac, and to Jacob, as God Almighty, but by my name the LORD I did not make myself known to them" (RSV). But what about those passages in which the Lord identifies himself to one of the patriarchs by precisely that name? Thus, Gen. 15:7: "And he said to him [i.e., Abraham], 'I am the LORD'" (RSV). Or those passages in which the narrator describes the Lord speaking to Abraham as Lord: "Now the LORD said to Abraham" (Gen. 12:1)? Or those passages that indicate some familiarity with the Lord? So, Gen. 12:8: "There he built an altar to the LORD and called on the name of the LORD" (RSV). The name "Yahweh" appears either by itself or in combination with another word 148 times in Genesis, most of which are by the narrator (ninety-six times). Eve is the first character in Genesis to use that name for God (Gen. 4:1). Abraham uses the name "Yahweh" as well (e.g., Gen. 14:22; 15:2, 8; 18:27, 30, 31, 32; 22:14).

Table 5

Response	Verse	
➤ "I am the LORD"	6	
1. "I will bring you out"	6	
2. "I will deliver you"	6	redemption
3. "I will redeem you"	6	
4. "I will take you for my people"	7	adoption
5. "I will be your God"	7	
6. "I will bring you into the land"	8	settlement
7. "I will give it to you for a possession"	8	
➤ "I am the LORD"	8	

It is unwarranted to assume, however, that all of the above flatly contradict Exod. 6:3, as if to suggest that there were conflicting traditions in Israel as to when God's people first knew him as Yahweh: in the days of the patriarchs and even before, the Yahwist (J) tradition, or not until the time of Moses, the Priestly (P) tradition, compiled several centuries after J. It may simply be the Lord's way of saying to Moses that the patriarchs never understood the full significance of God's personal name. To be sure, they knew it, used it, and recognized it as a vocable. Gleason Archer (1973: 113) states, "Exodus 6:3 teaches that God, who in earlier generations had revealed Himself as El Shaddai (God Almighty) by deeds of power and mercy, would now in Moses' generation reveal Himself as a covenant-keeping Jehovah by His marvelous deliverance of the whole nation of Israel."

But did Moses, his peers, and successors grasp the significance of the name? Would such a breakthrough have to wait until Jesus could say, "I have made your name known to those whom you gave me from the world" (John 17:6 NRSV)?

There are other possibilities for explaining the claim of Exodus 6 alongside the phenomena of Genesis. For example, Moberly (1992: 36–79) has suggested that the narratives in Genesis are the product of Yahwistic storytellers retelling and reshaping originally non-Yahwistic traditions in a Yahwistic context. So then, the use of "Yahweh/LORD" in Genesis by anyone (the narrator and especially the characters in the narrative) is anachronistic. The writers record not the characters' actual words, but the way that the characters would have said it had they lived in the time of the storytellers. Such a solution, while possible, opens the door to similarly interpreting other names or concepts and ideas in Genesis. Eslinger (1996: 194) has pointed out that prior to Exod. 5:2 no one is said to "know/not know" Yahweh, so in Genesis no individual literally "knows" Yahweh.

The second critical matter is the genealogy given in Exod. 6:14–27. We are particularly interested in the line of descent to Moses and Aaron. See figure 4.

Figure 4

Jacob (6:14)

|

Levi (6:16)

|

Kohath (6:16)

|

Amram (6:18)

|

Moses, Aaron (6:20)

Moses and Aaron are, then, the great-great-grandsons of Jacob. To phrase it differently, there are four generations between the descent into

Egypt and the exodus from Egypt. The duration of that period of time is given as 430 years in Exod. 12:40–41, as four hundred years in Gen. 15:13, and as "the fourth generation" in Gen. 15:16. Are four generations enough to cover four centuries?

Furthermore, Exod. 1:6 plainly says that the death of Joseph antedated the birth of Moses. However, Gen. 50:23 tells us that Joseph lived long enough to see his own great-grandchildren (Joseph, Ephraim, Machir, and unnamed children). These fourth-generation children would be as removed from Jacob as were Moses and Aaron, and probably younger than Moses and Aaron.

Two responses may be made. One is that we must assume that the genealogy of Moses and Aaron in Exod. 6:14–20 is selective, not complete or continuous. This is not unheard of either in the Bible or in other literature of the Mediterranean world (see Kitchen 1966: 54–55). Also, other portions of Scripture posit a minimum of ten generations between Joseph and Joshua. For example, 1 Chron. 7:20–29 lists (Joseph) Ephraim, Rephah, Resheph, Telah, Tahan, Ladan, Ammihud, Elishama, Nun, and Joshua. This latter fact confirms the selectivity of Exod. 6:14–27.

It is of interest that this genealogy discusses Aaron's children (v. 23) and one of his grandchildren (v. 25). Yet nothing is recorded of Moses' progeny. Moses, whose descent goes back to Levi, is followed by Joshua, whose descent goes back to Joseph. No caste is here inaugurated in which God chooses his leader on the basis of heredity. Kings and priests, yes. But prophetic spokesmen, no.

Exodus Commentaries and Major Studies

Ashby, G. 1998. *Go Out and Meet God: A Commentary on the Book of Exodus*. ITC. Grand Rapids: Eerdmans.

Beegle, D. 1972. *Moses, the Servant of Yahweh*. Grand Rapids: Eerdmans.

Binz, S. J. 1993. *The God of Freedom and Life: A Commentary on the Book of Exodus*. Collegeville, Minn.: Liturgical Press.

Birch, B. C. 1995. "Divine Character and the Formation of Moral Communities in the Book of Exodus." In *The Bible in Ethics: The Second Sheffield Colloquium*. Ed. J. W. Rogerson, M. Davies, and M. Daniel Carroll R. JSOTSup 207. Sheffield: Sheffield Academic Press. Pp. 119–35.

Brenner, A., ed. 1993. *A Feminist Companion to Exodus to Deuteronomy*. The Feminist Companion to the Bible 6. Sheffield: Sheffield Academic Press.

Brueggemann, W. 1994. "Exodus." In *The New Interpreter's Bible*. Vol. 1. Ed. L. E. Keck et al. Nashville: Abingdon. Pp. 675–981.

Cassuto, U. 1967. *A Commentary on the Book of Exodus*. Jerusalem: Magnes.

Childs, B. S. 1974. *The Book of Exodus: A Critical, Theological Commentary.* OTL. Philadelphia: Westminster.

Clements, R. E. 1972. *Exodus.* CBC. Cambridge: Cambridge University Press.

Clifford, R. J. 1990. "Exodus." In the *New Jerome Bible Commentary.* Ed. R. E. Brown, J. A. Fitzmyer, and R. E. Murphy. Englewood Cliffs, N.J.: Prentice Hall. Pp. 44–60.

Coats, G. W. 1988. *Moses: Heroic Man, Man of God.* JSOTSup 57. Sheffield: JSOT Press.

———. 1998. *Exodus 1–18.* FOTL 2A. Grand Rapids. Eerdmans.

Cole, R. A. 1973. *Exodus.* TOTC. Downers Grove, Ill.: InterVarsity Press.

Croatto, J. S. 1981. *Exodus: A Hermeneutic of Freedom.* Maryknoll, N.Y.: Orbis.

Daube, D. 1963. *The Exodus Pattern in the Bible.* All Souls Studies 2. London: Faber & Faber.

Davies, G. 1999. "The Theology of Exodus." In *In Search of True Wisdom: Essays in Old Testament Interpretation in Honour of Ronald C. Clements.* Ed. E. Ball. JSOTSup 300. Sheffield: Sheffield Academic Press. Pp. 137–52.

Dozeman, T. B. 1996. *God at War: Power in the Exodus Tradition.* Oxford: Oxford University Press.

Driver, S. R. 1911. *The Book of Exodus.* Cambridge Bible for Schools and Colleges. Cambridge: Cambridge University Press.

Durham, J. I. 1987. *Exodus.* WBC 3. Waco, Tex.: Word.

Ellison, H. L. 1982. *Exodus.* The Daily Study Bible. Philadelphia: Westminster.

Enns, P. 2000. "Exodus." The NIV Application Commentary. Grand Rapids: Zondervan.

Fokkelman, J. P. 1987. "Exodus." In *The Literary Guide to the Bible.* Ed. R. Alter and F. Kermode. Cambridge, Mass.: Belknap. Pp. 56–65.

Fox, E. 1986. *Now These Are the Names: A New English Rendition of the Book of Exodus.* New York: Schocken.

Fretheim, T. E. 1991a. *Exodus.* Interpretation. Louisville: John Knox.

———. 1991b. "The Reclamation of Creation: Redemption and Law in Exodus." *Int* 45:345–65.

———. 1996. "'Because the Whole Earth Is Mine': Theme and Narrative in Exodus." *Int* 50:229–39.

Gowan, D. E. 1994. *Theology in Exodus: Biblical Theology in the Form of a Commentary.* Louisville: Westminster John Knox.

Greenberg, M. 1969. *Understanding Exodus.* New York: Behrman.

———. 1971. "Exodus, Book of." *EncJud* 6:1050–67.

Gutzke, M. G. 1974. *Plain Talk on Exodus.* Grand Rapids: Zondervan.

Halpern, B. 2003. "Eye-witness Testimony: Parts of Exodus Written within Living Memory of the Event." *BAR* 29 (5):50–57.

Hoffmeier, J. K. 1986. "The Arm of God versus the Arm of Pharaoh in the Exodus Narratives." *Bib* 67:378–87.

Houtman, C. 1993–2002. *Exodus.* 4 vols. Historical Commentary on the Old Testament. Kampen: Kok; Leuven: Peeters.

Huey, F. B., Jr. 1977. *Exodus: A Study Guide Commentary.* Grand Rapids: Zondervan.

Hyatt, J. P. 1971. *Commentary on Exodus*. New Century Bible. London: Oliphants.

Jacob, B. 1992. *Exodus*. Trans. Y. Elman. Hoboken, N.J.: Ktav.

Janzen, J. Gerald. 1997. *Exodus*. WBComp. Louisville: Westminster John Knox.

Janzen, W. 2000. *Exodus*. Believers Church Bible Commentary. Scottdale, Pa.: Herald.

Johnstone, W. 1990. *Exodus*. OTG. Sheffield: Sheffield Academic Press.

Kitchen, K. A. 2003. "Lotus Eating and Moving On—Exodus and Covenant." In *On the Reliability of the Old Testament*. Grand Rapids/Cambridge: Eerdmans. Pp. 241–312.

Knight, G. A. F. 1976. *Theology as Narration: A Commentary on the Book of Exodus*. Edinburgh: Handsel.

Kugel, J. L. 1997. *The Bible as It Was*. Cambridge, Mass.: Belknap. Pp. 285–437.

Leder, A. C. 1999. "Reading Exodus to Learn and Learning to Read Exodus." *CTJ* 34:11–35.

———. 2001. "The Coherence of Exodus: Narrative Unity and Meaning." *CTJ* 36:251–69.

Levenson, J. D. 1991. "Exodus and Liberation." *HBT* 13:134–74.

Millard, A. 2000. "How Reliable Is Exodus?" *BRev* 26 (4):50–57.

Newsome, J. 1998. *Exodus*. Interpretation Bible Studies. Louisville: Geneva.

Nicholson, E. W. 1973. *Exodus and Sinai in History and Tradition*. Richmond: John Knox.

Noth, M. 1962. *Exodus: A Commentary*. OTL. Philadelphia: Westminster.

Pixley, G. V. 1987. *On Exodus: A Liberation Perspective*. Trans. R. R. Barr. Maryknoll, N.Y.: Orbis.

Plasteras, J. 1966. *The God of Exodus: The Theology of the Exodus Narratives*. Milwaukee: Bruce.

Propp, W. C. 1999. *Exodus 1–18: A New Translation with Introduction and Commentary*. AB 2. New York: Doubleday.

Radday, Y. T., and Y. Levi. 1985. *An Analytic Linguistic Key-Word-in-Context Concordance to the Book of Exodus*. The Computer Bible 28. Wooster, Ohio: Biblical Research Associates.

Ramm, B. 1974. *His Way Out: A Fresh Look at Exodus*. Glendale, Calif.: Regal.

Rendtorff, R. 1989. "'Covenant' as a Structuring Concept in Genesis and Exodus." *JBL* 108:385–93.

Sarna, N. 1986. *Exploring Exodus: The Heritage of Biblical Israel*. New York: Schocken.

———. 1991. *Exodus: The Traditional Hebrew Text with the New JPS Translation*. JPS Torah Commentary. Philadelphia: The Jewish Publication Society.

Smith, M. S. 1996. "The Literary Arrangement of the Priestly Redaction of Exodus: A Preliminary Investigation." *CBQ* 58:25–50.

Sternberg, M. 1998. *Hebrews between Cultures: Group Portraits and National Literature*. Bloomington: Indiana University Press.

Van Seters, J. 1994. *The Life of Moses: The Yahwist as Historian in Exodus–Numbers*. Louisville: Westminster John Knox.

Vervenne, M., ed. 1996. *Studies in the Book of Exodus: Redaction, Reception, Interpretation.* BETL 126. Leuven: Leuven University Press.

Exodus 1–6

Ackerman, J. S. 1974. "The Literary Context of the Moses Birth Story (Exodus 1–2)." In *Literary Interpretations of Biblical Narratives.* Vol. 1. Ed. K. R. R. Gros Louis, J. S. Ackerman, and T. S. Warshaw. Nashville: Abingdon. Pp. 74–119.

Archer, G. 1973. *A Survey of Old Testament Introduction.* Chicago: Moody.

Ashby, G. W. 1994–1995. "The Bloody Bridegroom: The Interpretation of Exodus 4:24–26." *ExpT* 106:203–5.

Barr, J. 1969. "The Symbolism of Names in the Old Testament." *BJRL* 52:11–29.

Bietak, M. 2003. "Israelites Found in Egypt: Four Room House Identified in Medinet Habu." *BAR* 29 (5):40–49, 82–83.

Carroll, R. P. 1994. "Strange Fire: Abstract of Presence Absent in the Text. Meditations on Exodus 3." *JSOT* 61:39–58.

Childs, B. S. 1962. *Myth and Reality in the Old Testament.* SBT 27. London: SCM Press. Pp. 59–65.

Coats, G. W. 1972. "A Structural Transition in Exodus." *VT* 22:129–42.

———. 1973. "Moses in Midian." *JBL* 92:3–10.

Davies, G. F. 1992. *Israel in Egypt: Reading Exodus 1–2.* JSOTSup 135. Sheffield: JSOT Press.

Dumbrell, W. 1972. "Exodus 4:24–26: A Textual Re-examination." *HTR* 65:285–90.

Eslinger, L. M. 1991. "Freedom or Knowledge? Perspective and Purpose in the Exodus Narrative (Exodus 1–5)." *JSOT* 52:43–60.

———. 1996. "Knowing Yahweh: Exod. 6:3 in the Context of Genesis 1–Exodus 15." In *Literary Structure and Rhetorical Strategies in the Hebrew Bible.* Ed. L. J. de Regt et al. Assen: Van Gorcum. Pp. 188–98.

Exum, J. C. 1983. "'You Shall Let Every Daughter Live': A Study of Exodus 1:8–2:10." *Semeia* 28:63–82.

Feliks, J. 1971. "Burning Bush." *EncJud* 4:1528–30.

Frolov, S. 1996. "The Hero as Bloody Bridegroom: On the Meaning and Origin of Exodus 4,26." *Bib* 77:520–23.

Fuchs, E. 2000. "A Jewish-Feminist Reading of Exodus 1–2." In *Jews, Christians, and the Theology of the Hebrew Scriptures.* Ed. A. O. Bellis and J. S. Kaminsky. SBLSymS 8. Atlanta: Society of Biblical Literature. Pp. 307–26.

Garr, W. R. 1992. "The Grammar and Interpretation of Exodus 6:3." *JBL* 111:385–408.

Gordon, C. H. 1965. *The Ancient Near East.* New York: Norton.

Gottlieb, I. B. 1998. "Law, Love, and Redemption: Legal Connotations in the Language of Exodus 6:6–8." *JANES* 26:47–57.

Hamlin, E. J. 1974. "The Liberator's Ordeal: A Study of Exodus 4:1–9." In *Rhetorical Criticism: Essays in Honor of James Muilenburg.* Ed. J. J. Jackson and M. Kessler. PTMS 1. Pittsburgh: Pickwick. Pp. 33–42.

Harris, R. L. 1974. "The Pronunciation of the Tetragrammaton." In *The Law and the Prophets: In Honor of O. T. Alis*. Ed. J. H. Skitton. Nutley, N.J.: Presbyterian and Reformed. Pp. 215–24.

Holmgren, F. C. 2002. "Exodus 2:11–3:15." *Int* 56:73–76.

Hughes, P. E. 1997. "Moses' Birth Story: A Biblical Matrix for Prophetic Messianism." In *Eschatology, Messianism, and the Dead Sea Scrolls*. Ed. C. A. Evans and P. W. Flint. Grand Rapids: Eerdmans. Pp. 10–22.

Isbell, C. 1982. "Exodus 1–2 in the Context of Exodus 1–14: Story Lines and Key Words." In *Art and Meaning: Rhetoric in Biblical Narrative*. Ed. D. J. A. Clines et al. JSOTSup 19. Sheffield: JSOT Press. Pp. 37–61.

Janzen, J. Gerald. 1979. "What's in a Name? 'Yahweh' in Exodus 3 and the Wider Biblical Context." *Int* 33:227–39.

Kitchen, K. A. 1966. *Ancient Orient and Old Testament*. Chicago: Inter-Varsity Press.

———. 1968. "Moses: A More Realistic View." *CT* 12:920–23.

———. 1976. "From the Brickfields of Egypt." *TynB* 27:137–47.

Kline, M. 1975. "Old Testament Origins of the Gospel Genre." *WTJ* 38:1–27.

Kunin, S. D. 1996. "The Bridegroom of Blood: A Structuralist Analysis." *JSOT* 69:3–16.

McCarthy, D. J. 1978. "Exodus 3:14: History, Philology and Theology." *CBQ* 40:311–22. Repr., in *Institution and Narrative: Collected Essays*. AnBib 108. Rome: Biblical Institute Press, 1985. Pp. 225–36.

Mendenhall, G. E. 1973. *The Tenth Generation: The Origins of the Biblical Traditions*. Baltimore: Johns Hopkins University Press.

Moberly, R. W. L. 1992. *The Old Testament of the Old Testament*. OBT. Minneapolis: Fortress.

Orlinsky, H. M. 1973. "Moses." In *Essays in Biblical and Jewish Culture and Bible Translation*. New York: Ktav. Pp. 5–38.

Patrick, D. 1994. "The Rhetoric of Revelation [Exodus 3–4]." *HBT* 16:20–40.

Phillips, A., and L. Phillips. 1998. "The Origin of 'I Am' in Exodus 3:14." *JSOT* 78:81–84.

Propp, W. H. 1993. "That Bloody Bridegroom (Exodus IV 24–26)." *VT* 43:495–518.

Robinson, B. P. 1986. "Zipporah to the Rescue: A Contextual Study of Exodus IV 24–26." *VT* 36:447–61.

———. 1997. "Moses at the Burning Bush." *JSOT* 75:107–22.

Seitz, C. 1999. "The Call of Moses and the 'Revelation' of the Divine Name: Source-Critical Logic and Its Legacy [Exodus 3, 1–4, 17; 6, 2–9]." In *Theological Exegesis: Essays in Honor of Brevard S. Childs*. Ed. C. Seitz et al. Grand Rapids: Eerdmans. Pp. 145–61.

Thompson, T. L. 1995. "How Yahweh Became God: Exodus 3 and 6 and the Heart of the Pentateuch." *JSOT* 68:57–74.

Tigay, J. H. 1978. "'Heavy of Mouth' and 'Heavy of Tongue': On Moses' Speech Difficulty." *BASOR* 231:57–64.

Weems, R. J. 1992. "'The Hebrew Women Are Not Like the Egyptian Women': The Ideology of Race, Gender and Sexual Reproduction in Exodus 1." *Semeia* 59:25–34.

Westermann, C. 1967. *Handbook to the Old Testament.* Trans. R. H. Boyd. Minne-
    apolis: Augsburg.

Zlotnick-Sivan, H. 2004. "Moses the Persian? Exodus 2, the 'Other' and Biblical
    'Mnemohistory.'" *ZAW* 116:189–205.

7

Plagues, Passover, and the Exodus

EXODUS 7:1–15:21

This section of Exodus is devoted principally to a description of the plagues that God sent on Egypt (7:14–11:10; 12:29–32), and of the exodus from Egypt via the Red (or Reed) Sea. Moses receives from the Lord, as preparation, this astounding word: "I make you as God to Pharaoh" (7:1 RSV). But before elation can set in, God also says, "Pharaoh will not listen to you" (7:4 RSV). A God who will not be listened to!

The Plagues (7–11)

The function of the plagues goes back to the word of Pharaoh (5:2 NRSV): "I do not know the LORD." The key word here is "know." It appears in:

> 6:7: "and you [Israel] shall know that I am the LORD your God" (RSV)
> 7:5: "and the Egyptians shall *know* that I am the LORD" (NRSV)

157

7:17: "by this you [Pharaoh] shall know that I am the LORD" (NRSV; the first plague)

8:10: "that you [Pharaoh] may know that there is no one like the LORD our God" (NRSV; the second plague)

8:22: "that you [Pharaoh] may know that I am the LORD in the midst of the earth" (RSV; the fourth plague)

9:14: "I will send all my plagues . . . that you [Pharaoh] may know that there is none like me in all the earth" (NRSV; the seventh plague)

9:29: "I [Moses] will stretch out my hands . . . there will be no more hail, that you [Pharaoh] may know that the earth is the LORD's" (RSV; also the seventh plague)

10:2: "that you [Moses and Israel] may tell . . . what signs I [the Lord] have done among them [Egyptians]; that you may know that I am the LORD" (RSV; the eighth plague)

11:7: "that you [Moses and Israel] may know that the LORD makes a distinction between the Egyptians and Israel" (RSV; the tenth plague)

14:4: "and I will get glory over Pharaoh . . . and the Egyptians shall *know* that I am the LORD" (RSV; crossing the sea)

14:18: "and the Egyptians shall *know* that I am the LORD, when I have gotten glory over Pharaoh, his chariots, and his horsemen" (RSV)

The use of this idiom continues in Exodus beyond this pericope, as indicated by 16:6, 12. In the wilderness Israel will "know" that he is the Lord God through his miraculous provisions. Elsewhere in the Pentateuch the phrase occurs only in Deut. 29:6. Beyond the Pentateuch its use is sporadic (1 Kings 20:13, 28; Isa. 45:3; 49:23, 26; 60:16; Hos. 2:20; Joel 2:27; 3:17). Of these the closest to those directed at Pharaoh ("so that you may know that I am the LORD") is Isa. 45:3, in which God uses the phrase in addressing Cyrus, king of Persia. The exception to the infrequency of this phrase in the Old Testament outside of Exodus is Ezekiel. It occurs there an incredibly high number of times, most of which are directed to the prophet's audience, the Judean exiles (e.g., Ezek. 5:13; 6:7, 14; 7:4, 9, 27; 11:10, 12; 12:15, 16; 13:9, 14, 21, 23). The difference between the popular use of this phrase in these two books is that in Exodus it is placed in a context of confinement and oppression that is about to give way to liberty, while in Ezekiel it is placed in a context where liberty has recently given way, or is about to give way, to confinement and oppression, thus the exact opposite of the Exodus setting.

The Purpose of the Plagues

This emphasis on knowing the Lord lifts the plagues beyond the function of chastisement. The plagues are not God's revenge on Pharaoh. The Lord's intention is not to leave behind in Egypt a bruised and bloodied Pharaoh, nor is the Lord interested in leaving the Egyptian king breathless via an exhibition of miracles.

The divine purpose is that Pharaoh and his people—to say nothing of the Israelites—will indeed acquire knowledge of the true God. They have an educative rationale. It will be knowledge based on observation and confrontation, not on hearsay. To know the Lord as Lord means to recognize and then submit to his authority. This is the choice that Pharaoh needs to make and is invited to make. To be sure, there is no reference in later chapters to Pharaoh saying, "I now know Yahweh," or "I now know who Yahweh is," and there is nothing remotely approaching Isaiah's prophecy vis-à-vis Egypt: "In that day five cities of Egypt will speak the language of Canaan and swear allegiance to the LORD Almighty" (Isa. 19:18 NIV).

Ten plagues are recorded:

1. 7:14–25: water to blood
2. 8:1–15: swarms of frogs
3. 8:16–19: gnats (or lice)
4. 8:20–32: swarms of flies (Hebrews spared [8:22])
5. 9:1–7: pestilence upon cattle (Hebrews' livestock spared [9:4, 6])
6. 9:8–12: boils on humans and animals
7. 9:13–35: hail, thunder, and lightning (except in the portion of territory assigned to the Hebrews [9:26])
8. 10:1–20: swarm of locusts
9. 10:21–29: three days of thick darkness
10. 11:1–12:36: death of the firstborn, both people and cattle (Hebrews exempted if the necessary preparations are taken [12:7, 13])

The suggestion often has been made that each of these plagues is aimed directly at some aspect of Egyptian religion. In several instances this is quite possible, but in others the connection is difficult to make. Indeed, Exod. 12:12 has the Lord saying, "And on all the gods of Egypt I will execute judgments" (RSV). See also Num. 33:4b: "For the LORD had brought judgment on their gods" (NIV). That does apply to some of the plagues:

1. Hapi, the god of the Nile, bringer of fertility
2. Hek/qet, the frog-headed goddess of fruitfulness

4. Kheper(a), in the form of a beetle (if that may be included among "swarms of flies"). He symbolizes the daily cycle of the sun across the sky.
5. Many Egyptian gods and goddesses are pictured in the hieroglyphs zoomorphically: Hathor, a cow-headed goddess, or a goddess with a human head adorned with horns or cow's ears; Khnum, a ram-headed male figure; Amon, king of the gods and patron deity of the Pharaohs, a male figure with a ram's head, or a ram wearing a triple crown; Geb, god of the earth, a goose or a male figure with his head surmounted by a goose; Isis, queen of the gods, a cow's or ram's horns on her head
7. Nut, the sky goddess, also protector of the dead
8. Serapia, protector from locusts
9. Re, the personification of the sun, king of the gods, and father of humankind
10. Possibly Taurt, goddess of maternity, who presided over childbirth; later a protective household deity

We should note that the biblical text gives no indication that the plagues are to be associated with Egyptian religion and deities. The similarities may, therefore, be coincidental. As far as the nature of the plagues is concerned, some of them, more than likely, would already have been experienced by the Egyptians (e.g., the red hue of the waters of the Nile, and a plague of frogs coming from the marshy banks of the river). Others of them probably were unprecedented, such as the plagues of hail and darkness, given Egypt's virtual lack of rain and its year-round bright, sunny days (except for windstorms that quickly blot out the light of the sun).

Some scholars have argued that the plagues can be explained chronologically within the ecosystem of Egypt, and so what one finds in Exodus 7–10 is a literal history of a succession of natural phenomena (see Hort 1957; 1958). Many other scholars reject the attempt to defend the account of the plagues as historically accurate and true information. But J. K. Hoffmeier (1992: 375) raises this interesting question: If the sequence of events outlined by Hort and others for the annual fall and rise of the Nile is on target, "how is it that a variety of traditions could be drawn together centuries later by a redactor that makes such good sense in Egypt, but certainly not in Palestinian locales?"

Z. Zevit (1976: 211) has looked for analogies to the plagues elsewhere. He has discovered similar terms and language in the pericope about the plagues and in the creation narratives of Genesis, and he suggests that Genesis 1–2 is the background, thematically, for the plagues. Thus, for example, in the plague of blood the phrase "all their pools of water"

(Exod. 7:19) is literally "every gathering of their waters," which is a parallel to the "waters that were gathered together" of Gen. 1:10. Zevit also connects the ten plagues with the tenfold "and he [God] said" of Gen. 1:3, 6, 9, 11, 14, 20, 24, 26, 28, 29.

The Hardening of Pharaoh's Heart

Terms Used to Describe Pharaoh's Heart

Terminology about the hardening of Pharaoh's heart appears twenty times in Exodus 4–14, and three different Hebrew verbs are used—*kābēd*, *ḥāzaq, qāšâ*—to describe the act of hardening. The basic meaning of *kābēd* is "to be heavy." In addition to describing the heart, the word *kābēd* can describe the eyes (Gen. 48:10), the ears (Isa. 6:10), or the mouth and the tongue (Exod. 4:10). All these references are to the malfunction of a particular organ, the malfunction being caused by either age or disease (Gen. 48:10; Exod. 4:10). Thus R. R. Wilson (1979: 22) says that in these passages the writer is "referring to an organ of perception that is no longer receiving outside stimuli."

The verb *ḥāzaq* means "to be strong, hard." The root is in the name "Hezekiah," meaning "the Lord is my strength," and in "Ezekiel," meaning "may God strengthen." Put in a negative context, perhaps our closest English equivalent is "bullheaded." The verb *qāšâ* means "to be hard, difficult, severe."

Following below are the passages from Exodus that use one of these Hebrew verbs. After each reference is a listing of the particular verb that is used and an indication of what stem that verb assumes there, the basic Qal stem or the Piel or Hiphil stems (put most simply, the Qal describes a state, "to be . . ."; the Piel and Hiphil describe a condition or situation that is caused, "to make . . ."). The translation is that of the NRSV. I include parallels from the Jerusalem Bible (JB) and the New English Bible (NEB) if they are different from the NRSV. These two modern versions of Scripture, which I consider to be among the best, show flexibility in choice of translation for one of the three Hebrew verbs listed above. Whenever a verse number is put in brackets, it is the verse number in the Hebrew text, which is at variance with the English text.

1. 4:21: "I will harden his heart"; "make him obstinate" (NEB); *ḥāzaq* in the Piel
2. 7:3: "I will harden Pharaoh's heart"; "I will make Pharaoh's heart stubborn" (NEB, JB); *qāšâ* in the Hiphil
3. 7:13: "still Pharaoh's heart was hardened"; "Pharaoh, however, was obstinate" (NEB); "stubborn" (JB); *ḥāzaq* in the Qal

4. 7:14: "Pharaoh's heart is hardened"; "obdurate" (NEB); "adamant" (JB); *kābēd* in adjectival form

5. 7:22: "Pharaoh's heart remained hardened"; "remained obstinate" (NEB); "was stubborn" (JB); *ḥāzaq* in the Qal

6. 8:15[11]: "Pharaoh . . . hardened his heart"; "he became obdurate" (NEB); "became adamant" (JB); *kābēd* in the Hiphil

7. 8:19[15]: "Pharaoh's heart was hardened"; "remained obstinate" (NEB); "was stubborn" (JB); *ḥāzaq* in the Qal

8. 8:32[28]: "Pharaoh hardened his heart"; "became obdurate" (NEB); "was adamant" (JB); *kābēd* in the Hiphil

9. 9:7: "the heart of Pharaoh was hardened"; "he remained obdurate" (NEB); "became adamant" (JB); *kābēd* in the Qal

10. 9:12: "the LORD hardened the heart of Pharaoh"; "made Pharaoh obstinate" (NEB); "made Pharaoh's heart stubborn" (JB); *ḥāzaq* in the Piel

11. 9:34: "he hardened his heart"; "became obdurate" (NEB); "became adamant" (JB); *kābēd* in the Hiphil

12. 9:35: "the heart of Pharaoh was hardened"; "remained obstinate" (NEB); "was stubborn" (JB); *ḥāzaq* in the Qal

13. 10:1: "I have hardened his heart"; "I have made him obdurate" (NEB); "stubborn" (JB); *kābēd* in the Hiphil

14. 10:20: "the LORD hardened Pharaoh's heart"; "made Pharaoh obstinate" (NEB); "made Pharaoh's heart stubborn" (JB); *ḥāzaq* in the Piel

15. 10:27: "the Lord hardened Pharaoh's heart"; "made Pharaoh obstinate" (NEB); "made Pharaoh's heart stubborn" (JB); *ḥāzaq* in the Piel

16. 11:10: "the LORD hardened Pharaoh's heart"; "made him obstinate" (NEB); "made Pharaoh's heart stubborn" (JB); *ḥāzaq* in the Piel

17. 13:15: "Pharaoh stubbornly refused to let us go"; "proved stubborn and refused to let us go" (NEB); "stubbornly refused to let us go" (JB); *qāšâ* in the Hiphil

18. 14:4: "I will harden Pharaoh's heart"; "make Pharaoh obstinate" (NEB); "make Pharaoh's heart stubborn" (JB); *ḥāzaq* in the Piel

19. 14:8: "the LORD hardened the heart of Pharaoh"; "made obstinate" (NEB); "made . . . stubborn" (JB); *ḥāzaq* in the Piel

20. 14:17: "I will harden the hearts of the Egyptians"; "make obstinate" (NEB); "make . . . stubborn" (JB); *kābēd* in the Piel

Of the three verbs, then, *ḥāzaq* is used most frequently (11x), followed by *kābēd* (7x) and *qāšâ* (2x).

Analyses of the Terminology

It is interesting to arrange these twenty verses on the basis of the subject of the verb. See table 6.

From these analyses at least several observations may be made. To be sure, there is the word from God to Moses in 4:21 and 7:3 that "I will harden Pharaoh's heart." Twice Moses hears this before the commencement of the plagues. But neither time does the announcement elicit either protest or a demand for an explanation from Moses. And we have already seen in the Exodus narrative (chs. 3–4) that Moses occasionally protests or presses God for additional facts. Here, however, he is compliant.

Table 6

God as Subject (10 References)

kābēd	ḥāzaq	qāšâ
10:1 Hiphil	4:21 Piel	7:3 Hiphil
14:17 Piel	9:12 Piel	
	10:20 Piel	
	10:27 Piel	
	11:10 Piel	
	14:4 Piel	
	14:8 Piel	

Pharaoh as Subject (4 References)

kābēd	ḥāzaq	qāšâ
8:15[11] Hiphil		13:15 Hiphil
8:32[28] Hiphil		
9:34 Hiphil		

Pharaoh's Heart as Subject (6 References)

kābēd	ḥāzaq	qāšâ
7:14 adjective	7:13 Qal	
9:7 Qal	7:22 Qal	
	8:19[15] Qal	
	9:35 Qal	

Is this, then, an indication that Moses has accepted his responsibilities and is confident enough that he does not question God? Or may we assume that on hearing such an enigmatic word from God, Moses engaged in even further remonstrations with God? May not such announcements be considered God's declaration of the outcome?

On examining the description of the plagues, one notices that references to God's hardening of Pharaoh's heart emerge only late in the narrative. Thus:

1. "Pharaoh's heart is hardened" (7:14)
2. "he hardened his heart" (8:15[11])
3. "Pharaoh's heart was hardened" (8:19[15])
4. "But Pharaoh hardened his heart" (8:32[28])
5. "But the heart of Pharaoh was hardened" (9:7)
6. "But the LORD hardened the heart of Pharaoh" (9:12)
7. "But Pharaoh hardened his heart" (9:34)
   "So the heart of Pharaoh was hardened" (9:35)
8. "I have hardened his heart" (10:1)
   "But the LORD hardened Pharaoh's heart" (10:20)
9. "But the LORD hardened Pharaoh's heart" (10:27)
10. "The LORD hardened Pharaoh's heart" (11:10)

What is noticeable is that there is no reference to God's hardening the heart of Pharaoh until after the sixth plague is well under way. There are only two references (9:34, 35) to Pharaoh hardening his own heart after God's hardening is done. And surely it is significant that even after God has hardened Pharaoh's heart (#6 [9:12]), Pharaoh, at least once more, can harden his own heart (#7 [9:34]). But after that God, and God alone, does the hardening (#8 [10:20]; #9 [10:27]; #10 [11:10]). It is as if Pharaoh's window of opportunity has slammed shut.

Moshe Greenberg (1969: 181) graphically captures Pharaoh's problem: "In this dramatic evolution of Pharaoh's reactions there is a consistency of principle—the core of his intransigence—namely the maintenance of his sovereignty. That is the crux of the matter; that is what cannot coexist with God's authority. Thus the opposition of Pharaoh is the archetypal opposition of human power, of human authority to the claims of God. Under pressure it will show flexibility and accommodation, even reversing itself—first by crying for help, then by confessing guilt and making concessions. But after all its retreats, it clings to its last redoubt, a core of self-assertiveness and independence, to surrender which would mean the end of its claim to ultimate, self-sufficient power. Here it resists, careless of the cost, unto death."

Can this be fortuitous? Or is the Scripture implying that Pharaoh, now so impervious to God, has forfeited his right to choose consciously and independently? May freedom be abrogated? At least for a while Pharaoh had control over his own choice, but never did he exercise control over the consequences of his choice.

A strong concentration on the hardening of Pharaoh's heart can cause us to miss the several clear ways in which God attempted to soften his heart:

1. By the prayers of Moses: "Pray to the LORD" (8:8[4]; 9:28; 10:17); "Pray for me" (8:28[24])
2. By the testimony of his own magicians: "This is the finger of God" (8:19[15])
3. By moving him to partial obedience: "I will let the people go to sacrifice to the LORD" (8:8[4]); "Go, sacrifice to your God within the land . . . I will let you go . . . only you shall not go very far away" (8:25–28[21–24]); "Go . . . only let your flocks and your herds remain behind" (10:24)
4. By moving him to partial penitence: "I have sinned this time; the LORD is in the right, and I and my people are in the wrong" (9:27); "I have sinned against the LORD your God, and against you. Now therefore, forgive my sin" (10:16). Putting together the "I have sinned" of 9:27 and the "he sinned yet again" of 9:34, Greenberg (1969: 161) notes, "He acknowledged guilt but went right on being guilty." Pharaoh needs to hear the word in Matt. 3:8: "Prove your repentance by the fruit it bears" (NEB).
5. By continually giving Pharaoh another chance: God is as long-suffering with Pharaoh as he was with Moses after the burning bush. Moses' repeated "I will not go" is matched by Pharaoh's repeated "I will not let you go." That God had to act ten times before Pharaoh acquiesced is neither unexpected nor surprising. After all, in terms of long-range effectiveness, or even for the first few generations after the deluge, how successful was the flood, another act of divine judgment?

Explanations about the Hardening of Pharaoh's Heart

Addressing the issue of the hardening of Pharaoh's heart, and similar events, Walther Eichrodt (1961–1967: 2:178–79) states:

The remarkable thing, however, is that this never led to a flat determinism, depriving Man of the responsibility for his actions. At all times the capacity for self-determination is insistently retained. The whole ethical exhortation of the prophets is based on the conviction that decision is placed in the hands of men. But the Law too . . . rests on this presupposition. The fundamental postulate of moral freedom is thus found in equal force alongside the religious conviction of God's effective action in all things; and no attempt is made to create a harmonizing adjustment between them. It is testimony to the compelling power of the Old Testament experience of God that it was able to affirm both realities at once, and to endure the tension between them, without discounting anything of their unconditional validity.

What God has joined together, let no one put asunder!

In the New Testament one finds further explanation of the motif in Romans 9–11. Paul refers to the hardening of Pharaoh's heart (9:17–18) and to the hardening of Israel (11:7, 25). Following Eichrodt, we will observe that the New Testament, no less than the Old, holds in tension God's divine sovereignty and humankind's moral freedom. This is precisely what emerges out of this Pauline passage.

Contending that physical descent from Abraham is insufficient to qualify one as a spiritual child of Abraham, Paul buttresses his case by appealing to Genesis. Both Isaac and Ishmael were physical sons of Abraham, but only one was the child of promise (9:7–9). Both Jacob and Esau were children of Isaac, but Esau was passed over in favor of Jacob (9:10–13). Paul thus has addressed the questions of God's fidelity (9:6) by showing God's principle of selectivity in operation in patriarchal history.

But if God is selective, does this imply injustice on God's part (9:14)? Were Ishmael and Esau indiscriminately rejected? To respond to that objection, Paul turns to Exodus and essentially says, "If you maintain that the God of the patriarchs is unjust, you must maintain the same about the God of Exodus." Here too selectivity was in operation. On Israel he showed mercy; Pharaoh's heart he hardened. (Note that in Romans "mercy" appears eleven times, nine of which are in chs. 9–11: 9:15 [2x], 16, 18, 23; 11:30, 31 [2x], 32.)

Crucial here is Rom. 9:17: "I have raised you [Pharaoh] up for the very purpose of showing my power in you . . ." (NRSV). This verse is a quotation of Exod. 9:16. The equivalent in Exodus to "I have raised you up" (in Romans) is "I have let you live." "Raising up," then, has nothing to do with being born or created. Rather, it means "I have not destroyed you" or "I have allowed you to continue to live." The raising up is itself an expression of God's mercy. And God's mercy and hardening both are expressions of his sovereignty (Rom. 9:18).

To underscore this idea of a sovereign God, Paul appeals to creation (God as potter), plus several quotes from Hosea and Isaiah (Rom. 9:19–29).

Where, then, does all of this place humankind? This is the concern of Rom. 9:30–10:21. It is important that we not stop with 9:29. God is sovereign, yes, but this does not negate human freedom. If there are Jews who are not justified, it is not because their unbelief was predetermined, but because they have "stumbled over the stumbling stone" (9:32 NRSV).

Many preachers and missionaries have used Rom. 10:14–15 ("How, then, can they call on the one they have not believed in? And how can they believe in the one of whom they have not heard? And how can they hear without someone preaching to them?" [NIV]) to appeal to people for their involvement in evangelism and world mission. This is appropriate as an application of the text beyond its context. But within the context, Paul is raising these questions ironically. The Jews to whom he writes have heard, and God has repeatedly sent messengers to them. So they cannot use ignorance as an excuse. There has been no lack of invitation on God's part: "All day long I have held out my hands to a disobedient and contrary people" (10:21 NIV). Thus we have, side by side, divine sovereignty (9:6–29) and human privilege and personal responsibility (9:30–10:21).

Turning from comments on Jews as individuals, Paul progresses to a discussion of Jews as a people, a community (Rom. 11:1–36). Although God has rejected individual Jews, he has never rejected his people in toto (11:2). In 11:7–25 Paul compares implicitly the hardening of Pharaoh and the hardening of Jews. In each case God uses the hardening redemptively. He hardened Pharaoh. The result? The Israelites were delivered from Egypt. He has hardened the Israelites. The result? Gentiles are allowed to enter God's kingdom. What, then, of the Jews, not just the remnant? Is the hardening permanent? Paul's answer is an emphatic no. "All Israel will be saved" (11:26 NIV)—a tantalizing expression upon which Paul does not elaborate.

The Passover (12:1–13:16)

Exodus 12 spells out the procedures in the observance of Passover. Further information is found in the cultic calendars of the Pentateuch: Lev. 23:5–8; Num. 28:16–25; Deut. 16:1–8. In these three passages, as well as in Exodus 12, Passover is closely linked with the Feast of Unleavened Bread. The Old Testament records the observance of five particular Passovers besides the original one: the Israelites in the wilderness (Num. 9:1–14); at Gilgal after the Israelites enter Canaan (Josh. 5:10–12); that celebrated by Hezekiah (2 Chron. 30:1–27, but no parallel in Kings); that celebrated by Josiah (an abbreviated account in 2 Kings 23:21–23, and an extended account in 2 Chron. 35:1–19); that celebrated in the postexilic community (Ezra 6:19–22).

The Hebrew word for "Passover" is *pesaḥ*. There is also a verb, *pāsaḥ* ("to pass over"), used three times in Exodus 12: "When I see the blood, I will pass over you" (12:13 NIV); "The LORD will pass over the door" (12:23 RSV); "It is the sacrifice of the LORD's passover, for he passed over the houses of the people of Israel in Egypt" (12:27 RSV).

But what is the meaning of "the LORD will pass over"? Does it mean that God will bypass the houses over whose door the blood is smeared? The clue is found in 12:23: "The LORD will pass over the door and will not allow the destroyer to enter your houses to slay you" (RSV). To "pass over," then, means "to protect," or as the NEB suggests in a footnote, "stand guard over." The Lord himself will block the entry of the destroyer. He will be a protective covering for his people. Their security is in his presence.

Most important here is the use of the blood. That blood is to be extracted from the lamb's body and then smeared over the doorposts and the horizontal beam atop the door (12:7, 13). Failure to take this action will result in disaster.

It is no wonder, then, that Moses, in relating God's word to his people (12:21–27), focuses exclusively on the role of the blood. As Brevard Childs (1974: 200) notes, "The literary effect of Moses' speech is one of tremendous telescoping." Moses says nothing about the meal in the home, the quality of the lamb to be chosen, when it is to be killed, how the meat is to be prepared, how much of it is to be eaten, or what type of clothing the people are to wear—all of which are included in God's directions to Moses (12:1–13).

Exodus 12 is concerned not only about the *when* of Passover, the *why* of Passover, the *how* of observing it, but also about *who* may participate (12:43–49). The observance of Passover is not an indiscriminate invitation to everyone. Who may participate? The congregation of Israel (v. 47); the slave (v. 44), if circumcised, who has the same privileges as a Hebrew; the stranger (v. 48), the non-Israelite who has become a believer in Yahweh. Who may not participate? The foreigner (v. 43), the pagan unbeliever; the sojourner (v. 45), either the resident alien or the visitor who will settle temporarily on Israelite soil; the hired servant (v. 45), one belonging to another nation but working in Israel. These distinctions are necessary because of the "mixed multitude" (12:38) leaving Egypt, and this is why instructions about eligibility for participation in Passover (12:43–49) come just after this "mixed multitude" leaves Egypt (12:37–39).

The New Testament writers deliberately move from the lamb to the Lamb, from the type to the antitype, for this is the fullness of God's plan. The prison now is a kingdom of darkness, not slavery in Egypt. The captive who is called forth is not Israel, but the world. Redemption is an ethical change rather than a geographical change.

As with the lamb in Egypt (Exod. 12:46), so not one bone of Jesus the Lamb was broken (John 19:36). The two explicit references in the epistolary literature of the New Testament to Christ the Passover Lamb are in 1 Cor. 5:7 ("Christ, our paschal lamb" RSV) and 1 Pet. 1:19 ("a lamb without blemish or spot" RSV). What is of interest in these passages is that both Paul and Peter are concerned more with the implications of redemption by the Lamb for holy living than they are in formulating a theological discourse on soteriology. That is, the apostles move beyond salvation into sanctification.

The immediate sequel to the Passover is Moses' transmission of further instructions to the Israelites about the Feast of Unleavened Bread (13:3–10) and the consecration of the firstborn (13:11–16). Each of these two sections stresses that God's redemption is both *from* and *into*. It is from Egypt, but into the land of the Canaanites (vv. 5, 11). Israel's possession of the new land will be the fulfillment of God's promises to the patriarchs. Suddenly the reader is taken back as far as Gen. 12:7. But once in the land, the people of Israel must share their testimony with the children whom God will give them (vv. 8, 14). God's faithfulness reverberates over three periods: the past (your ancestors); the present (you); the future (your children).

The Exodus (13:17–15:21)

Exodus 12:37 informs us that six hundred thousand men, besides women and children, left Egypt. The total number of Israelites leaving would have been in excess of two million. This same number is repeated substantially in Exod. 38:26; Num. 1:46; 2:32; 26:51. How should we deal with this astronomical number? Exodus 23:29–30 suggests that God will drive out the Canaanites gradually because Israel's population is too meager to repopulate Canaan: "Little by little I will drive them out from before you, *until you are increased.*" (See also table 12 in ch. 16.)

The Population of Israel

A great deal of discussion has surrounded the total number of those counted in the census: 603,550. This number excludes the Levites, all women, and all children under twenty years of age. The total size of the congregation would have been approximately two million people, perhaps as many as two and a half million.

Critics among biblical scholars have offered various explanations. One suggestion is that the figures are nothing short of fabulous, lacking any historical value. That is, they represent the unrestrained imagination of a later writer given to hyperbole. It is P, among the source documents (if one subscribes to this view), that is responsible for inventing these fictitious numbers, just as it is P that reports the astonishing longevity of those who lived prior to the flood in Genesis 5 (see Davies 1995: 465–67). G. A. Rendsburg (2001: 393) compares the Canaanite story from Ugarit in which Kret goes in search of his abducted wife accompanied by three million men (literally, "three hundred myriads"). A second suggestion is that the numbers have historical value but reflect a later census made during David's reign (see the totals in 2 Sam. 24:9; 1 Chron. 21:5).

A third suggestion involves the Hebrew word *ʾelep*, whose normal translation is "thousand." As early as 1905 the eminent archaeologist Flinders Petrie (1906: 209–11) suggested that the word should be translated not as "thousand" but as "family." In this he has been seconded in more recent years by Jacob Milgrom (1978: 79–80). Verses cited to support this thesis include Judg. 6:15, "my clan [*ʾelep*] is the weakest in Manasseh"; Num. 1:16, "the ones chosen . . . the leaders . . . the heads of the clans [*ʾelep*] of Israel" (KJV: "heads of thousands in Israel"); 1 Sam. 10:19, "present yourselves before the LORD by your tribes [*šēbeṭ*] and by your clans [*ʾelep*]" (NRSV, JB, NIV, RSV, KJV: "thousands"); 1 Sam. 10:21, "he brought the tribe [*šēbeṭ*] of Benjamin near by its families [*mišpāḥah*]." These latter two verses would seem to indicate that "clan" and "family" are synonyms. For other texts in which *ʾelep* means "clan," see Josh. 22:14, 21, 30; 1 Sam. 23:23; Isa. 60:22 (NIV: "a thousand"); Zech. 9:7; 12:5–6 (NRSV, NIV: "leaders"). Thus, according to this system Judah does not have a population of 74,600 (Num. 1:27); rather, it totals 74 families and 600 people.

A third suggestion is much like the one made by Petrie. George Mendenhall (1958) suggests that the word *ʾelep* designates not "family," "clan," or "tent," but a military unit within the clan (see Num. 1:3). Following this interpretation, we would paraphrase Num. 1:26–27 as, "Of the people of Judah registered by lineage in clans and ancestral homes: when all the males of twenty years or more who were fit for military service were polled, 74 units of the tribe were recorded, and from these 600 men were enrolled for military service."

In either case, the conclusion is the same. The number of men (twenty years or older) in the wilderness is reduced from 603,550 to 5,550. Evangelical scholars have in many instances accepted the rendering of *ʾelep* as "military unit" or "family." As C. J. Humphreys (1998: 199) has observed, "If the purpose of the Exodus account is to demonstrate the power of God in defeating the Egyptian army, greatly exaggerating the number of Israelites is hardly consistent with that purpose."

Additional support for the decreased number perhaps is found in the military records from the ancient Near East. If Ramses II (1304–1234 B.C.) is the Pharaoh of the exodus—a possibility, but still not a totally accepted suggestion—it is interesting to observe that at the famous battle at Kadesh in Syria, Pharaoh and the Hittite king Muwatallis each fielded approximately twenty thousand troops (Breasted 1906: 3:127, 129).

And these were the armies of the two titans of that day! By contrast the Israelites would have had, as they left Egypt, a group of males (twenty years and older) approximately one-fourth the size of the Egyptian and Hittite armies.

But is all of this explaining or explaining away the integrity of the biblical narrative? James Barr (1978: 250), focusing on this very section of Exodus and the opening chapters of Numbers, asks whether the modern conservative "is boldly upholding the accuracy of the Bible, relying on the power of God to sustain this great multitude by miraculous feedings? Not in the slightest. On the contrary, he is doing all he can to find a way to cut the numbers down." Anyone who might think that all evangelical Old Testament scholars have abandoned the traditional translation—one that is retained in all modern Bible versions—should read the comments of Gleason Archer (1973: 234–38) in defense of the credibility of the high numbers. A sufficiently large number of Israelites must be assumed to make sense of Pharaoh's words "Behold, the people of Israel are too many and too mighty for us" (Exod. 1:9 RSV). Also, the approximately six and one-half tons of precious metal donated to the tabernacle project by the Israelites (Exod. 38:21–31) presupposes a rather large base of people as contributors, to say nothing of how this was carried out of Egypt and into the wilderness.

The Crossing of the Reed Sea

The crossing of the Reed Sea (to be preferred to "Red Sea," which is based not on the Hebrew but on the Greek *erythra thalassa* and the Latin *mare rubrum*) is described miraculously. Reading the Hebrew *yām sûp* as "Reed Sea" rather than "Red Sea" reflects the fact that *sûp*, when used alone, refers to reeds or rushes, as in Exod. 2:3, "She placed the child in it and put it among the reeds [*sûp*] along the bank of the Nile" (NIV), or Exod. 2:5, "She saw the basket among the reeds [*sûp*] and sent her slave girl to get it" (NIV). The people of God pass through on dry land between two walls of water, walls of water that subsequently converged and submerged the retreating Egyptians.

To have the Red Sea divided would be no insignificant event. Today the Red Sea is approximately 1,200 miles in length (excluding the gulfs on Aqaba and Suez at the north). Its width varies from 124 to 155 miles. Its average depth is a bit more than 1,600 feet. Minimum depth is 600 feet, and maximum depth is 7,700 feet. In addition, the name "Sea of Reeds" (or "Rushes") presupposes fresh water, not salt water, in order for reeds to grow.

We conclude, then, that the Hebrews crossed not the Red Sea or the Gulf of Suez but rather some freshwater lake in northern Egypt (perhaps the southern tip of modern Lake Manzalah near Port Said). In no way, however, does this undercut the supernatural element in the story. Six hundred Egyptians were drowned, a fact that is not impossible, given this general area's proneness to earthquakes and possible tidal waves, as Knight (1976: 104–5) and Kitchen (1975: 47) point out. Whether passage was through a sea, a lake, or a lagoon, God had delivered his people from the claws of the largest lion in the world, Egypt. What for Egypt is destructive, is for God's people a rite of passage on their way to their God-given destiny (Dozeman 1996: 414). The means by which the Egyptians are drowned (Deut. 11:4; Josh. 24:6) are the means by which Israel is delivered (Deut. 1:40; 2:1; Josh. 4:21–24).

One might suspect that such a distinctive divine working would erase any suspicions that the Israelites might have entertained about God's ability to deliver them and Moses' ability to lead them. Such was not the case. As early as Exod. 16:2–3 the recently liberated people of God are yearning for Egypt. Freedom and pioneering are not as promising as bondage with the guarantee of three meals a day.

Exodus 14 concludes by observing, "The people feared the LORD; and they believed in the LORD and in his servant Moses" (v. 31 RSV). But such belief must be verbalized, for impression without expression leads to depression. Moses is coupled with the Lord at the end of ch. 14, but in the song of ch. 15 Moses is conspicuously absent.

It is fitting in this litany of praise in Exodus 15 that God is addressed primarily as Yahweh. Ten times the Tetragrammaton is used: vv. 1, 3 (2x), 6 (2x), 11, 16, 17, 18, 21. One time there is an abbreviated form of Yahweh, *yāh* (v. 2), one time the use of *ʾădōnāy* (v. 17), and two times *ʾēl* (v. 2). The hymn is, then, an affirmation of God's lordship. Some commentators (e.g., Fretheim 1991: 162) have observed that Exod. 1:1–15:21 follows the pattern found often in the psalms of lament—psalms composed either by communities or individuals in a time of threat when it seemed hard to believe that God was with his people. They move from describing the crisis and the crying out to God that it provokes (Exodus 1–2), to relating God's gracious intervention (what he says he plans to do [Exod. 3:1–7:7] and what he does do [Exod. 7:8–14:31]), ending with a doxology of some sort (15:1–21). Cry has turned to song.

In speaking of God, the hymn begins in the third person (vv. 1–5), shifts into the second person (vv. 6–17), then returns to and concludes with the third person (vv. 18–21). Preponderantly, then, this is a hymn addressed directly to God, the God "who dwells in the praises of his people."

The emphasis is primarily on what God has done. Israel does serve a God who acts, and acts decisively. To tamper with God's people is no small risk. As early as Genesis 12 an Egyptian Pharaoh discovered that truth. To wound the body is to wound the head. Indeed, the apostle Paul found out that to persecute the church was to persecute Christ.

The hymn celebrates not only the great acts of God but also his nature, who he is. He is "majestic in holiness" (v. 11). He is a God of covenant, and steadfast love (v. 13). He is incomparable (v. 11).

So, then, both God's acts and God's nature lend a predictability to the future (vv. 13–18). The Philistines, the Edomites, the Moabites, and the Canaanites too will fall as have the Egyptians. No exterior force can restrain the forward march of God's people. Only sin and disobedience can loom as a deterrent.

There is an interesting translation difference in the versions for some of the lines in vv. 13–18. Here is the NIV text, with the NRSV text in brackets:

1. 15:13: "You *will lead* [*led*] the people you have redeemed . . . you *will guide* [*guided*] them to your holy dwelling."
2. 15:14: "Nations *will hear and tremble* [*heard . . . trembled*]."
3. 15:15: "Chiefs of Edom *will be terrified* [*were dismayed*] . . . leaders of Moab *will be seized* [*seized*] . . . people of Canaan *will melt away* [*melted away*]."
4. 15:16: "Terror and dread *will fall* [*fell*] upon them . . . they *will be still* [*became still*] as a stone . . . until your people *pass by* [*passed by*] . . . until the people you bought *pass by* [*passed by*]."
5. 15:17: "You *will bring* them in and *plant* them [*brought . . . planted*]."

In other words, the NIV translates most of the verbs in vv. 13–18 as futures, while the NRSV (among many others) translates them as past or perfect verbs. A translation such as the NRSV renders the verbs as past tenses because that is their grammatical form (technically, preterites). A translation such as the NIV renders the verbs as future tenses because they tell of things that have not yet happened. What God has done (vv. 1–12), he will continue to do (vv. 13–17); and although future events have not yet taken place, they can be celebrated as "done deals." The incidents alluded to in vv. 13–18 could be either distant future events (e.g., the conquest of Canaan under Joshua, and David's capture of Jerusalem) or the anticipation of more immediate future events in the ensuing chapters of Exodus (the wilderness journeys, arrival at Sinai, the construction of the tabernacle).

The Plagues Account (Exodus 7–11)

Brueggemann, W. 1995. "Pharaoh as Vassal: A Study of Political Metaphor." *CBQ* 57:27–51.

Chisholm, R. B., Jr. 1996. "Divine Hardening in the Old Testament." *BSac* 153:410–34.

Eakin, F. E., Jr. 1977. "The Plagues and the Crossing of the Sea." *RevExp* 74:473–82.

Eichrodt, W. 1961–1967. *Theology of the Old Testament.* Trans. J. Baker. 2 vols. OTL. Philadelphia: Westminster.

Fretheim, T. E. 1991. "The Plagues as Ecological Signs of Historical Disaster." *JBL* 110:385–96.

Greenberg, M. 1969. *Understanding Exodus.* New York: Behrman.

———. 1971a. "Plagues of Egypt." *EncJud* 13:604–13.

———. 1971b. "The Redaction of the Plague Narrative in Exodus." In *Near Eastern Studies: In Honor of William Foxwell Albright.* Ed. H. Goedicke. Baltimore: Johns Hopkins University Press. Pp. 243–52.

Gunn, D. M. 1982. "The 'Hardening of Pharaoh's Heart': Plot, Character and Theology in Exodus 1–14." In *Art and Meaning: Rhetoric in Biblical Literature.* Ed. D. J. A. Clines et al. JSOTSup 19. Sheffield: JSOT Press. Pp. 72–96.

Hoffmeier, J. K. 1986. "The Arm of God versus the Arm of Pharaoh in the Exodus Narratives." *Bib* 67:378–87.

———. 1992. "Egypt, Plagues in." *ABD* 2:374–78.

Hort, G. 1957. "The Plagues of Egypt." *ZAW* 69:84–103.

———. 1958. "The Plagues of Egypt." *ZAW* 70:48–59.

Irwin, B. P. 2003. "Yahweh's Suspension of Free Will in the Old Testament." *TynB* 54:55–62.

Kuyper, L. J. 1974. "Hardness of Heart according to Biblical Perspective." *SJT* 27:459–74.

Lemmelijn, B. 1996. "Transformations in Biblical Studies: The Story of the History of Research into the 'Plague Narrative' in Exod. 7:14–11:10." *JNSL* 22:117–27.

Lowenstamm, S. E. 1971. "Number of Plagues in Psalm 105." *Bib* 52:34–38.

———. 1974. "An Observation on Source-Criticism of the Plague Pericope." *VT* 24:374–78.

Margulis, B. "Plagues Tradition in Ps. 105." *Bib* 50:491–96.

McCarthy, D. J. 1965. "Moses' Dealing with Pharaoh: Exodus 7:8–10:27." *CBQ* 27:336–47. Repr., in *Institution and Narrative: Collected Essays.* AnBib 108. Rome: Biblical Institute Press, 1985. Pp. 115–26.

———. 1966. "Plagues and the Sea of Reeds: Exodus 5–14." *JBL* 85:137–58.

Noegel, S. E. 1995. "The Significance of the Seventh Plague." *Bib* 76:532–39.

———. 1997. "Moses and Magic: Notes on the Book of Exodus." *JANES* 24:45–59.

Stieglitz, R. 1987. "Ancient Records and the Plagues of Egypt." *BAR* 13 (6):46–49.

Van Seters, J. 1986. "The Plagues of Egypt: Ancient Tradition or Literary Invention?" *ZAW* 98:31–39.

Wilson, R. R. 1979. "The Hardening of Pharaoh's Heart." *CBQ* 41:18–36.

Zevit, Z. 1976. "The Priestly Redaction and Interpretation of the Plague Narrative in Exodus." *JQR* 66:193–211.

———. 1990. "Three Ways to Look at the Plagues." *BRev* 6 (3):16–23, 42, 44.

Passover and the Exodus (Exodus 12–15:21)

Ackerman, S. 2002. "Why Is Miriam Also among the Prophets? (And Is Zipporah among the Priests?)." *JBL* 121:47–80.

Archer, G. L. 1973. *A Survey of Old Testament Introduction.* Chicago: Moody.

Barr, J. 1978. *Fundamentalism.* Philadelphia: Westminster.

Batto, B. 1983. "The Reed Sea: Requiescat in Pace." *JBL* 102:32–34.

Breasted, J. H. 1906. *Ancient Records of Egypt: Historical Documents from the Earliest Times to the Persian Conquest.* 5 vols. Chicago: University of Chicago Press. Repr., New York: Russell & Russell, 1962.

Childs, B. S. 1970. "A Traditio-historical Study of the Reed Sea Tradition." *VT* 20:406–18.

———. 1974. *The Book of Exodus: A Critical, Theological Commentary.* OTL. Philadelphia: Westminster.

Coats, G. W. 1969. "The Song of the Sea." *CBQ* 31:1–17.

———. 1975. "History and Theology in the Sea Tradition." *ST* 29:141–54.

Collins, J. J. 1995. "The Exodus and Biblical Theology." *BTB* 25:152–60.

Craigie, P. C. 1969. "Yahweh as a Man of Wars." *SJT* 22:183–88.

Davies, E. W. 1995. "A Mathematical Conundrum: The Problem of the Large Numbers in Numbers i and xxvi." *VT* 45:449–69.

Dozeman, T. B. 1996. "The *yam-sup* in the Exodus and the Crossing of the Jordan River." *CBQ* 58:407–16.

Francisco, C. T. 1977. "The Exodus in Its Historical Setting." *Southwestern Journal of Theology* 20:3–20.

Freedman, D. N. 1974. "Strophe and Meter in Exodus 15." In *A Light unto My Path: Old Testament Studies in Honor of Jacob M. Myers.* Ed. H. N. Bream et al. Gettysburg Theological Studies 4. Philadelphia: Temple University Press. Pp. 163–203.

Frerichs, E. S., and L. H. Lesko, eds. 1997. *Exodus: The Egyptian Evidence.* Winona Lake, Ind.: Eisenbrauns.

Gottwald, N. 1989. "The Exodus as Event and Process: A Test Case in the Biblical Grounding of Liberation Theology." In *The Future of Liberation Theology: Essays in Honor of Gustavo Gutierrez.* Ed. M. H. Ellis and O. Maduro. Maryknoll, N.Y.: Orbis. Pp. 250–60.

Grabbe, L. L. 2000. "*Adde praeputium praeputio magnus acervus erit:* If the Exodus and Conquest Had Really Happened." *BibInt* 8:23–32.

Heinzerling, R. 2000. "On the Interpretation of the Census Lists by C. J. Humphreys and G. E. Mendenhall." *VT* 50:250–52.

Hendel, R. 2001. "The Exodus in Biblical Memory." *JBL* 120:601–22.

Hoffmeier, J. K. 1997. *Israel in Egypt: The Evidence for the Authenticity of the Exodus Tradition.* Oxford: Oxford University Press.

Huddlestun, J. 1992. "Red Sea." *ABD* 5:633–42.

Humphreys, C. J. 1998. "The Number of People in the Exodus from Egypt: Decoding Mathematically the Very Large Numbers in Numbers i and xxvi." *VT* 48:196–213.

———. 2000. "The Numbers in the Exodus from Egypt: A Further Appraisal." *VT* 50:323–28.

Kitchen, K. A. 1975. "Red Sea." *ZPEB* 5:46–49.

Knight, G. A. F. 1976. *Theology as Narration: A Commentary on the Book of Exodus.* Edinburgh: Handsel.

———. 1995. *The Song of Moses: A Theological Quarry.* Grand Rapids: Eerdmans.

Levenson, J. D. 1991. "Exodus and Liberation." *HBT* 13:134–74.

Lowenstamm, S. E. 1969. "The Lord Is My Strength and Glory." *VT* 19:464–70.

Mann, T. W. 1971. "The Pillar of Cloud in the Reed Sea Narrative." *JBL* 90:15–30.

———. 1996. "Passover: The Time of Our Lives." *Int* 50:240–50.

McIntire, M. 1999. "A Response to Colin J. Humphreys's 'The Number of People in the Exodus from Egypt: Decoding Mathematically the Very Large Numbers in Numbers i and xxvi.'" *VT* 49:262–64.

Mendenhall, G. E. 1958. "The Census Lists of Numbers 1 and 26." *JBL* 77:52–66.

Milgrom, J. 1978. "Priestly Terminology and the Political and Social Structure of Pre-monarchic Israel." *JQR* 69:65–81. Repr., in *Studies in Cultic Theology and Terminology.* SJLA 36. Leiden: Brill, 1983. Pp. 1–17.

———. 1999. "On Decoding Very Large Numbers." *VT* 49:131–32.

Miller, P. D., Jr., 1973. *The Divine Warrior in Ancient Israel.* Cambridge, Mass.: Harvard University Press.

Oblath, M. D. 2000. "Of Pharaohs and Kings—Whence the Exodus?" *JSOT* 87:23–42.

Patterson, R. D. 1995. "The Song of Redemption." *WTJ* 57:453–61.

Petrie, F. 1906. *Researches in Sinai.* London: Murray.

Rendsburg, G. A. 2001. "An Additional Note to Two Recent Articles on the Number of People in the Exodus from Egypt and the Large Numbers in Numbers 1 and 26." *VT* 51:392–95.

Routledge, R. 2002. "Passover and Last Supper." *TynB* 53:203–21.

Snaith, N. 1965. "The Seed of Reeds: The Red Sea." *VT* 15:395–98.

Van Seters, J. 2001. "The Geography of the Exodus." In *The Land I Will Show You: Essays in the History and Archaeology of the Ancient Near East in Honor of J. Maxwell Miller.* Ed. J. A. Dearman and P. M. Graham. JSOTSup 343. Sheffield: Sheffield Academic Press. Pp. 255–76.

Vervenne, M. 1994. "The Sea Narrative Revisited." *Bib* 75:80–98.

Walsh, J. T. 1977. "From Egypt to Moab: A Source-Critical Analysis." *CBQ* 39:20–33.

Wolters, A. 1990. "Not Rescue but Destruction: Reading Exodus 15:8." *CBQ* 52:223–40.

8

Testing in the Wilderness

EXODUS 15:22–18:27

A dramatic change in atmosphere and mood occurs after 15:1–21 into 15:22–18:27. The celebration of 15:1–21 gives way to the complaining of 15:22–26. Grumbling replaces gratitude, and so soon after the doxologies of 15:1–21. In fact, one of the key words in this section of Exodus, *lûn* ("complain, grumble, murmur"), occurs in the Old Testament only in the wilderness stories of the Bible (Exod. 15:22–17:16; Num. 11:1–36:13). It appears in Exod. 15:24; 16:2, 7, 8; 17:3, and nine times in the comparable stories in Numbers (Num. 14:2, 27 [2x], 29, 36; 16:11, 41; 17:5, 10). The one time that the verb appears outside of the wilderness traditions is in Josh. 9:18: "the whole assembly *grumbled* against the leaders."

There are a number of vocabulary parallels between this section of Exodus and the plagues of an earlier section that tie the two together. (1) In 7:24 "they could not drink" the (bloodied) water of the river; in 15:23 "they could not drink" the (bitter) water of Marah. (2) In 9:18 and 22 God "rains" hail all over Egypt; in 16:4 God "rains" bread all over the Israelite camp. (3) In 10:14, 15 locusts "came up" (NIV: "invaded") and "covered" all the ground; in 16:13 quail "came up" (NIV: "came") and "covered" the camp. (4) In 7:20 Moses "struck" the Nile with his raised staff, and in 17:5–6 he "struck" the rock with the staff.

(5) The purpose of the plagues is that Pharaoh/Egypt "shall know that I am the LORD" (7:5, 17, and others NRSV); God supplies manna and quail so that his people may "know" who their deliverer and provider is (16:6, 8).

The three-month journey from Egypt to Sinai was not carefree, either for Moses or for the Israelites. During this brief part of their itinerary they confronted at least four crises: the bitter waters at Marah (15:22–27); the need for sufficient quantities of food (16:1–36); a lack of drinking water at Rephidim (17:1–7); the invasion of the Amalekites (17:8–16). A fifth crisis might be the state of Moses' health. He is evidently overtaxed. Can he continue at such a pace indefinitely? Might Israel lose its leader, now dangerously close to the point of complete physical exhaustion (18:1–27)? His hands are weary (17:12), and his schedule of appointments is hectic (18:13).

A key verb used throughout this section is *nāsâ*, "to prove, put to the test." It appears in 15:25 and 16:4 with God as subject and the Israelites as the object of the testing. It is the same verb used to describe God's putting Abraham to the test with Isaac (Gen. 22:1). *Nāsâ* is used similarly in the postlude to the Decalogue, Exod. 20:20 (see also Deut. 8:2, 16; 13:3; 33:8). Other places where God "tests" (using the same Hebrew verb) are Judg. 2:22; 3:1, 4; 2 Chron. 32:31; Ps. 26:2. Moberly (2000: 98) notes that with the exception of 2 Chron. 32:31 and Ps. 26:2, all other testings take place in contexts of considerable significance: (1) the climactic moment in Abraham's life (Gen. 22:1); (2) the start of Israel's destiny after their deliverance from Egypt (Exod. 15:25; 16:4); (3) to explain why God gave his people the Decalogue (20:20); (4) as a comment on the duration of Israel's four-decade-long wilderness wanderings (Deut. 8:2, 16); (5) the exercise of discernment in refusing to follow or be seduced by false prophets (Deut. 13:3); (6) an occasion when the Levites remained loyal to God and were rewarded with the priesthood (Deut. 33:8); (7) God leaving nations to test Israel in the Promised Land (Judg. 2:22; 3:1, 4).

Twice the verb is used in this unit with negative overtones (17:2, 7). Here subject and object are reversed. The Israelites are the subject and God is the object, as in Deut. 6:16. The implications in these two verses of ch. 17 are clear. God is not to be tested. His reliability is not something that needs to be established. A companion to testing God is murmuring (15:24; 16:2). To be sure, such murmurings are directed immediately at Moses, but to raise a question about God's servant is to raise a question about God (16:7–8; cf. "You did not lie to us but to God!" [Acts 5:4 NRSV]). Murmuring is a frame of mind in which one believes that in difficulties God is insufficient. The author of Hebrews, referring to the rebellion described in Exod. 17:1–7, suggests that murmuring leads to hardening of the heart, and that leads to forfeiting one's position in God's kingdom (Heb. 3:7–13).

There is here, then, precious little of letting requests be made known unto God with thanksgiving. Nevertheless, God is not piqued. He does respond, not because of the Israelites' murmurings, but in spite of their murmurings.

First, bitter waters become sweet after Moses throws a tree into the water (15:25). This happened in response to prayer by Moses. In the first plague water became blood. Here, brackish water becomes sweet water. In the New Testament water will become wine (John 2:9).

Second, the daily supply of bread and meat came in the form of manna and quail (16:1–36). Both foods have been described as typical at one time in the Sinai peninsula. Manna has been explained as a secretion from insects or lice produced when they puncture the fruit on the branches of tamarisk trees, the juice of which forms into white balls or flakes (hardly designed to whet the appetite!). Quail are the smallest member of the pheasant family. The Sinai peninsula is the natural stopping place for these birds when they fly north to Europe from Africa in the spring, and when they return to Africa in the fall.

Most interesting here is God's order not to gather in excess of one day's supply of manna (16:4). The only limitation is that the amount collected be consumable within the day (16:16, 18). None could be left until the next day (16:19). Predictably, some people disobeyed, and they had to suffer the embarrassing consequences (16:20). Each day God furnished a fresh supply of manna for his people. In this way God taught them about a relationship of trust, an attitude reflected later in words of Jesus, "Do not be anxious about your life, what you shall eat or what you shall drink. . . . Do not be anxious about tomorrow" (Matt. 6:25, 34 RSV), as well as in Jesus' teaching that we are to ask God for daily bread (Matt. 6:11). The Israelites are to trust God to meet their physical needs one day at a time. Tomorrow is God's concern and problem, not theirs.

In addition to the restriction on the amount, there is also a restriction about gathering manna on the Sabbath (16:25–26), for none will be available. God's bakeries shut down on that day. Once again, there were those who did not believe that Moses meant what he said. He meant what he said! The curious found nothing (16:27).

At the beginning of the narrative God informs Moses (16:5) that the gathering of manna on Fridays would result in the ingathering of a double portion. This is precisely what happened (16:22). But nowhere between vv. 5 and 22 is it recorded that Moses relayed this information to the people. Brevard Childs (1974: 290) comments, delightfully, "God gives Israel, as it were, a surprise party." Indeed, the comment in v. 22b—"and when all the leaders of the congregation came and told

Moses" (RSV)—confirms their happy surprise. Their mouths are opened in astonishment.

Finally, we note Moses' instruction to Aaron to put some manna in a jar and place it "before the testimony" (16:33–34). "Testimony" usually is a reference to the tables of the covenant inscribed with the Ten Commandments (see Exod. 31:18; 32:15; 34:29). Or it may refer to the ark into which the "testimony" was placed (see Exod. 25:22; 26:33–34). Exodus 25:16, 21 contain the actual commands to place the testimony into the ark.

Of course, there is no testimony (see Exod. 27:21; 30:6, 36) or ark or tabernacle yet in existence in Exodus 16. And yet how significant it is that the reader discovers that before there was any reference to putting God's law in the ark, there is the notice to put God's manna in front of, in, or on the ark. A God who has given us his law? Yes. But first a God who has mercifully and bountifully met our needs and shown himself to be faithful and graceful.

The third crisis is a lack of water at Rephidim (17:1–7). The first time there was undrinkable water (15:23). Now it is no water at all. God's solution to this dilemma is unusual. In v. 6 we read that God said to Moses, "I will stand before you there on the rock at Horeb; and you shall strike the rock" (RSV). And all this is to be done publicly, not privately (v. 6b).

Even to read that God stood before Moses is surprising. To stand before someone else sometimes indicates a state of subordination or servitude (e.g., Gen. 18:8; Deut. 1:38; 10:8; in KJV, 1 Sam. 16:22). Thus, possibly, Gen. 18:22, which reads, "but Abraham still stood before the LORD" (RSV), may once have read, "and the Lord still stood before Abraham." At least there is an indication that the later scribes emended certain passages of Scripture that they felt to be offensive in what was said or implied about God. Such changes in the text are called *tiqqune soferim*, "emendations of the scribes" (see Ginsburg 1966: 347–63, especially 352–53).

God stations himself on the rock that is to be struck, thus making himself vulnerable to injury. It is perhaps with this particular imagery in mind that Paul can say, "Our fathers . . . all ate the same supernatural food [Exodus 16] and all drank the same supernatural drink [Exodus 17]. For they drank from the supernatural Rock which followed them, and the Rock was Christ" (1 Cor. 10:1, 3–4 RSV).

Although on this occasion God had saved the Israelites from thirst, and death, the names given to this site recall not God's goodness but the people's faithlessness: Massah and Meribah ("proof" and "contention"). Their attitude overshadowed God's act.

Three times in succession God has performed a supernatural act. It is interesting to observe where miracles appear in the Bible. In substantial sections of Scripture there is no hint of miracle at all. The Wisdom literature is an obvious example. How many miracles does one read about, for example, in the prophecies of Isaiah or Jeremiah, the historical books of Samuel and Kings, the Pauline Epistles, or the Catholic Epistles? Actually, there are only three places where one finds a cluster of miracles: during the career of Moses, during the times of Elijah and Elisha, and during the ministry of Jesus and parts of Acts—that is, at the beginning, during the period of greatest temptation, and at the launching of the church. Miracle, yes, but not too much miracle. Too much miracle can be as debilitating as none at all. And surely it is of interest that when Jesus asked, "Who do people say that I am?" (he whose ministry certainly was marked by miracles), two of the three individuals whom the disciples named never performed even a single miracle that we know of: Jeremiah and John the Baptist (Matt. 16:13–16). So possibly, the essence of Jesus' ministry is to be discovered not in how many signs and wonders he could perform, but elsewhere.

The fourth crisis was a surprise invasion against the Israelite camp by the Amalekites (Exod. 17:8–16). In the first incident at Rephidim it was God who "stood" on the rock. Now Moses will "stand" on the top of the hill (17:8). The slashing rod (17:6) is still in Moses' hand (17:9), but it is his hands, not the rod, that are paramount.

Actually, the reference to the raising and lowering of Moses' hands, resulting respectively in either success or setback, is not explained in terms of purpose or function. Perhaps it is best to say that we do not know what Moses was doing. Was he giving encouragement, as some scholars have suggested? Was he simply raising the rod heavenward to invoke divine assistance? For two reasons, the traditional explanation that Moses assumes the posture of intercessor should not be dismissed lightly. One reason is the references in the Psalter to the raising of hands in prayer, twice as a gesture of adoration (Ps. 63:4; 134:2), once as a gesture of petition (Ps. 28:2). The other reason is the consistent picture that emerges of Moses as intercessor par excellence. Already we have read three times that Moses "cried" to the Lord: Exod. 14:15; 15:25; 17:4.

And while Moses is atop the hill holding "the staff of God" in his hand, Joshua is fighting below (17:13). Whatever Moses was doing, it did not eliminate the need to battle with the antagonist. The walls of Jericho will collapse, but not until the Israelites march around them. Jesus can turn the water into wine, but not before the servants fill the jugs with water.

The Amalekite attack is not the last of Israel's problems. On the contrary, all four crises described here have parallels in Israel's history after the people leave Sinai. The first and third crises, both having to do with water, have their parallel in the incident recorded in Num. 20:2–13, another Meribah. The second crisis, the need for food, is close to that recorded in Num. 11:4–35. The fourth crisis is paralleled by a subsequent invasion by the Amalekites (Num. 14:39–45).

There is, however, one major difference between the narratives in Exodus and those recorded in Numbers. In the former, the complainers suffer no personal consequences in spite of their attitude. In the latter, with the covenant now behind them, Moses is excluded from entry into Canaan (Num. 20:12); a number of Israelites die because of a God-sent plague (Num. 11:33); the Amalekites, unlike the first time, are victors over the Israelites (Num. 14:45). The difference between the two seems to suggest that there is a greater fallout from post-covenantal sins (e.g., death for adultery) than for pre-covenantal sins (e.g., financial compensation to the father for sexually seducing his virgin daughter).

The fifth crisis in this unit, if it can be called such, is precipitated by a visit of Moses' father-in-law, Jethro, to the Israelite camp (Exod. 18:5). The incentive for his visit is rumors that the Lord had brought Israel out of Egypt. Like the Queen of Sheba, who came to visit Solomon, Jethro must come to confirm the veracity of those rumors.

Moses is more than eager to testify (18:8). His testimony elicits praise from Jethro as well as either a new commitment or a deeper commitment by Jethro to following Yahweh (depending on how one interprets the phrase "now I know" of v. 11).

All of this sets the context for the overburdened Moses. Jethro's suggestion is that Moses delegate authority, not try to do everything himself. This is not an easy proposal for administrators to accept, especially if they have a messianic complex and feel the urge to monopolize. Realizing that they were unable to be involved in every issue, the apostles chose to concentrate on preaching and prayer, while the ministry to widows was delegated to seven deacons who met the spiritual qualifications (Acts 6:1–6).

What about Moses? Is he too condescending to take advice? Proverbs 12:15b says that "the wise listen to advice" (NRSV), and 13:10b that "wisdom is with those who take advice" (NRSV). This attitude is to be contrasted with that of the "old and foolish king who will no longer take advice" (Eccles. 4:13). Strange, too, it is that the suggestion comes from Jethro, a priest in Midian; it is not whispered into Moses' ear by the angel of the Lord. Are the children of this world sometimes wiser than the children of light (Luke 16:8)? If God speaks directly to Moses on most occasions, here is one time when he speaks to Moses through another person, and perhaps an unexpected person at that.

Happily, Moses approvingly accepts Jethro's idea. He will adjudicate the difficult cases, while the ordinary cases can be handled by his appointees. The narrative ends by reporting that Jethro said farewell to his son-in-law and returned to Midian. He had come as an enquirer. Now he departs contentedly, his curiosity satisfied, his questions answered. He now believes, not because of hearsay evidence, but because he has indeed heard for himself, and knows.

Testing in the Wilderness (Exodus 15:22–18:27)

Brueggemann, W. 1977. *The Land.* Philadelphia: Fortress. Pp. 28–44.

Carpenter, E. 1997. "Exodus 18: Its Structure, Style, Motifs and Function in the Book of Exodus." In *A Biblical Itinerary: In Search of Method, Form and Content; Essays in Honor of George W. Coats.* Ed. E. Carpenter. JSOTSup 240. Sheffield: Sheffield Academic Press. Pp. 91–108.

Childs, B. S. 1974. *The Book of Exodus: A Critical, Theological Commentary.* OTL. Philadelphia: Westminster.

Coats, G. W. 1968. *Rebellion in the Wilderness: The Murmuring Motif in the Wilderness Traditions of the Old Testament.* Nashville: Abingdon.

———. 1972. "The Wilderness Itinerary." *CBQ* 34:135–52.

———. 1975. "Moses versus Amalek: Aetiology and Legend in Exodus xvii 8–16." In *Congress Volume, Edinburgh 1974.* Ed. G. W. Anderson. VTSup 28. Leiden: Brill. Pp. 29–41.

Davies, G. I. 1974. "The Wilderness Itineraries: A Comparative Study." *TynB* 25:46–81.

Feliks, J. 1971a. "Mana." *EncJud* 11:883.

———. 1971b. "Quail." *EncJud* 13:1420.

Ferris, P. W. 1975. "Manna Narrative of Exodus 16:1–10." *JETS* 18:191–99.

Ginsburg, C. D. 1966 [1897]. *Introduction to the Massoretico-Critical Edition of the Hebrew Bible.* New York: Ktav.

Moberly, R. W. L. 2000. *The Bible, Theology, and Faith: A Study of Abraham and Jesus.* Cambridge: Cambridge University Press.

Smith, M. S. 1997. *The Pilgrimage Pattern in Exodus.* JSOTSup 239. Sheffield: Sheffield Academic Press.

Talmon, S. 1966. "The 'Desert Motif' in the Bible and in Qumran Literature." In *Biblical Motifs: Origins and Transformations.* Ed. A. Altmann. Cambridge, Mass.: Harvard University Press. Pp. 31–63.

Tigay, J. H. 1975. "Empirical Basis for the Documentary Hypothesis." *JBL* 94:329–42.

9

Law and Covenant

EXODUS 19–24

After three months of traveling, the Hebrews reached Mount Sinai, usually associated with Jebel Musa (Arabic, "the mountain of Moses"), which is about 7,500 feet in height. Moses constantly goes up and down the mountain: "and Moses went up to God" (19:3); "so Moses came [down]" (19:7); "Moses went up" (19:9 [implied]); "so Moses went down" (19:14); "Moses went up" (19:20); "Moses went down" (19:25) (see Arichea 1989).

If the Israelites arrive at Sinai in Exod. 19:1, they will not depart from there until Num. 10:11–12. They reached Sinai "in the third month" (Exod. 19:1) after they left Egypt. Numbers 10:11 reports that the Israelites moved on from Sinai on "the twentieth day of the second month of the second year." That is, the encampment at Sinai lasted about eleven months. Surely it is a monumental and defining moment in the lives of the people of God. According to Blenkinsopp (1992: 48), the events narrated over the Pentateuch cover 2,706 years. Only eleven months of these almost three millennia are spent at Sinai. And yet this unit (Exod. 19:1–Num. 10:10) takes up about one-third of the Pentateuch.

Schramm (2000: 328) provides these figures: Gen. 1:1–Exod. 18:27 = 2,028 verses; Exod. 19:1–Num. 10:10 = 1,972 verses; Num. 10:11–Deut. 34:12 = 1,849 verses.

The Covenant at Sinai (19)

The first time that Moses ascends Sinai, God speaks and Moses listens (vv. 3–6). It is, first of all, a reminder to Israel of God's faithfulness and concern. Israel has not come this far either by coincidence or aggressiveness (v. 4). But from the "what I did . . . I bore . . . and brought you" of v. 4 we pass to the "now . . . if you will obey" of v. 5 (RSV). We pass from cause to effects, from divine love to human responsibility, and then from effects to results: "you shall be" (v. 5).

1. Cause: "what I did to the Egyptians, . . . I bore you on eagle's wings and brought you to myself"
2. Effect: "if you will obey my voice and keep my covenant"
3. Results: "you shall be my treasured possession"; "you shall be to me a kingdom of priests"; "you shall be . . . a holy nation." Thus God's people are unique, separated from the world, but only that they may serve as ministers of reconciliation in that world.

The first of these three expressions we may call a word about privilege; the second, a word about responsibility (which is also a privilege); the third, a word about character. The phrase "treasured possession" (NRSV) reflects the Hebrew word *sĕgullâ* (used again to define the privileged status of Israel in Deut. 7:6; 14:2; 26:18; Ps. 135:4; Mal. 3:17). In 1 Chron. 29:3 and Eccles. 2:8 the word refers to royal wealth, and it marks the special treasure acquired by kings. The Vulgate correctly renders this word as *peculium*—that which is set apart, being of special value (and the origin of the KJV's famous rendering "my peculiar people," with "peculiar" in its meaning of "distinctive, special").

The second expression reminds God's people that they are called to be a servant people, a towel-and-basin community. The third phrase, "a holy nation," uses the word "holy" for the first time in the Bible in conjunction with people. Previously it has been used only to refer to certain times (Gen. 2:3) or certain places (Exod. 3:5). The expression appears regularly in Deuteronomy, except with "people" instead of "nation" (7:5; 14:2, 21; 26:19; 28:9). One difference between the two is that Exodus (19:6; 22:31) holds out holiness as a goal and an ideal ("you *shall be* a holy nation"), while Deuteronomy views holiness as an accomplished fact (e.g., 7:6: "you *are* a people holy to the LORD").

Perhaps all too quickly the people respond positively and enthusiastically (v. 8), without taking the time to think about the implications of their response.

The second time (vv. 10–13) there is again only monologue. To give verbal assent to obedience is one thing; to consecrate and purify oneself is another. Israel's response to God's first word at Sinai was words. Israel's response to God's second word is action: putting on clean clothes and avoiding physical contact with the mountain upon pain of death. To touch it is as fatal as touching a high-voltage wire today. Third, the people temporarily abstain from normal sexual activities (v. 5; cf. a similar injunction from Paul in 1 Cor. 7:5; and what Eve said to the snake, "Neither shall you touch it, lest you die" [Gen. 3:3]).

The people spend the better part of three days (v. 16) preparing to meet God. Nothing is casual or cavalier. There is no place for nonchalance. One does not rush precipitously into the presence of God; rather, it is something for which one prepares diligently and thoroughly. And most importantly, the worshipers must be sanctified or purified (v. 14). Known sins cannot deliberately be transported into the presence of God. Anything that is obnoxious to God must be purged.

The third time is prefaced by the descent of Yahweh to the peak of Mount Sinai (v. 18). Far from being his domicile, the mountain functions only as Yahweh's temporary abode. His revelation to his people is accompanied by thunder, lightning, a thick cloud, dense smoke, fire, a shaking of the mountain, and trumpet blasts. All of this is hardly intended to encourage the Israelites to press for too much familiarity. It is their *Lord* whom they are about to encounter. And for all the electrifying atmosphere present throughout this chapter—thunder, cloud, lightning, threat of death, and so on—the Israelites are not tempted to run and get as far away as possible, to put as much distance between themselves and Sinai as they can. The luminous and numinous presence of God attracts; it does not repel. Thus the people are told not to go too near to Sinai (19:12–13). As Gowan (1994: 27) notes, "It is important that they *can* take precautions, for this is not a danger to be escaped from, but to be approached as nearly as possible."

Walther Eichrodt (1961–1967: 1:16) points out how such theophanies are different from pagan counterparts. "In marked contrast to the Canaanite and Babylonian conceptions it is not those natural phenomena which are directly familiar to Man and welcomed by him as beneficent, such as sun and moon, springs and rivers, trees and woods, . . . but the natural forces which break out with startling suddenness to terrify men and to threaten them with destruction."

For a third time Moses ascends to the top of the mountain (v. 20). On this occasion the Lord adds a further restriction. Not even the priests are to approach God (v. 24). Only Aaron may accompany Moses. In anticipation of the tabernacle, the tip of Sinai has become a Holy of Holies—God's holy presence is there. It is forbidden to everyone except Moses and Aaron, who will eventually be the high priest.

Hebrews 12:18–29 is an interesting commentary on Exodus 19. It begins (vv. 18–24) by contrasting approaching God under the old covenant at Mount Sinai with approaching God under the new covenant at Mount Zion. Pyrotechnics give way to Jesus as an indication of God's presence. And yet such a change means not less accountability but greater accountability (vv. 25–29), for God not only *was* (at Sinai) but still *is* "a consuming fire." So while the medium of God's self-revelation has changed, God himself has not changed. He has not transformed himself from a holy God into a "consumer-friendly" God.

The Decalogue (20:1–21)

In all of the dealings between the Israelites and the Egyptians, while the former were in servitude to the latter, Moses' role was primarily that of mediator. God did not speak to Pharaoh, but he did send Moses to speak to Pharaoh. That role continued for Moses into the Passover ("Tell all the congregation of Israel" [12:3 rsv]) and into the exodus ("Tell the people of Israel" [14:2 rsv]). At Sinai his function still was to transmit God's word to the people ("These are the words which you shall speak to the children of Israel" [19:6 rsv]).

In the laws that follow the giving of the Ten Commandments (20:21–23:33), the mediatorial ministry of Moses is again underscored: "Thus you shall say to the people of Israel" (20:22 rsv). Similarly, God's word about the tabernacle reaches the people through Moses (25:1; 35:1).

By contrast, in the revelation of the Decalogue this theme is omitted. Moses joins his peers as listener. God now speaks directly to his people: "And God spoke all these words, saying" (20:1 rsv). Is this the Bible's way of informing us that when we read the Decalogue, we are face to face with the apogee or the summum bonum of God's will for his followers in terms of lifestyle and moral commitment? Note the sequel to the commandments: "I have talked with you from heaven" (20:22), not from Sinai.

When God speaks to the Israelites, he addresses them as individuals, not as a group. All the occurrences of "you" in the commandments are masculine singular, not plural. The Hebrew clearly distinguishes between the two. For example, the "You shall not make" of v. 4, *lōʾ taʿăśeh*, if plural, would be *lō taʿăśû*.

It is interesting to note that although God alone transmits the Decalogue, he speaks of himself in vv. 2–6 in the first person ("I am the LORD . . . before me . . . I the LORD your God . . . who hate me . . . who love me and keep my commandments" RSV). But in vv. 7–17 God speaks of himself in the third person (e.g., in v. 7, "The LORD will not hold anyone guiltless who takes his name in vain," where we might expect, "I the LORD will not hold anyone guiltless who takes my name in vain").

Characteristics of the Decalogue

Eight of the Ten Commandments are negative prohibitions. Only two are positive: "Remember the sabbath day. . . . Honor your father and your mother" (NRSV). This is not surprising in light of the fact that law is essentially restrictive. It functions as a deterrent. It is more proscriptive than it is prescriptive. Behavior in the community is regularized by the outlawing of certain types of activities.

Eight-tenths of the Decalogue are negative apodictic (i.e., categorical) prohibitions, put in the second-person singular. The Hebrew language has two ways of expressing a prohibition: (1) the negative particle ʾal with the jussive form of the verb (reproduced in the Septuagint usually by mē with the imperative or aorist subjunctive); (2) the negative particle lōʾ with the imperfect form of the verb (reproduced in the Septuagint usually by ou with the future indicative).

John Bright (1973) has analyzed the distribution of these two formulations of prohibitions in the Old Testament. As to the difference in nuance between the two, he concludes that ʾal with the jussive is the weaker of the two, and it is concerned with a specific command for a specific occasion, with no implication for the future. By contrast, lōʾ with the imperfect expresses a categorical prohibition of binding validity for the present and the future.

The first formulation predominates in Wisdom literature, where a prohibition is often justified by a motive clause: "Do not walk in the way with them . . . for their feet run to evil" (Prov. 1:15–16 RSV). The second is clearly the choice in the Pentateuch, especially in sections dealing with legal and cultic matters. Thus, in the four chapters of Exodus occupied with the laws of the covenant (21–23, 34), the first occurs but twice, while the second is used fifty-five times.

It is not incidental that the laws of prohibition in the Decalogue have been consistently couched in the strongest form of negation that the Hebrew language had available. The commandments are not open to review and/or revision by any advisory panel that may freely abandon them if convenience warrants. They have, linguistically, a built-in permanence. Obsolete they are not. Absolute they are.

Purpose of the Decalogue

George Mendenhall (1973: 200) lists six differences between covenant and law. We are interested here in how he states the difference between the two at the point of purpose. The purpose of covenant is to create a new relationship. The purpose of law is to regulate or perpetuate an existing relationship by orderly means. Similarly, Brevard Childs (1974: 383) comments, "The law defines the holiness demanded of the covenant people. . . . The measurement of holiness in terms of God's own nature prevents the covenant claim from being given a moralistic interpretation."

Chapter 19 of Exodus is concerned with the institution of the covenant. Then in ch. 20 and following are the laws. The purpose of the Decalogue is explicitly spelled out in 20:20: "Do not fear; for God has come to prove [test] you, and that the fear of him may be before your eyes, that you may not sin" (RSV). The verse appears almost to contain a contradiction: "do not fear . . . that the fear of him may be before your eyes." Hans W. Wolff (1974) has collected and analyzed all the "fear of God" passages in Genesis and Exodus. He translates Exod. 20:20 as "Do not fear: for God has come to prove you, and that the fear of him may do its work on you, that you may not sin."

One type of fear is condemned; another type of fear is indispensable. Which goes and which remains? That for which there is no permanent place is fear in the sense of terror and trembling. No relationship will be healthy if it is based only on fright. The glory of the Lord that appeared to the shepherds at the birth of Jesus produced dread in them—"they were filled with fear" (RSV)—and to calm them the angel had to say, "Be not afraid" (Luke 2:9–10). The angel's "Be not afraid" is the same as Moses' "Do not fear."

What, then, is the fear that is encouraged? It is fear in the sense of obedience to God's revealed law. God's purpose for his people in the giving of the Decalogue is "that you may not sin." The language brings to mind 1 John 2:1: "I am writing this to you so that you may not sin" (RSV). That is the divine standard. But John's fresh word is about divine sympathy: "But if any one does sin, we have an advocate with the Father, Jesus Christ the righteous" (NRSV). The connections of Exod. 20:20 with Abraham in Genesis 22 are especially important. These are the only two passages in the Old Testament in which we read of a divine testing (using the Hebrew verb nāsâ) whose purpose is to produce "fear of God" in the one being tested. Abraham was tested, and in obeying he demonstrated that he feared God. Israel is now to be tested via the Decalogue, and obedience to those commandments will evidence fear of God. Abraham thus becomes a model or example for Israel to emulate.

These, then, are God's ten commands. They are law. But is there promise here too? Are the commandments more than a code imposed from above? Does God provide not only the law but also the enablement to keep that law? No one is able to live up to this standard in his or her own power. Augustine's prayer is to the point here: "Command what thou wilt, and perform what thou commandest."

Structure of the Decalogue

The commandments are referred to (in Hebrew) as "ten words" in Deut. 4:13; 10:4; Exod. 34:28. Exactly where and how these ten words should be divided and distinguished is still open to question, as is evidenced by the different enumerations in different religious traditions. In Judaism alone the first commandment is Exod. 20:2: "I am the LORD your God, who brought you out of the land of Egypt" (NRSV). In Catholic and Protestant traditions this is considered a prologue to the Decalogue. To continue with Judaism, the instructions about "no other gods" (v. 3) and no "graven image" (vv. 4–6) are taken as one commandment, and together they constitute the second commandment. Commandments three through ten are the same as in most Protestant traditions.

In Roman Catholic and Lutheran traditions vv. 3–6 are considered the first commandment. The second commandment (v. 7, respecting the Lord's name) is in Protestant and Jewish tradition the third commandment. The difference of one continues through the ninth (or eighth) commandment (no false witness). What in Protestant and Jewish tradition is the final commandment (v. 17, no covetousness) is divided into two distinct commandments (17a, 17b) to form the ninth and tenth commandments in Catholic and Lutheran traditions (nine, "you shall not covet your neighbor's house"; ten, "you shall not covet your neighbor's wife . . ." NIV). In any subsequent reference to a particular commandment I will follow the numbering system generally used in Protestant traditions.

There is a deuterograph of the Exodus Decalogue in Deut. 5:6–21. Essentially the list is a duplicate, but there are three interesting variations in the wording of commandments four, five, and ten. For the fourth commandment, in Exodus to "remember" the Sabbath, Deut. 5:12 instead reads "observe," and it adds the motive clause "as the LORD your God commanded you." In addition, whereas Exod. 20:11 grounds the Sabbath in God's day of rest after the six days of creation, Deut. 5:15 roots the Sabbath in Israel's exodus from Egypt.

The second divergence is in the fifth commandment, about parents. Again Deut. 5:16 adds the phrase "as the LORD your God commanded you," and it inserts another phrase not found in Exodus, "that it may go well with you" (NRSV). Third, in the tenth commandment Exod. 20:17 prohibits first the coveting of the neighbor's house, and second the neighbor's wife, while Deut. 5:21 reverses the order of those two and also adds "field" to the list of untouchables. And while Exod. 20:17 uses "covet" (*ḥāmad*) for both clauses ("you shall not covet your neighbor's house/wife"), Deut. 5:21 uses two different verbs: "you shall not covet [*ḥāmad*] your neighbor's wife; you shall not crave [*ʾāwâ*] your neighbor's house."

It is quite obvious that the intent of the first four commandments is different from that of the last six. The first four are vertical in their orientation and have to do with one's relationship to God. The last six are horizontal and deal with one's relationships with fellow human beings. Perhaps it is significant that the commandment about parents is the first in those of horizontal dimension (see Cassuto 1967: 246). There is a shift from creator to procreator; one's life is owed to both.

When asked about the greatest commandment (as if they could be arranged in a hierarchy), Jesus quoted Deut. 6:5: "You shall love the Lord your God with all your heart, and with all your soul, and with all your mind" (Matt. 22:37 NRSV). That reduces into one sentence the first four commandments. And although not solicited for further information, Jesus goes on to say, "And a second is like it, You shall love your neighbour as yourself" (Matt. 22:39 RSV). That reduces into one sentence the last six commandments. Note that Jesus reinforces that love can be commanded. Is that not a violation of love? Is not love something voluntarily chosen? By putting love within the context of a demand, or even an ultimatum, Jesus is suggesting that love for God and for others is centered in the will, not in the emotions.

Following Jesus' word about keeping the commandments in order to enter life, the rich young ruler asked, "Which one[s]?" Jesus said nothing about the first four commandments, but drew only from the second category, and even his order of recital was interesting: six, seven, eight, nine, and five! Lack of love for one's brothers and sisters cancels out the possibility of love for God, and it turns expressions of love for God into a charade (one of the messages of 1 John).

Exposition of the Decalogue

The first commandment is "You shall have no other gods before me." The force of the expression "before me" most likely means "in addition to me." The temptation of Israel (and with us?) is not so much to abandon serving God in order to serve other gods, but to worship other gods in addition to the Lord. Unlike the second commandment, which addresses itself to the "how" of worship, this one speaks to the "who" to worship. God's people must allow nobody else and nothing else to exercise an ultimate claim over or demand an ultimate loyalty from them. The very fact that this prohibition exists, and even heads the list, assumes that members of the believing community are indeed prone to pay homage to surrogates for God. (This is not a word directed to the Moabites or to the Philistines, but to those who have embraced a covenantal relationship with God.) Similarly, in today's world the establishment of speed limits on highways is necessitated by (apart from energy conservation) the fact that without any restrictions many drivers would treat public roads like private racetracks.

The commandment to worship no other gods is senseless unless the alternative does indeed exist and is at times attractive, and unless human beings have a proclivity compelling them in that direction. It is a logical fact that one does not have to prohibit or discourage activities that most people are disinclined to do anyway. Thus, for example, there is no commandment saying, "Thou shalt not leap off high cliffs." Conversely, the opposite of prohibitive commandments—performative commandments—urge behavior that may not be predictable or chosen. Thus, Jesus "commands" his followers to "love another." Left to our own devices, we may choose simply to ignore, manipulate, or abuse one another.

The second commandment is "You shall not make for yourself a graven image." Old Testament religion is aniconic. To be sure, religious art with powerful symbolic significance is permitted—witness the adornments in the tabernacle and temple—but images of God, or any deity, are outlawed. For all the times that the patriarchs and Moses spoke "face to face" with God, not once did any of them give us any inkling of what they saw or what God looked like.

Abraham Heschel (1954: 118) draws a distinction between "real" symbols and "conventional" symbols. Using a national flag as an illustration of a conventional symbol, he suggests that this type of symbol represents a reality not because it possesses the inherent qualities of that reality, but because of the association, relationship, or convention suggested by it. A real symbol, on the other hand, is a "visible object that represents something invisible, something present representing something absent . . . he who has the image has the god."

The Bible is not lacking in parodies of idolatry. The latter chapters of Isaiah abound in them. For example, in Isa. 46:1–2 we read of the Babylonians fleeing Babylon at the invasion of Cyrus. They have placed their gods on the backs of their animals. Why? Are the gods in danger? Are the people responsible for their gods' safety? If the people do not look after their gods in this time of crisis, who will? And the gods are valuable, made as they were by people. Through this God says to his people, "You do not carry me on your back. I carry you on my back."

To have access to an image of God suggests almost that such a god can be controlled and manipulated. Perhaps we cannot improve on Augustine's definition of idolatry: "Idolatry is worshiping anything that ought to be used, or using anything that is meant to be worshiped."

The third commandment is "You shall not take the name of the LORD your God in vain." Presumably, what is proscribed here is more than just profanity or vulgarity in the modern sense. Also, the common statement that the command forbids false swearing or oath-taking in court is true, but it is not exhaustive of the meaning.

The Hebrew word for "vain" used here comes from a root meaning "to be empty" in the sense of "to be without substance, to be worthless." Any invocation of God's presence, any calling on his name that is simply perfunctory, is taking God's name in vain—that is, using the divine name for or in something that lacks vitality, reality, and substance. So Elton Trueblood (1972: 31) can say, "The worst blasphemy is not profanity, but lip service."

The fourth commandment is "Remember the sabbath day, to keep it holy." Childs (1974: 415) renders "to keep it holy" as a factitive Piel in Hebrew and translates it as "to make holy." Those legitimate concerns of the previous six days are to be laid aside momentarily for what Herman Wouk (1959: 60) colorfully calls "a retreat into restorative magic." Umberto Cassuto (1967: 415) points out the connection between the Sabbath, which is the seventh day, and the seven living beings called to observe it: you, your son, your daughter, your manservant, your maidservant, your cattle (even the animals observe the Sabbath!), the sojourner.

Too much should not be made of the different motive clauses in Exodus and Deuteronomy. We have already observed that Exodus links the Sabbath with the seventh day of rest after creation, while Deuteronomy connects it with the exodus from Egypt. As B. D. Napier (1963: 82) observes, "The fundamental sanction of the Sabbath in both statements of commandment is *creation*—in Deuteronomy the creation of a people, in Exodus the creation of the world."

Israel was not alone in the observance of special and sacred days. Not a little has been written about a possible connection between the biblical Sabbath and the Babylonian *shapattu*. Eichrodt (1961–1967: 1:132) writes:

In Babylonia the "seventh" days (i.e., the seventh, fourteenth, nineteenth, twenty-first and twenty-eighth of the month) had the character of a *dies nefastus* (Bab. *ûmu limnu*) on which special care had to be taken, the king in particular having to submit to all kinds of precautionary measures (e.g., not to mount his chariot, not to offer sacrifice, etc.). Of a general intermission of work there is no mention whatsoever. Only on the fifteenth day was work suspended in Babylonia; and far from this being due to the joyful, festal character of the day, it was obviously actuated by quite different motives, namely that on this particular day there was no luck to be had, and it was necessary to pacify the gods (whence the name *ûm nuḫ libbi:* "day of pacification of the heart") and to appease their anger by a kind of day of penitence and prayer.

In some ways this fourth commandment feeds off and naturally follows (and partially protects) the first two commandments. The proper observance of the Sabbath guards against people idolizing their own work and agendas. On this one day no work is to be done. In contrast to the days of public sacrifices when laborious or heavy work (*mĕleʾket ʿăbōdâ*) is forbidden (Num. 28:18, 25, 26; 29:1), only on the Sabbath and Yom Kippur/Day of Atonement is no work at all to be done (*kol-mĕlāʾkâ*). See Num. 29:7 and Lev. 23:3, 28.

Not only does the fourth commandment relate to the first two, but also it is a bridge into the last six, those dealing with one's relationship with other members of the community, for the Sabbath is a gift of God for everyone—children, slaves, the stranger, all those who otherwise might not be able to find rest.

The fifth commandment is "Honor your father and your mother." What the reader of the Bible might have expected is "Obey your father and mother." It is, however, easier to obey than to honor. One can hate but obey. One cannot both hate and honor.

The seriousness of the injunction is reinforced by the choice of the verb "honor." Several times it is used with God as the object (1 Sam. 2:30; Ps. 50:23; Prov. 3:9; Isa. 29:13; 43:20, 23). Both God and parents are worthy of honor. The underlying Hebrew word sometimes is translated as "glorify," and it describes how God is to be worshiped (Ps. 22:23; 50:15; 86:9, 12; Isa. 24:15).

This is not to say that parents are worthy of worship. Jesus quoted and endorsed the fifth commandment (Matt. 15:4; Mark 7:10; Paul also in Eph. 6:2), but he also said, "He who loves father or mother more than me is not worthy of me" (Matt. 10:37 RSV). Parents, as part of the "other gods" proscribed in the first commandment, make feeble gods indeed.

As in Lev. 19:3, but in opposite order, the commandments about keeping the Sabbath and honoring one's parents are in sequence. Possibly the connection between the two lies in the idea that observing the Sabbath is a way of honoring God, and thus is a counterpart to honoring one's parents.

The sixth commandment is "You shall not kill." Some scholars have translated the verb as "murder." That is, what is banned is not all forms of killing (such as the death penalty for certain crimes, or involvement in war), but the unnecessary taking of life out of anger or greed. Occasionally the verb describes nonculpable homicide (Num. 35:11; Deut. 4:42; Josh. 20:3, 5), indicated by the addition of some qualifier such as "unintentionally" or "in ignorance or unwittingly." Another illustration of this is Num. 35:27: an avenger of the blood who kills a manslayer who has wandered outside the limits of the city of refuge is not guilty.

But these are exceptions. The normal meaning is culpable homicide, and the commandment is thus best translated, "You shall not murder," especially in light of the negative particle *lō'*. Cain did this directly; David did it indirectly. God forbids one person from killing another, and also from taking his or her own life. Interestingly, there is only one clear-cut instance of suicide in the Old Testament, that of Ahithophel (2 Sam. 17:23).

Jesus extended the sixth commandment to include feelings of anger, verbal abuse of another person, or derogatory name-calling (Matt. 5:21–26). His admonition is "make friends quickly with your accuser" (RSV).

The seventh commandment is "You shall not commit adultery." If the previous commandment upheld the sanctity of life, and the one before that the sanctity of the home, this commandment upholds the sanctity of marriage. Marriage is not simply a relationship of convenience, nor is it to be tampered with. Infidelity carries with it the most serious of consequences.

Jesus expanded this prohibition to include the ocular as well as the physical (Matt. 5:27–30). Lust is possessive and self-gratifying. Witness David's behavior with Bathsheba. It reduces the other person to an object. Mutual obligation and commitment are nonexistent.

One suspects that a passage of Scripture such as Lev. 20:10–21, which deals with other forbidden sexual behaviors, is simply an extension of the law about adultery. There are ten commandments, not one thousand or ten thousand. The infractions cited in the Decalogue are representative, not exhaustive, what von Rad (1962: 1:194) has called "signposts on the margin of a wide sphere of life." The restriction of the Decalogue to ten statements plus a basic absence of sanctions eliminates it from being seen as the equivalent of a manual or textbook. Hence, its ongoing value is to be discovered in the basic principles and boundaries that it fosters.

The eighth commandment is "You shall not steal." The reference is to theft of property and possibly also kidnapping. The right of possession is affirmed. The attempt to get something for nothing is condemned. The commandment militates against the philosophy of "What is yours is mine, and I'm going to take it away from you."

The antidote for stealing is reflected in Paul's word to the church at Philippi: "And my God will supply every need of yours" (Phil. 4:19 RSV), but such a promise covers only needs, not greeds.

The ninth commandment is "You shall not bear false witness." Probably the original application of this commandment was to the offering of false, misleading testimony in court or at official transactions and exchanges in the marketplace. If the story of Ahab and Jezebel and Naboth's vineyard in 1 Kings 21 follows legal teaching (false accusation and testimony can be a means of depriving one's neighbor of what rightfully belongs to him or her), then perhaps it sheds light on why this commandment comes between the eighth and tenth commandments. Number eight refers to taking another's property by force or stealth. Number nine refers to taking another's property by false testimony. Number ten refers to coveting another's property.

But a broader and more general interpretation surely is permissible. The commandment extends to any malicious conversation, intentional or unintentional, that raises a question about the integrity of someone else's character. And character defamation is as ancient as Genesis 3.

Not without reason does James refer to the tongue as an arsonist. Uncontrolled, it becomes incendiary. Unchecked, it becomes the most lethal weapon in destroying the unity in a believing community.

Again we turn to Paul for the opposite of what this commandment forbids: "Count others better than yourselves" (Phil. 2:3). Such an attitude will restrain the temptation to be a false witness.

The tenth commandment is "You shall not covet." Quite obviously this commandment is different from the preceding nine, or at least the preceding five, in at least two ways. One is the way that it appears to prohibit even an inner, subjective attitude, while the others address specific, visible acts. What one thinks and feels, and not simply what one does, has moral consequences. The second involves the means by which one could establish guilt and then prosecute for coveting.

The first nine commandments present no problem in this regard.

One, "You shall have no other gods." Compare Exod. 22:20: "Whoever sacrifices to any god, save to the LORD only, shall be utterly destroyed" (RSV).

Two, "You shall not make for yourself a graven image." Compare the nearly catastrophic result after the incident of the golden calf (Exodus 32).

Three, "You shall not take the name of the LORD your God in vain." Note the remainder of the verse: "for the LORD will not hold anyone guiltless who misuses his name" (NIV).

Four, "Remember the sabbath day, to keep it holy." Compare Exod. 31:15: "The seventh day is a sabbath of solemn rest, . . . whoever does any work on the sabbath day shall be put to death" (NRSV).

Five, "Honor your father and your mother." Compare Exod. 21:15, 17: "Whoever strikes/curses his father or his mother shall be put to death" (RSV).

Six, "You shall not kill." Compare Exod. 21:12: "Whoever strikes a person mortally shall be put to death" (NRSV).

Seven, "You shall not commit adultery." Compare Deut. 22:22: "If a man is found lying with the wife of another man, both of them shall die" (RSV).

Eight, "You shall not steal." Compare Exod. 22:1–3: "When someone steals an ox or a sheep . . . the thief shall pay five oxen for an ox, and four sheep for a sheep" (NRSV). See also Exod. 21:16: "Whoever kidnaps a person . . . shall be put to death" (NRSV).

Nine, "You shall not bear false witness." Compare Deut. 19:18–19: "If the witness is a false witness, having testified falsely against another, then you shall do to the false witness just as the false witness had meant to do to the other" (NRSV).

The pattern is this: in the Decalogue there is a straightforward prohibition or admonishment, without reference to any penalty for violation. Subsequent to the Decalogue we encounter the violation posed as a possibility, and the consequences of such a violation are spelled out.

Could the pattern be made to continue into the last commandment: "Thou shalt not covet. . . . Anyone who covets . . . shall die/be put to death"? Such a verse would be surprising, but narratives to support the idea are not lacking. This is the story of Eve, of Achan, of Ahab and Jezebel over Naboth's vineyard, of Judas Iscariot.

Some exegetes have suggested that the verb "covet" includes actions as well as emotions, on the basis of verses such as Deut. 7:25, "You shall not covet the silver or the gold . . . or take it for yourselves" (RSV), and Mic. 2:2, "They covet fields, and seize them" (NRSV).

One suspects, however, that this explanation is dictated less by exegesis than by the desire to understand the prohibition in terms amenable to law enforcement. In addition, the two verbs for "covet" in the Deuteronomy Decalogue (Deut. 5:21) are different. The first is the same as that used twice in Exod. 20:17, *ḥāmad*. But the second is *ʾāwâ*: "You shall not *desire/crave* your neighbor's house." And the connotation of this verb, a synonym of *ḥāmad* in Deut. 5:21, concerns emotions, quite apart from any outward act. As Childs (1974: 427) remarks, "The Deuteronomic recension simply made more explicit the subjective side of the prohibition which was already contained in the original command."

Perhaps this is the reason why this particular commandment is placed last. It is the most comprehensive of all the commandments, and it includes what is absent from the rest of the Decalogue. And who will not recognize that behind much killing, adultery, stealing, and lying is covetousness? This is the root of the problem.

We have looked to Paul for some positive reformulations of the prohibitive commandments. Again we may appeal to him, and again the verse is from his letter to the Philippians: "I have learned, in whatever state I am, to be content" (4:11 RSV). This is the difference between ruling over one's desires and being a slave to them.

The Book of the Covenant (20:21–23:33)

The title given to this section of Exodus is taken from Exod. 24:7: "Then he took the book of the covenant, and read it in the hearing of the people" (NRSV).

Unlike the Decalogue, which God transmits directly to his people, this section of Exodus finds Moses once again in the ministry of mediation: "Thus you shall say to the people of Israel" (20:22 RSV). He is neither author nor collator, just transmitter. Indeed, it would not be inappropriate to apply here Peter's dictum that "no prophecy ever came by human will, but people moved by the Holy Spirit spoke from God" (2 Pet. 1:21). The Bible, and this section of Exodus especially, goes to great lengths to reinforce the idea that Moses is but a conveyor of truth, not the originator of truth.

And yet many Christians approach chs. 21–23 of Exodus in the same way as they eat fish. The bones are to be thrown away, and only the meat digested. To press the analogy, the Ten Commandments of ch. 20 are the meat, the "eternal word of God"; the following three chapters are the bones—the unedifying, the unpalatable, the anachronistic, and hence the disposable. That no such hierarchy appears in the biblical text itself is beside the point. It is, for example, difficult to conceive of these three chapters as a gold mine for expository preaching.

Types of Laws in the Book of the Covenant

The laws in this unit are as follows:

1. proscriptions of idols and the law about the altar (20:22–26)
2. the law for male and female slaves (21:1–11)

3. prohibitions against murder, physical and verbal abuse of parents, and kidnapping, all of which elicit the death penalty (21:12–17)
4. laws penalizing those who injure and maim others: a neighbor, a slave, a pregnant woman (violations that do not incur the death penalty) (21:18–26)
5. the law about the goring ox that tramples to death a human being, with culpability also attached to a careless owner (21:28–32)
6. the law about the uncovered pit into which an unsuspecting animal tumbles (21:33–34)
7. the law about one animal that is fatally injured by another, with blame going to the owner of the killer animal if necessary precautions were shirked (21:35–36)
8. prohibitions against thievery, mandating restitution (22:1–4)
9. the law about destroying the crops of another through illegal grazing of one's own animals or through arson (22:5–6)
10. laws pertaining to borrowers and to those entrusted with the belongings of others (22:7–15)
11. the law about seduction of a virgin, leading to premarital intercourse (22:16–17)
12. a collection of miscellaneous laws on religious and social matters, such as magic, bestiality, idolatry, mistreatment of aliens, and usury (22:18–31)
13. justice in the courtroom, both in the witness stand and on the judge's bench (23:1–9)
14. Sabbath laws (23:10–13)
15. a summons to observe the thrice-held festivals on the calendar (23:14–19a)
16. a prohibition against cooking a young goat in its mother's milk (23:19b)
17. epilogue (23:20–33)

Though it is futile to look for some significance in the sequence of the laws, perhaps it is not trite to observe that the first law and the last are parallel in subject matter. The code begins and ends with a call to worship, that which brings the devotee directly into the presence of God: worship in the right way (the law about the altar) and at the right time (the three annual festivals).

Although there is no particular pattern in the sequence of the laws, there is a distinct pattern in the literary forms in which the laws are couched. Note that the first law (the altar law [20:22–26]) is phrased much like one of the Ten Commandments: "You shall not make gods of silver . . . you shall not go up by steps to my altar" (RSV). I have previously referred to this type of law as apodictic law.

But beginning with 21:1 and continuing through 22:17, the laws are framed in a conditional way (the exceptions are the statements in 21:12, 15, 16, 17). This type of law usually is referred to as casuistic law. That is, instead of making a generalization, a casuistic law addresses itself to a specific situation. Accordingly, most of these laws first have a protasis, a section that deals with the specific situation at question. Normally a violation is described and is introduced by "when" or "supposing that": "when people quarrel," "when someone strikes a slave." Occasionally a legitimate transaction may be involved: "when you buy a Hebrew slave."

The second part of the law is called the apodosis. Usually this part spells out the consequence of the violation: "When a slaveowner strikes a slave . . . and the slave dies [protasis], . . . the owner shall be punished [apodosis]." Further qualification or extenuating circumstances often are included. The apodosis, if it follows a legitimate transaction, addresses the privileges of any parties involved.

Beginning with 22:18 and continuing to 23:19, there is a return to apodictic law: "You shall not permit a female sorcerer to live" (NRSV). Thus, the code begins with apodictic law (20:22–26), shifts to casuistic law (21:1–22:17), then returns to apodictic law (22:18–23:19). Exodus 21:1 introduces what follows with "These are the laws [mišpāṭîm] you are to set before them" (NIV). Exodus 24:3 begins by saying, "Moses went and told the people all the LORD's words [děbārîm] and laws [mišpāṭîm]" (NIV). Many commentators suggest that the word "laws" (mišpāṭîm) refers to the casuistic regulations of 21:1–22:17, while "words" (děbārîm) refers to the apodictic regulations of 20:22–26; 22:18–23:19.

One possible conclusion to draw from this is that 21:1–22:17, the casuistic laws, once existed separately from the rest of the code and was inserted secondarily by a redactor into its present position. Indeed, this is the prevailing view of biblical scholarship.

But perhaps another solution is possible. Cyrus Gordon (1965: 83) has drawn attention to the literary form of ancient Near Eastern literature, including parts of the Bible, an observation that warns against the premature dissecting of the text. Thus, for example, the Book of Job begins and ends in prose, with poetry in between, and the Book of Daniel begins and ends in Hebrew, with the middle section in Aramaic. Might not the same literary structure be found in the Book of the Covenant? The beginning and the end are identical in form; the middle section is different from both its predecessor and successor. (The Decalogue begins with three negative commandments, continues with two positive ones, then concludes with five negative commandments.)

Comparison of Biblical and Nonbiblical Legal Codes

It is not without advantage to compare biblical law with other legal codes composed in those nations that surrounded Israel in the second and first millennia B.C. The most important, in order of antiquity, are:

1. Code of Ur-nammu, named after the first king of the third dynasty of Ur (ca. 2100–2000 B.C.). This is the first law code known in history (ca. 2050 B.C.). It is written in Sumerian, and only portions have survived. This includes a prologue and twenty-nine laws, all of which are casuistic in form.
2. Code of Eshnunna, not a personal name but a place name. It is located near modern Baghdad and flourished between the fall of Ur (2000 B.C.) and the age of Hammurabi (1800–1600 B.C.). The laws, sixty-one in total, are the oldest ones written in Babylonian, and date back to ca. 1980 B.C.
3. Code of Lipit-Ishtar, a ruler of the first dynasty of Isin (ca. 2000–1900 B.C.), one of the prominent city-states to emerge after the fall of Ur. The code consists of three main parts: a prologue, the laws, and an epilogue. It too is written in Sumerian. Thirty-eight laws, in part or in whole, have survived, and all of these are casuistic in form. They date to ca. 1930 B.C.
4. Code of Hammurabi, who was the sixth king of the first dynasty of Babylon, with the years of his reign being 1792–1750 B.C. It is written, as is the Code of Eshnunna, in Babylonian and is the most famous of the extrabiblical law codes. It is structured, as is Lipit-Ishtar, in tripartite fashion: prologue, laws, epilogue. There are 282 casuistic laws in this code.
5. The Hittite Law Code, which is not precisely datable, although Hittitologist Harry Hoffner (1975: 1:800) states that "it is possible that the first recension of the Hittite laws dates from the reign of Telipinu (1525–1500 BC)." The laws are found on two tablets, each having one hundred laws.
6. The Middle Assyrian Laws, preserved on clay tablets. The tablets date from the time of the Assyrian king Tiglath-pileser I (1115–1077 B.C.), but the laws may predate the tablets by as much as three centuries. Some 116 laws are preserved on eleven different tablets, again in casuistic form. To a degree unseen in the previous law codes, penalties for violations often include all forms of bodily mutilation—for example, cutting off the nose or removing a finger.

The existence of such law codes does not mean that they were appealed to by courts or judges in the administration of justice. Never did they assume a normative status. On the contrary, they were all but ignored. The point is well made by two Assyriologists. Says Leo Oppenheim (1977: 158), "This code [of Hammurabi] . . . does not show any direct relationship to the legal practices of the time. Its contents are rather to be considered in many essential respects a traditional literary expression of the king's social responsibilities and of his awareness between existing and desirable conditions." Or, to quote William Hallo (1971: 176), "They [these law codes] made no attempt to provide universal criteria of culpability, nor were they cited, or even necessarily followed, in the determination of lawsuits. But they were studied in the schools . . . and must have formed part of the education of scribes and judges." Thus, the guides for legal decision are not codes but tradition, public opinion, and even common sense.

An examination of these laws shows in some cases an almost word-for-word correspondence with one of the laws in the Covenant Code of Exodus or the laws of Deuteronomy. Other laws are remarkably similar to those of Exodus, with changes only in terminology. Childs (1974: 462–63) is able to provide a parallel (or parallels) in pagan law codes to every unit in the Covenant Code, and Westbrook (1994b: 21) notes, "More than half of the Covenant Code's provisions have some parallel in one or more of the cuneiform codes, whether in the form of the same problem addressed or distinction applied, a similar rule, or an identical rule." For at least two reasons, the fact that some biblical law shares the precepts of other ancient Near Eastern legal corpora should not be surprising or unexpected, nor should it raise suspicions. First, a number of behaviors that the Covenant Code forbids are ones that all ancient societies would forbid—for example, murder. Thus Exod. 21:12, "Anyone who strikes a man and kills him shall surely be put to death" (NIV), is not significantly different from the Sumerian Ur-nammu code, paragraph 1: "If a man kills, that man shall be put to death." Second, just a few chapters back in Exodus (ch. 18), counsel on how to administer justice in Israelite society comes from a non-Israelite source, Moses' Midianite father-in-law, Jethro (see Olson 1996: 262).

The Law about Female Slaves

As an illustration I will use the law in Exod. 21:7–11 about a daughter sold into slavery by her father. The constituent parts are that unlike the male slave, she may not go free after six years; if she is unpleasing to her prospective husband, she is to be returned to her family; if she becomes her employer's daughter-in-law, she is to be treated as a daughter; if she is married to her employer, a subsequent marriage by the husband to another woman does not diminish the slave's status in any way; violation of any of these last four contingencies by the employer or husband results in the woman's freedom.

Here are the parallels.

Code of Hammurabi, 170, 171: "When a man's first wife bore him children and his female slave also bore him children, if the father during his lifetime has ever said 'my children!' to the children whom the slave bore him . . . after the father dies, the children of the first wife and the children of the slave shall share equally in the goods of the paternal state." Law 171 deals with the opposite situation of the father vis-à-vis the children of his female slave—"If he never said [of them] 'my children!' "—then the slave's offspring are not entitled to part of the paternal estate, but both slave and offspring are manumitted.

Code of Hammurabi, 119: "If an obligation came due against a man and he has accordingly sold his female slave who bore him children, the owner of the female slave may repay the money which the merchant paid out and thus redeem his female slave."

Code of Hammurabi, 146, 147: "A barren wife who provides her husband with a female slave may not sell the slave if the latter mothers a child by the wife's husband before and when the wife does."

Code of Eshnunna, 31: "If a man deprives another man's slave-girl of her virginity, he shall pay one-third of a mina of silver; the slave-girl remains the property of her owner."

Code of Eshnunna, 34: "If a slave-girl of palaces gives her son or her daughter to a palace or temple official for bringing him or her up, the palace may take back the son or the daughter whom she gave."

Hittite Code, 31 (tablet 1): "If a free man and a slave-girl are lovers and they cohabit, he takes her for his wife, they found a family and have children, but subsequently . . . they break up the family, the man receives the children, but the woman receives one child." Laws 32 and 33 deal respectively with the marriage of a male slave to a free woman, and a male slave to a female slave. In both laws, if a marital separation ensues, the consequences are the same as those in law 31.

Code of Lipit-Ishtar, 25, 26: "If a man married a wife and she bore him children, and those children are living, and a slave also bore children for her master, but the father granted freedom to the slave and her children, the children of the slave shall not divide the estate with the children of their former master." Law 26 covers the marriage of a widower to a slave girl with children produced from both the first and second marriages. The children of the first marriage are not negated as heirs.

The Law about an Ox That Gores

One more example of commonality in biblical and nonbiblical law codes will suffice. It concerns the law about the goring ox in Exod. 21:28–36.

Actually, this involves three laws presented as one extended law: (1) the case where an ox gores a human (21:28–32); (2) an intervening law dealing with a careless person who digs a pit and does not cover it, thus allowing an animal to fall into it and injure itself (21:33–34); (3) the case where an ox gores another ox (21:35–36). The particulars are that if an ox kills a person, it is put to death by stoning, but its flesh may not be eaten. No liability is attached to the owner of the ox. If, however, the ox is known to be temperamental, and warnings to the owner have gone unheeded, and if the ox kills a human being, the owner too is executed. If someone's ox falls into an open pit dug by another person, the latter must pay restitution to the owner of the deceased animal. If someone's ox kills an ox belonging to another person, they share the loss. If the owner knew that the ox was prone to goring and yet took no precautions, the owner of the goring ox assumes all the damages.

The parallels are:

Code of Hammurabi, 250: "If an ox, when it was walking along the street, gored a man to death, that case is not subject to claim."

Code of Hammurabi, 251: "If a man's ox was a gorer, and his city council made it known to him that it was a gorer, but he did not pad its horns or tie up his ox, and that ox gored to death a member of the aristocracy, he shall give one-half mina of silver."

Code of Eshnunna, 53: "If an ox gores another ox and causes its death, both ox owners shall divide [between themselves] the price of the live ox and also the equivalent of the dead ox."

Code of Eshnunna, 54: "If an ox is known to gore habitually and the authorities have brought the fact to the knowledge of its owner, but he does not have his ox dehorned, and it gores a man and causes his death, then the owner of the ox shall pay two-thirds of a mina of silver."

Finkelstein (1981: 36–39) perceives a significant difference in Exodus between the case where the ox gored a human (21:28–32) and the case where the ox gored another ox (21:35–36). By contrast, the parallel cases in the Code of Eshnunna are presented without any interruption such as one finds in Exod. 21:33–34. Damage to persons outweighs damages to property. This explains why in the Codes of Hammurabi and Eshnunna the owner of a rogue ox that kills someone is merely fined, whereas in the Covenant Code he is sentenced to death (Exod. 21:29).

Differences between Biblical and Nonbiblical Legal Codes

The point is well taken, then, that many biblical laws have almost precise counterparts in pagan literature. The absence of such parallels, rather than their presence, would raise suspicions about the integrity of the biblical laws. It is fair to say that all societies and cultures outlaw certain practices (e.g., murder, hate, oppression) and encourage the implementation of others (e.g., justice, compassion for the poor). In these areas Israel had no monopoly and often had no word from God that went beyond the practices of its neighbors.

This is not, however, to equate all ancient Mediterranean law codes. Even in those areas where similarity may be the greatest, differences between biblical and nonbiblical law are apparent. Consider, for example, the discussion about the various laws about the goring ox. The significant difference is, as we saw, the much more severe punishment mandated by the passage in Exodus. In the Codes of Hammurabi and Eshnunna the only concern is the economic compensation of the victim's family: "he shall give one-half mina of silver" (Hammurabi, 251); "the owner of the ox shall pay two-thirds of a mina of silver" (Eshnunna, 54). By contrast, Exod. 21:28 calls for the death of the ox (cf. Gen. 9:5–6) and abstention from eating its meat. Furthermore, if the owner has callously sloughed off previous warnings about the dangerous animal, and the latter kills someone, the owner dies too (Exod. 21:29), unless the victim's family is willing to settle for the imposition of a steep fine (Exod. 21:30). Note here the high value placed on human life. In taking another's life, a fine is no substitute for proper justice.

One observes also a distinct emphasis in the laws dealing with slaves. The particular verses in Exodus are concerned almost exclusively with the slave's privileges or the reparations that fall upon the owner if the slave is in any way abused or mishandled (21:1–11, 20–21, 26–27, 32). Surely it is not insignificant that laws on slavery in the Covenant Code come toward the beginning of that code, while those on this subject in the Code of Hammurabi come at the end (278–82).

Nowhere in the Covenant Code do punishments take the form of physical mutilation, except in the "eye for an eye, tooth for a tooth" passage in Exod. 21:23–25. By contrast, in the first millennium B.C. Middle Assyrian Laws, such penalties reach epidemic proportions. But even the Code of Hammurabi legislates for certain offenses the cutting off of half of the hair (127); the removal of the tongue (192), the eye (193), the ear of a slave (205), or the hand (218, 226, 253). Prisoners of war might be treated similarly. Witness Samson at the mercy of the Philistines (Judg. 16:21); the residents of Jabesh-gilead intimidated by Nahash the Ammonite (1 Sam. 11:2); the slain Saul and the Philistines (1 Sam. 31:9–10); David's troops in Ammonite territory (2 Sam. 10:4).

It is true that Scripture does mandate "an eye for an eye, and a tooth for a tooth" (Exod. 21:24–25). This is the famous lex talionis, and the parallel in the Code of Hammurabi is 197, "a bone for a bone," and 200, "a tooth for a tooth." Both of these laws, however, cover only assaults by a member of the aristocracy against a peer.

Primarily because of Jesus' reference to this particular law in Matt.
5:38–48 and a misunderstanding of the intent of that reference, many
people have assumed that this is a classic distinction between the spirits
of the Old and the New Testaments: the first teaches retaliation, while
the second teaches forgiveness. Such a dichotomy could not be further
from the truth. The Book of the Covenant itself (see Exod. 23:4–5) urges
that people exert themselves to help their enemy. What the law in Exodus
does teach is the principle of equal justice for all. That is, the penalty
must match the crime (an eye for an eye, or a tooth for a tooth). The
penalty must not exceed what the crime merits (thus prohibiting the
victimizing of the poor and underprivileged through overpenalization),
nor must the penalty fall below what the crime merits (thus prohibiting
the rich from escaping the law's demands because of position, contacts,
and bargaining money). What Jesus does in the Sermon on the Mount
is elevate the response to evil beyond the concern for simple justice to
voluntary assistance for the oppressor.

We may conclude that the distinctions between biblical and nonbiblical law should not be unduly magnified (see Jackson 1973a) or mini-
mized. Apart from any specific law, perhaps the most significant thing
to be observed, in terms of comparative studies, is the crucial position
that God assumes in this section of Exodus. First, God is the author
of these laws: "And the LORD said to Moses, 'Thus shall you say to the
people of Israel'" (Exod. 20:22 RSV); "These are the ordinances which
you shall set before them" (Exod. 21:1 RSV). True, the stela on which
the Code of Hammurabi is written is topped by a bas-relief showing
Hammurabi receiving the commission to write the law code from the
sun god, Shamash, the god of justice. And in both the epilogue and
prologue appeal is made to the stimulation and authority of Shamash
and Marduk. However, nowhere in the 282 laws does a god ever speak.
The same is true of the other law codes.

By contrast, God not only commissions Moses to speak, but also he
speaks in the first person throughout the section, especially in 20:22–26
and 22:20–23:19: "I have talked with you" (20:22 RSV); "An altar of earth
you shall make for me" (20:24 RSV) (the words "me" or "I" appear seven
times in the brief section of 20:22–26). Also, "I will appoint for you a
place" (21:13 RSV); "I will surely hear their cry" (22:23 RSV); "I will kill"
(22:24); "I will hear" (22:27); "I will not acquit" (23:7); "I have said"
(23:13); "I commanded you" (23:15); "Behold, I send" (23:20). Even in
the articulation of the laws, Moses, the law mediator, takes a subordinate
position to God, the lawgiver. God does not speak, then disappear, then
briefly reappear before the end.

If we wish to underline that Israel, as reflected in these law codes,
reached a higher moral sensitivity than did its neighbors, we nevertheless

must note that even in the Book of the Covenant inequities remain. Despite the privileges granted to slaves, they are treated as less than free people. Murder is a capital offense (Exod. 21:12). If a slave is murdered by an owner, the owner is "to be punished" (Exod. 21:20). The formula "shall be put to death" is not used. The *lex talionis,* with its expression of equal justice for all, does not include the slave (Exod. 21:26–27). The male slave may go free after six years (Exod. 21:2). Apparently no such provision was extended to the female slave, except in cases where she was subjected to physical abuse (Exod. 21:27). Only males may make pilgrimages to the thrice-held religious festivals (Exod. 23:17); females are excluded. This latter point does not necessarily provide evidence, as some have claimed, of the Old Testament's patriarchal and misogynistic agenda. Given the degrading role of women in the public fertility cults of the ancient Near East, where they functioned as shrine prostitutes, the exclusion of women from these Israelite festivals does not represent demotion to second-class status; rather, it is a way of protecting and valuing their honor and dignity as human beings. Then again, all that a verse like 23:17 may be saying is that attendance at these festivals is mandatory for men, while it is optional for women. Were they, say, pregnant or nursing, women would be exempt from participation.

If the Book of the Covenant rises above the Code of Hammurabi, we must also conclude that this early "sermon on the mount" anticipates a fuller word from the later Sermon on the Mount.

The Ceremony of Covenant Ratification (24:1–18)

It is not enough just to hear the word of the Lord, to be simply "hearers" but not "doers." Nor is nodding, halfhearted, token obedience acceptable. Perhaps prematurely, the people had said, after first reaching Sinai, "All that the LORD has spoken we will do" (Exod. 19:8 RSV). They thought that they were prepared to match God's challenge to them, recorded in Exod. 19:5–6: "Now therefore, if you will obey my voice . . ." (RSV).

Then follows the divine recitation of the Decalogue and the mediation of the Covenant Code laws through Moses (Exodus 20–23; 24:3a, 7), plus their inscription (24:4). Unanimously the people affirm their acceptance of and future loyalty to the word of the Lord—and not once, but twice (Exod. 24:3b, 7b)! That the commitment was made in total sincerity is without doubt (as was Peter's "Lord, I am ready to go with you to prison and to death"). However, as the events of ch. 32 confirm, such a profession of loyalty proved to be short-lived. But at no point does Moses raise a question about the people's integrity. He takes them at their word.

To clinch the covenant agreement, Moses builds an altar at the bottom of the mountain, as he did in 17:15, and he has the appropriate persons offer sacrifices to the Lord (the Hebrew word for "altar" means "place of sacrifice"). Half of the blood from the slain animals is thrown against this altar, and the other half is sprinkled over the people. This particular ritual probably speaks of commitment by both sides to this new relationship. The Lord, here represented by the altar, binds himself to his people. He will not be faithless. Similarly, the people commit themselves. After all, can there be any kind of meaningful relationship if the commitment is not mutual? As Janzen (1997: 187) suggests, "Blood also implies a life so committed to the covenant relation that it is prepared to lay itself down for the sake of that relation." There may be another explanation for this ritual where blood is sprinkled first on the altar (v. 6) and then on the people (v. 8). The one other occurrence of this is at the time of the consecration of the priests. The blood of the sacrifice is first sprinkled on the altar (Exod. 29:20; Lev. 8:24) and then on Aaron and his sons (Exod. 29:21; Lev. 8:30). Furthermore, both episodes also include eating scenes (Exod. 24:11b and Exod. 29:22–34; Lev. 8:31–36). As Gen. 26:30 and 31:54 indicate, covenants often were sealed and celebrated with a meal (as in a wedding reception of today). So, before God anoints and consecrates one (small) part of his people (the priestly clergy) to his service, he anoints and consecrates all of his covenant people to his service.

With this ceremony behind him, Moses is now free, along with a select group, to ascend the mount. The language is nothing short of astounding: "they saw the God of Israel . . . they beheld God" (Exod. 24:10–11 NRSV); and subsequently they were treated to a heavenly banquet: they "ate and drank." Not surprisingly, no conversation is recorded.

First, seventy-four men were distinguished from the people (Exod. 24:9). Then Moses is removed from this group (24:12), but only after waiting six days. What then happens brings us back into the milieu of ch. 19. God's glory as a devouring fire envelops the mountain, and Moses too. For Moses, the mountain's peak is his Holy of Holies, into which he enters, unaccompanied, surely with an accelerated heartbeat.

It is interesting to compare this situation, where Moses *"entered* the cloud" (v. 18) as he went up the mountain, with 40:35, which states that "Moses *could not enter* the Tent of Meeting because the cloud had settled upon it, and the glory of the LORD filled the tabernacle" (NIV). At Sinai (in contradistinction to the tabernacle, where Moses is not admitted into the divine cloud) he is admitted into the divine cloud. About the only way we can put these two side by side (permission granted, permission denied) is to assume that what Moses was allowed to do at Sinai was a one-time, unique, unrepeatable experience. Anytime Moses enters the tabernacle it is to hear the voice of God, not to see him, his view of the ark being blocked by the veil/curtain.

The Sinai Theophany and Covenant (Exodus 19–24)

Alexander, T. D. 1999. "The Composition of the Sinai Narrative in Exodus xix i–xxiv ii." *VT* 49:2–20.

Arichea, D. C., Jr. 1989. "The Ups and Downs of Moses: Locating Moses in Exodus 19–33." *BT* 40:244–46.

Blenkinsopp, J. 1992. *The Pentateuch: An Introduction to the First Five Books of the Bible.* New York: Doubleday.

———. 1997. "Structure and Meaning in the Sinai-Horeb Narrative." In *A Biblical Itinerary: In Search of Method, Form and Content; Essays in Honor of George W. Coats.* Ed. E. Carpenter. JSOTSup 240. Sheffield: Sheffield Academic Press. Pp. 109–25.

Brettler, M. Z. 2000. "The Many Faces of God in Exodus 19." In *Jews, Christians, and the Theology of the Hebrew Scriptures.* Ed. A. O. Bellis and J. S. Kaminsky. SBLSymS 8. Atlanta: Society of Biblical Literature. Pp. 353–67.

Dozeman, T. B. 1989a. "Spatial Form in Exodus 19:1–8a and in the Large Sinai Narrative." *Semeia* 46:87–101.

———. 1989b. *God on the Mountain: A Study of Redaction, Theology and Canon in Exodus 19–24.* SBLMS 37. Atlanta: Scholars Press.

Eichrodt, W. 1961–1967. *Theology of the Old Testament.* Trans. J. Baker. 2 vols. OTL. Philadelphia: Westminster.

Gowan, D. E. 1994. *Theology in Exodus: Biblical Theology in the Form of a Commentary.* Louisville: Westminster John Knox.

Hague, M. R. 2001. *The Descent from the Mountain: Narrative Patterns in Exodus 19–40.* JSOTSup 323. Sheffield: Sheffield Academic Press.

Hendel, R. S. 1989. "Sacrifice as a Cultural System: The Ritual Symbolism of Exodus 24,3–8." *ZAW* 101:366–90.

Hilber, J. W. 1996. "Theology of Worship in Exodus 24." *JETS* 39:177–89.

Mendenhall, G. E. 1990. "Covenant." *Encyclopaedia Britannica.* 15th ed. 32 vols. Chicago and London: Encyclopaedia Britannica. Vol. 5, pp. 226–30.

Muilenburg, J. 1959. "The Form and Structure of the Covenantal Formulations." *VT* 9:347–65.

Nicholson, E. W. 1974. "The Interpretation of Exodus xxiv 9–11." *VT* 24:77–97.

———. 1975. "The Antiquity of the Tradition in Exodus xxiv 9–11." *VT* 25:69–79.

———. 1976. "The Origin of the Tradition in Exodus xxiv 9–11." *VT* 26:148–60.

———. 1986. *God and His People: Covenant and Theology in the Old Testament.* Oxford: Clarendon.

Phillips, A. 1984. "A Fresh Look at the Sinai Pericope—Part 2." *VT* 34:282–94. Repr., in *Essays on Biblical Law.* JSOTSup 344. Sheffield: Sheffield Academic Press, 2002. Pp. 37–48.

Rad, G. von. 1962. *Old Testament Theology*. Trans. D. M. G. Stalker. 2 vols. New York: Harper & Row. Vol. 1, pp. 190–219.

Rendtorff, R. 1989. "'Covenant' as a Structuring Concept in Genesis and Exodus." *JBL* 108:385–93. Repr., in *Canon and Theology: Overtures to an Old Testament Theology*. Minneapolis: Fortress, 1993. Pp. 125–34.

Schramm, B. 2000. "Exodus 19 and Its Christian Appropriation." In *Jews, Christians, and the Theology of the Hebrew Scriptures*. Ed. A. O. Bellis and J. S. Kaminsky. SBLSymS 8. Atlanta: Society of Biblical Literature. Pp. 327–52.

Van Seters, J. 1988. "'Comparing Scripture with Scripture': Some Observations on the Sinai Pericope of Exodus 19–24." In *Canon, Theology and Old Testament Interpretation: Essays in Honor of Brevard S. Childs*. Ed. G. M. Tucker et al. Philadelphia: Fortress. Pp. 111–30.

Weinfeld, M. 1975. "Berith." *TDOT* 2:253–79.

The Ten Commandments (Exodus 20:1–21)

Barclay, W. 1974. *The Ten Commandments for Today*. New York: Harper & Row.

Bright, J. 1973. "The Apodictic Prohibition: Some Observations." *JBL* 92:185–204.

Brooks, R. 1990. *The Spirit of the Ten Commandments: Shattering the Myth of Rabbinic Legalism*. San Francisco: Harper & Row.

Brown, W. P., ed. 2004. *The Ten Commandments: The Reciprocity of Faithfulness*. Library of Theological Ethics. Louisville: Westminster John Knox.

Cassuto, U. 1967. *A Commentary on the Book of Exodus*. Jerusalem: Magnes.

Childs, B. S. 1974. *The Book of Exodus: A Critical, Theological Commentary*. OTL. Philadelphia: Westminster.

Clines, D. J. A. 1995. "The Ten Commandments, Reading from Left to Right." In *Words Remembered, Texts Renewed: Essays in Honour of J. F. A. Sawyer*. JSOTSup 195. Sheffield: Sheffield Academic Press. Pp. 97–112.

Curtis, E. M. 1985. "The Theological Basis for the Prohibition of Images in the Old Testament." *JETS* 28:277–87.

Greeley, A. M. 1975. *The Sinai Myth: A New Interpretation of the Ten Commandments*. New York: Doubleday.

Greenberg, M. 1971. "Decalogue." *EncJud* 5:1435–46.

Haggerty, B. A. 1978. *Out of the House of Slavery: On the Meaning of the Ten Commandments*. New York: Paulist Press.

Harrelson, W. 1980. *The Ten Commandments and Human Rights*. Philadelphia: Fortress.

Heschel, A. J. 1954. *Man's Quest for God: Studies in Prayer and Symbolism*. New York: Scribner.

Johnstone, W. 1988. "The Decalogue and the Redaction of the Sinai Pericope in Exodus." *ZAW* 100:361–85.

Mendenhall, G. E. 1973. *The Origins of the Biblical Tradition*. Baltimore: Johns Hopkins University Press.

Miller, P. D., Jr. 1989. "The Place of the Decalogue in the Old Testament and Its Law." *Int* 43:229–42.

Napier, B. D. 1963. *The Book of Exodus.* The Layman's Bible Commentary 3. Richmond: John Knox.

Nicholson, E. W. 1977. "The Decalogue as the Direct Address of God." *VT* 27:422–33.

Patrick, D. 1995. "The First Commandment in the Structure of the Pentateuch." *VT* 45:107–18.

Phillips, A. 1970. *Ancient Israel's Criminal Law: A New Approach to the Decalogue.* Oxford: Blackwell.

———. 1983. "The Decalogue—Ancient Israel's Criminal Law." *JJS* 34:1–20. Repr., in *Essays on Biblical Law*. JSOTSup 344. Sheffield: Sheffield Academic Press, 2002. Pp. 2–24.

———. 1984. "A Fresh Look at the Sinai Pericope—Part 1." *VT* 34:39–52. Repr., in *Essays on Biblical Law*. JSOTSup 344. Sheffield: Sheffield Academic Press, 2002. Pp. 25–37.

Provan, I. 2001. "'All These I Have Kept Since I Was a Boy' (Luke 18:21): Creation, Covenant and the Commandments of God." *Ex Auditu* 17:31–46.

Segal, Ben-Zion, ed. 1985. *The Ten Commandments in History and Tradition.* Jerusalem: Magnes.

Stamm, J. J., and M. E. Andrews. 1967. *The Ten Commandments in Recent Research.* Naperville, Ill.: Allenson.

Tappy, R. E. 2000. "The Code of Kingship in the Ten Commandments." *RB* 107:321–33.

Trueblood, E. 1972. *Foundations for Reconstruction.* Waco, Tex.: Word.

Weinfeld, M. 1973. "The Origin of the Apodictic Law: An Overlooked Source." *VT* 23:63–75.

Williams, J. G. 1971. *Ten Words of Freedom: An Introduction to the Faith of Israel.* Philadelphia: Fortress.

Wolff, H. W. 1974. "The Elohistic Fragments in the Pentateuch." In *The Vitality of Old Testament Traditions,* by H. W. Wolff and W. Brueggemann. Atlanta: John Knox. Pp. 67–82.

Wouk, H. 1959. *This Is My God.* New York. Doubleday.

The Covenant Code (Exodus 20:22–23:33)

Anderson, C. B. 2004. *Women, Ideology, and Violence: Critical Theory and the Construction of Gender in the Book of the Covenant and Deuteronomic Law.* New York: Continuum.

Blenkinsopp, J. 1995. *Wisdom and Law in the Old Testament: The Ordering of Life in Israel and Early Judaism.* Rev. ed. New York: Oxford University Press. Pp. 94–102.

Carmichael, C. M. 1972. "A Singular Method of Codification in the *Mishpatim.*" *ZAW* 84:19–25.

———. 1992. *The Origins of Biblical Law: The Decalogues and the Book of the Covenant.* Ithaca, N.Y.: Cornell University Press.

Elison, H. L. 1973. "The Hebrew Slave: A Study in Early Israelite Society." *EvQ* 45:30–35.

Fensham, F. C. 1976. "The Role of the Lord in the Legal Sections of the Covenant Code." *VT* 26:262–74.

Finkelstein, J. J. 1981. *The Ox That Gored*. Transactions of the American Philosophical Society 71.2. Philadelphia: American Philosophical Society.

Fuller, R. 1994. "The Miscarriage Interpretation and the Personhood of the Fetus." *JETS* 37:169–84.

Gordon, C. H. 1965. *The Ancient Near East*. New York: Norton.

Greenberg, M. 1960. "Some Postulates of Biblical Criminal Law." In *Yehezkel Kaufmann Jubilee Volume*. Ed. M. Haran. Jerusalem: Magnes. Pp. 5–28.

Greengus, S. 1992. "Law." *ABD* 4:242–65.

———. 1976. "Law in the Old Testament." *IDBSup* 532–37.

———. 1994. "Some Issues Relating to the Comparability of Laws and the Coherence of the Legal Tradition." In *Theory and Method in Biblical and Cuneiform Law: Revision, Interpolation and Development*. Ed. B. M. Levinson. JSOTSup 181. Sheffield: Sheffield Academic Press. Pp. 60–87.

Hallo, W. W., and W. K. Simpson. 1971. *The Ancient Near East: A History*. New York: Harcourt Brace Jovanovich.

Hanson, P. D. 1977. "The Theological Significance of Contradiction within the Book of the Covenant." In *Canon and Authority*. Ed. G. W. Coats and B. O. Long. Philadelphia: Fortress. Pp. 110–31.

Haran, M. 1979. "Seething a Kid in Its Mother's Milk." *JJS* 30:23–35.

Hoffner, H. A., Jr. 1975. "Hittites." In *Wycliffe Bible Encyclopedia*. Ed. C. F. Pfeiffer, H. F. Vos, and J. Rea. 2 vols. Chicago: Moody. Vol. 1, pp. 799–801.

Jackson, B. S. 1972. *Theft in Early Jewish Law*. New York: Oxford University Press.

———. 1973a. "Reflections on Biblical Criminal Law." *JJS* 24:8–38.

———. 1973b. "The Problem of Exod. xxi 22–25 (ius talionis)." *VT* 23:273–304.

———. 1975. *Essays in Jewish and Comparative Legal History*. SJLA 10. Leiden: Brill.

———. 1979. "Legalism." *JJS* 30:1–22.

Kline, M. 1977. "Lex Talionis and the Human Fetus." *JETS* 20:193–201.

Lemeche, N. P. 1975. "The Hebrew Slave: Comments on the Slave Law, Ex xxi 2–11." *VT* 25:129–44.

———. 1976. "Manumission of Slaves—The Fallow Year—The Sabbatical Year—The Yobel Year." *VT* 26:38–59.

Levinson, B. M., ed. 1994a. *Theory and Method in Biblical and Cuneiform Law: Revision, Interpolation and Development*. JSOTSup 181. Sheffield: Sheffield Academic Press.

———. 1994b. "The Case for Revision and Interpolation within the Biblical Legal Corpora." In *Theory and Method in Biblical and Cuneiform Law: Revision, Interpolation and Development*. Ed. B. M. Levinson. JSOTSup 181. Sheffield: Sheffield Academic Press. Pp. 37–59.

Lowenstamm, S. E. 1977. "Exodus xxi 22–25." *VT* 27:352–60.

Malul, M. 1990. *The Comparative Method in Ancient Near Eastern and Biblical Legal Studies*. AOAT 227. Neukirchen-Vluyn: Neukirchener Verlag.

McKay, J. W. 1971. "Exodus xxiii 1–3, 6–8: A Decalogue for the Administration of Justice in the City Gate." *VT* 21:311–25.

Mendenhall, G. E. 1954. "Law and Covenant in Israel and in the Ancient Near East." *BA* 17 (2):26–46.

Olson, D. T. 1996. "The Jagged Cliffs of Mount Sinai: A Theological Reading of the Book of the Covenant (Exod. 20:22–23:19)." *Int* 50:251–63.

Olyan, S. M. 1996. "Why an Altar of Unfinished Stones? Some Thoughts on Ex 20,25 and Dtn 27,5–6." *ZAW* 108:161–71.

Oppenheim, A. L. 1977. *Ancient Mesopotamia: Portrait of a Dead Civilization*. 2nd ed. Chicago: University of Chicago Press.

Patrick, D. 1973. "Casuistic Law Governing Primary Rights and Duties." *JBL* 92:180–87.

———. 1977. "The Covenant Code Source." *VT* 27:145–57.

———. 1978. "I and Thou in the Covenant Code." In *SBLSP 1978*. Ed. P. J. Achtemeier. Missoula, Mont.: Scholars Press. Vol. 1, pp. 71–86.

———. 1985. *Old Testament Law*. Atlanta: John Knox.

Paul, S. 1970. *Studies in the Book of the Covenant in the Light of Cuneiform and Biblical Law*. VTSup 18. Leiden: Brill.

———. 1971. "Book of the Covenant." *EncJud* 4:1214–17.

Sprinkle, J. M. 1993. "The Interpretation of Exodus 21:22–25 (*lex talionis*) and Abortion." *WTJ* 55:233–53.

———. 1994. *The Book of the Covenant: A Literary Approach*. JSOTSup 174. Sheffield: Sheffield Academic Press.

Tate, M. 1977. "The Legal Traditions of the Book of Exodus." *RevExp* 74:483–509.

Van Seters, J. 1996. "The Law of the Hebrew Slave." *ZAW* 108:534–46.

Wenham, G. J. 1971. "Legal Forms in the Book of the Covenant." *TynB* 22:95–102.

Westbrook, R. 1986. "Lex Talionis and Exodus 21, 22–25." *RB* 93:52–69.

———. 1988. *Studies in Biblical and Cuneiform Law*. Cahiers de la Revue biblique 26. Paris: Gabalda.

———. 1994a. "The Deposit Law of Exodus 22, 6–12." *ZAW* 106:390–404.

———. 1994b. "What Is the Covenant Code?" In *Theory and Method in Biblical and Cuneiform Law: Revision, Interpolation and Development*. Ed. B. M. Levinson. JSOTSup 181. Sheffield: Sheffield Academic Press. Pp. 15–36.

Wright, D. P. 2003. "The Laws of Hammurabi as a Source for the Covenant Collection (Exodus 20:23–23:19)." *Maarv* 10:11–87.

10

Tabernacle, the Golden Calf, and Covenant Renewal

EXODUS 25–40

Quite possibly the last major unit of Exodus (that dealing with the tabernacle) seems anticlimactic, maybe even tedious, for many modern readers of the Old Testament. Who, having made some general observations about these chapters, might have an abiding interest in their content except perhaps an interior decorator or architect? Nevertheless, Scripture has given us an intricate description of the tabernacle, a description that ranges over sixteen chapters, from divine orders to build (25–31), to interruption and delay of implementation because of apostasy (32–34), to final execution of the divine mandate (35–40). The movement is from instruction (25–31) to interruption (32–34) to implementation (35–40). Sandwiched in between two sections (25–31 and 35–40) that deal with proper worship of God and building what God wants his people to build is a section (32–34) that deals with improper worship of God and building/making what God does not want his people to build/make. One may also discern that Exodus begins and ends with Israelites building something. At the beginning they are forced to build store cities for Pharaoh (1:11); at the end they choose to build a portable place of worship where God may dwell in their midst.

The Tabernacle (25–31; 35–40)

Most of the concerns of biblical scholarship vis-à-vis the tabernacle have been with historical questions, to the virtual neglect of theological analysis. The late-nineteenth-century formulation of Julius Wellhausen has been revised but not abandoned. It was his contention that the account in Exodus about the tabernacle is fictional, that indeed no such edifice ever existed during the wilderness period. Rather, the story was composed in the late exilic period, using the Solomonic temple as a model.

Historical Analysis

Wellhausen based his conclusions on the following considerations. First, can we believe that the Israelites had available in the desert sufficient quantities of the necessary metals and fabrics? To be sure, verses such as Exod. 12:35–36 (also 3:21, 22; 11:2–3) inform us that the Israelites did not leave Egypt empty-handed. Exodus 38:21–31 summarizes the amounts of gold, silver, and bronze used. Following R. B. Y. Scott on Hebrew weights and their approximate modern equivalents, Brevard Childs (1974: 637) calculates 1,900 pounds of gold, 6,437 pounds of silver, and 4,522 pounds of bronze as the respective amounts of precious metals used in the building of the tabernacle—altogether, slightly less than 13,000 pounds, or 6.5 tons, of metal.

As an extension of this, Wellhausen doubted whether the Israelites possessed the necessary skills to work with these metals in the wilderness, to say nothing of engineering and carpentry skills. This is a stronger objection when it is recalled that considerably later Solomon had to import Phoenician artisans as construction supervisors to build the temple (1 Kings 7:13–14) rather than use indigenous laborers.

Second, Wellhausen observed the virtual silence of Scripture on the role of the tabernacle after the conquest. The references are indeed few, and these are limited primarily to identifying where it was erected in Palestine (Josh. 18:1; 19:51; 1 Sam. 1:7; 2:22). This paucity of allusions raised suspicions in his mind about the historicity of a tabernacle in the wilderness, if indeed it was as pivotal as Exodus would lead us to believe.

For various reasons modern scholars have divorced themselves from the total skepticism of Wellhausen on this subject. The consensus now is that probably there did exist in the time of Moses some kind of simple tent shrine, reflected in the key text Exod. 33:7–11. Here the reference is to a much smaller edifice, situated outside, not in the middle, of the camp. The details in Exodus 25–31 and 35–40 are then dismissed as a much later exaggerated priestly tale of an unspectacular tent. But one may wonder if the tent mentioned in 33:7–11 ever functioned as *the* designated place of worship and the place from which God spoke to his people. Could it be that this tent is a provisional substitute for the more permanent tent in the middle of the camp, brought on by the idolatry in the preceding chapter (Moberly 1983: 63–66, 171–77)? In the preceding paragraph (33:1–6) God has spoken of the removal of his presence from the people because of their sinful idolatry, and so perhaps we should see this tent in that context. The fact that this tent is spoken of twice in one verse (v. 7) as "outside the camp," and is further qualified as being "some distance away/farther away," reinforces such an interpretation of this tent in the larger context of chs. 32–33.

Innumerable suggestions have been made in an attempt either to mesh P's ornate tabernacle and E's simple tent (i.e., two mutually exclusive descriptions of the same phenomenon) or to distinguish between the two structures in terms of purpose and provenance. The latter approach is the minority approach. However, the assumption that we are dealing with two different phenomena—and no text in Exodus demands that the two are interchangeable—obviates the need for much hypothetical reconstruction of the history of the tabernacle (Feinberg 1975: 582).

Theological Analysis

We may make the following observations about the tabernacle as described in these chapters of Exodus.

In the tabernacle there are seven pieces of furniture, if we assume that the carved cherubim are decorative extensions of the mercy seat. Can the number of furniture pieces be fortuitous?

The articles of clothing worn by those officiating in the tabernacle number eight, four of which are worn by the high priest alone (the ephod [28:6–12]; the breastpiece of judgment [28:15–30]; the ephod's robe [28:31–35]; a turban [28:36–38]), and four more that are worn by all the priests (a coat, girdle, cap, and linen breeches [28:40–42]). The only part of the human body not covered is the feet, perhaps indicating that the priests performed their tasks barefooted (compare God's command to Moses and Joshua to remove their shoes in his presence [Exod. 3:5; Josh. 5:15]).

Figure 5

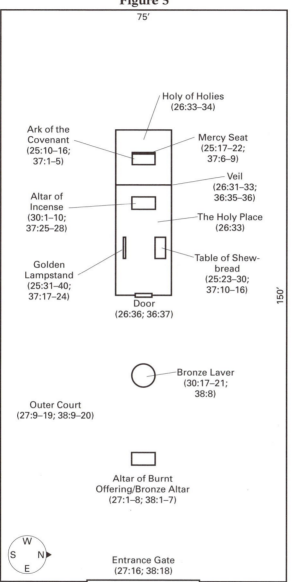

God does not delegate the responsibility for designing the tabernacle to any building or advisory committee. He alone is architect. The tabernacle, no less than the Decalogue, is rooted in divine revelation. Therefore, one is not surprised to encounter the frequently repeated phrase "he [or 'they'] did [or 'put'] . . . as the Lord had commanded Moses" in the closing chapters of Exodus. It appears ten times in ch. 39 (vv. 1, 5, 7, 21, 26, 29, 31, 32, 42, 43) and eight times in ch. 40 (vv. 16, 19, 21, 23, 25, 27, 29, 32). It also appears twice in ch. 36 (vv. 1, 5). Thus God's commands are for execution and implementation, not for consideration and discussion.

The materials necessary for the tabernacle and the priestly vestments are to come from the freewill offerings of the people. No one is taxed or assigned dues or apportionments. The giving is voluntary (25:1–7, especially v. 2). The response to Moses' appeal was overwhelming. Unlike many clergy who often beg and cajole for monies, Moses had to restrain the people from further giving—a magnanimous spirit on the part of the congregation indeed (36:2–7)!

The description of the furniture of the tabernacle starts with the pieces at the center and works outward, but not consistently so. And in the sections dealing with the actual construction, the order of completion is different from the order of instruction. See table 7.

Table 7

Instruction			Completion		
Holy of Holies	ark	25:10–16	ark	37:1–5	**Holy of Holies**
	mercy seat	25:17–22	mercy seat	37:6–9	
The Holy Place	table of shew-bread	25:23–30	table of shew-bread	37:10–16	**The Holy Place**
	lampstand	25:31–40	lampstand	37:17–24	
Outer Court	bronze altar	27:1–8	altar of incense	37:25–28	**Outer Court**
The Holy Place	altar of incense	30:1–10	bronze altar	38:1–7	**The Holy Place**
Outer Court	laver	30:17–21	laver	38:8	**Outer Court**

In the left-hand column what is most intriguing is the separation by two chapters (28–29) of the command to build the incense altar (30:1–10) from the previous commands about the furniture. Responding to scholars who view this particular paragraph as a later interpolation, Menahem Haran (1978: 228–29) remarks, "No doubt the literary form in which P has come down to us does not satisfy the requirements of classical taste . . . but such phenomena . . . cannot be taken as an argument for splitting up the sources into different strata." There may be, however, an explanation in the text as to why the description of the incense altar is not joined with that of the other inner sancta in ch. 25. Jacob Milgrom (1991: 236–37) observes that God's instructions to Moses fall into two parts: the tabernacle in blueprint (25:1–27:19) and the tabernacle in operation (27:20–30:38). The incense altar comes in the second section because it is described functionally (30:7–8). The same explanation applies as to why the laver in the courtyard is delayed until later in chs. 26–31 (30:17–21), where its use or purpose is revealed.

The text of Exodus itself should caution us against reading too much symbolic interpretation into the tabernacle. To detect in each piece of furniture, in each fabric, in each curtain ring, in each color some hidden meaning is more speculative than exegetical.

Similarly, modern attempts to assert the superiority of the tent or tabernacle over the later temple seem liable to the same charge. Thus Walter Brueggemann (1979: 169–70) states, "The old tradition of 'tent' asserts a claim of mobility and freedom for God. The 'house' tradition . . . stresses the abiding presence of Yahweh to Israel. . . . Now the notion of presence is primary and God's freedom is severely constricted." I respond by asking, Does the Old Testament clearly delineate such a tension? Is such friction the transparent witness of Scripture?

There is symbolism in the portrayal of the tabernacle. The symmetrical dimensions bear this out. The length of the court is twice that of the width. The Holy Place is twice the size of the Holy of Holies. The latter is a cube of ten cubits.

The choice of metals is indicative of greater degrees of sanctity: the more crucial the object, the more precious the metal used to make it. The term "pure gold" is applied only to the furniture of the tabernacle proper: the ark (25:11), the mercy seat (25:17), the table of shewbread (25:24), the lampstand (25:31, 36, 38, 39), the altar of incense (30:3). By contrast, the altar and the laver in the court are made of bronze or copper (27:2, 4, 6; 30:17). Ordinary gold was used for the moldings, the rings and the poles (the latter used for carrying objects such as the ark). In the case of the ark, these poles were never to be pulled out of the rings (25:15). The use of silver was limited to objects such as the base of a pillar near the veil (26:32) or rods joining the pillars around the edge of the court (27:10).

The same gradation applies to fabrics. The most crucial piece of fabric is the veil, separating the Holy Place from the Holy of Holies. Primarily it is made of blue, purple, and crimson wools, along with fine linen (26:31). The tabernacle curtains are just the opposite: primarily a fine linen product, along with the blue, purple, and crimson wool (26:1). Last are the curtains of goat's hair (26:7).

Parallels between the Passages about Creation and the Tabernacle

In the discussion of Joseph's story in Genesis I showed some parallels between the beginning and end of the Book of Genesis. Some scholars have suggested parallels between the beginning of Genesis and the end of Exodus, or more specifically, between creation and tabernacle. Thus, P. J. Kearney (1977) relates the seven divine speeches in chs. 25–31 (25:1; 30:11; 30:17; 30:22; 30:34; 31:1; 31:12) to the seven days of creation, noting parallels between each day and each corresponding divine speech in Exodus about the tabernacle. Some of these parallels appear forced, while others appear to have validity, especially those involving days six and seven and speeches six and seven. Exodus 25–31 is creation. Exodus 32–33 is the fall. Exodus 34–40 is the restoration.

Somewhat differently, Joseph Blenkinsopp (1976: 280; 1977: 62) unites the two by isolating vital parallel phrases in both the creation and tabernacle sections. With Blenkinsopp's argument as a guide, it is convenient to structure the passages as I have done in figure 6.

Further, binding the two together is the reference to "the Spirit of God" in both the creation of the world and the creation of the tabernacle (Gen. 1:2; Exod. 31:3; 35:31). It should not escape us that the first individual filled with God's Spirit was not a patriarch, a lawgiver, a prophet, or a judge, but an artisan, Bezalel, supervisor of the tabernacle project.

Parallels between Mount Sinai and the Tabernacle

Apart from the relationship of the tabernacle to creation, what, if any, is the relationship of the tabernacle to Sinai? It appears that Israel's experience of God at Sinai in 19–24 is an archetype of the tabernacle. What the peak of Mount Sinai is in 19–24, the Holy of Holies is in 25–40. Only Moses may ascend to the former, and only Aaron may enter the latter. The very sight of Sinai's summit is punishable by death (Exod. 19:21), and so is its tabernacle counterpart (Lev. 16:2). Joshua, Aaron, and seventy of the elders may go partway up Sinai's slopes (Joshua going a bit higher than the others, possibly to the cloud perimeter [24:13]), but no farther. Only the priests may enter the Holy Place, but no farther. The third division is "at the foot of the mountain" (24:4 NIV). Here is where all the people assemble and where Moses builds an altar. Its equivalent in the tabernacle is the forecourt area of the courtyard, where the people bring their sacrifices.

First, the tabernacle perpetuates Mount Sinai. At the conclusion of the revelation at Sinai we read, "The glory of the LORD settled on Mount Sinai, and the cloud covered it six days" (24:16 RSV); when the tabernacle was finished, "The cloud covered the tent of meeting, and the glory of the LORD filled the tabernacle" (40:34 NRSV). God's presence, once on Sinai, is now over the tabernacle.

Figure 6

And God saw everything that he had made, and behold, it was very good. (Gen. 1:31)	And Moses saw all the work, and behold, they had done it; as the LORD had commanded, so had they done it. (Exod. 39:43)
Thus the heavens and the earth were finished. (Gen. 2:1)	Thus all the work of the tabernacle of the tent of meeting was finished. (Exod. 39:32)
God finished his work which he had done. (Gen. 2:2)	So Moses finished the work. (Exod. 40:33)
So God blessed the seventh day. (Gen. 2:3)	And Moses blessed them. (Exod. 39:43)

Second, the tabernacle intensifies Mount Sinai. At the peak of Mount Sinai Moses "entered the cloud" (24:18). But when the same divine glory enshrouded the tabernacle, Moses "was not able to enter the tent of meeting" (40:35 NRSV). At Sinai the divine presence is penetrable; at the tabernacle the divine presence is initially impenetrable.

Third, the tabernacle completes Mount Sinai. Sinai is a marriage, the start of a new relationship. Now the partners must start to live together. In Sinai God has said, "I have chosen you"; in the tabernacle God has said, "I will dwell among the people of Israel, and will be their God" (29:43–46 RSV). Of course, it is precisely this divine presence that imparts sanctity to the tabernacle, not the gold or expensive fabrics or presence of the Levites. The tabernacle is holy only because it is the dwelling place of the holy God. If he leaves, all sanctity leaves.

Fourth, the tabernacle extends Mount Sinai. The Israelites cannot take a mountain with them when it is time to break camp, but they can take along a portable tent. To leave Sinai behind is not to leave the God of Sinai behind. The God whose presence at Sinai is restricted to the top of Sinai, where it is enshrouded in cloud, will be the God who will dwell in the midst of his people.

The tabernacle is the place where God and people can be closest to each other. Here God meets with his people (29:42–43). As such, the tabernacle is, as Davies (1962: 506) notes, "the principal bridgehead in the OT to the doctrine of the Incarnation." God, who once dwelt among his people in an edifice, now dwells among us in Jesus Christ (John 1:14: "the Word made his dwelling [tabernacled] among us"; Col. 1:19: "For in him [the Son] all the fullness of God was pleased to dwell" [NRSV]).

For the author of Hebrews, the tabernacle or tent is a prefigurement of the heavenly tent. (Revelation 21:16 makes the same equation. "The holy city, the new Jerusalem" and the Holy of Holies are the only two things in Scripture explicitly said to be cubic in dimensions.) The latter is greater and more perfect. It is not made with hands (Heb. 9:11). Its officiating high priest is Jesus Christ. The point, then, of the New Testament use of the tabernacle is twofold: the dwelling of God in Jesus Christ in the incarnation, and the dwelling of God in heaven. In both the believer is brought into proximity with God.

The Golden Calf and Covenant Renewal (32–34)

Exodus 32 relates how, in the absence of Moses, the Israelites and Aaron built a golden calf at the foot of Sinai, an act of flagrant apostasy. These are the same people who recently had said, not once but twice, "All the words that the LORD has spoken we will do" (24:3, 7 NRSV). Converts and committed believers had become casualties, almost overnight. An affirmation of obedience was forgotten.

Clearly, Aaron emerges as the villain in the story. As far back as the preexodus days the Lord had said to Moses about Aaron, "Is there not Aaron? . . . I know that he can speak well. . . . He shall be a mouth for you" (4:14, 16 RSV); "Aaron your brother shall be your prophet" (7:1 RSV). This proved to be no understatement! Aaron talked so well and so convincingly that he became the leader in soliciting materials for the idolatrous calf (32:2–3) and in the actual construction (32:4)—and all this coated with religious praxis (32:5–6)! The setting is perfect for a prophet to intrude and say, "Has the LORD as great delight in burnt offerings and sacrifices, as in obeying the voice of the LORD?" (1 Sam. 15:22 NRSV).

To make matters worse, when confronted by his younger brother, Aaron is prepared to place all the blame on the people at large: "You know the people, that they are set on evil" (32:22 RSV). He is also audacious enough to gloss over his own participation in this fiasco: "They gave it [the gold] to me, and I threw it into the fire, and out came this calf!" (32:24 NRSV). The parallels between Aaron and Adam in Genesis 3 are obvious. Both claim that they did what they did because someone else incited them by giving them something ("The woman . . . she gave me some fruit . . . and I ate it" [Gen. 3:12 NIV]; "They gave me the gold, and I threw it into the fire" [Exod. 32:24b]). Some scholars are not prepared to say that Aaron was not telling the truth, but rather that the story indeed presupposes that the calf emerged from the flame self-produced (see Loewenstamm 1967; 1975). This can hardly be the case, and besides, such an interpretation badly misses one of the points of the chapter: the contrast between the faithful Moses and the conniving Aaron.

If Aaron is villain, then Moses is hero. He is first intercessor. In language almost without equal for boldness in the Old or New Testaments, he urges God not to follow through on his intentions to wipe out his people (32:12). And to Moses' pleadings God accedes: "And the LORD repented of/relented of/changed his mind about the evil that he thought to do to his people" (32:14). Said Pascal, "God instituted prayer to lend His creatures the dignity of causality." Yehezkel Kaufmann (1960: 284–85) remarks that Moses does not "avert God's wrath from Israel by rousing them to repentance; he intercedes on their behalf, invoking God's promise to the patriarchs, and the glory of his name." Such intercession is carried to the extent that Moses risks his own relationship with God: "If not, blot me out of the book that you have written" (32:32 NRSV; cf. Paul's expression in Rom. 9:3).

The Old Testament uses the verb *nāḥam* (repent? relent? change one's mind?) thirty-four times with God as subject. Two texts (Num. 23:19; 1 Sam. 15:29) teach that God, unlike human beings, never needs to repent of sin. And he never repents of his choice of David (Ps. 110:4). But in the other thirty-plus passages that speak of God repenting/relenting, many times God is said to repent of "evil" (not sin!), which in a version such as the NIV is rendered as "calamity" or "disaster." Sometimes God repents/relents of evil in response to somebody's repentance (e.g., Jer. 18:8; 26:3; Jon. 3:9–10). At other times God repents/relents in response to somebody's intercession on behalf of the guilty, as here in Exodus 32 and in Amos 7:3, 6. Extremes of interpretation should be avoided here. On the one hand, the note about divine repentance in Exodus 32 suggests that God, although sovereign, is not unbending and unyielding, that he takes our intercessions seriously, and that in his love and mercy he is unchangeable. On the other hand, the note about divine repentance in Exodus 32 should not be used to suggest that in intercessory prayer God can be won over to our side by a good argument and be persuaded to do what we would do if we were God. As Master (2002) has reminded us, Exodus 32 must be placed in the context of the message and argument of the whole book of Exodus. For example, a God who is open to changing his mind and who is looking for a willing, enthusiastic, obedient individual to lead his people out of Egypt certainly would have changed his mind about the Moses of chs. 3–6. And in chs. 7–14 God's will is to liberate the Israelites, with or without the cooperation of Pharaoh. And in chs. 15–18 God will continue to lead the people toward Canaan and graciously meet their needs, their sin of grumbling notwithstanding. In ch. 32 God's words to Moses about Israel's future are couched more in the form of threatened judgment than decree, and as such they invite and stimulate a prophetic intercessory response from Moses. Thus what God does in Exodus 32 is best characterized by mercy, than by change of mind (Master 2002: 595).

But Moses is more than intercessor. There is no concession made to the people. In a fit of rage, not unlike Jesus in the temple, he casts the divinely made and inscribed tablets to the ground upon observing this scenario. After the calf is ground to powder, it is mixed with water, and the people are made to drink (32:20). It is still something of a mystery how, according to v. 20, one can (1) burn gold (unless "burn" in this instance means "smelt"), (2) grind gold to powder, and (3) grind to powder what has been burnt. Possibly the calf was encased in wood, or sat on a wooden pedestal, and that is what was burnt. But there is no clear support for that in the text. But there is no mystery in why Moses then made them "drink" the gold, now burnt and ground to powder, once he had scattered it on the waters. In another setting (Num. 5:11–31), a wife whose husband is suspicious of her fidelity is made to drink water taken (presumably) from the laver and mixed with dirt from the floor of the tabernacle (Num. 5:16–22). Imbibing such a potion will produce some kind of physical manifestation of guilt. The purpose of Moses making the people drink the mixture is not stated, but it may well be a means/ordeal to distinguish the innocent from the guilty, for how else would the Levites have known whom to strike down (Exod. 32:26–29)? Another item connecting Num. 5:11–31 and Exodus 32 is that both deal with the betrayal of an exclusive relationship: the (possibly) adulterous wife, and idolatrous Israel (see Janzen 1990: 607).

Still, it is for the people's redemption and reclamation that Moses is ultimately concerned (32:30). In the presence of the people and Aaron he is critic, fulminator, and antagonist. In the presence of God he is mediator, intercessor, and protagonist.

Far from obliterating his people, God commands Moses to lead the congregation on, but God will supply a surrogate for his presence (32:34; 33:1–5). God's refusal to be in the midst of his people is reinforced by the reference to the tent "outside the camp" to which Moses goes alone (33:7–11). God has become aloof.

If God is not finished with Israel, Moses is not finished with God. The intercessions of Moses, begun in ch. 32, continue into ch. 33. Moses asks of God, "Show me your ways. . . . Show me your glory" (vv. 13, 18 NRSV).

It is hard to miss the glaring contrast between "I will not go up among you" (33:3 NRSV) and "My presence will go with you" (33:14 NRSV). Childs (1974: 595) has caught the implication in Moses' request: "God has said: 'My presence will go with you.' Moses replies: 'If thy presence will not go, then do not make us leave this place.' The effect is to minimize the partial concession in order to press for the full request. Indeed, what Moses is really after comes out clearly in his repetition of the phrase 'I and thy people.' God's response had continued to attach itself to Moses himself. Moses shakes it off and demands that the response include the people."

To both of Moses' requests there is an answer. To the first, "Show me your ways," the answer is, "My presence will go with you." To the second, "Show me your glory," the answer is, "I will make all my goodness pass before you [i.e., a visual revelation], and will proclaim before you my name [i.e., a conceptual revelation]" (33:19 RSV). The promise is then dropped and picked up in 34:6: "The LORD passed before him, and proclaimed, 'The LORD, the LORD, a God merciful and gracious. . . .'" (NRSV). What follows is a description of God's character, often referred to in Jewish tradition as the "thirteen attributes of God," a list reflected in texts such as Num. 14:18; Neh. 9:17, 31; Ps. 86:15; 103:8; 145:8; Jer. 32:18; Joel 2:13; Jon. 4:2; Nah. 1:3. God is seen in what he does and how he acts.

Before, God himself had stood on the rock at Horeb (17:6); now, it is Moses' turn to stand in a cleft of the rock and catch a fleeting glimpse of God's back (33:23), much as Elijah did at Horeb/Sinai when the Lord passed by (1 Kings 19:11–13).

By ch. 34 we are prepared for covenant renewal. The language is reminiscent of Exodus 19: "Be ready in the morning. . . . No one shall come up with you . . . let no flocks or herds feed in front of that mountain. . . . The LORD descended in the cloud" (34:2–5).

Moses is still concerned about his congregation: "Go in the midst of us . . . pardon our iniquity and our sin and take us for thy inheritance" (34:9 RSV). There is no boastfulness here, nor is Moses attempting to exonerate himself. He identifies fully with his people.

Verses 10–26 are God's words to all Israel, a kind of short version of the Covenant Code in 20:22–23:19. In both an "angel" figures prominently (23:20–23; 32:34; 33:1–2). First, God commands intolerance toward all pagan forms of worship (vv. 11–16). There is to be no yoking with unbelievers. Then follows in vv. 17–26 a selective sample of laws from both the Decalogue (34:17, 21) and the Book of the Covenant (34:23, 26). Of special interest is the law of 34:17: "Do not make cast idols." Although it bears resemblance to the first two commandments of the Decalogue, it bears most directly on what happened with the golden calf in ch. 32. In other words, says God, let there be no repetition of the incident of the golden calf. These particular prohibitions or admonitions fall into one of two general categories: the prohibition of apostasy, and the observance of the cultic calendar. These are precisely the areas in which Israel trespassed in building the golden calf: erecting a forbidden idol, followed by a religious festival.

Fittingly, the chapter concludes with Moses' descent from Sinai, his face aglow—a fact that becomes readily apparent to everyone except

Moses himself (34:29–30). And how different is Moses' descent from the mountain with tablets in hand in ch. 34 from his descent from the mountain with tablets in hand in ch. 32 (v. 15)! A beaming and radiant face replaces a face exuding rage. Childs (1974: 619) remarks, "The biblical story is concerned that the divine glow on Moses' face should not be understood as a type of metamorphosis. Moses did not himself become a deity. He was unaware of any transformation. The whole point of the story emphasizes that his was only a reflection of God's glory." Indeed, this is the point of Psalm 8: human beings are made a little less than God and are crowned with glory and honor. Humankind is a reflection of God, but never an equal.

Verses 29–35 fall into two distinct units: what happened on this particular occasion (vv. 29–33), and what happens on all future occasions whenever Moses enters into God's presence and mediates that revelation to Israel (vv. 34–35). Moses is the one through whom God's glory shines, and he is the one through whom God's word comes forth. To be sure, Moses is not made divine, but he is set apart from all his peers, including his older, priestly brother, Aaron. And all this is a gift of God. As Dozeman (2000: 29) comments, "Authority arises not from his [Moses'] own personality or charisma but only in his role as a channel for divine teaching."

When the text says that Moses' face was "radiant, shone" (vv. 29, 30, 35), it uses a verb that suggests "became horned." Thus some scholars have argued that what happened here is that Moses wore a mask with horns, or he was disfigured in some way through too much access to the divine glory (Propp 1987)—that is, his face blistered and looked like little horns. That is hardly the case. It is likely that the writer chose a verb that refers to "horns" to describe Moses' shining face in order to recall the golden calf/bull of ch. 32 and its horns. God is making Moses what the people wanted the calf to be, a mediator and representative of God's presence (Moberly 1983: 109). The apostle Paul's use of this incident (2 Cor. 3:7–18) teaches, among other things, that all disciples of Jesus reflect God's glory ("we, who with unveiled faces all reflect the Lord's glory" NIV). A privilege once reserved for an extraordinary servant of God is now extended to even the most ordinary follower of the Messiah, in whose face God's glory shines (2 Cor. 4:6).

The Tabernacle (Exodus 25–31; 35–40)

Abrahams, I. 1971. "Tabernacle." *EncJud* 15:679–88.

Blenkinsopp, J. 1976. "The Structure of P." *Bib* 38:275–92.

———. 1977. *Prophecy and Canon: A Contribution to the Study of Jewish Origins.* SJCA 3. Notre Dame, Ind.: University of Notre Dame Press. Pp. 54–79.

Brueggemann, W. 1979. "Trajectories in OT Literature." *JBL* 98:161–85.

Childs, B. S. 1974. *The Book of Exodus: A Critical, Theological Commentary*. OTL. Philadelphia: Westminster.

Cross, F. M., Jr. 1981. "The Priestly Tabernacle in the Light of Recent Research." In *Temples and High Places in Biblical Times*. Ed. A. Biran. Jerusalem: Nelson Glueck School of Biblical Archaeology of Hebrew Union College-Jewish Institute of Religion. Pp. 169–80.

Davies, G. Henton. 1962. "Tabernacle." *IDB* 4:498–506.

Elnes, E. E. 1994. "Creation and Tabernacle: The Priestly Writers' 'Environmentalism.'" *HBT* 16:144–55.

Feinberg, C. 1975. "Tabernacle." *ZPEB* 5:572–83.

Freidman, R. E. 1992. "Tabernacle." *ABD* 6:292–300.

Gutmann, J. 1971. "The History of the Ark." *ZAW* 83:22–30.

Haran, M. 1965. "The Priestly Image of the Tabernacle." *HUCA* 36:191–226.

———. 1971a. "Priestly Vestments." *EncJud* 13:1063–69.

———. 1971b. "Shewbread." *EncJud* 14:1394–96.

———. 1978. *Temples and Temple Service in Ancient Israel*. Oxford: Clarendon.

Hurowitz, V. 1985. "The Priestly Account of Building the Tabernacle." *JAOS* 105:21–30.

Jackson, J. J. 1995. "The Ark and Its Making." *HBT* 17:117–22.

Kearney, P. J. 1977. "Creation and Liturgy: The P Redaction of Exodus 25–40." *ZAW* 89:375–87.

Klein, R. W. 1996. "Back to the Future: The Tabernacle in the Book of Exodus." *Int* 50:264–76.

Lewis, J. 1977. "The Ark and the Tent." *RevExp* 74:28–44.

Longacre, R. E. 1995. "Building for the Worship of God: Exodus 25:1–30:10." In *Discourse Analysis of Biblical Literature: What It Is and What It Offers*. Ed. W. R. Bodine. SemeiaSt. Atlanta: Scholars Press. Pp. 41–49.

McEvenue, S. E. 1974. "The Style of a Building Instruction." *Semitica* 4:1–9.

Milgrom, J. 1991. *Leviticus 1–16*. AB 3. New York: Doubleday.

Motyer, J. A. 1974. "The God Who Is Sufficient: The Indwelling God (Exodus 25:1–40:38)." *The Keswick Week*, 111–21.

Rodriguez, A. M. 1986. "Sanctuary Theology in the Book of Exodus." *AUSS* 24:29–37.

Woudstra, M. H. 1970. "The Tabernacle in Biblical-Theological Perspective." In *New Perspectives on the Old Testament*. Ed. J. Barton Payne. Waco, Tex.: Word. Pp. 88–103.

The Golden Calf and Covenant Renewal (Exodus 32–34)

Bailey, L. R. 1971. "The Golden Calf." *HUCA* 42:97–115.

Brichto, H. C. 1983. "The Worship of the Golden Calf: A Literary Analysis of a Fable on Idolatry." *HUCA* 54:1–44.

Coats, G. W. 1977. "The King's Loyal Opposition: Obedience and Authority in Exodus 32–34." In *Canon and Authority*. Ed. G. W. Coats and B. O. Long. Philadelphia: Fortress. Pp. 91–109.

Dozeman, T. B. 2000. "Masking Moses and Mosaic Authority in Torah." *JBL* 119:21–45.

Frankel, D. 1994. "The Destruction of the Golden Calf: A New Solution." *VT* 44:330–39.

Halpern, B. 1976. "Levitic Participation in the Reform Cult of Jeroboam I." *JBL* 95:31–42.

Hanson, A. 1976. "John 1:14–18 and Exodus 34." *NTS* 23:90–101.

Honeycutt, R. L., Jr. 1977. "Aaron, the Priesthood, and the Golden Calf." *RevExp* 74:523–35.

Irvin, W. H. 1997. "The Course of the Dialogue between Moses and Yhwh in Exodus 33:12–17." *CBQ* 59:629–36.

Janzen, J. G. 1990. "The Character of the Calf and Its Cult in Exodus 32." *CBQ* 52:597–607.

Kaufmann, Y. 1960. *The Religion of Israel*. Trans. M. Greenberg. Chicago: University of Chicago Press.

Knoppers, G. N. 1995. "Aaron's Calf and Jeroboam's Calves." In *Fortunate the Eyes That See: Essays in Honor of David Noel Freedman in Celebration of His Seventieth Birthday*. Ed. A. B. Beck et al. Grand Rapids: Eerdmans. Pp. 92–104.

Laney, J. C. "God's Self-Revelation in Exodus 34:6–8." *BSac* 158:36–51.

Loewenstamm, S. E. 1967. "The Making and Destruction of the Golden Calf." *Bib* 48:481–90.

———. 1975. "The Making and Destruction of the Golden Calf—A Rejoinder." *Bib* 56:330–43.

Master, J. 2002. "Exodus 32 as an Argument for Traditional Theism." *JETS* 45:585–98.

McCann, J. C., Jr. 1990. "Exodus 32:1–14." *Int* 44:277–81.

Moberly, R. W. L. 1983. *At the Mountain of God: Story and Theology in Exodus 32–34*. JSOTSup 22. Sheffield: JSOT Press.

Newing, E. G. 1993. "Up and Down—In and Out: Moses on Mount Sinai; The Literary Unity of Exodus 32–34." *ABR* 41:18–34.

Oswalt, J. 1973. "The Golden Calves and the Egyptian Concept of Deity." *EvQ* 45:13–20.

Perdue, L. G. 1973. "The Making and Destruction of the Golden Calf—A Reply." *Bib* 54:237–46.

Propp, W. H. 1987. "The Skin of Moses' Face—Transfigured or Disfigured?" *CBQ* 49:375–86.

Sasson, J. M. 1968. "Bovine Symbolism in the Exodus Narrative." *VT* 18:380–87.

Sommer, B. D. 2001. "Conflicting Constructions of Divine Presence in the Priestly Tabernacle." *BibInt* 9:25–40.

PART THREE

Leviticus

11

The Sacrificial System

LEVITICUS 1–7

One would assume that the Book of Leviticus, the crucial middle section of the fivefold Pentateuch, is so called because it is all about the Levites. To be sure, there are copious references to "priests" throughout Leviticus (in fact, 194 of them); indeed, some chapters are devoted exclusively to priestly issues (e.g., 8–10; 21–22). By contrast, there is only one brief reference in Leviticus to Levites, and that is in 25:32–33 in conjunction with the Jubilee Year ("The Levites always have the right to redeem their houses in the Levitical towns . . . so the property of the Levites is redeemable . . . because the houses in the towns of the Levites are their property among the Israelites" NIV). However, in Numbers there are whole sections or units devoted to the role of the "Levites": 1:47–53 (census of the Levites); 2:17, 33; 3:1–4:49 (role of the Levites); 7 (see especially vv. 4–5); 8:5–26; 16 (a Levitical-inspired revolt against Moses); 17:1–3 (Aaron's name on the staff of Levi); 18 (duties of and offerings for priests and Levites); 26:57–62 (census of the Levites); 31:47 (spoils of war for the Levites); 35:1–4 (Levitical towns). In some ways, then, "Leviticus" would be a more appropriate name for Numbers than for Leviticus—that is, if "Leviticus" specifically earmarks the Levites. More than likely, however, the word "Leviticus," which comes to us as a title for this third pentateuchal book from the Greek Septuagint and the Latin Vulgate, originally was not a designation in those languages for the Levites as a specific group of clergy, but rather was a more general term meaning something like "priestly-related." As such, it is an appropriate title for this book of the Bible. Such an understanding of "Leviticus" accords with the postbiblical, rabbinic name for Leviticus, which is *torat kohanim,* "instruction for/by priests."

Leviticus divides naturally into five units:

1. laws about sacrifice (1–7)
2. laws about priestly ordination (8–10)
3. laws about physical and moral impurities (11–16)
4. laws about physical and moral holiness (17–26)
5. laws about vows (27)

Norman Geisler (1977: 66) has suggested that Leviticus be understood as a two-part book: (1) the way to the Holy One (1–10), that way being by sacrifice (1–7) and priesthood (8–10); (2) the way to holiness (11–27), that way involving sanitation (11–16) and sanctification (17–27).

Leviticus underscores that the material found in its chapters is divinely revealed content. No hint is given that any institution described is incorporated from another religious system. Nor is there any indication that the substance of the book is the product of a committee on liturgy that imposes on the community its recommended means of worshiping God.

The revelatory nature of the material in Leviticus is underlined by the fact that twenty of the twenty-seven chapters begin with the formula "the LORD said unto Moses." The exceptions are chs. 2, 3, 5, 7, 9, 10, and 26. And some of these simply continue the emphasis of the preceding chapter (hence the absence of the formula), or else they contain this formula in the body of the chapter instead of at the beginning.

Leviticus is addressed to the members of a believing community. The covenant is in the past, and the marriage relationship is well under way. Exodus ended by devoting a good bit of attention to *where* God is to be worshiped—in the tabernacle. Leviticus extends the theme to include *how* God is to be worshiped. In Exodus the emphasis is on locality. In Leviticus the emphasis is on attitude and proper relationships.

More than any other Old Testament book, at least in terms of prominent vocabulary, Leviticus summons Israel to a holy life. Precisely what is involved in the holy life will surface as we make our way through the book. But for starters, we note that the word "holy" occurs in this book of the Bible more often than in any other. Strong's *Exhaustive Concordance,* based on the KJV, lists ninety uses of "holy" in Leviticus, and fifty of these occur in chs. 19–27. Strong also cites seventeen uses of the verb "sanctify," and again a majority of these are in chs. 19–27 (fourteen of seventeen). If we concentrate exclusively on the Hebrew root q-d-$š$, we discover, using Mandelkern's or Evan-Shoshan's Hebrew concordances, that some form of this root, in adjectival, nominal, or verbal structure, appears 150 times in Leviticus (about 20 percent of all occurrences in the Old Testament).

And lest it be thought that Leviticus addresses the holiness demanded exclusively, or even primarily, of the priest, we should observe that just the opposite is the situation. Precious little in this book is directed exclusively at the clergy (these exceptions are chs. 8–10, 16 partially, and 21:1–22:16). The remainder is addressed to all the people. So Leviticus is describing a holiness that applies to everyone, not a holiness just for the religious hierarchy—a holiness within the reach of all, out of the reach of none.

Description of the Sacrifices

The first seven chapters are devoted to a description of the sacrifices ordained by God that bear on the perpetuation of the relationship of humankind with God. Worship without sacrifice is inconceivable. Wherever sin has driven a wedge between God and humankind, both sacrifice (the outer act) and penitence (the inner attitude) become incumbent upon the sinner. But as we will see, some sacrifices have nothing to do with sin and atonement. And we also should note that the sacrifices described in chs. 1–7 are not an exhaustive listing. For example, there is nothing in these seven chapters on the incense offering (Exod. 30:7–8) or the drink offering (Exod. 29:38–41). The emphasis in these opening chapters of Leviticus is on private offerings/sacrifices versus public ones—that is, the sacrifices that the common Israelite would have offered to God most repeatedly.

The five sacrifices are:

1. the whole burnt offering (Leviticus 1): called in Hebrew the ʿōlâ, "that which goes up," and in the Septuagint, "holocaust"
2. the cereal offering (Leviticus 2): involving here exclusively cereal products
3. the peace/fellowship/well-being offering (Leviticus 3): perhaps a covenant meal
4. the sin offering (Lev. 4–5:13): a sacrifice of repentance for sins
5. the guilt/reparation offering (Lev. 5:14–6:7): also a sacrifice of repentance for sins, but additionally underscoring the need of restitution; thus, a special kind of sin offering

Immediately one can distinguish between points 1–3 and 4–5. The first three climax, in their respective narration, with the impact that such a sacrifice has on God. Such a sacrifice, when offered, becomes "a pleasing odor to the LORD" (ten references):

1. 1:9, 13, 17 (whole burnt)
2. 2:2, 9, 12; 6:15, 21 (cereal)
3. 3:5, 16 (peace)

In connection with the last two sacrifices the phrase appears only in 4:31.

By contrast, a unique phrase occurs repeatedly in the narration of the last two sacrifices: "the priest shall make atonement for him/them and he/they shall be forgiven" (nine references):

4. 4:20, 26, 31, 35; 5:10, 13 (sin)
5. 5:16, 18; 6:7 (guilt)

The first three sacrifices move to their climax in indicating their result on God: to him it is a pleasing odor. The Hebrew word for "pleasing" comes from the verb *nûaḥ* ("rest, be at ease, experience comfort/plea-sure" [the same verb behind the name "Noah" in Gen. 5:29]). In receiving these offerings God experiences pleasure. The last two sacrifices move to their climax in indicating their result on the one who gives the offer-ing: that person is forgiven.

There is a second difference between the two categories of sacrifices. None of the first three sacrifices is identified with either an occasion that prompts the sacrifice or a particular violation that elicits it. They are to be spontaneous acts, sacrifices offered to God in praise and thanks-giving. To be sure, we read in 1:4 that the burnt offering is "to make atonement" for the individual. We also need to observe that the phrase "it shall be acceptable in your behalf" (NRSV) is unique, occurring in neither the sin nor the guilt offerings, and the significant phrase "shall be forgiven" is absent here.

By contrast, the latter two sacrifices are identified with a specific oc-casion: "If anyone sins unwittingly in any of the things which the LORD has commanded not to be done . . ." (4:2 RSV). This sacrifice covers the inadvertent violation of God's prohibitive laws. The guilt offering also addresses itself to inadvertent violations, not in the area of the prohibitive laws, but in the area of "any of the holy things of the LORD" (5:15). "Holy things" could refer to the sacred furniture in the tabernacle (e.g., Num. 4:4: "This is the work of the Kohathites in the Tent of Meeting: the care of the most holy things" [NIV]), metals or artifacts to be donated to the sanctuary treasury, firstborn animals and firstfruits, the tithe, and so forth. The first would cover sins of commission, and the second would cover sins of omission. Quite clearly, then, the latter two sacrifices, unlike the first three, are expiatory or propitiatory in nature. Explicitly, sin and its forgiveness are the issues.

From this distinction there emerges in the biblical narration a third difference between the two categories of sacrifices. This distinction involves the use of the blood. In the first three sacrifices (really only in the whole burnt offering and the peace offering) the blood of the sacrificed animal is thrown/sprinkled (*zāraq*) by the priests against the outer altar, the bronze altar (1:5, 11; 3:2, 8, 13), or drained out (*māṣâ* [1:15]) against the side of this altar. The same procedure is followed in the sin offering of one of the rulers or tribal chieftains (4:25), and in the sin offering of one of the common people (4:30, 34). But even here, instead of the priest sprinkling (*zāraq*) the blood against the side of the outer altar, he "puts" (*nātan*) some of the blood on the horns of the altar and "pours out" (*šāpak*) the remainder of the blood at the altar's base.

However, in the case of the sin offering of either the priest or the whole congregation the picture is changed. In these two situations the blood is brought by the priest into the tent of meeting. Some of the blood is then "sprinkled" (and the verb here for "sprinkle" is *nāzâ* rather than *zāraq*, although the two seem essentially synonymous) seven times before the veil that separates the Holy Place from the Holy of Holies. Some is put (*nātan*) on the horns of the altar of incense (i.e., the inner altar). The remainder is poured (*šāpak*) at the base of the outer, brazen altar (4:5–7, 16–18). This is the Bible's way of saying that the greater the offender, the greater the offense. In addition, Lev. 6:30 specifically prohibits the eating of the flesh of the sin offering if the animal's blood has been brought into the tent of meeting. Here incineration, not consumption, is the mandate. (In anticipation of the discussion about the Day of Atonement [Leviticus 16], let it be briefly noted that on that day the blood of the sacrificial victim is brought into the Holy of Holies [Lev. 16:14–15], a procedure not permitted in any of the sacrificial rituals of Leviticus 1–7.)

Yet a fourth distinction is another set of vocabulary words that are very prominent in the first three sacrifices but are much less frequent in the latter two. The first of these is the emphasis in the first three sacrifices on "bringing, presenting" one's sacrifice before the Lord (*qārab*, literally, "bring near"). This verb occurs as follows:

whole burnt (6x): 1:3 (2x), 10, 14; 7:8 (2x)
cereal (7x): 2:1, 4, 12, 14 (2x); 6:14 (MT 6:7), 20 (MT 6:13)

peace (15x): 3:1 (2x), 6, 7 (2x), 12; 7:11, 12 (2x), 13, 14, 16, 18, 25, 29
sin (3x): 4:3, 14; 5:8
guilt (1x): 7:3

Similarly, the Hebrew word for "offering" (*qorbān*, "that which is brought near," from the verb *qārab*) appears many more times with the first three sacrifices than with the latter two:

whole burnt (4x): 1:3, 10, 14 (2x)
cereal (8x): 2:1 (2x), 4, 5, 7, 13 (2x); 6:20 (MT 6:13)
peace (12x): 3:1, 2, 6, 7, 8, 12, 14; 7:13, 14, 15, 16, 29
sin (4x): 4:23, 28, 32; 5:11
guilt (none)

Thus the verb for "present/bring near" a sacrifice before God appears twenty-eight times in the nonexpiatory, voluntary sacrifices, but only four times in the expiatory, mandatory sacrifices. And the noun for "offering" occurs twenty-four times in the first three sacrifices, but only four times in the latter two.

The preponderant use of this verb/noun in the sacrifices that fall into the category of gift to God as an act of devotion and thanksgiving rather than the category of gift to God as a prelude to seeking forgiveness may indicate that the primary purpose of sacrifice is not atonement. Rather, it is a means of expressing the reality and dynamics of one's relationship with God via a gift as a part of entering God's presence.

Surely it is not unintentional that Lev. 1:1–6:7 begins not with offerings whose explicit purpose is forgiveness of sin, but with offerings whose explicit purpose is expressing one's devotion to God. Leviticus does not begin with restoration to God and then move on to celebration; rather, it starts with celebration and then moves on to the possibility of restoration to God, if and when needed.

Thus far we have observed four significant differences between sacrifices that may be termed voluntary and those that may be termed propitiatory or expiatory. Another relationship in these sacrifices needs to be emphasized. This has to do with the connection between 1:1–6:7, the sacrificial system, and 6:8–7:38, supplementary instructions on the sacrifices.

Two things need to be observed. First, 1:1–6:7 spells out primarily the responsibilities of those who give the offerings. Thus we read in 1:2, "Speak to the people of Israel" (NRSV). On the other hand, 6:8–7:38 deals with the responsibilities of the officiants. Thus the opening statement of 6:9 is "Command Aaron and his sons" (NRSV). One section addresses the laity, while the other section addresses the clergy. A shirking of responsibility by either renders the sacrifice void.

Instructions about the Sacrifices

The second observation deals with the order of the sacrifices in both sections. See table 8.

Table 8

1:1–6:7	6:8–7:38
whole burnt	whole burnt
cereal	cereal
peace	sin
sin	guilt
guilt	peace

Anson Rainey (1970: 486–87) has called the first grouping a didactic order, a kind of pedagogical classification in which the offerings are grouped according to their logical or conceptual association. The second grouping he terms an administrative order, the order in which the administrative details of the sacrifices were entered in the record books of the temple. Gordon Wenham (1979: 118–19) suggests that the first grouping is governed by theological motivations. The food offerings precede those offerings that deal with the forgiveness of sin. The second grouping is arranged in order of frequency, from the regular daily sacrifices to those that were optional.

Nowhere does Leviticus 1–7 arrange these offerings in any hierarchy. There is no indication in the biblical text itself that we are progressing from the less important to the more important or vice versa, any more than a hierarchy is suggested by Paul in the New Testament in his listing of the gifts or fruit(s) of the Spirit. To designate some of these sacrifices as the pith and marrow of biblical thought while assigning others to only marginal significance is unwarranted.

I believe that Rainey (1970: 494–98) has correctly discerned a third order in the sacrifices. This he calls the procedural order. To illustrate, in the ceremony of the ordination of the priests (Leviticus 8), the sin offering *precedes* the burnt offering—an order different from anything in Leviticus 1–7—which then is followed by the wave (peace) offering (8:14–17; 8:18–21; 8:22–29). The next chapter covers the commencement of Aaron's high priesthood. Again the order is interesting. To make atonement for himself, Aaron offered first a sin offering, then a burnt offering (9:8–11; 9:12–14). The order of the people's offerings was sin (9:15), burnt (9:16), cereal (9:17), and peace (9:18–21).

The order is brought out strikingly in the case of the Nazirite. From the perspective of what he is to bring to the Lord, the order is a burnt offering, a sin offering, and a peace offering (Num. 6:14–15), but the order in which they are presented to the Lord by the priest is sin offering, burnt offering, and peace offering (Num. 6:16–17). In Hezekiah's cleansing of the temple, sin offerings come first (2 Chron. 29:20–24), then burnt offerings (29:25–30), then other sacrifices (29:31–35). Consistently the sin offering has priority of place. The point is that sin has to be dealt with first. To talk about consecration and fellowship with God while ignoring unconfessed sin is a priori impossible and impermissible.

But this point needs qualification. In some ways the translation "sin offering" is most justifiable in 4:1–5:13 and 6:24–30 (MT 6:17–23). But once one moves beyond these two passages, the rendering of the Hebrew word might better be "purification offering." The reason for this is that on most occasions when one presents a "sin" offering before God, it is clear that no sin has been perpetrated. For example, the Nazirite's "sin" offering that he presents on leaving his office (Num. 6:14) certainly is not because of some trespass, any more than is the "sin" offering brought by the new mother (Lev. 12:6–7).

Common Elements among the Sacrifices

The majority of the sacrifices here prescribed in Leviticus have several common denominators.

The Worshiper Brings a Gift

The worshiper never comes into the presence of God empty-handed. The sentiment expressed in the hymn "Nothing in My Hand I Bring" would find little echo in Leviticus. Worshipers come either with their gifts or with God's gift.

The Meaning of the Gift

The gift that is brought is frequently described as a *qorbān*, usually translated as "offering" (on this word see the brief comments above). It is used at least once to describe each of the five sacrifices except the guilt offering. Leviticus and Numbers have a monopoly on this word. It appears 38 times in Numbers, 39 times in Leviticus (31 of which are in chs. 1–7), and only twice more in the Old Testament (a Greek transliteration of the word appears also in Mark 7:11). A more literal translation of the word than "offering" is "a thing brought near." The sacrifices thus are concerned with the issue of how one can live in nearness to God. Leviticus is answering the question "Can there be proximity and propinquity between God and humankind?"

The Description of the Gift

The offering overwhelmingly is a domesticated animal—bull, goat, or sheep. Occasionally grains are offered. The offering of grains rather than animals seems to depend on the range of one's financial resources. Yet it is that which is most costly, most valuable, that is given to God. And that is not all: the animal that is offered is to be without blemish.

The same Hebrew word used to describe the sacrificial animal, *tā-mîm*, can describe Noah (Gen. 6:9), Abraham (Gen. 17:1), Job (Job 12:4), or any worshiper hoping to enter God's presence (Ps. 15:2). The word, then, encompasses both physical purity and moral purity. The Old Testament itself seems to shift its emphasis, in terms of sacrifice, from the sacrificial animal without physical impurities (Leviticus) to the sacrificial servant, a person without moral impurities. This certainly is the message of Isaiah 53, the servant who bore our griefs, who was wounded for our transgressions and iniquities, yet who did not open his mouth. The scene for the New Testament message could not be more beautifully and ideologically prepared (see 1 Pet. 1:19).

It is well known that the prophets inveighed against the abuse of sacrifices. Their ire was raised whenever they saw the people of God being faithful in their observance of ritual but faithless in their lifestyles. Sacrifice must never be used as a smoke screen for ethical depravity. Outward conformity must be matched by inner holiness. To support this, one thinks of passages such as Isa. 1:11–17; Hos. 6:6; Amos 5:21–24; Mic. 6:6–8—voices from the eighth and early seventh centuries B.C. Later in the seventh and into the sixth centuries B.C. the emphasis is found again in Jeremiah (e.g., 6:20), especially his famous temple sermon (7:1–15). Such sentiments are reflected even in the Psalter (see Ps. 51:16–17).

Perhaps the clearest analogy to the theme of unblemished sacrificial victim is in the message of the postexilic prophet Malachi. Not only are the people's offerings *incomplete* ("You are robbing me" [3:8]) and their lives *impure* ("You have wearied the LORD" [2:17]), but also their sacrifices to God are *imperfect* ("The priests despise my name" [1:6]). The animals presented are lame, blind, or sick, in such poor condition that the people would not dare to give them to their earthly leader (1:8b).

It is not particularly distant from this stress on the purity of the victim to the teaching of Paul when he says, "Present your bodies as a living sacrifice [not dead *or* alive, but dead *and* alive!], holy and acceptable to God" (Rom. 12:1 NRSV). And Paul inserts that we are able to do this only "by the mercies of God."

The Gift Depends on One's Resources

In most of the sacrifices in Leviticus, that which is to be presented is graded according to the donor's ability and resources. For example, the burnt offering may be a bull (1:3–5), a sheep or goat (1:10), or a bird (1:14). No exorbitant demands are placed on those of meager means. Jacob Milgrom has suggested that the cereal offering, the one sacrifice in which animals do not play a part, eventually became the burnt offering given by poor people.

In the sacrifices of expiation similar gradations appear, but there they are in the spectrum of more serious perpetrator to less crucial perpetrator. Thus, in the sin offering the priest or the whole congregation brings a young bull (4:3, 14); the ruler presents a male goat (4:23); one of the common people brings a female goat (4:28), a female lamb (4:32), or birds (5:7). Nowhere is there any indication that God desires to deprive his followers. They are to give as has been given to them. The principle seems to be this: not equal offering, but equal sacrifice. The widow's mites may be every bit as sacrificial as the philanthropist's millions.

The Donor Participates in the Ritual

The person who brings an offering is actively involved in the ritual and is not a passive spectator. The donor presents the sacrificial victim and, in doing so, lays a hand on the animal's head (1:4; 3:2, 8, 13; 4:4, 15, 24, 29, 33). The Hebrew word for "lay (the hand)," *sāmak*, is one that normally means to apply some pressure rather than merely to touch. The verb appears in, for example, Judg. 16:29 to refer to Samson reaching toward the two central pillars of the Philistine temple and "bracing himself/leaning" against them. It occurs as the verb with "hand(s)" as object twenty-four times in the Old Testament. The absence of such a procedure in the cereal offering is dictated by at least two facts. First, how would it be possible for one to both present and then place hands on flour or grain? Second, the procedure is limited to blood offerings, and hence it is inapplicable to the cereal offering.

But what purpose is served by the imposition of a hand? Leviticus 1–7 does not attempt to answer this question. It merely states the procedure and avoids a rationale. Elsewhere the laying on of hands (two hands, that is) is connected with either the transmission of blessing (Gen. 48:13–14) or of curse and judgment (Lev. 24:14), or the transference and removal of sin (Lev. 16:21), or an act of commissioning (Moses of Joshua in Num. 27:23; Deut. 34:9). Numbers 8:9–10 is perhaps the closest parallel. Moses is "to present" (the root is *q-r-b,* the same as in Lev. 1–7) the Levites to the congregation, who in turn lay their hands on the Levites. The latter are substitutes for the congregation's firstborn: "For they are wholly given to me from among the people of Israel; instead of all that open the womb. . . . I have taken the Levites instead of all the firstborn" (Num. 8:16, 18 RSV).

If indeed this is a parallel, then the laying on of hands on the animal signifies that the animal is a substitute. Can we assume, then, that involved in this is the transference of sin from the worshiper to the sacrificial victim? Not necessarily. In the Day of Atonement ritual the laying of Aaron's hands on the live goat does signify the transference of sins: "Aaron shall lay both his hands upon the head of the live goat . . . and he shall put them [sins, iniquities, and transgressions] upon the head of the goat" (Lev. 16:21 RSV). However, this goat is not then offered to God as a sacrifice, with its flesh to be either burnt or eaten. Instead it is sent to the wilderness. Other than that, nothing happens to it. It does not die. Most likely the laying on of a hand signifies ownership. It is a way of the donor saying, "This is my gift, my offering; I relinquish ownership."

The Worshiper's Responsibilities

After the animal is brought to the place of worship, the worshiper, not the priest, kills the animal (by slitting its throat?). The Hebrew word that is used for "kill" is *šaḥaṭ.* Its use is normally restricted to ritual killing, and it appears eighty-four times in the Old Testament, thirty-six of which are in Leviticus. For Roland de Vaux (1964: 452), the significance of this killing (and subsequent burning) is that it makes the offering useless except for consumption, and therefore the offering is an irrevocable gift, given to God, and therefore withdrawn from profane use.

In addition to slaying the victim, the worshiper was responsible for skinning and dissecting the animal and washing the entrails (1:6–9, 12–13).

The Priest's Responsibilities

The sacrificial victim's blood is drained and then scattered around or on either the outer or the inner altar, depending on which sacrifice is involved. This is specifically a priestly duty (e.g., 1:5, 11, 15; 3:2, 8, 13; 4:5–7).

Interestingly, Leviticus 1–7 nowhere points out the significance of this act or of the role of the blood in the ritual. The rite is simply described, without commentary or theological analysis. The rationale is provided by Lev. 17:11: "For the life of the flesh is in the blood; and I have given it for you upon the altar to make atonement for your souls; for it is the blood that makes atonement, by reason of the life" (RSV).

Some of the problems inherent in this crucial verse become evident simply by comparing widely different translations that have been proposed by competent scholars of Hebrew linguistics.

> For the life of the flesh is in the blood, and I have assigned it to you to serve as expiation for your lives on the altar; for the blood may expiate according to the value of life. (Levine 1974: 68)

> The life-essence of flesh is in the blood and I for my part have on your behalf designated it (to be put) on the altar to serve as compository payment, for it is the blood which serves as compository payment for the life (taken). (Brichto 1976: 23, 28)

> For the life of the flesh is the blood, and it is I who have assigned it to you upon the altar to expiate for your lives, for it is the blood, as life, that expiates. (Milgrom 1971a: 156; 1971b: 1041)

> For the life of the flesh is in the blood; and I have given it for you upon the altar to make atonement for your souls; for it is the blood that makes atonement, by reason of the life (that is in it). (Rainey 1971: 600)

Perhaps it is debatable whether Lev. 17:11 may serve as *the* basis for a substitutionary theory of sacrifice. Why does Leviticus 1–7 contain no reference to a substitutionary rationale? Why is there no 17:11 in chs. 1–7? What is the relationship of 17:11 to its immediate context, 17:1–16, a paragraph dealing with restrictions upon the slaughter of animals? And what is to be made of the fact that these verses deal with the peace offering (17:5), the one sacrifice that has nothing to do with atonement and forgiveness of sin?

Perhaps the heavy emphasis on the role of blood in Leviticus 1–7 highlights not the idea of substitution per se, but rather the simple idea that sacrifice involves death.

The Sacrifice and Its Meaning

After the animal is offered, killed, quartered, and cleaned, and its blood is drained, either all or selected parts of it are placed on the altar and burned (1:9, 13, 17; 3:5, 11, 16; 4:10, 19, 26, 31, 35). The same holds true for the cereal offering (2:2, 9, 16). The Hebrew text consistently uses the verb q-t-r to describe the burning on the altar.

To describe the burning of animal flesh "outside the camp," the Hebrew uses the more usual word for "burning," ś-r-p (cf. the seraphim, śĕrāpîm, "the burning ones"): 4:12, 21; 8:17; 9:11. This verb is limited in Leviticus to the sin offering of the high priest or the whole community. It connotes the rapaciousness with which fire consumes, and it is perhaps best translated as "incinerate," thus contrasting with q-t-r, a slower, more gradual, and controlled burning.

It is not unexpected that those sacrifices burned on the altar by the priest are described as a "pleasing odor to the LORD." What should we do with a phrase such as this? Were the sacrifices food for God, a source of nutrition? Have we here vestiges of myth? To my mind, Yehezkel Kaufmann (1960: 111) has provided the best explanation. Calling such phrases "petrified linguistic survivals," he quotes identical phrases or ideas in the writings of the prophets, and then he adds:

> That the classical prophets felt free to use these phrases is the best testimony to their innocence. Had the people at large believed that sacrifice was food for the deity, the prophets and legislators—who surely did not hold this view—would hardly have used such expressions which could only have lent support to what they must consider a gross error. Indeed they would have combated this notion.

In the light of the sacrifices as a pleasing odor to God, we can more fully understand Paul's treatment in Eph. 5:2 of Christ's death: "And walk in love, as Christ loved us and gave himself up for us, a fragrant offering and sacrifice to God" (RSV).

Disposing of the Sacrificial Victim

Various procedures were followed in the disposition of the sacrificial victim. In the burnt offering the entire animal was consumed (1:9, 13) except for the hide, which went to the priest (7:8). Some of the cereal offering was given to the priest for food (2:3, 10; 6:16, 18). In the sin offering some of the animal was burned on the altar by the priest. This included the choice entrails and the suet over and on the entrails (4:8–10). In the case of the sin offering of the priest and the congregation, the carcass and the remaining entrails were burned outside the camp as refuse (4:11, 12, 21), but not in the case of the laity's sin offering. Additionally, we are informed that the priest could not eat the flesh of the sin offering brought by himself or the congregation (6:30).

Again we see the principle illustrated: the greater the offender, the greater the offense.

The peace offering is unique. It is the one sacrifice that has multiple ways of disposition of the meat. Part is consumed on the altar (3:3–5). Another part is given to the priests (7:31–35). The third element is the most radical departure. The person who gave the offering also ate part of the sacrificial victim (7:15–21). This is the only sacrifice in which that permission is granted. It is for this reason that warnings about "eating blood" come in the context of the peace offering (3:17; 7:26, 27; 17:10, 12, 14). In eating the meat, the worshiper must be certain that all the blood has been drained. In this one instance God invites his people into his presence to share a meal with him and with one another. In other words, the fellowship hall is as much a part of worship as the sanctuary.

The Forgiveness of Sin

I have stated that the last two sacrifices—sin and guilt—deal exclusively with the forgiveness of sin. Yet there is a qualification made. These two sacrifices are aimed to forgive sins committed "unwittingly," "in ignorance," "inadvertently," or "unintentionally." The expression is applied to all four levels of the sin offering (4:2, 13, 22, 27; but not in 5:1–13, although it does use the phrases "even though he is unaware of it" [vv. 2, 3, 4] and "when he learns of it" [vv. 3, 4]), as well as to the guilt offering (5:14, 18).

Leviticus 4:1–5:13 suggests that we risk sinning unintentionally in seven different ways (this formulation I owe to my colleague Lawson Stone):

1. when we cross an unrecognized boundary (4:1–12): "When anyone sins unintentionally and does what is forbidden in any of the LORD's commands . . ." (NIV).
2. when we run with the herd (4:13–21): "If the whole Israelite community sins unintentionally . . ." (NIV).
3. when we think that our responsibilities exempt us (4:22–26): "When a leader sins unintentionally . . ." (NIV).
4. when we think that our insignificance excuses us (4:27–35): "If a member of the community sins unintentionally . . ." (NIV).
5. when we neglect doing something right (5:1–3): "If a person sins because he does not speak up when he hears a public charge to testify regarding something he has seen or learned about . . ." (NIV).
6. when we act or speak on impulse (5:4–13): "Or if a person thoughtlessly takes an oath to do anything . . ." (NIV).

7. when we thoughtlessly trivialize the sacred (5:14–16): "When a person commits a violation and sins unintentionally in regard to any of the Lord's holy things . . ." (NIV).

Two conclusions often have been drawn from this contingency. The first is that the Old Testament sacrificial system makes provisions only for accidental sins, not for those perpetrated deliberately. Besides the material in Leviticus, Num. 15:27–31 explicitly states that there is provision of atonement for the one who sins inadvertently, but then it adds, "But whoever acts high-handedly . . . affronts the Lord, and shall be cut off from among the people . . . and bear the guilt" (NRSV).

Second, as an extension of the first conclusion, many Christian intepreters of Leviticus have concluded that it is precisely here that the superiority of Christ's sacrifice emerges, for in his death there is full atonement—provision for all sins, both accidental and deliberate. Although this line of thought is inviting, one might suspect that such conclusions rest on faulty exegesis. Even the contention that there is no sacrificial provision in Leviticus for deliberate sin is seriously open to question, as I will attempt to show shortly.

But first, what is the intent of the qualification about inadvertent sin? Why does Leviticus make such a distinction? Can this be the Old Testament's way of saying that sin, any kind of sin, both premeditated and unintended, is disastrous, an affront to God, and not a chance for him to display his capabilities? The Old Testament is as vehement in its repudiation of the antinomian spirit as is the New Testament. The Old Testament believer, no less than the New Testament believer, can affirm that "where sin increased, grace abounded all the more" (Rom. 5:20 NRSV). But that beautiful truth must not be perverted into a license for sinning.

To return to Leviticus 1–7, is there anything in the sacrificial system that militates against the idea of there being no forgiveness for deliberate sins? The clue is found in an examination of the guilt offering (5:14–6:7), introduced also by the qualifying comment "If any one commits a breach of faith and sins unwittingly" (5:15 RSV). The analysis of this particular sacrifice has been skillfully done by Jacob Milgrom (1976b: 84–128), and here I am basically following his argument.

The common denominator for this sacrifice is that it covers those cases in which the sin committed results in another party suffering some kind of loss in regard to rightful ownership. The wronged or deprived party may be God himself (the point of the two cases given in 5:14–16 and 5:17–19) or another human being (6:1–4). For this reason restitution, plus 20 percent, is at the heart of this sacrifice (see 5:16; 6:5).

An examination of the particular situations covered in 6:1–7 (sins against another person) shows that these cannot possibly be sins done inadvertently. For example, refusing to return something that an acquaintance has placed in one's safekeeping, or stealing from someone, or lying about finding something that was lost by another can hardly be called inadvertent sins! Yet these are precisely the areas covered in 6:1–7. And to compound the problem, the sinner issues a false statement ("swearing falsely" [6:3, 5]) in an attempt to establish innocence or to cover up the otherwise blatant sin.

To solve the dilemma—how can deliberate sins be forgiven?—we may turn to a variant of Lev. 5:14–6:7, which is Num. 5:6–8. What is novel and crucial in the text in Numbers is that confession is essential in the case of a deliberate sin. It must succeed conviction and precede restitution (Num. 5:7). Thus the sin moves into the category of inadvertent sins and may be expiated.

To quote Milgrom (1976b: 109–10), "A more correct understanding of this priestly postulate [i.e., that only involuntary wrongdoers are eligible for sacrificial atonement] would be that sacrificial atonement is barred to the unrepentant sinner," or (1976: 124), "It is not the deliberate sinner who is excluded from sacrificial expiation but the unrepentant sinner."

To say this is to echo exactly what is said in the Epistle to the Hebrews. Compare the language of Heb. 6:4, 6: "For it is impossible to restore again to repentance . . . if they then commit apostasy, since they crucify the Son of God" (RSV); or Heb. 10:26: "If we sin deliberately after receiving the knowledge of the truth, there no longer remains a sacrifice for sins" (RSV). It is the absence of confession and contrition that bars the way of the backslider into restored, redemptive fellowship with Christ.

Leviticus Commentaries and Major Studies

Bamberger, B. J. 1979. *Leviticus*. The Torah: A Modern Commentary. New York: Union of American Hebrew Congregations.

Bellinger, W. H., Jr. 1998. "Leviticus and Ambiguity." *Perspectives in Religious Studies* 25:217–25.

Bonar, A. A. 1966. *A Commentary on Leviticus*. Repr., London: Banner of Truth.

Budd, P. J. 1996. *Leviticus: Based on the New Revised Standard Version*. NCBC. London: Marshall Pickering; Grand Rapids: Eerdmans.

Carroll, M. P. 1985. "One More Time: Leviticus Revisited." In *Anthropological Approaches to the Old Testament*. Ed. B. Lang. IRT 8. Philadelphia: Fortress. Pp. 117–26.

Childs, B. S. 1979. *Introduction to the Old Testament as Scripture.* Philadelphia: Fortress. Pp. 180–89.

Clements, R. E. 1970. "Leviticus." In *The Broadman Bible Commentary.* Vol. 2. Ed. C. J. Allen. Nashville: Broadman. Pp. 1–74.

Damrosch, D. 1987. "Leviticus." In *The Literary Guide to the Bible.* Ed. R. Alter and F. Kermode. Cambridge, Mass.: Belknap. Pp. 66–77.

Douglas, M. 1995. "Poetic Structure in Leviticus." In *Pomegranates and Golden Bells: Studies in Biblical, Jewish and Near Eastern Ritual, Law, and Literature in Honor of Jacob Milgrom.* Ed. D. P. Wright, D. N. Freedman, and A. Hurvitz. Winona Lake, Ind.: Eisenbrauns. Pp. 239–56.

———. 1999. *Leviticus as Literature.* Oxford: Oxford University Press.

Fabry, H.-J. 2000. "The Reception of the Book of Leviticus in Qumran." In *The Dead Sea Scrolls—Fifty Years after Their Discovery: Proceedings of the Jerusalem Congress, July 20–25, 1997.* Ed. L. H. Schiffman et al. Jerusalem: Israel Exploration Society. Pp. 74–81.

Gerstenberger, E. S. 1996. *Leviticus.* OTL. Louisville: Westminster John Knox.

Goldberg, L. 1980. *Leviticus: A Study Guide Commentary.* Grand Rapids: Zondervan.

Gorman, F. H., Jr. 1990. *The Ideology of Ritual: Space, Time, and Status in Priestly Theology.* JSOTSup 91. Sheffield: JSOT Press.

———. 1997. *Divine Presence and Community: Leviticus.* ITC. Grand Rapids: Eerdmans.

Grabbe, L. L. 1993. *Leviticus.* OTG. Sheffield: JSOT Press.

———. 1997. "The Book of Leviticus." *CurBS* 5:91–110.

Harrison, B. 1999. "The Strangeness of Leviticus." *Judaism* 48:208–28.

Harrison, R. K. 1980. *Leviticus: An Introduction and Commentary.* TOTC. Downers Grove, Ill.: InterVarsity Press.

Hartley, J. E. 1992. *Leviticus.* WBC 4. Dallas: Word.

Hayes, J. H. 1998. "Atonement in the Book of Leviticus." *Int* 52:5–15.

Jensen, P. P. 1992. *Graded Holiness: A Key to the Priestly Conception of the World.* JSOTSup 106. Sheffield: JSOT Press.

Kaiser, W. C., Jr. 1994. "The Book of Leviticus: Introduction, Commentary and Reflections." In *The New Interpreter's Bible.* Vol. 1. Ed. L. E. Keck et al. Nashville: Abingdon. Pp. 983–1191.

Kinlaw, D. F. 1969. "Leviticus." In *Beacon Bible Commentary.* Vol. 1. Kansas City, Mo.: Beacon Hill Press. Pp. 317–95.

Klawans, J. 2003. "Ritual Purity, Moral Purity, and Sacrifice in Jacob Milgrom's *Leviticus.*" *RelSRev* 29:19–28.

Knohl, I. 1995. *The Sanctuary of Silence: The Priestly Torah and the Holiness School.* Minneapolis: Fortress.

Kugler, R. A. 1997. "Holiness, Purity, the Body, and Society: The Evidence for Theological Conflict in Leviticus." *JSOT* 76:3–27.

Leder, A. C., and D. A. Vroege. 1999. "Reading and Hearing Leviticus." *CTJ* 34:431–42.

Levine, B. 1989. *Leviticus: The Traditional Hebrew Text with the New JPS Translation.* JPS Torah Commentary. Philadelphia: The Jewish Publication Society.

Milgrom, J. 1971. "Leviticus." *EncJud* 11:138–47.

———. 1976. "Leviticus." *IDBSup* 541–45.

———. 1989. "Leviticus." In *The Books of the Bible*. Ed. B. W. Anderson. 2 vols. New York: Scribner. Vol. 1, pp. 63–70.

———. 1991. *Leviticus 1–16: A New Translation with Introduction and Commentary*. AB 3. New York: Doubleday.

———. 2000. *Leviticus 17–22: A New Translation with Introduction and Commentary*. AB 3A. New York: Doubleday.

———. 2001. *Leviticus 23–27: A New Translation with Introduction and Commentary*. AB 3B. New York: Doubleday.

Noordtzij, A. 1982. *Leviticus*. Bible Student's Commentary. Trans. R. Togtman. Grand Rapids: Baker.

Poorthuis, M. J. H. M., and J. Schwartz, eds. 2000. *Purity and Holiness: The Heritage of Leviticus*. Jewish and Christian Perspective Series 2. Leiden: Brill.

Rendtorff, R., and R. A. Kugler, eds. 2003. *The Book of Leviticus: Composition and Reception*. VTSup 93. Leiden: Brill.

Rooker, M. F. 2000. *Leviticus*. NAC 3A. Nashville: Broadman & Holman.

Ross, A. P. 2002. *Holiness to the Lord. A Guide to the Exposition of Leviticus*. Grand Rapids: Baker.

Sawyer, J. F. A., ed. 1996. *Reading Leviticus: A Conversation with Mary Douglas*. JSOTSup 227. Sheffield: Sheffield Academic Press.

Sherwood, S. K. 2002. *Leviticus, Numbers, Deuteronomy*. Berit Olam. Collegeville, Minn.: Liturgical Press. Pp. 1–94.

Smith, C. R. 1996. "The Literary Structure of Leviticus." *JSOT* 69:17–32.

Tidball, D. 1996. *Discovering Leviticus*. Leicester: Crossway.

Waltke, B. K. 1975. "Leviticus." *ZPEB* 3:913–20.

Walton, John H. 2001. "Equilibrium and the Sacred Compass: The Structure of Leviticus." *BBR* 11:293–304.

Warning, W. 1999. *Literary Artistry in Leviticus*. BIS 35. Leiden: Brill.

Wenham, G. 1979. *The Book of Leviticus*. NICOT. Grand Rapids: Eerdmans.

Wevers, J. W. 1986. *Text History of the Greek Leviticus*. MSU 19. Göttingen: Vandenhoeck & Ruprecht.

Wright, D. P. 1999. "Holiness in Leviticus and Beyond: Differing Perspectives." *Int* 53:351–64.

Leviticus 1–7

Abba, R. 1977. "The Origin and Significance of Hebrew Sacrifice." *BTB* 7:123–38.

Anderson, G. A. 1987. *Sacrifices and Offerings in Ancient Israel: Studies in Their Social and Political Importance*. HSM 41. Atlanta: Scholars Press.

Baker, D. W. 1979. "Division Markers and the Structure of Leviticus 1–7." In *Studia Biblica 1978*. Ed. E. A. Livingstone. 3 vols. JSOTSup 11. Sheffield: JSOT Press. Vol. 1, pp. 9–15.

———. 1987. "Leviticus 1–7 and the Punic Tariffs: A Form Critical Comparison." *ZAW* 99:188–97.

Brichto, H. C. 1976. "On Slaughter and Sacrifice, Blood and Atonement." *HUCA* 47:19–56.

Collins, J. J. 1977. "The Meaning of Sacrifice: A Contrast of Methods." *BRes* 22:19–37.

Davies, D. 1977. "An Interpretation of Sacrifice in Leviticus." *ZAW* 89:387–98. Repr., in *Anthropological Approaches to the Old Testament*. Ed. B. Lang. IRT 8. Philadelphia: Fortress. Pp. 151–62.

Eichrodt, W. 1961–1967. *Theology of the Old Testament*. Trans. J. Baker. 2 vols. OTL. Philadelphia: Westminster. Vol. 1, pp. 141–72.

Freeman, H. E. 1963. "The Problem of the Efficacy of the Old Testament Sacrifices." *Grace Journal* 3:21–28.

Geisler, N. 1977. *A Popular Survey of the Old Testament*. Grand Rapids: Baker.

Goodsir, R. 1979. "Animal Sacrifices—Delusion or Deliverance?" In *Studia Biblica 1978*. Ed. E. A. Livingstone. 3 vols. JSOTSup 11. Sheffield: JSOT Press. Vol. 1, pp. 157–60.

Gray, G. B. 1970 [1925]. *Sacrifice in the Old Testament: Its Theory and Practice*. Repr., New York: Ktav.

Jensen, P. P. 1995. "The Levitical Sacrificial System." In *Sacrifice in the Bible*. Ed. R. T. Beckwith and M. J. Selman. Grand Rapids: Baker. Pp. 25–40.

Kaufmann, Y. 1960. *The Religion of Israel*. Trans. M. Greenberg. Chicago: University of Chicago Press.

Kiuchi, N. 1987. *The Purification Offering in the Priestly Literature: Its Meaning and Function*. JSOTSup 56. Sheffield: JSOT Press.

Leach, E. 1985. "The Logic of Sacrifice." In *Anthropological Approaches to the Old Testament*. Ed. B. Lang. IRT 8. Philadelphia: Fortress. Pp. 136–50.

Levine, B. 1974. *In the Presence of the Lord: A Study of Cult and Some Cultic Terms in Ancient Israel*. SJLA 5. Leiden: Brill.

Marx, A. 2003. "The Theology of Sacrifice according to Leviticus 1–7." In *The Book of Leviticus: Composition and Reception*. Ed. R. Rendtorff and R. A. Kugler. VTSup 93. Leiden: Brill. Pp. 103–20.

McCarthy, D. J. 1969. "The Symbolism of Blood and Sacrifice." *JBL* 88:166–76.

———. 1973. "Further Notes on the Symbolism of Blood and Sacrifice." *JBL* 92:205–10.

Milgrom, J. 1967–1968. "The Cultic *ŠᵉGĀGĀ* and Its Influence in Psalms and Job." *JQR* 58:115–25.

———. 1971a. "A Prolegomenon to Leviticus 17:11." *JBL* 90:149–56.

———. 1971b. "Kipper." *EncJud* 10:1039–44.

———. 1971c. "Sin Offering and Purification Offering." *VT* 21:237–39.

———. 1972. "The Alleged Wave-Offering in Israel and in the Ancient Near East." *IEJ* 22:33–38.

———. 1975a. "The Priestly Doctrine of Repentance." *RB* 82:186–205.

———. 1975b. "The Compass of Biblical Sancta." *JQR* 65:205–16.

———. 1976a. "Two Kinds of *Hatta'ṭ.*" *VT* 26:333–37.

———. 1976b. *Cult and Conscience: The ASHAM and the Priestly Doctrine of Repentance.* SJLA 18. Leiden: Brill.

———. 1976c. "Atonement in the OT." *IDBSup* 78–82.

———. 1976d. "Sacrifices and Offerings, OT." *IDBSup* 763–71.

———. 1990. "The *Modus operandi* of the *hatta'ṭ:* A Rejoinder." *JBL* 109:111–13.

———. 1991. "The *hatta'ṭ:* A Rite of Passage?" *RB* 98:120–24.

———. 1993. "On the Purification Offering in the Temple Scroll." *Revue de Qumran* 16:99–101.

———. 1996. "Further on the Expiatory Sacrifices." *JBL* 115:511–14.

Miller, P. D., Jr. 2000. *The Religion of Ancient Israel.* Louisville: Westminster John Knox. Pp. 106–30.

Rad, G. von. 1962. *Old Testament Theology.* Trans. D. M. G. Stalker. 2 vols. New York: Harper & Row. Vol. 1, pp. 250–62.

Rainey, A. 1970. "The Order of Sacrifices in Old Testament Ritual Texts." *Bib* 51:485–98.

———. 1971. "Sacrifice." *EncJud* 14:599–607.

———. 1975. "Sacrifice and Offerings." *ZPEB* 5:194–211.

Schenker, A. 1997. "Once Again, the Expiatory Sacrifices." *JBL* 116:697–99.

Snaith, N. H. 1957. "Sacrifices in the Old Testament." *VT* 308–17.

———. 1963. "Wave Offering." *ExpT* 74:127.

———. 1965. "Sin-Offering or Guilt-Offering?" *VT* 15:73–80.

———. 1970. "The Sprinkling of Blood." *ExpT* 82:23–24.

Vaux, R. de. 1964. *Studies in Old Testament Sacrifice.* Cardiff: University of Wales Press.

———. 1965. *Ancient Israel.* Trans. J. McHugh. 2 vols. New York: McGraw-Hill. Vol. 2, pp. 415–56.

Watts, J. W. 2003. "The Rhetoric of Ritual Instruction in Leviticus 1–7." In *The Book of Leviticus: Composition and Reception.* Ed. R. Rendtorff and R. A. Kugler. VTSup 93. Leiden: Brill. Pp. 79–100.

Wenham, G. J. 1995. "The Theology of the Old Testament Sacrifice." In *Sacrifice in the Bible.* Ed. R. T. Beckwith and M. J. Selman. Grand Rapids: Baker. Pp. 75–87.

Wright, D. P. 1986. "The Gesture of Hand Placement in the Hebrew Bible and in the Hittite Literature." *JAOS* 106:433–46.

Zimmerli, W. 1977. *Old Testament Theology in Outline.* Trans. D. E. Green. Atlanta: John Knox. Pp. 148–55.

Zohar, N. 1988. "Repentance and Purification: The Significance and Semantics of *ht'ṭ* in the Pentateuch." *JBL* 107:609–18.

12

Priestly Ordination

LEVITICUS 8–10

I have already suggested that Lev. 6:8–7:38 is not only a supplement to the information given in 1:1–6:7, but also specific instructions to the priests concerning their obligations in the sacrificial ceremonies. What is it, however, that qualifies the priest to perform his sacerdotal functions, and where does it all get started?

Ordination of the Priests (8)

Everything in ch. 8 takes place publicly at the "entrance to the tent of meeting" (vv. 3, 4, 33, 35), the large, open courtyard area that leads up to the entrance to the inner tent. As Klingbeil (1995: 64, 79) has noted, at this stage the priests are in a medial, liminal state. They have not yet been ordained and so cannot offer sacrifices, but clearly they are not laity. The means is consecration, involving washing (vv. 5–6), robing (vv. 7–9), anointment (vv. 10–13), and then the offering of sacrifices, specifically the sin, burnt, and peace or ordination offerings, in that order (vv. 14–29). The instructions for this installation ceremony are found in Exodus 29; the ceremony is implemented in Leviticus 8.

There is a literary comparison to the tabernacle sections of Exodus. Exodus 25–31 gives the instructions for the tabernacle, and Exodus 35–40 narrates their implementation. The movement from instruction to implementation in both instances is clear: the tabernacle in Exodus 25–31 and Exodus 35–40, and the priesthood in Exodus 28–29 and Leviticus 8. Similarly, the implementation section climaxes both times with the same phraseology: "he did . . . as the LORD commanded." We have already noted the proliferation of this phrase in Exodus 39–40 especially. To this add Lev. 8:4, 5, 9, 13, 17, 21, 29, 34, 36. To be more precise, in each of these three chapters we read seven times that Moses or somebody did "as the LORD commanded him": Exodus 39 (the priestly garments), vv. 1, 5, 7, 21, 26, 29, 31; Exodus 40 (the setting up of the tabernacle), vv. 19, 21, 23, 25, 27, 29, 32; Leviticus 8 (the ordination of the priests), vv. 4, 9, 13, 17, 21, 29, 36. There is also a contrast in both sections between the right and the wrong way of doing something: how to worship God (Exodus 25–31) and how not to worship God (Exodus 32); how to officiate properly (Leviticus 8–9) and how to officiate improperly (Lev. 10:1–2, 16–20).

The Hebrew words for "consecration" or "ordination" and "ordain" are closely related. The word for "consecration" is millū'îm, "a filling," translated in the Septuagint as "completion" or "perfection." The verb "ordain" is rendered by a Hebrew expression, "to fill the hand," millē' yād.

The ordination offering is discussed in 8:22–29, with the parallel in Exod. 29:19–34. Several things are especially noteworthy. First, not only in this chapter but also in the next two, Moses is the supervisor, and Aaron is the subordinate (see Wenham 1979: 132). Thus Jacob Milgrom (1971: 142; 1976b: 542) comments, "Strikingly, the superiority of prophet over priest is insisted upon by the priestly document."

A second interesting fact is that again there is a more extensive use of the blood than there is in the peace offering of Leviticus 3. The blood of the ram is daubed on the tip of the priest's right ear, the thumb of his right hand, and the large toe of his right foot. Why these parts of the anatomy? Was the priest one who was to be especially sensitive to the Lord, thus able to *hear* God's word? Was the priest indeed the one who needed clean *hands* to enter the presence of God, as the psalmist suggested (Ps. 24:4)? Was the priest the one who, par excellence, *stood* in God's holy place (Ps. 24:3) and must *walk* blamelessly (Ps. 15:2)?

The expression for "ordain" appears in 8:33. The verse may be read, "And you shall not go out from the door of the tent of meeting for seven days, until the day of the filling of the days of your filling, for within seven days he will fill your hand." The same expression for priestly ordination appears in Exod. 28:41; 29:9, 33, 35; 32:29; Lev. 16:32; 21:10; Num. 3:3; Judg. 17:5, 12; 1 Kings 13:33.

To become a priest, then, meant to have one's hand filled. But what can the meaning of such a passage be? Does it refer to a salary that the priest is to receive; is he given the right to a portion of the revenues and offerings brought to the sanctuary, as suggested by de Vaux (1965: 2:346–47) and Cody (1969:153–54)? This inference is made on the basis of cuneiform texts from Mari that deal with the distribution of booty. For example, slaves taken as booty from a conquered city "fill the hand" (*mil qati*) of the conquerors.

Perhaps it is impossible to discover precisely the antecedents of the Hebrew phrase. Could it be that the filled hands of the priest symbolize the fact that his life was to be filled with nothing except holy things? Priesthood is a preoccupation, not a pastime. Like Jesus, the priests must be about their Father's business. It is interesting to speculate on the meaning of Lev. 9:17: "And he presented the cereal offering and filled his hand [*wayĕmāllē' kappô*] from it, and burned it upon the altar" (RSV). Does this mean that he took a fistful (as in Lev. 2:2: "and he shall take from it a handful," *wĕqāmaṣ miššām mĕlō' qumṣô*), or does it mean that he celebrated his first sacrifice?

The Hebrew verb "to fill" is used in nonclerical contexts where the emphasis again is on total consecration to God's work. Moses says of Caleb, "He has wholly followed the LORD" (Deut. 1:36 RSV). The Hebrew reads, literally, "He completely filled [himself] after the Lord." The phrase is used again for Caleb's level of devotion in Num. 32:11–12; Josh. 14:8, 9, 14.

The ordination of the priests is to be a public ceremony (8:3–4). But before either Aaron and his sons are anointed (vv. 10–13) or any sacrifices are offered (vv. 14–35), it is important that Aaron be outfitted in the proper priestly regalia (vv. 5–9). Two of the puzzling pieces are the Urim and Thummim (v. 8). Whatever they are, they are mentioned again in Exod. 28:30; Num. 27:21; Deut. 33:8; 1 Sam. 14:41; 28:6; Ezra 2:63; Neh. 7:65. The consensus is that these were two flat pieces, stones perhaps, that functioned as sacred lots by which the priest could receive guidance from God. The word "Urim" is related to the Hebrew verb meaning "to curse" (thus, a no from God?), and "Thummim" is related to the Hebrew verb meaning "to be perfect, blameless" (thus, a yes from God?).

Some scholars (e.g., Kaufmann 1960: 89) have contended that the Urim and Thummim are unique to Israel and Old Testament practice. Others (e.g., Lipinski 1970: 496) have suggested an approximate counterpart in pagan religions. Whether we are dealing here with adoption, adaption, or innovation, Walther Eichrodt (1961–1967: 1:114) has a keen insight:

It is a significant indication of the spirit of the Yahweh religion that it should never have absorbed into its system any but this, the simplest technical device for inquiring the will of God. Because of this the control of the priest over the divine decisions, which is bound up with the development of a science of divination incomprehensible to the layman, was prevented for all time.

Throughout ch. 8 Moses is the active one. Aaron and his sons are completely passive. Aaron and his sons are brought forward, washed, robed, anointed, have three different sacrifices offered on their behalf by Moses, are anointed again, and finally are given some concluding instructions by Moses. That is to say, before Aaron and his sons can do anything, something must be done to/for them. Before God can minister through them, God must minister to them.

The Commencement of Priestly Ministry (9)

Chapter 8 has described the seven-day-long consecration and ordination of Aaron and his sons. With this behind him, Aaron is ready for the first offering on behalf of the congregation. Aaron's ministry on behalf of others begins "on the eighth day" (v. 1), much as circumcision takes place on the eighth day, after seven days of life outside the womb. The expression "seven days" occurs eighty-five times in the Old Testament, seventy of which occur in contexts of some aspect of worship, and in many of these the reference is to a time of restoration, or to a time of separation and transition, what today we would call a rite of passage (see Klingbeil 1997: 509). But that will have to wait until the second half of ch. 9. Verses 1–14 are for Aaron himself. Only in vv. 15–21 does he become celebrant.

Leviticus 9 seems to stress that the priest's ministry to others is useless unless his own relationship to God is above reproach. The chapter is also reminding the priest that although he is the occupant of a holy office and holds holy orders, he is still a flawed human being, one who needs constantly to be purified.

That there has been a sin and burnt offering at Aaron's consecration is good but insufficient (8:14–21). The whole process must be repeated before the recently ordained clergyman can become mediator. Again, he must offer the sin offering for himself (9:8–11), then the burnt offering (9:12–14).

Perhaps to make the situation even more dramatic, Moses tells Aaron to take a *calf* for his sin offering, and a *ram* for his burnt offering (9:2, 8). A calf? The last calf that Aaron had seen was the golden calf he fashioned at the foot of Mount Sinai (Exodus 32). And a ram? Was this not the substitute that God supplied for Abraham in place of Isaac (Gen. 22:13)? The calf, a reminder of recent disobedience, and the ram, a reminder of distant obedience!

Only after Aaron's own needs are met is he able to become to the congregation all that he is meant to be. He oversees the presentation to God of four congregational sacrificial offerings: sin, burnt, cereal, and peace (9:15–21). The chapter observes at least three times that the offering of sacrifices brings the presence of God near. Note the repetition of "for today the LORD will appear to you" or "and the glory of the LORD will appear to you" in vv. 4, 6, 23 (RSV). The first two are promises ("will appear"), while the last one is fulfillment ("appeared").

The order of events, then, in ch. 9 is a mandate from Moses; priestly sacrifices; congregational sacrifices; the appearance of the glory of God; worship in praise and prostration—"and when all the people saw it, they shouted and fell on their faces" (v. 24 NRSV). The glory of God, manifested in all its awe, makes a congregation fall prostrate in worship. The same happens in the life of an individual. Witness Ezekiel (Ezek. 1:28; 3:23), Daniel (Dan. 8:17), Paul (Acts 9:4), and John (Rev. 1:17).

Correct and Incorrect Procedures (10)

Chapter 9 ended with an emphasis on worship. What a jolt it is, then, to move into ch. 10, whose emphasis, at least at the beginning, is divine judgment. Two of Aaron's sons, Nadab and Abihu, offered "strange fire" to the Lord, and for this trespass they paid with their lives. To lose two sons, both of whom are ordained clergy, is blow enough. In addition, Aaron and his two surviving sons must abstain from any public demonstration of grief or mourning over these deceased relatives (10:6).

What precisely was the nature of the sin, a sin so enormous as to merit death? A specific answer to that question escapes us. From the times of the rabbinical writings to the present numerous suggestions have been offered. *Leviticus Rabbah*, a homiletical commentary written in the fifth century A.D. in Palestine, tries to answer the question. Were Nadab and Abihu drunk? Did they enter the sanctuary without washing their hands? Were they schemers and opportunists who said, "When will those two old men [Moses and Aaron] die, so that we can exercise control over the community?"

Perhaps the error was in some incorrect ritual procedure. This is the view adopted by much of modern scholarship. Thus, J. C. H. Laughlin (1976: 561) and M. Haran (1978: 183, 232) suggest that the sin was making incense with fire taken from a source other than the fire on the altar. J. Milgrom (1991a: 598) renders the phrase as "unauthorized coals," and he observes, "This can only mean that instead of deriving from the outer altar . . . the coals came from a source that was 'profane' . . . or 'outside' . . . such as an oven."

G. Robinson (1978: 308–9) goes a step further. On the basis of passages in Scripture that prohibit kindling a fire on the Sabbath (Exod. 35:2–3; Num. 15:32–36), a sin meriting the death penalty, and passages that refer to the use of fire in the worship of false gods (e.g., Jer. 44:15–23), he concludes, "This may suggest that the crime in question has to do with apostasy, with idolatrous worship."

The point of the narrative is that the priest follows orders. Disobedience and departure from the divinely revealed way have catastrophic repercussions. After all the instances in ch. 8 of Moses doing what the Lord commanded, it is boldly contrastive to read about two of Aaron's sons doing something that the Lord had not commanded. Doing something that the Lord "did not command" is, outside of Leviticus 10, unique to Jeremiah (see Beal and Linafelt 1995: 25). God never commanded anybody to sacrifice his or her children (Jer. 7:31; 19:5; 32:35), and he never commanded adultery or dishonesty (Jer. 29:33).

But not all trouble is past. Soon Moses finds himself in an altercation with Aaron over his two surviving sons, Eleazar and Ithamar (Lev. 10:16–20). Between these two scenes is the note that Aaron is to *teach* the people of Israel all the statutes of the Lord (v. 11). The irony is hard to miss: he is failing with his own family and is unable to teach them!

The two sons stumble over the sin offering brought to them by the people. In such a case the sacrifice is to be eaten by the priests (6:26, 29). This they refused to do (10:17). But why should such an omission lead to a heated argument? I believe that Milgrom (1976a: 337) has correctly assessed the point:

> When the P code prescribed that every *ḥaṭṭāʾt* except that brought for severe sins should be eaten by the priests, it took a giant step towards eviscerating the magical and demonic elements from Israelite ritual. For it must be assumed in keeping with the evidence from the ancient Near East, that ritual detergents were always destroyed after they were used lest their potent remains be exploited for purposes of black magic. By requiring that the *ḥaṭṭāʾt* be eaten, Israel gave birth to a new and radical idea: the sanctuary is purged not by any inherent power of the ritual but only by the will of God. Thus, when Aaron and his sons burned an ordinary *ḥaṭṭāʾt* instead of eating it, they engendered the suspicion that they were afraid to eat it, possibly opening the flood-gates to a reincursion of magical practices and beliefs.

Nadab and Abihu are incinerated for their infraction. Their two brothers, Eleazar and Ithamar, are not. Even though Moses is "angry" over the sin of omission of the two remaining sons, he is "satisfied" at the explanation that Aaron provides. Although it is difficult to determine the thrust of Aaron's explanation to Moses (the death of his two other sons and their corpses polluted the sanctuary and, by extension, the sacrifice?), his words "but such things as this have happened to me" (v. 19) suggest that the sons' motive for disregarding ritual procedure was not defiance (as with Nadab and Abihu); rather, it was the circumstance of the moment—the loss of two siblings. Although public grieving is outlawed for the priest, the private sobbing of bereavement is healthy, necessary, and never out of line. That Moses accepts this explanation means that not every deviation is a black-and-white one that can be resolved routinely by legalistic mechanisms.

Leviticus 8–10

Anderson, G. A., and S. M. Olyan, eds. 1991. *Priesthood and Cult in Ancient Israel.* JSOTSup 125. Sheffield: JSOT Press.

Beal, T. K., and T. Linafelt. 1995. "Sifting for Cinders: Strange Fire in Leviticus 10:1–5." *Semeia* 69–70:19–32.

Bibb, B. D. 2001. "Nadab and Abihu Attempt to Fill a Gap: Law and Narrative in Leviticus 10:1–7." *JSOT* 96:83–99.

Cody, A. 1969. *A History of Old Testament Priesthood.* AnBib 35. Rome: Pontifical Biblical Institute.

Eichrodt, W. 1961–1967. *Theology of the Old Testament.* Trans. J. Baker. 2 vols. OTL. Philadelphia: Westminster.

Fleming, D. 1998. "The Biblical Tradition of Anointing Priests." *JBL* 117:401–14.

Greenberg, M. 1998. "The True Sin of Nadab and Abihu." *Jewish Bible Quarterly* 26:263–67.

Haran, M. 1971. "Priests and Priesthood." *EncJud* 13:1069–86.

———. 1978. *Temples and Temple Service in Ancient Israel.* Oxford: Clarendon.

Houston, W. 2000. "Tragedy in the Courts of the Lord: A Socio-Literary Reading of the Death of Nadab and Abihu." *JSOT* 90:31–39.

Kaufmann, Y. 1960. *The Religion of Israel.* Trans. M. Greenberg. Chicago: University of Chicago Press.

Klingbeil, G. A. 1995. "Ritual Space in the Ordination Ritual of Leviticus 8." *JNSL* 21 (1):59–82.

———. 1996. "The Syntactic Structure of the Ritual of Ordination (Leviticus 8)." *Bib* 77:509–16.

———. 1997. "Ritual Time in Leviticus 8 with Special Reference to the Seven Day Period in the Old Testament." *ZAW* 109:500–513.

Laughlin, J. C. H. 1976. "The 'Strange Fire' of Nadab and Abihu." *JBL* 95:559–65.

Leithart, P. J. 1999. "Attendants of Yahweh's House: Priesthood in the Old Testament." *JSOT* 85:3–24.

Levine, B. 1993. "Silence, Sound, and the Phenomenology of Mourning in Biblical Israel." *JANES* 22:89–106.

Lipinski, E. 1970. "Urim and Thumim." *VT* 20:495–96.

Milgrom, J. 1971. "Leviticus." *EncJud* 11:138–47.

———. 1976a. "Two Kinds of *haṭṭaʾt*." *VT* 26:333–37.

———. 1976b. "Leviticus." *IDBSup* 541–45.

———. 1991a. *Leviticus 1–16*. AB 3. New York: Doubleday.

———. 1991b. "The Consecration of the Priests: A Literary Comparison of Leviticus 8 and Exodus 29." In *Ernten, was man sät: Festschrift für Klaus Koch zu seinem 65. Geburtstag*. Ed. D. R. Daniels, U. Glessmer, and M. Rösel. Neukirchen-Vluyn: Neukirchener Verlag. Pp. 273–86.

Moore, M. S. 1996. "Role Pre-emption in the Israelite Priesthood." *VT* 46:316–29.

Nelson, R. 1993. *Raising Up a Faithful Priest: Community and Priesthood in Biblical Theology*. Louisville: Westminster John Knox.

Robinson, G. 1978. "The Prohibition of Strange Fire in Ancient Israel." *VT* 28:301–17.

Sabourin, L. 1973. *Priesthood. A Comparative Study*. Studies in the History of Religion 25. Leiden: Brill.

Segal, P. 1989. "The Divine Verdict of Leviticus x 3." *VT* 39:91–95.

Vaux, R. de. 1965. *Ancient Israel*. Trans. J. McHugh. 2 vols. New York: McGraw Hill. Vol. 2, pp. 345–57.

Wenham, G. 1979. *The Book of Leviticus*. NICOT. Grand Rapids: Eerdmans.

13

Clean and Unclean

LEVITICUS 11–15

In the midst of ch. 10 we were informed that one of the functions of the priest is "to *distinguish* between the holy and the common, and between the unclean and the clean; and . . . to *teach* . . . all the statutes which the LORD has spoken" (10:10–11 RSV). The priest, then, is both celebrant and educator, both liturgist and instructor.

Even here the subordinate role of Aaron to Moses is clear. The distinctions between holy and common and clean and unclean that follow in these three chapters are not Aaron's ideas. Nor were the distinctions hammered out in committee by the priestly triumvirate of Aaron, Eleazar, and Ithamar. They are to teach what the Lord has spoken to Moses (10:11). The chapter beginnings are either "the LORD said to Moses and Aaron" (11 and 13) or "the LORD said to Moses" (12 and 14). Moses may be addressed alone. Aaron is spoken to only with Moses.

Four key Hebrew words appear in Lev. 10:10 that will dominate in these five chapters: (1) "holy" (*qōdeš*); (2) "common" (*ḥōl*); (3) "unclean/impure" (*ṭāmēʾ*); and (4) "clean/pure" (*ṭāhôr*), especially the latter two. Two speak of the desirable (holy and clean/pure), two of the undesirable (common and unclean). "Holy" and "clean/pure," the two positive words, are not exactly synonyms, any more than "common" and "unclean/

259

impure" are. We can know that the first two are not interchangeable because although the Bible calls God "holy" (*qōdeš*), it never calls him "pure" (*ṭāhôr*). There are verses in which God says, "Be holy, for I, the LORD your God, am holy." There is no verse that says, "Be pure, for I, the LORD your God, am pure." To be sure, nothing or nobody is holy that is not also clean and pure. Nothing or nobody can be holy and impure simultaneously. By contrast, something or somebody that is "common" can be either pure or impure.

It is debatable whether the better opposite of "holy" is "common" or "unclean." Some argue for "common" as the better antonym (and see Lev. 10:10), while others argue for "unclean/impure." Miller (2000: 150) has found an appealing middle ground: "while holiness had its *opposite* in the common or profane (*ḥol*), it encountered its *opposition* in the presence of impurity (*ṭame˒*)."

One needs to keep in mind that impurity is not synonymous with sinfulness, although sinfulness can produce impurity. This distinction can be observed by contrasting the use of the verb *kāpar* ("make atonement for") in the sacrificial section (chs. 1–7) and in the purity-impurity section (chs. 11–15), and especially by what other phrase follows it. In the sacrificial section, where the phrase "the priest shall make atonement for them/him" occurs, it is always followed by the phrase "and they/he shall be forgiven" (4:20, 26, 31, 35; 5:6, 10, 13, 16, 18, 26 with the exception of 5:6). By contrast, in the purity-impurity section, where the phrase "the priest shall make atonement for her/him/it" occurs (12:7, 8; 14:18, 19, 20, 21, 29, 31, 53; 15:30), when it is followed immediately by another verb, the verb is "be clean" (12:7, 8; 14:20, 53). Those with sin need forgiveness (always in the passive voice); those with impurity who, along with their clergy, engage in appropriate ritual procedures are declared clean (always in the active voice; they are not said to be "cleansed").

The overwhelming number of situations or actions that engender impurity are perfectly natural and normal ones: eating, birth of a child, ailments and infections, dying and death, sexual intimacy with one's spouse, bodily discharges. This much larger group Wright (1992: 730) calls "permitted" impurities, to be distinguished from the "prohibited" impurities that arise, according to Wright (1992: 733), from "mismanagement of permitted impurities or other moral breaches." In the case of the permitted impurities the effects are minimal, the duration short-lived ("until evening"), and bathing and/or laundering one's clothes suffice. Miller (2000: 271–72) prefers the term "tolerated" impurities to "permitted" impurities because "any impurity, while allowed, was not necessarily encouraged and was to be generated as infrequently as possible, because any impurity threatened the holy and everything that pertained to it."

Clean and Unclean Animals (11)

The entire eleventh chapter is consumed with one issue: the Israelites' diet—what they may and may not eat. Five areas are examined in table 9.

It is immediately clear that nowhere are any fruits or vegetables listed as unacceptable food—only certain types of meat. God's first dietary directive to humankind supplies the reason: "Behold, I have given you every plant yielding seed which is upon the face of all the earth, and every tree with seed in its fruit; you shall have them for food" (Gen. 1:29 RSV). The same holds true for creatures on the land and of the air (Gen. 1:30).

Table 9

Reference	Reference	Reference	Reference	Reference
1–8 land animals	9–12 fish	13–23 birds and winged insects	24–40 uncleanness transmitted by contact with dead or unclean animals	41–44 swarming things
1–3 permitted	9 permitted	13–19 outlawed birds	24–28 to a person via nonedible land animals	41–44 outlawed
4–8 outlawed	10–12 outlawed	20, 23 outlawed winged insects	29–38 to a nonhuman entity via "swarming things"	
			39–40 to a person via edible land animals	
				45–47 conclusion
				45 rationale for abstinence
				46–47 summarizing statement

Only after the flood does humankind change from herbivorous to carnivorous (see Gen. 9:3–5). Only after the serpent is cursed does an apron of fig leaves (Gen. 3:7) give way to a covering of skins (Gen. 3:21).

Several suggestions have been made to justify the list of clean and unclean animals, suggestions that, by and large, are not in the biblical text itself. At least four rationales have been offered repeatedly. One is the ethical explanation. This approach is reflected in a quotation from Aristeas, a first-century B.C. Egyptian Jew: "The dietary laws are ethical, since abstention from the consumption of blood tames man's instinct for violence by instilling in him a horror of bloodshed." It is interesting to observe that Noah, at God's command, took aboard the ark both clean and unclean animals (Gen. 7:2). The unclean animals are also objects of God's mercy.

A second is the aesthetic. Animals whose very appearance is repulsive are unlikely to find themselves on the dinner table.

A third reason is the theological. Animals associated with pagan religions were taboo for Israel, just as were, for example, pagan mourning customs.

Perhaps the most frequently cited rationale is the hygienic. As more likely carriers of disease, some animals are automatically eliminated. Maimonides, the twelfth-century Jewish philosopher and theologian, illustrates this emphasis: "These ordinances seek to train us in the mastery of our appetite. . . . All the food which the Torah has forbidden us to eat have some bad and damaging effect on the body" (*Guide to the Perplexed* 3:48).

A novel suggestion has been put forward by anthropologist Mary Douglas. She first appeals to the morphological criteria listed in Leviticus 11 itself. Mammals that part the hoof and chew the cud are permitted. Aquatic creatures must have fins and scales. Says Douglas (1975: 266), "It [the dietary code] rejects creatures which are anomalous, whether in living between two spheres, or having defining features of members of another sphere, or lacking defining features." The clean species must have all the necessary criteria of its class (Douglas 1975: 284). It is not difficult to project the criteria of anomaly from the animal to the human. If God rejects the animal that lacks the crucial and distinguishing characteristics of its species, then all the more will he reject a person who tries to live in two worlds, the anomalous believer.

In more recent writings Douglas (1993; 1999) has focused on the forbidden "swarming/creeping/crawling" creatures of Leviticus 11 (vv. 20, 21, 23, 31–33, 41, 42, 43, 44, 46). Every one of these verses, except v. 21, forbids the ingestion of these creatures, whether they live on the land or in the sea or fly in the air. However, in Genesis 1 these same creeping/swarming creatures are created by God and are called "good" (Gen. 1:24–25). They too perish in the flood (Gen. 7:21), but they are part of God's postdiluvian re-creation process (Gen. 8:17). For Douglas (1993: 18), such nonpredatory, vulnerable creatures represent "victims of predation"—that is, the poor and oppressed and marginal in society. Not eating such creatures is a reminder to show justice and compassion to those who do not dwell in the cultural mainstream. Leaving aside this allegorical explanation, one wonders if there might be another explanation for placing crawling creatures off-limits to human consumption: a kind of guilt by association.

Each of these forbidden-for-eating creatures "moves on its belly [*gāḥôn*]" (Lev. 11:42), just as the serpent was condemned by God to "crawl on [its] belly [*gāḥôn*]" all the days of its life for its part in seducing humankind into disobedience and away from God (Gen. 3:14).

It is no accident that every time food regulations appear in the Pentateuch, the word "holy" is not far away. Exodus 22:31 reads, "You are to be my holy people. So do not eat the meat of an animal torn by wild beasts; throw it to the dogs" (NIV; see also Lev. 20:25–26; Deut. 14:21). The best example is in the chapter that we are examining, especially 11:44: "consecrate yourselves . . . be holy . . . I am holy" (NIV). Jacob Milgrom (1963: 291–92) rightly says, "Relatively few individual statutes of the Bible are coupled with the demand for holiness. And none of these have the demand with the same staccato emphasis and repetition as do the food prohibitions."

That this was no trivial matter to the Jew is evidenced by Ezekiel's personal testimony (Ezek. 4:14). Daniel, although invited to sit at a king's table and eat a meal suitable for royalty, chose to follow the dietary restrictions (Dan. 1:8). Peter, now a follower of Jesus and filled with the Holy Spirit at Pentecost, never was able to extricate himself from the prohibitions of Leviticus 11 (Acts 10:14). Peter's statement "I have never eaten anything impure or unclean" (Acts 10:14 NIV) is his fourth "never" statement addressed to Jesus, and on each occasion Jesus rebukes him in the next verse. Compare Peter saying, "This shall never happen to you" (Matt. 16:22 NIV), "Even if all fall away on account of you, I never will" (Matt. 26:33 NIV), and "You shall never wash my feet" (John 13:8 NIV) with his "never" statement in Acts 10.

It is crucial to observe that holiness is reflected in one's life by conduct at the dinner table. One does not honor God by bringing the unclean into God's temple, and one does not honor God by taking the unclean into another temple, one's body (1 Cor. 3:16; 6:19–20). It is a holiness put into practice among family members and behind closed doors. It is a holiness faithfully lived out even when no one is watching.

Uncleanness from Childbirth (12)

This chapter deals with the procedures mandated for a mother after the delivery of a child. First, she must remain in seclusion for a week (v. 2); after the child's circumcision she remains in seclusion for another month (v. 4). Her first trip out of the home is to the tent of meeting (v. 6). Feminists who decry the patriarchal imbalance of much of the Old Testament cite the fact that in the case of the birth of a girl, the mother's length of seclusion is doubled (one week to two weeks, thirty-three days to sixty-six days). It is not clear why a daughter's birth doubles the purification period of the new mother. It does not seem to be an affront against anything female. More than likely the doubling represents a concern to safeguard the new daughter and her potential fertility, given the fact that quite likely she will one day be a new mother herself.

It is only after, not before or during, these forty to eighty days of purification have passed that the mother brings a burnt offering and a sin offering to the Lord. Does the bringing of such offerings imply that sex is sinful, and that procreation is a trespass requiring expiation? Hardly. If that were so, then Leviticus 12 would refute everything else Scripture teaches on this subject.

We note that in connection with both male and female bodily discharges both the burnt and sin offering are required (Lev. 15:13–15, 29–30). Defilement during a Nazirite vow requires these two sacrifices also (Num. 6:10–11). It would be rather ridiculous and far-fetched to link any of these occasions with sin in the life of the person involved. It is much more correct to describe these offerings as purification rituals. It is the postnatal flow of blood that is the cause of the uncleanness.

To be sure, much of this type of ritual is unknown in a modern Christian church or in the maternity section of a hospital. But Dennis Kinlaw (1969: 1:355) correctly observes, "In a society like ours where much of the danger of childbirth has been removed by modern medicine and the mystery removed by biological knowledge, who is to say that some customs are not needed to restore the element of gracious mystery and sacredness to such events?"

We know both from antiquity and from our own times that an approaching birth, the moment of birth, and the days immediately after birth are fraught with both anticipation and anxiety, a hope that all will go well for both the newborn and the new mother. By declaring the new mother impure (in more modern medical terms read "susceptible"), Leviticus seeks to protect and shelter both mother and infant from any harm that might come to either one (see Levine 1989: 249).

In contrast to ritual (i.e., ceremonial isolation as a means of protecting two vulnerable people from harm), pagan religion advocates the use of spells and incantations to ward off demonic spirits. One thinks of, for example, the amulet from Arslan Tash in northern Syria (seventh century B.C.) with this Phoenician text on it: "Incantations against the Flyers [winged demons?], the goddesses, (against) Sasm son of Padrishisha, the god, and against the Strangler of the Lamb. The house I enter, you shall not enter. The court I tread you shall not tread. . . . Against the Flyers: From the dark chamber pass away! At once! At once, O night demons . . ." (translation by P. Kyle McCarter in *The Context of Scripture: Monumental Inscriptions from the Biblical World* [ed. W. W. Hallo and K. Lawson Younger Jr.; 3 vols.; Leiden: Brill, 1997–2002], 2:222–23).

Leprosy (13–14)

Two full chapters of Leviticus are devoted to a discussion of leprosy, its diagnosis (ch. 13) and the cleansing of the leper (ch. 14). We can safely assume that the word "leprosy" is a generic term that covers a number of skin diseases, most of which would be noncontagious (for studies of the Hebrew word for "leprosy" see Harrison 1962; Hulse 1975; Sawyer 1976; Wilkinson 1977; 1978). That the disease in question can affect both clothing and buildings seems to imply a range of meanings that would cover even rot, fungus, and mildew.

Table 10 outlines the areas covered in this section of Leviticus.

Table 10

Reference	Reference
13:1–59 diagnosis	14:1–57 cleansing and further diagnosis
1–28, 38–39 skin	1–32 ritual for rehabilitation
24–37 hair	33–53 diagnosis of leprosy in houses
40–44 scalp	
45–46 quarantine	
47–59 deteriorating garments	
	54–57 summarizing statement

Quite predictably, the priestly sections of Scripture address themselves to the issue of purity—that is, cleanness and uncleanness, purity and impurity. The Hebrew word for "clean" or "pure" occurs more than two hundred times in the Old Testament. Ninety-three of these occurrences (about 43 percent of the total) are in Leviticus and Numbers. The word for "unclean" or "impure" appears more than 280 times in the Old Testament. Of these occurrences, 182 (about 64 percent of the total) are in Leviticus and Numbers (see the charts in Neusner 1973: 26).

There is a threefold ritual in which the leper must be involved in order to remove the "uncleanness" and be reintroduced into the community. There is a ceremony for the first day (14:2–8). It is important to observe that the purpose of this ritual is not to cleanse the disease, but rather to witness to the fact that the disease is already healed. This is the plain intent in 14:3: "if the leprous disease is healed" (RSV). Thus the ritual is symbolic and religious, not therapeutic. Nor does the priest ever function as healer or physician. If anything, he is an ecclesiastical public health official (Milgrom 1971a: 35).

There are also a second ceremony for the seventh day (14:9) and a third ceremony for the eighth day (14:10–32), with the focus here on the offering of the appropriate sacrifices. As in Leviticus 1–7, revisions occur in the sacrificial requirements if the leper is poor.

It would be wide of the mark to say that the Old Testament considers leprous diseases to be the result of sin (although stories such as the one about Miriam in Numbers 12 and King Uzziah in 2 Chron. 27:16–21 do show leprosy to be a manifestation of divine judgment). As in the case of a woman after the birth of her child, a period of absence from the community is mandated for those with blemishes on their bodies. The offering of sacrifices allows readmittance into community activities. Ostracism is replaced by fellowship.

It is extremely difficult, if not impossible, to make the case that leprosy is a "type" of sin in the Bible. Leviticus is saying that leprosy is like sin but is not itself sin or a sign of sin. It is like sin in that it bars people from cultic fellowship with God. Of course, leprosy, like sin, is insidious, progressive, pervasive, benumbing, and loathsome. Why allegorists (as early as *Leviticus Rabbah,* a rabbinic and homiletical commentary on Leviticus redacted sometime in the fifth century A.D. in Israel but containing much earlier material) have made the analogy appears obvious. Additionally, passages such as Num. 12:9–11 and 2 Chron. 26:19 teach that God might afflict someone with leprosy as a punishment for sin. And in Exod. 15:26 God says to his people, "If you pay attention to his commands and keep all his decrees, I will not bring on you any of the diseases I brought on the Egyptians" (NIV), which clearly shows that God is capable of sending diseases as a judgment against sin.

Not a few of Jesus' miracles involved lepers. Interestingly, the blind are healed, the crippled are healed, but the lepers are "cleansed" (*katharizō*). In other contexts this same Greek verb takes on a very distinct moral nuance: Acts 15:9; 2 Cor. 7:2; Eph. 5:26; James 4:8; 1 John 1:7, 9.

Uncleanness and Bodily Discharges (15)

Specifically, emissions from the genital area of the body are the concern in this section of Leviticus.

1. abnormal emissions from men (15:1–15)
2. normal emissions from men (15:16–18)
3. normal emissions from women (15:19–24)
4. abnormal emissions from women (15:25–33)

Note that for the second and the third emissions bathing is sufficient to remove the impurity (15:18, 21). In the case of the first and the fourth emissions the offering of sacrifices is required (15:14–15, 29–30), with a difference in praxis for men and women. A man is to "take" his sacrificial animals and "come before the LORD to the entrance to the Tent of Meeting and give them to the priest" (v. 14 NIV). A woman is to "take" her sacrificial animals and "bring them to the priest at the entrance to the Tent of Meeting" (v. 29 NIV). Unlike a man, a woman is not said to "come before the LORD." The failure to mention that the woman too comes "before the LORD" indicates either that it is assumed, having already been stated in the case of a male, or that it reflects the fact that women could not enter the divine presence to the degree that men could (Wegner 2003).

A more precise way of outlining the chapter is as follows:

A introduction (vv. 1–2a)
  B abnormal emissions of men (vv. 2b–15)
    C normal emissions of men (vv. 16–17)
      D sexual intercourse (v. 18)
    C′ normal emissions of women (vv. 19–24)
  B′ abnormal emissions of women (vv. 25–30)
A′ summary (vv. 31–33)

This way of discerning the chapter's structure highlights v. 18 as the central verse in the chapter, the one that deals with sexual intimacy between a married couple, and the one verse in the chapter that deals simultaneously with male and female uncleanness. Even the most intimate and private moment between a man and a woman is impacted by one's religious beliefs. What I believe about my faith determines to a degree how I behave sexually with my spouse. And in the case of Leviticus 15, because sexual congress produces impurity in both partners, there would be a veto on sex before the Sabbath, especially if one is headed for the sanctuary. As Levine (1989: 92, 96) has pointed out, such abstinence from sexual relationships is the opposite of most other ancient Near Eastern religions, where "everything that pertained to sexuality had a role in cult and ritual."

The explanation for this type of legislation is found in 15:31: "Thus you shall keep the people of Israel separate from their uncleanness, lest they die in their uncleanness by defiling my tabernacle that is in their midst" (RSV). Responding to this rationale, Jacob Neusner (1973: 20) says, "Here in a single sentence is the complete priestly ideology of purity. All matters of purity attain importance because of the cult. No other occasion for attaining or preserving purity is considered."

The area covered here finds further reflection in Jesus' healing of the woman with the issue of blood (Mark 5:25–34). She wanted to touch his garments. But what made the difference was not so much Jesus' garments as the woman's faith. Jesus did not say, "My garments have made you well." Nor did he even say, "I have made you well." What he said was, "Your faith has made you well." What is involved here is not superstition, but the exercise of faith.

By way of summary, almost all the categories of clean or unclean spelled out in Leviticus 11–15 fall into the area of the nonmoral. With the exception of the dietary code, all the applications of the purity laws address events in one's life that are normal or unavoidable: childbirth, diseases, and bodily emissions.

In the discussion of leprosy we saw that the New Testament uses the same Greek word to describe cleansing from leprosy and cleansing from sin. That is, purity is both a physical and a moral matter.

This is not, however, an innovation with the New Testament. Strikingly, the Old Testament had already extended the idea of purity beyond the cult to include the concept of moral blamelessness. For example, David's prayer on one occasion was, "Purge me . . . and I shall be clean . . . create in me a clean heart" (Ps. 51:7, 10 NRSV). And God promises to cleanse the iniquities of restored Israel (Ezek. 36:33). Consistently, then, the Old Testament's emphasis on moral cleansing takes its vocabulary directly from ritual language. What is the force of this adaptation? In my judgment, Geerhardus Vos (1948: 182) has made the most astute observation. In explaining the parallels, he states, "God teaches people to feel about sin as they are accustomed to feel about an ignominious and uncomfortable exclusion from the ritual service." Moral uncleanness, no less than physical uncleanness, erects a barrier between God and humankind. The divine remedy is nothing short of cleansing.

Leviticus 11–15

Brin, G. 1977. "Firstlings of Unclean Animals." *JQR* 68:1–15.

Childs, B. S. 1985. *Old Testament Theology in a Canonical Context.* Philadelphia: Fortress. Pp. 84–91.

Davies, M. L. 1987–1988. "Levitical Leprosy: Uncleanness and the Psyche." *ExpT* 99:136–39.

Douglas, M. 1966. *Purity and Danger. An Analysis of Concepts of Pollution and Taboo.* London: Routledge & Kegan Paul.

———. 1972. "Deciphering a Meal." *Daedelius* 101:61–81.

———. 1975. *Implicit Meanings: Essays in Anthropology.* London: Routledge & Kegan Paul.

———. 1993. "The Forbidden Animals in Leviticus." *JSOT* 59:3–23.

———. 1999. *Leviticus as Literature.* Oxford: Oxford University Press. Pp. 134–75.

Firmage, E. B. 1990. "The Biblical Dietary Laws and the Concept of Holiness." In *Studies in the Pentateuch.* Ed. J. A. Emerton. VTSup 41. Leiden: Brill. Pp. 177–208.

Frymer-Kensky, T. 1983. "Pollution, Purification, and Purgation in Biblical Israel." In *The Word of the Lord Shall Go Forth: Essays in Honor of David Noel Freedman in Celebration of His Sixtieth Birthday*. Ed. C. L. Meyers and M. O'Connor. Winona Lake, Ind.: Eisenbrauns. Pp. 399–414.

Gorman, F. H., Jr. 1990. *The Ideology of Ritual: Space, Time and Status in the Priestly Theology*. JSOTSup 91. Sheffield: JSOT Press. Pp. 151–79.

Harrison, R. K. 1962. "Leprosy." *IDB* 3:111–13.

Houston, W. 1993. *Purity and Monotheism: Clean and Unclean Animals in Biblical Law*. JSOTSup 140. Sheffield: JSOT Press.

———. 2003. "Towards an Integrated Reading of the Dietary Laws of Leviticus." In *The Book of Leviticus: Composition and Reception*. Ed. R. Rendtorff and R. A. Kugler. VTSup 93. Leiden: Brill. Pp. 142–61.

Hulse, E. V. 1975. "Nature of Biblical Leprosy and the Use of Alternative Medical Terms in Modern Translations of the Bible." *PEQ* 107:87–105.

Jenson, P. P. 1992. *Graded Holiness: A Key to the Priestly Conception of the World*. JSOTSup 106. Sheffield: JSOT Press.

Kass, L. R. 1994. "Why the Dietary Laws?" *Commentary* 46:42–48.

Kinlaw, D. F. 1969. "Laws Concerning Uncleanness." In *Beacon Bible Commentary*. Vol. 1. Kansas City, Mo.: Beacon Hill Press. Pp. 353–62.

Klawans, J. 2000. *Impurity and Sin in Ancient Judaism*. New York: Oxford University Press.

Levine, B. 1989. *Leviticus: The Traditional Hebrew Text with the New JPS Translation*. JPS Torah Commentary. Philadelphia: The Jewish Publication Society.

Magonet, J. 1996. "'But If It Is a Girl, She Is Unclean for Twice Seven Days . . .': The Riddle of Leviticus 12:5." In *Reading Leviticus: A Conversation with Mary Douglas*. Ed. J. F. A. Sawyer. JSOTSup 227. Sheffield: Sheffield Academic Press. Pp. 144–52.

Meier, S. 1989. "House Fungus: Mesopotamia and Israel (Lev. 14:33–53)." *RB* 96:184–92.

Milgrom, J. 1963. "The Biblical Diet Laws as an Ethical System." *Int* 17:288–301.

———. 1971a. "Leprosy." *EncJud* 11:33–36.

———. 1971b. "Sin-Offering or Purification Offering?" *VT* 21:237–39.

———. 1990. "Ethics and Ritual: The Foundations of the Biblical Dietary Laws." In *Religion and Law: Biblical-Judaic and Islamic Perspectives*. Ed. E. R. Firmage, B. G. Weiss, and J. W. Welch. Winona Lake, Ind.: Eisenbrauns. Pp. 159–91.

———. 1991. "The Composition of Leviticus, Chapter 11." In *Priesthood and Cult in Ancient Israel*. Ed. G. A. Anderson and S. M. Olyan. JSOTSup 125. Sheffield: JSOT Press. Pp. 182–91.

———. 1993. "The Rationale for Biblical Impurity." *JANES* 22:107–11.

Miller, P. D., Jr. 2000. *The Religion of Ancient Israel*. Louisville: Westminster John Knox.

Moskala, J. 2001. "Categorization and Evaluation of Different Kinds of Interpretation of the Laws of Clean and Unclean Animals in Leviticus 11." *BRes* 46:5–41.

Neusner, J. 1973. *The Idea of Purity in Ancient Judaism; With a Critique and a Commentary by Mary Douglas*. SJLA 1. Leiden: Brill. [See especially chapter 1, "The Biblical Legacy."]

Rabinowicz, H. 1971. "Dietary Laws." *EncJud* 6:26–46.

Rad, G. von. 1962. *Old Testament Theology*. Trans. D. M. G. Stalker. 2 vols. New York: Harper & Row. Vol. 1, pp. 272–79.

Rendsburg, G. A. 1993. "The Inclusio of Leviticus xi." *VT* 43:418–21.

Sawyer, J. F. A. 1976. "A Note on the Etymology of *saraʿat*." *VT* 26:241–45.

Schearing, L. S. 2003. "Double Time . . . Double Trouble? Gender, Sin and Leviticus 12." In *The Book of Leviticus: Composition and Reception*. Ed. R. Rendtorff and R. A. Kugler. VTSup 93. Leiden: Brill. Pp. 429–50.

Selvidge, M. 1984. "Mark 5:25–34 and Leviticus 15:19–20: A Reaction to Restrictive Purity Regulations." *JBL* 103:619–23.

Toombs, L. 1962. "Clean and Unclean." *IDB* 1:641–48.

Vos, G. 1948. *Notes on Biblical Theology*. Grand Rapids: Eerdmans.

Wegner, J. R. 2003. "'*Coming before the Lord*': The Exclusion of Women from the Public Domain of the Israelite Priestly Cult." In *The Book of Leviticus: Composition and Reception*. Ed. R. Rendtorff and R. A. Kugler. VTSup 93. Leiden: Brill. Pp. 451–65.

Wenham, G. J. 1981. "The Theology of Unclean Food." *EvQ* 53:6–15.

———. 1983. "Why Does Sexual Intercourse Defile (Lev 15, 18)?" *ZAW* 95:432–34.

Whitekettle, R. W. 1995. "Leviticus 12 and the Israelite Woman: Ritual Process, Liminality and the Womb." *ZAW* 107:393–408.

———. 1996. "Levitical Thought and the Female Reproductive Cycle: Wombs, Wellsprings and the Primeval World." *VT* 46:376–91.

Wilkinson, J. 1977. "Leprosy and Leviticus: The Problem of Description and Identification." *SJT* 30:153–70.

———. 1978. "Leprosy and Leviticus: A Problem of Semantics and Translation." *SJT* 31:153–66.

Wright, David P. 1987. *The Disposal of Impurity: Elimination Rites in the Bible and in Hittite and Mesopotamian Literature*. SBLDS 101. Atlanta: Scholars Press.

———. 1990. "Observations on the Ethical Foundations of the Biblical Dietary Laws: A Response to Jacob Milgrom." In *Religion and Law: Biblical, Jewish, and Islamic Perspectives*. Ed. E. R. Firmage, B. G. Weiss, and J. W. Welch. Winona Lake, Ind.: Eisenbrauns. Pp. 193–98.

———. 1991. "The Spectrum of Priestly Impurity." In *Priesthood and Cult in Ancient Israel*. Ed. G. A. Anderson and S. M. Olyan. JSOTSup 125. Sheffield: JSOT Press. Pp. 150–81.

———. 1992. "Unclean and Clean (OT)." *ABD* 6:729–41.

14

The Day of Atonement

LEVITICUS 16

One full chapter in Leviticus is given to a description of the Day of Atonement. Leviticus 23:26–32, part of a sacred calendar, is a further reference to this particular day, called there "a day of [the] atonement[s]," *yôm (hak)kippûrîm*. In rabbinic literature it is simply called "the day" or "the great day" (see the Mishnah tractate *Yoma*). The New Testament is similarly brief in the title it uses: "the Fast": "because even the Fast had already gone by" (Acts 27:9).

There are two additional pieces of information in Lev. 23:26–32 about the Day of Atonement not found in ch. 16. One is that 23:26–32 uses the strongest language possible about consequences for failing to properly observe the day through fasting and self-denial: "And anyone who does any work during that entire day, such a one I will destroy from the midst of the people" (v. 30 NRSV).

To attribute punishment directly to God in the priestly codes is rare. The closest parallel is where the uncommon "I [God] will cut that person off from the people" (17:10; 20:3, 5, 6) replaces the more common passive form "that person shall be cut off from the people" (Lev. 7:20, 21, 25, 27; 17:4, 9; 18:29; 19:8; 20:17, 18; 22:3; 23:29).

The second unique element is the mention in 23:32 that the observance of this day is to last "from the evening of the ninth day . . . until the following evening" (NIV), the only special day, including the Sabbath, that the Old Testament so describes. This chronological note provides the background for what became the standard starting time in Judaism for all the holy days: the evening prior to the day itself.

Critics' Views about the Day of Atonement

The preoccupation of most commentaries is the literary dissection of ch. 16. Two conclusions about the chapter's integrity enjoy virtually universal acceptance among the critics. One conclusion is that the Day of Atonement, as such, never existed in the time of Moses. That is to say, where it stands now is blatantly anachronistic, equivalent to the claim of a day honoring Martin Luther King Jr. in the time of Abraham Lincoln. More than likely, say the critics, the Day of Atonement emerged only relatively late in Israel's history—not only postexilic, but even after the time of Ezra and Nehemiah!

This particular interpretation is based primarily on the argument from silence (see de Vaux 1965: 2:509–10). No preexilic text—nothing in the historical books or in the prophetic corpus—mentions the day. Therefore, it did not exist then. One should, however, use the argument from silence hesitatingly, and the interested reader should refer for this particular case to the comments of Yehezkel Kaufmann (1960: 210 n. 17) and Jacob Milgrom (1976a: 83). This is not to deny that the observance of the Day of Atonement may have undergone modifications over time, and that Leviticus 16 represents the form of observance near the end of the biblical period. We recall, for instance, how Christian observance of Christmas Sunday or Easter Sunday has changed over the centuries, while a certain fundamental core of emphasis has never changed.

The second widely accepted conclusion is that Leviticus 16 is a heterogeneous unit, divisible into multiple literary strands. Martin Noth's comment (1977: 117) is illustrative:

> It is evident at the first glance that the chapter is in its present form the result of a probably fairly long previous history that has left its traces in a strange lack of continuity and unity about the whole. The material is indeed so complicated that all attempts hitherto at factual and literary analysis have not led to at all convincing results. But the fact itself, that the chapter came into being through an elaborate process of growth, is generally recognized and accepted.

Reasons advanced for this idea include the appearance of doublets or repetitions. Thus we read in v. 6, "And Aaron shall offer the bull as a sin offering for himself and shall make atonement for himself and for his house" (RSV), which is repeated in v. 11. Does the repetition indubitably prove the case for dual traditions? Could not vv. 6–10 be considered a general outline of the events? Verses 11–28 then would be a close-up, detailed account of those same events.

A second reason for discerning mixed sources in this chapter is the conclusion, vv. 29–34, which appears to be a later appendix. Besides other information in these verses, the reader learns that the Day of Atonement is to be observed annually on the tenth day of the seventh month, which is Tishri (v. 29). Usually the date or day for observing the rituals comes at the beginning of a section, but here it is at the end. The conclusion? The author of this appendix is different, at least from the author who described the festivals in Leviticus 23. (Could one therefore cogently argue, to cite a New Testament illustration, that because Paul's prayers customarily appear at the beginning or by the middle of his epistles, the prayer recorded in 1 Thess. 5:23–24 must be non-Pauline? Order or placement seem to have little to do with authenticity.)

Aspects of Atonement

Perhaps it is not an accident that the expression "Day of Atonement" reads literally in Hebrew, "day of atonements." Atonement covers three areas in this chapter: the high priest, the sanctuary, and the people.

Through the use of repetition, at least of key phrases, Leviticus 16 emphasizes some crucial ideas. Before anything redemptive can happen, the high priest must deal with his own sins. "Aaron shall offer . . . a sin offering for himself . . . make atonement for himself . . . a sin offering for himself . . . make atonement for himself . . . a sin offering for himself . . . has made atonement for himself . . . make atonement for himself" (vv. 6, 11, 17, 24 RSV). Thus the phrase "for himself," used seven times, underscores the absolute necessity that the ranking clergyman first rectify his own errors. That a high priest could be above this requirement would be unthinkable and heretical.

Hebrews 9 tells us that Jesus broke the pattern. He entered once, not annually, into the holy place, and with his own blood, not that of an animal (Heb. 9:11–14). Jesus has no sin to acknowledge and no need to make atonement for himself.

It is interesting to observe that not only people, but inanimate objects as well, need atonement on this day. Compare the following: "he shall make atonement for the holy place" (v. 16 RSV); "he shall go out to the altar . . . and make atonement for it" (v. 18 RSV); "cleanse it and hallow it" (v. 19 RSV); "when he has made an end of atoning for the holy place and the tent of meeting and the altar" (v. 20 RSV); "he shall make atonement for the sanctuary . . . for the tent of meeting, and for the altar" (v. 33 RSV).

In a very real sense, then, judgment does begin at God's house (cf. 1 Pet. 4:17). The sanctuary does need to be cleansed, which Jesus did. Is the Old Testament suggesting here that sin is almost substantival, something that creeps into God's presence because of the sins of God's people and wraps itself around the holy vessels in the sanctuary?

The use of the Hebrew verb *kāpar*, "to expiate, make atonement," is interesting. Hebrew linguists widely disagree about the nuances implicit in the verb. A moderate suggestion is that the verb means "to rub." Something can be either rubbed off (e.g., sin is wiped off or purged) or rubbed on (e.g., sin is covered). It is significant that the Targum of Leviticus from Qumran (second century B.C.?), in which several verses from Leviticus 16 are all that have survived, translates the Hebrew word *kappōret* ("mercy seat, propitiatory") with the Aramaic word *ksy*ʾ, meaning "cover, lid" (see Fitzmyer 1978: 15–17; 1980: 17–18). Among Hebrew scholars today the preference is for "rub off, remove" rather than "rub on, cover."

What we are particularly interested in here is how the Hebrew language handles an object after this verb. Seldom, especially in liturgical literature, is a person the direct object of the verb *kāpar*. In Leviticus, at least, the subject of this verb is the priest, never God. If the object is a person, the noun is preceded by some preposition: "for," "on behalf of," "with respect to." The person is not the object of the rites of expiation—blood is not poured or daubed on the person—but rather is the beneficiary of those rites of expiation.

By contrast, inanimate objects may be direct objects of the verb *kāpar* with no intervening preposition. Leviticus 16:33 (NRSV) illustrates the difference between the two: "he shall make atonement for the sanctuary, and . . . for the tent of meeting and for the altar [*kāpar* plus direct object, indicated by the untranslated particle ʾ*et*], and . . . for the priests and for all the people of the assembly" (*kāpar* plus the preposition ʿ*al* before "priests" and "all the people").

B. A. Levine (1974: 66) speculates that Leviticus, and related literature, avoided the construction of the verb *kāpar* plus a direct object, if a person, to negate the association that it is the rites themselves that are automatically effective. The acts are prerequisite, but not causational. They are only means to an end. God himself gives forgiveness and grants atonement.

Use of the Blood

In the examination of Leviticus 1–7 we observed the frequent references to blood in the sacrifices of expiation. The one distinguishing fact about Leviticus 16 is that on the Day of Atonement, and only on that day, the blood is carried into the Holy of Holies, the innermost sanctuary of the tabernacle. The biblical phrases are "within the veil . . . on the front of . . . and before the mercy seat" (vv. 12–15 RSV). Figure 7 clarifies the procedures mentioned in these verses.

One wonders why on this particular day the blood is carried into the tabernacle's most hallowed precinct. Perhaps the answer lies in a strategic word that occurs in this chapter, "transgressions," in vv. 16, 21. Gerhard von Rad (1962: 1:263 n. 177) observes that of the eighty-six occurrences of this word in the Old Testament, only two are in that sizable section of Scripture designated by the critics as P. Those two are Lev. 16:16, 21. They appear nowhere else in Leviticus. The word is taken from the language of politics and international relationships. As such, the word conveys the idea of revolt or rebellion. Von Rad goes on to say that "it [peša⁣c] is unquestionably the gravest word for sin, especially on the lips of the prophets."

Figure 7

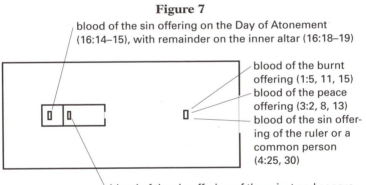

blood of the sin offering on the Day of Atonement (16:14–15), with remainder on the inner altar (16:18–19)

blood of the burnt offering (1:5, 11, 15)
blood of the peace offering (3:2, 8, 13)
blood of the sin offering of the ruler or a common person (4:25, 30)

blood of the sin offering of the priest and congregation (4:6, 7, 17–18), with remainder poured at the outer altar (4:7b, 18b)

This kind of sin is precisely the opposite of sin committed inadvertently. For this reason, on the Day of Atonement, given to deal with sin in its most gross manifestation, the blood is carried as close to the presence of God as possible. Neither the outer brazen altar nor the inner incense altar will suffice here as the main receptacle for the blood.

If Leviticus 16 is the one chapter in the priestly literature in which the word "transgressions" occurs twice in proximity (16:16, 21), the

Joseph story provides another instance of this word occurring twice in succession (although the NIV obscures this point). The brothers of Joseph, claiming to quote their late father Jacob, say to him, "'Forgive your brothers' transgressions [NIV: 'wrongs'] and their sin.' Now please forgive the transgressions [NIV: 'sins'] of the servants of the God of your father" (Gen. 50:17). As Carmichael (2000: 171) has pointed out, it is possibly this parallel that led to the tradition in later Judaism (as in, e.g., *Jubilees*) to connect the Joseph story with the Day of Atonement. As on this one day Joseph's brothers sought his forgiveness for their sins of transgression, the Israelites are to seek God's forgiveness for their sins of transgression on Yom Kippur. Joseph is dispatched to Egypt, the scapegoat into the wilderness.

Actually, this is a day for the removal, either through sacrifice or through riddance, of just about any kind of sin. Note the frequent use of the word "all" before each of the sin words: "*all* the wickedness and rebellion of the Israelites—*all* their sins" (v. 21 NIV); "be clean from *all* your sins" (v. 30 NIV); "for *all* the sins of the Israelites" (v. 34 NIV). God in his mercy has set aside one day in the year when his people can unload all the junk and garbage in their lives, much as many communities have a day or two per year where they bring in extra dumpsters and permit people to put out in the trash items that they normally could not dispose of. The Day of Atonement is what Kawashima (2003: 372) has called a "cultic drainage system." As Brueggemann (1997: 666) has stated, "Yahweh has granted to Israel a reliable, authorized device whereby Israel can be restored to a full relationship with Yahweh."

The Scapegoat

The presentation of the blood of the slain sin offering is one-half of the ceremony of the Day of Atonement. The second half is again unique to this particular occasion. One of the goats for the congregation's sin offering is to be kept alive (vv. 5, 10, 20). Unlike the procedures described in chs. 1–7, in this ritual it is Aaron, not the worshiper, who lays his hands on the head of the goat (v. 21). The officiating priest then "confesses" Israel's sins and transgressions. Again, this is a departure from Lev. 5:5, where the worshiper must "confess" personal sin. The goat then "bears" the iniquities to the wilderness. (The reader should note that the ideas of "to bear or carry" and "to forgive" are covered by the same verb in Hebrew.) This idea of carrying sin away is the antecedent for Isaiah's song about the Suffering Servant, who "has borne our griefs" (Isa. 53:4 RSV) and who "bore the sin of many" (Isa. 53:12 NRSV), and for John the

Baptist's exclamation "Behold, the Lamb of God, who takes away the sin of the world" (John 1:29 RSV). The typological significance of this event is expounded in Heb. 6:19–20; 9:7–14.

The problem of interpretation can be focused by comparing the translations of the NRSV and the NIV in the following verses:

16:8:   "And Aaron shall cast lots on the two goats, one lot for the LORD and the other lot *for Azazel*." (NRSV)

"He is to cast lots for the two goats—one lot for the LORD and the other *for the scapegoat*." (NIV)

16:10:   "But the goat on which the lot fell *for Azazel* shall be presented alive before the LORD to make atonement for it, that it may be sent away into the wilderness *to Azazel*." (NRSV)

"But the goat chosen by lot as *the scapegoat* shall be presented alive before the LORD to be used for making atonement by sending it into the desert *as a scapegoat*." (NIV)

The difference between the two versions is obvious. For the NRSV, the Hebrew word ʿăzāʾzēl is the name of an individual (or place?) to whom the live goat is sent. For the NIV, the Hebrew word refers to the live goat itself.

The translation of the NRSV carries the day among most scholars. For this reason the prevailing interpretation is that Azazel is a supernatural power, probably demonic, whose haunt is the wilderness. The idea is that the most efficient way to get rid of evil is by banishing it to its original source.

Further support for this idea usually is located in two places. First, appeal is made to a few other verses in the Old Testament that suggest a belief that the wilderness was inhabited by demons. Leviticus 17:7 refers to the offering of sacrifices to "goat-demons" (śĕʿîrîm) in the open field. The most frequently quoted passage is Isa. 34:14, in which the prophet, in speaking of God's destruction of Edom, says that the land will turn into a wilderness filled with wild animals and birds. Among the creatures mentioned here are goat-demons (same Hebrew word as in Lev. 17:7) and Lilith (RSV: "the night hag"), the female night-demon famous, or infamous, in incantations. A third reference to goat-demons as objects of worship is found in 2 Chron. 11:15. The idea of the wilderness as the haunt of unclean spirits also appears in the New Testament, in Matt. 12:43; Luke 11:24.

The second area of support for the equation of Azazel with a demonic force is found in apocryphal literature. In *1 Enoch* Azazel is identified as the leader of the angels who, as recorded in Genesis 6, wanted the daughters of men (see *1 En.* 8:1; 9:6; 10:4–8; 13:1). Eventually, Azazel is bound by Raphael and cast into a dark wilderness.

Are we dealing, then, with a vestige of myth that never was censored from Israel's religious history? Can we believe that a major part of such a critical event, whenever it arose, included dispatching an animal to a demon's den?

Gordon Wenham (1979: 234) quotes J. H. Hertz on this, an observation I believe to be pungent. "The offering of sacrifices to 'satyrs' [goat-demons] is spoken of as a heinous crime in the very next chapter (17:7); homage to a demon of the wilderness cannot, therefore, be associated with the holiest of the Temple-rites in the chapter immediately preceding." Could Scripture affirm in one chapter the activity of Baal in the storm, then in an adjacent chapter have the Shema?

Where, then, does the NIV obtain its translation "scapegoat"? First, the Hebrew word ʿăzāʾzēl is made up of two Semitic words, the Hebrew word for "goat" and the Aramaic verb "to go." Hence, Azazel is the goat that goes, the scapegoat, the go-away goat. The rendering "scapegoat" comes to us from Tyndale's translation of the Scriptures into English in 1530, in which he coins the term "escapegoat." In a sense this is an excellent translation contextually, for unlike the other goat, which does not survive but is sacrificed, this goat does survive, is not sacrificed, escapes death, and is set free into the "wilderness, desert," a place where goats are much more hardy than sheep (see Douglas 2003). Second, this is the way the word was understood by many of the ancient versions, particularly the Septuagint and the Vulgate. The Septuagint, for example, translates the Hebrew word in vv. 8, 10, 26 in three different but similar ways: "the one sent away" (vv. 8, 10); "the one sent away for release" (v. 10); "the goat which is determined for release" (v. 26).

As Kaufmann (1960: 114) notes, Azazel, if he is the destination of the goat, plays no active role. "Unless the sin is expelled the deadly wrath of YHWH may be aroused, but no harm will come from Azazel. . . . The value of the rite does not lie in exorcising a dangerous demonic power, but in fulfilling a commandment of God." (Levine's [1974: 79–83] criticism of Kaufmann's interpretation of Azazel centers mostly on the translation of Lev. 16:10 and advocates a much greater magical objective than Kaufmann observes in the ritual.)

The Role of the People

The congregation has played only a minimal role in the ceremonies. Aaron selects the two male goats. Aaron places his hands on the live goat. The other goat Aaron kills as a sin offering for the people. Aaron alone enters the sanctuary.

What of the people? Are they passive and uninvolved? Hardly. The point of vv. 29, 31 is that the Day of Atonement is to function as a Sabbath. Not only are the people to abstain from work, but also they are "to afflict/deny themselves." This certainly does not mean self-laceration or self-flagellation. It means that the Day of Atonement, for the laity, is to be a national day of prayer, fasting, and repentance, a time of ruthless self-examination and transparency. See also Lev. 23:27–32 for the idea of "afflicting" oneself on the Day of Atonement.

The ceremonies in the tabernacle are appropriate and God-ordained, but they become effective only if accompanied by genuine contrition in the community of believers. The Bible nowhere accepts the idea that its rituals are *ex opere operato*.

But God's way is not a religion of nothing but self-denial and self-discipline. It includes those, but it is more than that. It surely is no accident that in the sacred calendar of which Leviticus 23 speaks, the Day of Atonement in the seventh month (23:26–32) is followed immediately by the Feast of Booths/Tabernacles (23:33–44) in the seventh month. On this occasion one is to "rejoice before the LORD your God for seven days" (v. 40b NRSV), and it is the only festival in Leviticus 23 that calls for rejoicing. So, says Leviticus, get right with God, let God remove from your life everything antithetical to him, everything you have messed up, and then enjoy a party!

Leviticus 16

Ahituv, S. 1971. "Azazel." *EncJud* 6:111–19.

Brueggemann, W. 1997. *Theology of the Old Testament: Testimony, Dispute, Advocacy.* Minneapolis: Fortress.

Carmichael, C. 2000. "The Origin of the Scapegoat Ritual." *VT* 50:167–82.

Douglas, M. 2003. "The Go-Away Goat." In *The Book of Leviticus: Composition and Reception.* Ed. R. Rendtorff and R. A. Kugler. VTSup 93. Leiden: Brill. Pp. 121–41.

Eichrodt, W. 1961–1967. *Theology of the Old Testament.* Trans. J. Baker. 2 vols. OTL. Philadelphia: Westminster. Vol. 1, pp. 130–31.

Fitzmyer, J. A. 1978. "The Targum of Leviticus from Qumran Cave 4." *Maarav* 1 (1):5–23.

———. 1980. "The Aramaic Language and the Study of the New Testament." *JBL* 99:5–21.

Gorman, F. H., Jr. 1990. *The Ideology of Ritual: Space, Time and Status in the Priestly Theology.* JSOTSup 91. Sheffield: Sheffield Academic Press. Pp. 61–102.

Grabbe, L. L. 1987. "The Scapegoat Tradition: A Study of Early Jewish Interpretation." *JJS* 18:152–67.

Hasel, G. 1981. "Studies in Biblical Atonement II: The Day of Atonement." In *The Sanctuary and the Atonement*. Ed. A. V. Wallenkampf and W. R. Lesher. Washington, D.C.: Review and Herald Publishing Association. Pp. 115–33.

Helm, R. 1994. "Azazel in Early Jewish Tradition." *AUSS* 32:217–26.

Janowski, B. 1995. "Azazel." In *Dictionary of Deities and Demons in the Bible*. Ed. K. van der Toorn et al. Leiden and New York: Brill. Pp. 240–47.

Jenson, P. P. 1992. *Graded Holiness: A Key to the Priestly Conception of the World*. JSOTSup 106. Sheffield: Sheffield Academic Press. Pp. 197–209.

Kaufmann, Y. 1960. *The Religion of Israel*. Trans. M. Greenberg. Chicago: University of Chicago Press.

Kawashima, R. S. 2003. "The Jubilee Year and the Return of Cosmic Purity." *CBQ* 65:370–89.

Kraus, H. J. 1966. *Worship in Israel*. Richmond: John Knox. Pp. 68–70.

Levine, B. A. 1974. *In the Presence of the Lord: A Study of Cult and Some Cultic Terms in Ancient Israel*. SJLA 5. Leiden: Brill.

Lyonnet, S., and L. Sabourin. 1970. *Sin, Redemption, and Sacrifice: A Biblical and Patristic Study*. AnBib 48. Rome: Biblical Institute Press. Pp. 61–184.

McClean, B. H. 1991. "The Interpretation of the Levitical Sin Offering and the Scapegoat." *SR* 20:345–56.

Milgrom, J. 1976a. "Atonement, Day of." *IDBSup* 82–83.

———. 1976b. "Atonement in the OT." *IDBSup* 78–80.

Noth, M. 1997. *Leviticus*. Trans. J. E. Anderson. Rev. ed. OTL. Philadelphia: Westminster.

Rad, G. von. 1962. *Old Testament Theology*. Trans. D. M. G. Stalker. 2 vols. New York: Harper & Row. Vol. 1, pp. 262–72.

Rodriguez, A. M. 1996. "Leviticus 16: Its Literary Structure." *AUSS* 34:269–86.

Roo, C. R. Jacqueline de. 2000. "Was the Goat for Azazel Destined for the Wrath of God?" *Bib* 81:223–42.

Rudman, D. 2004. "A Note on the Azazel-goat Ritual." *ZAW* 116:396–401.

Tawil, H. 1980. "Azazel, the Prince of the Steppe: A Comparative Study." *ZAW* 92:43–59.

Vaux, R. de. 1965. *Ancient Israel*. Trans. J. McHugh. 2 vols. New York: McGraw-Hill. Vol. 1, pp. 507–10.

Wenham, G. 1979. *The Book of Leviticus*. NICOT. Grand Rapids: Eerdmans.

Wright, David P. 1992a. "Azazel." *ABD* 1:536–37.

———. 1992b. "Day of Atonement." *ABD* 2:72–76.

Zatelli, I. 1998. "The Origin of the Biblical Scapegoat Ritual: The Evidence of Two Eblaite Texts." *VT* 48:254–63.

15

A Holiness Manifesto

LEVITICUS 17–27

The critical view is that these last chapters of Leviticus, excluding ch. 27, once existed as an independent legal code, and only later were they grafted into P, much as the Book of the Covenant is considered to be an insertion into the text of Exodus.

This "discovery" was made in the late nineteenth century by German scholar August Klostermann, and to this unit of Leviticus he gave the title *Heiligkeitsgesetz*, "Holiness Code" (with the symbol "H" now commonly used to designate this source).

Until recently the consensus was that the Holiness Code appeared first, and the Priestly writers later appended it to their own writings to form what is now the second half of Leviticus. Some scholars now, thanks to the spearheading interpretation of Knohl (1995), reverse the chronological order of P and H to suggest that the Priestly traditions are earlier than the Holiness Code and that the latter represents a redactional supplement to, if not a "correction" of, P. Those advocating this position inevitably move up significantly the traditional date assigned to P's composition, from during or just after the Babylonian exile to as early as the time just after Solomon's building of the temple. Thus one ends up with a JEPD theory instead of a JEDP theory.

Regardless of how one feels about the critical assessment of these last chapters of Leviticus, the observation certainly is valid that the reader finds an explicit emphasis on holiness as a motivation for conduct and lifestyle to a degree not found in chs. 1–16. Furthermore, all references to "holy/consecrate/sanctify/hallow" in chs. 1–16 refer to the sanctuary, or to something in the sanctuary, or to the clergy who serve in the sanctuary. The lone exception is 11:44–45, a reference to holiness modeled in the people of God by what they eat or do not eat. By contrast, the restricted circle of holiness emphases of 1–16 is expanded to cover all Israelites in 17–27. We might call it a "laicization" of holiness as a lifestyle incumbent upon all. This is not unexpected if the primary focus of 1–16 is on how the people of God are to worship: at God's holy sanctuary through the ministry of God's holy/consecrated servants. In chs. 17–27 the primary focus is not so much on how God's people are to worship as on how they are to live; those who worship a holy God will aspire to live holy lives and appropriate the resources that a holy God makes available to them to so order their lives. I have already mentioned that the Hebrew root *q-d-š* occurs 150 times in Leviticus (as a verb, noun, or adjective). The breakdown is interesting. See table 11.

It is self-evident that there is a much greater use of *q-d-š*-related words in the last eleven chapters of Leviticus than in the first sixteen. And within this unit (in descending order), chs. 27, 22, 21, and 23 employ the root most often (sixty-six of eighty-five times). Neither of the first two chapters in this pericope, 17 and 18, uses the root.

Several times in Leviticus the people of God receive a call to holiness in the form of a divine ultimatum—for example: 11:44–45, "Consecrate yourselves therefore, and be holy, for I am holy" (RSV); 19:2, "You shall be holy, for I the LORD your God am holy" (NRSV); 20:7, "Consecrate yourselves therefore, and be holy; for I am the LORD your God" (NRSV); 20:26, "You shall be holy to me; for I the LORD am holy" (NRSV). That these verses are not time-conditioned or eclipsed by a fuller revelation is documented by Peter's freedom to place these verses, without change, in the context of his Christian message to a community of believers (see 1 Pet. 1:15–16).

Table 11

Chapter(s)	Occurrence	Total
1–16	65	
17–27	85	150
17	0	
18	0	
19	5	

Chapter(s)	Occurrence	Total
20	7	
21	13	
22	19	
23	12	
24	3	
25	2	
26	2	
27	22	85

In the four instances cited in the preceding paragraph we observe that each summons to holiness has attached to it a motivational clause: "for I am the LORD your God" or "for I the LORD am holy." It is no accident that these commands are always given by the Lord himself, speaking directly in the first person. Never in Leviticus does Moses or Aaron say, "You shall be holy, for God is holy." God himself establishes the standard. And Peter quotes God, not Moses! It would be wide of the mark to read any of these statements as a threat: "You had better be holy or else!" Rather, we should read them as a word of divine invitation. To be sure, there are consequences for intentionally choosing an unholy agenda for one's life. God's way, however, is not to frighten or intimidate people into holiness, but to lure them into it by lifting up his own nature as the benchmark and model.

Of course, the phrase "you shall be holy as God is holy" does not mean "you shall be *as* holy as God is holy." The idiom is known elsewhere in Scripture. For example, Jesus says, "You, therefore, must be perfect, as your heavenly Father is perfect" (Matt. 5:48 RSV). Such comparisons abound in 1 John: "If we walk in the light, as he is in the light . . ." (1:7 NIV); "Whoever says, 'I abide in him,' ought to walk just as he walked" (2:6 NRSV); "And all who have this hope in him purify themselves, just as he is pure" (3:3 NRSV); "Everyone who does what is right is righteous, just as he is righteous" (3:7 NRSV); "We should believe . . . love . . . just as he has commanded us" (3:23 NRSV).

Certainly Leviticus is claiming that God alone is holy intrinsically. He is the origin and the source of all that is holy. In addition, affirms Leviticus, God not only delivers the people from captivity and grants them a new land but also desires to produce in them a pattern of living that is worthy of the follower of a holy God. If Exodus covered the area of salvation and deliverance, it also laid the foundations for the sanctification (see Exod. 19:6; 22:31) now accentuated in these chapters of Leviticus. What specifically is involved in this holy life will emerge as we make our way through this unit.

For all these differences in emphases between chs. 1–16 and 17–27, one should also be sensitive to their similarities. Certain units in each larger section parallel each other. For example, chs. 1–7 (acts of worship) line up with 23–25 (times of worship); chs. 8–10 (priestly ministry) parallel 21–22 (priestly rules); chs. 11–15 (clean living) go with 18–20, 26–27 (holy living).

Additionally, there are other themes common to both larger sections. One of these is the repeated emphasis on circumstances that render a person unclean/impure, and usually, but not always, with a statement of measures to be taken for removal of such impurity. An impurity condition in Leviticus emerges first in 5:2–3, last in 22:4–8, and in many chapters in between. But they are not all identical. In some ways the circumstances that produce uncleanness in 17–27 seem more severe than those in 1–16. As Kugler (1997: 26) has noted, impurity concerns in 1–16 deal for the most part with what enters or exits or touches one's body. By contrast, impurity concerns in 17–27 deal mostly with what one does with one's body. This may explain the placement of the penalty for an infraction in this area: the offender is to be "cut off" (either the offender's line of descendants will cease, or the offender is barred from "being gathered to his fathers" in the afterlife). In 1–16 this use of the verb *kārat*, "cut off," occurs only four times (7:20, 21, 25, 27), whereas in 17–27 it occurs thirteen times (17:4, 9, 10, 14; 18:29; 19:8; 20:3, 5, 6, 17, 18; 22:3; 23:29). And 17–27 is the only section to have the more severe, active form of the verb: "I [God] will cut that person off" (17:10; 20:3, 5, 6). Or to mention one more phrase, the expression "profane the name of God" occurs six times in 17–27 (18:21; 19:12; 20:3; 21:6; 22:2, 32), but never in 1–16.

Eating Meat, but with a Caution (17)

Appropriately, this section of Leviticus, dealing with practical holiness, begins with some legislation about diet. Although no form of the Hebrew root *q-d-š* occurs in this particular chapter, we have already observed in other scriptural contexts (see the discussion of Leviticus 11) the sanctity that is attached to one's choice of edible foods.

Chapter 17 following 16 seems purposeful. First, in both chapters there is a strong emphasis on the place of the blood (of an animal). Chapter 16 deals with the most sacred use of the blood: taking it into the Holy of Holies. Chapter 17 deals with the most profane use of the blood: ingesting it while eating meat. Second, Lev. 16:29 is the first verse in Leviticus to teach that the particular issue at hand applies to everyone, "whether native born or alien." Although this phrase, or a form of it, appears throughout 18–25 (18:26; 19:10, 33–34; 20:2; 22:18; 23:22; 24:16, 22; 25:23, 35, 47), it surfaces most frequently in ch. 17 (vv. 8, 10, 12, 13, 15).

As Menahem Haran (1971: 821) has observed, the laws in this section of Leviticus are concerned with the everyday affairs of the community and/or the individual. Ritual matters and explanations are minimal. Leviticus 17 illustrates this. How is the believer to eat meat (a luxury item anyway?), and where is the believer to bring sacrifices?

Two principal restrictions are given. First, no domestic sacrificial animals are to be slaughtered outside the sanctuary (vv. 3–4). Much has been made of the contrast between these two verses and Deut. 12:15, "you may slaughter and eat flesh within any of your towns" (RSV), and similar sentiments in Deut. 12:21, "you may eat within your towns" (NRSV). What Leviticus prohibits, Deuteronomy allows.

The critical view that places P after D is faced here with an oddity, or at least a priestly rule that could be labeled as patent nonsense. In effect, the law would ban the eating of meat for the majority of Israel. It would be tantamount to saying that only in Saint Peter's Basilica could a Mass be celebrated. What, then, about Catholics living far from Rome?

Gordon Wenham (1979: 243) correctly observes, "This law [i.e., Lev. 17:3–7] could be effective . . . when everyone lived close to the sanctuary as during the wilderness wanderings. After the settlement it was no longer feasible to insist that all slaughtering be restricted to the tabernacle. It would have compelled those who lived a long way from the sanctuary to become vegetarians."

In the wilderness God was teaching his people that his tabernacle was a special place, unique and set apart from every other edifice in the camp. It was the heart of that organism. Sacrifices could not be offered casually, indifferently, or at any place that the worshiper deemed appropriate or convenient. Only one house was God's house. (On this topic, the interesting comments by Yehezkel Kaufmann [1960: 180–82] are worth pursuing.) The two passages can be harmonized if one understands the Leviticus 17 passage to be speaking of the sacrificing/slaughtering of animals explicitly as offerings to be brought to God, while the Deuteronomy 12 passage speaks of the sacrificing/slaughtering of animals for consumption in one's home.

The second restriction placed on the slaughter of animals was that before consumption, the blood had to be drained. The prohibition is against eating, not drinking, blood. This rule has already been sounded in Leviticus (3:17; 7:26; cf. Deut. 12:16, 23). Actually, this prohibition appears as early as Gen. 9:4, and is binding upon all humanity, not just Israelites. This may explain why James and others at the apostolic council in Jerusalem, in addressing the needs of non-Jewish Christians, did away with mandatory observance of the dietary laws of Leviticus and Deuteronomy, but not with the blood prohibition (Acts 15:20, 29).

It is a moot question whether Lev. 19:26 speaks to the same issue: "You shall not eat any flesh with the blood in it" (RSV). This is, however, quite a free translation. The Hebrew says simply, "You shall not eat over the blood." The same expression appears in 1 Sam. 14:32–33 and Ezek. 33:25. Perhaps this refers to a pagan rite in which blood was offered to underground deities (Milgrom 1971b), or pouring sacrificial blood on the ground instead of on the altar.

Sexual Purity (18–20)

Chapter 18 is replete with the phrase "you shall not." Chapter 19 is equally filled with the phrase "you shall," as well as "you shall not" and "do not." Thus, the idea of holiness is formulated both negatively and positively. Chapter 20 contains the penalties for the infringement of any of the illicit relationships covered in chs. 18 (sexual) and 19 (magical). These penalties include being put to death by the community, or by God if the community defaults, for worshiping of Molech (20:2–5), or being put to death by God for engaging in prohibited magical practices (20:6); for illicit sexual unions the penalty may be death at the hands of the community ("they shall be put to death" [20:10–16]), death brought by God ("they shall be cut off" [20:17–19]), or childlessness ("they shall die childless" [20:20–21]). It is possible that when the text says that God "cuts off" somebody (vv. 3, 5, 6), it is not referring to God terminating someone's life. This is especially true in verses 2 and 3 where after we read that "the people of the land shall stone them to death" (v. 2 NRSV), we find this, "And [I] will cut them off from the people" (v. 3 NRSV). Hence, being "cut off" may be different from being "put to death," the first being done by God, the second by humans. To be "cut off [by God]" then would either be (a) to lose one's posterity (Ps. 109:13) or (b) to be denied life in the hereafter and reunion with one's ancestors.

Once again the emphasis is that the Israelites' conduct is to be morally superior to that of their pagan neighbors (18:3). Israel does not look to Egypt or Canaan for sexual standards. Unbelievers do not establish the moral criteria by which the believers live in community.

Something of the understanding and approach to sexual matters in nonbiblical religions can be gleaned from this comment by Cyrus Gordon (1965: 125): "The modern student must not make the mistake of thinking that the ancient easterner had any difficulty in reconciling the notion of divinity with carryings on that included chicanery, bribery, indecent exposure for a laugh, and homosexual buffoonery." And if this describes life at the divine level, can life at the human level be far behind, especially if people portray their gods as resembling themselves?

It would be wrong to conclude that these prohibitions are basically reactions against practices of Israel's geographical neighbors. Addressing the subject of homosexuality, John Oswalt (1979: 59–60) observes, "The rationale behind that ethic [of Leviticus 18 and 20] is not simply a reaction to a life style that happens not to be Hebrew. . . . Rather these activities are prohibited because they grow out of and lead to a world view that is radically opposed to that of the Bible. . . . They represent one common outlook on sex and the world, that is, the denial of boundaries."

Most of ch. 18 is devoted to a listing of incestuous relationships (vv. 6–18), but other sexual offenses are also included (vv. 19–23): intercourse with a woman during her menstrual period (because it cannot lead to conception?) (v. 19); adultery (v. 20); giving children as a sacrifice to Molech, a deity worshiped by some of Israel's neighbors (v. 21; cf. 2 Kings 23:10); male homosexuality (v. 22); bestiality (v. 23).

We note that at least two of the prohibited relationships in vv. 6–18 were not always prohibited. Leviticus 18:9 states, "You shall not uncover the nakedness of your sister" (NRSV). Yet Abraham was married to Sarah, his half-sister (Gen. 20:12; cf. 2 Sam. 13:13, where Tamar says to her brother Amnon, "He [King David] will not withhold me from you" NRSV). Leviticus 18:18 states, "You shall not take a woman as a rival wife to her sister, uncovering her nakedness while her sister is yet alive" (RSV). Yet this is precisely what Jacob did (Gen. 29:16–30). This is indirect proof of the antiquity of the patriarchal traditions. What was once legal now became illegal (see Kaufmann 1960: 318–19).

The seriousness of these offenses in chs. 18 and 20 is brought out by the use of the verb "vomit" in both, the same verb used to describe what the fish did with Jonah (Jon. 2:11): "So I punished it for its sin, and the land vomited out its inhabitants" (18:25 NIV); "Keep all my decrees . . . so that the land where I am bringing you to live may not vomit you out" (20:22 NIV).

Leviticus moves without fanfare from its apodictic pronouncements against illicit sex (ch. 18) to equally apodictic pronouncements about positive holiness (ch. 19). Basically, ch. 19 is a collection of ethical and ritual laws, many of which conclude with the phrase "I am the LORD your God." This phrase is used fourteen times in this chapter (as opposed to five times in ch. 18 and only two in ch. 20). The repeated use of this phrase underscores the fact that these laws are rooted in God and in his holy character. They are not a product of some assembly or theological clique.

Holiness is defined in this chapter in terms of social holiness. That is to say, the demonstration of holiness will emerge most clearly in one's relationships. Little in this chapter is private and monastic. Holiness covers relationships to parents (v. 3), to children (v. 29), to God (vv. 4–8, 26–28, 30–31), to the poor and the stranger (vv. 9–10, 15, 33–34), to women (vv. 20–22), to one's neighbor or kin (vv. 11–18, 35–36), to the aged (v. 32), to animals (v. 19), to the soil (vv. 19, 23–25), and to the disabled (v. 14).

Each section denotes a different response from the holy life: obedience to parents and God; respect for the elderly; meeting the physical needs of the poor; telling the truth; rising above the temptations of injustice.

The most memorable verse in this chapter is v. 18b, "You shall love your neighbor as yourself" (NRSV). This is quoted nine times in the New Testament (Matt. 5:43; 19:19; 22:39; Mark 12:31, 33; Luke 10:27; Rom. 13:9; Gal. 5:14; James 2:8). The sentiment is also contained in verses such as 1 John 4:20: "Those who say, 'I love God,' and hate their brothers or sisters, are liars" (NRSV). But, according to Leviticus 19, it is not enough to love one's neighbor as oneself. One must also love the stranger or sojourner as oneself (vv. 33–34). The outsider is not to be kept psychologically on the outside.

Priestly Purity (21–22)

It is the priest as human being, as citizen, who is discussed in these two chapters. The following items are highlighted: restrictions on the number of people for whom the priest may mourn, and the categories of women from which he may not choose a prospective bride (21:1–9); these restrictions are even more stringent for the high priest (21:10–15); physical blemishes, which in most cases are permanent, prohibit a priest from officiating (21:16–24); the priest may not eat any of the sacrificial food when he is temporarily unclean, as spelled out in chs. 13–15 (22:1–9); who in the priest's family has a right to eat priestly food (22:10–16); blemished animals are unacceptable for sacrifice (22:17–30).

It is interesting that ch. 21, before treating any other fact related to the priesthood, first addresses death and mourning and then speaks about marriage. One might have expected the order to be reversed: first marriage and then death and mourning. And the order is the same for both priest and high priest—priest: death and mourning (21:1–6), marriage (21:7); high priest: death and mourning (21:10–12), marriage (21:13–15). Possibly the reason why Leviticus 21 begins with restrictions on those for whom the clergy may grieve (in the case of the high priest, even for his own parents!) is to dissociate biblical faith from either worship of the dead or contacting the dead—a pervasive concept in the ancient Near East, and one in which the priests played a prominent role.

The common denominator in all these regulations is that God has "sanctified/made holy" the priest (21:8, 15, 23; 22:9, 16, 32). Therefore he is to be "holy." By and large these are unique standards imposed only on Israel's clergy. Certainly in any age God's summons to holiness must be exemplified unquestionably in the life of those who "bear the vessels of the Lord." If they do not set and implement the standard, how will the congregation ever exemplify the holy life?

In these priestly regulations we again see that one does not achieve holiness by withdrawing from society. Holiness has to do with one's relationship to family, spouse, and household employees, and with one's own physical appearance.

Holy Festivals (23)

People may be holy. Priests may be holy. Buildings and particular sites may be holy. This section adds to that list certain holy days and festivals on the calendar. The list includes the Sabbath (v. 3); Passover and the Feast of Unleavened Bread (vv. 4–8); the offering by farmers of a sheaf of barley, the first grain to ripen in the spring, to God, who receives his portion of the new crop before any of his people may have access to it (vv. 9–14); the Feast of Weeks or Pentecost (vv. 15–22); the Feast of Trumpets (vv. 23–24); the Day of Atonement (vv. 26–32); the Feast of Tabernacles (vv. 33–44). Part of living the holy life is, according to Leviticus 23, giving God control over one's time weekly (v. 3) and seasonally (vv. 4–44), orienting one's work around worship, not vice versa.

These holy days are to be happy days. Too often these two ideas are kept worlds apart. One can be holy but at the same time unhappy, or happy but at the same time unholy. The people of God are "to rejoice before the LORD," at least on the Festival of Weeks/Pentecost (v. 40).

On the majority of these days normal manual labor (NIV: "regular work") is suspended (vv. 7, 8, 21, 25, 35, 36)—that is, work related to one's occupation and livelihood, but not lighter work, say, around one's house. But on the Sabbath (v. 3) and the Day of Atonement (vv. 28, 30, 31) any and all kind of work is outlawed. It is a time for families to be together. It is a time to be generous in assisting the poor (v. 22).

The claim that all days are holy probably would evolve into the concept that no days are holy. Something of the significance of these festivals to Judaism can be seen in the postexilic prophets. For seventy years God's people had been in captivity. They had not celebrated Passover, Pentecost, or Tabernacles for three-quarters of a century. Imagine a Christian who is denied the privilege of observing Christmas, Good Friday, or Easter for that length of time! Then the Lord sent to the community two interesting prophets whose names were symbolic of their messages. One was Zechariah, "the Lord has remembered." Has he? Can we be sure that he has not forgotten us? The second prophet was Haggai, "my feasts." Imagine having a new pastor named Reverend Feasts when you have not celebrated one of your feasts in seventy years! Both names speak of promise and divine faithfulness.

The Holy Place and the Holy Name (24)

Two areas are discussed with regard to the tabernacle. The first is the necessity of using pure oil for the lighting in the tabernacle (vv. 1–4). The second is that the shewbread, consisting of twelve wheat loaves (for the twelve tribes), set in two rows of six, be replaced every Sabbath (vv. 5–9). Four times (vv. 2, 3, 4, 8) we read that these procedures in the tent of meeting are to be done "continually, regularly" (*tāmîd*)—that is, daily in the case of vv. 1–4 (the lighting of the menorah from evening to morning), and weekly in the case of vv. 5–9 (the priests are eating the provided holy bread).

Then comes a story of a man of mixed parentage who cursed the Name (vv. 10–16), an infraction mandating the death penalty, a penalty enforced by the community, not by a hooded executioner (vv. 14, 16).

The chapter concludes with a catena of laws. It is clear why the first of these laws, the one about one person killing another (v. 17), comes here. It follows the account of the blasphemer who is stoned to death for his crime. Not all taking of human life is illegal. Of special interest here is the resurfacing of the *lex talionis* for maiming (vv. 19–20; cf. Exod. 21:23–24), and its extension to apply to both the sojourner and the native (v. 22). Jacob Milgrom (1971: 146) remarks, "That *lex talionis* . . . was extended to the stranger is one of the great moral achievements of P's legislation. Not only is every distinction eradicated between the powerful and the helpless but even between the Israelite and the non-Israelite." Holiness that is authentic overcomes the parochialisms and provincialisms that are so much a part of unholy life.

The Sabbatical and Jubilee Years (25)

Two strategic years are discussed in this chapter: the Sabbatical Year (vv. 1–7), which occurs every seventh year; and the Jubilee Year (vv. 8–55), which occurs every fiftieth year.

The emphasis on the Sabbatical Year is that the land is to lie fallow every seventh year. Other emphases are stated elsewhere in Scripture. Exodus 23:10–11 says the Sabbatical Year is for the sake of the poor. Deuteronomy 15:1–11 says this year is for debtors and the remission of their debts. In leaving the land fallow for one year out of every seven, the people of God are being reminded that the land, God's gift to his people, needs a Sabbath rest occasionally as much as they do weekly. They are also learning how to trust God to provide for their food needs over that year. As Kawashima (2003a: 385) has observed, the promise in vv. 5–7 that everybody (owners, slaves, laborers, animals) will eat the same food, the food that grows naturally during the Sabbatical Year, recalls the setting of Genesis 1, where all living things shared in the same God-provided bounty. Thus, the Sabbatical Year is not a famine year, but a return-to-paradise year, thanks to God's faithful provision for the needs of all.

The name "Jubilee" is an Anglicized transliteration of the Hebrew word *yôbēl* (v. 10), which translates both as "ram" and as "ram's horn," the sounding of which proclaims the start of the Jubilee Year. As in the Sabbatical Year, land must lie fallow (vv. 11–12). Landed property is returned to the original owner (vv. 25–55) without compensation to the current owner. Land ownership is to be equalized every fifty years. The theological basis for this is found in v. 23: "for the land is mine." He is the Lord of land and of economics.

In a way beyond that of the Sabbatical Year, in the Jubilee observance God is putting his people in an even more potentially devastating situation in which they need to trust him. There is no sowing of seed in the forty-ninth or fiftieth years. What if the forty-eighth year has been a year of drought? Will God sustain his people through three lean years (cf. vv. 20–21)? There is a parallel in the manna story of Exodus 16, where God instructs his people not to gather manna on the Sabbath, and instead he provides a double supply on the sixth day to carry them through the seventh.

The kin of anyone who, for some reason or other, understandable or not, becomes poor should redeem that person (vv. 25–28, 35–38, 47–55). There is a ban on taking interest for room or board by a creditor (vv. 35–38). Nor is the debtor to be treated as a slave (vv. 39–46) if the debtor was forced by poverty into self-enslavement.

Verses 24–55 use the words "redeem, redemption, redeemable" eighteen times (vv. 24, 25, 26 [2x], 29 [2x], 30, 31, 32, 33, 48 [2x], 49 [3x], 51, 52, 54). The verb *gāʾal* ("redeem") and the nouns *gōʾēl* and *gĕʾullâ* ("redeemer" and "redemption") appear in Leviticus again only in ch. 27 (nine times: vv. 13, 15, 19, 20 [2x], 27, 28, 31, 33—actually twelve times if we include the double use of this root in vv. 13, 19, 31, a feature not apparent in English translation). Mixed in with all these references to redemption in 25:24–55 are scattered references to the Jubilee Year (vv. 28 [2x], 30, 31, 33, 40, 50, 52, 54). In obvious ways the law of redemption seems a better option than the Jubilee Year. For example, it seems preferable to retrieve land as soon as one is financially able to do so, or has a close relative willing to do so, rather than wait until the next Jubilee Year, especially if it is decades away.

Ronald Sider (1977: 89) points out tellingly, "It is surely more than coincidental that the trumpet blast announcing the Jubilee sounded forth on the day of atonement (Lev. 25:9)! Reconciliation with God is the precondition for reconciliation with brothers and sisters. Conversely, genuine reconciliation with God leads inevitably to a transformation of all other relationships." Once again, genuine holiness spills over into one's relationship with others—in this case, especially the poor, the indebted, or the enslaved.

The Two Ways (26)

The two ways are the lifestyle that brings the blessing of God (vv. 3–13) versus the lifestyle that brings the wrath of God (vv. 14–46). Leviticus 26 might be labeled as the "altar call" of Leviticus, and it functions in Leviticus as Deuteronomy 27–28 does in Deuteronomy. Blessings are threefold: sufficient rains for the harvest (v. 4), peace in the land (v. 6), and, most of all, the presence of God (v. 11). The wrath of God includes circumstances ranging from disease and sickness (v. 16) to war (vv. 23–29), whose by-products are plague, famine, and cannibalism.

Religious Vows (27)

It would be more accurate to say that this chapter deals with the retraction of, not the making of, religious vows. Is there room in Old Testament faith for legitimate desanctification? This chapter answers yes, in certain instances.

1. Persons may be redeemed (vv. 1–8).
2. Only impure animals may be redeemed (vv. 9–13), not pure animals that are offerable.
3. Houses may be redeemed (vv. 14–15).
4. Land may be redeemed (vv. 16–25).
5. Only unclean firstlings may be redeemed (vv. 26–27).

6. No "devoted thing" (person, animal, land) may be redeemed (vv. 28–29).

7. The tithe from crops may be redeemed, but the animal tithe may not (vv. 30–33), for it is offerable (as in number 2).

In each case, if one desires to reclaim what has been given to God, the added fee is 20 percent more than the value of the item (vv. 13, 15, 19, 27, 31). This must be the Bible's way of saying that the taking of a vow, giving something or somebody to God, is, like marriage, "not to be entered into lightly or unadvisedly." The chapter may be an addendum to 17–26 as many scholars suggest, for 26:46 sounds like a conclusion. But if it is an addendum, it is a great and appropriate addendum, not only to 17–26 but also to 1–26. The focus of ch. 26 is on rewards/punishment for obedience/disobedience. But there is not a word in ch. 27 about rewards. There is no "Anyone who makes a special vow will receive my blessing." Here Leviticus ends on the priceless privilege of pure acts of adoration and devotion to one's God, motivated not by any promise of prosperity in return (in fact, you will be 20 percent poorer!), but simply by one's love for the Lord and his sanctuary.

Chapter 26 has articulated God's vows to people. How appropriate it is that Leviticus follows this with a chapter about people's vows to God. At the heart of religion and holiness are promise and commitment: God's to me, mine to God.

The Holiness Code (Leviticus 17–27)

Eichrodt, W. 1961–1967. *Theology of the Old Testament*. Trans. J. Baker. 2 vols. OTL. Philadelphia: Westminster. Vol. 1, pp. 270–82.

Eissfeldt, O. 1965. *The Old Testament: An Introduction*. Trans. P. R. Ackroyd. New York: Harper & Row. Pp. 233–39.

Gammie, J. G. 1989. *Holiness in Israel*. OBT. Minneapolis: Fortress.

Haran, M. 1971. "Holiness Code." *EncJud* 8:820–25.

Joosten, J. 1996. *People and Land in the Holiness Code*. VTSup 67. Leiden: Brill.

Kaufmann, Y. 1960. *The Religion of Israel*. Trans. M. Greenberg. Chicago: University of Chicago Press.

Knohl, I. 1995. *The Sanctuary of Silence: The Priestly Torah and the Holiness School*. Minneapolis: Fortress.

Kugler, R. A. 1997. "Holiness, Purity, the Body, and Society: The Evidence for Theological Conflict in Leviticus." *JSOT* 76:3–27.

Milgrom, J. 1971. "Lev. 17–26, The Holiness Source." *EncJud* 11:143–47.

———. 1976. "Sanctification." *IDBSup* 782–84.

Schwartz, B. J. 1999. *The Holiness Legislation: Studies in the Holiness Code*. Jerusalem: Magnes.

Wenham, G. 1979. *The Book of Leviticus*. NICOT. Grand Rapids: Eerdmans.

Wright, David P. 1992. "Holiness (OT)." *ABD* 3:237–49.

———. 1999. "Holiness in Leviticus and Beyond: Differing Perspectives." *Int* 55:351–64.

Leviticus 17

Brichto, H. C. 1976. "On Slaughter and Sacrifice, Blood and Atonement." *HUCA* 47:22–36.

McCarthy, D. J. M. 1969. "The Symbolism of Blood and Sacrifice." *JBL* 88:166–76.

Milgrom, J. 1971a. "A Prolegomenon to Lev. 17:11." *JBL* 90:149–56.

———. 1971b. "Blood." *EncJud* 4:1115–16.

———. 2000. "Does H Advocate the Centralization of Worship [Lev. 17:1–7]?" *JSOT* 88:59–76.

Schwartz, B. J. 1991. "The Prohibitions concerning the 'Eating' of Blood in Leviticus 17." In *Priesthood and Cult in Ancient Israel*. Ed. G. A. Anderson and S. M. Olyan. JSOTSup 125. Sheffield: JSOT Press. Pp. 34–66.

———. 1996. "'Profane' Slaughter and the Integrity of the Priestly Code." *HUCA* 67:15–42.

Snaith, N. H. 1974. "The Meaning of *se'irim*." *VT* 24:115–18.

———. 1975. "The Verbs *Zabah* and *Shahat*." *VT* 25:242–46.

Wood, B. G. 1973. "In the Blood Is Life—A Common Belief in Ancient Times?" *Bible and Spade* 2:105–18.

Leviticus 18–20

Bigger, S. 1979. "The Family Laws of Leviticus 18 in Their Setting." *JBL* 98:187–203.

Carmichael, C. M. 1982. "Forbidden Mixtures." *VT* 32:394–415.

———. 1994. "Laws of Leviticus 19." *HTR* 87:239–56.

———. 1997. *Law, Legend, and Incest in the Bible: Leviticus 18–20*. Ithaca, N.Y.: Cornell University Press.

Day, J. 1989. *Molech: A God of Human Sacrifice in the Bible*. University of Cambridge Oriental Publications 41. Cambridge: Cambridge University Press.

Douglas, M. 1999. "Justice as the Cornerstone: An Interpretation of Leviticus 18–20." *Int* 53:341–50.

Frymer-Kensky, T. 1989. "Law and Philosophy: The Case of Sex in the Bible." *Semeia* 45:89–102.

Gordon, C. H. 1965. *The Common Background of Greek and Hebrew Civilizations*. New York: Norton.

Green, A. R. W. 1975. *The Role of Human Sacrifice in the Ancient Near East*. Missoula, Mont.: Scholars Press.

Hartley, J. E., and T. Dwyer. 1996. "An Investigation into the Location of the Laws on Offering to Molek in the Book of Leviticus." In *"Go to the Land I Will Show You": Studies in Honor of Dwight S. Young*. Ed. J. E. Coleson and V. H. Matthews. Winona Lake, Ind.: Eisenbrauns. Pp. 81–94.

Heider, G. C. 1985. *The Cult of Molek: A Reassessment*. JSOTSup 43. Sheffield: JSOT Press.

Hoffner, H. A., Jr. 1973. "Incest, Sodomy and Bestiality in the Ancient Near East." In *Orient and Occident: Essays Presented to Cyrus H. Gordon on the Occasion of His Sixty-fifth Birthday*. Ed. H. A. Hoffner. Neukirchen-Vluyn: Neukirchener Verlag. Pp. 81–90.

Horton, F. L. 1973. "Form and Structure in Laws Relating to Women: Leviticus 18:6–18." In *SBLSP 1973*. Ed. G. W. MacRae. Cambridge, Mass.: Society of Biblical Literature. Pp. 20–33.

Houtmann, C. 1984. "Another Look at Forbidden Mixtures." *VT* 34:226–28.

Johnson, L. T. 1982. "The Use of Leviticus 19 in the Letter of James." *JBL* 101:391–401.

Kaiser, W. C., Jr. 1971. "Leviticus 18:5 and Paul: Do This and You Shall Live (Eternally?)." *JETS* 14:19–28.

Magonet, J. 1983. "The Structure and Meaning of Leviticus 19." *Hebrew Annual Review* 7:151–67.

Malmat, A. 1990a. "'Love Your Neighbor as Yourself': What It Really Means." *BAR* 16 (4):50–51.

———. 1990b. "'You Shall Love Your Neighbor as Yourself': A Case of Misinterpretation [Lev 19,18]?" In *Die Hebräische Bibel und ihre zweifache Nachgeschichte: Festschrift für Rolf Rendtorff zum 65. Geburtstag*. Ed. E. Blum, C. Macholz, and E. W. Stegemann. Neukirchen-Vluyn: Neukirchener Verlag. Pp. 111–15.

McKeating, H. 1979. "Sanctions against Adultery in Ancient Israelite Society, with Some Reflections on Methodology in the Study of Old Testament Ethics." *JSOT* 11:52–72.

Meachem, T. 1997. "The Missing Daughter: Leviticus 18 and 20." *ZAW* 109:254–59.

Milgrom, J. 1977. "The Betrothed Slave-Girls: Leviticus 19:20–22." *ZAW* 89:43–50.

———. 1995. "The Most Basic Law in the Bible." *BRev* 11 (4):17, 48.

———. 1996a. "Law and Narrative and the Exegesis of Leviticus xix 19." *VT* 46:544–48.

———. 1996b. "The Changing Concept of Holiness in the Pentateuchal Codes, with Emphasis on Leviticus 19." In *Reading Leviticus: A Conversation with Mary Douglas*. Ed. J. Sawyer. JSOTSup 227. Sheffield: JSOT Press. Pp. 65–75.

Mohrmann, D. C. 2004. "Making Sense of Sex: A Study of Leviticus 18." *JSOT* 29:57–79.

Olyan, S. 1994. "'And with a Male You Shall Not Lie the Lying Down of a Woman': On the Meaning and Significance of Leviticus 18:22 and 20:13." *Journal of the History of Sexuality* 5:179–206.

Oswalt, J. 1979. "The Old Testament and Homosexuality." In *What You Should Know about Homosexuality.* Ed. C. W. Keysor. Grand Rapids: Zondervan. Pp. 17–77.

Phillips, A. 1973. "Some Aspects of Family Law in Pre-exilic Israel." *VT* 23:349–61.

———. 1980. "Uncovering the Father's Skirt." *VT* 30:38–43.

Schwartz, B. J. 1986. "A Literary Study of the Slave Girls Pericope—Leviticus 19:20–22." *Scripta hierosolymitana* 31:241–55.

Snaith, N. H. 1966. "The Cult of Molech." *VT* 16:123–24.

Stager, L. E. 1985. "The Archaeology of the Family in Ancient Israel." *BASOR* 260:370–72.

Tosato, A. 1984. "The Law of Leviticus 18:18: A Reinvestigation." *CBQ* 46:199–214.

Walsh, J. T. 2001. "Leviticus 18:22 and 20:13: Who Is Doing What to Whom?" *JBL* 120:201–9.

Leviticus 21–22

See also the bibliography at the end of Leviticus 8–10.

Levine, B. A. 1976. "Priests." *IDBSup* 687–90.

Milgrom, J. 1976. *Cult and Conscience: The ASHAM and the Priestly Doctrine of Repentance.* SJLA 18. Leiden: Brill. Pp. 63–66.

Zipor, M. 1987. "Restrictions on Marriage for Priests (Lev 21, 7, 13–14)." *Bib* 68:259–67.

Leviticus 23

Andreason, N. E. 1978. *Rest and Redemption: A Study of the Biblical Sabbath.* Andrews University Monographs 11. Berrien Springs, Mich.: Andrews University Press.

Eichrodt, W. 1961–1967. *Theology of the Old Testament.* Trans. J. Baker. 2 vols. OTL. Philadelphia: Westminster. Vol. 1, pp. 119–33.

Haran, M. 1972. "The Passover Sacrifice." In *Studies in the Religion of Ancient Israel.* VTSup 23. Leiden: Brill. Pp. 86–116.

Hui, T. K. 1990. "The Purpose of Israel's Annual Feasts." *BSac* 147:143–54.

Kaiser, W. C., Jr. 1985. *The Uses of the Old Testament in the New.* Chicago: Moody. Pp. 145–76.

Kaufmann, Y. 1960. *The Religion of Israel.* Trans. M. Greenberg. Chicago: University of Chicago Press. Pp. 305–9.

Kraus, H. J. 1966. *Worship in Israel.* Richmond: John Knox. Pp. 32–35.

Milgrom, J. 1997. "The First Fruits Festival of Grain and the Composition of Leviticus 23:9–21." In *Tehillah lᵉ-Moshe: Biblical and Judaic Studies in Honor of Moshe Greenberg.* Ed. M. Cogan et al. Winona Lake, Ind.: Eisenbrauns. Pp. 81–89.

Robinson, G. 1980. "The Idea of Rest in the Old Testament and the Search for the Basic Character of Sabbath." *ZAW* 92:32–42.

———. 1988. *The Origin and Development of the Old Testament Sabbath: A Comprehensive Exegetical Approach.* Beiträge zur biblischen Exegese und Theologie 21. Frankfurt am Main and New York: Lang.

Siker-Gieseler, J. 1981. "The Theology of the Sabbath: A Canonical Approach." *Studia Biblica et Theologica* 11:5–20.

Stewart, R. 1971. "The Jewish Festivals." *EvQ* 43:149–61.

Vaux, R. de. 1965. *Ancient Israel.* Trans. J. McHugh. 2 vols. New York: McGraw-Hill. Vol. 2, pp. 475–83.

Leviticus 24

Hutton, R. R. 1999. "The Case of the Blasphemer Revisited (Lev xxiv 10–23)." *VT* 49:532–41.

Master, J. R. 2002. "The Place of Chapter 24 in the Structure of the Book of Leviticus." *BSac* 159:415–24.

Mittwock, H. 1965. "The Story of the Blasphemer Seen in a Wider Context." *VT* 15:386–89.

Weingreen, J. 1972. "The Case of the Blasphemer (Leviticus xxiv, 10ff.)." *VT* 22:118–23.

Leviticus 25

Bergsma, J. 2003. "The Jubilee: A Post-Exilic Priestly Attempt to Reclaim Lands?" *Bib* 84:225–46.

Brueggemann, W. 1977. *The Land.* Philadelphia: Fortress.

Carmichael, C. M. 1999. "The Sabbatical/Jubilee Cycle and the Seven-Year Famine in Egypt." *Bib* 80:224–39.

Casperson, L. W. 2003. "Sabbatical, Jubilee, and the Temple of Solomon." *VT* 53:283–96.

Fager, J. 1993. *Land Tenure and the Biblical Jubilee: Uncovering Hebrew Ethics through the Sociology of Knowledge.* JSOTSup 155. Sheffield: JSOT Press.

Gamaron, H. 1971. "The Biblical Law against Loans on Interest." *JNES* 30:127–34.

Gnuse, R. 1985. "Jubilee Legislation in Leviticus: Israel's Vision of Social Reform." *BTB* 15:43–48.

Habel, N. 1995. *The Land Is Mine: Six Biblical Land Ideologies.* OBT. Minneapolis: Fortress.

Hoenig, S. 1969. "Sabbatical Years and the Year of Jubilee." *JQR* 59:222–36.

Hudson, M. 1999. "'Proclaim Liberty throughout the Land': The Economic Roots of the Jubilee." *BRev* 15 (1):26–33, 44.

Kawashima, R. S. 2003a. "The Jubilee Year and the Return of Cosmic Purity." *CBQ* 65:370–89.

———. 2003b. "The Jubilee, Every 49 or 50 Years?" *VT* 53:117–20.

Kinsler, F. Ross. 1999. "Leviticus 25." *Int* 53:395–99.

Lang, H. 1986. "The Jubilee Principle: Is It Relevant for Today?" *Ecumenical Review* 38:437–43.

Lemeche, N. 1976. "Manumission of Slaves—the Fallow Year—the Sabbatical Year— the Jobel Year." *VT* 26:38–59.

Maloney, F. J. 2000a. "The Scriptural Basis of Jubilee, Part I: The First Testament—The End of Servitude." *ITQ* 65:99–110.

———. 2000b. "The Scriptural Basis of Jubilee, Part II: The Second Testament—At What Price?" *ITQ* 65:231–44.

Maloney, R. 1974. "Usury and Restrictions on Interest-Taking in the Ancient Near East." *CBQ* 36:1–20.

Milgrom, J. 1995. "The Land Redeemer and the Jubilee [Lev 25, 33a 39–43]." In *Fortunate the Eyes That See: Essays in Honor of David Noel Freedman in Celebration of His Seventieth Birthday*. Ed. A. B. Beck et al. Grand Rapids: Eerdmans. Pp. 66–69.

North, R. 1954. *Sociology of the Biblical Jubilee*. AnBib 4. Rome: Pontifical Biblical Institute.

———. 2000. *The Biblical Jubilee . . . after Fifty Years*. AnBib 145. Rome: Pontifical Biblical Institute.

Ringe, S. H. 1985. *Jesus, Liberation, and the Biblical Jubilee: Images for Ethics and Christology*. OBT. Philadelphia: Fortress.

Schenker, A. 1998. "The Biblical Legislation on the Release of Slaves: The Road from Exodus to Leviticus." *JSOT* 78:23–41.

Sider, R. J. 1977. *Rich Christians in an Age of Hunger: A Biblical Study*. Downers Grove, Ill.: InterVarsity Press. Pp. 88–92.

Sutherland, J. R. 1982. "Usury: God's Forgotten Doctrine." *Crux* 18:9–14.

Ucko, H., ed. 1997. *The Jubilee Challenge: Utopia or Possibility? Jewish and Christian Insights*. Geneva: WCC Publications.

Vaux, R. de. 1965. *Ancient Israel*. Trans. J. McHugh. 2 vols. New York: McGraw-Hill. Vol. 1, pp. 173–77.

Weinfeld, M. 1985. "Freedom Proclamations in Egypt and in the Ancient Near East." In *Pharaonic Egypt: The Bible and Christianity*. Ed. S. Israelit-Groll. Jerusalem: Magnes. Pp. 317–27.

———. 1990. "Sabbatical Year and Jubilee in the Pentateuchal Laws and Their Ancient Near Eastern Background." In *The Law in the Bible and in Its Environment*. Ed. T. Veijola. Publications of the Finnish Exegetical Society 51. Göttingen: Vandenhoeck & Ruprecht. Pp. 39–62.

———. 1995. *Social Justice in Ancient Israel and in the Ancient Near East*. Minneapolis: Fortress.

Westbrook, R. 1971a. "Jubilee Laws." *ILR* 6:209–26.

———. 1971b. "Redemption of Land." *ILR* 6:367–75.

———. 1991. *Property and the Family in Bibical Law.* JSOTSup 113. Sheffield: JSOT Press. Pp. 36–57.

Westphal, M. 1978. "Sing Jubilee." *The Other Side* 14 (March): 29–35.

Wright, C. J. H. 1984. "What Happened Every Seven Years in Israel? Old Testament Sabbatical Institutions for Land, Debts and Slaves." *EvQ* 56:129–38, 193–201.

———. 1992. "Jubilee, Year of." *ABD* 3:1024–27.

Leviticus 26

Milgrom, J. 1997. "Leviticus 26 and Ezekiel." In *The Quest for Context and Meaning: Studies in Biblical Intertextuality in Honor of James A. Sanders.* Ed. C. A. Evans and S. Talmon. BIS 25. Leiden: Brill. Pp. 57–62.

Leviticus 27

Gehman, H. S. 1975. "The Oath in the Old Testament: Its Vocabulary, Idiom, and Syntax; Its Semantics and Theology in the Masoretic Text and the Septuagint." In *Grace upon Grace: Essays in Honor of Lester J. Kuyper.* Ed. J. I. Cook. Grand Rapids: Eerdmans. Pp. 51–63.

Milgrom, J. 1976. *Cult and Conscience: The ASHAM and the Priestly Doctrine of Repentance.* SJLA 18. Leiden: Brill. Pp. 44–63.

Wenham, G. J. 1978. "Leviticus 27,2–8 and the Price of Slaves." *ZAW* 90:264–65.

PART FOUR

Numbers

16

Preparations for Departure from Sinai

NUMBERS 1:1–10:10

If in some ways "Leviticus" seems an odd title for the third book of the Pentateuch, the same could be said about the common English title for this fourth book of the Pentateuch. We owe the title "Numbers" to the Vulgate's *Numeri*, taken from the Septuagint's *Arithmoi*. There are, to be sure, number lists and totals scattered throughout Numbers (e.g., the census lists of chs. 1 and 26, and the census of the Levites in chs. 3 and 4), but these number chapters are uncommon in Numbers.

The title for this book in the Hebrew Bible is "In the Wilderness," taken from the fourth word in the Hebrew text of Num. 1:1 ("and-spoke Yahweh to-Moses in-the-wilderness-of Sinai . . ."). The wilderness, that relatively unpopulated stretch of land between Egypt and Canaan first entered by Israel in Exod. 15:22, is the geographical setting for Numbers. As such, it will be a place where God's people will either deepen their trust in the power of their God to supply their needs or doubt their God's abilities and resources. Wilderness will represent for Israel either possibilities or problems as they move through this buffer zone "between liberation and landedness" (Fretheim 2001: 111).

It is almost a consensus that the Book of Numbers leaves much to be desired and has much that is puzzling in the presentation of its material. Thus B. A. Levine (1976: 634) sees it as "the least coherent of all the Torah books." R. C. Dentan's (1962: 567) view is similar: "Since the book has no real unity and was not composed in accordance with any logical, predetermined plan, whatever outline may be imposed on it will have to be recognized as largely subjective and arbitrary." To cite but one example, commentators try to make sense of why ch. 15, a compendium of miscellaneous laws, comes between the account of the spies/scouts (chs. 13–14) and the account of Korah's rebellion (ch. 16).

Dissenters from this evaluation are few, but among them is Brevard Childs. His thesis is that all the materials in Numbers—the cultic, legal, narrative, and even the statistical information—revolve around the overarching theme of holiness. Childs (1979: 199) remarks, "In spite of its diversity of subject matter and complex literary development the book of Numbers maintains a unified sacerdotal interpretation of God's will for his people which is set forth in a sharp contrast between the holy and the profane." I am more inclined to accept the evaluation of Childs than of those who view Numbers as a random collection of J/E and mostly P materials.

Perhaps it is best to begin by observing the divisions within the book, based on geographical and chronological notations.

> 1:1–10:10—Preparations for Departure from Sinai
> 1:1: "The LORD spoke to Moses in the wilderness of Sinai . . . on the first day of the second month, in the second year after they had come out of the land of Egypt" (NRSV).
> 10:11–20:21—Departure from Sinai and Arrival at Kadesh
> 10:11: "In the second year, in the second month, on the twentieth day of the month, the cloud was taken up from over the tabernacle of the testimony" (RSV).
> 20:22–36:13—Journey from Kadesh to Moab
> 20:22: "And they journeyed from Kadesh" (RSV).

Table 12 lists the chronology of each section.

We should note that not all commentators agree on precisely where the second section ends and the third section begins. Both M. Noth and R. C. Dentan conclude the second section at 20:13. G. B. Gray (*A Critical and Exegetical Commentary on Numbers* [1903]) ends the second section at 21:9. The New Oxford Annotated Bible (RSV [1973]), in editorial notes, terminates the second section at 21:13. F. L. Moriarty (1968) suggests 22:1 as the conclusion to the unit.

Table 12

Duration	Reference	Cross-reference
20 days	1:1–10:10	Num. 1:1; 10:11
38 years	10:11–20:21	Num. 33:38 (date of Aaron's death)
6 months	20:22–36:13	Num. 33:38; Deut. 1:3

Dennis Olson, in several studies (1985, 1996, 1997), has suggested dividing Numbers into two sections. Using the two lay censuses of ch. 1 and ch. 26 as his key, his first unit is 1–25, his second 26–36. The first unit covers the first generation of Israelites who came out of Egypt, all of whom (except for Joshua and Caleb) never made it to Canaan. They perished in the wilderness because of incessant sinfulness and disobedience. The second unit covers the "wilderness-baby generation," the second generation, those to whom Deuteronomy is addressed and who will enter Canaan under Joshua's leadership. Thus for Olson, Numbers is about the death of the old (chs. 1–25) and the birth of the new (chs. 26–36), and God having to start over.

There are some powerful contrasts between 1–25 and 26–36, all of which put those of the second part in a better light than those of the first part. In the first military encounter that the Israelites fight in 1–25, they lose (14:45). In the one post–chapter 26 military encounter that the second-generation Israelites fight in 26–36, they win (ch. 31). Elsewhere in 1–25 Israel either wants to avoid confrontation (13:31–32) or veers away from confrontation (20:21). Where Israel is victorious in 1–26—the accounts of destroying Arad in 21:1–3 and defeating Sihon and Og in 21:21–35—the victories probably should be credited to the second generation. That reading is more likely than believing that the first generation of Israelites, under the judgment of God and destined to be obliterated shortly, are the triumphant warriors. W. W. Lee, in a perceptive study (2000), disagrees with Olson, suggesting that 21:1–3 rather than ch. 26 marks the transition from the old to the new generation.

A second contrast between the two units is that many Israelites die or suffer in 1–25, but none die or suffer in 26–36:

1. 11:1: "fire from the LORD . . . consumed some of the outskirts of the camp" (NIV)
2. 11:33: "he [the LORD] struck them with a severe plague" (NIV)
3. 12:10: "there stood Miriam—leprous, like snow" (NIV)
4. 14:37: "these men . . . were struck down and died of a plague" (NIV)
5. 16:32: "the earth opened its mouth and swallowed them" (NIV)

6. 16:35: "fire came out from the LORD and consumed the 250 men" (NIV)
7. 16:49: "14,700 people died from the plague" (NIV)
8. 20:28: "Aaron died there on top of the mountain" (NIV)
9. 25:8: "he [Phinehas] drove the spear through both of them" (NIV)
10. 25:9: "those who died in the plague numbered 24,000" (NIV)

I have labeled the first unit in Numbers as "Preparations for Departure from Sinai." It covers 1:1–10:10. The Israelites have not moved geographically from Mount Sinai. What are the preparations for departure?

Census and Tribal Arrangement (1–2)

In terms of pure excitement and dramatic effect on the reader, the material presented in the first two chapters of Numbers does not measure up to the impact created by the clashing thunder and smoke that engulfed Sinai, followed by the revelation of God's will. Have we gone from the miraculous to the mundane, from the terrific to the trite?

In these two chapters Moses is told by God to take a census of the congregation of Israel (1:1–3). He is assigned a representative from each tribe, except that of Levi, to assist in the taking of this census (1:4–16). The census is taken (1:17–46). The Levites are exempted from this particular census (1:47–54). An area is assigned to each of the tribes on the east, south, west, or north side of the tent of meeting, an area of residence that is to be maintained whether the people are encamped or on the march (2:1–34).

There are, nonetheless, a few things here that merit our attention. The census is to include all males aged twenty years and older, "all in Israel who are able to go forth to war" (1:3). Israel is being sent forth as a sheep among wolves. Military activity, for either preservation or conquest, will be inevitable. The previous encounter with the Amalekites (Exod. 17:8–16) is a harbinger of experiences ahead. What inevitably lies immediately ahead in the journeyings of Israel is brought out by the use of the phrase "able to serve in the army" fifteen times in ch. 1 (vv. 3, 18, 20, 22, 24, 26, 28, 30, 32, 34, 36, 38, 40, 42, 45). The presence of God over/among/at the head of his people as they march on does not render the need for a prepared army superfluous. God works not outside of his people, but through his people, to see them realize his destination for them.

We note here that the initiative for taking the census is from God, as was the sending out of the scouts to look over Canaan (13:1–2). Moses does not suddenly feel the need to increase the number of military personnel. The reader fails to detect in Moses any attitude similar to that ascribed by Joab to David and his census-taking: "But why does my lord the king delight in this thing?" (2 Sam. 24:3 RSV, with an added word evidenced by the parallel, 1 Chron. 21:3).

Previously I mentioned the theme of holiness in Numbers. It is in the last paragraph of ch. 1 (vv. 47–54) that this particular theme emerges. To be sure, we are informed that the Levites are not to be numbered in the census involving the nonclerical tribes. Are they left out completely? Numbers 1:50–51 assigns three duties to the Levites: transporting the tabernacle, dismantling it, and reassembling it. But then follows this awesome note: "Anyone else who goes near it shall be put to death" (1:51b NIV). To trespass on another's responsibilities brings death.

Yet there is more. Two verses later we read, "The Levites shall encamp around the tabernacle of the testimony, that there may be no wrath upon the congregation of the people of Israel; and the Levites shall keep charge of [or, 'shall do guard duty for'] the tabernacle of the testimony" (1:53 RSV). The Levites are sacerdotal guards who must strike down any intruder who attempts to violate a prohibition with regard to tabernacle service. If the intruder is not stopped, the whole community falls under God's judgment.

Thus the Israelites cannot be nonchalant in meeting their enemy ahead (vv. 1–46). But neither can they be careless or indifferent in their worship of God (vv. 47–54). An enemy can wipe them out, but so can God's wrath! They must avoid at all costs the attitude that says, "I'll do it my way."

As G. S. Ogden (1996: 425) has observed, Numbers 2 in our modern Bibles is arranged so as to emphasize the centrality of God's presence among his people via the either assembled or disassembled tent in the middle of the camp. On each of its four sides stand the priests and Moses (east), the Kohathite Levites (south), the Gershonite Levites (west), and the Merari Levites (north), and behind each of these four groups there lay three tribes on each side:

2:1–2: instructions for the camp (2 verses)

2:3–9: Judah between Issachar and Zebulon on the east (7 verses)

2:10–16: Reuben between Gad and Simeon on the south (7 verses)

2:17: Levites and the tent in the middle (1 verse)

2:18–24: Ephraim between Benjamin and Manasseh on the west (7 verses)

2:25–31: Dan between Asher and Naphtali on the north (7 verses)

2:32–33: summary and totals (2 verses)

[2:34: a statement of compliance]

Two Levitical Censuses (3–4)

Most of the content in these two chapters is devoted to a description of the numbers and duties of the Levites. But even before readers encounter the results of the first census, they are greeted with a reminder of Aaron's two sons Nadab and Abihu, who "died before the LORD when they offered unholy fire before the LORD . . . and they had no children" (3:4 RSV). There is a right way to worship the Lord, an infraction of which brings disastrous consequences for both laity (1:51) and clergy (3:4).

But that is not all. Two more times in ch. 3 the ominous threat of execution for trespass in the worship of God is highlighted: "anyone else who comes near shall be put to death" (vv. 10, 38). Jacob Milgrom (1970: 17–18) has shown convincingly that the translation "come near" or "approach" is not what the text is prohibiting; rather, the word can only mean "to exceed one's privileges" or "to usurp the responsibilities of another," or "to encroach." The Israelites, including the Levites, were to know what they must do and must not do, and they were not to confuse the two. Otherwise, they must accept the consequences.

Why were there two Levitical censuses (3:14–39; 4:1–49)? Actually, the two are quite distinct from one another. A clue in discerning the distinction is found in the first census in 3:15: "Number the sons of Levi . . . every male from a month old and upward" (RSV). By contrast, the second census includes those "from thirty years old up to fifty years old" (4:3 NRSV). Thus the first census starts with those in infancy and is open-ended, while the second is limited to those falling within the twenty years from age thirty to fifty.

Might we assume, then, that the Levites included in the first census are being earmarked for service that will be lifelong? Thus there is no age restriction. On the other hand, the second census includes Levites who are to be inducted into a ministry for which there is a time restriction: the twenty years after adolescence and young manhood, and before the beginning of advanced age.

The text itself affirms the reason for the limitation of service in Numbers 4. Here it is physical labor that is being described. Specifically it involves assembling, dismantling, and carrying the tabernacle. It is not wide of the mark to translate the word "service/work" (4:3, 23, 24, 27, 30, 31, 33, 35, 39, 43, 47) as "strenuous physical labor." For that reason a retirement age is prescribed, fifty, and a starting age is prescribed, thirty. It is interesting that the minimum age in ch. 1 for eligibility to serve in the army is twenty, but in ch. 4 the minimum age for eligibility to serve as a Levite vis-à-vis the sanctuary is thirty. Ten more years of maturation are required for those who would enter the Lord's service as opposed to those who would enter the Lord's army.

The responsibilities are threefold and are divided among the sons of Levi. The responsibilities for the Kohathites are spelled out in 4:4–20. They have the special distinction of carrying "the holy things" of the tabernacle (vv. 15, 19). For that reason two extra items are added. First, the chapter says that the actual work of dismantling these most sacred parts of the tabernacle is the responsibility of Aaron and his sons, not the Kohathites at all (vv. 5–14)! The Kohathites are transporters, not dismantlers.

Second, to give the injunction force, it is noted that the Kohathites will die (vv. 15, 18, 20) if they overstep their boundaries. At least so far, Numbers seldom has missed the opportunity to inject, in the midst of statistical reports and work assignments, the somber note about the consequences of disobedience. God, in his holiness, will have it no other way.

The second group of Levites is the Gershonites (vv. 21–28). Their work primarily is to carry the tabernacle curtains, or at least to stand guard by the wagons on which the curtains are carried. Absent here is any note, as with the Kohathites, that they operate under priestly directive or that usurpation is a capital offense.

The third group of Levites is the Merarites (vv. 29–33). Like the Gershonites, they stand guard over a portion of the tabernacle carried in wagons. This time the material is the wooden frames and pillars.

One can see that the Kohathites have the greatest privilege. They also have the greatest responsibilities. To whom much is given, much is required. Those who climb highest may fall farthest.

Keeping the Camp Holy (5)

Numbers began by devoting two chapters to the laity in Israel (1–2). Two chapters were given to the clergy, the Levites (3–4). Now there is a return, for two more chapters, to the laity (5–6), in each section of which the clergy play a significant role. They deal with impurity concerns (5:1–4); they may be the beneficiary of the restitution, in the absence of family, for someone against whom sin was committed (5:5–10); they officiate at the ritual of a wife suspected of adultery (5:11–31); they play a major role in the life of a Nazirite, especially as he or she prepares to exit that office (6:1–21); they prayerfully bless the people (6:2–27).

The first four chapters have underscored the sanctity of the tabernacle, either in place assignment or in role assignment. It is God's dwelling place, and all is to be observed and implemented as he has spoken. It is not without significance that these first four chapters all end on the same note: "Thus did the people [or, 'Moses'] according to the word of the Lord, as the Lord commanded" (1:54; 2:34; 3:51; 4:49).

Having thus delineated this idea, it is natural for the text to follow these directives with various ordinances that will help to maintain the camp as holy. The first four chapters have been positive: this is where you station yourself; this is what you are supposed to do. By contrast, Numbers 5 is negative in its emphasis. It deals with putting out of the camp those who defile it or detract from its sacred character. Thus the leper is banned (cf. Lev. 13:46), as is the one with any kind of a discharge (cf. Leviticus 15, which, however, unlike Leviticus 13, does not use the expression "sent/live outside the camp"). To be sure, the person is not executed, put to death like a Kohathite, but is exiled from the community.

Only with the knowledge of a stipulation like this is one able to appreciate fully Jesus' actions in "touching" a leper (Mark 1:41). If the disciples were present to observe this, it is not hard to believe that they protested, "Lord, you've just contaminated yourself!" Might it be possible that Jesus, to prove the contrary, immediately pressed his hand flat on the flesh of one of his disciples, probably Peter?

If certain types of physical impurities defile God's camp (5:1–4), what then of deliberate sin and its baleful effects? This question is addressed by 5:5–10 (essentially an elaboration of the guilt-offering section in Lev. 5:14–6:7). Wherever sin surfaces in the community, it must be openly acknowledged by the perpetrator, for to sin against another child of God is to sin against God himself. Therefore oral confession is indispensable—"that person incurs guilt and shall confess the sin that has been committed"—as is full restitution plus 20 percent more than the value of what was taken or stolen. All of this precedes the atonement ritual performed by the priest.

There is also a new note added in this paragraph. If the victim of the crime is deceased and has no relatives, this does not cancel obligations of restitution. Far from it. Now the monies are to be turned over to the priest and the sanctuary (vv. 8–10). Once again the note is sounded: God's camp is to be a holy place, a pure place. Neither Levitical nor lay deviations from the divine plan will be tolerated. Unclean people must be excluded. Sin against a neighbor must be articulated by the perpetrator and repented of, thus paving the way for full restitution both with the offended party and with God.

The third paragraph in the chapter (vv. 11–31) continues the theme of the maintenance of holiness among God's people. Here the issue is alleged/actual adultery by a wife. The husband suspects her infidelity, but there were no witnesses, nor was the wife apprehended in an embarrassing situation.

The previous paragraph had discussed actual sin between two people. This paragraph discusses potential sin between two spouses. One item that connects 5:5–10 with 5:11–31 is that both deal with unfaithfulness, unfaithfulness to God in 5:6 and unfaithfulness to one's spouse in 5:12. In both cases the Hebrew expresses an act of infidelity with *māʿal maʿal* (cognate verb and noun), which carries the idea of committing sacrilege against or breaking faith with someone. It is intriguing that even suspected sin must be investigated. If the suspicion turns out to be nothing but that, so be it; but if disturbing and aberrant factors are uncovered, they must be dealt with.

The modern reader of Scripture may come away from such a story with second thoughts about its legitimacy. Why is there a trial only for the suspected wife? What if the woman suspects her husband of infidelity? Does she have any options? Then again, does such a procedure give the husband the right to force his wife through an ordeal any and every time he entertains illusions about possible escapades on her part? Must she imbibe this unpalatable "mixed drink" just to satisfy his curiosity?

The following observations may be made. First, we may safely assume that the husband resorts to this trial procedure only if he is unable to eradicate his suspicions. Nagging doubts will not go away, and so in that case something must be done. It is unlikely that an insanely jealous and highly insecure husband would be allowed to continually test his wife. S. K. Sherwood (2002: 146) wonders whether this law was ever actually put into practice. Indeed, nowhere does Scripture record a case of it being enforced. But if it was enforced, Sherwood comments that after such a shameful display as the law prescribes, even if the wife is proven innocent, not only would the wife lose her respect and honor in the community, but the husband likewise would lose his. Accordingly, any husband would think long and hard before putting his wife through such a trial.

Second, it is inaccurate to call the procedure to which the wife is subjected a trial by ordeal. The accused adulteress is not forced to plunge her hand into hot water, nor must she walk barefoot on spikes, nor is she submerged in water over her head. Such are the tests used in trial by ordeal. For example, Law 132 of the Code of Hammurabi, regarding an issue like that in Num. 5:11–31, reads, "If a finger has been pointed at a man's wife because of another man, but she has not been caught lying with that other man, she shall leap into the River for the sake of her husband." That is, if guilty, she sinks and drowns, and if innocent, she survives. In the Code of Hammurabi the danger is quite real; in Numbers it is hypothetical. (And indeed, in Num. 5:27 what does it mean that the imbibed water "shall . . . cause bitter pain, and her body shall swell, and her thigh shall fall away" [RSV]? Is this physical atrophy, sterility, or something else?) Another reason that negates the idea of a trial by ordeal is that in such a trial the accused is assumed guilty unless proven innocent. As both H. C. Brichto (1975: 66) and J. Sasson (1972: 251) observe, the ritual in Numbers 5 is just the opposite: it judges on the innocence, not the guilt, of the accused. Frymer-Kensky (1984: 24) points out that in true trials by ordeal the god's decision on the situation is manifested immediately, which is not the case in Numbers 5.

A third observation grows out of the preceding paragraph. Far from dehumanizing the woman by making her accountable to every whim of a capricious husband, the procedure urges just the opposite. Says Brichto (1975: 67), after observing the often disadvantaged place of women in the Old Testament, "The ritual . . . is a ploy in her favor—it proposes that the husband 'put up or shut up.'" If he is suspicious of his wife's integrity, then let him be brave enough to initiate a scheme that will establish the truth one way or the other; if he is not brave enough to move from imagination to implementation, then let him drop the charges and stop the insinuations.

The Nazirite (6)

Except for vv. 21–27, which feature the Aaronic benediction, this entire chapter is given over to a description of the Nazirite. We are familiar with this office because of those auspicious individuals in Scripture who were Nazirites. This includes such notables as Samson, Samuel, and John the Baptist (Luke 1:15). These three were leaders in their respective periods. Samson and Samuel were outstanding military chieftains or prophets leading Israel's armies against the Philistines. In their activities they resemble more a West Point graduate than they do a member of a monastic community.

Yet in Numbers 6 none of these positive elements emerges. The chapter is more concerned to describe what the Nazirite may not do than what he or she (see below) is to do. I suggest that this is in keeping with the emphasis seen so far in Numbers vis-à-vis God's demands for holiness. His laws are not to be sidestepped. Also, given the use throughout the chapter of phrases such as "as long as he is a Nazirite" (v. 4 NIV), "during the entire period of his vow of separation" (v. 5 NIV), "when the period of his separation is over" (v. 13 NIV), and "this is the law of the Nazirite . . . in accordance with his separation" (v. 21 NIV), Numbers 6 is primarily about the temporary Nazirite as opposed to lifelong Nazirites such as Samson or Samuel. One thinks of a parallel in our times that is often made between "short-term" missionaries and "career" missionaries.

Three restrictions are placed on Nazirites. First, they are to abstain from wine, strong drink, vinegar, grapes, and grape juice. Second, they are not to cut their hair. Third, they are to avoid contact with the deceased, including members of their own family. So Nazirites are to be disciplined in their appetites, distinctive in their appearance, discreet in their associations.

If a Nazirite does become contaminated through accidental contact with a corpse, atonement proceedings become mandatory (vv. 9–12). Even at the completion of the Nazirite vow the individual brings a burnt offering, a sin offering, and a peace offering. The offerings are then presented to the Lord in this order: sin offering, burnt offering, peace offering (vv. 13–20).

Chapter 5 began with a note regarding the presence of the unclean in the camp of God. They are to be quarantined, both male and female (5:3). The chapter continued with the emphasis, "When a man or a woman commits any of the sins. . . ." The remainder of the chapter dealt with husband-wife relationships. In the same way the Nazirite office is open to "either a man or a woman." Neither sex has a monopoly on this position.

That such an office was available to women becomes even more startling when one realizes that the proscriptions for the Nazirite parallel most closely those for the high priest as opposed to the lower echelons of the priesthood. For example, a Nazirite must avoid self-contamination contracted through contact with the corpse of a family member (Num. 6:7). This is true also for the high priest (Lev. 21:11), but not for the ordinary priests (Lev. 21:1–4). The Nazirite is to abstain from intoxicants (Num. 6:4). This is true also for Aaron and his sons when they "go into the tent of meeting" (Lev. 10:9). Parallel to the injunction against cutting the hair is an injunction regarding the hair directed toward the high priest (Lev. 10:6; 21:10) and the anointing of his head with oil (Lev. 21:10; Exod. 29:7). No one is barred from Nazirite ministry on the basis of gender, unlike the Levitical and priestly ministries, for which only males are eligible.

Perhaps the last paragraph, the Aaronic benediction in vv. 21–27, is to be connected with the information about the Nazirite by the notation that the Nazirite is to be "holy to the LORD" (v. 8 NRSV). This is true of the priests too. They are "to be holy to their God" (Lev. 21:6–7). Also, the section about Nazirites is introduced by "Say to the people of Israel" (v. 2 RSV). To Aaron and his sons Moses is to say, "Thus you shall bless the people of Israel" (v. 23 RSV).

It is important to note that it is not Aaron who blesses. He is transmitter, not author. It is the Lord, and only the Lord (note the threefold use of the Tetragrammaton in the blessing), who blesses. The Lord's work is to "bless and keep" his people. The verb "bless" is familiar enough to readers of the Bible. The meaning of the verb "keep" is less known. This verb is used about 450 times in the Bible, and according to Paul Riemann (1970: 483), "Nowhere is there a single instance where a man's keeping another man is an expressed covenant norm or even a recognized social obligation." The Lord, and the Lord alone, is the keeper.

He also "makes his face to shine" and "lifts up his countenance" upon his people. One wonders here if perhaps what is involved in this blessing is the deliberate use of court imagery. God as king graciously grants his subjects an audience with royalty. He is not aloof. The expression "to lift up one's face" is used elsewhere in Scripture with a definite connotation. Thus, Job 42:8–9: "My servant Job shall pray for you, and I will accept his prayer. . . . The Lord accepted Job's prayer" (NIV). In both instances "to accept" is literally "to lift up the face." For God to "lift up his face" on his people is for him to accept them, to raise the features of his face into a smile, to look upon them with favor. Similarly, Jacob hopes that the gift he is sending to Esau will move Esau to "receive" him—literally, "lift up his face" toward Jacob (Gen. 32:20 [MT v. 21]). By contrast, "to drop one's face" is "to frown" (see Gen. 4:6; Jer. 3:12).

It is interesting to note that in the Hebrew the length of each of the three lines of the blessing increases by two words:

> v. 24: The-Lord bless-you and-keep-you (3 words)
>
> v. 25: The-Lord make-shine his-face upon-you and-be-gracious-to-you (5 words)
>
> v. 26: The-Lord turn his-face toward-you and-give you peace (7 words)

Perhaps Numbers 1–6 has been describing a cause-to-effect movement. When there is obedience and a commitment to holy living (1:1–6:21), the result is the presence of a blessing God (6:22–27).

"Offerings before the Lord" (7:1–10:10)

The information that follows in ch. 7 antedates the information in chs. 1–6 by one month. The year, month, and day on which Moses finished setting up the tabernacle (Num. 7:1) was the second year, *first* month, and first day (see Exod. 40:17). Numbers 1 is dated a month later than this: the second year, *second* month, and first day. But there is a tie-in between the end of ch. 6 and the beginning of ch. 7. Chapter 6 ends by emphasizing what God wants to do for his people; ch. 7 emphasizes what the people want to do for God. The God who gives blessing at the end of ch. 6 is the God who receives in ch. 7. That the gift *to* God follows the gift *from* God shows that any gifts to God are a response to his gift and not a means of earning that gift of blessing.

Chapter 7 is the longest chapter in the Pentateuch. It is concerned with the offerings from the tribal leaders for the Lord. Verses 12–88 identify the tribal leader and the offering brought for the tabernacle. The list starts with Judah and ends with Naphtali. In every instance the individual is to bring not only commodities (a silver plate or a golden dish), but also various animals for the following offerings: cereal, burnt, sin, and peace, always in that order. Worship is more than handing God a gratuity. It is fellowship through sacrifice.

The part of ch. 7 about offerings (vv. 12–88) is preceded once again by a note not lacking in gravity or a reminder of God's holiness (vv. 1–11). The Israelite leaders are to present wagons for the transportation of tabernacle equipment (vv. 1–8). The exception is for the "holy things" of the tabernacle that are to be carried on the shoulders of the Kohathites (v. 9). Numbers 4:1–15 informed us that the Kohathites must not dismantle the "holy things." That is left to the priests. But neither must the "holy things" be piled on wagons. Human porterage is necessary.

The chapter concludes (v. 89) with the observation that God spoke with Moses from the Holy of Holies. The text simply says, "He [Moses] heard the voice" (NIV). It does not say that he saw the Lord. God's communion with Moses is aural, not visual. The Lord is heard, not seen, and that is because Moses does not enter the Holy of Holies. He stops at the curtain/veil that separates the Holy Place from the Holy of Holies. To be sure, Yahweh communes with Moses in a way he communes with no other, but even for Moses there are restrictions.

Chapter 8 deals with the consecration of the Levites, a chapter much like Leviticus 8, which covers the ordination of the Aaronic priests, but with one main distinction. The priests, when ordained, are "consecrated/sanctified" (Exod. 29:1, 21, 23; Lev. 8:12, 30). The Levites, when they start their service, are "purified" (Num. 8:7 [2x], 15, 21 [2x]). The possible connection between chs. 7 and 8 is that both chapters are about "gifts." Chapter 7 describes the people's gifts to God (see 7:3); ch. 8 describes God's gifts to his priests—that is, the Levites (see 8:19). The description of the actual consecration service (vv. 5–22) is preceded by a brief paragraph (vv. 1–4) noting the responsibility of the Aaronic priests for the lighting of the lamps in the tabernacle (see Exod. 25:31–40; 27:20–21; Lev. 24:2–4). Thus for a second time Numbers has placed a prelude directed at the priests before information for the Levites (see 4:5–15a, priests; 4:15b–49, Levites).

Almost exclusively the consecration rite of the Levites is a purification ceremony. The Levites need "cleansing" (vv. 6–7 [2x], 15, 21). They
must "purify themselves" (v. 21). A burnt offering and a sin offering
are mandated (v. 12). Much like the sacrificial animal, the Levite is a
substitute for the firstborn, and as such receives the laying on of hands
(vv. 10, 11, 16, 18). Their function is to avert divine wrath from consuming Israel (v. 19). This they do by turning back any encroacher (see
also 1:53; 18:5).

Jacob Milgrom (1970: 74 n. 271) has explained the rationale for the
emphasis on atonement in Levitic consecration, and his explanation
focuses on the use of the word "work" in vv. 11, 15, 19, 22, 24, 26: "I
submit that 'service' in Num. ch. 8 means removal labor in all cases. . . .
This view alone can explain the need for purificatory rites accompanying
the induction service of the Levites. For guard duty performed around
and at a distance from the Tabernacle contact with sancta is entailed;
removal operations, on the other hand, being the sole Levitic function
for the direct handling of sancta would require purificatory aspergings
and sacrifice."

To review the material in Numbers from the perspective of the addressee, we have the following: chs. 1–2, laity; 3–4, clergy; 5–6:21, laity;
6:22–27, clergy; 7:1–89, laity; 8, clergy.

Numbers 9:1–14 brings us back to the laity and particularly to the
subject of the postponed Passover. In certain instances the Passover may
be observed one month later—that is, the second month instead of the
first month (vv. 3, 5, 11). What are the legitimate reasons for postpone-
ment of Passover observance? Two situations are listed. If someone is
on a long-distance journey or is unclean through contact with a corpse
(v. 10), delay becomes mandatory. Refusal to observe Passover in the first
month for any other reason than those two results in the culprit being
"cut off" from the people. Once again a note of warning, caution, and
somberness has been sounded. If you are unclean and thus unworthy
of being in God's presence, then delay; otherwise, do not try to sidestep
your responsibilities to God in worship.

The provision of information about Passover observance just before
the people leave Mount Sinai for Canaan parallels the same sequence
of the provision of information about the first Passover (Exod. 12:1–28)
just before the people leave Egypt for Mount Sinai (Exod. 12:29–51). On
both occasions, before the people of God pass on, they are to celebrate
that day on which their God passed over them.

The conclusion to ch. 9 is much like that of ch. 6. There the emphasis
was on the divine presence that blesses. It is God's face that shines. Here
the emphasis (vv. 15–23) is on the divine presence that guides. It is the
hovering cloud that indicates encampment. It is the ascending cloud that

indicates that the Israelites were to move forward. The frequent use of the word "cloud" in these verses (it appears eleven times in vv. 15–23) suggests that the Israelites did their journeying during daylight hours, when, of course, the clouds in the sky are visible (but see v. 21b). Logically it might have made more sense to travel mostly under the cover of darkness, both for protection from enemies and for protection from the blazing sun in the wilderness. But seldom is God bound by ways of human logic and practicality.

The section concludes (10:1–10) with a reference to two silver trumpets. These instruments were to be blown at certain feasts, at the beginning of the year, for summoning the congregation, or breaking camp. Verses 5–7 emphasize that the trumpets sound an alarm, something like a military siren. Thus the trumpets are more for emergencies than for worship or concerts. Musical instruments have an almost negligible role in the ministry of the priests (see Kaufmann 1960: 11 n. 304). The Book of Leviticus, much of which is about the place of individual and community worship, especially chs. 1–16, never once mentions anything about music.

Numbers Commentaries and Major Studies

Ackerman, J. S. 1987. "Numbers." In *The Literary Guide to the Bible*. Ed. R. Alter and F. Kermode. Cambridge, Mass.: Belknap. Pp. 78–91.

Allen, R. B. 1990. "Numbers." In *The Expositor's Bible Commentary*. Vol. 2. Ed. F. E. Gaebelein. Grand Rapids: Zondervan. Pp. 657–1008.

Ashley, T. R. 1993. *The Book of Numbers*. NICOT. Grand Rapids: Eerdmans.

Brown, R. 2002. *The Message of Numbers*. The Bible Speaks Today. Downers Grove, Ill.: InterVarsity Press.

Budd, P. J. 1984. *Numbers*. WBC 5. Waco, Tex.: Word.

Caine, I. 1971. "Numbers, Book of." *EncJud* 12:1249–54.

Childs, B. S. 1979. *Introduction to the Old Testament as Scripture*. Philadelphia: Fortress. Pp. 190–201.

Cole, R. D. 2000. *Numbers*. NAC 3B. Nashville: Broadman & Holman.

Davies, E. W. 1995. *Numbers*. NCBC. Grand Rapids: Eerdmans.

Dentan, R. C. 1962. "Numbers, Book of." *IDB* 3:567–71.

Douglas, M. 1993. *In the Wilderness: The Doctrine of Defilement in the Book of Numbers*. JSOTSup 158. Sheffield: JSOT Press.

Dozeman, T. B. 1998. "The Book of Numbers: Introduction, Commentary and Reflections." In *The New Interpreter's Bible*. Vol. 2. Ed. L. E. Keck et al. Nashville: Abingdon. Pp. 1–168.

Fretheim, T. E. 2001. "Numbers." In *The Oxford Bible Commentary*. Ed. J. Barton and J. Muddiman. Oxford: Oxford University Press. Pp. 110–54.

Harrison, R. K. 1992. *Numbers: An Exegetical Commentary*. Wycliffe Exegetical Commentary. Grand Rapids: Baker.

Knierim, R. P. 1990. "The Book of Numbers." In *Die Hebräische Bibel und ihre zweifache Nachgeschichte: Festschrift für Rolf Rendtorff zum 65. Geburtstag*. Ed. E. Blum, C. Macholz, and E. W. Stegemann. Neukirchen-Vluyn: Neukirchener Verlag. Pp. 155–63.

Kugel, J. L. 1997. *The Bible as It Was*. Cambridge, Mass.: Belknap. Pp. 461–500.

Lee, W. W. 2000. "The Transition from the Old Generation to the New Generation in the Book of Numbers: A Response to Dennis Olson." In *Reading the Hebrew Bible for a New Millennium: Form, Concept, and Theological Perspective*. Vol. 2, *Exegetical and Theological Studies*. Ed. W. Kim et al. SAC. Harrisburg, Pa.: Trinity. Pp. 201–20.

Levine, B. A. 1976. "Numbers, Book of." *IDBSup* 631–35.

———. 1993. *Numbers 1–20: A New Translation with Introduction and Commentary*. AB 4A. New York: Doubleday.

———. 2000. *Numbers 21–36: A New Translation with Introduction and Commentary*. AB 4B. New York: Doubleday.

L'Heureux, C. E. 1990. "Numbers." In *The New Jerome Biblical Commentary*. Ed. R. E. Brown, J. A. Fitzmyer, and R. E. Murphy. Englewood Cliffs, N.J.: Prentice-Hall. Pp. 80–93.

Maarsingh, B. 1987. *Numbers: A Practical Commentary*. Trans. J. Vriend. Text and Interpretation. Grand Rapids: Eerdmans.

Milgrom, J. 1970. *Studies in Levitical Terminology*. Vol. 1, *The Encroacher and the Levite: The Term ʿAboda*. University of California Publications, Near Eastern Studies 14. Berkeley: University of California Press.

———. 1990. *Numbers: The Traditional Hebrew Text with the New JPS Translation*. JPS Torah Commentary. Philadelphia: The Jewish Publication Society.

———. 1992. "Numbers, Book of." *ABD* 4:1146–55.

Moriarty, F. L. 1968. "Numbers." In *The Jerome Biblical Commentary*. Ed. R. E. Brown, J. A. Fitzmyer, and R. E. Murphy. 2 vols. in 1. Englewood Cliffs, N.J.: Prentice-Hall. Vol. 1, pp. 86–100.

Noth, M. 1969. *Numbers: A Commentary*. Trans. J. D. Martin. Philadelphia: Westminster.

Ogden, G. S. 1996. "The Design of Numbers." *BT* 47:420–28.

Olson, D. T. 1985. *The Death of the Old and Birth of the New: The Framework of Numbers and the Pentateuch*. BJS 71. Chico, Calif.: Scholars Press.

———. 1996. *Numbers*. Interpretation. Louisville: John Knox.

———. 1997. "Negotiating Boundaries: The Old and New Generations and the Theology of Numbers." *Int* 51:229–40.

Oswalt, J. 1975. "Numbers, Book of." *ZPEB* 4:461–69.

Ringe, S. H. 1999. "Reading Back, Reading Forward." *Semeia* 88:189–94.

Sakenfeld, K. D. 1989. "Numbers." In *The Books of the Bible*. Ed. B. W. Anderson. 2 vols. New York: Scribner. Vol. 1, pp. 71–87.

———. 1995. *Journeying with God: A Commentary on the Book of Numbers*. ITC. Grand Rapids: Eerdmans.

Sherwood, S. K. 2002. *Leviticus, Numbers, Deuteronomy.* Berit Olam. Collegeville, Minn.: Liturgical Press. Pp. 95–195.

Snaith, N. H. 1967. *Leviticus and Numbers.* The Century Bible. London: Nelson. Pp. 179–347.

Sturdy, J. 1976. *Numbers.* CBC. Cambridge: Cambridge University Press.

Wenham, G. J. 1981. *Numbers: An Introduction and Commentary.* TOTC. Downers Grove, Ill.: InterVarsity Press.

———. 1997. *Numbers.* OTG. Sheffield: Sheffield Academic Press.

Wevers, J. W. 1982. *Text History of the Greek Numbers.* MSU 16. Göttingen: Vandehoeck & Ruprecht.

Williams, G. 1994. "The Verb *qarab* 'Come Near' in Numbers." *BT* 45:245–47.

Numbers 1:1–10:10

Kaufmann, Y. 1960. *The Religion of Israel.* Trans. M. Greenberg. Chicago: University of Chicago Press.

Milgrom, J. 1997. "Encroaching on the Sacred: Purity and Polity in Numbers 1–10." *Int* 51:241–53.

Numbers 1–2

In the bibliography for Exodus 12–15:21 see Davies 1995; Heinzerling 2000; Humphreys 1998; 2000; Milgrom 1999; Rendsburg 2001.

Archer, G. L. 1973. *A Survey of Old Testament Introduction.* Chicago: Moody. Pp. 234–38.

Mayes, A. D. H. 1974. *Israel in the Period of the Judges.* Naperville, Ill.: Allenson. Pp. 16–34.

Milgrom, J. 1978. "Priestly Terminology and the Political and Social Structure of Pre-Monarchic Israel." *JQR* 69:65–81.

Sasson, J. 1978. "A Genealogical 'Convention' in Biblical Chronography?" *ZAW* 90:171–85.

Wenham, J. W. 1967. "Large Numbers in the Old Testament." *TynB* 18:19–53.

Numbers 3–4

Abba, R. 1962. "Priests and Levites." *IDB* 3:876–89.

Cody, A. 1969. *A History of Old Testament Priesthood.* AnBib 35. Rome: Pontifical Biblical Institute. Pp. 29–38.

Milgrom, J. 1970. *Studies in Levitical Terminology.* Vol. 1, *The Encroacher and the Levite: The Term ʿAboda.* University of California Publications, Near Eastern Studies 14. Berkeley: University of California Press.

Spencer, J. R. 1998. "PQD, the Levites, and Numbers 1–4." *ZAW* 110:535–46.

Vaux, R. de. 1965. *Ancient Israel.* Trans. J. McHugh. 2 vols. New York: McGraw-Hill. Vol. 2, pp. 358–71.

Numbers 5

Verses 5–10

Milgrom, J. 1974. *Cult and Conscience: The ASHAM and the Priestly Doctrine of Repentance.* SJLA 18. Leiden: Brill. Pp. 104–6.

Verses 11–31

Bach, A. 1993. "Good to the Last Drop: Viewing the Sotah (Numbers 5,11–31) as the Glass Half Empty and Wondering How to View It Half Full." In *The New Literary Criticism and the Hebrew Bible.* Ed. J. C. Exum and D. J. A. Clines. JSOTSup 143. Sheffield: JSOT Press. Pp. 26–54.

Brichto, H. C. 1975. "The Case of the Śōtā and a Reconsideration of Biblical Law." *HUCA* 46:55–70.

Fishbane, M. 1974. "Accusations of Adultery: A Study of Law and Scribal Practice in Numbers 5:11–31." *HUCA* 45:25–45.

Frymer-Kensky, T. 1976. "Ordeal, Judicial." *IDBSup* 638–40.

———. 1984. "The Strange Case of the Suspected Sotah (Numbers V 11–31)." *VT* 34:11–26.

McKane, W. 1980. "Poison, Trial by Ordeal and the Cup of Wrath." *VT* 30:474–92.

Milgrom, J. 1981. "The Case of the Suspected Adulteress, Numbers 5:11–31: Redaction and Meaning." In *The Creation of Sacred Literature: Composition and Redaction of the Biblical Text.* Ed. R. E. Friedman. University of California Publications in Near Eastern Studies 22. Berkeley: University of California Press. Pp. 69–75.

———. 1985. "On the Suspected Adulteress (Numbers V 11–31)." *VT* 35:368–69.

Pardee, D. 1985. "Marim in Numbers V." *VT* 35:112–15.

Phillips, A. C. 1970. *Ancient Israel's Criminal Law: A New Approach to the Decalogue.* Oxford: Blackwell. Pp. 118–21.

Sasson, J. 1972. "Numbers 5 and the 'Waters of Judgment.'" *BZ* 16:249–51.

Ward, E. F. de. 1977. "Superstition and Judgment." *ZAW* 89:1–19.

Numbers 6

Verses 1–21

Diamond, E. 1997–1998. "An Israelite Self-Offering in the Priestly Code: A New Perspective on the Nazirite." *JQR* 88:1–18.

Eichrodt, W. 1961–1967. *Theology of the Old Testament*. Trans. J. Baker. 2 vols. OTL. Philadelphia: Westminster. Vol. 2, pp. 303–6.

Milgrom, J. 1971. "Nazirite." *EncJud* 12:907–9.

———. 1974. *Cult and Conscience: The ASHAM and the Priestly Doctrine of Repentance*. SJLA 18. Leiden: Brill. Pp. 66–70.

Rainey, A. 1970. "The Order of Sacrifices in Old Testament Ritual Texts." *Bib* 51:485–98.

Riemann, P. 1970. "Am I My Brother's Keeper?" *Int* 24:482–91.

Vaux, R. de. 1965. *Ancient Israel*. Trans. J. McHugh. 2 vols. New York: McGraw-Hill. Vol. 2, pp. 466–67.

Verses 22–27

Brichto, H. C. 1971. "Priestly Blessing." *EncJud* 13:1060–61.

Freedman, D. N. 1975. "The Aaronic Benediction." In *No Famine in the Land: Studies in Honor of John L. McKenzie*. Ed. J. W. Flanagan and A. W. Robinson. Missoula, Mont.: Scholars Press. Pp. 411–42.

———. 1980. "The Aaronic Benediction (Numbers 6:24–26)." In *Pottery, Poetry and Prophecy: Studies in Early Hebrew Poetry*. Winona Lake, Ind.: Eisenbrauns. Pp. 229–42.

Korpel, M. C. A. 1989. "The Poetic Structure of the Priestly Blessing [Numbers 6,24–26]." *JSOT* 45:3–13.

Miller, P. D., Jr. 1975. "The Blessing of God: An Interpretation of Numbers 6:22–27." *Int* 29:240–51.

Westermann, C. 1978. *Blessing in the Bible and the Life of the Church*. Trans. K. R. Crim. OBT. Philadelphia: Fortress. Pp. 42–45.

17

From Sinai to Kadesh

NUMBERS 10:11–20:21

The Israelites have heard much from both God and Moses since reaching Sinai. Instructions, rules, and exhortations have been abundant. But now is the time to break camp and move on. Sinai is no more God's geographical goal for his people than would be the Mount of Transfiguration for Peter, James, and John. It should, however, nerve God's people for the future by giving them a deeper exposure of God.

From Marching to Murmuring (10:11–12:16)

Frank Cross (1973: 308–17) has observed the proliferation of the phrase "and the children of Israel journeyed from . . ." in Exodus and Numbers, and he compares it with the phrase "these are the generations of . . ." that appears ten times in Genesis. Seven of these "and they journeyed from . . ." phrases are in Exodus: 12:37; 13:20; 14:2; 15:22; 16:1; 17:1; 19:2.

The remaining five phrases are in Numbers: 10:12; 20:1, 22; 21:10; 22:1. But the departure from Sinai is unique. The Israelites will take with them from there memories that they cannot forget. The scene in

322

10:11–36 is dramatic, pulsating. Flags are flying. God's presence is distinctly manifest. Conquest is on everyone's mind. It may come as a bit of a surprise that Moses asks his father-in-law, Hobab, to accompany them (vv. 29–32, especially v. 31) as they leave Sinai, since, says Moses to his Midianite father-in-law, "You know where we should camp in the desert, and you can be our eyes." So, who is to guide Israel: the divine presence in the fire cloud (9:15–23), or Hobab, or both? If it is both, then the passage illustrates the importance in biblical thought of both God's work and human work as vital parts in the advancement of God's will. For a parallel, one thinks of Joshua sending out the spies to scout out Jericho in Joshua 2 right after God has unilaterally guaranteed victory to Joshua ("No one shall be able to stand up against you") in Joshua 1. If Hobab did agree to go after his first refusal (Num. 10:30), and that is not at all certain, then no subsequent text highlights any contribution of his. In the narratives that follow there is honor for Yahweh, but none for Moses' father-in-law.

The reader is hardly prepared for the rude shock, then, that comes in chs. 11 and 12. Far from a mood of optimism and gallantry, there is instead the ugly spectacle of divisiveness, complaints, depression, and bewilderment, with divine judgment as the appropriate response.

Three different scenes are presented in this debacle. First, there is a general complaining about "misfortunes/hardships." The Hebrew form used for "complained" (the Hithpael) may suggest that this is not an isolated instance, but rather a pattern of behavior. God responds with a consuming fire on the fringes of the camp. Only the intercessory prayers of Moses terminate the punishment (11:1–3). Second, not satisfied with a one-dish menu—manna—the people cry to God for diverse food (11:4–34). Third, Miriam challenges both the sagacity of Moses in the choice of a wife and the credibility of his unique relationship to God (12).

The immediate purpose of these events is to contrast the God who is present in his camp to bless (chs. 1–10) with the God who is present in his camp to judge whenever a group or an individual attempts to shatter the harmony of the community (chs. 11–12). Thus, a fire consumes (11:1); a plague breaks out (11:33); an accuser becomes leprous (12:10).

The role of Moses in each of the three incidents is interesting. In the first he is successful intercessor. He raises no question, offers no rebukes. In the second, however, the craving of the "rabble" for meat is another matter. If "Moses prayed" in 11:2, he is "displeased/troubled" in 11:10. Moses assumes that the people's complaining and memories of the food in Egypt are an indictment against him. He is distraught and wants no more responsibility for this ungrateful, unresponsive congregation. Even death is preferable to further ministry (v. 15). Murmuring is contagious. Moses is lowering himself to the level of his congregation, adopting its mentality.

God's response to Moses (vv. 16–23) is one of both respite and rebuke. Respite is provided in that Moses no longer needs to function alone. God will provide him with seventy elders who will share the burden of leadership. It is as if Moses has more than enough "Spirit" to share. His own portion of Spirit is not thereby reduced, any more than one candle loses any of its flame when it lights another candle (Sommer 1999: 610). But it is also a word of rebuke. If Moses wants to leave, that is allowed, but first let him choose any seventy of the congregation. God will then put on them "the Spirit" that he has put on Moses. Moses is not indispensable, but the presence of God's Spirit is. Only the gift of the divine Spirit can explain Moses' abilities.

All of this transpired in the tent of meeting (vv. 16b, 24). The Spirit, however, is not confined to a cubicle. The Spirit also rests on two others, Eldad and Medad, in the camp (v. 26). But orthodox Joshua wants that to cease (v. 28). Rigidity dies hard. This attitude is reflected in words of the disciple John to Jesus: "Master, we saw a man casting out demons in your name, and we forbade him, because he does not follow with us" (Luke 9:49 RSV). But Moses does not share Joshua's narrow perspective. Moses' "I wish that all the LORD's people were prophets and that the LORD would put his Spirit on them!" (Num. 11:29 NIV) shows a truly catholic spirit. (A very few commentators treat Moses' statement in v. 29 as a more cynical one: "I wish that all God's people were prophets and that they would be put through the wringer just as I have been, and then let's see how they feel!")

God did honor the people's urge for seasoned dishes. Unlike in Exodus 16, however, there is a price to be paid. At the very moment the people are enjoying these succulent morsels, a plague is unleashed (v. 33). In the commentary of Ps. 106:15, "He gave them what they asked, but sent a wasting disease among them" (NRSV). God acquiesces, but he does not acquit. The Hebrew word for the "wind" that brought the quail (v. 31) that eventually led to the severe plague is the same as the Hebrew word for the "Spirit" that came upon the seventy elders and moved them to prophesy (v. 25): *rûaḥ*. Numbers 11:4–34 powerfully illustrates the potential for either blessing bordering on ecstasy or catastrophe bordering on obliteration when the divine *rûaḥ* is active.

The third incident is in ch. 12. If in ch. 11 Moses was indirectly challenged, here the attack is frontal. In 11:1–3 God heard the complaining (see v. 1) (and told it to Moses?); in 11:4–34 Moses heard the complaining (see v. 10) and told it to God. In both 11:1–3 and 11:4–34 God is the one under attack; in 12:1–16 Moses is the one under attack. The first innuendo is leveled against the propriety of Moses' choice of a spouse.

He has married a "Cushite" woman (12:1). The charge seems to come more from Miriam than from Aaron, as 12:1 says, literally, "And she spoke, Miriam, and Aaron, against Moses." The verb is third-person, feminine, singular, not plural. (The same construction is found in Judg. 5:1: "Then she sang, Deborah, and Barak.") Robinson (1989: 432) goes so far as to call Aaron "Miriam's stooge."

Perhaps this is why Miriam becomes leprous, although Aaron also is implicated when God says, "Why then were you [plural] not afraid to speak against my servant Moses?" (12:8 NIV). Cross (1973: 204) points out that if the term "Cushite" implies blackness, or an Ethiopian, as it does usually in the Bible, then the story renders "the whitened skin of Miriam a singularly fit punishment for her objections to the Cushite wife."

On the other hand, Num. 12:1 may simply be saying that Moses' wife was from the tribe of Cushan, an area parallel to that of Midian in Hab. 3:7: "I saw the tents of Cushan in distress, the dwellings of Midian in anguish" (NIV). This would accord perfectly with Exod. 2:21—Moses married Zipporah, a Midianite—rather than forcing the assumption that the reference in Numbers 12 is to a second marriage for Moses.

Moses knows all about someone becoming leprous as a result of doing or saying something displeasing to God. It happened to him when for a third time he tried to evade going obediently to Egypt (see Exod. 4:1–9, especially vv. 6–7).

Interestingly, Aaron can ask mercy only from Moses (vv. 11–12). It is Moses who again intercedes (v. 13). Thus we are brought back to the Moses of 11:1–3, a Moses whose prayers result in the mitigation, but not the cancellation, of the divine sentence. There is no word of remonstration against either Miriam or Aaron. He adopts a policy of silence toward his detractors. In fact, as Ackerman (2002: 80) has observed, in the rest of Numbers Moses and Aaron seem to get along quite well (13:26; 14:2, 5, 26; 15:33; 16:3, 11, 16–22, 36–40, 41–50; 17:1–11; 18:1–7; 19:1; 20:2, 6, 8, 10). By contrast, Miriam appears but once in Numbers after ch. 12, and that is only to die (20:1b).

Not only is Moses' relationship to a unique wife questioned, but so is his unique relationship to God: "Has the LORD indeed spoken only through Moses?" (12:2 RSV). Is he the only vehicle of revelation? Does he have a monopoly on God's pronouncements? Is Moses God's vicar on earth, a kind of papal figure? God's answer is simple: yes (see vv. 6–8).

Chapter 11 of Numbers casts Moses in a different light than does ch. 12. In ch. 11 the emphasis is on a ministry that Moses shares with others. God will put the same Spirit on seventy elders that he has put on Moses. It is a divine resource on which Moses has no monopoly. By contrast ch. 12 focuses on the uniqueness of Moses' ministry (see

vv. 6–8). God speaks only with Moses face to face. Moses is unique not only in his ministry but also in his character: he is very "humble" (v. 3). This is the only time that this word appears in the Hebrew Bible in the singular. Elsewhere, in the plural, it refers to the "afflicted" who cry out to God. A key to Moses' successful leadership, as with any of God's leader servants, is to have both a ministry gladly shared with others and a ministry for which God has uniquely gifted him and set him apart. And although Scripture may teach the priesthood of all believers, it does not seem to teach the "prophethood" of all believers.

As Brevard Childs (1979: 198) has pointed out, these stories, and those that follow, perpetuate the theme of 1:1–10:11: the absolute necessity for holiness among God's people. The sacred character of the community is impugned when the fabric of that community is torn by dissension and nitpicking. It compels God to move from blessing to judgment.

All too often critical studies have been preoccupied with the attempt to detect two different stories, now untidily combined, in both chs. 11 (the quail and the elders) and 12 (Moses' wife, and his relationship to God). See, for example, the studies by George Coats, heavily influenced as they are by Martin Noth, the scholar who emphasizes the history of traditions. To be applauded is the intensive work of David Jobling (1977; 1978), which goes beyond the genetic approach to Scripture—what is the prehistory of the text?—and deals with the final form of the text.

In such a study the commonality of theme in these two chapters becomes transparent. In each narrative there is a main program: God is giving to Israel the Promised Land of Canaan. Then there is a counterprogram, instigated by the people against the march, by the rabble against the food, by Moses against his role, by Miriam and Aaron against Moses. Finally there is a counter-counterprogram from God, the purpose of which is to restore unity. The instigators are punished. God's will is one people, one food, and one leader.

Shall We Go Up or Shall We Not? (13:1–14:15)

These two chapters discuss the dispatching of spies from Kadesh or Kadesh-barnea (the extreme southern border of Canaan [Num. 34:4], some forty miles south of Abraham's Beersheba) to Canaan to determine the advisability of attacking Canaan, the reports brought back, and the repercussions. We should note that the original plan is God's: "The LORD said to Moses, 'Send men to spy out the land of Canaan'" (NRSV). One might think that God could have supplied the information about Canaan directly and thus have saved all the time and bother of this adventure. Nevertheless, the people must do the searching and the investigation.

The modern Bible critics agree unanimously that these two chapters represent a weaving together of two stories. There is the original event, traceable to J/E. Subsequently this story was reworked and supplemented by another narrative, this one from P.

The criterion for supposing the heterogeneity of the text here is the presence of indubitable doublets that are mutually exclusive. Thus, the spies survey only the area of the southern Negeb and the area of Hebron (13:22 [J/E]). Or did they survey the whole land of Canaan, "to Rehob, near the entrance of Hamath" (RSV), way up in northern Canaan (13:21 [P])? Is it only Caleb who protests the negative report (13:30 [J/E]), or is it both Caleb and Joshua (14:6 [P])? Is it only Caleb who is to enter the Promised Land (14:24 [J/E]), or is it Caleb and Joshua (14:30 [J/E, or a gloss on J/E?])?

The critical reconstruction (with minor variations) is approximately as follows:

13:1–7a P	13:25–26 P	14:5–10 P
13:7b–20 J/E	13:27–31 J/E	14:11–25 J/E
13:21 P	14:1–3 P	14:26–38 P
13:22–24 J/E	14:4 J/E	14:39–45 J/E

It is debatable, however, that the contradictory doublets are indeed that. But before we examine that issue, we do well to recall C. S. Lewis's caveat about the whole area of biblical criticism. In *Christian Reflections* (Grand Rapids: Eerdmans, 1967 [pp. 159–66]) Lewis observes that reviewers of his own works, whenever they attempted to answer questions about why he wrote something, what influenced him, and what his purpose was in writing—areas not always specifically addressed or annotated by the author—invariably were wrong. Still, to the uninformed reader of the review, these comments might be so convincing as to be accepted as entirely truthful.

Turning specifically to the issue of "reconstructing" how an ancient book was written, Lewis (p. 161) says:

> The superiority in judgement and diligence which you are going to attribute to the Bible critics will have to be almost super human if it is to offset the fact that they are everywhere faced with customs, language, race-characteristics, class-characteristics, a religious background, habits of composition, and basic assumptions, which no scholarship will ever enable any man now alive to know as surely and intimately and instinctively as the reviewer can know mine. And for that very same reason,

remember, the Biblical critics can never be crudely proved wrong. St Mark is dead. When they meet St Peter there will be more pressing matters to discuss.

In the case of Numbers 13–14 it seems possible that one story has been laid over an earlier one. Doublets, if that is what they really are, could be a giveaway for such an arrangement. The next step would be to isolate the two stories from each other (as I have done above, following the consensus). That is as far as older biblical criticism went. More recent trends have been to treat suggestively the implications of this editorial process (see, e.g., McEvenue 1971: 117–27).

Logic impels us to ask whether Numbers 13–14 is indeed laced with contradictions. Are there other explanations that are equally viable? The twelve spies would not likely travel as a group. Clandestine operations necessitate separation. How much would the phrase "Negeb" mean to Hebrew spies who had known only two places in their lives, Egypt and part of the Sinai peninsula? Might "Negeb" be a designation for Canaan in the sense of *pars pro toto*?

The opposition of Caleb on the first day alongside the opposition of Caleb and Joshua on the second day is understandable. In ch. 13 the opposition is from the spies, but in ch. 14 that spirit of morbidity has engulfed all the congregation. A. MacRae (1970: 179) observes about ch. 13, "It would be more effective for Caleb to do this, since Joshua was so closely associated with Moses that he would not be so readily accepted as an independent witness."

The salvation of Caleb stands over against the perdition of the unbelieving spies (14:24). The salvation of Caleb and Joshua stands in stark contrast with that of the "wicked congregation" (14:27, 30).

Should we try to wring from these "contradictions" all that is possible or implicit? What, then, would we do with this: "Not one shall come into the land where I swore that I would make you dwell, except Caleb . . . and Joshua" (14:30 RSV)? How far do we want to press "not one" against "except Caleb and Joshua"? Are Moses and Aaron also condemned by this incident? Certainly not.

What is to be said about the two chapters in their final form, whether homogeneous or composite? In the first place, it should be obvious that they perpetuate the point of the narratives of chs. 11 and 12. There the sin of unbelief wreaked havoc on God's camp: death by fire, plague, leprosy. Similarly, in these two chapters the results of the sin of unbelief are disastrous: immediate death (14:37), premature death and exclusion from the land of promise (14:22–23, 29–30), defeat (14:45). The Israelites have an even record against the Amalekites: a pre-Sinai victory (Exod. 17:8–14) and a post-Sinai defeat.

Again, the two chapters abound in inner contrasts. Chapter 13 focuses on the negative response of the spies, ch. 14 on the negative response of the whole congregation. The report of the spies is defeatist and pessimistic, that of Caleb is positive (13:25–33). The fruit in the land is huge (13:23, 24, 27b), but its occupants are bigger still (13:28, 31, 33). The people debate about returning to Egypt (14:1–5) or fighting to possess Canaan (14:6–9). God threatens to destroy these people (14:11–12); Moses pleads with him not to (14:13–19). The narrator relates, "All the people of Israel murmured against Moses and Aaron" (14:2 RSV); God asks, "How long shall this wicked congregation murmur against me?" (14:27 RSV). Caleb and Joshua will enter Canaan; none of their peers will (14:28–30). The children of the faithless spies will enter Canaan (14:31), but they also must suffer for their fathers' faithlessness (14:33). The unbelievers wanted to stone Moses, Aaron, Caleb, and Joshua (14:10); Moses seeks his antagonists' forgiveness and pardon (14:19). God metes out immediate chastisement (14:37), and he promises delayed chastisement (14:29, 32, 34).

T. E. Fretheim (2001: 120–21) has pointed out the number of ways that what the people wanted, ironically, they got, so that God grants a desired result, or as Yahweh says in 14:28, "I will do to you the very things I heard you say" (NIV). They say that they want to die right there in the wilderness (14:2), and they will get their wish (14:32). Joshua tries to convince the people that "the LORD is with us" (14:9), but they discover that that is not so (14:42). Forty days of scouting out Canaan (13:25) lead into forty years of judgment (14:34). The people's desire not to be brought into "this land" by God (14:3) is granted: "not one of you will enter the land" (14:30 NIV).

We have become accustomed, thus far in our pentateuchal studies, to those situations that call for the death penalty for a violation of the accepted norms of behavior. The list has included murder, idolatry, sexual aberrations, and illicit physical contact with sancta. The implementation of justice is directed toward individual trespassers of covenant regulations.

But here the entire congregation is indicted for faithlessness, not just selected individuals within the larger group. Only a few survive unscathed, like Noah in an earlier generation.

And as surely as Noah had to tolerate the majority opinion of his day, so do Caleb and Joshua. The faith of these leaders in the integrity of God's promise gives Noah victory over sarcasm, and Caleb and Joshua victory over hostility. The taunters and the incredulous, on the other hand, are denied the ark and the land.

Further Revolts against Moses (15–18)

Chapter 15 breaks sharply into the narrative of Numbers, having no immediate observable relationship to what follows and what precedes. It is a unit given completely to cultic matters, and it is sandwiched between incidents of murmuring against Moses (13–14; 16–18). As a comparable example, imagine an elaborate disquisition on the preparation of wine for the Eucharist by Luther squeezed in between his descriptions of his altercations with the leadership of the Roman Catholic Church.

To dismiss the placement of the chapter as a pointless insertion and intrusion is unwarranted, however. Five issues are broached in the chapter: additional information about the first three sacrifices spelled out in Leviticus—whole burnt, cereal, and peace (vv. 1–16); an offering of firstfruits (vv. 17–21); supplementary and repeated information about the sin offering, revolving around the theme of sins of ignorance or inadvertence (vv. 22–31); an instance of the death penalty for violation of the Sabbath—specifically, gathering sticks (vv. 32–36); wearing tassels on one's clothing (vv. 37–41). The importance of the tassel ornament in later Judaism can be gauged by the two references to it in Matthew: "the fringe of his [Jesus'] garment" (9:20 RSV) and "they [the scribes and the Pharisees] make . . . their fringes long" (23:5 NRSV).

Numbers 15 seems to be related to its immediate context in several possible ways. Conceivably, it serves as a pause in the drama (see Caine 1971: 1250), but why is such a pause needed, and what is accomplished thereby? Is the law of (general) association at work here? Chapter 14 dealt with the sin of the congregation; ch. 15 (vv. 22–26) provides, via the sin offering, atonement for the whole congregation. Or does the incident in chs. 13–14 provide a powerful illustration of the wording of 15:30–31 about those who "sin defiantly"? For them there is no atonement. They will be "cut off."

May the law of contrast be also evident here? At the end of ch. 14 Israel is unable to attack Canaan and thus has to abort plans to penetrate Canaan from the south (vv. 39–45); at the beginning of ch. 15 we read, "When you come into the land you are to inhabit . . ." (v. 2 NRSV). Judgment, yes, but that is neither God's goal nor ultimate word.

The first three sacrifices of the Levitical code, addressed in 15:1–16, are not the expiatory sacrifices, but those that are voluntary, spontaneous, given to God in gratitude and praise. One finds precious little gratitude and praise in Numbers 13, 14, and 16!

The whole issue of inadvertent sin, both of the congregation (15:22–26) and of the individual (15:27–29), contrasts vividly with sin done "high-handedly/defiantly" (15:30). The scenario described in 13–14 and 16 is the latter type. For these there are no sacrificial provisions. Only the intercessory prayers of Moses save the perpetrators (14:13–19; 16:22), and even then not completely.

The tassels (vv. 37–41) on the clothing are a way for God to communicate to Israel that they are to be holy to their God—not a moralistic holiness, but a holiness rooted in obedience (15:40). If holy living is God's moral goal for his people, the chapters surrounding this summons have displayed the exact antinomy of that lifestyle.

With the beginning of ch. 16 we find more criticism of Moses. Thus far, opposition to him has come from the congregation (ch. 11), his family (ch. 12), and the spies (ch. 13). We now add to that list clerical opposition (ch. 16).

The instigator is Korah, a Levite of the Kohathite branch. Joined by two laypersons, Dathan and Abiram, plus 250 prominent men of the congregation, Korah attacks Moses (16:3).

Does Moses have a monopoly on sanctity? asks Korah. What makes Korah's rebuke hard for Moses to take is that Korah is Moses' first cousin. According to Exod. 6:14–25, Moses' father, Amram, and Korah's father, Izhar, are brothers, and both fathers are sons of Kohath, one of Levi's three sons. So the opposition directed at Moses in ch. 12 from siblings continues in ch. 16 with opposition stemming from a first cousin on the father's side. And it is also understandable why Korah, a Kohathite Levite, and two laypersons from the tribe of Reuben would join forces. Numbers 3:29 informs us that the Kohathites were to camp on the south side of the tabernacle. Right behind them on that south side is the tribe of Reuben (Num. 2:10). Not only does misery love company, but so do big egos—people who believe that they deserve something bigger than what they currently have.

The criticism is strong, but is it legitimate or is it a falsification? In one sense Korah is quite correct. All of God's people are holy. God himself says so in Exod. 19:6 ("you will be . . . a holy nation" [NIV]) and in passages such as Deut. 7:6 ("for you are a people holy to the LORD your God" [NRSV]). Restraining any impulse to defend himself, Moses is willing to leave the matter to God's adjudication (vv. 5–7). As in the contest with Elijah and the prophets of Baal at Carmel (1 Kings 18), the Lord will distinguish between truth and error, between prophet and prevaricator. As at Carmel, the confrontation is between the one and the many. Thus Moses says, "Hear now, you sons of Levi" (16:8 RSV). He does not say, "Hear now, Korah." Korah is simply spokesman for the larger group.

The motivation behind Korah's protest is discovered in 16:8–10. Why be content with being a parish priest when a bishopric is a possibility?

God is not quite as patient as Moses is! God wants to solve the impasse in blitzkrieg fashion (v. 21). Moses and Aaron, however, make intercession for the transgressor (v. 22). Let any necessary punishment be limited to the culprit instead of something pervasive. And that is precisely what happens: Korah and his kin are swallowed up by the earth (vv. 31–33). All "swallowing" scenes in the Bible are in contexts of divine judgment and triumph. Besides this passage, we think of Aaron's staff swallowing the staffs of his Egyptian competitors (Exod. 7:12), or Moses' and Miriam's hymnic celebration of the earth swallowing Pharaoh and the Egyptians (Exod. 15:12), or the great fish swallowing the derelict Jonah (Jon. 1:17), or death being swallowed up in the victory of Christ (1 Cor. 15:54). Surely it is ironic that the Levites, who are supposed to keep God's "wrath" (qeṣep) from falling on the community because of misbehavior (Num. 1:53), now become the object of that wrath because of their misbehavior: "Will you be angry/wrathful [qeṣep] with the entire assembly when only one man sins?" (Num. 16:22 NIV). As Magonet (1982: 10) notes, Num. 16:22 has the first use of "wrath/qeṣep" in Numbers after its use in 1:53.

The sin of Korah is twofold. It consists of an attitude of defiance plus the actual performance of duties not apportioned to him. The earth's swallowing of Korah and his accomplices is "to be a reminder to the people of Israel, so that no one who is not a priest, who is not of the descendants of Aaron, should draw near to burn incense before the LORD" (v. 40 RSV). Once again Numbers has underscored the fact that God has assigned different responsibilities to different groups. The trouble starts when one group says, contrary to the attitude of the apostle Paul, "I have *not* learned in whatsoever state I am to be content" (cf. Phil. 4:11).

The seriousness of this arrangement is enforced in 18:3: "They [the tribe of Levi] . . . must not approach either the vessels of the sanctuary or the altar, otherwise both they and you [Aaron and the priests] will die" (cf. 18:7 NRSV). That particular ultimatum we have already encountered in Num. 1:51; 3:10; 3:38; 4:20. One looks in vain here for any concept of the priesthood of all believers. Authority has been established. Boundaries have been set. Ministries have been defined. Activities have been regulated.

The complaint of Dathan and Abiram against Moses is different from that of Korah. For Korah, it is his impression that Moses is arrogant, someone who thinks that he is a cut above everybody else. Dathan and Abiram, the ringleaders of the political faction of the revolt, complain about Moses' ineffective leadership and his leadership style (vv. 13–14). Their words "And now you also want to lord it over us?" (v. 13b NIV) recall words uttered at Moses earlier by some of his own people, "Who made you ruler . . . over us?" (Exod. 2:14 NIV). The Hebrew word *śārar*, "become prince/lord over," appears only in Num. 16:13. Exodus 2:14 employs the cognate noun *śar*, which is derived from the verb *śārar*, "lord, prince, chief" (see Magonet 1982: 7).

One of the characteristics of murmuring is that it is highly contagious. Having already faced one tête-à-tête, Moses must now endure another. One might think that the survivors, having seen the earth swallow up all of Korah's collaborators and having seen God's fire incinerate 250 incense offerers, might be hesitant to continue to grumble. It is they, not just Moses and Aaron, who should be falling on their faces. But it is difficult to halt a spirit of complaining when it has reached avalanche proportions. Surprisingly, Moses is blamed for something that God has done: "You have killed the people of the LORD" (v. 41 [Heb. 17:6] NRSV). (The division for chs. 16 and 17 in the Hebrew Bible differs from that in English translations. English 16:1–35 = Hebrew 16:1–35; English 16:36–50 = Hebrew 17:1–15; English 17:1–13 = Hebrew 17:16–28.) If Moses' intercession saved the people earlier (v. 22), here he saves them from chaos (vv. 46–48 [Heb. 17:11–13]). But on this occasion it is Aaron who is the means of the people's deliverance at Moses' suggestion. Moses, the prophet, uses prayerful intercession to save his people. Aaron, the priest, uses God-ordained ritual to save his people. Aaron's offering of incense (v. 47 [MT 17:12]) that leads to atonement for the renegades contrasts boldly with those who early in ch. 16 also offered incense and perished nonetheless. There is a world of difference between offering incense on behalf of somebody else and their welfare, and offering incense in order to advance and promote oneself. Once again Moses placates God, even when Moses has been the butt of the vilification. Here Moses is imitating his wife, whose quick action earlier saved him from divine wrath (Exod. 4:25).

Chapter 17 [MT 17:16–28] relates in several ways to what preceded. Through the incident of Aaron's budding rod the attempt is made to establish Aaron's position of preeminence. In both chs. 16 and 17 the theme of divine selection is sounded. The key word is "choose." In one case the acceptance of an incense offering (16:7) establishes the one whom God has chosen as holy, and in the other case the acceptance of a rod (17:5 [MT v. 20]) establishes the one whom God has chosen as his priest. The decision is left to God. God's clear response on the second issue should stifle further murmuring.

What is the emotional response by the people to the aperture in the earth, the demise of Korah, the plague, and the divine attestation placed on Aaron? They are shocked, dumbfounded, filled with terror, and are about as eager to approach the sanctuary as was Daniel to walk into the lion's den. Why precipitate one's death (17:12–13 [MT vv. 27–28])?

I suggest that the purpose of ch. 18 is to show God's response to this outbreak of chagrin and phobia. After all, can there be genuine corporate worship if God's house is perceived as a trap that lures the unsuspecting to their deaths? In what follows, the line of argument that I pursue is heavily indebted to Jacob Milgrom (1970: 18–35).

The purpose of 18:1–7 (and for that matter, vv. 21–23) is to alleviate the people's concern. Here we are informed that the priests "shall bear iniquity in connection with the sanctuary . . . in connection with your priesthood" (18:1 RSV). Later we are told that the "Levites shall do the service of the tent of meeting, and they shall bear their iniquity" (18:23 RSV). The purpose is stated in 18:5: "so that wrath will not fall on the Israelites again" (NIV).

The interpretation of the key phrase of 18:23, "they shall bear their iniquity," is problematic. What is the identification of "they" and "their"? Is it "they [the Israelites] shall bear their [own] iniquity"? Hardly. Is it "they [the Levites] shall bear their [own] iniquity"? Possibly. Or is it "they [the Levites] shall bear their [the Israelites'] iniquity"? That is, one party bears the guilt of a second party. If that is the case, then Numbers 18, especially vv. 21–23, is saying that the Levites are vicariously culpable for the sins of the laity. Milgrom (1970: 32–33), after defending the third interpretation, states:

> Whereas the doctrine of collective responsibility is a cornerstone of P's theology for all sins against God, within the sanctuary there is an attempt to limit its destructive impact to the clergy alone. Herein lies the magnitude of the solace offered the panicky Israelites: henceforth, this cardinal doctrine of collective responsibility shall be compromised for their sakes so that they may worship at the sanctuary without fear.

Chapter 18 focuses on privileges and duties of priests (vv. 1–19) and Levites (vv. 20–32). God communicates most of this information directly to Aaron. Outside of Lev. 10:8, Num. 18:1, 8, and 20 are the only places where God reveals his directives to Aaron. Normally God speaks either to Moses, who then speaks to Aaron or to the people, or to Moses and Aaron simultaneously. Only toward the end of the chapter (v. 25), when discussing the tithe of the tithe that the Levites give to the priests, does God speak to and through Moses. This shift probably has a practical explanation. The concern in vv. 25–32 is the tithe that Aaron and his priestly colleagues receive from the Levites. God reveals this matter about intramural clergy responsibilities to Moses, who will not benefit from this tithe. He is a disinterested third party.

Two Types of Impurity (19:1–20:21)

Chapter 19 is concerned with one type of impurity: ritual impurity contracted by touching something deceased (vv. 11–13, 16) or by being in proximity to something deceased (v. 14). The theme of death was prominent in the previous unit (chs. 16–18), the victims including Korah and his fellow insurrectionists (16:35), and the 14,700 casualties of the plague (16:49 [MT 17:14]). Aaron stands between the dead and the living (16:48 [MT 17:13]). There is a fear of death (17:12–13 [MT 17:27–28]), and the possibility of death for encroachment (18:3, 7, 22) or improprieties in tithing (18:32).

A person who is contaminated by contact with a corpse is provided with the possibility of cleansing. The ritual involves the sprinkling of the blood of a red heifer/cow that is slaughtered outside the camp. The ashes of the incinerated heifer/cow are mixed with water and sprinkled on the unclean person on the third and seventh days after the contamination (19:17–19).

This is not the first time in Numbers we have met with contamination through contact with a corpse. Numbers 5:2–3 says explicitly that "one that is unclean through contact with the dead" is to be put out of the camp, but no such directive is given for the similar situation discussed in Numbers 19. Why? Must we resort to source criticism? Not necessarily. Perhaps the "discrepancy" can be explained by the fact that Numbers 5 deals with the camp in the wilderness, the immediate situation, whereas Numbers 19 is concerned with the future only: "and it shall be a perpetual statute for them" (19:21)—that is, when Israel is settled in Palestine (see Milgrom 1978: 516).

If that is the case, then there is a perceptible pattern in this part of Numbers. Present history, usually disastrous, is followed by a chapter regarding a future time for which God has made redemptive provision. Thus, chs. 11–14 deal with divine judgment in the present; ch. 15 includes cultic regulations for the future (15:15, 21, 23), underlining God's grace to cover human sin. Again, chs. 16–18 are concerned with divine judgment in the present; ch. 19 sets forth cultic regulations for the future, again underlining God's power to cleanse people from uncleanness. Surely it is significant that this chapter, which focuses on purification from contamination by physical contact with or in proximity to a deceased person, comes in between the record of the deaths of Korah, Dathan, Abiram, and many others in chs. 16–17 and the deaths of Miriam and Aaron in ch. 20 (vv. 1, 22–29).

In some ways impurity coming from contact with a corpse is like other contracted impurities. For example, the statement in 19:11 that anybody involved in such circumstances is unclean for seven days parallels other impurities for which a week of purification is required (the mother who has recently given birth [Lev. 12:2]; the individual with an infectious skin disease [Lev. 14:8]; a person with an abnormal bodily discharge [Lev. 15:13, 28]). But in all these situations the individual must present at the end of the purification period a sin/purification offering (Lev. 12:6–8; 14:19; 15:14–15, 29–30). That is not the case here. This omission would seem to place this particular impurity more in the category of the less severe than the more severe. Thus Numbers 19 avoids extremes: do not treat death lightly, but do not become obsessed or paranoid about it either.

The second type of impurity, although not called such, centers on the complaint about the absence of water (cf. Exod. 17:1–7). The imbroglio is ringed by the report of the death of Miriam (Num. 20:1) and the death of Aaron (20:22–29).

Interestingly, unlike in Numbers 11, the people suffer no consequences. But Moses does! He is to be excluded from the Promised Land because, as God says to him, "You did not trust in me enough to honor me as holy in the sight of the Israelites" (20:12 NIV). When the people were in trouble, Moses interceded for them. But who will pray for Moses? Does he have a mediator? If nothing else, the story illustrates the principle "To whom much is given, much is required." One might apply God's statement to Israel, "You only have I known of all the families of the earth; therefore I will punish you" (Amos 3:2 NRSV), to Moses. This could be paraphrased, "You alone have I chosen among the people as leader; therefore I will punish you."

The text does not give us the specific nature of Moses' and Aaron's sin. The indicting language of 20:12 is simply, "You did not trust in me." The Hebrew for "trust in" is exactly the same as that with which the Lord indicts his people in 14:11: "How long will they refuse to believe [trust] in me?" (NRSV). The first generation did not trust/believe in Yahweh, and so they will not enter the land. Moses and Aaron also did not trust/believe in Yahweh, and so they will not enter the land. What Abraham did (Gen. 15:6, with, as in Num. 20:12, the Hiphil of *ʾāman* followed by the preposition *bĕ*), neither Abraham's descendants nor Aaron and Moses did, and it cost them dearly. The text does not elaborate on the evidence or manner of Moses' distrust. Did he strike the rock rather than speak to the rock? Did he hit the rock twice instead of once? Did he speak too abrasively to his people ("Listen, you rebels")? If it is this last suggestion—and this is most unlikely—then the charge that Moses hurls at his people ("Listen, you rebels") is the same one that Yahweh directs at Aaron and Moses ("Both of you rebelled against my command" [v. 24b]). So who is the greater rebel: the congregants or those set aside by God as leaders of the congregants?

Right after the section citing God's rejection of Moses and denial of his opportunity to lead the people into Canaan-land (vv. 1–13) comes the story of Israel, under Moses' leadership still, trying to get Edom's green light to pass through their territory (20:14–21). Moses continues to lead his people in spite of the bad news that he has just received. He is not immediately relieved of his responsibilities, nor does he shirk from ministry. That will continue until God says, "This far, but no further."

Numbers 10:11–36

Childs, B. 1979. *Introduction to the Old Testament as Scripture*. Philadelphia: Westminster.

Coats, G. W. 1972. "Wilderness Itinerary." *CBQ* 34:135–52.

Cross, F. M. 1973. *Canaanite Myth and Hebrew Epic: Essays in the History of the Religion of Israel*. Cambridge, Mass.: Harvard University Press. Pp. 308–17.

Leiman, S. Z. 1974. "The Inverted '*Nuns*' at Numbers 10:35–36 and the Book of Eldad and Medad." *JBL* 93:348–55.

Levine, B. 1976. "More on the Inverted *Nuns* of Num. 10:35–36." *JBL* 95:122–24.

Numbers 11–12

Ackerman, S. 2002. "Why Is Miriam Also among the Prophets? (And Is Zipporah among the Priests?)" *JBL* 121:47–80.

Anderson, B. W. 1994. "Miriam's Challenge." *BRev* 10 (3):16, 55.

Ben-Amos, D. 1990. "Comments on R. C. Culley's 'Five Tales of Punishment in the Book of Numbers.'" In *Text and Tradition: The Hebrew Bible and Folklore*. Ed. S. Niditch. SemeiaSt. Atlanta: Scholars Press. Pp. 35–45.

Burns, R. J. 1987. *Has the Lord Spoken Only through Moses? A Study of the Biblical Portrait of Miriam*. SBLDS 84. Atlanta: Scholars Press. Pp. 41–79.

Butler, T. C. 1979. "An Anti-Moses Tradition." *JSOT* 12:9–15.

Coats, G. W. 1968. *Rebellion in the Wilderness: The Murmuring Motif in the Wilderness Traditions of the Old Testament*. Nashville: Abingdon. Pp. 96–115, 124–27, 261–64.

———. 1982. "Humility and Honor: A Moses Legend in Numbers 12." In *Art and Meaning: Rhetoric in Biblical Literature*. Ed. D. J. A. Clines, D. M. Gunn, and A. J. Hauser. JSOTSup 19. Sheffield: JSOT Press. Pp. 97–107.

Culley, R. C. 1990. "Five Tales of Punishment in the Book of Numbers." In *Text and Tradition: The Hebrew Bible and Folklore*. Ed. S. Niditch. SemeiaSt. Atlanta: Scholars Press. Pp. 25–34.

Dawes, S. B. 1990. "Numbers 12,3: What Was Special about Moses?" *BT* 41:336–40.

DeVries, S. J. 1975. "The Time Word *mahar* as a Key to Tradition Development." *ZAW* 87:65–79.

Jobling, D. 1977. "A Structural Analysis of Numbers 11 and 12." In *SBLSP 1977*. Ed. P. J. Achtemeier. Cambridge, Mass.: Society of Biblical Literature. Pp. 171–204.

———. 1978. *The Sense of Biblical Narrative: Three Structural Analyses in the Old Testament*. JSOTSup 7. Sheffield: Department of Biblical Studies, University of Sheffield.

Kselman, J. S. 1976. "Notes on Numbers 12:6–8." *VT* 26:500–505.

Leveen, A. B. 2002. "Variations on a Theme: Differing Conceptions of Memory in the Book of Numbers." *JSOT* 27:201–21.

Robinson, B. P. 1989. "The Jealousy of Miriam: A Note on Num. 12." *ZAW* 101:428–32.

Rogers, C. 1986. "Moses: Meek or Miserable?" *JETS* 29:257–63.

Sommer, B. D. 1999. "Reflecting on Moses: The Redaction of Numbers 11." *JBL* 118:601–24.

Trible, P. 1989. "Bringing Miriam out of the Shadows." *BRev* 10 (3):14–25, 34.

———. 1995. "Eve and Miriam: From the Margins to the Center." In *Feminist Approaches to the Bible*. Ed. H. Shanks. Washington, D.C.: Biblical Archaeology Society. Pp. 15–24.

Wilkinson, J. 1999. "The Quail Epidemic of Numbers 11:31–34." *EvQ* 71:195–208.

Numbers 13–14

Beck, J. A. 2000. "Geography and the Narrative Shape of Numbers 13." *BSac* 157:271–80.

Brin, G. 1980. "The Formula 'From . . . Onward/Upward' (*m . . . whlʾh wmʿlh*)." *JBL* 99:161–71.

Coats, G. W. 1968. *Rebellion in the Wilderness: The Murmuring Motif in the Wilderness Traditions of the Old Testament*. Nashville: Abingdon. Pp. 137–56.

Condie, K. 2001. "Narrative Features of Numbers 13–14 and Their Significance for the Meaning of the Book of Numbers." *Reformed Theological Review* 60:123–27.

Flanagan, J. W. 1976. "History, Religion, and Ideology: The Caleb Tradition." *Horizons* 3:175–85.

Fretheim, T. E. 2001. "Numbers." In *The Oxford Bible Commentary*. Ed. J. Barton and J. Muddiman. Oxford: Oxford University Press. Pp. 110–54.

Lerner, B. D. 1999. "Timid Grasshoppers and Fierce Locusts: An Ironic Pair of Biblical Metaphors." *VT* 49:545–48.

MacRae, A. 1970. "Numbers." In the *New Bible Commentary*. Ed. D. Guthrie and A. J. Motyer. Rev. ed. Grand Rapids: Eerdmans.

McEvenue, S. E. 1969. "A Source-Critical Problem in Nm 14,26–38." *Bib* 50:453–65.

———. 1971. *The Narrative Style of the Priestly Writer*. AnBib 50. Rome: Pontifical Biblical Institute. Pp. 90–144.

Newing, E. G. 1987. "The Rhetoric of Altercation in Numbers 14." In *Perspectives on Language and Text: Essays and Poems in Honor of Francis I. Andersen's Sixtieth Birthday.* Ed. E. W. Conrad and E. G. Newing. Winona Lake, Ind.: Eisenbrauns. Pp. 211–28.

Sakenfeld, K. D. 1975. "The Problem of Divine Forgiveness in Numbers 14." *CBQ* 37:317–30.

Vaux, R. de. 1978. *The Early History of Israel.* Philadelphia: Westminster. Pp. 523–26.

Numbers 15

Caine, I. 1971. "Numbers, Book of." *EncJud* 12:1249–54.

Fox, M. V. 1974. "The Sign of Covenant Circumcision in the Light of Priestly ʾot Etiologies." *RB* 81:481–523.

Knohl, I. 1991. "The Sin Offering Law in the 'Holiness School' (Numbers 15:22–31)." In *Priesthood and Cult in Ancient Israel.* Ed. G. A. Anderson and S. M. Olyan. JSOTSup 125. Sheffield: JSOT Press. Pp. 192–203.

Robinson, G. 1978. "The Prohibition of Strange Fire in Ancient Israel: A New Look at the Case of Gathering Wood and Kindling Fire on the Sabbath." *VT* 28:301–17.

Numbers 16–18

Alter, R. 1981. *The Art of Biblical Narrative.* New York: Basic Books. Pp. 104–7.

Coats, G. W. 1968. *Rebellion in the Wilderness: The Murmuring Motif in the Wilderness Traditions of the Old Testament.* Nashville: Abingdon. Pp. 156–84.

Levine, B. 1996. "Offerings Rejected by God: Numbers 16:15 in Comparative Perspective." In *"Go to the Land I Will Show You": Studies in Honor of Dwight W. Young.* Ed. J. E. Coleson and V. H. Matthews. Winona Lake, Ind.: Eisenbrauns. Pp. 107–16.

Magonet, J. 1982. "The Korah Rebellion." *JSOT* 24:3–25.

Mann, T. W. 1987. "Holiness and Death in the Redaction of Numbers 16:1–20:13." In *Love and Death in the Ancient Near East.* Ed. J. H. Marks and R. M. Good. Guilford, Conn.: Four Quarters. Pp. 181–90.

Milgrom, J. 1970. *Studies in Levitical Terminology.* Vol. 1, *The Encroacher and the Levite: The Term ʿAboda.* University of California Publications, Near Eastern Studies 14. Berkeley: University of California Press. Pp. 18–35.

———. 1988. "The Rebellion of Korah, Numbers 16–18: A Study in Tradition History." In *SBLSP 1988.* Ed. David J. Lull. Atlanta: Scholars Press. Pp. 570–78.

Pierce, R. W. 1987. "Male/Female Leadership and Korah's Revolt: An Analogy?" *JETS* 30:3–10.

Snaith, N. H. 1973. "Notes on Numbers 18:9." *VT* 23:373–75.

Wenham, G. J. 1981. "Aaron's Rod (Numbers 17, 16–28)." *ZAW* 93:280–81.

Numbers 19

Etkin, W. 1979. "The Mystery of the Red Heifer: A Scientific Midrash." *Judaism* 28:353–56.

Milgrom, J. 1978. "Studies in the Temple Scroll." *JBL* 97:501–23.

———. 1981. "The Paradox of the Red Cow (Num xix)." *VT* 31:62–72.

Wold, D. J. 1979. "The Kareth Penalty in P: Rationale and Cases." In *SBLSP 1979*. Ed. P. J. Achtemeier. Missoula, Mont.: Scholars Press. Pp. 1–45.

Numbers 20:1–21

Beck, J. A. 2003. "Why Did Moses Strike Out? The Narrative—Geographical Shaping of Moses' Disqualification in Numbers 20:1–13." *WTJ* 65:135–41.

Coats, G. W. 1976. "Conquest Traditions in the Wilderness Theme." *JBL* 95:177–90.

Freund, R. A. 1994. "'Thou Shalt Not Go Thither': Moses and Aaron's Punishment and Varying Theodicies in the MT, LXX and Hellenistic Literature." *SJT* 8:105–25.

Margaliot, M. 1983–1984. "The Transgression of Moses and Aaron: Numbers 20:1–13." *JQR* 74:196–208.

Propp, W. H. 1988. "The Rod of Aaron and the Sin of Moses." *JBL* 107:19–26.

Sakenfeld, K. D. 1985. "Theological and Redactional Problems in Numbers 20.2–13." In *Understanding the Word: Essays in Honour of Bernhard W. Anderson*. Ed. J. T. Butler, E. W. Conrad, and B. Ollenburger. JSOTSup 37. Sheffield: JSOT Press. Pp. 133–54.

18

From Kadesh to Moab

NUMBERS 20:22–36:13

This unit opens with a narration of Aaron's death (20:22–29), an event that is recalled in 33:38–39 and Deut. 32:50. Moses has already lost one member of his family, his sister Miriam (20:1). Again the story is reflective of a prevalent theme in Numbers: sin cannot go unchecked. In collusion with Moses, Aaron did not "believe" in God (20:12) but rather "rebelled" against his command (20:24)—both verbs are second-person, masculine plural.

Surprisingly, perhaps, it is Moses who is informed of Aaron's imminent death. Moses is to "take" Aaron and his son Eleazar up to Mount Hor and transfer Aaron's high-priestly clothing to Eleazar. Such transfer of priestly leadership from the first generation to the second generation, from father to son, symbolizes the larger dynamic of this fortieth year of wilderness wandering: the transition from the exodus generation to their children's generation. The scene is reminiscent of Abraham and Isaac at Beersheba (Genesis 22). Abraham is to "take" Isaac, who does not know about the mission's purpose, to Mount Moriah. A fully cooperative, unquestioning Abraham parallels a fully cooperative, unquestioning Moses. Both are prepared to say a final good-bye to a close relative.

Moses knew only too well the reason for Aaron's demise. But there is no indication that Moses felt constrained to make a public disclosure of the reason, nor did he capitalize on the opportunity to turn a funeral into an evangelistic opportunity, replete with warnings and exhortations.

Some Early Opposition and Victories (20:22–21:35)

Three conflicts are presented in ch. 21. The first is a battle with some Canaanites in the Negeb area. The Israelites are delivered from subjugation after they "vowed a vow" to the Lord (21:2), a theme that shortly will occupy the entire chapter of Numbers 30. Moses is conspicuously absent from the narrative of this battle—a sure sign that his pivotal role is winding down since God's word in 20:12 about his exclusion from Canaan. Surely it must be the second generation that gets the credit for this victory rather than the condemned exodus generation. Once more the Israelites complain of no food or water (21:4–9). Also, the Israelites encounter opposition on the way to Moab from Sihon, king of the Amorites (21:21–32 [see Deut. 2:24–37 for a retelling]), and Og, king of Bashan (21:33–35 [see Deut. 3:1–11 for a retelling]). Israel must fight not only to get *into* the Promised Land but also to get *to* the Promised Land.

The second conflict adds some interesting new developments. This time God does not send water or food. Before Moses can do or say anything, God sends "fiery/venomous serpents." The Hebrew word for "serpent" here is the same as that for the serpent of Genesis 3: "bronze one[s]." The Hebrew word for "fiery/venomous" here is śārāp, which is used to describe the angelic creatures in the temple in Isaiah's vision (Isa. 6:2).

Faced with the prospect of death through snakebite, the people confess, "We have sinned," and then they ask for a suspension of the plague. The language is a reminder of earlier language in Exodus. Pharaoh says, "Entreat the LORD to take away the frogs" (Exod. 8:8 RSV). Here the Israelites say, "Pray that the LORD will take the snakes away from us" (21:7 NIV).

God's response to the people's request is interesting. Moses does pray, but God does not take away the serpents. He provides a cure, a fiery serpent that is to be raised on a pole. The presence of this elevated serpent does not guarantee immunity from attack. Its presence does become therapeutic, however, when an individual, if bitten, looks at it.

One can easily see how the New Testament is able to draw a parallel to this event: "And as Moses lifted up the serpent in the wilderness, so must the Son of Man be lifted up, that whoever believes in him may have eternal life" (John 3:14–15 RSV).

God did not get rid of the serpents. He also had not (yet!) abolished the presence of sin. But he had provided relief from the problem, a relief that is like the problem yet different from it. The New Testament equivalent of the Old Testament "to look" is "to believe." Here they are synonymous terms. Faith, then, is, as A. W. Tozer (1948: 89) has said, "The gaze of the soul upon a saving God."

In this particular incident perhaps the wrong prayer has been prayed. Instead of asking, "Take away the serpents from us," the people should have prayed, or at least gone on to pray, "Take away from us the attitudes that do not glorify and honor your name." Respite, not reformation, is their concern. Centuries later King Hezekiah broke this bronze snake into pieces because it had become an idolatrous icon (2 Kings 18:4). What God provides for our healing is to be appropriated but not venerated. When God's gifts are themselves worshiped, idolatry in one of its most sinister forms has erupted.

Verses 10–20 of ch. 21 provide an itinerary of Israel's further trek through the wilderness. The journey itself is uneventful, but it is noteworthy by virtue of the two poetic sections in the unit, one a quote from a lost book identified as the "Book of the Wars of the LORD" (vv. 14–15 NRSV)—evidence of real rather than hypothetical sources behind the Pentateuch—and the other, which we may call, for convenience, the "Song of the Well" (vv. 17–18).

The remainder of the chapter describes Israel's confrontation with Sihon of the Amorites (vv. 21–32) and Og of Bashan (vv. 33–35), with much greater detail for the battle with Sihon than for that with Og. The former is treated in twelve verses, the latter in three.

The people of God have no interest in the territory of Sihon. Rather, their sights are set on something else: a better land "whose builder and maker is God" (cf. Heb. 11:10). To that end, the Israelites desire only to pass through (is this theme similar to that of *Pilgrim's Progress*?) to a greater destination. That simple courtesy Sihon refused to grant. An easy-enough yes from Sihon, and there would have been no storm. Instead, there is a recalcitrant no, and Sihon sees his cities, especially Heshbon, pass from his control into the control of Israel. Jesus, much later, found himself in a similar situation. He wanted passage through a Samaritan village. The request was denied. The Samaritans acted as Sihon had. But instead of routing the Samaritans, Jesus rebuked those who wanted precisely that to happen (Luke 9:51–56). Rather than pressing the issue, Jesus took an alternate route, as Moses had done earlier with the Edomites (Num. 20:21; Luke 9:56). Circumvention is, most of the time, preferable to confrontation.

And perhaps Israel would have done the same with Sihon and the Amorites had not Sihon rushed his military forces into action (21:23). The Israelites had no choice but to respond militarily, and this they did quite well.

The event is sealed and justified by the recitation of a poem (vv. 27–30), the contents of which deal at least in part with Sihon's former capture of Heshbon from the Moabites (see v. 29). But now Sihon has surrendered his gains. To be sure, there are extremely difficult problems in translating the poem. For instance, who recites this poem (v. 27)? The KJV has "they that speak in proverbs"; the NIV has "this is why the poets say"; the NRSV has "therefore, the ballad singers say." Or could the Hebrew *mōšĕlîm* be translated as "taunters"? In addition, v. 30, a key verse, is puzzling, as is indicated by divergences in both the ancient and modern versions of the Bible. Is v. 30 a further description of Sihon's victory over Moab, or a description of Israel's victory over Sihon?

At least the whole story, and the poem in particular, says that gains can become losses, new frontiers can be forfeited. Stubbornness may be nothing more than stupidity.

There are two other scriptural accounts of the battle against Sihon: Deut. 2:24–37; Judg. 11:19–26. In attempting to relate these three narrations, biblical scholars have drawn one of two conclusions: (1) Numbers is the original account, and the account in Deuteronomy 2 and Judges 11 is derived from it (J. R. Bartlett, Roland de Vaux); (2) the account in Deuteronomy is the oldest of the three, and Num. 21:21–31 is a later adaptation of it (John Van Seters).

Van Seters seeks not only to make the Numbers story post-Deuteronomic but also to make the whole episode fictional! In part he bases his conclusions on the differences between the accounts in Numbers and Deuteronomy.

Indeed, there are differences. One significant difference is "then Israel sent messengers to Sihon" (Num. 21:21 RSV) versus "so I [Moses] sent messengers . . . to Sihon" (Deut. 2:26 RSV). Was it Moses who sent the couriers to Sihon, or was it the people? As an extension of this we note that Moses is mentioned nowhere in Num. 21:21–31. He assumes no role in the narrative.

Unlike the account in Numbers, the account in Deuteronomy 2 is replete with references to divine activity. Note this material unique to Deuteronomy: "I have given into your hand Sihon . . . engage him in battle" (v. 24 NIV); "This day I will begin to put the dread and fear of you upon the peoples" (v. 25 NRSV); "For the LORD your God hardened his spirit" (v. 30 RSV); "And the LORD said to me, 'Behold, I have begun to give Sihon and his land over to you'" (v. 31 RSV); "And the LORD our

God gave him over to us" (v. 33 RSV); "The LORD our God gave all into our hands" (v. 36 RSV).

What implications may be drawn from these differences? Van Seters (1972: 196) is prepared to say that Numbers, "if anything, secularizes the other accounts." But could there not be another reason for deemphasizing the role of Moses and the activity of God in Numbers, a reason that does justice to the larger context?

The story about Sihon is not particularly removed from the incident at the rock in which Moses is informed by God that his activity is unacceptable. Moses is to be barred from entering into the land of promise (20:12). Aaron was already denied entrance (20:29), and he is dead. The silence about Moses' role in Num. 21:21–30 may be a reflection of the incident in 20:12; Moses, therefore, will have only a minimal role to play in the acquisition of land (see Coats 1976: 189–90).

I also find myself nonplussed by Van Seters's assertion (1972: 197) that these accounts "have a highly ideological character which makes these episodes historically untrustworthy." On what basis can we claim that the ideological is nonhistorical, and the nonideological is historical? The logic of that escapes me.

Balaam the Diviner (22–24)

This particular section of Numbers is among the best known of the whole book. The Israelites' reputation precedes them, causing panic in Balak, Moab's head of state. It is not evident why Balak's father, Zippor, is frequently named, especially in ch. 22 (22:2, 4, 10, 16; 23:18), but could there be an intended comparison between Balak, whose father is Zippor, leading Moab, and Moses, whose wife is Zipporah, leading Israel? "Zippor" means "bird," so it is the son of a bird versus the husband of a bird. Earlier in Numbers it was Israel who was afraid of the people (13:33). Now it is Israel who has become, figuratively, the "Anakim" and the "Nephilim." The Moabites are the grasshoppers.

Israel, when in distress, yearned for a return to Egypt. But where can the Moabites go? Where is their security? Military resistance is a risky option. A person inundated in fear can only speak in hyperbole. For Balak, the Israelites are so numerous as to "cover the face of the earth" (22:5). In so speaking about the Israelites, his concerns parallel those of the Pharaoh of the oppression/exodus (Exod. 1:9–10).

In such a crisis perhaps one's trump card is magic. To that end, Balak sends an urgent message to Balaam, who lives a considerable distance from Moab, at Pethor, south of Carchemish on the Euphrates. If it is this Pethor to which Balak sends his delegation, then it is a trip of approximately four hundred miles, one that would take the better part of a month to complete.

Balaam's job, should he decide to accept it, is simple enough. He is to pronounce a curse on the Israelites that will immobilize them, making them especially vulnerable to defeat by Balak. To make the offer as tempting as possible, Balak throws in an almost irresistible honorarium (22:7, 17). Behind this approach is the idea that religious power can be purchased, that it is a commodity, a marketable item. In the time of the apostles, Simon the magician thought that the power of the Spirit for one's life could be bought for cash, as if it were an item on a menu (Acts 8:18–19). And really good diviners do not come cheap!

Balaam eventually accepts Balak's offer, and he goes to Moab on the back of a donkey to await Balak's palm leaves and hosannas. It may surprise the reader that Balaam first rejects the offer because God told him to (22:12). But when the delegation returns the second time with a much more generous offer, Balaam seems to fudge a bit (22:19). In 22:20 God gives Balaam the green light to go with the messengers, only to be angry two verses later with Balaam for going (22:22)! Maybe it is not clear to Balaam that when God gives permission, that is not necessarily the same thing as God giving sanction. The episode about Balaam's donkey (22:21–35) seems humorous to everyone except Balaam. Only the physical manifestation of the angel of the Lord restrains Balaam from precipitous action against his beast of burden. Confronted by the divine, Balaam can only fall on his face (22:31), as Joshua later would do before the angel of the Lord (Josh. 5:14). Balaam also says, "I have sinned," a confession that parallels the people's confession in the preceding chapter, "We have sinned" (21:7).

Balaam does not appear in any way shocked by his donkey's capacity for human speech. As Robert Alter (1981: 106) puts it, "Balaam in his wrath hardly seems to notice the miraculous gift of speech as though he were accustomed to having daily domestic wrangles with his asses." Animals often play a key role in biblical dramas. One thinks of Abraham's ram, Jonah's fish, Daniel's lions, Peter's rooster, and Jesus' colt.

The closest parallel to Balaam's donkey is the serpent that seduces Eve (Genesis 3). Numbers 22 and Genesis 3 are the only two narratives in the OT in which an animal communicates in human speech. The parallels between the two chapters do not stop there, however (Savran 1994). Both the donkey's and the serpent's first spoken word is a question (Num. 22:28; Gen. 3:1b), but the purpose of the serpent's deceptive question is to create confusion and doubt, while the purpose of the donkey's honest question is to clarify confusion. In Genesis 3 the movement is from blessing to curse; in Numbers 22–24 the movement is from curse to blessing. Balaam's words to Balak, "Even if Balak gave me his palace . . . I could not do anything of my own accord, good or bad/evil" (Num. 24:13 NIV), recall the prominence of the tree of the "knowledge of good and bad/evil" in Genesis 2–3.

The rest of the story involves Balak and Balaam together, with the latter delivering orally four oracles: 23:7–10; 23:18–24; 24:3–9; 24:15–24. These four messages are called "discourse[s]." The Hebrew word for this is *māšāl*, and it may provide another connecting link with the previous unit in Numbers, the song sung by the *mōšělîm* (21:27). The first three oracles Balaam gives in response to Balak's request, and the fourth he delivers spontaneously. Perhaps we should see a correspondence between three scenes involving Balaam and the donkey (22:21–23, 24–25, 26–28), each resulting in increasing discomfort for Balaam, and the three scenes involving Balaam and Balak (23:1–12, 13–26; 23:27–24:14), each resulting in increasing discomfort for Balak, as the seer's prophecies of Israel's future become more lavish. The donkey's question to Balaam, "What have I done to you?" (22:28), is the reverse of Balak's question to Balaam, "What have you done to me?" (23:11).

What Balak hears from Balaam is precisely the opposite of what he had hoped to hear. These were words of blessing, not curse; benediction, not malediction. No one was more surprised than Balaam himself. There is no indication that he was being duplicitous with Balak and that all along he intended to bless Israel. There are two equally miraculous events in this story, and both have to do with talking. One is for God to make Balaam's donkey talk, and the other is to make Balaam a speaker of blessing rather than a spewer of blasphemy on Israel. Two tongues are divinely touched. We should note, however, that before God touches Balaam's tongue, he touches his eyes by opening them (22:31). The Lord did the same with Hagar (Gen. 21:19), with the servants of Elisha when they were surrounded by the enemy (2 Kings 6:17), and with the two disciples who unknowingly walked with the resurrected Christ to Emmaus and sat at the table with him (Luke 24:31). All of these persons could sing, "I once was blind, but now I see," for an encounter with God has the potential to be an eye-opener.

Addressing Balaam's speech (with the approval of the Lord), Gerhard von Rad (1960: 72–73) says:

> God lets the magician go on his way. He does not bar the road before him; He does not strike him down in His wrath; He will merely direct the word that Balaam is to utter. Here our story gives expression to

something that is very important in the faith of the Old Testament; God does not guide history and the destiny of men by continually opposing men in the projects that they have taken in hand. On the contrary, he lets them act. To all appearance, they are acting simply according to His plan.

Balaam is not an Israelite. Raymond Brown (1988) compares Balaam to the "wise men" who came with their gifts for the Christ child (Matt. 2:1–12). As a non-Israelite diviner, Balaam is what would have been called in Jesus' time a *magus*. Both come from the east (Num. 23:7; Matt. 2:1). Both speak of or follow an important star (Num. 24:17; Matt. 2:2), one star pointing to David, the other to Jesus. In both cases God gives a revelation to Gentiles. Balaam seems to know more about Israel's future than does Israel, and the magi, who have only God's incomplete revelation (a star in the heavens), worship the Christ child, while those who have God's final revelation in the Scriptures (Herod, chief priests, scribes) do not worship him. More than likely Balaam is not a monotheist, at least by upbringing and tradition. His vocation is a vice in Israel. True, the Lord does guide those who do not know him, as in the case of Cyrus of Persia (Isa. 45:4b). But Balaam knows the Lord, or knows of him. He uses the name "Yahweh/Lord" thirteen times. God speaks to him (22:9, 12, 20). He speaks of the Lord as "my God" (22:18). He recognizes the angel of the Lord (22:31). The Lord meets with Balaam (23:16) and "put[s] a word in his mouth" (23:5, 16). Balaam even shows some spiritual metamorphosis as he gradually sloughs off the old pagan techniques of which he is master (24:1). The Spirit of God rests upon him (24:2).

Some interpreters, religiously pluralistic, have seized this as one of the more significant points in the story as far as contemporary value and application are concerned: here the unbeliever, the man of another religion (or no religion), speaks the truth of God. Thus A. E. Zannoni (1978: 18), under his discussion of the story's "implications for the Church," says, "It is not unknown in our times that secular institutions have 'preached the gospel' while the church, the new Israel, has remained thunderously silent." George Coats (1972: 29), in his concluding remarks about "Balaam the Saint," hints at the same point.

But before we cite the story as a score for pluralism and tolerance and a blow against confessionalism and dogmatism, let us observe that Balaam makes no reference to any other gods. He knows only Yahweh of Israel. What he says about Israel does not (necessarily) represent his own opinions on the subject. He probably loathes the Israelites—an attitude shown by his active role in the Israelite apostasy at Baal-peor (Numbers 25, and especially 31:16). Also, we need to recall Yehezkel

Kaufmann's (1960: 294) observation that while Scripture tells us of individual non-Israelites who knew God intimately, it also says that outside of Israel no nation knows him.

What is the relationship of this story to the larger context of Numbers? Two items seem apparent. In the first place, Moses once again is conspicuously absent from these three chapters. He is not a part of the drama at all. We saw this in ch. 21 in the incident involving Arad, Sihon, and Heshbon and there related it to God's sentence of condemnation on Moses. His inconsequential role continues into the story of Balak and Balaam. Of course, in this particular story all of Israel, not just Moses, is uninvolved. Presumably they are unaware of any of the machinations of Balak and Balaam. This may explain why in the opening chapters of Deuteronomy Moses retells the spy story of Numbers 13–14, the circumvention of Edom in Numbers 20, and the battles against Sihon and Og in Numbers 21 but says nothing about the Balaam incident in Numbers 22–24.

This latter point raises the question of how Moses is privy to the content of Balaam's oracles if he is not geographically involved. The critics can be expected to dismiss the question as ludicrous on the grounds that the whole story is from the ninth to eighth century B.C., the Yahwist and the Elohist. (A few scholars, such as Van Seters [1997], attribute all of Numbers 22–24 to the J source [except for the donkey narrative and a few other passages], a source that Van Seters dates to the late postexilic period.) The four oracles would antedate the narrative framework by a century or two (if one follows the conclusion of W. F. Albright's linguistic analysis of Balaam's oracles).

On the other hand, perhaps a case can be made that when Balaam was apprehended for his involvement in the Baal-peor debacle, part of his defense was to retell his oracles to Moses (as is suggested by Seerveld 1980: 73 n. 10). That he had blessed Israel and spoken of Israel's future prosperity, maybe even a messiah (24:17?), would be in his favor, so he may have thought.

Returning to the relationship of the story to Numbers, we may note another connection. Almost ad nauseam Numbers has related (and will relate) stories in which Israel's existence is threatened. But why? Consistently the reason for potential demise has been internal: Israel has been its own worst enemy; Israel may destroy itself.

Israel need not fear, says this story, the incantations of an international wizard. This is not where the potential hazard is. But Israel should begin to do some deep soul-searching when a critical spirit, faultfinding, and backbiting emerge. These compare to the threats of a Balaam as does cancer to an upset stomach.

Baal-peor (25)

The Israelites have now reached Shittim, east of the Jordan and almost directly across the river from Jericho. This is the place from which Joshua sent out the two spies (Josh. 2:1). Numbers 31:16 informs us that Balaam devised the scheme to get the Israelites involved in sexual debauchery with "the daughters of Moab." He is as eminently success-ful in this as he was unsuccessful in his attempts to place a curse on Israel. Where the potency of spell fails, the potency of seduction suc-ceeds. Where the indirect approach falters, the frontal attack takes over. Ruth, a Moabite, later provides a stunning contrast with the Moabite women of Numbers 25.

The Israelites, again reflecting their insensitivity to matters moral and spiritual, are only too happy to become involved with the daugh-ters of Moab (possibly virgins, as in biblical Hebrew the expression "daughters of" followed by a place-name may designate unmarried women; see Gen. 36:2; 2 Sam. 1:20, 24; Isa. 3:16). Thus an unholy alliance is created between the sons of God and the daughters of men (Gen. 6:1–4). It is even more tragic that the account of Israel's engaging in adulterous sexual relations with foreigners should come right on the heels of a foreigner's prophecy of great blessing for the future. Just about everything that Balaam says about Israel (e.g., "I see a people who live apart" [23:9 NIV]; "The LORD their God is with them" [23:21 NRSV]; "How beautiful are your tents, O Jacob" [24:5 NIV]; "A star will come out of Jacob" [24:17 NIV]) is contradicted by the immorality of ch. 25.

God's first response is anger against Israel. (In the story about Balaam and Balak, God's anger was kindled against Balaam [22:22], Balaam's anger against his donkey [22:27], and Balak's anger against Balaam [24:10].) Divine anger eventually leads to the outbreak of a plague (v. 9), but the narrative indicates that the repercussions might have been sig-nificantly reduced had the divine mandate been followed. Some scholars are bothered by the fact that the Lord's directive "Take all the chiefs of the people, and hang them in the sun before the LORD" (25:4 RSV) is ignored by Moses. He orders the judges to kill those who have "yoked themselves/joined in worship to Baal of Peor [god of fire]" (v. 5). In other words, what Moses orders has nothing at all to do with what God has ordered.

It is possible to suggest that there is some disarray in the text, although the critics assign both vv. 4 and 5 to the non-P materials in Numbers. Taking the text as it stands, I suggest there are no gaps here in the logical development of the story. Precisely because Moses did not implement the word of the Lord, many who might have been spared (v. 4b) were not (v. 9). If that is the case, then we have another illustration of Moses attempting to improve on God's plan, or at least revise it (see Num. 20:10–12). Both times the consequences are tragic.

Why does the Lord specify that the "chiefs of the people" should be impaled? Two possibilities come to mind. This may be an example of vicarious punishment in which the innocent suffer for the guilty, here the innocent being those with social power who did not restrain those under their authority—that is, the sins of the children being visited upon the fathers. Or it may be that the "chiefs of the people" were indeed the ringleaders, one of whom is identified as Zimri the Simeonite (v. 14). More than likely the daughters of Moab would try to entice the leaders. Also, the woman in the story, Cozbi, is identified as a member of a prominent Midianite family (v. 15). Her name comes from a Hebrew/Semitic root *kāzab*, which means "lie, deceive." Balaam used this verb in 23:19 when he said, "God is not a human being, that he should lie [*kāzab*]."

More than half of the chapter, vv. 6–15, is given to the act of unfaithfulness by one Israelite, Zimri, and the intuitive response to that apostasy by one Israelite, Phinehas, grandson of Aaron. (The source critics are unable to agree whether this part of the chapter is from P.) Here the focus is on the individual trespasser, not the people, and on the individual vindicator, not Moses and the judges.

Zimri's crime was to bring a Midianite woman into "the inner room" (NIV, NRSV: "tent") (v. 8), presumably for sexual intercourse. The word in Hebrew for "inner room" is used only here in the Old Testament. De Vaux (1978: 569) translates this word as "pavilion, tent, or alcove," and suggests that it may have been used for sacred prostitution. The whole affair took place in the sight of Moses and the people, who "were weeping at the door of the tent of meeting." This may imply that the act was perpetrated near Israel's sanctuary.

If so, Phinehas's leap into action becomes quite comprehensible. Three times (3:10, 38; 18:7) Numbers has said that one of the responsibilities of the priesthood was "to put to death any unauthorized person who comes near" the sacred things of the tabernacle. This passage would then serve as an illustration of that principle in operation (see Milgrom 1970: 48–49).

Twice the text comments on Phinehas's zeal (vv. 11, 13). That Phinehas is said to be "zealous/jealous" for the Lord connects him with that same trait in Elijah (1 Kings 19:10, 14). And we might note the use of this word to describe the pre-Christian Saul of Tarsus (Acts 22:3; Gal. 1:14; Phil. 3:6). What all three individuals have in common is a passionate desire to live out and maintain the truth of the faith, and a willingness to engage in violent actions against those they think are sabotaging the faith (Zimri and Cozbi, the prophets of Baal, followers of Jesus the Messiah).

This section of the chapter also serves to contrast the amendment-oriented Moses and the action-oriented Phinehas. Earlier it was Moses who made atonement on Israel's behalf (see, e.g., Exod. 32:30), or Moses who urged Aaron to make atonement on behalf of the congregation (Num. 16:46–48), thus arresting the divine plague. Moses is not involved at all here. It is Phinehas who makes atonement for Israel (v. 13).

It is hard not to take the Lord's speech to Moses as a rebuke: "Phinehas . . . has turned back my wrath from the people of Israel" (v. 11 RSV).

A Second Census and Questions about Inheritance (26–27)

On the heels of an act of apostasy (ch. 25) comes an extended census, a second one akin to that described in ch. 1. Registrants in this census include those who are the descendants of the Israelites who came out of Egypt (v. 4b), but who are aged twenty and older, the minimum age for inclusion in the first census. The NIV's "these were the Israelites who came out of Egypt" cannot be referring to that first generation, as vv. 64–65 expressly say that none of that generation, except Caleb and Joshua, are included. It is possible to run all of v. 4 together to say "those twenty years old or more, just as the LORD had commanded the (first generation of) Israelites who came out of Egypt." The immediate purpose of this survey is to provide statistical data for allotting the land after it has been conquered (vv. 52–56). That in itself is interesting, since there is formidable opposition ahead.

God's look to the future is different from that of the spies. The spies say, "We are unable to take the land"; God says, "You will take the land." To that end, Israel can confidently begin preparations and sense nothing premature in doing so. For a comparable situation, imagine a presidential candidate choosing a running mate and cabinet members even before the primaries have begun.

The totals for each tribe are fairly close to each other in chs. 1 and 26, so there has been neither a boom nor a bust in terms of population. The two exceptions are the tribe of Simeon, which has declined from a total of 59,300 (1:23) to 22,200 (26:14), and the tribe of Manasseh, which has expanded from 32,200 (1:35) to 52,700 (26:34). Possibly Simeon is amalgamating with Judah, and hence its lower numbers (see Josh. 19:1; Judg. 1:3), while Manasseh is expanding (see Josh. 17:11, 16, which speak of Manasseh's growing pain—too many people for one place, so they must extend their borders).

The results of the census create one problem, however. There is one family in which Zelophehad, the father, is deceased; there are no sons, only five daughters (Num. 27:1), a point to which the preceding census has already drawn attention (26:33). The problem is that women do not normally inherit property (see Deut. 21:15–17). Are they then to be totally without patrimony? It is true that the three daughters of Job received an inheritance (Job 42:15), but that situation is different because there the father is still alive. This delegation of five women coming before a male in a public place ("the entrance to the tent of meeting") to seek a legal decision from that presiding male is comparable to the two women/harlots who sought a legal decision from a presiding male (King Solomon) as to which of them was the true mother of a baby (1 Kings 3:16–28).

Perhaps the subordinate role of women is emphasized here even by the Hebrew construction that is used. We read that the daughters of Zelophehad "drew near/approached" (*qārab*) and "stood before" (*lipnê*) Moses and the priest (Num. 27:1–2). Joshua 17:4 simply says that the daughters "came before" (*qārab lipnê*) Eleazar. There is one other instance in Numbers in which a person "came before" (*qārab lipnê*) Moses: when those who were unclean through contact with a corpse approached him. In both instances there is proximity but not contact. Both the contaminated and the daughters of Zelophehad are to keep their distance.

What is the solution to an apparent conundrum? This is the fourth and final case in Leviticus–Numbers in which an issue comes up that previous legislation has not addressed, and for which Moses seeks counsel from God. The other three cases are (1) the blasphemer (Lev. 24:10–23, especially v. 12); (2) the delayed Passover (Num. 9:1–14, especially v. 8); (3) the Sabbath-breaker (Num. 15:32–35, especially v. 34). Such incidents demonstrate that God's revelation to his people was not necessarily a "done deal," nor was it one that exhaustively covered all possible topics. In addition to God's definitive and primary revelation there is room for further disclosures as the need arises, but they are always disclosures that complement the Sinai revelation rather than contradict it. God's word is simple and direct. A new law is initiated. Inheritance may pass not only to sons but also, where circumstances dictate, to daughters (v. 8), to brothers of the deceased (v. 9), to uncles of the deceased (v. 10), or to the nearest living relative (v. 11)..

And this law is to become binding for future generations rather than being a temporary measure (v. 11b). Note again the prospect of a guaranteed future. The census of ch. 26 anticipates occupation of the land of Palestine. The juridical innovation of ch. 27 likewise looks into the future with optimism. As Sakenfeld (1988a: 42) has observed, while the incident reinforces the point that females may inherit property only in the absence of male offspring, it also makes clear that this ruling is not a onetime exception, but rather is generalized to provide opportunity for other such women anytime in the future when similar circumstances might arise.

The second half of the chapter deals with the commissioning of Joshua to succeed Moses (27:12–23). Its position at this point in Numbers is quite natural. The census detailed the second generation. The daughters of Zelophehad are the successors to their father. Moses too needs an heir, not biologically but functionally. The first generation will become casualties in the wilderness because of their sins. God has raised up a second generation to set foot in the land of promise. Similarly, the first leader will join the first generation outside of that land. Joshua is a new leader for a new generation.

The appointment of Joshua also serves as a guarantee, as did the census and the incident of Zelophehad's daughters, of where God is taking his people. Natural qualifications do not commend Joshua for the job. He is supernaturally prepared, for in him is the Spirit (v. 18).

It is noteworthy that Moses makes the suggestion to God about a successor (v. 16). His magnanimous spirit shows through in his concern that Israel not "be as sheep which have no shepherd" (v. 17 RSV). To the end, and even under divine judgment, his spirit remains pastoral. Might an indication of Moses' zeal be evidenced by the Lord's instruction to Moses to lay "your hand" (singular) upon Joshua (v. 18), to which Moses responded by laying "his hands" (plural) on him (v. 23)?

God describes Joshua in v. 18 as "a man in whom is the spirit," or "a man in whom is (a) spirit," or "a man in whom is spirit" (NIV footnote). (The Hebrew language does not distinguish between uppercase and lowercase letters.) If we do not capitalize "spirit," or even if we do, God's reference is most likely to Joshua's skill/spirit as a God-gifted leader, as in the Gen. 41:38 reference to Joseph's skill/spirit in dream interpretation, or the Exod. 31:2 reference to Bezalel's God-given skill/spirit to be supervisor of the tabernacle project. Sometimes "spirit/rûaḥ" is a synonym for "courage," as in Josh. 2:11 ("When we heard of it . . . everyone's courage failed" NIV) and Josh. 5:1 ("Now when all the Amorite kings . . . heard . . . their hearts sank and they no longer had the courage to face the Israelites" NIV). In either case, God does not call, then equip; rather, God equips, then calls.

A Religious Calendar and Vows (28–30)

The first two chapters of this unit describe *ad seriatim* the various offerings that Israel is to give the Lord. In all, eight different occasions are highlighted. I list them in the left-hand column of table 13, with their parallels from one of the other cultic calendars in the Pentateuch (Exod. 23:10–19; 34:18–24; Lev. 23:1–44; Deut. 16:1–17). The second generation receives in chs. 28–29 a reminder that "My times are in your hand" (Ps. 31:15 NRSV). Worship is to punctuate everyone's schedule daily (Num. 28:1–8), weekly (28:9–10), monthly (28:11–15), seasonally (28:16–29:40).

Israel's offerings to the Lord are to be in the form of animals, fine flour, oil, and wine. Numbers 28–29 provide us with an exact number of each, or quantity of each, that is to be given for the specific occasion. The sacrifices of animals are listed in table 14.

The number of animals offered as whole burnt offerings outnumbers those offered as sin offerings in approximately a 40:1 ratio. In the studies of Leviticus we saw that the whole burnt offering, unlike the sin offering, is not primarily expiatory in purpose; rather, it is an expression of praise and gratitude. This, then, earmarks the outstanding characteristic of Hebrew worship.

It is also interesting to observe that for the Feast of Tabernacles alone there is a specific number, and a decreasing number, of animals specified for each day. This one feast accounts for approximately 60 percent of the total of young bulls, 40 percent of the total of rams, and 36 percent of the total of goats.

Once again, as we have seen in the immediately preceding chapters, Numbers establishes policies for the Israelites to follow once they are settled in Palestine. The land will be divided (ch. 26), Joshua will be leader (ch. 27), and Israel's life will be permeated by worship (chs. 28–29).

It is of some interest that the thrice-noted "three times in the year shall all your males appear before the LORD God" in these calendars (Exod. 23:17; 34:23; Deut. 16:16) does not appear in Numbers 28–29 in its discussion of Unleavened Bread, Pentecost, and Tabernacles. "Women's rights" have already been discussed in Num. 27:1–11.

It is somewhat unexpected, therefore, to read in ch. 30, the last part of this unit, that a father may overrule an unmarried daughter's vows to the Lord (vv. 3–5). (The mention of vows at the end of ch. 29 [v. 39] provides a smooth bridge into the larger discussion of vows in ch. 30.) Similarly, a husband may nullify the religious vows of his wife, even if the wife made the vow while unmarried and still living with her father (vv. 6–8). The exception to this is the widow or the divorcée (v. 9). The fourth ruling in this chapter on vows is that a husband can annul any vow his wife makes if he does so on the day he learns of it (vv. 10–12).

Table 13

Numbers 28–29		Exodus 23:10–19	Exodus 34:18–24	Leviticus 23:1–44	Deuteronomy 16:1–17
1. 28:3–8	daily offering	(29:38–42)			
2. 28:9–10	Sabbath offering	12*	21*	1–3*	
3. 28:11–15	offering at first of month				
4. 28:16–25	offering at Passover and Unleavened Bread	15	18–20, 25	5–8	1–8
5. 28:26–31	offering at Pentecost (Weeks/First-fruits)	16a	22a, 26	15–22	9–12
6. 29:1–6	offering at New Year			23–25	
7. 29:7–11	offering on Day of Atonement			26–32	
8. 29:12–38	offering at Tabernacles	16b	22b	33–36, 39–43	13–15

*No offering is prescribed. The Sabbath observance is enjoined.

Table 14

		Type of Offering			
		Whole Burnt			Sin
Occasion	Frequency per Year	Young Bulls	Rams	Male Lambs	Goats
1. Daily					
morning	365			1	
evening	365			1	
2. Sabbath	52			2	
3. First of Month	12	2	1	7	1
4. Unleavened Bread	7	2	1	7	1
5. Pentecost	1	2	1	7	1
6. New Year	1	1	1	7	1
7. Day of Atonement	1	1	1	7	1
8. Tabernacles	1				
Day one		13	2	14	1

Occasion	Frequency per Year	Type of Offering			
		Whole Burnt			Sin
		Young Bulls	Rams	Male Lambs	Goats
Day two		12	2	14	1
Day three		11	2	14	1
Day four		10	2	14	1
Day five		9	2	14	1
Day six		8	2	14	1
Day seven		7	2	14	1
Day eight		1	1	7	1
Annual totals		113	37	1,093	30

Table 14 is based on the work of Anson Rainey, "The Order of Sacrifices in Old Testament Ritual Texts," *Bib* (1970): 492–93. Used by permission. I have changed the totals for the columns regarding rams and male lambs.

There is one thing in the woman's favor: the husband or father must respond negatively, if he chooses to do so, on the very day he hears about his wife's or daughter's vow (vv. 5, 8, 12, 14). To delay a response to some later time means that the man becomes vicariously culpable: "he shall bear her iniquity" (v. 15 RSV). The right of a male (father, husband) to overrule a vow of a female (daughter, wife) seems to reinforce the headship of men over women in Old Testament times. Two other observations may be made, however. First, the reason why a father/husband may annul a daughter's/wife's vow is that in the majority of instances ultimate responsibility for fulfilling them would fall upon the father/husband, since in most cases a vow is fulfilled through a sacrifice (Olson 1997: 237). Second, as with many legal arrangements in the Old Testament, there is no reference in biblical narrative to any husband/father actually overruling a vow of a wife/daughter. For example, Hannah vowed her baby Samuel to the Lord's service (1 Sam. 1:11), presumably a vow that her husband, Elkanah, could have vetoed but did not. One would think that Jephthah's daughter would have liked to have had the right to cancel her father's vow (Judg. 11:30–31)!

Concluding Events in Moab (31–36)

I will briefly note the last events covered in Numbers. The first subunit is God's command to conduct a holy war against Midian (ch. 31) as retaliation for the latter's seduction of Israel into acts of harlotry and idolatry (and the fourth of Israel's military victories [21:1–3; 21:21–31; 21:22–35]). The reason is that the Lord's "vengeance" may be displayed against Midian (31:2–3). "Vengeance" does not mean revenge or pique, but rather the legitimate expression of divine authority when that authority is challenged (Mendenhall 1973: 99). Two major concerns dominate this chapter. One is the concern for the ritual purity of the soldiers (vv. 19–24, 50), a concentrated theme in different contexts in Numbers. In an otherwise gruesome chapter, where only young virgin girls may be spared (v. 18 [cf. Judg. 19:21]), and not even young boys are exempted (v. 17 [cf. Exod. 1:16]), Numbers 31 makes the point that war is a defiling activity. Labeling such a concept "an ethical perception of sorts," Niditch (1993b: 87, 89) states, "Numbers 31 expresses genuine ambivalence concerning the ethics of war. The cause is holy, the war is ritualized, but the killing defiles. Thus as one enters war ritually one must exit with separation, cleansing, and sacrifices of atonement." A second concern is that a percentage of the spoil taken in war is to go to both the sanctuary and the Levites (vv. 25–54), with the soldiers contributing 0.2 percent of their share, and the rest 2 percent of their share.

The second subunit is ch. 32. Various territories east of the Jordan are allotted to Reuben, Gad, and half of the tribe of Manasseh, with the proviso that they assist the other tribes in the conquest of Canaan. If Canaan is to be taken, all of God's people must participate. There is no room for spectators, only for soldiers. In both chs. 31 and 32 Moses becomes angry over the people's failure to do something. In 31:4 he is angry because the people did not carry the war far enough. In 32:14 he is angry (or believes that God will be angry) because the Transjordan tribes seem unwilling to fight in concert with their compatriots on the west side of the Jordan.

The third subunit is ch. 33, a stage-by-stage description (at least vv. 1–49) of Israel's itinerary from Egypt to the plains of Moab. This is one chapter whose orientation is principally toward the past, and as such, it is surrounded by materials whose orientation is principally toward the future. True, the chapter is narrated without commentary or homiletical addenda, but the facts speak for themselves. The God who guided will guide. But this must not encourage complacency in the people, hence the concluding exhortation in vv. 50–56. The possibility of "thorns" in Israel's future (v. 55) recalls the certainty of thorns in sinful Adam's future (Gen. 3:18).

The fourth subunit is ch. 34. It describes the boundaries of the Promised Land (vv. 1–15) and identifies the individuals who are to oversee the division of the land among the tribes (vv. 16–29). Most interesting is the extension of the northern boundary to Lebo-Hamath (v. 8 [a good bit north of the traditional northern boundary city Dan]) and the extension of the southern boundary to Kadesh-barnea (v. 4 [a good bit south of the traditional southern boundary city of Beersheba]). More than likely the north-south border "from Dan to Beersheba" covers only the arable land. Equally interesting is the omission of any land east of the Jordan (v. 12)—an interesting fact coming on the heels of two and one-half of the tribes requesting permanent settlement on the east side of the Jordan (ch. 32). This is all rather irrelevant for Moses. He will play no part in this. His successor has already been selected. Yet it is he who transmits the divine instructions. He is still leader!

The fifth subunit is ch. 35. Once in Canaan, the Israelites are to set up forty-eight Levitical cities (vv. 1–8), as well as six cities of refuge (vv. 9–15) to which a manslayer may flee to escape blood revenge (vv. 16–34; see also Exod. 21:13). Once again the ultimate concern voiced here is that of purity and holiness. If God's regulations on the taking of life are not enforced, the land will be polluted (v. 33) and defiled (v. 34).

The last subunit is ch. 36, which deals with potential problems when the family inheritance goes not to a male heir but to a female heir. What if she marries outside her tribe (v. 3)? Sakenfeld (1988a: 43) remarks that "possession of arable land would make any woman in Israel extremely desirable as a marriage prospect." As in ch. 27 (giving their father's inheritance to the daughters of Zelophehad), a new law is formulated to meet this contingency. Tribal intermarriage is to be denied to a woman if she is an heir (vv. 6–8). Subsequently, the daughters of Zelophehad are held up as paragons of obedience (vv. 10–12)—a refreshing change from many of the lackluster and sorry models that we have encountered thus far, and on this positive note Numbers concludes. That they happily marry their paternal first cousins (v. 11) shows that they had a much more positive relationship with them than did Moses with his paternal first cousin Korah (ch. 16).

Presumably, 36:1–13 could have come right after 27:1–11 (inheritance of property by females, followed immediately by marriage options for such women). How might we explain the separation of ch. 36 from ch. 27? Had the elders been brooding over Moses' edict in ch. 27 for some time, or did it suddenly dawn on them that the solution to the problem in ch. 27 now created a new problem whose loophole must be closed? Or might we have here what biblical scholars call an "inclusio," a kind of matching set of bookends, usually involving repetition, to a discourse unit of Scripture that highlight a theological point (as in Psalm 8 beginning and ending with the same verse emphasizing the majesty of God's name)? The two narratives about these five daughters "frame the intermediary hortatory material with a real life illustration of dynamic confidence in God" (Ulrich 1998: 537). The women are not passive; they are bold. They believe that faithfulness to God rather than

gender guarantees the blessing of land inheritance to the next generation. Unlike the so-called prodigal son (Luke 15:12), they do not ask that
their share of the estate be given to them now. They will wait for God's
timing, and so they wait until Josh. 17:36.

Numbers 20:22–21:35

Bartlett, J. R. 1969. "Historical Reference of Numbers XXI:27–30." *PEQ* 101:94–
   100.

———. 1970. "Sihon and Og of the Amorites." *VT* 20:257–77.

———. 1978. "Conquest of Sihon's Kingdom: A Literary Re-examination." *JBL*
   97:347–51.

Borass, R. S. 1978. "Of Serpents and Gods." *Dialog* 17:273–79.

Christensen, D. L. 1974. "Numbers 21:14–15 and the Book of the Wars of Yahweh."
   CBQ 36:359–60.

Coats, G. W. 1968. *Rebellion in the Wilderness: The Murmuring Motif in the Wilderness
   Traditions of the Old Testament.* Nashville: Abingdon. Pp. 115–24.

———. 1976. "Conquest Tradition in the Wilderness Theme." *JBL* 95:177–90.

Culley, R. C. 1976. *Studies in the Structure of Hebrew Narrative.* Semeia Supplements
   3. Philadelphia: Fortress. Pp. 102–4.

Fretheim, T. E. 1978. "Life in the Wilderness." *Dialog* 17:266–72.

Gunn, D. M. 1974. "'Battle Report': Oral or Scribal Convention?" *JBL* 93:513–18.

Joines, K. R. 1974. *Serpent Symbolism in the Old Testament: A Linguistic, Archaeological, and Literary Study.* Haddonfield, N.J.: Haddonfield House.

Tozer, A. W. 1948. *The Pursuit of God.* Harrisburg, Pa.: Christian Publications.

Van Seters, J. 1972. "The Conquest of Sihon's Kingdom: A Literary Examination."
   JBL 91:182–97.

———. 1976. "Oral Patterns or Literary Conventions in Biblical Narrative." *Semeia*
   5:139–54.

———. 1980. "Once Again—The Conquest of Sihon's Kingdom." *JBL* 99:117–19.

Vaux, R. de. 1978. *The Early History of Israel.* Philadelphia: Westminster. Pp. 551–
   67.

Yohanan, A. 1976. "Nothing Early and Nothing Late: Re-writing Israel's Conquest."
   BA 39:55–76.

Numbers 22–24

Albright, W. F. 1944. "The Oracles of Balaam." *JBL* 63:207–33.

———. 1971. "Balaam." *EncJud* 4:121–23.

Alter, R. 1981. *The Art of Biblical Narrative.* New York: Basic Books. Pp. 104–7.

Barre, M. L. 1997. "The Portrait of Balaam in Numbers 22–24." *Int* 51:254–66.

Brown, R. E. 1988. *An Adult Christ at Christmas*. Collegeville, Minn.: Liturgical Press. Pp. 10–14.

Clark, I. 1982. "Balaam's Ass: Suture or Structure?" In *Literary Interpretations of Biblical Narratives*. Vol. 2. Ed. K. R. R. Gros Louis and J. S. Ackerman. Nashville: Abingdon. Pp. 137–44.

Coats, G. W. 1972. "Balaam: Sinner or Saint?" *BRes* 17:21–29. Repr., in *Saga, Legend, Tale, Novella, Fable: Narrative Genres in Old Testament Literature*. Ed. G. W. Coats. JSOTSup 34. Sheffield: JSOT Press, 1985. Pp. 56–62.

———. 1982. "The Way of Obedience. Traditio-Historical and Hermeneutical Reflections on the Balaam Story." *Semeia* 24:53–79.

Craigie, P. C. 1969. "The Conquest and Early Hebrew Poetry." *TynB* 20:76–94.

Daube, D. 1973. *Ancient Hebrew Fables*. Oxford: Oxford University Press. Pp. 14–16.

Dijkstra, M. D. 1995. "Is Balaam Also among the Prophets?" *JBL* 114:43–64.

Goldin, J. 1990. "In Defense of Balak: Not Entirely Midrash." *Judaism* 40:455–60.

Greene, J. T. 1992. *Balaam and His Interpreters: A Hermeneutical History of the Balaam Traditions*. BJS 244. Atlanta: Scholars Press.

Hackett, J. 1984. *The Balaam Text from Deir ʿAlla*. HSM 31. Chico, Calif.: Scholars Press.

———. 1986. "Some Observations on the Balaam Tradition at Deir ʿAlla." *BA* 49:216–22.

———. 1992. "Balaam." *ABD* 1:569–72.

Hoftijzer, J., and G. van der Kooij, eds. 1976. *Aramaic Texts from Deir ʿAlla*. Documenta et monumenta Orientis antiqui 19. Leiden: Brill.

———. eds. 1991. *The Balaam Text from Deir ʿAlla Re-evaluated*. Leiden: Brill.

Horowitz, V. 1992. "The Expression *uqsamim beyadam* (Numbers 22:7) in Light of Divinatory Practices from Mari." *HS* 33:5–15.

Kaiser, W. C., Jr. 1996. "Balaam Son of Beor in Light of Deir ʿAlla and Scripture: Saint or Soothsayer?" In *"Go to the Land I Will Show You": Studies in Honor of Dwight W. Young*. Ed. J. Coleson and V. Matthews. Winona Lake, Ind.: Eisenbrauns. Pp. 95–106.

Kaufmann, Y. 1960. *The Religion of Israel*. Trans. M. Greenberg. Chicago: University of Chicago Press. Pp. 84–91.

Layton, S. C. 1992. "Whence Comes Balaam? Num 22,5 Revisited." *Bib* 73:32–61.

Long, B. O. 1971. "Two Question and Answer Schemata in the Prophets." *JBL* 90:129–39.

Lutsky, H. 1999. "Ambivalence toward Balaam." *VT* 49:421–25.

McCarter, P. K. 1980. "The Balaam Texts from Deir ʿAlla: The First Combinations." *BASOR* 239:49–65.

Moberly, R. W. L. 1999. "On Learning to Be a True Prophet: The Story of Balaam and His Ass." In *New Heaven and New Earth: Prophecy and the Millennium; Essays in Honor of Anthony Gelston*. Ed. P. J. Harland and C. T. R. Hayward. VTSup 77. Leiden: Brill. Pp. 1–17.

Moore, S. M. 1990a. *The Balaam Traditions: Their Character and Development*. SBLDS 113. Atlanta: Scholars Press.

————. 1990b. "Another Look at Balaam." *RB* 97:359–78.

Rad, G. von. 1960. *Moses*. New York: Association Press. Pp. 71–80.

Safren, J. D. 1988. "Balaam and Abraham." *VT* 38:105–13.

Savran, G. 1994. "Beastly Speech: Intertextuality, Balaam's Ass and the Garden of Eden." *JSOT* 64:33–55.

Seerveld, C. G. 1980. *Balaam's Apocalyptic Prophecies: A Study in Reading Scripture.* Toronto: Wedge Publishing Foundation.

Smick, E. C. 1974. "A Study of the Structure of the Third Balaam Oracle." In *The Law and the Prophets: In Honor of O. T. Allis*. Ed. J. H. Skilton. Nutley, N.J.: Presbyterian and Reformed. Pp. 242–52.

Tosato, A. 1979. "The Literary Structure of the First Two Poems of Balaam." *VT* 29:98–106.

Van Seters, J. 1994. *The Life of Moses: The Yahwist as Historian in Exodus–Numbers.* Louisville: Westminster John Knox. Pp. 405–35.

————. 1997. "From Faithful Prophet to Villain: Observations on the Tradition History of the Balaam Story." In *A Biblical Itinerary: In Search of Method, Form and Content; Essays in Honor of George W. Coats*. Ed. E. Carpenter. JSOTSup 240. Sheffield: Sheffield Academic Press. Pp. 126–32.

Vermes, G. 1973. "The Story of Balaam: The Scriptural Origin of the Haggadah." In *Scripture and Tradition in Judaism*. Ed. G. Vermes. 2nd ed. Studia post-biblica 4. Leiden: Brill. Pp. 127–77.

Westermann, C. 1978. *Blessing in the Bible and the Life of the Church*. Trans. K. R. Crim. OBT. Philadelphia: Fortress. Pp. 49–53.

Zannoni, A. E. 1978. "Balaam: International Seer/Wizard Prophet." *St. Luke's Journal of Theology* 22:5–19.

Numbers 25

Lutsky, H. 1997. "The Name 'Cozbi' (Numbers xxv 15, 18)." *VT* 47:546–49.

Mendenhall, G. E. 1973. *The Tenth Generation: The Origins of the Biblical Tradition.* Baltimore: Johns Hopkins University Press. Pp. 105–21.

Milgrom, J. 1970. *Studies in Levitical Terminology*. Vol. 1, *The Encroacher and the Levite: The Term ʿAboda*. University of California Publications, Near Eastern Studies 14. Berkeley: University of California Press.

Reif, S. C. 1971. "What Enraged Phinehas? A Study of Numbers 25:8." *JBL* 90:200–206.

Seebass, H. 2003. "The Case of Phinehas at Baal Peor in Num 25." *BN* 117:40–46.

Sivan, H. Z. 2001. "The Rape of Cozbi (Numbers xxv)." *VT* 51:69–80.

Stern, E. 1971. "Phinehas." *EncJud* 13:465–67.

Van Unnik, W. C. 1974. "Josephus' Account of the Story of Israel's Sin with Alien Women in the Country of Midian." In *Travels in the World of the Old Testament: Studies Presented to Professor M. A. Beek on the Occasion of His 65th Birthday*. Ed.

M. S. H. G. Heerma van Voss, P. H. J. Houwink ten Cate, and N. A. van Uchelen. Studia Semitica Neerlandica 16. Assen: Van Gorcum. Pp. 241–61.

Vaux, R. de. 1978. *The Early History of Israel*. Philadelphia: Westminster. Pp. 568–70.

Numbers 26–27; 36

Ben-Barak, Z. 1980. "Inheritance by Daughters in the Ancient Near East." *Journal of Semitic Studies* 25:22–33.

Coats, G. W. 1977. "Legendary Motifs in the Moses Death Reports." *CBQ* 39:34–44.

Davies, E. W. 1981. "Inheritance Rights and Hebrew Levirate Marriage." *VT* 31:138–44, 257–68.

Sakenfeld, K. D. 1988a. "Zelophehad's Daughters." *Perspectives in Religious Studies* 15:37–47.

———. 1988b. "In the Wilderness Awaiting the Lord: The Daughters of Zelophehad and Feminist Interpretation." *Princeton Seminary Bulletin* 9:179–86.

Snaith, N. H. 1966. "The Daughters of Zelophehad." *VT* 16:124–27.

Ulrich, D. R. 1998. "The Framing Function of the Narratives about Zelophehad's Daughters." *JETS* 41:529–38.

Weingreen, J. 1966. "The Case of the Daughters of Zelophechad." *VT* 16:518–22.

Westbrook, R. 1985. "Biblical and Cuneiform Law Codes." *RB* 92:247–64.

Numbers 28–30

Fisher, L. R. 1970. "New Ritual Calendar from Ugarit." *HTR* 63:485–501.

———. 1975. "Literary Genres in the Ugaritic Texts." In *Ras Shamra Parallels: The Texts from Ugarit and the Hebrew Bible*. Vol. 2. Ed. L. R. Fisher. Analecta orientalia 50. Rome: Pontifical Biblical Institute. Pp. 131–52.

Olson, D. T. 1997. "Negotiating Boundaries: The Old and New Generations and the Theology of Numbers." *Int* 51:229–40.

Numbers 31

Niditch, S. 1993a. "War, Women and Defilement in Numbers 31." *Semeia* 61:39–57.

———. 1993b. *War in the Hebrew Bible*. Oxford: Oxford University Press. Pp. 78–89.

Wright, D. P. 1985. "Purification from Corpse Contamination in Numbers xxxi 19–24." *VT* 35:212–13.

Numbers 32

Jobling, D. 1980. "'The Jordan a Boundary': A Reading of Numbers 32 and Joshua 22." In *SBLSP 1980*. Ed. P. J. Achtemeier. Chico, Calif.: Scholars Press. Pp. 183–207.

Vaux, R. de. 1965. *Ancient Israel*. Trans. J. McHugh. 2 vols. New York: McGraw Hill. Vol. 2, pp. 366–67.

Numbers 33

Davies, G. I. 1974. "The Wilderness Itineraries: A Comparative Study." *TynB* 25:46–81.

———. 1979. *The Way of the Wilderness: A Geographical Study of the Wilderness Itineraries in the Old Testament*. Cambridge: Cambridge University Press.

Numbers 35

Greenberg, M. 1962. "City of Refuge." *IDB* 1:638–39.

———. 1968. "Idealism and Practicality in Numbers 35:4–5 and Ezekiel 48." *JAOS* 88:59–66.

———. 1971. "Levitical Cities." *EncJud* 11:136–38.

Spencer, J. R. 1992a. "Levitical Cities." *ABD* 4:310–11.

———. 1992b. "Refuge, Cities of." *ABD* 5:657–58.

Vaux, R. de. 1965. *Ancient Israel*. Trans. J. McHugh. 2 vols. New York: McGraw-Hill. Vol. 2, pp. 366–67.

PART FIVE

Deuteronomy

19

Remember the Past

DEUTERONOMY 1:1–4:40

Qoheleth was quite correct when he said, "Of making many books there is no end" (Eccles. 12:12 NRSV). Had Qoheleth had access only to studies about Deuteronomy, he would not have had to revise or retract his statement. Compared with work that has been done on, for example, Leviticus or Numbers, the research on Deuteronomy has been, and continues to be, enormous.

Analyses of Deuteronomy

In relationship to the rest of the Pentateuch, Deuteronomy is considered something of an oddity. For one thing, so the suggestion goes, its theology and themes are distinctly different from its pentateuchal neighbors. Thus the kerygma of the Deuteronomist is to be seen as a part of the theology of the Pentateuch, but it is not to be considered as representative of the whole. It becomes understandable, then, why one encounters articles about themes in Genesis through Numbers adjacent to those about themes in Deuteronomy and Deuteronomic literature.

Or perhaps the reader will encounter preaching and proclamation commentaries on only Genesis through Numbers in one volume.

The Documentary Hypothesis

Part of the reason for considering Deuteronomy apart from the rest of the Pentateuch has to do with several points of the Documentary Hypothesis. One of the basic tenets of this theory is that the hypothetical sources J, E, and P are to be found in an amalgamated fashion throughout Genesis to Numbers. But next to nothing of D has intruded into these four biblical books. Conversely, next to nothing of J, E, and P has made its way into the text of Deuteronomy.

This latter point in no way suggests that the Book of Deuteronomy is viewed by critical exegetes as a homogeneous unit. Quite the contrary. In only two areas of Deuteronomic studies is there anything that approaches unanimity. One of these "assured results" is that Deuteronomy is not the work of Moses, although "Mosaic elements" may surface here and there. The attribution of the book to Moses is how the author of Deuteronomy hopes to gain special sanctity for his composition and the ideas he advances therein. Rather than use his own and much less influential name, he uses the pseudonymn of the legendary Moses. Scholars make this conclusion in spite of the fact that Deuteronomy, of all the books of the Pentateuch, claims most adamantly to be the work of Moses—for example: "and Moses wrote this law" (31:9 RSV). The Pentateuch is replete with instances of Moses speaking, but references to his scribal activities are minimal.

Defenders of partial, substantial, or ultimate Mosaic authorship are not lacking. These writers include Protestant conservative scholars such as P. C. Craigie, R. K. Harrison, K. A. Kitchen, M. Kline, G. T. Manley, S. J. Schultz, and J. A. Thompson, all of whom are referred to in the bibliography. They are joined by Jewish writers such as J. H. Hertz (1940) and M. H. Segal (1961). Along similar lines, Max Margolis (1922: 102–15), a brilliant Jewish biblical scholar and textual critic with special interest in the Septuagint, suggested that Josiah's "Book of the Law," to be fully intelligible, must have included not only Deuteronomy but also Exodus through Numbers—a legitimate observation that runs counter to the trend of twentieth-century scholarship about Deuteronomy. Substantially the same point is made by Cyrus Gordon (1965a: 150; 1965b: 213).

The second area of consensus, one that is related to the question of authorship, is the heterogeneous nature of the book. That is, Deuteronomy grew by stages and underwent editorial revisions until it reached the final form in which it is now preserved in our Bibles. A corollary of this has been the attempt to identify what precisely constituted "Ur-Deuteronomy," the original nucleus to which the additions were appended. Those who have addressed this issue usually have settled on chs. 5–26 and 28 as the kernel, or simply the laws of chs. 12–26 with a brief introduction and conclusion. Few authors have attempted to deal with the significance of the "final form" of Deuteronomy—how the parts relate to each other and to the whole—but perhaps the writings of Brevard Childs and Robert Polzin (see the bibliography) are reflective of a new trend in studies of Deuteronomy, whether through canonical criticism (Childs) or structural analysis (Polzin).

Modern surveys of studies in the history of Scripture usually identify the early-nineteenth-century scholar W. M. L. De Wette as the forerunner of current analyses. His work on Deuteronomy, the exact conclusions of which are accepted by hardly any scholars today, paved the way for a host of biblical specialists to follow. And the issue is far from settled. It is common for contemporary scholars, after outlining "the current issues," to say that no final conclusion has been reached. As far as Deuteronomy is concerned, it is difficult to perceive that there will ever be a final, unanimous conclusion on matters of date, authorship, and provenance.

De Wette's analysis of Deuteronomy was as follows. Deuteronomy was written *after* the reforms of the Judean king Josiah (late seventh century B.C.). Some individuals, sympathetic to the Josianic reforms (e.g., cult centralization and riddance of pagan icons), penned Deuteronomy, using Moses as an alias and the plains of Moab as the fictional setting, and conveniently placed it in the temple ruins. There it was discovered by those repairing the temple and subsequently "baptized" and "justified" the agenda of Josiah. After all, was not Josiah implementing Moses' words and laws, standards that had been dormant for centuries?

This theory spawned the famous phrase that Deuteronomy essentially is "a pious fraud." According to this theory, the book is pious in the sense that it attempted to provide historical precedent for religious reform; it is fraudulent in the sense that the whole book was artificially produced, akin to Hitler's chaplains writing a book, using an apostolic name, that reeked with anti-Jewish rhetoric and then placing it in one of the confessional booths of Notre Dame before the invasion of France.

More recently, some critics have attempted to soften De Wette's view. Whether they have softened that view or simply revised it is, in my opinion, debatable. For instance, in various publications Moshe Weinfeld has insisted that Deuteronomy, contra P, reflects a trend toward humanism and secularization. By this Weinfeld (1973: 230) does "not refer to an atheistic trend or to any opposition to religion or religious institutions, but to a general tendency to free religious institutions and ways of thinking from strict adherence to the rules of taboo, etc., and thus to give them a more secular appearance." Nevertheless, De Wette's "pious" Deuteronomy has become Weinfeld's "humanistic" Deuteronomy.

It would be unfair to modern scholars to suggest they have maintained De Wette's hypothesis. In their views, by and large, the only thing counterfeit about Deuteronomy is the contention that the historical recitations, hymns, and laws were spoken and reduced to writing by Moses in the plains of Moab after thirty-eight years in the wilderness, sometime in the thirteenth century B.C. Granting the spurious nature of this alone, the critics were willing to grant the authenticity of Deuteronomy.

Julius Wellhausen (*Prolegomena to the History of Israel* [1885]), as much as anyone, gave Deuteronomy a new anchor. His exposition of documentary sources in the Pentateuch was to become definitive and classical. The foundation of Wellhausen's theory, on which every other tenet might be constructed, was the intrinsic connection of Deuteronomy and Josiah's reform, a connection that led to Wellhausen's conclusion that Deuteronomy (chs. 12–26, anyway) was written just prior to the reforms, around 622 B.C.

So important for his overall source theory did Wellhausen consider the dating of Deuteronomy that he labeled it "the fulcrum" of his literary reconstruction of the Pentateuch. The year 622 B.C. became for Wellhausen what the Hijrah of A.D. 622 became for Muslims, the first fixed date in Islamic history. As for Muslims, for whom everything is either ante-Hijrah or post-Hijrah, so for Wellhausen, scripturally speaking, everything is either ante-Deuteronomy or post-Deuteronomy.

It is safe to say that nearly all higher-critical scholars accept Wellhausen's dating of Deuteronomy in the seventh century B.C. A departure from classical Wellhausianism would be the suggestion that some parts of Deuteronomy antedate the seventh century B.C. and were added later to Ur-Deuteronomy. (A further departure is reflected by those scholars who, on exegetical grounds, would reverse Wellhausen's view and date P *before* D, not after D, as did Wellhausen. See, for example, the writings of Yehezkel Kaufmann and his student Weinfeld, and comments of Jacob Milgrom scattered throughout his many publications.)

Although, as I have said, a majority of scholars place Deuteronomy's composition in the seventh century B.C., they have followed various routes to arrive at that conclusion.

To begin with, there are commentators who think that Deuteronomy had its origin in the northern Israelite community, and not in Judah at all. This is the interpretation of the celebrated nestor of studies in Deuteronomy, Gerhard von Rad. His basic observation was that Deuteronomy is more sermonic than it is anything else. Even the laws, and the way they were promulgated, would be more appropriate in the pulpit than in the courtroom. Who would be the most likely group of homileticians who could blend historical recitation and exhortation? In von Rad's view it was the northern Levites who fled from northern Israel to Judah to escape the disasters about to befall Israel from the Assyrian invaders. It was they who brought these traditions with them to southern Judah after Israel's demise at the hands of the Assyrians in 721 b.c. In cooperation with some concerned laypersons, seventh-century Levites, living in Judah, "produced" Deuteronomy in the hope of providing a stimulus for religious revival.

Very close to von Rad's view is that of E. W. Nicholson. He too posits the origin of Deuteronomy in the north, but with a difference. The authors of Deuteronomy are not the Levites, but representatives of the northern prophetic groups who also fled to the south after the Assyrian takeover in the north. As for an actual time for composition, Nicholson suggests the reign of Manasseh, the grandfather of Josiah. The idea behind this suggestion is that reform movements, as reflected in Deuteronomy, arise on the heels of periods of debauchery and immorality, eras that lack even traces of religious zeal. The reign of Manasseh meets that qualification nicely. Thus, out of the murkiness emerges either a Levitical or prophetical Martin Luther.

On the other side of the coin are those scholars who fully agree with the dating of Deuteronomy to the seventh century. Their distinction, however, is their emphatic point that Deuteronomy originated in the south, not in the north. It is Judean, not Israelite.

Most prolific in their writings have been the German Jesuit Norbert Lohfink and the Jewish scholar Moshe Weinfeld, both of whom see the language of Deuteronomy as having more affinities with court language and wisdom language than with any other. Hence, the Judean or Jerusalemic background of the book.

For Lohfink (1977: 12–21), Deuteronomy, which was composed in several stages, functioned first as an underground text, a voice of protest against a growing Assyrian hegemony over Judah that went back at least as far as Hezekiah's father, Ahaz. For it was Ahaz who gave the order to build an Assyrian-like altar for the Jerusalem temple (2 Kings 16:10–16). The reaction of Judah to this upheaval was culture shock. Deuteronomy represents part of this reaction. Only under Josiah did Deuteronomy begin to assume the status of official law. It also legitimated the independence movement of Josiah (a return to De Wette?).

Weinfeld (1972) produced a most original and provocative treatment of Deuteronomy in *Deuteronomy and the Deuteronomic School*, much of which he has reproduced in the first volume of his Anchor Bible commentary on Deuteronomy 1–11 (1991). His position is that Deuteronomy was written by sages and scribes who were connected with the royal house of Judah from the time of Hezekiah to that of Josiah. For further evidence to buttress his position, Weinfeld claimed that the composition of Deuteronomy was influenced by the literary model of seventh-century B.C. Assyrian state treaties, particularly the treaty between Esarhaddon, king of Assyria (680–669 B.C.), and his eastern vassals. Who, then, in Judah would be more informed about such models than the narrow circle of scribes within the court?

One of Weinfeld's key observations was born out of his comparison between the legal sections of Deuteronomy and the counterparts in the rest of the Pentateuch. For example, observing that Deuteronomy permits profane slaughter—"you may slaughter your animals in any of your towns and eat as much of the meat as you want" (12:15, 21), unlike Lev. 17:1–9, which legislates that animals for food be sacrificed at the sanctuary—he concluded that Deuteronomy is reflective of a seventh-century trend to secularization and demythologization.

It appears that Weinfeld's treatment of Deuteronomy is suspect on three grounds. In the first place, a good case can be made that the literary structure of Deuteronomy parallels more closely the second-millennium B.C. covenants than it does the first-millennium B.C. covenants. To illustrate, the later covenantal forms, unlike the earlier ones, lack a historical prologue and a listing of promised blessings (to match the threatened curses). Deuteronomy displays both of these phenomena.

A second criticism challenges the wisdom influence on Deuteronomy, which Weinfeld claims to see. Why, for example, if the hand of the scribes and sages is so evident in Deuteronomy, is there no legislation covering their activities, as there is for king, prophet, and judge? Why would they omit themselves? Again, if Deuteronomy is the work of the sapientialists, how did they usurp the authority to write Torah literature, and was this control retained in the Second Temple period, or did it revert to the priests (see Rofé 1974: 204–9)?

Third, are the differences between the laws of Deuteronomy and the counterparts to be explained as a movement toward secularization? Scholars embracing the traditional interpretation of Deuteronomy would explain the differences as necessitated by a change from a wilderness and nomadic milieu to a territorial and sedentary milieu. That is, the differences are to be explained chronologically, not sociologically, as Weinfeld has done.

But even apart from this contention it can be demonstrated that Deuteronomy moves in precisely the opposite direction from secularization (see Milgrom 1973: 156–61; Weinfeld 1973: 230–33). For example, Deuteronomy emphasizes that Israel already *is* holy (7:6; 14:2, 21). By contrast, Leviticus lays holiness before Israel as a goal: "You shall be holy" (Lev. 19:2). Again, it is in Deuteronomy alone that the priest functions beyond the temple area. He accompanies the troops into battle as a chaplain (Deut. 20:1–4); he sits on a supreme tribunal to hear cases of homicide and assault (17:8–13) and thus assumes a new judicial role not specified for him elsewhere.

Having briefly examined some current ideas about Deuteronomy's place of origin, authorship, and raison d'être, we see that there is anything but a consensus. It is unlikely that any future monograph will ever silence all contrary views. For some, this is the genius of biblical scholarship. It is a scientific discipline in which one can speak only about the current state of knowledge. For others, such a smorgasbord of opinions reduces biblical scholarship to an exercise in novelty. Concerning Deuteronomy, there are really only two options on the issues: the classical position or some form of De Wette *redivivus*.

The Traditional View

On what grounds does the classical position rest? First, there is the claim of Deuteronomy itself, such as, "These are the words that Moses spoke to all Israel beyond the Jordan" (1:1 NRSV); "Moses undertook to explain this law, saying" (1:5 RSV); "And Moses wrote this law" (31:9 RSV). Such statements must either be accepted as authentic or dismissed as spurious.

Second, the New Testament also pairs Deuteronomy and Moses. Jesus refers to Moses' law on divorce (Matt. 19:8; cf. Deut. 24:1–4). Paul speaks of the muzzled ox in the "law of Moses" (1 Cor. 9:9; cf. Deut. 25:4). The author of Hebrews mentions the "law of Moses" about the testimony of witnesses at a trial (Heb. 10:28; cf. Deut. 17:2–6). These Mosaic references agree with the talmudic witness (*Baba Bathra* 14b–15a) about Deuteronomy.

What is to be done with such references? For the higher critics they are meaningless and irrelevant. These references are dismissed immediately because, so goes the argument, Jesus and the others are not making a historical judgment, but rather are making a concession to the traditional beliefs of the time. We would be led to believe, then, either that Jesus knew that Deuteronomy was Josianic but chose not to raise this ancillary issue lest it lead him and his audience away from the subject at hand, or that nineteenth- and twentieth-century biblical scholarship has made Jesus look uninformed, a child of his times, whenever he cited historical sources. Another reason that the witness of post–Old Testament literature must be ignored, it is argued, is that if such a witness is valid, it means that a substantial percentage of the modern work done on Deuteronomy would be discredited, and multiple theories would have to be laid to rest.

Third, many evangelical writers, especially Kline and Kitchen, have made a strong case for the fact that the literary structure of Deuteronomy resembles most closely that of second-millennium B.C. political treaties between suzerain and vassal. These are from Hittite archives, and the structural items include title or preamble (equivalent to Deut. 1:1–5); historical prologue (Deut. 1:6–4:49); stipulations, both general (Deuteronomy 5–11) and specific (Deuteronomy 12–26); blessings for obedience and curses for disobedience (Deuteronomy 27–28); deposit of the text in a place accessible to the vassal (Deut. 31:26) and periodic public reading (Deut. 31:9–13); and the presence of witnesses for ratification (Deut. 30:19; 31:19, 26).

Not all writers are predisposed, however, to say that this settles the issue. For Weinfeld, as we have seen, the parallels with first-millennium B.C. treaties are more inviting. George Mendenhall, the first to point out the identical sequence in nonbiblical and biblical treaties, has not suggested, thereby, that Deuteronomy is essentially a Mosaic piece of work. Reflective of how tenaciously some refuse to surrender a late date for Deuteronomy is a quotation in Craigie (1976: 26 n. 23) from K. Baltzer: "It remains however, a striking and historically unexplained fact that the Old Testament resembles most closely the highly developed formulary of the Hittite treaty."

W. F. Albright (1957: 314–33) has observed, with documentation, that in the seventh century B.C. there was throughout the Middle East a nostalgic turn to the past. Judah was no exception, as is reflected in a Josianic Deuteronomy that recalled the golden days of Moses. For that reason, Albright has no problem dating "late" books such as Job and Proverbs that are filled with linguistic parallels to Canaanite literature produced six to nine hundred years earlier. If indeed there was a revival of Canaanite literature during the seventh century, then to be consistent we would have to maintain that there was a revival of Hittite treaty forms at the same time.

A fourth pillar in the evangelical position is an alternative explanation to the laws of Exodus 21–23 that appear again in Deuteronomy 12–26. I will discuss some of these later, but such amplifications, as found in Deuteronomy, are necessitated by the shift from Israel in the wilderness to Israel now about to be settled permanently in Canaan. This is at least as plausible as the explanation that the laws in Deuteronomy are adaptations to the monarchic period.

Fifth, one may challenge the contention that one of the main themes in Deuteronomy is centralization of worship, and thus is a product of the time of Hezekiah and Josiah (see Manley 1957: 122–36). Rather, Deuteronomy's main theme is opposition to idolatry, a sin on which no chronological period has a monopoly. Does it not seem probable that if Deuteronomy wanted to reinforce the point of centralization, then somewhere "the place which the LORD your God will choose" (Deut.

12:5 RSV) would be identified as Jerusalem? In fact, Jerusalem is *never* mentioned in the book. Does this absence mean that Deuteronomy was reduced to writing before Jerusalem assumed prominence, or does Deuteronomy reflect the northern provenance of Proto-Deuteronomy, or does the absence of the name lend "a certain timelessness to a theology of place," as suggested by Sheehan (1977: 61)?

Finally, a word may be said about the ideas common to Deuteronomy and the prophets Hosea and Isaiah, especially Hosea. Weinfeld (1972: 366–70) devotes an entire appendix to affinities between Deuteronomy and Hosea. When A resembles B, did B take material from A, or vice versa? Or did both have access to the same tradition? Ostensibly, any of the three positions could be argued cogently, but certain factors suggest that Deuteronomy was the source from which Hosea the northern prophet drew his emphases and even phraseology (see Manley 1957: 143–45; McCurley 1974: 298–302).

In his Deuteronomy commentary Patrick Miller (1990: 5–10) advances the view that Deuteronomy reflects different contributors. Along with von Rad he senses a deep priestly/Levitical interest in Deuteronomy. In agreement with Nicholson he observes the prophetic spirit in Deuteronomy. Along with Weinfeld he affirms the humaneness and social morality of the wisdom teachers in Deuteronomy. If Deuteronomy harbors an amalgam of such differing perspectives (priestly, prophetic, wisdom), perhaps it is because "Moses is the only person in Israel's history who may have represented all three interests" (Block 2001: 389).

The Deuteronomic History

Biblical scholars recognize Martin Noth for his seminal studies of the "Deuteronomic History." This particular term, as used by Noth and others, designates Joshua, Judges, 1–2 Samuel, 1–2 Kings, and limited parts of Deuteronomy, specifically chs. 1–4 and perhaps 29 and 30. It is suggested that these form a theological treatise, most likely written by one person, around the time of the exile, about 550 B.C. Its purpose is to explain to those dispersed from their land why the exile happened. And the explanation offered is informed by the religious emphases of Ur-Deuteronomy (chs. 5–26, 28).

Specifically, Noth suggested that the Deuteronomist produced his work in order to inform both the exiled Judeans and the motley group left in Judah (those who had escaped either execution or deportation) that what had happened in 587 B.C. occurred because of their disobedience to God and his covenantal demands. What had just transpired was the manifestation of covenant curse on covenant disobedience. After all, was this not the negative side of Ur-Deuteronomy's theology: obedience leads to blessing, disobedience leads to curse?

As far as Noth interpreted the evidence, he failed to see any hope in the narration of this large portion of Scripture that he labeled as the Deuteronomic History. As such, the Deuteronomist represents the quintessence of morbidity. His role would be akin to that of a rabbi in the 1940s and 1950s fulminating against European Jews who survived the genocidal pogroms of the Third Reich, claiming that such horrors occurred because European Jewry had been unfaithful to God. No word of hope is offered, only unmitigated gloom.

More recent studies of the Deuteronomic History have attempted to salvage some positive emphases within that history. All is not gloom or hopelessness. In the midst of his articulation of history the Deuteronomist reminds the audience that God is good, that he can be trusted even by a landless people (Walter Brueggemann), and that he summons the bewildered and the exiled to repent and return to him (H. W. Wolff).

It must be admitted that the whole idea of a Deuteronomic History, as reconstructed by Noth et al., is plausible and possible. It is not as easy to say that the reconstruction is probable. For one thing, as D. N. Freedman (1976: 226) reminds us, "In the last analysis . . . it must be admitted that DH is not a given part of the Hebrew Bible as we have it; this caution must be kept in mind throughout."

Equally reasonable as the theory of an exilic composition is the idea of a thirteenth-century B.C. Deuteronomy—something that the book specifically underlines. This is followed by Joshua, the events described therein being reduced to writing anytime between the death of the one after whom the book is named and the days of the early monarchy. The whole book would serve as an impressive illustration of the blessings of God that come on the heels of a committed and God-honoring life. There is no generation that does not need to hear and be reminded of that, be they newcomers, old, or the dispossessed.

By contrast, the Book of Judges would make clear to these relative newcomers or pioneers the consequences of the attempt to evade the will of God. And so we could continue through Kings.

Finally, we may question the validity of the concept of a peculiar Deuteronomic theology that applies to only one part of the Old Testament in contradistinction to other Old Testament theologies; and even granting the legitimacy of a distinctive Deuteronomic theology, why must it be an exilic phenomenon only? In terms of the first point, we need to note that probably all of the Old Testament is Deuteronomic. Is, for example, Chronicles diametrically different from Samuel and Kings in the theology it espouses when dealing with covenantal matters? Are not the patriarchal narratives informed by a Deuteronomic substratum?

As far as the second point is concerned, it is sufficient to say that Israel had no monopoly on Deuteronomism. Sentiments very close to some of those expressed in Deuteronomy can be found in Near Eastern literature in hymns, prayers, and wisdom texts that date from the third millennium to the first millennium B.C. This literature comes from Egypt, Mesopotamia, Asia Minor, and Canaan. To illustrate, writing about "the good life" in Mesopotamia, cuneiform specialist Thorkild Jacobsen (1964: 220) can say, "The way of obedience, of service and worship is the way to achieve protection; and it is also the way to earthly success, to the highest values in Mesopotamian life: health and long life, honoured standing in the community, many sons, wealth." Why must we assume that Israel produced a theological construct parallel to that of its neighbors, but a millennium or two later?

The Book of Deuteronomy plays a large role, a programmatic role, in all discussions of Deuteronomistic history. As far as the opening three or four chapters of Deuteronomy are concerned, it was Noth's contention that they were written not by the author of Deuteronomy, but by the author of the Deuteronomic History. As such, Deuteronomy 1–4 must be identified as "deuteronomistic." Deuteronomy 5–26 must be identified as "deuteronomic."

One of Noth's principal reasons for such a cleavage was that there are "two introductions" (chs. 1–4 and chs. 5–11) to Deuteronomy. A doublet in a biblical book, especially at the beginning, is always suspect. (Note how the first two chapters of Genesis have been scissored.)

In the nineteenth century Wellhausen, then the doyen of biblical studies, suggested that chs. 1–4 and 5–11 were parallels, each from different editions of the book. Noth suggested that they are not parallels, but rather that chs. 5–11 are the real introduction to Deuteronomy. By and large, this has been embraced by contemporary Old Testament scholars (although I am not aware of any commentary on Deuteronomy that starts with ch. 5).

Noth's attempt to divorce chs. 1–4 from 5–11 has three immediate effects. First, if the divorce is granted, then it becomes all but impossible and even extraneous to relate chs. 1–4 to the rest of Deuteronomy. It is placed where it is for convenience, but beyond that it plays only a minimal role for understanding the shape of Deuteronomy, being the orphan that it is.

Second, the removal of chs. 1–4 from the whole destroys the literary structure of Deuteronomy, which fits in toto almost perfectly the form of the second-millennium B.C. covenants. To wrench chs. 1–4 from their setting is to strip away the preamble (1:1–5) and the historical prologue with exhortations (1:6–4:40). In essence, then, Noth has taken a literary unit that structurally is typical and conforms to all Near Eastern analogues and artificially disunited it.

Third, this reconstruction, if valid, vitiates the book's own witness about its organization. The first thirty chapters represent three distinct speeches of Moses, each introduced by a distinct formula: "These are the words that Moses spoke to all Israel" (1:1 [RSV and 1:5] for 1:6–4:40); "And Moses summoned all Israel, and said to them" (5:1 [RSV] for chs. 5–28); "And Moses summoned all Israel and said to them" (29:2 [RSV] for chs. 29–30 [or perhaps through 31:6]). The rest of the book represents a collection of Moses' discourses, which are mostly poetic (chs. 32–33), plus the description of several concluding events of Moses' life (31:7–29; 34:1–12).

Moses' First Speech (1:1–4:40)

The Book of Numbers covered a good bit of time and history, approximately forty years (compare the first date in Numbers, which is "the first day of the second month of the second year after the Israelites came out of Egypt" [1:1 NIV], with the last date in Numbers, which is "he [Aaron] died on the first day of the fifth month of the fortieth year after the Israelites came out of Egypt" [33:38 NIV]). By contrast, Deuteronomy seems to cover events that happened within a twenty-four-hour span. That can be seen by comparing the following two verses:

> Deut. 1:3: "In the fortieth year, on the first day of the eleventh month, Moses proclaimed. . . ." (NIV)
> Deut. 32:48: "On that same day the LORD told Moses. . . ." (NIV)

However, since 1:5 states only that Moses "began" to expound the law on the first day of the eleventh month, and not that he "finished" it on that day as well, we may assume that "that same day" of 32:48 refers to the events narrated in ch. 32, and that Moses' death occurred sometime in the twelfth month. It is unlikely, but not impossible, that Moses would deliver three addresses (1:5–4:40; 5:1–28:68; 29:1–30:20), give a sermonette to Joshua (31:7–8), compose and deliver two poems (32; 33), and then die, all within the space of twenty-four hours.

The bulk of Deuteronomy is most like Exodus 19–Numbers 10:11, in which Israel is camping at Sinai. In Deuteronomy Israel is camping in Moab. In Exodus 1–18 Israel is moving toward Sinai. In Num. 10:11–36:13 Israel is moving toward Moab. The two resting times are the times when God speaks (mostly through his servant Moses) definitively and extensively to his people. It is in these camping, less hectic times that God's people learn to be still, listen, and discern the voice of God for their lives and future.

The first speech of Moses, then, constitutes the first four chapters of Deuteronomy. Clearly, it has two divisions: (1) chs. 1–3, which are a historical review of Israel's odyssey, beginning with the departure from Sinai, followed by the wilderness wanderings; (2) ch. 4, which is primarily an exhortation. So the orientation of chs. 1–3 is the past, framed in the indicative mood. The emphasis is on recollection. The orientation of ch. 4 is the present and the future, framed in the imperative mood: "give heed . . . do . . . go in . . . take possession." In chs. 1–3 Moses is panoramist; in ch. 4 he is preacher. The narrator becomes exhorter; the historian is also analyst.

We should observe that these words of Moses are addressed to "all Israel" (1:1). The significance of this phrase is underscored not only by its proliferation in Deuteronomy (fourteen times, eleven of which are in the framework sections) but also by the fact that the same phrase appears only two times in the rest of the Pentateuch: Exod. 18:25; Num. 16:34 (see Flanagan 1976–1977: 162). There is no one who does not need to hear this divine word and then respond appropriately.

Reminiscence

In this speech, Moses recalls eight events:

1. 1:9–18: Moses' burdens reduced by the appointment of judges who will function as assistants (cf. Exod. 18:13ff.; Num. 11:10ff.)
2. 1:19–46: The story of the spies sent out to gather data about the land of Canaan (cf. Num. 13–14)
3. 2:1–8a: Israel's passage around the territory of Edom (cf. Num. 20:14–21)
4. 2:8b–25: Israel's passage through the territory of Moab (cf. Num. 21:4–20)
5. 2:26–37: Israel's victory over Sihon of Heshbon (cf. Num. 21:21–32)
6. 3:1–7: Israel's victory over Og of Bashan (cf. Num. 21:33–35)
7. 3:8–22: The distribution of tribal territories east of the Jordan (cf. Numbers 32)
8. 3:23–29: Moses' request to enter Canaan and the denial of permission (cf. Num. 27:12–14, although the two are different incidents)

We note that the first and last items in the list deal with provisions that concern only the Israelites. In both instances Moses' burdens will be lifted. Assistants will lighten his load. Not going beyond Pisgah will put the burden on someone else, namely, Joshua. Every other event deals with Israel's international relationships, either potential (3) or real (4–6).

Moses' recall of the past is not merely repetitive; it is also interpretive. New insights are inserted. Earlier events may even be ignored—for example, the incident in Numbers involving Balak and Balaam. A quick look at the seven events of Deuteronomy 1–3 bears this out.

First, to be sure, Deut. 1:9–18 is a blend of two earlier biblical events, one pre-Sinai (Exod. 18:13–27, the only pre-Sinai event in this pericope; see especially Deut. 1:13–17), and one post-Sinai (Deut. 1:9–12; Num. 11:14–17). That being the case, we observe there is no hint in Deuteronomy about the role of Jethro, whose idea it was that Moses reduce his workload and parcel out the responsibilities, nor is there any reference to the Lord's word to Moses to choose seventy elders. In Numbers God is the addressee of Moses' complaint "I am not able to carry all this people alone" (Num. 11:14 NRSV); in Deuteronomy it is the people who are addressed by Moses' statement "At that time I said to you, 'I am not able alone to bear you'" (Deut. 1:9 RSV).

Second, the account about sending the spies, and their report, is substantially the same as that of Numbers 13–14. However, the narration in Deuteronomy includes the intriguing observation "The LORD was angry with me [i.e., Moses] also on your account, and said, 'You also shall not go in there'" (Deut. 1:37 RSV)—a point reiterated in 3:26 and 4:21. Missing from Deuteronomy is Moses' great prayer of intercession recorded in Num. 14:13–19.

The most startling difference between the two accounts is that Num. 13:1–2 attributes the scouting expedition to God: "The LORD said to Moses, 'Send some men to explore the land of Canaan'" (NIV), while Deut. 1:22–23 suggests that it was the people's idea, not God's: "Then all of you came to me and said, 'Let us send men ahead to spy out the land.' . . . The idea seemed good to me" (NIV). It is possible to reconcile these variations by suggesting that in retelling the spy story Moses intentionally revised it to place blame on the people instead of suggesting that God was responsible for authoring and authorizing an expedition that turned into a fiasco and the death of the first generation in the wilderness. It is doubtful, however, that Moses is trying to protect God and "get him off the hook" by absolving him of something that backfired. A better clue may be found in the Samaritan Pentateuch, which places Deut. 1:20–23a at the head of Numbers 13. Thus, "[Deut. 1:20–2:3a] Then I [Moses] said to you. . . . Then all of you came to me and said. . . . The idea seemed good to me. [Num. 13:1] The LORD said to Moses, 'Send some men to explore the land.'"

Thus, the idea originally was Israel's, Moses presumably sounded out God, and God permitted the incident. To be sure, the Samaritan Pentateuch rendering is an attempt to harmonize, but it correctly captures the spirit of the two references, for why would a redactor leave such a blatant contradiction in the narrative? It also provides a parallel to 1 Samuel 8 and following: the idea of a king comes initially from the people, Samuel sounds out God, God permits the request, and disastrous consequences result.

Third, before Moses reached Edom, he sent an advance group to the Edomites to obtain permission for passage. That permission was denied, and so Israel was forced to circumvent Edom (Num. 20:14–21). Deuteronomy does not record the activities of an advance party or the denial of permission. What is novel here is God's command to make no militaristic moves against Edom, and also God's reference to the fact that he has apportioned land to the Edomites too (Deut. 2:5).

Fourth, the Lord gives a similar word to the Israelites about Moab, as recorded in Deuteronomy. Avoid military confrontation, they are told, for the Moabites too hold their land by right of Yahweh's allotment (Deut. 2:9). One can only wonder about the psychological effect on the Israelites after hearing that other nations also received their land from Israel's God. (Amos 9:7 suggests that the God of Israel not only brought Israel out of Egypt but also directed other nations' exoduses as well.) Did such ideas inflate or deflate Israel? The latter seems likely.

In some Bibles vv. 10–12 are placed in parentheses, while in others they are indented. Someone after Moses must have added these verses, as v. 12b assumes that the conquest of Canaan is completed: "They destroyed the Horites . . . just as Israel *did* in the land the LORD gave them as their possession" (NIV). So even a commitment to Mosaic authorship of Deuteronomy makes room for significant post-Mosaic contributions to the final composition.

Fifth, in Israel's encounter with Sihon of Heshbon, Deuteronomy explains Sihon's refusal to grant Israel passage as due to the Lord hardening his heart (Deut. 2:30). God gave to Edomites, Moabites, and Ammonites land, but to Sihon he gave a hardened heart and spirit. Others whose heart Yahweh hardened are, of course, Pharaoh in Exodus (Exod. 9:12; 10:1, 20, 27; 11:10) and the Canaanites in Joshua so that they would not surrender to Israel but instead would fight and surely lose (Josh. 11:20). In all cases God overrules the free will of individuals who have already chosen a path of self-sovereignty for themselves.

Sixth, the victory over Og of Bashan (a mountainous area in the territory of modern Syria south of Damascus) occupies eleven verses in Deuteronomy versus three verses in Numbers. Like 2:10–12, 3:11, a reference to King Og's enormous bed (see Millard 1988), is a post-Mosaic addition. The language of 3:11c establishes this: "It is *still* in Rabbah of the Ammonites" (NIV).

Seventh, in the last event we have a further notation about Moses the vicarious sufferer (3:26, a restatement of 1:37). And although he was afflicted, he opened not his mouth. Or did he? We need to take a second look at whether Deuteronomy and Numbers are as far apart in their explanations of Moses' exclusion from the land of promise as many commentators suggest they are. Does Numbers attach personal responsibility to Moses—"you did not believe in me" (20:12 RSV), "you rebelled against my word" (27:14 NRSV)—while Deuteronomy exonerates Moses and pictures him as the one who, although innocent, bears the penalty for the sins of others?

Are not the three passages in Deuteronomy (1:37; 3:26; 4:21) simply saying that Israel was Moses' stumbling block? Indeed it was precisely on account of their constant bickering and complaining that Moses was driven to his tantrum, and thus the divine condemnation. Note that 3:26, God's sentence of exclusion, is followed by the command to transfer authority to Joshua (3:28)—precisely the sequence in Num. 27:12–23: the sentence of exclusion (vv. 12–14) and the transfer of authority to Joshua (vv. 15–23).

Exhortation

We have already observed the shift in ch. 4 toward exhortation and away from the exclusively historical reminiscences of chs. 1–3. But even within ch. 4 there is still some historical recital, evidenced by the reference to the incident at Baal-peor (v. 3; cf. Numbers 25), and God's self-revelation at Sinai/Horeb (vv. 9–14; cf. Exodus 19–20). This movement from recollection to appeal is further underscored by the frequent use of direct discourse in chs. 1–3 and indirect discourse in ch. 4, as Polzin (1980: 39–40) has pointed out. Note these places in the first three chapters where Moses quotes God directly: 1:6–8, 35–36, 37b–40, 42; 2:3–7, 9, 13, 18–19, 24–25, 31; 3:2, 26–28. In the following passages Moses quotes himself directly: 1:9–13, 16–17, 20–21, 29–31; 2:27–29; 3:18–22, 24–25. In the following passages Moses quotes the people directly: 1:14, 22, 25b, 27–28, 41a. By contrast, in ch. 4 Moses quotes God directly only in v. 10, and he never quotes himself or the people in a past reference.

Moses' particular concern in this chapter is that the Israelites, once in Canaan, will find the temptation of idolatry irresistible (vv. 15–19, 23, 25). It is particularly interesting that when Moses lists the forms of graven images prohibited (vv. 16–19), his sequence is exactly the opposite of the creation sequence of Gen. 1–2:4a (Fishbane 1972: 349): male and female, beast and animal, bird, creeping things, fish, sun, moon, and stars, all the host of heaven. For Israel to abandon the Lord and engage in idolatry would so reverse his will for their lives. It would be a reversal equal to the undoing, the *bouleversement,* of God's creation.

Moses is also urging the Israelites to learn not only from prehistory and history but also from his personal experience. Moses wants Israel to live (v. 1), although he must die (v. 22). A fourth stimulus to obedience is the character of God. He is jealous, a devouring/consuming fire (v. 24).

A final basis for Moses' appeal for obedience is the threat of exile. The Lord who drove out nations before Israel (v. 38) will drive out Israel as well (v. 27). It is an accepted axiom of critical biblical studies that any reference in Scripture to an exile of Israel presupposes that the writer lived after the Babylonian devastation of Judah and Jerusalem in 587 B.C. Gerhard von Rad's comment (1966: 50) is illustrative: "It [4:25ff.] gives a clue for dating the whole, since this preacher knows already of the exile of 587."

But this conclusion surely avoids the simple fact that Israel, except for a brief period of glory during David's time, lived perpetually under the shadow of much mightier neighbors, and so exile or loss of independence was always a possibility (witness the testimony of Judges). Additionally, this hypothesis completely skirts the evidence from the second and first millennia B.C. in which we read of the capture of a place, followed by the deportation of its citizenry (see Kitchen 1970: 4–7). Must everything and anything predictive or prophetic in the Old Testament be reduced to a *vaticinium ex eventu?*

Threat, however, is never the ultimate word. Indeed, God is jealous/impassioned, a devouring fire (v. 24). There is no other besides him (v. 35). He is heard, but not seen (v. 12). But also he is "merciful/compassionate" and never "will fail you . . . or forget" (v. 31). The conclusion to this great summons of Moses is a promise about "the land which the LORD your God gives you for ever" (v. 40 RSV).

And because God is merciful, even the apostate and the exiled may "return" (v. 30) to him. If the door to the reestablishment of communion with God is closed, it is humankind who insists on that, not God. God's people may "forget" God and his precepts (v. 9), but God will never "forget" his people (v. 31).

Deuteronomy Commentaries and Major Studies

Achtemeier, E. 1987. "Plumbing the Riches: Deuteronomy for the Preacher." *Int* 41:269–81.

Albright, W. F. A. 1957. *From the Stone Age to Christianity: Monotheism and the Historical Process.* 2nd ed. New York: Doubleday.

Biddle, Mark E. 2003. *Deuteronomy*. Smyth & Helwys Bible Commentary. Macon, Ga.: Smyth & Helwys.

Blenkinsopp, J. 1968. *Deuteronomy, the Book of the Covenant: A Scripture Discussion Outline*. London: Sheed & Ward.

———. 1968. "Deuteronomy." In *The Jerome Biblical Commentary*. Ed. R. E. Brown, J. A. Fitzmyer, and R. E. Murphy. 2 vols. in 1. Englewood Cliffs, N.J.: Prentice-Hall. Vol. 1, pp. 101–22.

———. 1990. "Deuteronomy." In *The New Jerome Biblical Commentary*. Ed. R. E. Brown, J. A. Fitzmyer, and R. E. Murphy. Englewood Cliffs, N.J.: Prentice-Hall. Pp. 94–109.

———. 1995. "Deuteronomy and the Politics of Post-Mortem Existence." *VT* 45:1–16.

Block, D. I. 2001. "Recovering the Voice of Moses: The Genesis of Deuteronomy." *JETS* 44:385–408.

Braulik, G. 1994. *The Theology of Deuteronomy: Collected Essays of George Braulik*. Trans. U. Lindblad. BIBAL Collected Essays 2. North Richland Hills, Tex.: BIBAL.

Brueggemann, W. 2002. *Deuteronomy*. AOTC. Nashville: Abingdon.

Cairns, I. 1992. *Word and Presence: A Commentary on the Book of Deuteronomy*. ITC. Grand Rapids: Eerdmans.

Carmichael, C. M. 1974. *The Laws of Deuteronomy*. Ithaca, N.Y.: Cornell University Press.

Childs, B. S. 1979. In *Introduction to the Old Testament as Scripture*. Philadelphia: Fortress. Pp. 202–25.

Christensen, D. L. 1991. *Deuteronomy 1–11*. WBC 6A. Dallas: Word.

———. 1992. "New Evidence for the Priestly Redaction of Deuteronomy." *ZAW* 104:197–201.

———, ed. 1993. *A Song of Power and the Power of Song: Essays on the Book of Deuteronomy*. SBTS 3. Winona Lake, Ind.: Eisenbrauns.

Clements, R. E. 1969. *God's Chosen People: A Theological Interpretation of the Book of Deuteronomy*. Valley Forge, Pa.: Judson.

———. 1989. *Deuteronomy*. OTG. Sheffield: JSOT Press.

———. 1998. "Deuteronomy." In *The New Interpreter's Bible*. Vol. 2. Ed. L. E. Keck et al. Nashville: Abingdon. Pp. 269–538.

———. 2003. "A Dialogue with Gordon McConville on Deuteronomy. The Origins of Deuteronomy: What Are the Clues?" *SJT* 56:508–16.

Craigie, P. C. 1976. *The Book of Deuteronomy*. NICOT. Grand Rapids: Eerdmans.

Flanagan, J. W. 1976–1977. "The Deuteronomic Meaning of the Phrase *kol yisra'el*." *SR* 6:159–68.

Freedman, D. N. 1976. "Deuteronomic History, The." *IDBSup* 226–28.

Gordon, C. H. 1965a. *The Ancient Near East*. New York: Norton.

———. 1965b. *The Common Background of Greek and Hebrew Civilizations*. New York: Norton.

Harrison, R. K. 1969. *Introduction to the Old Testament*. Grand Rapids: Eerdmans. Pp. 635–62.

Hertz, J. H. 1940. "Deuteronomy: Its Antiquity and Mosaic Authorship." *Journal of the Transactions of the Victoria Institute* 72:88–103.

Hoppe, L. J. 1983. "The Levitical Origins of Deuteronomy Reconsidered." *BRes* 28:27–36.

Jacobsen, T. 1964. *Before Philosophy.* Repr., Baltimore: Penguin Books.

Kaufmann, Y. 1960. *The Religion of Israel.* Trans. M. Greenberg. Chicago: University of Chicago Press. Pp. 172–211.

Kitchen, K. A. 1970. "Ancient Orient, 'Deuteronomism,' and the Old Testament." In *New Perspectives on the Old Testament.* Ed. J. Barton Payne. Waco, Tex.: Word. Pp. 1–24.

———. 1979. *The Bible in Its World.* Downers Grove, Ill.: InterVarsity Press. Pp. 79–85.

Kline, M. 1963. *Treaty of the Great King: The Covenant Structure of Deuteronomy.* Grand Rapids: Eerdmans.

Levinson, B. M. 1990. "McConville's Law and Theology in Deuteronomy." *JQR* 80:396–404.

———. 1997. *Deuteronomy and the Hermeneutics of Legal Innovation.* New York and Oxford: Oxford University Press.

———. 2000. "The Hermeneutics of Tradition in Deuteronomy: A Reply to J. G. McConville." *JBL* 119:269–86.

———. 2004. "Deuteronomy." In *The Jewish Study Bible.* Ed. A. Berlin and M. Z. Brettler. Oxford: Oxford University Press. Pp. 356–450.

Lohfink, N. 1976. "Deuteronomy." *IDBSup* 229–32.

———. 1977. "Culture Shock and Theology: A Discussion of Theology as a Cultural and Social Phenomenon Based on the Example of Deuteronomic Law." *BTB* 7:12–21.

Lundblom, J. 1996. "The Inclusio and Other Framing Devices in Deuteronomy i–xxviii." *VT* 46:296–315.

Manley, G. T. 1957. *The Book of the Law: Studies in the Date of Deuteronomy.* Grand Rapids: Eerdmans.

Mann, T. W. 1995. *Deuteronomy.* WBComp. Louisville: Westminster John Knox.

Margolis, M. 1922. *Hebrew Scriptures in the Making.* Philadelphia: Jewish Publication Society.

Mayes, A. D. H. 1981. *Deuteronomy.* NCBC. Grand Rapids: Eerdmans.

———. 1993. "On Describing the Purpose of Deuteronomy." *JSOT* 58:13–33.

McBride, S. D., Jr. 1987. "Polity of the Covenant People: The Book of Deuteronomy." *Int* 41:229–44.

McCarthy, D. J. 1978. *Treaty and Covenant.* 2nd ed. AnBib 21. Rome: Pontifical Biblical Institute.

McConville, J. G. 1979. "God's 'Name' and God's 'Glory.'" *TynB* 30:149–63.

———. 1984. *Law and Theology in Deuteronomy.* JSOTSup 33. Sheffield: JSOT Press.

———. 1993. *Grace in the End: A Study in Deuteronomic Theology.* Studies in Old Testament Theology. Grand Rapids: Zondervan.

———. 2001. "Metaphor, Symbol and the Interpretation of Deuteronomy." In *After Pentecost: Language and Biblical Interpretation*. Ed. C. Bartholomew et al. Scripture and Hermeneutics 2. Carlisle: Paternoster. Pp. 329–51.

———. 2002a. "Singular Address in the Deuteronomic Law and the Politics of Legal Administration." *JSOT* 97:19–36.

———. 2002b. *Deuteronomy*. Apollos Old Testament Commentary. Leicester, England: Apollos; Downers Grove, Ill.: InterVarsity Press.

———. 2003. "A Dialogue with Gordon McConville on Deuteronomy: A Response from Gordon McConville." *SJT* 56:525–31.

McConville, J. G., and J. G. Millar. 1994. *Time and Place in Deuteronomy*. JSOTSup 179. Sheffield: Sheffield Academic Press.

McCurley, F. R., Jr. 1974. "The Home of Deuteronomy Revisited: A Methodological Analysis of the Northern Theory." In *A Light unto My Path: Old Testament Studies in Honor of Jacob M. Myers*. Ed. H. N. Bream, R. D. Heim, and C. A. Moore. Gettysburg Theological Studies 4. Philadelphia: Temple University Press. Pp. 298–302.

Merrill, E. 1994. *Deuteronomy*. NAC 4. Nashville: Broadman.

Milgrom, J. 1973. "The Alleged 'Demythologization' and 'Secularization' in Deuteronomy." *IEJ* 23:151–56.

———. 1976. "Profane Slaughter and a Formulaic Key to the Composition of Deuteronomy." *HUCA* 47:1–17.

Millar, J. Gary. 1999. *Now Choose Life: Theology and Ethics in Deuteronomy*. New Studies in Biblical Theology. Grand Rapids: Eerdmans.

———. 2002. "'A Faithful God Who Does No Wrong': History, Theology, and Reliability in Deuteronomy." In *The Trustworthiness of God: Perspectives on the Nature of Scripture*. Ed. P. Helm and C. R. Trueman. Grand Rapids/Cambridge: Eerdmans. Pp. 3–17.

Miller, P. D., Jr. 1987. "'Moses My Servant': The Deuteronomic Portrait of Moses." *Int* 41:245–55. Repr., in *A Song of Power and the Power of Song: Essays on the Book of Deuteronomy*. Ed. D. L. Christensen. SBTS 3. Winona Lake, Ind.: Eisenbrauns, 1993. Pp. 301–12.

———. 1990. *Deuteronomy*. Interpretation. Louisville: John Knox.

———. 1999. "Deuteronomy and Psalms: Evoking a Biblical Conversation." *JBL* 118:3–18.

Moberly, R. W. L. 2003. "A Dialogue with Gordon McConville on Deuteronomy: Theological Interpretation of an OT Book: A Response to Gordon McConville's Deuteronomy." *SJT* 56:516–25.

Moran, W. L. 1963. "The Ancient Near Eastern Background of the Love of God in Deuteronomy." *CBQ* 25:77–87.

———. 1969. "Deuteronomy." In *A New Catholic Commentary on Holy Scripture*. Ed. R. C. Fuller. Camden, N.J.: Nelson. Pp. 256–76.

Nicholson, E. W. 1967. *Deuteronomy and Tradition*. Philadelphia: Fortress.

———. 1986. *God and His People*. Oxford: Clarendon; New York: Oxford University Press.

O'Brien, M. A. 1995. "The Book of Deuteronomy." *CurBS* 3:95–128.

Olson, D. T. 1994. *Deuteronomy and the Death of Moses: A Theological Reading*. OBT. Minneapolis: Fortress.

———. 1995. "Deuteronomy as De-Centering Center: Reflections on Postmodernism and the Quest for a Theological Center of the Hebrew Scriptures." *Semeia* 71:119–32.

Payne, D. F. 1985. *Deuteronomy*. The Daily Study Bible. Old Testament. Philadelphia: Westminster.

Philips, A. C. 1973. *Deuteronomy*. CBC. Cambridge: Cambridge University Press.

Polzin, R. 1980. *Moses and the Deuteronomist: A Literary Study of the Deuteronomic History*. New York: Seabury. Pp. 25–72.

———. 1987. "Deuteronomy." In *The Literary Guide to the Bible*. Ed. R. Alter and F. Kermode. Cambridge, Mass.: Belknap. Pp. 92–101.

———. 1993. "Reporting Speech in the Book of Deuteronomy: Toward a Compositional Analysis of the Deuteronomic History." In *A Song of Power and the Power of Song: Essays on the Book of Deuteronomy*. Ed. D. L. Christensen. SBTS 3. Winona Lake, Ind.: Eisenbrauns. Pp. 355–74.

Rad, G. von. 1953. *Studies in Deuteronomy*. London: SCM Press.

———. 1962. "Deuteronomy." In *Old Testament Theology*. Trans. D. H. G. Stalker. 2 vols. New York: Harper & Row. Vol. 1, pp. 219–31.

———. 1966. *Deuteronomy: A Commentary*. Trans. D. Barton. OTL. Philadelphia: Westminster.

Richter, S. L. 2002. *The Deuteronomistic History and the Name Theology: lešakkēn šemô šām in the Bible and the Ancient Near East*. Berlin: de Gruyter.

Rofé, A. 1974. Review of M. Weinfeld, "Deuteronomy and the Deuteronomic School." *Christian News from Israel* 24:204–9.

———. 1988. *Introduction to Deuteronomy: Part I and Further Chapters*. SBLDS 96. Atlanta: Scholars Press.

Romer, T. 1994. "The Book of Deuteronomy." In *The History of Israel's Traditions: The Heritage of Martin Noth*. Ed. S. L. McKenzie and M. P. Graham. JSOTSup 182. Sheffield: Sheffield Academic Press. Pp. 178–212.

Sanders, J. A. 1989. "Deuteronomy." In *The Books of the Bible*. Ed. B. W. Anderson. 2 vols. New York: Scribner. Vol. 1, pp. 89–102.

Schultz, S. J. 1971. *Deuteronomy*. Everyman's Bible Commentary. Chicago: Moody.

Segal, M. H. 1961. "The Composition of the Pentateuch—A Fresh Examination." *Scripta hierosolymitana* 8:68–114.

Sheehan, John F. X. 1977. *Let the People Cry Amen!* New York: Paulist Press.

Sherwood, S. K. 2002. *Leviticus, Numbers, Deuteronomy*. Berit Olam. Collegeville, Minn.: Liturgical Press. Pp. 197–292.

Sonnet, J.–P. 1997. *The Book within the Book: Writing in Deuteronomy*. BIS 14. Leiden: Brill.

Thompson, J. A. 1978. *Deuteronomy: An Introduction and Commentary*. TOTC. Downers Grove, Ill.: InterVarsity Press.

Tigay, J. H. 1996. *Deuteronomy: The Traditional Hebrew Text with the New JPS Translation*. JPS Torah Commentary. Philadelphia: The Jewish Publication Society.

Vervenne, M., and J. Lust, eds. 1997. *Deuteronomy and Deuteronomic Literature: Festschrift C. H. W. Brekelmans.* BETL 133. Leuven: Leuven University Press.

Weinfeld, M. 1961. "The Origin of Humanism in Deuteronomy." *JBL* 80:241–47.

———. 1971. "Deuteronomy." *EncJud* 5:1573–83.

———. 1972. *Deuteronomy and the Deuteronomic School.* Oxford: Clarendon.

———. 1973. "On 'Demythologization' and 'Secularization' in Deuteronomy." *IEJ* 23:230–33.

———. 1991. *Deuteronomy 1–11: A New Translation with Introduction and Commentary.* AB 5. New York: Doubleday.

———. 1992. "Deuteronomy, Book of." *ABD* 2:168–83.

———. 1996. "Deuteronomy's Theological Revolution." *BRev* 12 (1):38–41, 44–45.

Wright, C. J. H. 1996. *Deuteronomy.* NIBCOT 4. Peabody, Mass.: Hendrickson.

Wright, G. E. 1953. "Deuteronomy: Introduction." In *The Interpreter's Bible.* Vol. 2. Ed. G. A. Buttrick. Nashville: Abingdon. Pp. 311–31.

Deuteronomy 1:1–4:40

Brueggemann, W. 1968. "The Kerygma of the Deuteronomistic Historian: Gospel for Exiles." *Int* 22:387–402.

Cazelles, H. 1967. "Passages in the Singular within Discourse in the Plural of Dt 1–4." *CBQ* 24:207–19.

Christensen, D. L. 1985a. "Form and Structure in Deuteronomy 1–11." In *Das Deuteronomium: Entstehung, Gestalt und Botschaft.* Ed. N. Lohfink. BETL 68. Leuven: Leuven University Press. Pp. 135–44.

———. 1985b. "Prose and Poetry in the Bible: The Narrative Poetics of Deuteronomy 1,9–18." *ZAW* 97:179–89.

Davies, G. I. 1979. "The Significance of Deut. 1:2 for the Location of Mt. Horeb." *PEQ* 111:87–101.

Fishbane, M. 1972. "Varia Deuteronomica." *ZAW* 84:349–52.

Glatt-Gilad, D. A. 1997. "The Re-Interpretation of the Edomite-Israelite Encounter in Deuteronomy 11." *VT* 47:441–55.

Kallai, Z. 1995. "Where Did Moses Speak (Deuteronomy i 1–5)?" *VT* 45:188–97.

Kitchen, K. A. 1970. "Ancient Orient, 'Deuteronomism,' and the Old Testament." In *New Perspectives on the Old Testament.* Ed. J. Barton Payne. Waco, Tex.: Word. Pp. 1–24.

Lindars, B. 1968. "Torah in Deuteronomy." In *Words and Meanings: Essays Presented to David Winton Thomas on His Retirement from the Regius Professorship of Hebrew in the University of Cambridge, 1968.* Ed. P. R. Ackroyd and B. Lindars. London: Cambridge University Press. Pp. 117–36.

Mayes, A. D. H. 1981. "Deuteronomy 4 and the Literary Criticism of Deuteronomy." *JBL* 100:23–51. Repr., in *A Song of Power and the Power of Song: Essays on the Book of Deuteronomy.* Ed. D. L. Christensen. SBTS 3. Winona Lake, Ind.: Eisenbrauns, 1993. Pp. 195–224.

Millard, A. R. 1988. "King Og's Bed and Other Ancient Ironmongery." In *Ascribe to the LORD: Biblical and Other Essays in Memory of Peter C. Craigie*. Ed. L. Eslinger and G. Taylor. JSOTSup 67. Sheffield: JSOT Press. Pp. 481–92.

Moran, W. L. 1963. "The End of the Unholy War and the Anti-Exodus." *CBQ* 44:333–42. Repr., in *A Song of Power and the Power of Song: Essays on the Book of Deuteronomy*. Ed. D. L. Christensen. SBTS 3. Winona Lake, Ind.: Eisenbrauns, 1993. Pp. 147–55.

Polzin, R. 1980. *Moses and the Deuteronomist: A Literary Study of the Deuteronomic History*. New York: Seabury. Pp. 25–43.

Slater, S. 1999. "Imagining Arrival: Rhetoric, Reader, and Word of God in Deuteronomy 1–3." In *The Labour of Reading: Desire, Alienation, and Biblical Interpretation*. Festschrift for Robert C. Culley. Ed. F. C. Black, R. Boer, and E. Runions. SemeiaSt. Atlanta: Society of Biblical Literature. Pp. 107–22.

Summer, W. A. 1968. "Israel's Encounters with Edom, Moab, Ammon, Sihon, and Og according to the Deuteronomist." *VT* 18:216–28.

Vaux, R. de. 1978. *The Early History of Israel*. Philadelphia: Westminster. Pp. 555–60.

Veijola, T. 1993. "Principal Observations on the Basic Story in Deuteronomy 1–3." In *A Song of Power and the Power of Song: Essays on the Book of Deuteronomy*. Ed. D. L. Christensen. SBTS 3. Winona Lake, Ind.: Eisenbrauns. Pp. 137–46.

Wolff, H. W. 1975. "The Kerygma of the Deuteronomic Historical Work." In *The Vitality of Old Testament Traditions*, by H. W. Wolff and W. Brueggemann. Atlanta: John Knox. Pp. 83–100.

20

Be Careful in the Future

D E U T E R O N O M Y 4:41–11:32

This unit begins with a brief paragraph (4:41–43) about the three cities of refuge that Moses established east of the Jordan, a topic that Moses discusses again in 19:1–13, but on that occasion he speaks of three more cities of refuge on the west side of the Jordan. Here is the second reference in the third person to Moses in Deuteronomy, the first being 1:1, 5. We instinctively ask why this particular notation is placed here. Is it an awkward addition inserted by a later editor with no discernable relationship to its immediate context? Perhaps. On the other hand, throughout the preceding chapters and in ch. 4 Moses has been expatiating on God's law and statutes. If observed and implemented, they lead to life. The faithful adherent of God's laws will not die, but will have prolonged life. This paragraph likewise deals with death and life, life for the one who takes another's life unintentionally. Are God's word and revelation a city of refuge itself? To leave it is to make oneself a target.

We will see later in the discussion of the laws of chs. 12–26 that apparently unrelated laws are conjoined simply because of a key word in each, or a phrase similar to both, or an ultimately common theme in both. Not only does 4:41–43 serve as a transition between the first and second speeches of Moses; it also highlights the theme of life, a theme underscored in the immediately preceding and succeeding chapters of Deuteronomy.

The Theme of Oneness (5–6)

Moses' second address starts with 5:1, a summons to "all Israel" to listen, not to the advice or reflections of a sage, but to the recitation of God's standards. This second speech of Moses begins and ends with the importance of "today": "Hear, O Israel, the decrees and laws I declare in your hearing *today*" (5:1 NIV); "Be sure that you obey all the decrees and laws I am setting before you *today*" (11:32 NIV). The two verses are nearly identical.

Two things are of interest here. First is Moses' reminder to his audience that at Horeb (i.e., Sinai) the Lord made a covenant "with us . . . not with our ancestors" (5:2–3 NRSV). Moses is addressing people who either were infants at that time or were born after the event. Also, he clearly refers in 4:31 to "the covenant with your ancestors that he swore to them" (NRSV).

Thus we are confronted with a paradox: "covenant with your ancestors" (4:31) and "not with our ancestors" (5:3). Precisely here is a clue to how this material in Deuteronomy functions. To be sure, God did make a covenant with that first generation. He is not about to make another covenant with the next generation. In fact, the word "covenant" never appears in the Old Testament in the plural. "Covenants" does not exist. What Moses is appealing for is that his contemporaries fully appropriate that earlier covenant for themselves. God's word to the first generation is to be appropriated by the next generation. Nowhere does Moses even hint that God needs to do something more or that his work is unfinished. God has done everything necessary to make possible the obedience of every generation.

The second point of interest in this chapter is the second reading of the Ten Commandments (cf. the first version in Exod. 20:1–17). There are indeed differences, some major, some minor, between Deuteronomy's version of the Decalogue and the version in Exodus. Most of these we reviewed in the section about Exodus. Here, however, we need to ask what specific role is played by the repetition of the Decalogue at this point in Deuteronomy. Thus far we have encountered the recalling of history; now we encounter the recalling of Sinaitic law.

Is this repetition Moses' way of reminding his audience that God's law is immutable and eternal? God does not issue revised versions of his will about idolatry, murder, theft, and coveting. To be sure, there is adaptation in some particulars to new circumstances. There are amendments to the constitution. But the revelatory truths of the Decalogue are firmly set for the next generation and generations thereafter. To erase the prohibition against coveting or disrespect to one's parents is no more possible than to strike the phrase "all men are created equal" from the Declaration of Independence.

Thus, for this new generation the simple recitation of that old law is sufficient. But that old law must become *my* law, the standard and authority by which I measure my life and my lifestyle. The issue, then, is making past history present history. There are many generations, but only one law.

Of course, this is precisely what happens when Christians observe the sacraments, or when the Israelites observed the Old Testament sacraments such as Passover. To observe the sacrament is to reenact previous history in such a way that it has a bearing on my history. A person who relives the Passover experiences an exodus by reenacting this history, not simply because he or she says, "Yes, God did deliver the people back there." To partake of the Eucharist means to relive and reenact the death of Christ, and it is the appropriation of that death for the participant.

Following the recital of the Decalogue, Moses reminds the people of tremors that they experienced when God did speak (5:23–27), and how they were only too happy to select Moses to stand in the breach between themselves and God. God consented to this arrangement (5:28–29). Interestingly, in v. 29 God can only hope and desire that his people will fear him and keep his commandments ("Oh, that their hearts would be inclined to fear me and keep all my commands" NIV). Obedience and conformity are not something he can control. Jeffrey Tigay (1996: 74) quotes an ancient rabbinical sentence from the Talmud: "All is under the control of Heaven except for the fear of Heaven."

The immediate function of these verses is to emphasize Moses' unique mediatorial position. He alone stands between God and Israel. His credentials are both congregational appointment and divine approval. As such, this position confers on him the role of teacher and invests his announcements with authority.

The repetition of the Decalogue had impressed on Israel the idea of one divine law. The theme of oneness is then continued into the second half of ch. 5. Not only is there *one law,* there also is only *one mediator.*

This elevation of Moses to preeminence is indicated further by the relationship between Moses' use of "our God" and "your God" (in direct discourse) in his first and second speeches. Table 15 indicates this distinction.

It can be seen that Moses' use of "our God," used frequently in chs. 1–4, becomes almost nonexistent in the next twenty-four chapters. By contrast, in the second speech Moses' "your God" is used copiously, almost exclusively. Observing this psychological shift, Robert Polzin (1980: 49) remarks, "Moses at chapter 5 leaves off speaking to his audience as a fellow Israelite, and henceforth (apart from 5:2 and 6:4) speaks only from the viewpoint of his role as teacher."

Chapter 6 is best known for its celebrated v. 4: "Hear, O Israel: the LORD our God is one LORD" (RSV), frequently referred to as the "Shema" (a transliteration of the Hebrew imperative "Hear!"). There are indeed translation problems with even this basic verse, as a look at the commentaries will show (see also Moberly 1990). One might render the Hebrew text as "The LORD is our God, the LORD alone" or "The LORD is our God, the LORD is one," in which case the phrase draws attention to the special relationship between Yahweh and Israel. Or one might render it as "The LORD our God is one LORD" or "The LORD our God, the LORD is one," in which case the phrase is a statement describing the nature and character of God. Regardless of which translation one prefers, and especially if one goes with the latter two options, the verse remains a *locus classicus* for the biblical doctrine of monotheism.

Table 15

"Our God"			"Your God"		
Chapter	**Verse**	**Frequency**	**Chapter**	**Verse**	**Frequency**
(1–4) 1	6, 19, 20, 25	4	(1–4) 1	10, 21, 26, 30, 31, 32	6
2	29, 33, 36, 37	4	2	7 (2x), 30	3
3	3	1	3	18, 20, 21, 22	4
4	7	1	4	2, 3, 4, 10, 19, 21, 23 (2x), 24, 25, 29, 30, 31, 34, 40	15
Total		10			28
(5–28) 5	2	1	(5–28)		approx. 250
6	4	1			
Total		2			±250

So again the idea of oneness, sounded in ch. 5, is perpetuated in ch. 6. The progression is *one law, one mediator,* and now *one Lord.*

Why must there be at this point a reference to one God? For one thing, much of ch. 6 is an elaboration of the first commandment, or a spelling out of the implications of 5:6–10: "you shall love the LORD your God" (6:5 NRSV) and "thousands of those who love me" (5:10 RSV); "who brought you out of the land of Egypt" (6:12 NRSV) and "who brought you out of the land of Egypt, out of the house of bondage" (5:6 RSV); "you shall not go after other gods" (6:14 RSV) and "you shall have no other gods" (5:7 NRSV); "the LORD your God . . . is a jealous God" (6:15 NRSV) and "I the LORD your God am a jealous God" (5:9 NRSV); "you shall diligently keep the commandments of the LORD" (6:17 RSV) and "who . . . keep my commandments" (5:10 NRSV).

Here and elsewhere Deuteronomy juxtaposes love for God (6:5) and following God's commandments (6:6). Note the similar joinings in 10:12; 11:1, 13, 22; 19:9; 30:16. It is as if Deuteronomy makes the case that one loves God by obeying and honoring him and by making a commitment to holy living. W. L. Moran (1963) has demonstrated from ancient Near Eastern texts of the second and first millennia B.C. that a king is to "love" his vassal—that is, provide for the vassal's needs and effectively lead his subjects. The vassal likewise is to "love" his king—that is, serve him loyally. How the vassal "loves" his royal head is how, in such texts in Deuteronomy, the child of God is to "love" his or her Lord. This is, of course, quite close to Jesus' statement "If you love me, you will obey what I command" (John 14:15). Love as obedience does not suggest, however, that Deuteronomy advocates an emotionless version of loyalty. If passionate feelings without actions are unacceptable, so are actions devoid of feelings of love (Lapsley 2003).

When discussing the concept of one law, I noted that the duplication of the Decalogue serves to make the point of one law to transcend and serve as a grand *depositum* for every succeeding generation. One wonders, as an extension of that, if the intent of 6:4 is more than simply to affirm belief in one God versus many gods, monotheism versus polytheism, one Yahweh versus a plurality of Baals.

I suspect that the Old Testament's (and Deuteronomy's in particular) concept of monotheism is to be understood not ontologically, but historically. That is, the emphasis is not with one being or more than one being, but whether this being acts in a way that is consistent. A god who does one thing in a certain situation one time and does a different thing in that same situation another time leaves us with two gods. A god who is inconsistent is historically polytheistic. This point is beautifully illustrated by Paul in Rom. 3:21–31, the aim of which is to show that all people—Jew and Gentile alike—are justified through faith. Inserted into this theological argument is the statement "since God is one" (Rom. 3:30). If with the Gentiles God does one thing and with the Jews he does another, then we have two gods. But God does not do that. The problem is the same for both Jew and Gentile, and so is God's solution. God is one. P. D. Miller (1984: 22) similarly remarks, "'Yahweh is one' serves to underscore that the one who receives our ultimate allegiance is consistent. . . . We do not encounter the reality of God in one time or place of experience that is not wholly conformable with all moments and experiences. The presence of God in the world and in shaping history is not in one guise now and another guise elsewhere."

In Deut. 6:4 Moses lifts monotheism and the nature of God beyond arithmetic and numbers and places them into the realm of ethics—a God who is always consistent with himself and with us. And that is true for any generation that chooses to follow him. For this reason Moses is able to add to his monotheistic statement the exhortation to "love the LORD your God with all your heart, and with all your soul, and with all your might" (6:5 NRSV).

There seems to be no logical relationship between 6:4, "God is one," and 6:5, "love the LORD your God," if monotheism is limited to the concept of the one and the many. If, however, Moses is saying that as God's law is the same from generation to generation, so God himself is the same from generation to generation, then this means that God is not fickle, capricious, or unpredictable. God can be loved enthusiastically because he is lovable and consistent.

Love for God, if genuine, inevitably entails obedience to the word of God. One cannot love God with all one's heart and be lukewarm toward God's word. Thus Moses follows the injunction to love God with the injunction to put God's word "upon your heart" (6:6 RSV). The word of God is indispensable and therefore must be passed on to the next generation at all costs (6:7a). This word is to become a conversation piece, almost a preoccupation (6:7b). To place the word on the hands (6:8) and on the doorposts of the house (6:9) is desirable, but only after it has been placed in the heart. External performance cannot substitute for inner vitality.

Moses consistently reminds his people that their appropriate response to God—love, fear, obey—is indeed just that, a response. They were delivered from Egypt by grace. They were preserved in the wilderness by grace. They will receive the land of promise by grace. Chapter 6 illustrates the proper perspective. Verses 1–9 and 12–19 emphasize human responsibility; vv. 10–11 and 20–23 emphasize divine grace, especially the gratuitous gift of land.

A Call to Remembrance (7–11)

If Israel needs a proper relationship to God (ch. 6), it is also incumbent upon the people to have a proper relationship to those among whom they will live (ch. 7)—Israel is something of a dwarf surrounded by giants. Moses' counsel is clear: do not fraternize with your neighbors

(7:1–5). His second counsel is equally clear: do not live in fear of them (7:17–26).

The reason for such advice is twofold. What Israel has in its favor is not impressive size—"you were the fewest of all peoples" (7:7 NRSV)—but a life of holiness that mandates separation from everything impure (7:6). Elsewhere in the Pentateuch Israel is urged and invited to holiness ("you shall be holy/a holy nation"), as in Exod. 19:6; 22:31; Lev. 11:44–45; 19:2; 20:7, 26, but Deuteronomy describes Israel as already holy (Deut. 7:6; 14:2, 21; 26:19; 28:9). Elsewhere in the Pentateuch holiness is a prospect; in Deuteronomy it is a possession. But even more importantly, Israel is the object of God's love and the recipient of the divine promise that the nations are God's problem, not Israel's (7:8–9, 20–24). Indeed, the Israelites do need, as 6:6 had urged, to put God's word in their hearts. For if they do so with their own word—"if you say in your heart" (7:17)—the result is fright, anxiety, and consternation.

So the Israelites need to know both who the Lord is and the power of his word (ch. 6). They need to know who the enemy is and where to draw the line (ch. 7). They also need to make sure that they know who they are, and who they are not (ch. 8).

Perhaps in this eighth chapter Moses is suggesting that the Israelites should fear their enemies less than they fear themselves. The Israelites may become a more lethal weapon than any group of Hittites or Canaanites. To that end, 8:2 is a call to the Israelites to remember what the Lord did for them in the wilderness, in contrast to 7:18, which is a call to remember what the Lord did to Pharaoh in Egypt. The Lord humbled Pharaoh, but he also humbled Israel, as the incident in Exodus 16 illustrates.

The language in Deut. 8:2, that Israel should "remember how the Lord your God led you all the way in the desert . . . to *test* you in order to *know* what was in your heart" (NIV), recalls similar language used in Genesis 22 when Abraham went to sacrifice Isaac. Again the words "test" and "know" occur: "Some time later God *tested* Abraham. . . . Now I *know* that you fear God" (Gen. 22:1; 22:12b NIV). On both occasions God "tests" someone in order to "know" something. Both passages are similar to Deut. 13:3b, the larger context of which is instigation by a prophet or dreamer to serve other gods (13:2–6): "The Lord your God is testing you to find out whether you love him with all your heart and with all your soul" (NIV). Some interpreters would use such passages to deny that the Bible unequivocally teaches God's omniscience, to argue that God in fact makes new discoveries and gleans fresh information. However, there are other possibilities. For example, R. W. L. Moberly (2000: 106–7) grants that in these three passages of testing/knowing or finding out, the primary emphasis is upon Abraham's/Israel's response to the divine testing. And yet "God is engaged with the encounter in such a way that the outcome is a genuine divine concern. . . . The divine pronouncement 'now I know' . . . indicates that the deepened relationship [between Abraham/Israel and God] is in some way an intrinsic concern of God."

In a sense, God is taking a risk in sending his children into a garden of Eden (8:7–10). The contrast between the wilderness and the resources of this land could not be drawn more strongly, for once a person has succeeded, it becomes fatally easy to forget help received along the way. Few people know how to handle affluence.

Gerhard von Rad (1966: 73) observes that phrases such as "my power and the might of my hand" (8:17 RSV) on the lips of God's people sound very much like Lucifer's language in Isa. 14:12–14 and Ezek. 28:1–10. If Lucifer was cast down for his arrogance and presumption, the Israelites likewise will be cast out for theirs if they capitulate to that temptation. The way to avoid such a humiliation is for them to remember the Lord who brought them out of bondage (8:14), who led them through the wilderness (8:15), who fed them in the wilderness (8:16), who has given them power (8:18).

If we were to ask Moses, as we hear him speak throughout Deuteronomy 8, "What things might we do that cause our relationship with God to go askew?" he would answer:

1. let memory fail you (v. 2, "remember"; v. 11, "do not forget")
2. let vanity possess you (v. 14, "your heart will become proud" [NIV])
3. let prosperity intoxicate you (v. 13, "your herds and flocks grow large and your silver and gold increase" [NIV])
4. let security deceive you (v. 19, "if you . . . follow other gods and worship and bow down to them" [NIV])

Almost everything in Deut. 9:1–10:11 recalls the incident of the golden calf (Exodus 32). Chronologically this event precedes just about every historical event alluded to in Moses' first address, yet it is placed in his second address. In 5:22–27 we observed how Deuteronomy gives special attention to Moses' ministry of mediation. He stands between God and Israel. This particular story returns to that motif and provides another illustration of the critical contribution of Moses to Israel's well-being. The keys to Israel's continued existence are not its own power (8:17) and its own righteousness (9:4); the keys are a gracious God and a gifted Moses.

A quick look at 9:1–10:11 reveals that it is more a free retelling of Exodus 32–34 than an exact recounting. To illustrate, if we were to arrange the two accounts in parallel columns, the following differences (among others) would emerge. Exodus 32 records Moses' first intercessory prayer before he descends the mountain (Exod. 32:11–14), while Deuteronomy records his first prayer after he descends the mountain (Deut. 9:18–20), and it includes the notice of a special prayer for Aaron (9:20).

Also, before Deuteronomy records Moses' second intercessory prayer (Deut. 9:25–29, much like Exod. 32:11–14), it inserts three other incidents of aberrant living on the part of Israel: Taberah, Massah, and Kibroth-hattaavah (v. 22), probably to show that Israel's flagrant disobedience in building the golden calf was, unfortunately, part of a persistent pattern rather than an isolated faux pas. Finally, in the reestablishment of the covenant (Deut. 10:1–5 and Exodus 34) Moses not only receives orders to carve out two new tablets of stone; he is also told to make an ark of wood in which the tablets will be deposited. This latter piece of information was not recorded in Exodus.

What is accomplished by Moses' recalling the event of the golden calf and the renewed covenant (Exodus 32–34)? It is one of two stories from Exodus–Numbers on which Moses comments at some length in these opening chapters of Deuteronomy. The other is the spy story of Numbers 13–14 recounted in Deut. 1:19–46. These are the two great sins of the first generation of Israelites, idolatry and unbelief (Deut. 9:12), for which God either threatens to destroy Israel and start over with a new generation (Exod. 32:10) or actually says that he will do so (Num. 14:23). I suggest that it sets into even bolder relief the contrast between Moses and Israel. For one thing, Deuteronomy 9 falls into an A-B-A'-B' pattern: the disobedience of the people (9:7–17); the intercession of Moses (9:18–21); the disobedience of the people (9:22–24); the intercession of Moses (9:25–29).

The "insertion" of 9:22–24 is anything but haphazard. In Deut. 9:22 Moses refers to Israel's past disobedience at Taberah (Num. 11:1–3), Massah (Exod. 17:1–7), and Kibroth-hattaavah (Num. 11:31–34). Chronologically, the order should be Massah, Taberah, and Kibroth-hattaavah. The prayers of Moses saved them at Taberah (Num. 11:2), and thus fittingly it is first in the list. At Kibroth-hattaavah the people died of plague. Perhaps there will be another Kibroth-hattaavah, as Deut. 9:25 suggests: "because the LORD had said he would destroy you" (NIV). Unless Moses prays! Interestingly, Moses does not repeat his words to God as recorded in Exodus 32: "repent/relent" (32:12) and "blot me . . . out of thy book" (32:32 RSV). The omissions may be insignificant. But then again, it is not too difficult to imagine Moses, upon reflection, saying to himself, "Did I really order God to repent? Was I really audacious enough to put my own relationship with him in jeopardy?"

What is added to the whole by the new piece of information about the wooden ark (Deut. 10:1–5), of which mention is made in Deuteronomy only here and in ch. 31 (for the possible implications of this see Fretheim 1968)? Commentators such as von Rad have made much of the fact that the ark in Deuteronomy functions only as the receptacle of the tablets of law, and not as the place of divine residence or divine glory. The implication drawn about this perceived shift from the numinous to the mundane for the ark is that Deuteronomy has indeed undergone a process of demythologization. One can question, however, whether the role of the ark in Deuteronomy has been demoted to something less significant. To meet God in his word is no less spectacular than to meet him occupying a cloud or sitting between cherubim.

By adding information about the ark here (material omitted from Exodus 34), Moses emphasizes that the covenant is secure, inaccessible, permanent, and available only as Moses will give teaching from it and about it (see Peckham 1975: 51). Also, the mention of the ark at the end of this retelling of the debacle of the golden calf is appropriate in that it provides a stunning contrast about how one conceptualizes God's presence. The ark is a legitimate symbol of God's presence among his people; the calf is an illegitimate symbol of God's presence among his people. Once again the arrangement or introduction of new material serves to reinforce the unique, mediatorial ministry of Moses and the unchanging God who has issued an unchanging covenant: "and there they are" (10:5 NRSV).

The remainder of ch. 10 through 11:32 is a concluding hortatory section built primarily around a series of exhortations followed by motivations for obedience (e.g.: exhortation [10:12–13]; motivation [10:14–15]; exhortation [10:16]; motivation [10:17–18]).

Of special interest here is Moses' concern that the people "circumcise therefore the foreskin of your heart" (10:16 RSV). Thus, even as early as Deuteronomy the point is made that true circumcision is of the heart, not simply an incision into the external flesh. This particular exhortation resonates with Moses' restatement in 11:18–21 of 6:6–8. The law must be put on one's heart first, then on the hands, the eyes, the gates, and the doorposts. One wonders if Jeremiah, when he spoke of the new covenant, one feature of which was the divine writing of the law on the heart (Jer. 31:33), was not deliberately using a bit of irony. For, after all, much of the new covenant is old, unless one has strayed so far from its precepts that even the old sounds new.

Deuteronomy 11:26–32 serves as a transition between the preaching of chs. 5–11 and the list of laws that begins in ch. 12. As Moran (1969: 267) has observed, the three items listed here are in inverse order to their actual treatment in the subsequent chapters: blessing and curse (11:26–

28 and ch. 28); the ceremony at Shechem, between Ebal and Gerizim (11:29–31 and ch. 27); the laws of the Lord (11:32 and chs. 12–26). Now the stage is set for the announcement of the laws of Deuteronomy.

Deuteronomy 4:11–11:32

Begg, C. T. 1985. "The Destruction of the Calf (Exod 33,20/Deut 9, 21)." In *Das Deuteronomium: Entstehung, Gestalt und Botschaft*. Ed. N. Lohfink. BETL 68. Leuven: Leuven University Press. Pp. 208–51.

Brekelmans, C. 1985. "Deuteronomy 5: Its Place and Function." In *Das Deuteronomium: Entstehung, Gestalt und Botschaft*. Ed. N. Lohfink. BETL 68. Leuven: Leuven University Press. Pp. 164–73.

Childs, B. S. 1979. *Introduction to the Old Testament as Scripture*. Philadelphia: Fortress. Pp. 215–17.

Crump, W. 1974. "Dt. 7: A Covenant Sermon." *RestQ* 17:222–35.

Eslinger, L. 1987. "Watering Egypt (Deuteronomy xi 10–11)." *VT* 37:85–90.

Fretheim, T. E. 1968. "The Ark in Deuteronomy." *CBQ* 30:1–14.

Gammie, J. G. 1970. "The Theology of Retribution in the Book of Deuteronomy." *CBQ* 32:1–12.

Hoffman, Y. 1999. "The Deuteronomistic Concept of the Herem [Deut 7,1–7; 20,15–18]." *ZAW* 111:196–210.

Horowitz, H. L. 1975. "The Sh'ma Reconsidered." *Judaism* 24:476–81.

Isbell, C. 2003. "Deuteronomy's Definition of Jewish Learning." *JBQ* 31:109–16.

Ishida, T. 1979. "The Structure and Historical Implications of the Lists of Pre-Israelite Nations." *Bib* 60:461–90.

Janzen, J. G. 1987. "On the Most Important Word in the Shema (Deuteronomy vi 4–5)." *VT* 37:85–90.

Jones, R. C., Jr. 1992. "Deuteronomy 10:12–22." *Int* 46:281–85.

Lapsley, J. E. 2003. "Feeling Our Way: Love for God in Deuteronomy." *CBQ* 65:350–69.

McBride, S. D. 1973. "The Yoke of the Kingdom: An Exposition of Deuteronomy 6:4–5." *Int* 27:273–306.

McKay, J. W. 1972. "Man's Love for God in Deuteronomy and the Father/Teacher-Son/Pupil Relationship." *VT* 22:426–35.

Miller, P. D., Jr. 1984. "The Yoke of the Kingdom." *Iliff Review* 41:17–29.

Moberly, R. W. L. 1990. "'Yahweh Is One': The Translation of the Shema." In *Studies in the Pentateuch*. Ed. J. A. Emerton. VTSup 41. Leiden: Brill. Pp. 209–15.

———. 1999. "Toward an Interpretation of the Shema." In *Theological Exegesis: Essays in Honor of Brevard S. Childs*. Ed. C. Seitz and K. Greene-McCreight. Grand Rapids: Eerdmans. Pp. 124–44.

———. 2000. *The Bible, Theology, and Faith: A Study of Abraham and Jesus*. Cambridge: Cambridge University Press.

Moran, W. L. 1963. "The Ancient Near Eastern Background of the Love of God in Deuteronomy." *CBQ* 25:77–87.

———. 1967. "Conclusion of the Decalogue: Ex. 20:17–Dt. 5:21." *CBQ* 29:543–54.

———. 1969. "Deuteronomy." In *A New Catholic Commentary on Holy Scripture*. Ed. R. C. Fuller. Camden, N.J.: Nelson. Pp. 256–76.

Nelson, R. D. 1987. "Deuteronomy 5:1–15." *Int* 41:282–87.

———. 1997. "*Herem* and the Deuteronomic Social Conscience." In *Deuteronomy and Deuteronomic Literature: Festschrift C. H. W. Brekelmans*. Ed. M. Vervenne and J. Lust. BETL 133. Leuven: Leuven University Press. Pp. 39–54.

Nicol, G. G. 1988. "Watering Egypt (Deuteronomy xi 10–11) Again." *VT* 38:347–48.

O'Connell, R. H. 1990. "Deuteronomy viii 1–20: Asymmetrical Concentricity and the Rhetoric of Providence." *VT* 40:437–52.

———. 1992a. "Deuteronomy vii 1–26: Asymmetrical Concentricity and the Rhetoric of Conquest." *VT* 42:248–65.

———. 1992b. "Deuteronomy ix 7–x 7, 10–11: Panelled Structure, Double Rehearsal, and the Rhetoric of Covenant Rebuke." *VT* 42:492–509.

Orel, V. 1997. "The Words on the Doorpost." *ZAW* 109:614–17.

Peckham, B. 1975. "The Composition of Deuteronomy 9:1–10:11." In *Word and Spirit: Essays in Honor of David Michael Stanley, S.J., on His 60th Birthday*. Ed. J. Plevnik. Willowdale, Ont.: Regis College Press. Pp. 3–59.

Polzin, R. 1980. *Moses and the Deuteronomist: A Literary Study of the Deuteronomic History*. New York: Seabury.

Pressler, C. 1999. "The *Shema*ᶜ: A Protestant Feminist Reading." In *Escaping Eden: New Feminist Perspectives on the Bible*. Ed. H. C. Washington, S. L. Graham, and P. Thimmes. New York: New York University Press. Pp. 41–52.

Rad, G. von. 1966. *Deuteronomy: A Commentary*. Trans. D. Barton. OTL. Philadelphia: Westminster.

Tigay, J. H. 1996. *Deuteronomy: The Traditional Hebrew Text with the New JPS Translation*. JPS Torah Commentary. Philadelphia: The Jewish Publication Society.

Walsh, M. F. 1977. "Shema Yisrael: Reflections on Deuteronomy 6:4–9." *TBT* 90:1220–25.

Willis, J. T. 1973. "Man Does Not Live by Bread Alone: Dt. 8:3 and Mt. 4:4." *RestQ* 16:141–49.

Willoughby, B. E. 1977. "A Heartfelt Love: An Exegesis of Deuteronomy 6:4–19." *RestQ* 20:73–87.

Zipor, M. A. 1996. "The Deuteronomic Account of the Golden Calf and Its Reverberation in Other Parts of Deuteronomy." *ZAW* 108:20–33.

21

The Laws of Deuteronomy

Deuteronomy 12–26

The next fifteen chapters of Deuteronomy represent a long series of laws, some of which are duplicates from other legal sections of the Pentateuch, some of which are adaptations of other pentateuchal laws, and some of which are novel. As far back as 1:5 we read, "Moses undertook to explain this law" (RSV); however, what follows is not law but four chapters of historical review followed by an exhortation.

A phrase similar to that of 1:5 is repeated in 4:44, "This is the law which Moses set before the children of Israel" (RSV), but once again, what follows through ch. 11 is an amalgamation of historical reminiscences and appeals for obedience. (To be sure, the Sinaitic Decalogue is repeated in ch. 5.) What this historical background accomplishes is the provision of a foundation on which the laws themselves may be superimposed. The God who speaks a word of law (chs. 12–26) does so only after he has spoken a word of grace (chs. 1–11). The divine standards are not placed in a vacuum but are set against the bountiful resources of a gracious God. Additionally, Israel is to obey these laws not to *become* holy, but rather, because Israel *is* holy. The observance of law is a by-product of holiness, not a means of attaining holiness.

A perpetually vexing problem for interpreters has been the mostly futile attempts to decipher some significant order in the arrangement of the laws. Laws that seemingly have nothing to do with each other are placed in sequence. This phenomenon is particularly true in the last few chapters of this unit.

Earlier scholarship dismissed the issue as unsolvable. All that could be said of chs. 12–26 is that they were "without form and void," one massive tōhû wābōhû. The haphazardness of the Deuteronomic corpus was attributed to endless editorial activity. Subsequently, scholars began to see form where before only formlessness was apparent. But even here the attempt ended with mixed results.

For example, Gerhard von Rad (1962: 1:226 n. 86) divided the unit as follows: 12:1–16:17, cultic laws; 16:18–18:22, laws concerning officials (judge, king, priest, prophet); 19:1–21:9, laws for criminal cases; 21:10–22:30, regulations concerning families. Von Rad then put chs. 23–26 aside, for they had no demonstrable unity, no common theme to tie them together.

Similarly, the editor who, along with Moshe Weinfeld (1971: 1573), contributed the article on Deuteronomy to the *Encyclopaedia Judaica*, suggested the following outline: 12:1–16:17, ceremonial laws (agreeing with von Rad); 16:18–18:22, civil laws (again agreeing with von Rad); 19:1–21, criminal laws. But in this outline the cutoff point is ch. 20, for in chs. 20–26 there is no discernable order.

Jeffrey Tigay (1996: 446–49) has tried to see some basic units in all of 12–26. His divisions are: 12:2–16:17, the sanctuary and other religious matters; 16:18–18:22, civil and religious authorities; 19:1–21:9, judicial and military matters; 21:10–25:29, miscellaneous laws, mostly about civil and domestic life; 26:1–15, liturgical declarations.

Philosopher and conservative Norman Geisler (1977: 79) has proposed this outline: 12:1–16:17, ceremonial duties (agreeing with the other three suggested outlines); 16:18–20:20, civil duties; ch. 21, social duties to one's family; ch. 22, social duties to one's friends; chs. 23–25, social duties to the whole fellowship of Israel and strangers. The latter part of the outline is especially forced. For instance, if the point of ch. 22 is social duties to one's friends, what does this have to do with the law of a woman dressing like a man (22:5), or the law about the bird's nest with the mother bird and her young inside (22:6–7)?

Two studies appeared that either broke new ground for exploration or resurrected and refined long-abandoned ideas. Calum Carmichael (1974) believes that the laws of Deuteronomy are "the work of one hand and demonstrate a remarkable system of order and presentation." His proposal is to see within this unit a series of laws in which the arrangement proceeds on the same principle of arrangement as that in the Covenant Code (Exod. 21:2–23:19). Thus Carmichael detects in Deuteronomy 12–26 a series of Edomite laws, Egyptian laws, "rest" laws, and so forth.

Few scholars now consider the problem solved as a result of Carmichael's studies (see particularly the response of Levinson 1990). Interestingly, his proposal of the organizing principles within the legal corpus of Deuteronomy has been dismissed as much too arbitrary and fanciful. (To be sure, his thesis is quite ingenious at times, but should this disqualify his work from serious consideration, and is his thesis any more fanciful than others?)

A much more sober criticism of Carmichael than that of fanciful ingenuity is the observation that he still views chs. 12–26 as a group of unrelated segments, with no unity to the whole.

Stephen Kaufman has suggested that the arrangement of the laws is linked to the sequence of the Ten Commandments as listed in Deuteronomy 5. Kaufman (1979: 108–9, 147) states, "The thesis presented here is that the Law of Deuteronomy (chaps. 12–26) is a highly structured composition whose major topical units are arranged according to the order of the laws in the Decalogue. . . . It is a unified masterpiece of jurisprudential literature created by a single author . . . an expanded Decalogue."

Kaufman's divisions are as follows:

1. Commandments 1 and 2 (Deut. 5:6–10): no other gods and no idols = Deut. 12:1–28
2. Commandment 3 (Deut. 5:11): no misuse of Yahweh's name = Deut. 13:1–14:27
3. Commandment 4 (Deut. 5:12–15): keep the Sabbath day = Deut. 14:28–16:17
4. Commandment 5 (Deut. 5:16): honor parents = Deut. 16:18–18:22
5. Commandment 6 (Deut. 5:17): no homicide = Deut. 19:1–22:8
6. Commandment 7 (Deut. 5:18): no adultery (and illicit mixtures) = Deut. 22:9–23:18
7. Commandment 8 (Deut. 5:19): no theft (and other property violations) = Deut. 23:19–24:7
8. Commandment 9 (Deut. 5:20): no false testimony against a neighbor = Deut. 24:8–25:4
9. Commandment 10A (Deut. 5:21a): no coveting a neighbor's wife = Deut. 25:5–12
10. Commandment 10B (Deut. 5:21b): no coveting a neighbor's house = Deut. 25:13–16

Braulik (1993) also suggests that the key to the sequence of laws in chs. 12–26 is the sequence of the Decalogue, especially those laws that start in ch. 19 and thereafter. (Keep in mind that Braulik combines the first and second commandments into one, and he splits what is in most Protestant traditions the tenth commandment into numbers nine and ten.) His suggested divisions are:

1. Commandment 1 (Deut. 5:6–10) = Deut. 12:1–13:19
2. Commandment 2 (Deut. 5:11) = Deut. 14:1–21
3. Commandment 3 (Deut. 5:12–15) = Deut. 14:22–16:17
4. Commandment 4 (Deut. 5:16) = Deut. 16:18–18:22
5. Commandment 5 (Deut. 5:17) = Deut. 19:1–21:23
   [Transition: 22:1–12]
6. Commandment 6 (Deut. 5:18) = Deut. 22:13–23:14
   [Transition: 23:15–24:5]
7. Commandment 7 (Deut. 5:19) = Deut. 24:6–7
8. Commandment 8 (Deut. 5:20) = Deut. 24:8–25:4
9. Commandments 9 and 10 (Deut. 5:21) = Deut. 25:5–16

My preference is Kaufman's analysis. Indeed, some of the relationships seem stronger than others, and perhaps at times a proposed relationship between laws themselves and how the unit relates to a particular commandment may be forced. But Kaufman's thesis does "unify" chs. 12–26, and it connects these specific laws to the Sinaitic Decalogue sounded in ch. 5, thus suggesting even a larger degree of homogeneity for this second speech of Moses (chs. 5–26).

Worship in the Right Way (12)

Perhaps more has been written about this particular chapter than any other in the legal corpus of Deuteronomy. The reason for this is the frequently made assertion that the core theme of Deuteronomy—centralization of worship—is most clearly articulated in this chapter. Indeed, the phrase "the place which the LORD will choose" appears six times: 12:5, 11, 14, 18, 21, 26 (plus three times in ch. 14 [vv. 23, 24, 25], one time in ch. 15 [v. 20], six times in ch. 16 [vv. 2, 6, 7, 11, 15, 16], two times in ch. 17 [vv. 8, 10], one time in chs. 18 [v. 6], 26 [v. 2], and 31 [v. 11]—a total of twenty-one occurrences).

Added to this prominent phrase is the extended phrase "to put [śûm] his name there" (12:5, 21; also 14:24) or "to make his name dwell [šākan] there" (12:11; also 14:23; 16:2, 6, 11; 26:2). Isaiah 18:7 reflects such phraseology when it refers to Mount Zion as "the place of the Name of the LORD Almighty."

Much has been made of the emphasis on both the "cult centralization" and "name theology" of Deuteronomy. Those who hold tenaciously to the dominance of centralization in Deuteronomy feel, of course, that the place where God puts his name is Jerusalem. Solomon later says as much (1 Kings 8:29), and so does Yahweh to Solomon (1 Kings 9:3) on the occasion of the dedication of the Solomonic temple in Jerusalem. It has been proposed that Josiah used religious reform as a cover for his real motives in supporting this centralization reform. For part of the reform involves "bringing there your burnt offerings and your sacrifices, your tithes and your donations" (12:6 NRSV). In the words of W. G. Claburn (1973: 15), "How does an ambitious king get his hands on the largest possible proportion of the peasantry's agricultural surplus? By reforming the fiscal system so that he brings into the capital a larger proportion of the taxes already being assessed." Thus, in one sweep Claburn portrays Josiah as a racketeer and a charlatan, a characterization not borne out by the material in Kings and Chronicles. I cite this as an illustration of the possibilities for flights of exegetical imagination when centralization is made the core theme of Deuteronomy. Even von Rad (1966: 89) points out that "there are, after all, a large number of ordinances which neither mention the demand for centralization nor even seem to be at all aware of it."

The name theology of Deuteronomy—"he will put his name there"—is intriguing. It is God's name, not God himself, that is there. Is this an attempt on the part of Deuteronomy to moderate more explicit references elsewhere in Scripture to the effect that God himself dwells in the tabernacle or temple? Von Rad's (1966: 90) comment is again illustrative: "The idea must therefore be understood as a protest against popular conceptions of the actual presence of Yahweh at the sanctuary." Weinfeld (1972: 193–209) seconds the interpretation and utilizes the name theology as an additional indication of the demythologization process at work in Deuteronomy. According to this analysis, the emphasis on name theology is essentially a polemic against corporeal conceptions of God.

But is that so? The phrase "to put one's name," or a variation of it, is not unique to Scripture. Gordon Wenham (1971: 113) observes that in cuneiform literature the expression has at least three nuances, being used in (1) an affirmation of ownership, the equivalent of taking possession; (2) in texts describing conquests, also associated with the erection of victory monuments; (3) in the inscription of a name on the foundation stones of sanctuaries.

Any one of these three is applicable to Deuteronomy. The place where God is to be worshiped is his possession. Is the shift from something as God's dwelling place to that same thing as God's possession really a move away from the anthropomorphic? And what could be more suitable than for God to put his own signature on the place of worship? For God is "a cornerstone chosen and precious, and whoever believes in him will not be put to shame" (1 Pet. 2:6).

J. G. McConville (1979) suggests that the idiom of Deuteronomy vis-à-vis God's dwelling is simply a complementary way of speaking about God's presence found elsewhere in Scripture. To take but one example, when the Bible speaks of dramatic, exceptional revelations of God, it tends to speak of God's "glory." When the Bible speaks of times of regular devotion and meeting with God, it tends to use God's "name." So why does Deuteronomy use "name" many times and "glory" only once (5:24)? The reason is, according to McConville (1979: 161), "Deuteronomy deals with what is to be the routine of worship in daily life in the new land," for which the placing of God's name rather than God's glory is more appropriate.

Finally, if Deuteronomy attempts to establish that it is only God's name, not God himself, that dwells in the place of worship, what are we to do with phrases such as "the LORD your God walks in the midst of your camp" (23:14 RSV); "he shall dwell . . . in your midst" (23:16 RSV); "your males shall appear before the LORD your God" (16:16 NRSV); "you shall set it down before the LORD your God" (26:10 NRSV)? God's name does not walk in the camp; God's name does not dwell in the midst; one does not appear before the name of the Lord or present an offering before the name of the Lord.

Chapter 12 is a series of contrasts. First, there is the contrast between "here" (v. 8) and "there" (v. 7). Once they are in the land of promise, the Israelites will undergo changes: "You shall not act as we are acting here today, all of us according to our own desires" (v. 8 NRSV). Second, there is a contrast between "their gods" (v. 2) and "your God" (v. 4), between "their name" (v. 3) and "his name" (v. 5), and between all the "places" of false worship (vv. 2–3) and "the place" that the Lord will choose.

This second contrast seems to suggest that the real issue in this chapter is not one sanctuary versus many sanctuaries, but rather pure worship versus false worship. To that end, the chapter begins (vv. 2–4) and ends (vv. 29–31) with notes about pagan icons and religious practices. Israel's worship must have neither. Israel's religious observance is to be characterized by rejoicing (vv. 7, 12, 18), ostensibly because it has nothing of the macabre in it.

And in the midst of a chapter given over to concerns about worship—and what more appropriate subject with which to begin the legal corpus?—there is also a substantial discussion of observances at home (vv. 15–28). For example, "You may . . . eat flesh . . . as much as you desire" (vv. 15, 21 RSV). Even the verb used for "kill" is *zābaḥ*, a verb used 129 times in the Old Testament and almost exclusively for sacrificial slaughter (see Milgrom 1976: 1). May we infer from this that even eating in one's home with one's family, enjoying the physical blessings of God, is also a sacrament? For even here God has a directive to give: in worship, eliminate the false gods; in eating, eliminate the blood (vv. 16, 23). Raze the false altars and pillars, and pour the blood on the ground.

The Temptation of Idolatry (13)

In this chapter the concern of Moses is still with purity of worship. In ch. 12 the emphasis was on idolatry; here the emphasis is on the idolater. In the case of the former, Israel is to demolish all places and relics associated with idolatry. But what if the temptation is not from one of the silent Asherim or cult images, but instead is from a vocal prophet (13:1–5), a family member (13:6–11), or evangelistic rabble-rousers (13:12–18)? In each instance Israel's response is to be quick and decisive: such persons "shall be put to death" (vv. 5, 9–10, 15–17). Even a whole community may be the object of a holy war if it allows itself to be swayed. There is no indication that subsequent repentance is an option that alleviates the recrimination.

In each of the three paragraphs a different reason is given that makes the temptation all the more enticing. In vv. 1–5 the impressive thing is that the temptation is accompanied by a sign or a wonder. Might Jesus have had this passage in mind when he spoke of forthcoming false messiahs and prophets who would show great signs and wonders that appear so authentic as to befuddle even the elect (Matt. 24:24)?

In the second paragraph (vv. 6–11) it is the source of the temptation that is powerful to resist. Indeed, foes may arise from within one's own household, or inner circle of friends, or relatives, to whom one may have to say: "Get behind me, Satan!" (cf. Mark 8:33). Chapter 12 highlights the home as a place of worship, rejoicing, and festivity. Chapter 13 presents a darker side of the home. It may be a place of temptation, a stumbling block rather than a stepping-stone.

The third possibility that makes the temptation to idolatry so alluring is statistics (vv. 12–18). The masses have adopted the heretical teachings of the "base fellows," or "wicked fellows," or literally, "sons of worthlessness." Can they all be wrong? Can a whole community be swayed? Can there be mass apostasy? Yes. But mass sin must inevitably lead to mass repercussions, if indeed all the facts and allegations have been thoroughly checked ("you shall inquire and make search and ask diligently" [v. 14 RSV]) and found to be true. Pentateuchal law makes provision, via a sin offering, for the forgiveness of the sins of a "whole Israelite community" (Lev. 4:13 NIV), but only for sins perpetrated unintentionally. Idolatry and apostasy do not fall into that category.

Holiness and Stewardship (14)

The movement in ch. 14 is from cause to effect. The cause is "You are the children of the LORD your God" (v. 1a NIV); the effect is your response to death (v. 1b), your eating habits (vv. 3–21), and your handling of your possessions (vv. 22–29).

In half a verse (v. 1b) the Mosaic law prohibits a pagan mourning custom: self-laceration or the shaving of a bare spot on the forehead. Might the insertion of this prohibition here be related to the notes of the previous chapter regarding putting to death or putting to the sword those who inspire or embrace idolatry? Especially in the case of the enticing relative, the extra warning is given that "your eye shall not pity" such a person. The strong language of ch. 13 is "must be put to death" (vv. 5, 9) and "destroy completely" (v. 15).

The chapter is still concerned with the idea that Israel is to be distinctive, different in many ways from neighbors (see v. 2). In ch. 12 the temptation is from idolatrous objects that are quite visible. In ch. 13 the temptation takes the form of verbal encouragement from an apostate. In ch. 14, however, there are no enticers encouraging the Israelites to shave their foreheads or eat forbidden foods. Israel is to get rid of the pillars (12:3) of the Canaanites, but not the pelicans (14:17).

The concern of this chapter, then, is that Israel shun not only the blatantly wicked things (chs. 12–13) but also the apparently more innocent and innocuous things: showing respect for the dead via a particular gesture, or avoiding certain meats. It is of no little significance that the section on clean animals is introduced with this phrase: "You shall not eat any detestable thing" (14:3 NASB). The Hebrew word for "detestable thing" is *tôʿēbâ*, which most often in Deuteronomy is used in reference to Canaanite practices, where the translation usually is "an abomination." For other references to *tôʿēbâ* in Deuteronomy that involve some kind of idolatry or Canaanite practices, see 7:25–26; 13:14; 18:12; 20:18; 22:5 (?); 23:18; 27:15; 32:16. By contrast, in Leviticus *tôʿēbâ* refers only to forms of unlawful sexual relations (Lev. 18:22, 26, 27, 29, 30; 20:13). The parallel chapter in Leviticus (ch. 11) about food laws uses the word *šeqeṣ* for "abomination," not the word used here. Thus Deuteronomy 14 deliberately uses a word that elsewhere in the book primarily designates acts of perversion by the Canaanites. Presumably the list of permitted and prohibited animals for food has something to do with that lifestyle, but beyond that we are unable to go.

We observe that the sequence of forbidden foods is identical in Leviticus 11 and Deuteronomy 14:3–21:

> four-footed land animals (Lev. 11:2–8; Deut. 14:4–8)
>
> water creatures (Lev. 11:9–12; Deut. 14:9–10)
>
> birds (Lev. 11:13–19; Deut. 14:11–18)
>
> flying insects (Lev. 11:20–23; Deut. 14:19–20)

The second half of the chapter is concerned with tithing: the annual tithe (vv. 22–27) and the triennial tithe (vv. 28–29; and see 26:12–14). In a seven-year cycle the first was presented in the first, second, fourth, and fifth years. The second was given in the third and sixth years. There is no tithe from the produce of the ground in the seventh year, for in that year there is neither planting nor harvesting (Exod. 23:10–11; Lev. 25:2–7). The concern is still with food, except that the emphasis has moved from meat to seed and grains. There is also a shift from the negative (do not worship that, or do not eat that) to the positive (tithe).

The tithe is in the form of produce, but under certain conditions (a far distance to travel to the central sanctuary) the tithe could be converted into money, which was easier to carry (v. 25). The pilgrim is even given a traveling allowance: "eat the tithe" (v. 23), and "spend the money for whatever you desire" (v. 26 RSV).

Sacred and festive celebrations must not become a time only for self and family. This is a time for opening the doors and inviting to one's table the penny-scraping Levite, the indigent sojourner, the fatherless, the widow. Getting rid of the wrong company brings God's blessing (13:17–18), and welcoming the right company brings God's blessing (14:29b).

The *Personae Miserabiles* (15)

Three items are discussed in this chapter: the Sabbatical Year (vv. 1–11); guidelines for owners of slaves (vv. 12–18); and the sacrifice of firstlings, (vv. 19–23), a law whose current positioning in the corpus might at first sight seem out of place and somewhat intrusive.

Deuteronomy 14:22 spoke of what Israel is to do with possessions "year by year." Deuteronomy 14:28 mentioned what Israel is to do with possessions "every three years." This emphasis on time continues into ch. 15: "at the end of every seven years" (15:1), and then follows a commentary on observance of the Sabbatical Year.

This particular year was initially described in Exod. 23:10–11. There the emphasis was on allowing the land to lie fallow for the sake of the poor and the animals, but it said nothing about remitting the debts of the poor (as does Deut. 15:1–6) or lending to the poor (as does Deut. 15:7–11). A second emphasis is found in Lev. 25:1–7. The land, or rotating portions thereof, is to lie fallow every seventh year. It is to be a rest for the land that "I [the LORD] give" (Lev. 25:2). The crop that grows by itself will provide the necessary food for both the family and the indigent (Lev. 25:6).

Chapter 15 of Deuteronomy adds yet another factor. In the Sabbatical Year there is to be a remission of debts (15:2). Presumably, this particular directive would be applicable only to a number of people, for in any given society what is the ratio between creditors and population? The additional stipulation about debt cancellation also envisions more clearly a people who are about to move into a more complex, highly developed society in which economics will play a larger role than before. This will include the accumulation of equity, financial security, and the borrowing, lending, and investment of money.

Moses once again becomes something of an exhorter. His caution to Israel is, "Take heed lest there be a base thought in your heart" (15:9 RSV). This is rather close to earlier warnings: "Beware lest you say in your heart, 'My power . . .'" (8:17 RSV) and "Do not say in your heart, . . . 'It is because of my righteousness . . .'" (9:4 RSV).

There is more to the Sabbatical Year than the cancellation of debts. It is insufficient simply to erase the financial obligations that others owe. There must be a sharing of one's possessions with the poor (15:7–8). This becomes particularly important as a Sabbatical Year approaches (15:9). It would be possible at this time to refuse a loan to someone in need. But Deuteronomy says to the Israelites: if a person in need requests a loan on the last day of the sixth year, the eve of the Sabbatical Year, meet that person's needs, even if it means having to cancel the debt the next day.

Few passages in Deuteronomy, or elsewhere, remind us more forcibly of the difference between the ideal world (in which we may wish to live) and the sinful, fallen world (in which we do live) than does 15:1–11. Verse 4 states, on the one hand, that "there should be no poor among you" (NIV). Verse 7 says, on the other hand, "if there is a poor person in your community," and v. 11 says that "there will always be poor people in the land" (NIV, quoted by Jesus in Matt. 26:11; Mark 14:7). Thus in one paragraph the Scripture can say almost in one breath that "there should not be any poor" and that "there will always be the poor." This juxtapositioning of mutually exclusive statements is a reminder that biblical law is addressed to people where they are rather than where they ought to be. The larger context for biblical law is not only a redeemed, paradisaical society but also a fallen society "curved in on itself" (*curvatus in se*), to use a phrase from Luther.

From a discussion of the Sabbatical Year we turn to a law about slavery in vv. 12–18. At many points it is similar to the law of Exod. 21:2–11, but at other points it is distinctly different. First, the Exodus law treats male slaves and female slaves separately (Exod. 21:2–6, 7–11), but here they are treated together: "a Hebrew man or a Hebrew woman" (Deut. 15:12 NRSV). Second, the version in Exodus holds out release for the male slave after six years, but not for the female slave: "she shall not go out as the male slaves do" (Exod. 21:7 NRSV; cf. 21:2).

Third, if the male slave decides to remain, he has that option in Exod. 21:5. In Deut. 15:17b ("do the same for your maidservant" NIV) that privilege is extended to the female slave. Fourth, and an extension of the third point, the male slave who agrees to stay with his master is to have his ear pierced (Exod. 21:6). That ceremony is also for the remaining female slave in Deut. 15:17b: "do the same for your maidservant." Fifth, in Exod. 21:6 the master pierces his servant's ear only after "he has brought him to God" (the KJV and the NIV have "judges" rather than "God" for *'ĕlōhîm*). This note is absent in this account. Yet a sixth difference is that the master must provide his servant with a gift rather than release the servant empty-handed (vv. 13–14). Exodus 21:2 says nothing about this.

More light (or complication?) is thrown on the whole area of slavery by the emphatic note in Lev. 25:39b that an Israelite could not make a fellow Israelite serve as a slave. Slaves were to be taken only from the nations and non-Israelites in Canaan (Lev. 25:44–45). In only two instances could an Israelite become the servant of another Israelite: voluntarily, by selling oneself because of abject poverty (Lev. 25:39a), or compulsorily, in the case of a thief who is unable to make restitution and thus must be sold to pay for the theft (Exod. 22:3).

Two ramifications follow from this. First, the law of Exod. 21:2–11, "when you buy a Hebrew slave" (RSV), may refer not to a Hebrew slave, but to a Habiru slave, those second-millennium B.C. migratory peoples who often hired themselves out as mercenaries or servants. Certainly Israelites could "buy" slaves from this stock.

Second, the emphasis of Lev. 25:39a, "he sells himself," demonstrates that the NRSV translation of Deut. 15:12, "if your brother, a Hebrew man, or a Hebrew woman, is sold to you" (cf. KJV, NKJV), is incorrect. It can only be "if your brother sells himself to you." The Hebrew *yimmākēr* translates naturally with reflexive nuance, rather than passive nuance, in this instance. If the passive voice of the verb is retained, then the most likely reference would be to an indigent father who unavoidably has had to sell his son or daughter.

Thus, the slave law of Deuteronomy 15 is concerned with the Israelite who has slipped to the bottom rung of the economic ladder. He must sell himself to another Israelite. But he is not to become automatically his wealthier compatriot's permanent ward or possession. In seven years he is to be freed and to be provided for liberally. So the slave law perpetuates the theme, started in this chapter by the teaching about the Sabbatical Year, that the covenant community is to make a special place within its gates for the poor. They must not be abused. They must not be abandoned. They are to be helped financially, and not with parsimonious pinches.

The third paragraph deals with the sacrifice of firstlings of the herd and flock (vv. 19–23). Why place this law here, especially when there has already been a reference to firstlings in 12:17? Stephen Kaufman (1979: 132) makes three interesting associations. Only Deuteronomy mentions that the firstling is not to be "worked" (15:19), an appropriate reference on the heels of the law about slaves who have "worked" for a fellow Israelite (15:12, 18). Deuteronomy 15:19 limits the firstlings of the "herd and flock," the same animals to be used in the Passover (16:2). (Exodus 12:5 limited the animals to yearling sheep or goats.) Deuteronomy 15:21 prohibits the consecration of animals that are, among other things, "lame." The Hebrew word for "lame" is *pissēaḥ*, very close in sound to *pesaḥ*, Passover, the item under discussion in the next chapter.

Also, this section is part of a longer one concerning things that are to be done a certain number of times each year or every certain number of years:

Tithe: "each year" (14:22)
Triennial tithe: "at the end of every three years" (14:28)
Debt remission: "at the end of every seven years" (15:1)
Slave release: "in the seventh year" (15:12)
Sacrifice of firstlings: "each year" (15:20)
Pilgrimage festivals: "three times a year" (16:16)

There are also a number of parallels between 14:22–29 (the tithe law) and 15:19–23 (offering of firstlings). Both describe something that is to be done "each year" (14:22; 15:20). Both refer to "the firstborn of herds and flocks" (14:23; 15:19). Both refer to something that is to be done "at the place God will choose" (14:23, 24, 25; 15:20). Both mention that the donor of the tithes/firstlings may "eat" what is brought to God (14:23; 15:22).

Thus a nice A-B-B′-A′ arrangement of two groups of related laws appears in 14:22–15:23:

A Giving of the tithe (14:22–24)
B Release of debts (15:1–11)
B′ Release of slaves (15:12–18)
A′ Giving of firstlings (15:19–23)

Three Sacred Feasts (16)

Clusters of three are frequent in this immediate section of Deuteronomy. We have seen three references to years: every year, every third year, every seventh year (chs. 14 and 15). Clean and unclean animals are from the categories of land creatures, birds, and fish (ch. 14). Three possible sources of idolatry are presented (ch. 13). There are three references to not eating the blood (12:16, 23; 15:23). In both chs. 12 and 16 there are six uses of the phrase "the place which the LORD your God will choose" (also three times in ch. 14).

Chapter 16 continues this emphasis by again drawing attention to the three major festivals to be observed throughout the year: the Feast of Passover and Unleavened Bread (vv. 1–8), the Feast of Weeks (vv. 9–12), and the Feast of Tabernacles (vv. 13–15). Then follows a summarizing statement in vv. 16–17: "Three times a year all your males shall appear before the LORD . . ." (NRSV). Just as one is not to let a slave leave the home "empty-handed" (15:13), neither is one to appear before the Lord "empty-handed" (16:16). Giving to the poor (15:7–11) is matched by giving to the Lord (16:17). Not only is there a triennial tithe for the Levite, the sojourner, the fatherless, and the widow (14:28–29); there is also the communal celebration of the Lord's feasts (16:11, 14). There is the offering for the poor, but there is also joint worship with the poor. Male and female, free and servant, rich and poor, married and single are all together under one roof in worship.

The actual description of the festivals in this chapter is fairly close to, but not exactly identical with, that in other books of the Pentateuch (for which see Exod. 12:1–28, 43–49; 23:14–19; 34:18–26; Lev. 23:1–43; Num. 9:1–14; 28:1–29:39). In the Passover Moses' directions about the employment of the blood of the lamb, spelled out quite clearly in Exodus 12, are omitted from this chapter (for the obvious reason that observance has moved from private homes to the sanctuary), but so are a number of other items. Commentators such as Moshe Weinfeld use such comparisons to buttress their point that Deuteronomy represents a move to secularization. On the other hand, if indeed Deuteronomy demonstrates this trend, what is to be said for the fact that Deuteronomy repeats what Exod. 23:17 and 34:24 mention about Passover being an observance limited to the place that God will choose, instead of being a home observance as spelled out in Exod. 12:3–4, 7? This hardly seems to be a move toward secularization.

Three other differences especially between Passover in Exodus 12 and here are as follows: (1) Exod. 12:9 says that the Passover sacrifice is not to be "cooked/boiled" (*bāšal*) in water, but "roasted." By contrast, Deut. 16:7 says that the sacrifice is to be "cooked/boiled" (*bāšal*). Second Chronicles 35:13 mentions that King Josiah boiled/roasted (*bāšal*) the Passover animals "over the fire," suggesting that *bāšal* refers to any kind of cooking preparation, boiling or roasting. (2) Exodus 12:3–5 limits the Passover sacrifice to a lamb from one's flock, whereas Deut. 16:2 permits "an animal from your flock and herd." This difference likewise has an explanation. Possibly the animals from the herd are for additional sacrifices made on this occasion. Tigay (1996: 153–54) offers two other suggestions. One is that while the Israelites were in Egypt, with celebration in the home, a small animal would suffice for most families. Deuteronomy anticipates a time when hosts of families will celebrate together, hence the need for a larger animal. Or, maybe in Egypt the Israelites owned primarily sheep and goats, but Deuteronomy anticipates a time when larger cattle will be raised as well. (3) A third, and more important, difference is that Exodus 12 treats Passover and the Feast of Unleavened Bread as two distinct events (12:1–13 and 12:14–20). Deuteronomy 16 combines and splices them: Passover (16:1–2); Unleavened Bread (16:3–4a); Passover (16:4b–7); Unleavened Bread (16:8). While almost all commentators agree on this amalgamation, there is disagreement over whether Deuteronomy reflects a very early combination of two originally separate celebrations for the first time (McConville 2000), or whether Deuteronomy reflects a much later combination of these two, say, around the time of King Josiah in the late 600s B.C. (Levinson 2000).

The summarizing statement in v. 16 that "three times a year all your *men* must appear before the LORD" (NIV) is a repeat of Exod. 23:17. It cannot mean that women are excluded from corporate worship. For one thing, vv. 11 and 14 include "your daughters" and "your maidservants" as co-celebrants on these festal occasions. Furthermore, Deut. 12:12, 18 include the same groups in community worship, while Deut. 12:7 speaks of the participation of "you and your families," and Deut. 14:26 speaks of "you and your household." Perhaps the participation of adult males was mandatory, and that of other members of the household voluntary, especially for at-risk individuals such as young children or pregnant/nursing mothers, for whom a long pilgrimage to the sanctuary would be too taxing. It is also likely that this emphasis on "men/males" highlights the major role of the father in such household/communal celebrations at the sanctuary.

Chapter 16 concludes with two brief paragraphs that might more appropriately be discussed under ch. 17. One paragraph is about the appointment of judges (vv. 18–20); the other is a note about avoiding pagan worship practices (vv. 21–22).

Indeed, vv. 18–20 deal partly with the selection of judges, who are to "judge the people with righteous judgment" (RSV). But most of the paragraph is about the people themselves, not the judges—"you," not "they." All Israelites are to be judgelike in their behavior, above partiality or bribes, and followers of justice.

Public Officials (17)

As we saw, the laws about administrative personnel began in 16:18 with the directive to appoint judges and officers. Then come three statements about false worship: do not plant a tree as an Asherah (16:21); do not set up a pillar (16:22); do not sacrifice a blemished animal (17:1). This is followed by a statement about the penalty for idolatry after a thorough investigation of the allegation and the provision of testimony from at least two witnesses (17:2–7); next comes the description of a supreme tribunal that is to handle cases that are too complex for local judges (17:8–13).

It might appear that the three laws about improper worship in 16:21, 22 and 17:1 interrupt the flow of 16:18–20 (the appointment of local judiciaries) and 17:2–7 (the implementation of justice at the local level), and would fit better somewhere in 12:1–16:17, with its emphasis on proper worship. This is hardly the case. There are some prominent vocabulary links between the sections. Both 17:1 and 17:4 speak of something that is "detestable" or a "detestable thing," the Hebrew word for which is *tôʿēbâ*. Again, in 17:1 the Hebrew for "flaw" is *dābār rāʿ*, while the Hebrew for "evil deed" in 17:5 is *haddābār hārāʿ*. But more importantly, as Stephen Kaufman (1979: 133–34) has observed, there is a natural flow in the material: (1) a general prescription to provide honest local judges (16:18–20); (2) prohibitions against false worship (16:21–17:1); (3): a case law instructing the judges in regard to worship violations (17:2–7). Thus, the arrangement of the legal materials so far is worship (12:1–16:17), justice (16:18–20), worship (16:21–17:1), justice

(17:2–7, 8–13). These are the two foci that make the people of God a true and faithful community. Worship without justice is Pharisaical; justice without worship leads to legalism.

Thus the order is the appointment of local judges (16:18–20); forbidden pagan methods of worship (16:21–17:1); the trial, conviction, and sentencing of idolaters before local courts (17:2–7); a tribunal at the central sanctuary, with both clergy and laity as members, to adjudicate complex legal disputes (17:8–13). The last few verses of the chapter (vv. 14–20) constitute Deuteronomy's law of the king. The first official described in this unit is the judge, who is to be appointed by the people (16:18), voted into office. By contrast, the king is chosen by the Lord (17:15).

It seems unnecessary to say that this unique law could have been composed only long after the Judean and Israelite monarchy was in existence, and in a decaying state at that. This is, of course, the position taken by almost all critical scholars. Is it not reasonable that somewhere in the space of this 120 years Moses had ample opportunities, both inside and outside Egypt, to observe the theatrics of oriental despots who reveled in their luxurious lifestyles? This observation of Moses becomes the basis and the background for the qualifying restrictions placed on the Israelite monarch, whose activity is described first negatively (vv. 15–17), then positively (vv. 18–20).

Von Rad (1966: 120) observes correctly, "Deuteronomy sees in kingship not an office which Yahweh could use for the welfare of the people, but only an institution in which the holder must live in a sphere of extreme peril because he is tempted by his harem or his wealth either to turn away from Yahweh or 'to lift up his heart above his brethren.'" A heart turned away from the Lord will produce a heart lifted up above one's people. Earlier, the people of Israel as a whole had been warned about saying in their heart, "My power has gotten me this wealth" (8:17). Both Israel and its head of state are potentially vulnerable at this point.

Positively, the king is to write, then read, regularly from "a copy of this law" (v. 18). P. C. Craigie (1976: 256) suggests three possibilities for "this law": the law of Deuteronomy, Deuteronomy as a whole or a certain section of it, or the original document of the Sinai covenant (Exodus 20–24). Regardless of which it is, the purpose of such a document is to remind the king of his subordinate status. He is not autonomous. He is not God, but only an instrument of God.

This law about the king is structured much like the law about worship in ch. 12, as Carmichael (1974: 104–5) has observed. In these two instances the people, once in the land, will make public an intention or request: "I would like some meat" (12:20 NIV); "Let us set a king over us" (17:14 NIV). God grants permission: "You may eat as much flesh as you desire" (12:20b RSV); "You may indeed set as king over you" (17:15 RSV). But there is a qualification attached to the permission: "You must not eat the blood" (12:16 NIV); "He must not multiply horses/wives/large amounts of silver and gold" (17:16–17). Thus some continuity is provided between these laws and the order and structure of their formulation. Carmichael calls it "repetition."

The placement of the law of the king (17:14–20) on the heels of a lengthy discussion of worship and justice (12:1–17:13) is interesting. We might expect some part of 17:14–20 to address the responsibilities of the king in these two areas. Normally in the ancient biblical world the king supervised both the public worship and the system of jurisprudence practiced throughout the land. The lack of such provisions in Deuteronomy 17 is an illustration of how Scripture presents not just a revised picture of Israel's monarchy, but a radical revision of such an institution that is hardly recognizable by its counterparts.

Priests and Prophets (18)

From the "secular" offices of judge and king Deuteronomy now turns to a discussion of the "religious" offices of priest (vv. 1–8) and prophet (vv. 9–22). All four offices illustrate the two ways in which individuals assumed prominent positions: charismatic (judge); hereditary (king); hereditary (priest and Levite); charismatic (prophet).

Unlike the previous two chapters, which emphasized mostly the necessary qualities of those holding the position of judge or king, ch. 18 says nothing about the quality of life for the priest and the Levite. Instead, the preoccupation of these verses is how these religious workers will be provided for. Since they have no patrimony, how will they live? As such, a word is spoken about all Levites (vv. 1–2), Levites who are also priests at the sanctuary (vv. 3–5), and nonpriestly provincial Levites (vv. 6–8). Consistently the emphasis is on their privileges of ministry and what the people are to give them as their dues. Just as Israel is totally dependent upon God for their well-being, so the priests and Levites are totally dependent upon the people of God for their well-being. Israel may have no other god(s), and the Levitical priests may have no other means of livelihood. Elsewhere Deuteronomy does spell out the responsibilities of the Levite. He is to carry the ark (10:8; 31:9, 25), and he has charge of the written law that guides the king (17:18). The closest that the actual law of the priest or Levite comes to outlining specific responsibilities is: "he may minister in the name of the LORD his God" (18:7 NRSV). But principally the law is for the benefit of the laity, not the clergy.

Before discussing the law of the prophet, Deuteronomy first lists various techniques employed by paganism for obtaining divine oracles (vv. 9–14). These are not the ways by which Israel will detect the voice of the Lord. What these banned items have in common is that they fall into the category of human wisdom and ingenuity. Yehezkel Kaufmann (1960: 43) rightly calls divination "a science of cosmic secrets," and the diviner "a 'scientist' who can dispense with 'divine revelation.'"

By contrast, the Lord will raise up as his medium of revelation a prophet. Like the king, he is to be from among the Israelite community (18:15; 17:15). He is able to speak only because God has put his word in his mouth (17:19; quite close to what the Lord later would say to a balking Jeremiah [Jer. 1:9]). That God, so to speak, feeds his word into the mouth of his prophets explains why so many of them introduce their pronouncements with "The word of the Lord came unto me" or "Thus says the Lord." By contrast, it is rare for anyone else in Scripture, Old and New Testaments, to preface and validate their remarks with this formula. It is one thing to affirm the inspiration of Scripture; it is another thing to understand how God inspired Scripture. But with the prophets there is no doubt: God inspired the prophets by dictating to them his word, by putting his word in their mouth so that what a prophet says, God says.

This prophet will resemble Moses. Here is one of the very few instances in the legal section of Deuteronomy where Moses speaks about himself as if he is a paradigm: "The Lord your God will raise up for you a prophet like me. . . . 'I [God] will raise up for them a prophet like you'" (18:15, 18 nrsv). This is the one office described by Moses in which he specifies a particular model—himself. He is the prototype. Moses here is either exhibiting the height of arrogance or telling the truth about himself, his uniqueness, and his influence as a model of future generations. Understandably, then, Peter's preaching at Pentecost points to the second Moses (Acts 3:20–25; see also 7:37). And just as the people dare ignore the first Moses only at their peril (Deut. 18:19), so to turn against the second Moses will bring even a greater retribution, but a retribution that can be mitigated by repentance.

One might assume from reading Deut. 12:1–16:17 that worship is all about the individual's direct access to God—Yahweh and me, or Yahweh and my family. Chapter 18, however, reminds us that no one goes it alone. The legitimate truth of the "priesthood of all believers" does not make superfluous those servants of God set apart by God to help the rest of us get to God and hear from God. We need a priest who will represent us before God (18:1–8), and we need a prophet who will represent God before us (18:14–22). Along with judges and kings they are parental figures whom we are to honor.

Dealing with Crime and Violence (19)

Verses 1–13 prescribe the setting up of six cities of refuge, three immediately on the west side of the Jordan, with the possibility of adding three additional cities in the future (v. 9b)—something, by the way, that never happened, ostensibly because of disobedience. This phenomenon has already been described briefly in Exod. 21:12–14 (where the emphasis is on altar asylum rather than city asylum), and at greater length in Num. 35:9–28. Deuteronomy 4:41–43 has already covered the placement of three asylum cities in the Transjordan. These cities provide asylum for the manslayer but not for the murderer. The previous chapter distinguished between the true prophet and the false prophet, who is to be put to death. This idea of distinction is then carried into ch. 19, the distinction being between the unintentional murderer and the intentional murderer, for whom, as with the presumptuous prophet, the penalty is death. Once again, the laws of Deuteronomy presuppose a future Israel, components of which will be sinful Israel. Even among the elect and holy nation there will be, regrettably, crimes of passion and violence displaying utter contempt for the sanctity of the life of others.

Weinfeld (1972: 236–37) makes much of the fact that Deuteronomy, unlike Numbers 35, does not specify how long the manslayer must remain in the city of refuge: "and he shall live in it until the death of the high priest" (Num. 35:25, 28 RSV). Not only does Weinfeld see this as further secularization in Deuteronomy; he also speculates that the silent assumption of the Deuteronomic law is that the individual must remain in asylum "until the rage of the avenger subsides." But what if that never happens? Can the subjective mood of a person provide the basis for a law? May not Deuteronomy simply reproduce the law concerning asylum without also reproducing the high priest's part (Milgrom 1973: 159)?

From its discussion of the law about asylum, Deuteronomy proceeds to a one-sentence law about not removing a neighbor's landmark (v. 14) and a law about the evidence of witnesses, especially malicious witnesses (vv. 15–21). The thrust of the (at least) two-witnesses requirement is to prevent the possibility of anyone being falsely charged and condemned merely on the basis of hearsay or spurious testimony by a felonious witness. The first part of this chapter (vv. 1–13) is designed to restrain immediate and illegal blood vengeance against a person who has accidentally taken the life of another. The second half of the chapter (vv. 15–21) is designed to restrain wrongful conviction resulting from lack of sufficient verifiable and incriminating testimony. The penalty for false and malicious testimony is rather severe, as vv. 18–21 make clear. To be sure, there are some specific scenarios that this law does not address. For example, we know from the story in 1 Kings 21:9–14 that the (false) witness of two individuals could result in the execution of a completely innocent person (Naboth). So the presence of two witnesses does not guarantee accuracy and confirmation. Again, if a crime is witnessed by only one person, as often would have been the case, does that mean that the perpetrator(s) could not be brought to trial and punished?

The law about removing landmarks (an attempt by the rich to oppress the poor?) is found again in 27:17 and also in Wisdom literature (Prov. 22:28; 23:10). But how can it be related to the law that precedes and follows, and do the three laws in this chapter—asylum, removing landmarks, and witnesses—fit together?

Perhaps in the case of the first two laws there is some common vocabulary to tie them together. "You shall prepare the roads to them and divide into three parts the area [gĕbûl] of the land" (19:3 RSV), and "You shall not [re]move your neighbor's boundary stone [gĕbûl], which your predecessors have set [gābal]" (19:14).

Stephen Kaufman (1979: 137) suggests the following organization: how to deal with homicide (vv. 1–13); how to prevent homicide (v. 14); how to deal with the accusation of homicide (vv. 15–21). Obviously, the laws about both asylum and testimony have a common concern, that innocent blood not be shed, either by an avenger of blood or by a witness who commits perjury against a defendant.

War Exemptions and Executions (20)

Chapter 19 discussed the taking of life when one kills a neighbor unintentionally or in hate, and a civil procedure against a malicious witness. The theme now continues into ch. 20, in which the general theme is war.

The first half of the chapter (vv. 1–9) is composed primarily of an exhortation by the priest—here in a unique role outside the sanctuary—to the soldiers to be courageous (vv. 2–4), and an offer by the officers to allow some to disqualify themselves for military service (vv. 5–9).

The list of those exempted from serving in the army is interesting: a man who has recently built a new house that has not yet been dedicated, or in which he has not yet started to dwell; a man who has planted a vineyard and has not enjoyed its harvest yet; a man who is engaged to be married; and those who are fearful and fainthearted (see Gideon's words to the fearful in Judg. 7:3). The first three categories of exemption are quite normal. It is somewhat unexpected to find an able-bodied man reclassified as unfit for service simply on the basis of being afraid. But who would want to serve in the trenches with a man given to panic under duress? He is best exempted from duty or assigned to a noncombat position. Nowhere does the Book of Joshua, when describing the wars of conquest in Canaan in chs. 6–11, ever mention such deferrals. But why should it? The purpose of Joshua 6–11 is to narrate military triumphs, not military exemptions.

Of particular interest is the possible impact of this part of Deuteronomy on the Gospel of Luke. In *Studies in the Gospels*, C. F. Evans (1955: 37–53) suggested that Luke 9:51–18:14 is a Christian Deuteronomy, patterned on the material in Deuteronomy 1–26. The suggestion has been applied specifically to Deut. 20:5–8 and Luke 14:16–20 (see Ballard 1972; Sanders 1974: 254–59). The parallel is the list of those exempted from military service in Deuteronomy and the list of excuses given by those who declined the invitation to the banquet in Luke (see table 16). But why use a battle or war (Deuteronomy 20) in association with a banquet (Luke 14)? Is it possibly because a good bit of Scripture points to two phenomena at the end of the age, a battle and a banquet, the great and terrible day of our Lord and the marriage supper of the Lamb?

The second half of Deuteronomy 20 (vv. 10–20) moves from military personnel to military strategies. A non-Palestinian city is first offered by Israel the chance to surrender (vv. 10–15). A city within Palestine is to be completely destroyed (vv. 16–18). A better way to formulate this is that vv. 10–15 state the customary way of treating defeated peoples, while vv. 16–18 deal with an exception to that general rule: treating defeated peoples in the Promised Land. In any siege, trees that bear edible fruit are not to be cut down (vv. 19–20). The two kinds of trees in vv. 19–20 parallel the two kinds of nations in vv. 10–18. Some nations are not to be destroyed, and some trees are not to be cut down; some nations are to be destroyed, and some trees may be cut down (for an example of Israel doing this to Moab, see 2 Kings 3:19, 25). Chapter 20 makes the point that one must not arbitrarily lump all the nations together, nor must one arbitrarily lump all the land's natural resources together. This is in line with ch. 19, which says that one must not too quickly lump all taking of human life together. Both chapters caution against taking impulsive action, generalizing too broadly, and painting every person or place with the same brush.

Interestingly, in vv. 10–18 victory is assumed. There is no indication that defeat or stalemate is a possibility. Israel is pictured as a powerful nation that will either intimidate its opposition into submission or stride unmolested and unchallenged into its opponents' cities and destroy "everything that breathes."

Table 16

Deuteronomy 20	Luke 14
house built, not yet dedicated (20:5)	field bought, not yet seen (14:18)
vineyard planted, fruit not yet enjoyed (20:6)	oxen bought, not yet examined (14:19)
man engaged to be married (20:7)	man recently married (14:20)

The chapter began with a list of those exempted from military service. The chapter concludes with a designation of what is to be spared from military destruction: the land's natural resources.

Life and Death (21)

I suggested at the beginning of this chapter that the last few chapters of the Deuteronomic legal corpus may be the most amorphous of all. Some scholars have been content to put everything in chs. 21–25 under the one heading of miscellaneous laws. Chapter 21 seems to confirm that, for we find the following: a law about the expiation of homicide when the murderer has not been apprehended (vv. 1–9); a law about marrying a (unmarried?) woman captured in war (vv. 10–14); a law about the inheritance upholding the right of the firstborn in a bigamous/polygamous household (vv. 15–17); a law about a stubborn and rebellious son (vv. 18–21); a law about the burial of the body of an executed criminal (vv. 22–23).

Carmichael (1979) contends that what all these laws have in common is that they dramatically associate death with life: the unworked heifer, the unplowed land, and the person slain in the open country. The woman captured in war is forcibly removed from her parents, for whom she mourns for one month, for presumably she will see them no more; but then she becomes the wife of an Israelite—a celebration of a new life. A father approaching death must not sidestep his eldest son's future well-being, his life. Wise parents try to preserve life through concern for and chastisement of their son, but they must turn him over for the punishment of death when all hope is gone and the son is incorrigible. The interment of an impaled criminal before nightfall will mean an undefiled land for Israel, a land that is alive, not sterile or stained. It is obvious that this particular polarity—life and death—is held out to the Israelites throughout all of Deuteronomy.

There may be other reasons for the arrangements of the laws in ch. 21. For example, the issue about marriage to a woman captured in war (vv. 10–14) might have better appeared somewhere in ch. 20, which contains laws about warfare. It is in ch. 21, however, because its primary concern is related to marriage, as are the next verses (vv. 15–17). Again, the section about the insubordinate son (vv. 18–21) and the section about the exposure of a criminal's corpse (vv. 22–23) both focus on execution. Finally, the first law in ch. 21 (vv. 1–9) and the last (vv. 22–23) address major consequences that may befall the whole community if they fail to take appropriate action over a human body found murdered in a field and a human body left hanging on a gibbet.

The first law in this chapter addresses the community; the last law also is directed to the community. Both deal with a corpse in open view, for which immediate action must be taken. In the first law the body is that of a victim; in the last it is the body of a criminal.

In the case of an unsolved murder a ritual is mandated, all parts of which are not apparent to us in terms of their significance. The heifer is no substitute for anybody's sin. Its blood is not shed; only its neck is broken. This must be the case, for the elders, after they break the heifer's neck, say, "Our hands did not shed this blood." To make sense, the "blood" has to be the blood of the victim, not of the heifer. All this does not mean that Deuteronomy has a unique view of sacrifice, as is argued by Weinfeld (1972: 210–17), but simply that the ceremony is *not* sacrificial. That is why the priests perform no ritual, and why in the ceremony the priests enter the story *after* the neck is broken.

The ceremony concludes with a handwashing ritual (v. 6) that probably amounts to a symbolic expression of innocence (cf. Pilate's handwashing at the trial of Jesus [Matt. 27:24]), and with a liturgical recitation (vv. 7–8) that amounts to a negative confession of innocence.

The next three laws of this chapter are concerned with the family, and the progression is interesting: wife (vv. 10–14); wife and son (vv. 15–17); son (vv. 18–21). The first of these three laws repeats Deut. 20:10–15, where we discovered that in a battle against a non-Palestinian city the women, children, and livestock were to be taken captive, not killed. Here it is added that the Israelite may take a wife from such a city. Presumably she is unmarried, for she is allowed to mourn for one month for her parents, not a husband. She is not to be treated like a slave.

The second law of this section forbids a man who has two wives, one of whom he favors, from arbitrarily assigning the inheritance to a son by the favored wife rather than leaving it to his firstborn son by the unfavored wife. Undoubtedly the law reflects the incident in Genesis in which Jacob bypasses Reuben, his firstborn by Leah (although Jacob did not bypass Reuben's firstborn rights arbitrarily).

This law stipulates that the firstborn, regardless of who his mother is, is to receive a "double portion/share." That expression is the same as one that Elisha speaks to Elijah: "Let me inherit a double share of your spirit" (2 Kings 2:9 NRSV). The expression often is interpreted erroneously to see Elisha asking for twice as much of the spirit as Elijah had. Rather, Elisha is asking Elijah—and here is his boldness—to declare him to be the primary successor. If there are two successors, then Elisha is requesting two-thirds of Elijah's spirit, with one-third to go to the other successor; if there are three successors, then Elisha is requesting one-half of Elijah's spirit, with one-fourth for each of the other two successors—and so forth.

The third law in this subunit deals with the case of the son who is persistently stubborn, rebellious, and refuses correction, and possibly the kind of son, if he is the firstborn, to whom the father of vv. 15–17 would not be very excited about giving the "double share." He is to be turned over to the authorities and stoned to death, but both parents must agree that this is the only course of action left. Few laws in Deuteronomy have as striking parabolic application to Israel as does this one, for the terms used here to describe the son—"stubborn and rebellious"—are consistently applied elsewhere in Scripture to Israel (Bellefontaine 1979: 18–19). To be more precise, both words appear frequently, but independently, throughout Scripture. The only other places where both Hebrew words occur in tandem as descriptors of Israel (or anyone) are Ps. 78:8, "They should not be like their ancestors, a stubborn and rebellious generation" (NRSV), and Jer. 5:23, "But these people have stubborn and rebellious hearts" (NIV). Does Israel too reach an incorrigible state where God has no disciplinary choice but exile (albeit with purification and redemption ultimately in view)?

Lawful and Unlawful Relationships (22)

There are fifteen laws in this chapter, nine in vv. 1–12, six in vv. 13–29 [v. 30 in the Hebrew Bible is v. 1 of ch. 23]. At least all the laws in vv. 13–30 fall into one general category: chastity. The first twelve verses, however, cannot be so neatly packed together. These twelve verses include laws about one's responsibilities when finding something lost that belongs to a neighbor, or assisting a neighbor's pack animal that has collapsed under its load (vv. 1–4) (and perhaps a law that provides Old Testament background for Jesus' parable about lost things [see Derrett 1979]); transvestism (v. 5); discovery of a bird's nest, either fallen or in a tree, with the mother bird and her young in it (vv. 6–7); how to properly build a house, especially the roof (v. 8); avoiding three kinds of mixtures (vv. 9–11); how to ornament one's cloak (v. 12).

There are three possibilities here. One is to view vv. 1–12 as a collection of heterogeneous laws. A second approach is to attempt to relate some of the laws at least to each other by a common word or theme, as is done by Stephen Kaufman (1979: 136). Thus 22:3, "so you shall do with his garment" (RSV), and 22:5, "nor shall a man put on a woman's garment" (NRSV). The emphasis on garments is continued into the laws about wool and linen (22:11), tassels on the cloak (22:12), and the menstrual garment (22:17). Or one can make this connection: a fallen animal (22:4), a fallen nest (22:6), a fallen person (22:8).

A third possibility, advanced by Carmichael (1974), is that 22:1–8 deals with procedures of wartime. When at war, it is wrong for someone to express anger against an enemy or compatriot by taking it out on their animals—one is not at war with the animals. And one should treat the occupants of a bird's nest as one would the fruit-producing trees: spare them. The interesting law about transvestism Carmichael takes to mean that a woman must not put on the weapons of a man of war or dress like a man in order to seek clandestine admission to the army. Nor should men attempt to avoid military conscription by dressing as women. Finally, in time of peace, prized as those moments are, one does not want to spill another's blood through careless house construction. In my view, Carmichael's explanations, though quite ingenious, especially his explanation of the law about transvestism, are unlikely. Why does the author of Deuteronomy 22 not speak more directly if indeed the concern here is wartime conduct? There is no indication in the first half of the chapter that the laws refer to wartime. In previous chapters (e.g., 20:1) the author specifically wrote, "When you go forth to war."

The remainder of the chapter (vv. 13–30) is about sexual relations, or more accurately, the violation of those relations. Perhaps the three brief laws about not mixing (two kinds of seeds, the ox and the ass, wool and linen [vv. 9–11]) serve as a prelude to these laws on chastity, which also deal with unlawful mixing at the sexual level. Also, the Numbers version of the tassel law (Num. 15:37–41; cf. Deut. 22:12) says that the purpose of these ornaments is to remind the Israelites of God's commands so that they will not "prostitute" themselves by pursuing the "lusts" of their own heart and eyes (Num. 15:39). It seems that a good bit of Deut. 22:13–30 is about going after the lusts of one's heart and eyes. Six situations are discussed: (1) a charge of infidelity brought by a husband against a wife that turns out to be false (vv. 13–19); (2) procedures to be followed if such a charge is substantiated (vv. 20–21); (3) adultery with a married woman (v. 22); (4) intercourse with an engaged virgin in the city (vv. 23–24); (5) intercourse with an engaged virgin in the countryside (vv. 25–27); (6) intercourse with an unengaged virgin (vv. 28–29). The first three of these have as their focus married women; the last three are concerned with unmarried women. (Verse 30 of ch. 22, noted above, is the first verse of ch. 23 in the Hebrew Bible.)

We may note three things about the penalties imposed. First, to whom is culpability attached? In only one instance the woman alone is punished: number 2 (v. 21). Twice both man and woman are condemned: numbers 3 and 4 (vv. 22, 24). Three times the man alone is judged: numbers 1 (vv. 18–19), 5 (v. 25), and 6 (v. 29).

In arranging the violations in this particular order, a deliberate literary sequence is created in which the punishments are arranged chiastically, as observed by Wenham and McConville (1980: 250):

A damages of one hundred shekels to woman's father
B woman executed
C woman and man executed
C' woman and man executed
B' man executed
A' damages of fifty shekels to woman's father

There is a significant difference between adultery and fornication. The penalty for adultery for both people is death (vv. 21–22). For fornication there is no death penalty. Instead, the man must pay a fine of fifty shekels to the woman's father (v. 29). For that reason, the man and a *betrothed* virgin are also stoned to death if they cohabit (v. 24), the exception being rape in the countryside. The explanation in the difference of the penalty is that Scripture treats the marriage relationship most seriously and honorably. The two have indeed become one flesh, and nothing is allowed to become a wedge between them in that unity.

Conspicuous here is one major difference between the laws of vv. 1–12 and those of vv. 13–30, all of which deal with marital and sexual misconduct. There is no penalty stated for violating the laws of vv. 1–12 beyond general phrases such as "the LORD your God detests anyone who does this" (v. 5b NIV), or "so that you may not bring the guilt of bloodshed on your house" (v. 8 NIV). What if one wears wool and linen together? What if one plows with an ox and donkey yoked together? No penalties are stated for such actions. By contrast, sins that involve sexual misconduct have consequences that are explicit and severe, ranging from major punitive damages to death.

Exclusion, Cleanliness, and Possession (23)

This chapter contains a potpourri of laws, perhaps without an overarching theme. The first eight verses deal with who may enter and who may not enter God's community. Each of the laws begins with the negative particle *lōʾ*: "not shall a man take" (22:30 [23:1 in the Hebrew text]); "not shall enter" (23:1); "not shall enter" (23:2); "not shall enter" (23:3); "not seek a treaty" (23:6); "not abhor . . . not abhor" (23:7). Membership in the legislature ("the assembly of the LORD") is not open to everyone, although resident rights are. Excluded from the governing body are Ammonites and Moabites, both of whom are products of an incestuous relationship (see Gen. 19:30–38), children born of adulterous/incestuous unions (v. 2), and the physiologically disqualified (v. 1). Included are the Egyptians, probably because despite their later mistreatment of the Hebrews they provided in the days of Joseph shelter and food for the famine-struck Hebrews and Edomites.

Verses 9–14 discuss the need for physical cleanliness in the camp and, to that end, who needs to go outside the camp: those who have a seminal discharge (v. 10; cf. Lev. 15:16) and those who have to relieve bodily needs at a latrine (vv. 12–13). It is unlikely that there is anything more than a hygienic concern here. Cleanliness in the camp is required because "the LORD your God moves about in your camp" (v. 14 NIV). So far the progression in the chapter is (1) those who must be kept out (vv. 1–8), and (2) those who must get out (vv. 12–14).

Also, the community is to allow escaped slaves to "dwell . . . in your midst" (v. 16 RSV). Provocatively, such slaves are allowed to dwell "any place they choose in any one of your towns" (NRSV). We recall that this is a divine prerogative throughout Deuteronomy. Is Israel, then, to welcome escaped slaves while excluding the Ammonites and Moabites (from membership involvements) and tolerating the Egyptians and Edomites ("the third generation")?

A law forbidding religious prostitution (vv. 17–18), part of which is concerned with money, specifically the donation of income to the sanctuary by prostitution (v. 18), is followed by one that prohibits loans with interest to fellow Israelites (vv. 19–20). The next law also is in the general area of money and possessions (vv. 21–23). A vow to the Lord needs to be paid in the right way. Verse 18 tells the wrong way to finance the vows! In a sense, the last law of this chapter is in the same area. Do not turn an act of good will by your neighbor to support the indigent into an act of thievery by yourself. There is to be no "what is yours is mine" (vv. 24–25). The sequence, then, of the second half of the chapter is: no exploitation of slaves (vv. 15–16), no sexual exploitation of others (vv. 17–18), no economic exploitation of one's kin (vv. 19–20), no exploitation of religious promises (vv. 21–23), no exploitation of Israel's support system for the poor (vv. 24–25).

Marriage and Poverty (24)

The first law in this chapter (vv. 1–4) is one that has evoked considerable discussion. Its subject is divorce and, more specifically, the remarriage of a woman to her first husband after either the death of her second husband or a divorce from her second husband. The crux in this passage is the explanation of the reason for the divorce: "he finds something indecent about her" (NIV), literally, "the nakedness of a thing." Does this refer to adultery or some other type of mischievous sexual conduct on the part of the wife? If so, then why are the woman and her companion not stoned to death, as 22:22 stipulated? We would expect execution, not divorce.

Also, the Hebrew expression for "something indecent" is found in 23:14 in a context dealing with proper toilet facilities in the camp: "that he [God] may not see anything indecent among you" (NRSV). Clearly, no moral connotation is attached to the phrase there—it refers to what is unbecoming, but certainly not what is immoral. There is no evidence in the Old Testament that human excrement per se is defiling.

What, then, are the options if sexual indulgence is ruled out? Perhaps we can adopt the other extreme and suggest that the ambiguity of the phrase gave to the husband the right to divorce his wife for whatever reason he wished (Phillips 1973: 355). This is not to suggest that the husband had license to dissolve a marriage Hollywood-style. Rather, it suggests that divorce is a domestic issue, not a concern of the courts, and therefore no legal body is able to issue or impose criteria on individuals vis-à-vis divorce regulations.

There is nothing in the law to indicate that divorce is illegal. Nor is there anything to suggest that the remarriage of a divorcée is illegal. What is anathema is the remarriage of two people formerly married to each other. Again, no reason is stated for the prohibition. Those who interpret a second marriage as adultery per se appeal for that meaning in the words "she has been defiled." To remarry one who is defiled is out of the question. That idea may be echoed in Jer. 3:1a. The issue in Jer. 3:1–5 is whether or not Israel, as Yahweh's bride, may return to Yahweh after committing religious apostasy, and whether or not Yahweh, Israel's "husband," may take her back or return to her. According to Deut. 24:4, a husband may not legally return and marry his first wife under the conditions that vv. 1–4 spell out. (For the interplay of these two texts, see Fishbane 1985: 307–10.) It appears in the Jeremiah passage that God is willing to risk humiliation and defilement, something that Deuteronomy 24 teaches takes place if a husband remarries his former wife after her second marriage to another husband. Walter Brueggemann (1998: 43 n. 4) quotes W. Sibley Towner vis-à-vis a passage in Daniel: "The . . .

question is whether God is trapped by the immutability of his own law. . . . God's law is immutability, and yet God himself can suspend it if compassion so demands."

Gordon Wenham (1979: 40) suggests that the reason for prohibiting remarriage has nothing to do with adultery, but instead is concerned with incest. To become a bride is to become a sister. To marry the same woman a second time is therefore tantamount to marrying one's sister. Wenham's suggestion has possibilities, but his explanation skirts the emphasis in the law on the second marriage to someone else. The concern of the law is neither the first nor the second marriage, but the third. And having said that, it is reasonable to ask how prevalent such a custom would be. In very few societies, at least in the West, does a remarriage of spouses take place.

Those who have explored the role of women in the Old Testament draw attention to the fact that nowhere does Old Testament Scripture permit a woman to take the initiative in divorce proceedings. This observation becomes more significant and critical when we realize that pagan cultures around Israel permitted both man and woman to start the proceedings, although Jesus' words in Mark 10:12, "and if she divorces her husband and marries another man" (NIV), suggest that it was more acceptable in his era. For instance, Law 142 of the Code of Hammurabi says, "If a woman so hated her husband that she declared, 'You may not have me,' her record shall be investigated at her city council, and if she was careful and was not at fault, even though her husband has been going out and disparaging her greatly, that woman, without incurring any blame at all, may take her dowry and go off to her father's house" (translation in James B. Pritchard, ed., *Ancient Near Eastern Texts Relating to the Old Testament* [2nd ed., Princeton, N.J.: Princeton University Press, 1955], 172).

Are we to conclude from this that women in other cultures had a greater degree of independence than women in Israel had? Was a woman a person in Mesopotamian society, but only a possession in Israelite society? I am persuaded that the answer to those questions is a definite no, a conclusion that is borne out by a full examination of all the literary evidence in both civilizations.

What, then, are we to make of the divorce procedure? The best answer to that question may be found in an interesting remark by Walther Eichrodt (1961–1967: 1:81):

> In general, it may indeed be said, that wherever a highly developed culture dissolves, or merely loosens, the cement of family and clan, then intensified legal protections for the individual normally become necessary. The Israelite kingdoms, however, were for the greater part of their existence

peasant, agricultural states. . . . In such simpler conditions the strength of the family and clan affords the individual a powerful support, which takes the place of many legal measures. . . . If this great importance of the clan right into the monarchical period is borne in mind, then the absence of these Babylonian-type legal stipulations in Israel becomes easier to understand.

Interestingly, a divorce/remarriage law is followed by a law on the maintenance of marriage (v. 5). A man is allowed to spend the first year of marriage completely with his wife. This law is close to that of 20:7, except that 20:7 refers to a premarital deferral from military service. Both statements reflect Deuteronomy's sensitivity to the feelings and needs of the wife or wife-to-be. Loneliness and separation should not be enforced on her (20:7), and she too is entitled to "happiness" (24:5), a term that includes all the pleasures that newlyweds share, including conjugal ones. Although the next law moves to the subject of taking a millstone as a pledge (v. 6), the sexual imagery of the two preceding laws lingers here. Just as the newly married husband is not to be separated from his wife, so also the "upper millstone," the one that moves over the stone underneath, is not to be separated from its partner. Stephen Kaufman (1979: 156 n. 108) notes the association of the word for "mill" with "bridegroom" and "groom" in Jer. 25:10: "I will banish from them the sounds of joy and gladness, the voices of bride and bridegroom, the sounds of millstones" (see also Job 31:10). In today's courts, what this law forbids would be called extortion, seizing something from somebody that is of little value to you but of great value to the owner as collateral for a loan on which one has defaulted.

The following catena of laws rounds out the chapter: kidnapping (like the law of v. 6, one of unlawful seizure) (v. 7); leprosy (remember Miriam) (vv. 8–9); another word on loans and treatment of debtors (vv. 10–13); oppression of the poor and immediate payment of their wages "before sunset," as in the preceding law in v. 13 (vv. 14–15); individual responsibility for violation of criminal and civil law (collective responsibility remains for sins against God, as in the second commandment in 5:9) (v. 16); justice for the defenseless (vv. 17–18); leaving food for the poor (vv. 19–22). This last law parallels the last law of chapter 23. When you are a guest, do not presume on your host's hospitality (23:24–25). When you are the host, or gathering in your crops, do not harvest the fields clean. Most of this last part of the chapter is concerned with laws concerning the poor (vv. 6, 7, 10–15, 17–22). Any attempt to control, manipulate, oppress, or starve them puts one's relationship to God in jeopardy.

A deterrent to behavior that is inappropriate for those who bear the name of Yahweh is memory. Three times the chapter calls the reader to remember: "remember what the Lord your God did to Miriam" (v. 9 NIV); "remember that you were slaves in Egypt" (vv. 18, 22 NIV). The old adage still stands: those who forget the past are bound to repeat its mistakes. For other references in Deuteronomy besides 24:9, 18, 22 that call on the people to remember, see 5:15; 7:18; 8:2; 9:7; 15:15; 16:3, 12; 25:17; 32:7. The Israelites are to remember things about themselves about which they cannot boast, and things about Yahweh about which they cannot help but boast.

Litigation and Justice (25)

This chapter contains mostly laws about pairs: a dispute between two persons (vv. 1–3); an ox and its owner (v. 4); "if brothers dwell together" (vv. 5–10); two men fighting (vv. 11–12); two kinds of weights (vv. 13–16); Israel and Amalek (vv. 17–19).

The first law involves a legal dispute between two contestants. The purpose of the law is not primarily to prescribe corporal punishment, but to limit it. The maximum number of blows on the guilty party is not to exceed forty (cf. Paul's thirty-nine lashes, one less than the limit [2 Cor. 11:24]).

Verse 4, a separate law, is about the illicit muzzling of an ox, a verse quoted by the apostle Paul in 1 Cor. 9:9 and 1 Tim. 5:18. It may indeed serve as an introduction to the law that follows (vv. 5–10). Just as the ox is entitled to eat while it works in the fields, so also is a childless widow entitled to bear a son who will carry on the name of her deceased husband (see Carmichael 1974: 239).

Clearly, the law of vv. 5–10 is a reflection of levirate marriage. The concern is not with a widow, but with a childless widow. Also the concern is that the woman not remarry "outside the family to a stranger." The law does leave some questions unanswered. For example, what is meant by the phrase "if brothers dwell together"? Do we take it literally, that they live under the same roof or on the same family estate, or more generally to mean in the same general vicinity? Is the levirate marriage limited only to the firstborn son? What if the other brothers are already married? If after a man fathers a child by his sister-in-law (a relationship normally forbidden [see Lev. 18:16]), is he allowed to marry another woman, or does he for all practical purposes disinherit himself? What if there are no other brothers? The story of Genesis 38 has the father-in-law as the levir, and in the Book of Ruth it is Boaz, one of Ruth's relatives, who "redeems" her.

One thing that this law does make clear is that a man could not be forced against his will to impregnate his sister-in-law. To be sure, his refusal to do so brought public humiliation—she is directed to "spit in his face and pull off one of his sandals" (the significance of which is not transparent)—but nothing beyond that. Additionally, this act by the woman was performed "in the presence of the elders," but they function only as interrogators and observers. Beyond that they play no role (unlike the judges in the law of vv. 1–3). As with the divorce law of 24:1–4, we may have another instance of family law. For the court to act would be for it to venture into unauthorized areas.

The fourth law in this chapter is also concerned with a family situation. A wife comes to the rescue of her husband who is being assaulted. She tries to put a stop to things, following her instincts, by grabbing the antagonist's genitals. For that, she is to lose her hand, of special interest because only here in biblical law is mutilation mandated as a fitting punishment for a crime. It is hard to believe that this law was implemented regularly, if at all. A law dealing with a woman's actions that possibly incapacitate a man from fathering children is a natural one to follow a law dealing with a situation in which a wife is incapacitated from having children. The reference in this law to a man's "private parts" (NIV) may resonate in the following law in the phrase "two weights in your bag" (v. 13).

The fifth law (vv. 13–16) shifts from people to possessions, in this instance two kinds of weights and measures. What is forbidden here is deception—or perhaps more precisely, even the possession of items by which fraud may be perpetrated: "you shall not *have* . . . two kinds of weights . . . two kinds of measures" (NRSV). The best way to fight temptation is to avoid situations in which the temptation most easily can move from thought to act. Thus even the appearance of evil is to be shunned.

The last paragraph in the section (vv. 17–19) perhaps ought to be included with the next chapter. It is Moses' reminder to Israel to show no mercy to the Amalekites, and as such it is not really one of the laws of the Deuteronomy corpus. What is found here, but not in Exod. 17:8–15, is the fact that Amalek attacked only the weary and faint of Israel, those most helpless and defenseless. May the simple addition of the fact be a parable without commentary to Israel? The Israelites run the risk of perpetually inciting God's wrath if they offend one of these weaker ones of their group. This last law in chapter 25 forms a frame with the second law in the chapter by the repeat of a phrase. The purpose of levirate marriage is that "his name [of the deceased married brother] will not be blotted out from Israel" (v. 6b NIV). The last law of the chapter commands Israel to "blot out the memory of Amalek" (v. 19b NIV). One blotting out is discouraged, another is encouraged.

Thanksgiving and Obedience: This Day! (26)

The legal corpus of Deuteronomy concludes with this chapter, and it may be divided quite transparently into three sections. First is a liturgy for the presentation of the firstfruits (vv. 1–11) (cf. the previous discussion of this in 14:22–27). A substantial part of this unit is comprised of the credo that the Israelites are to proclaim once they are settled in Palestine and the Lord has chosen the place at which he will establish his name (vv. 5–10). Essentially Moses says to Israel, "In your future do not forget your past."

The second part of the chapter is another liturgy for the presentation of the triennial tithe (vv. 12–15) (cf. the previous discussion of this in 14:28–29). The confession of vv. 5–10 emphasized what God had done for Israel, for "us." The confession within this liturgy (vv. 13–15) emphasizes what each person has done or not done. Apparently the believer is expected to be able to live a life of obedience and purity, to be able to stand before the Lord and say, "I have lived by your standards, Master." The first recitation climaxes by drawing attention to the obedient actions of the individual ("and now I bring the firstfruits of the soil that you, O Lord, have given me" [v. 10 NIV]). The second recitation climaxes with a prayer ("Look down from heaven . . . and bless your people Israel" [v. 15 NIV]).

The last paragraph (vv. 16–19) is the third section, and it is a concluding challenge from Moses to the people. It is a logical extension of the prayer for God's blessing uttered in v. 15. Verses 16–17 are the way to that blessing ("follow these decrees and laws" [NIV]). Verse 19 lists manifestations of that blessing ("set you in praise, fame and honor high above all the nations . . . a people holy to the LORD" [NIV]), with v. 18 being a transition and overlap between the two emphases (v. 18a goes with v. 19; v. 18b goes with vv. 16–17). Of special interest here is the emphasis on the "this day": "This day the LORD your God commands you. . . . You have declared this day. . . . And the LORD has declared this day" (vv. 16–18 RSV).

The phrase is a crucial one throughout all Deuteronomy. The expression, or one very close to it, appears at least fifty-nine times in Deuteronomy, almost half of which are in the formula "the commandments which I am commanding you this day."

Simon DeVries (1974: 316) has done an interesting study of this expression. His conclusion regarding the urgency evoked by the formula is worth noting: "His revelation is *now*. He is very alive and present. Israel must respond one way or another, because the voice of God is near. The word they must obey is not far off in the heavens or belonging to remote antiquity. Therefore, do not defer your choice to still another 'today.'"

What we are to give to God is twofold: thanksgiving (vv. 5–10) and obedient, faithful living (vv. 13–14, 16–17, 18b). But what we give to God pales in comparison to what God gives to us. Note that of the eight uses of "give" in vv. 1–15, God's people are the subject of just one (v. 12). God, on the other hand, is the giver seven times (vv. 1, 2, 3, 10, 11, 13, 15). God gives land, freedom, blessing, grace, his word, and his commands.

Deuteronomy 12–26

Blenkinsopp, J. 1995. "Deuteronomy and the Politics of Post-Mortem Existence." *VT* 45:1–16.

Braulik, G. 1993. "The Sequence of Laws in Deuteronomy 12–26 and in the Decalogue." In *A Song of Power and the Power of Song: Essays on the Book of Deuteronomy*. Ed. D. L. Christensen. SBTS 3. Winona Lake, Ind.: Eisenbrauns. Pp. 313–35.

Carmichael, C. 1967. "Deuteronomic Laws, Wisdom and Historical Traditions." *JJS* 12:198–206.

———. 1974. *The Laws of Deuteronomy*. Ithaca, N.Y.: Cornell University Press.

———. 1985. *Law and Narrative in the Bible: The Evidence of the Deuteronomic Laws and the Decalogue*. Ithaca, N.Y.: Cornell University Press.

Eslinger, L. 1984. "More Drafting Techniques in Deuteronomic Laws." *VT* 34:221–26.

Geisler, N. 1977. *Popular Survey of the Old Testament*. Grand Rapids: Baker.

Kaufman, S. 1979. "The Structure of Deuteronomic Law." *Maarav* 1 (2):105–58.

Knight, D. A. 2000. "Whose Agony? Whose Ecstasy? The Politics of Deuteronomic Law." In *"Shall Not the Judge of the Earth Do What Is Right?" Studies on the Nature of God in Tribute to James L. Crenshaw*. Ed. D. Penchansky and P. L. Redditt. Winona Lake, Ind.: Eisenbrauns. Pp. 97–112.

Levinson, B. M. 1990. "Calum M. Carmichael's Approach to the Laws of Deuteronomy." *HTR* 83:225–57.

Patrick, D. 1985. *Old Testament Law*. Atlanta: John Knox. Pp. 97–144.

———. 1995. "The Rhetoric of Collective Responsibility in Deuteronomic Law." In *Pomegranates and Golden Bells: Studies in Biblical, Jewish, and Near Eastern Ritual, Law, and Literature in Honor of Jacob Milgrom*. Ed. D. P. Wright, D. N. Freedman, and A. Hurvitz. Winona Lake, Ind.: Eisenbrauns. Pp. 421–36.

Pressler, C. 1993. *The View of Women Found in Deuteronomic Family Laws*. BZAW 216. Berlin: de Gruyter.

Rad, G. von. 1962. *Old Testament Theology*. Trans. D. M. G. Stalker. 2 vols. New York: Harper & Row.

Rofé, A. 1988. "The Arrangement of the Laws in Deuteronomy." *ETL* 64:265–87.

Steinbert, N. 1991. "The Deuteronomic Law Code and the Politics of State Centralization." In *The Bible and the Politics of Exegesis: Essays in Honor of Norman K. Gottwald on His Sixty-fifth Birthday*. Ed. D. Jobling, P. L. Day, and G. T. Sheppard. Cleveland: Pilgrim Press. Pp. 12–26.

Stulman, L. 1990. "Encroachment in Deuteronomy: An Analysis of the Social World of the Deuteronomic Code." *JBL* 109:613–32.

Tigay, J. H. 1996. *Deuteronomy: The Traditional Hebrew Text with the New JPS Translation.* JPS Torah Commentary. Philadelphia: The Jewish Publication Society. Pp. 446–59.

Weinfeld, M. 1971. "Deuteronomy." *Enc Jud* 5:1573–83.

Wenham, G. J., and J. G. McConville. 1980. "Drafting Techniques in Some Deuteronomic Laws." *VT* 30:248–52.

Deuteronomy 12

Claburn, W. G. 1973. "The Fiscal Basis of Josiah's Reforms." *JBL* 92:11–22.

Gutmann, J. 1977. "Deuteronomy: Religious Reformation or Iconoclastic Revolution." In *The Image and the Word: Confrontations in Judaism, Christianity and Islam.* Ed. J. Gutmann. Religion and the Arts 4. Missoula, Mont.: Scholars Press. Pp. 5–25.

Halpern, B. 1981. "The Centralization Formula in Deuteronomy." *VT* 31:20–38.

Kaufmann, Y. 1960. *The Religion of Israel.* Trans. M. Greenberg. Chicago: University of Chicago Press. Pp. 180–82.

Levinson, B. M. 1997. *Deuteronomy and the Hermeneutics of Legal Innovation.* Oxford: Oxford University Press. Pp. 23–52.

McConville, J. G. 1979. "God's 'Name' and God's 'Glory.'" *TynB* 30:149–63.

Milgrom, J. 1976. "Profane Slaughter and a Formulaic Key to the Composition of Deuteronomy." *HUCA* 47:1–17.

Nicholson, E. 1963. "The Centralisation of the Cult in Deuteronomy." *VT* 13:380–89.

Rad, G. von. 1966. *Deuteronomy: A Commentary.* Trans. D. Barton. OTL. Philadelphia: Westminster.

Rofé, A. 1972. "The Strata of the Law about the Centralization of Worship in Deuteronomy and the History of the Deuteronomic Movement." In *Congress Volume, Uppsala 1971.* VTSup 22. Leiden: Brill Pp. 221–26.

Roth, M. W. 1976. "The Deuteronomic Rest Theology: A Redactional-Critical Study." *BRes* 21:5–14.

Tigay, J. H. 1996. *Deuteronomy: The Traditional Hebrew Text with the New JPS Translation.* JPS Torah Commentary. Philadelphia: The Jewish Publication Society. Pp. 459–64.

Weinfeld, M. 1964. "Cult Centralization in Israel in the Light of a Neo-Assyrian Analogy." *JNES* 23:202–12.

———. 1972. *Deuteronomy and the Deuteronomic School.* Oxford: Clarendon.

Wenham, G. J. 1971. "Deuteronomy and the Central Sanctuary." *TynB* 22:103–18. Repr., in *A Song of Power and the Power of Song: Essays on the Book of Deuteronomy.* Ed. D. L. Christensen. SBTS 3. Winona Lake, Ind.: Eisenbrauns, 1993. Pp. 94–108.

Deuteronomy 13

Dion, P. E. 1991. "Deuteronomy 13: The Suppression of Alien Religious Propaganda in Israel during the Late Monarchial Era." In *Law and Ideology in Monarchic Israel.* Ed. B. Halpern and D. W. Hobson. JSOTSup 124. Sheffield: Sheffield Academic Press. Pp. 147–216.

Hamilton, J. M. 1998. "How to Read an Abhorrent Text: Deuteronomy 13 and the Nature of Authority." *HBT* 20:12–32.

Levinson, B. M. 2001. "Textual Criticism, Assyriology, and the History of Interpretation: Deuteronomy 13:7a as a Test Case in Method." *JBL* 120:211–43.

Polzin, R. 1980. *Moses and the Deuteronomist: A Literary Study of the Deuteronomic History.* New York: Seabury. Pp. 57–65.

Weinfeld, M. 1976. "The Loyalty Oath in the Ancient Near East." *UF* 8:389–90.

Deuteronomy 14

Craigie, P. C. 1977. "Deuteronomy and Ugaritic Studies." *TynB* 28:155–69.

Haran, M. 1979. "Seething a Kid in Its Mother's Milk." *JJS* 30:23–29.

Milgrom, J. 1990a. *Numbers: The Traditional Hebrew Text with the New JPS Translation.* JPS Torah Commentary. Philadelphia: The Jewish Publication Society. Pp. 432–36.

———. 1990b. "The Foundations of the Biblical Dietary Laws." In *Religion and Law: Biblical-Judaic and Islamic Perspectives.* Ed. E. R. Firmage, B. G. Weiss, and J. W. Welch. Winona Lake, Ind.: Eisenbrauns. Pp. 159–91.

———. 1991. *Leviticus 1–16: A New Translation with Introduction and Commentary.* AB 3. New York: Doubleday. Pp. 698–704.

Ratner, R., and B. Zuckermann. 1986. "'A Kid in Milk'? New Photographs of KTU 1. 23 Line 14." *HUCA* 57:15–60.

Weinfeld, M. 1971. "Tithe." *EncJud* 15:1156–62.

Wright, D. P. 1990. "Observations on the Ethical Foundations of the Biblical Dietary Laws: A Response to Jacob Milgrom." In *Religion and Law: Biblical-Judaic and Islamic Perspectives.* Ed. E. R. Firmage, B. G. Weiss, and J. W. Welch. Winona Lake, Ind.: Eisenbrauns. Pp. 193–98.

Deuteronomy 15

Hamilton, J. M. 1990. *Social Justice and Deuteronomy: The Case of Deuteronomy 15.* SBLDS 136. Atlanta: Scholars Press.

Houston, W. 1995. "'You Shall Open Your Hand to Your Needy Brother': Ideology and Moral Formation in Deuteronomy 15:1–18." In *The Bible in Ethics: The Second Sheffield Colloquium.* Ed. J. W. Rogerson, M. Davies, and M. Daniel Carroll R. JSOTSup 207. Sheffield: Sheffield Academic Press. Pp. 296–314.

Kaufman, S. 1984. "A Reconstruction of the Social Welfare Systems of Ancient Israel." In *In the Shelter of Elyon: Essays on Ancient Palestinian Life and Literature in Honour of G. W. Ahlstrom.* Ed. W. B. Barrick and J. R. Spencer. JSOTSup 31. Sheffield: JSOT Press. Pp. 277–86.

———. 1985. "Deuteronomy 15 and Recent Research on the Dating of P." In *Das Deuteronomium: Entstehung, Gestalt und Botschaft.* Ed. N. Lohfink. BETL 68. Leuven: Leuven University Press. Pp. 273–76.

Lemeche, N. P. 1976. "The Manumission of Slaves—the Fallow Year—the Sabbatical Year—the Yobel Year." *VT* 26:38–59.

Lindenberger, J. M. 1991. "How Much for a Hebrew Slave? The Meaning of *Mishneh* in Deuteronomy 15:18." *JBL* 110:479–98.

Mendelsohn, I. 1949. *Slavery in the Ancient Near East.* New York: Oxford University Press.

Tsevat, M. 1994. "The Hebrew Slave according to Deut. 15:12–18: His Lot and the Value of His Work, with Special Attention to the Meaning of *mishneh.*" *JBL* 113:587–95.

Weingreen, J. 1976. "The Deuteronomic Legislator—A Proto-Rabbinic Type." In *From Bible to Mishna: The Continuity of Tradition.* Manchester: Manchester University Press. Pp. 132–42.

Deuteronomy 16

Bokser, B. M. 1992. "Unleavened Bread and Passover, Feast of." *ABD* 6:755–65.

Cooper, A., and B. R. Goldstein. 1992. "Exodus and *Massot* in History and Tradition." *Maarav* 8:15–37.

Gaster, T. H. 1953. *Festivals of the Jewish Year: A Modern Interpretation and Guide.* New York: Sloane.

Goldstein, B. R., and A. Cooper. 1990. "The Festivals of Israel and Judah and the Literary History of the Pentateuch." *JAOS* 110:19–31.

Levinson, B. M. 1995. *Deuteronomy and the Hermeneutics of Legal Innovation.* Oxford: Oxford University Press. Pp. 53–97.

———. 2000. "The Hermeneutics of Tradition in Deuteronomy: A Reply to J. G. McConville." *JBL* 119:269–86.

McConville, J. G. 2000. "Deuteronomy's Unification of Passover and *Massot:* A Response to Bernard M. Levinson." *JBL* 119:47–58.

Wharton, J. A. 1987. "Deuteronomy 16:1–8." *Int* 41:287–91.

Deuteronomy 17

Craigie, P. C. 1976. *The Book of Deuteronomy.* NICOT. Grand Rapids: Eerdmans.

Daube, D. 1971. "One from among Your Brethren Shall You Set King over You." *JBL* 90:480–81.

Dutcher-Walls, P. 2002. "The Circumscription of the King: Deuteronomy 17:16–17 in Its Ancient Social Context." *JBL* 121:601–16.

Greenberg, M. 1990. "Biblical Attitudes toward Power: Ideal and Reality in the Law and Prophets." In *Religion and Law: Biblical-Judaic and Islamic Perspectives*. Ed. E. R. Firmage, B. G. Weiss, and J. W. Welch. Winona Lake, Ind.: Eisenbrauns. Pp. 101–12.

Hagedorn, A. S. 2003. "Deut 17, 8–13. Procedure for Cases of Pollution?" *ZAW* 115:538–56.

Halpern, B. 1981. *The Constitution of the Monarchy in Ancient Israel*. HSM 25. Chico, Calif.: Scholars Press. Pp. 216–49.

Knoppers, G. N. 1996. "The Deuteronomist and the Deuteronomistic Law of the King." *ZAW* 108:329–46.

Levinson, B. M. 1997. *Deuteronomy and the Hermeneutics of Legal Innovation*. Oxford: Oxford University Press. Pp. 98–143.

Lohfink, N. 1993. "Distribution of the Functions of Power: The Laws concerning Public Offices in Deuteronomy." In *A Song of Power and the Power of Song: Essays on the Book of Deuteronomy*. Ed. D. L. Christensen. SBTS 3. Winona Lake, Ind.: Eisenbrauns. Pp. 336–52.

McConville, J. G. 1998. "King and Messiah in Deuteronomy and the Deuteronomistic History." In *King and Messiah in Israel and the Ancient Near East: Proceedings of the Oxford Old Testament Seminar*. Ed. J. Day. JSOTSup 270. Sheffield: Sheffield Academic Press. Pp. 271–95.

Milgrom, J. 1983. "The Ideological and Historical Importance of the Judge in Deuteronomy." In *Essays on the Bible and the Ancient World: Isaac Leo Seeligmann Volume*. Vol. 3, *Non-Hebrew Section*. Ed. Y. Zakovitch and A. Rofé. Jerusalem: Rubinstein. Pp. 129–39.

Rad, G. von. 1966. *Deuteronomy: A Commentary*. Trans. D. Barton. OTL. Philadelphia: Westminster.

Van Seters, J. 1989. "The Creation of Man and the Creation of the King." *ZAW* 101:333–42.

Weingreen, J. 1976. "Deuteronomy, a Proto-Mishna." In *From Bible to Mishna: The Continuity of Tradition*. Manchester: Manchester University Press. Pp. 143–54.

Deuteronomy 18

See in the bibliography for Deuteronomy 17 Halpern 1981; Lohfink 1993.

Abba, R. 1977. "Priests and Levites in Deuteronomy." *VT* 27:257–67.

Cody, A. 1969. *A History of the Old Testament Priesthood*. AnBib 35. Rome: Pontifical Biblical Institute.

Duke, R. K. 1987. "The Portion of the Levite: Another Reading of Deuteronomy 18:6–8." *JBL* 106:193–201.

Haran, M. 1971. "Priests and Priesthood." *EncJud* 13:1069–86.

Kaufmann, Y. 1960. *The Religion of Israel*. Trans. M. Greenberg. Chicago: University of Chicago Press.

Paul, S. 1971. "Prophets and Prophecy." *EncJud* 13:1150–75.

Polzin, R. 1980. *Moses and the Deuteronomist: A Literary Study of the Deuteronomic History*. New York: Seabury. Pp. 57–65.

Tigay, J. H. 1975. "Empirical Basis for the Documentary Hypothesis." *JBL* 94:329–42.

Tucker, G. M. 1987. "Deuteronomy 18:15–22." *Int* 41:292–97.

Wilson, R. 1980. *Prophecy and Society in Ancient Israel*. Philadelphia: Fortress.

Deuteronomy 19

Greenberg, M. 1959. "The Biblical Conception of Asylum." *JBL* 67:125–32.

———. 1962a. "Avenger of Blood." *IDB* 1:321.

———. 1962b. "Bloodguilt." *IDB* 1:449–50.

———. 1962c. "City of Refuge." *IDB* 1:638–39.

Milgrom, J. 1973. "The Alleged 'Demythologization' and 'Secularization' in Deuteronomy." *IEJ* 23:151–56.

———. 1990. *Numbers: The Traditional Hebrew Text with the New JPS Translation*. JPS Torah Commentary. Philadelphia: The Jewish Publication Society. Pp. 504–11.

Rofé, A. 1986. "The History of the Cities of Refuge in Biblical Law." In *Studies in Bible*. Ed. S. Japhet. Scripta Hierosolymitana 31. Jerusalem: Magnes. Pp. 205–39.

Weinfeld, M. 1972. *Deuteronomy and the Deuteronomic School*. Oxford: Clarendon.

Deuteronomy 20

Ballard, P. H. 1972. "Reason for Refusing the Great Supper." *JTS* 23:341–50.

Craigie, P. C. 1976. *The Problem of War in the Old Testament*. Grand Rapids: Eerdmans.

Eph'al, I. 1983. "On Warfare and Military Control in Ancient Near Eastern Empires: A Research Outline." In *History, Historiography and Interpretation*. Ed. H. Tadmor and M. Weinfeld. Jerusalem: Magnes. Pp. 88–106.

Evans, C. F. 1955. *Studies in the Gospels*. Oxford: Blackwell.

Longman, T., and D. G. Reid. 1995. *God Is a Warrior*. Studies in Old Testament Biblical Theology. Grand Rapids: Zondervan.

Rofé, A. 1985. "The Laws of Warfare in the Book of Deuteronomy: Their Origin, Intent and Positivity." *JSOT* 32:23–44.

Sanders, J. A. 1974. "The Ethic of Election in Luke's Great Banquet Parable." In *Essays in Old Testament Ethics*. Ed. J. Crenshaw and J. T. Willis. New York: Ktav. Pp. 245–71.

Yadin, Y. 1963. *The Art of Warfare in Biblical Lands*. 2 vols. New York: McGraw-Hill.

Deuteronomy 21

Bellefontaine, E. 1979. "Deuteronomy 21:18–21: Reviewing the Case of the Rebellious Son." *JSOT* 13:13–31.

Callaway, P. R. 1984. "Deuteronomy 21:18–21: Proverbial Wisdom and Law." *JBL* 103:341–52.

Carmichael, C. 1979. "A Common Element in Five Supposedly Disparate Laws." *VT* 29:129–42.

Davies, E. W. 1986. "The Meaning of *pi sᵉnayim* in Deuteronomy xxi 17." *VT* 36:341–47.

Fleishman, J. F. 2003. "Legal Innovation in Deuteronomy xxi 18–20." *VT* 53:311–27.

Hagedorn, C. A. 2000. "Guarding the Parent's Honor—Deuteronomy 21.18–21." *JSOT* 88:101–21.

Lieu, J. M. 1995. "Reading in Canon and Community: Deuteronomy 21:22–23, a Test Case for Dialogue." In *The Bible in Human Society: Essays in Honour of John Rogerson*. Ed. M. Daniel Carroll R., D. J. A. Clines, and P. R. Davies. JSOTSup 200. Sheffield: Sheffield Academic Press. Pp. 317–34.

Marcus, D. 1981. "Juvenile Delinquency in the Bible and in the Ancient Near East." *JANES* 13:31–52.

Rotenberg, M., and B. L. Diamond. 1971. "The Biblical Conception of Psychopathy: The Law of the Rebellious Son." *Journal for the History of the Behavioral Sciences* 7:29–38.

Weinfeld, M. 1972. *Deuteronomy and the Deuteronomic School.* Oxford: Clarendon.

Wright, D. P. 1987. "Deuteronomy 21:1–9 as a Rite of Elimination." *CBQ* 49:387–403.

Zevit, Z. 1976. "*ᶜegla* Ritual of Deuteronomy 21:1–9." *JBL* 95:377–90.

Deuteronomy 22

Carmichael, C. 1974. "A Time for War and a Time for Peace: The Influence of the Distinction upon Some Legal and Literary Material (in Dt)." *JJS* 25:50–64.

———. 1995. "Forbidden Mixtures in Deuteronomy xxii 9–11 and Leviticus xix 19." *VT* 45:433–48.

Derrett, J. D. M. 1978. "2 Cor 6:14: A Midrash on Dt 22:10." *Bib* 59:231–50.

———. 1979. "Fresh Light on the Lost Sheep and the Lost Coin." *NTS* 26:36–60.

Fishbane, M. 1980. "Biblical Colophons, Textual Criticism and Legal Analogies." *CBQ* 42:438–49.

Harland, P. J. 1998–1999. "Menswear and Womenswear: A Study of Deuteronomy 22:5." *ExpT* 110:73–76.

Hiebert, R. J. V. 1994. "Deuteronomy 22:28–29 and Its Premishnaic Interpretations." *CBQ* 56:203–20.

Kaufman, S. 1979. "The Structure of the Deuteronomic Law." *Maarav* 1 (2):105–58.

Tigay, J. H. 1971. "Adultery." *EncJud* 2:313–15.

————. 1993. "Examination of the Accused Bride in 4Q159: Forensic Medicine at Qumran." *JANES* 22:129–34.

Wenham, G. J., and J. G. McConville. 1980. "Drafting Techniques in Some Deuteronomic Laws." *VT* 30:248–52.

Deuteronomy 23

Craigie, P. C. 1977. "Deuteronomy and Ugaritic Studies." *TynB* 28:155–69.

Fishbane, M. 1985. *Biblical Interpretation in Ancient Israel.* Oxford: Clarendon. Pp. 114–53.

Fisher, E. J. 1976. "Cultic Prostitution in the Ancient Near East." *BTB* 6:225–36.

Gruber, M. 1986. "Hebrew Qedesah and Her Canaanite and Akkadian Cognates." *UF* 18:133–48.

Milgrom, J. 1983. *Studies in Cultic Theology and Terminology.* SJLA 36. Leiden: Brill. Pp. 1–17.

Phillips, A. C. 1980. "Uncovering the Father's Skirt." *VT* 30:38–43.

Toorn, K. van der. 1989. "Female Prostitution in Payment of Vows in Ancient Israel." *JBL* 108:193–205.

————. 1992. "Cultic Prostitution." *ABD* 5:510–13.

Weinfeld, M. 1971. "Congregation." *EncJud* 5:893–96.

Deuteronomy 24

Brewer, D. I. 1998. "Deuteronomy 24:1–4 and the Origin of the Jewish Divorce Certificate." *JJS* 49:230–43.

Brueggemann, W. 1998. *A Commentary on Jeremiah: Exile and Homecoming.* Grand Rapids: Eerdmans.

Eichrodt, W. 1961–1967. *Theology of the Old Testament.* Trans. J. Baker. 2 vols. OTL. Philadelphia: Westminster.

Fishbane, M. 1985. *Biblical Interpretation in Ancient Israel.* Oxford: Clarendon. Pp. 307–12.

Hobbs, T. R. 1974. "Jeremiah 3:1 and Deuteronomy 24:1–4." *ZAW* 86:23–29.

Laney, J. C. 1992. "Deuteronomy 24:1–4 and the Issue of Divorce." *BSac* 149:3–15.

Lipinski, E. 1981. "The Wife's Right to Divorce in Light of an Ancient Near Eastern Tradition." *Jewish Law Annual* 4:103–27.

Phillips, A. 1973. "Some Aspects of Family Law in Pre-exilic Israel." *VT* 23:349–61.

Warren, A. 1998. "Did Moses Permit Divorce?" *TynB* 49:39–56.

Wenham, G. J. 1979. "The Restoration of Marriage Reconsidered." *JJS* 30:36–40.

Westbrook, R. 1986. "The Prohibition on Restoration of Marriage in Deuteronomy 24:1–4." In *Studies in Bible.* Ed. S. Japhet. Scripta Hiersolymitana 31. Jerusalem: Magnes. Pp. 387–405.

Deuteronomy 25

Carmichael, C. 1974. *The Laws of Deuteronomy.* Ithaca, N.Y.: Cornell University Press.

———. 1977. "Ceremonial Crux: Removing a Man's Sandal as a Female Gesture of Contempt." *JBL* 96:321–36.

Cohn, H. H. 1971. "Flogging." *EncJud* 6:1348–49.

Eslinger, L. 1981. "The Case of the Immodest Lady Wrestler in Deuteronomy 25:11–12." *VT* 31:269–81.

Frick, F. 1994. "Widows in the Hebrew Bible." In *A Feminist Companion to Exodus to Deuteronomy.* Ed. A. Brenner. The Feminist Companion to the Bible 6. Sheffield: Sheffield Academic Press. Pp. 139–51.

Kaiser, W. C., Jr. 1978. "Current Crisis in Exegesis and the Apostolic Use of Deuteronomy 25:4 in 1 Cor. 9:8–10." *JETS* 21:3–18.

Kruger, P. A. 1996. "The Removal of the Sandal in Deuteronomy xxv 9: 'A Rite of Passage'?" *VT* 46:534–39.

Noonan, J. T. 1980. "The Muzzled Ox." *JQR* 70:172–75.

Wilson, P. E. 1997. "Deuteronomy xxv 11–12—One for the Books." *VT* 47:220–35.

Deuteronomy 26

DeVries, S. J. 1974. "The Development of the Deuteronomic Promulgation Formula." *Bib* 55:301–16.

Eades, K. L. 2000. "Divine Action and Human Action: A Comparative Study of Deuteronomy 26:1–11 and Haggai 2:10–19." In *Reading the Hebrew Bible for a New Millennium: Form, Concept, and Theological Perspective.* Vol. 1, *Theological and Hermeneutical Studies.* Ed. W. Kim et al. SAC. Harrisburg, Pa.: Trinity. Pp. 103–23.

Janzen, J. G. 1994. "The 'Wandering Aramean' Reconsidered." *VT* 44:359–75.

Millard, A. 1980. "A Wandering Aramean." *JNES* 49:153–55.

Rice, G. 1961. "Egypt, the Desert, and Canaan (Three Themes in Dt 26:5–10)." *Journal of Religious Thought* 18:23–25.

Steiner, R. C. 1997. "The 'Aramean' of Dt 26:5: *Peshat* and *Derash*." In *Tehillah le-Moshe: Biblical and Judaic Studies in Honor of Moshe Greenberg.* Ed. M. Cogan, B. L. Eichler, and J. H. Tigay. Winona Lake, Ind.: Eisenbrauns. Pp. 127–38.

22

Blessings and Curses

DEUTERONOMY 27–30

The four chapters to be studied in this unit constitute the last two chapters of Moses' second address (chs. 27–28), and Moses' brief third address (chs. 29–30).

Moses has finished placing before Israel the law of the Lord. Toward this law no believer can be neutral. One will choose either to live by it or to ignore it. What Moses seeks to establish here is the fact of consequences, or retribution, a divine response that is commensurate with the choice made by the individual.

If that choice is obedience, the consequence is blessing; if that choice is disobedience, the consequence is curse. And particularly in the third address (see 29:27) the curse includes a future exile from the land—a theme first sounded in 4:27–31. Robert Polzin (1980: 70) captures the shift in emphasis from Moses' second address to his third: "The emphasis there [the second address, chs. 5–28] was on the immediate future and what Israel had to do to *remain* in the land God was giving them. Here in the third address, emphasis is on the far-distant future of the exile and on what Israel has to do to *regain* the land."

We may outline this section as follows:

1. 27:1–10: a covenant-renewal ceremony at Shechem
2. 27:11–26: a proclamation by the Levites of twelve prohibitions, with appropriate congregational response (the repeated "amen" amounts to an oath by the respondents to eschew such activities)
3. 28:1–14: blessings
4. 28:15–68: curses
5. 29:1–29: an exhortation to commitment and faithfulness
6. 30:1–10: hope for restoration even in exile and anticipation of a new covenant later announced in Jer. 31:31–34 and Ezek. 36:24–28
7. 30:11–20: the options: life and death—choose!

It is obvious, from a look at the sections involving results or consequences, that far more space is devoted to curse than to blessing. In ch. 27 we note that representatives of six of the tribes stand on Mount Ebal to curse (v. 13), and representatives of the remaining six tribes stand on Mount Gerizim to bless (v. 12). Yet we read of no blessings in the last half of the chapter, only curses. (This is one of the reasons why many interpreters think that ch. 27 is an insertion that separates ch. 26 from ch. 28, and one that has undergone a long literary development. The arguments on this question can be followed in the commentaries.)

This imbalance between curse and blessing is not unexpected. P. C. Craigie (1976: 340 n. 15) quotes Kenneth Kitchen on this phenomenon in other corpora. In the Code of Lipit-Ishtar curses outnumber blessings by a ratio of approximately 3:1. In the Code of Hammurabi the proportion of curses to blessings is approximately 20:1. This emphasis continues into the first-millennium B.C. Assyrian treaties (e.g., the seventh-century B.C. treaty of Esarhaddon, in which 250 of 674 lines are given to curses).

The exclusive use of "cursed" in 27:14–26 and the much greater use in ch. 28 of "cursed" (vv. 15–68) than "blessed" (vv. 1–14) may be more than simply a parallel with ancient Near Eastern treaties. The preponderance of one over the other may be Deuteronomy's way of "explicitly acknowledging an expectation that Israel's future lies under curse and not blessing" (Barker 1998: 284). The only "blessed" section of chs. 27–28 (28:1–14) is bracketed by "cursed" sections (27:14–26; 28:15–68). So understood, the heavy emphasis on maledictions in Israel's future in chs. 27–28 is not all that different from ch. 32, "the Song of Moses," one that at places envisions apostasy in Israel's future.

Left to their own devices, then, God's elect do not have a promising horizon. If satisfied to trust only in their own abilities to be steadfast, the Israelites do indeed have much reason to "worry about tomorrow" (cf. Jesus' words that his followers need not do so [Matt. 6:34]). It surely is important that as we move through Deuteronomy, we observe that calls for Israel's faithfulness in earlier parts (e.g., "circumcise your hearts [10:16]) are replaced by divine promises in later portions of the book (e.g., "The LORD your God will circumcise your hearts" [30:6 NIV]). Limits of human ability are contrasted with the unlimited faithfulness and resources of God (Olson 1995: 122). An Israel whose future is one under law is also an Israel whose future is one under grace.

Perhaps that is one reason for the geographical emphasis in ch. 27 on Mounts Ebal and Gerizim, both near the city of Shechem. Shechem is the first Canaanite city that Abraham enters, a place where God first promises land to his offspring, and where Abraham constructs his first altar (Gen. 12:7). Jacob buys real estate there (Gen. 33:19), and Joseph's remains are interred there (Josh. 24:32). In other words, what God is going to do in Israel's future, as envisioned in ch. 27, is fulfill the promise made to the patriarchs (see Deut. 1:6–8; 34:4). He is a God who is more a keeper of promises than one who doles out rewards for compliance. Furthermore, he is a God who anticipates failure and noncompliance, and to that end he mandates the placing of an altar (27:4–7), not on Mount Gerizim, from which the blessings are pronounced (27:12), but on Mount Ebal, from which the curses are pronounced (27:13). God's broken law and God's broken heart exist in tandem, as do divine anger and divine atonement. It is more than interesting that in a book that so emphasizes worshiping and coming before God only "in the place he will choose and cause his name to dwell," one can seek God and return to him from the most remote, alien, God-forsaken places (4:29; 30:4).

The theological issue sounded in these chapters is one that provided a basis for serious theological reflection in Scripture itself, and it is an issue that continues to the present day. I refer here to what is commonly called "Deuteronomic theology." That is, those who follow the Lord may anticipate blessing in the form of children, health, prosperity, conquest over the enemy, or ideal climatic conditions in which to produce agricultural crops. Conversely, the absence of these benefits, or the presence of their antithesis, is a result of disobedience to covenantal norms. Thus, Deuteronomy 28 puts the curses of God on Israel's disobedience into the categories of sickness and drought (vv. 20–24); military defeat (vv. 25–26); diseases of mind and body and loss of one's wife and livestock (vv. 27–35); a dreary, unproductive life in exile (vv. 36–46); and siege by the enemy (vv. 47–57).

The system, then, appears to be simple, straightforward, black and white. Those who follow the Lord rightly can instantly expect blessings at every material level; those who repudiate Yahweh's lordship over their lives can expect heartaches, setbacks, sterility, and so forth.

The question I wish to pursue is to what degree Deuteronomic theology informs the rest of the Old Testament. Are there sections of the Old Testament that challenge a facile equation at this point? Does Deuteronomy itself forbid the reader from oversimplifying the relationship between one's character and one's circumstances? What about the teachings of Jesus and Paul?

Or, if the Deuteronomic emphasis is perverted, what are the possibilities for ruin, harm, and misrepresentation? G. K. Chesterton speaks to this: "When once people have begun to believe that prosperity is the reward of virtue, their next calamity is obvious. If prosperity is regarded as the reward of virtue, it will be regarded as the symptom of virtue. Men will leave off the heavy task of making good men successful. They will adopt the easier task of making out successful men good" (quoted in Glatzer 1969: 236–37).

I have already had occasion to refer to the studies of Martin Noth and his contention that the narratives in Joshua and Kings function primarily as a historical witness to the truthfulness of Deuteronomy's theology vis-à-vis obedience, disobedience, and consequences. In the Book of Joshua, for example, those who engage in war in the way God instructs will win (Joshua 6), while those who engage in war in ways contrary to God's instructions will lose (Joshua 7). Think of what happens to a Saul, a David, or a Solomon when they violate God's laws. Conversely, think of God's blessings that come to a Hezekiah or a Josiah when they obey those laws.

To these historical books we may also add much from the oracles of the prophets. It is, for example, not an exaggeration to say that almost all the preaching of the eighth-century B.C. prophet Amos is based on Deuteronomy 28, or something very close to it. Such a backdrop makes even more intelligible his rhetorical questions, such as, "Does evil befall a city, unless the LORD has done it?" (3:6b RSV). In the very next chapter (4:6–11) Amos lists the following as illustrations of God's trying to bring Israel to an awakening: shortage of food, no rains for the harvest, lack of adequate drinking water, disease that wiped out the precious produce of gardens and vineyards, and war and pestilence. Thus, every conceivable misfortune is the product of the Lord's wrath.

A second support of this emphasis is a number of the psalms. One has only to think of texts such as Psalm 1, a contrast between the righteous person, who prospers in every effort, and the wicked person, who perishes. Again, one recalls David's testimony: "I have not seen the righteous forsaken or their children begging bread" (Ps. 37:25 NRSV); "Many are the torments of the wicked, but steadfast love surrounds those who trust in the LORD" (Ps. 32:10 NRSV). To be sure, the psalms of lament, especially those written by a righteous, law-abiding individual who feels abandoned by God (e.g., Psalm 22), or is bewildered by the prosperity of the ungodly (e.g., Psalm 73), or is on the receiving end of some damaging abuse (e.g., Psalm 109), show that good things do not always happen to good people. But those who inscribed such prayerful cries believed that they should be appropriately rewarded for their behavior, for their theology is the theology of Deuteronomy 27–28. The teaching of 2 Tim. 3:12 ("Everyone who wants to live a godly life in Christ Jesus will be persecuted" [NIV]) is light years removed from the world of Deuteronomy 27–30.

Parallel to some of these "wisdom psalms" are similar reverberations in Proverbs. The first nine chapters alone provide ample illustrations of the rewards for those who fear the Lord. They will be delivered, but the wicked will be cut off and rooted out (2:12, 21–22). To fear the Lord is a guarantee that "your barns will be filled with plenty, and your vats will be bursting with wine" (3:10 NRSV). One may add to these longer units aphoristic sayings in Proverbs such as, "Whoever sows injustice will reap calamity" (22:8 NRSV). (I am not concerned here with the debate on whether Wisdom literature views the retribution to be something imposed on the person from outside or above, or something that is inward and necessary, growing out of the act itself. I am simply establishing the fact of the principle that each act has a consequence.) There are many references in Proverbs to the topic of poverty (e.g., 6:9–11; 10:4; 14:23; 20:13; 24:30–34). Without exception, says Proverbs, poverty is the result of laziness or some other dysfunctional behavior. And laziness, immortalized in the famous "sluggard," is a sin. Proverbs never offers a hint that other factors may cause one to be engulfed in poverty.

So deeply entrenched was this idea that it was still prevalent among Jesus' disciples. Encountering a man with congenital blindness, they ask, "Who sinned, this man or his parents, that he was born blind?" (John 9:2 NRSV). After his conversation with the rich young ruler, Jesus added the following for the benefit of his disciples: "It will be hard for a rich man to enter the kingdom of heaven" (RSV). A camel will squeeze through the needle's eye before that happens (Matt. 19:23–24). Their response? "Who then can be saved?" After all, was not wealth one of the prime evidences of God's blessing (although the Old Testament recognizes that some individuals possess ill-gotten riches)? Their theology also explains why they could not accept the Lord's forthcoming crucifixion.

Yet we need to observe that for all the truthfulness of the treaty curses and blessings of Deuteronomy, they present only part of the picture. Any conclusions that we may want to draw need to be tempered by a study of all Scripture. The following observations are important.

First, the historical books themselves present something of a mixed picture. In war "the sword devours now one and now another" (2 Sam.

11:25 NRSV), so that the innocent suffer along with the guilty. Witness the untimely death of Abner (2 Sam. 3:33–34), the priests of Nob (1 Sam. 22:18), and the brothers of Abimelech (Judg. 9:5). These are instances in which death has nothing at all to do with retributive justice. On the other side of the ledger one has only to think of the many kings, both Judean and Israelite, who basked in luxury and opulence in spite of their God-defying attitudes and actions.

Second, the prophets do not baptize the Deuteronomic theology uncritically. In an emphasis reminiscent of parts of Deuteronomy, Hosea states that in spite of the infidelity of God's people, God has given them "the grain, the wine, and the oil" and has "lavished . . . silver and gold" upon them (Hos. 2:8 NRSV). Here are gifts of divine blessing, although by all accounts such gifts should have been withheld. Perhaps the parade example in prophetic literature is the Suffering Servant of Isaiah 53. The Servant of the Lord is rejected, afflicted, and treated with contempt. He does not prosper. And this is simply an extension, but in much greater intensity, of the suffering experienced by most of the prophets, especially Jeremiah. Few, if any, escaped persecution and harassment. But at no point is the suggestion made that these trials are a divine rebuke leveled at God's spokesmen.

Third, although many psalms do indeed support a traditional understanding of reward and punishment, just as many, if not more, challenge the traditional view. Limiting himself to the wisdom psalms, J. K. Kuntz (1977: 232) divides these psalms into three categories according to what they espouse about the doctrine of reward and punishment. These categories are the traditional; the realistic; and the futuristic, which hopes in the prospects of immortality. Add to this the large number of lament psalms (almost one-third of the Psalter), a few of which move into imprecation, and we are forced to look more deeply rather than accept a facile understanding of the act-and-consequence relationship.

Fourth, some entire books within the Old Testament canon protest against a frozen interpretation of Deuteronomy. The best examples are Ecclesiastes and Job. As the writer of Ecclesiastes observes, the same fate comes to both the wise and the foolish (2:14; 9:2). Both are forgotten quickly (2:16). Human beings have no advantage over beasts (3:19). God gives wealth and honor to some people, but others who are undeserving eat from them like scavengers (6:2). The experience of Job is well known. Job's friends were reflecting the theology of Deuteronomy accurately ("You are suffering, Job, because you have sinned deliberately, and the way to healing is repentance"), but their application of it to Job was inaccurate and thus irrelevant.

Fifth, the witness of the New Testament is interesting. Jesus certainly taught the *eventual* relationship of character to destiny; what he repudiated was the *immediate* relationship of character and circumstance. Thus, the case of the lad being born blind had nothing at all to do with sin (John 9:3). The eighteen who were crushed to death by the falling tower in Siloam were not quintessential sinners (Luke 13:1–5). Jesus taught that God sends rain and sunshine on believers and unbelievers alike (Matt. 5:45), an assertion that is especially poignant in light of Deut. 28:12, which pinpoints rain as one of God's blessings on the obedient. Jesus' pronouncement of blessing on the poor (Matt. 5:3), the mourners (Matt. 5:4), and the persecuted (Matt. 5:10) is characteristically non-Deuteronomic.

Two experiences from Paul's life buttress the instances taken from the Gospels (see Thompson 1979). Paul's experience on the Mediterranean during a storm (Acts 27) may be compared with Jonah's experience much earlier on the same sea and in the same kind of weather. Both Jonah and Paul are traveling on the same sea in an east-to-west direction. On both boats there is one famous passenger and hosts of other unknown passengers. Death by drowning seems imminent in both cases. Someone or something is thrown overboard to prevent casualties. There is one major difference, however. For Jonah the storm is sent from God to break down his disobedience and reluctance to go to Nineveh; for Paul the storm is simply a phenomenon of weather. Paul might add that the faithful believer can avoid Jonah's storm, but not Paul's storm. In the life of even the most devoted servant of God there may be a great deal of turbulence. That surely was true in the life of Paul, and supremely so in the life of Jesus, the most righteous individual ever to grace our planet.

The second illustration revolves around Rom. 8:31–39. Paul mentions certain experiences that Deuteronomy 28 lists precisely as treaty curses: tribulation, distress, persecution, famine, nakedness, peril, and sword. In the midst of his argument Paul quotes Ps. 44:22, "For your sake we face death all day long" (NIV), but he does not need to quote the next verse, Ps. 44:23, "Awake, O LORD! Why do you sleep?" (NIV). Rather, Paul can say, "In all these things we are more than conquerors" (NRSV). The basis for Paul's assurance is not his experiences, but the death and resurrection of Christ (Rom. 8:32–34).

A final point that can be made is that Deuteronomy itself (see Gammie 1970) gives us something of a double picture. Moses reminds the people that God humbled Israel in the wilderness not because of any specific sin, but to teach and to test them (Deut. 8:2–3). It was a way of disciplining Israel (Deut. 8:5). Moses also reminds the people that Israel's wealth is a gift of God, not something that they earned (Deut. 8:18). God is not giving the blessing of land and conquest to the Israelites because they are more righteous than the other nations (Deut. 9:4–6).

Israel avoided the wrath of God in the episode of the golden calf only because Moses prayed (Deut. 9:25–29), thus Israel is spared by the virtue of another, not because of any inherent virtue of its own. In the penultimate chapter of Deuteronomy (ch. 33) Moses pronounces exclusively future blessings on each of the tribes of Israel. Interestingly, unlike the preceding chapter (32), here not one word of warning is issued against potential departures from the law of Yahweh, nor is there any "God will bless you if you. . . ." See the quote from B. Childs on p. 460. So even the Book of Deuteronomy cautions against the oversimplification of a highly complex area of walking with God.

No one would ever question that every page of the New Testament reinforces the basic idea of Deuteronomy's theology: God honors obedience and looks with disdain upon disobedience. That is as much new-covenant truth as it is old-covenant truth. What new-covenant truth uniquely affirms is that some of the manifestations of God's blessings will be deferred until the era of the New Jerusalem—no more death, mourning, crying, or pain (Rev. 21:4).

Deuteronomy 27–30

Anbar, M. 1985. "The Story about the Building of an Altar on Mt. Ebal: The History of Its Composition and the Question of the Centralization of the Cult." In *Das Deuteronomium: Entstehung, Gestalt und Botschaft*. Ed. N. Lohfink. BETL 68. Leuven: Leuven University Press. Pp. 304–9.

Barker, P. A. 1998. "The Theology of Deuteronomy 27." *TynB* 49:277–303.

Bellefontaine, E. 1975. "The Curses of Deuteronomy 27: Their Relationship to the Prohibitives." In *No Famine in the Land: Studies in Honor of John L. McKenzie*. Ed. J. W. Flanagan and A. W. Robinson. Missoula, Mont.: Scholars Press. Pp. 49–61. Repr., in *A Song of Power and the Power of Song: Essays on the Book of Deuteronomy*. Ed. D. L. Christensen. SBTS 3. Winona Lake, Ind.: Eisenbrauns, 1993. Pp. 256–68.

Brettler, M. Z. 1999. "Predestination in Deuteronomy 30, 1–10." In *Those Elusive Deuteronomists: The Phenomenon of Pan-Deuteronomism*. Ed. L. S. Schearing and S. L. McKenzie. JSOTSup 268. Sheffield: Sheffield Academic Press. Pp. 171–88.

Brichto, H. C. 1963. *The Problem of "Curse" in the Hebrew Bible*. Philadelphia: Society of Biblical Literature.

Budd, P. J. 1973. "Priestly Instruction in Pre-exilic Israel." *VT* 23:1–14.

Craigie, P. C. 1976. *The Book of Deuteronomy*. NICOT. Grand Rapids: Eerdmans.

Eichrodt, W. 1961–1967. *Theology of the Old Testament*. Trans. J. Baker. 2 vols. OTL. Philadelphia: Westminster. Vol. 1, pp. 258–69.

Fensham, F. C. 1962. "Malediction and Benediction in Ancient Near Eastern Vassal-Treaties and the Old Testament." *ZAW* 74:1–9. Repr., in *A Song of Power and the*

Power of Song: Essays on the Book of Deuteronomy. Ed. D. L. Christensen. SBTS 3. Winona Lake, Ind.: Eisenbrauns, 1993. Pp. 247–55.

Gammie, J. G. 1970. "The Theology of Retribution in the Book of Deuteronomy." *CBQ* 32:1–12.

Glatzer, N., ed. 1969. *The Dimensions of Job: A Study and Selected Readings.* New York: Schocken.

Hill, A. E. 1988. "The Ebal Ceremony as Hebrew Land Grant? [Deut 17,1–26]." *JETS* 31:399–406.

Kaufmann, Y. 1960. *The Religion of Israel.* Trans. M. Greenberg. Chicago: University of Chicago Press. Pp. 329–38.

Kearney, P. J. 1973. "The Role of the Gibeonites in the Deuteronomic History." *CBQ* 35:1–19.

Kuntz, J. K. 1977. "The Retribution Motiv in Psalmic Wisdom." *ZAW* 89:223–33.

Lewy, I. 1962. "The Puzzle of Dt xxvii: Blessings Announced, but Curses Noted." *VT* 12:207–11.

Olson, D. T. 1995. "Deuteronomy as De-centering Center: Reflections on Postmodernism and the Quest for a Theological Center of the Hebrew Scriptures." *Semeia* 71:119–32.

Patrick, D. 1972. "The Word Is Near at Hand." *Encounter* 33:385–92.

Polzin, R. 1980. *Moses and the Deuteronomist: A Literary Study of the Deuteronomic History.* New York: Seabury. Pp. 69–71.

Rad, G. von. 1973. *Wisdom in Israel.* Trans. J. D. Martin. Nashville: Abingdon. Pp. 128–37.

Rofé, A. 1993. "The Covenant in the Land of Moab (Deuteronomy 28:69–30:20): Historico Literary, Comparative, and Formcritical Considerations." In *A Song of Power and the Power of Song: Essays on the Book of Deuteronomy.* Ed. D. L. Christensen. SBTS 3. Winona Lake, Ind.: Eisenbrauns. Pp. 269–80.

Schley, D. G., Jr. 1985. "'Yahweh Will Cause You to Return to Egypt in Ships' (Deuteronomy xxviii 68)." *VT* 35:369–72.

Thompson, D. L. 1979. "The Godly and the Good Life: The Relationship between Character and Circumstance in Biblical Thought." *Asbury Seminarian* 34:28–46.

Towner, W. S. 1971. "Retribution Theology in the Apocalyptic Setting." *USQR* 26:203–14.

Weinfeld, M. 1978. *Deuteronomy and the Deuteronomic School.* Oxford: Clarendon. Pp. 104–46.

Wolff, H. W. 1974. "The Kerygma of the Deuteronomic Historical Work." In *The Vitality of Old Testament Traditions,* by H. W. Wolff and W. Brueggemann. Atlanta: John Knox. Pp. 93–100.

23

Moses' Farewell

DEUTERONOMY 31–34

Two major chapters of this unit are poems: the "song of Moses" (ch. 32) and "the blessing of Moses" (ch. 33). Prefacing these poems is a list of a few events toward the end of Moses' life: the writing of the law, a concern for its periodic reading, the presentation of Joshua before the Lord (ch. 31). Following the poems is a final chapter, mostly about the death of Moses (ch. 34).

Apart from this mixture of narrative and poetry, three other items set chs. 31–34 apart. One is that there is a shift in emphasis away from what Moses says in chs. 1–30 to what Moses does, especially in ch. 31.

A second item is that these last few chapters of Deuteronomy provide a good contrast with the opening three chapters in that in Deuteronomy 1–3 Moses begins with a backward look as he recalls and retells earlier events in Israel's history after leaving Egypt; by contrast, in chapters 31–34 he ends with a forward look as he anticipates the future of Israel and the ministry of Joshua after his own demise. Thus Deuteronomy begins with reflection on a past of which Moses was a part, and it ends with reflection on a future in which Moses will have no part.

A third unique item about this section is that it provides the only occasions in Deuteronomy where God speaks directly (31:14b; 31:16b–21;

31:23b; 32:49–52; 34:4b; and portions of the poem in ch. 32). This is unlike the first four books of the Pentateuch, where God's voice is heard throughout. This does not imply any evaluative difference between the plethora of divine speech elsewhere in the Pentateuch and the paucity of divine speech in Deuteronomy. Deuteronomy is as much a divine word as any other Torah portion, except in this case the divine word lies behind the human words of Moses to a degree not seen elsewhere in the Pentateuch. If, for example, the psalms are originally a human word (they are prayers addressed to God) that become a divine word, Deuteronomy is a divine word delivered through a human instrument and a human word.

No small amount of ink has been expended on the two poems. For one thing, they are replete with translation problems and some unusual vocabulary and Hebrew grammar. The reader can check the verse-by-verse treatment in the commentaries or the studies of Frank Cross and D. N. Freedman and others in order to see some of the issues here.

Another concern has been the dating of these poems. The theories suggest the time of Samuel as the earliest possibility to the time of the exile as the latest possibility. I know of no critical scholar who has suggested a pre-Samuel or Mosaic date for composition (except for Umberto Cassuto, who dates both poems to the time of the judges). Nor am I aware of any critical scholar who does not endorse the idea that most of this latter unit is secondary, added much later to Ur-Deuteronomy.

The conservative response would be at least threefold. First, the critical reconstruction, if plausible, must simply avoid the witness of these chapters themselves about their origin: "Then Moses recited the words of this song" (31:30 NRSV); "Moses came and spoke all the words of this song" (32:44 NASB); "This is the blessing with which Moses the man of God blessed the children of Israel before his death" (33:1). Can such a witness be so easily ignored?

Second, the language of the poems is sufficiently archaic to be viewed as an authentic representation of late-second-millennium B.C. Canaanite. George Mendenhall (1975: 66) even goes so far to suggest a number of linguistic correlations between Deuteronomy 32 and the syllabic texts from Byblos, which he dates to not much later than 2000 B.C., if not earlier.

Third, as the "final" text stands, we have an almost perfect structure for a second-millennium B.C. covenant. These last few chapters would include the following parts of that structure: the deposition of the text ("Take this book of the law and place it beside the ark of the covenant of the LORD your God" [31:26 NASB]); the periodic public recital of the contents of the covenant ("At the end of every seven years . . . read this law before all Israel in their hearing" [31:10–11 RSV]); the presence of witnesses to observe the covenant event ("that this song may be a witness for me against the people of Israel" [31:19 RSV]; "this song shall confront them as a witness" [31:21 RSV]; "this book of the law . . . that it may be there for a witness against you" [31:26 RSV]; "and call heaven and earth to witness against them" [31:28 NRSV]). The question is this: which is more likely, a homogeneous creation by an individual cognizant of contemporary patterns of expression and covenant making, or a creation by bits and pieces of a perfect structure patterned nostalgically after forms that essentially have long ceased to exist?

Joshua the Successor (31)

This chapter contains seven speeches, four by Moses and three by the Lord:

1. Moses to Israel (vv. 1–6): Israel will conquer Canaan, even without Moses.
2. Moses to Joshua (vv. 7–8): Away with fear! The Lord will be with you.
3. Moses to priests and elders (vv. 9–13): Read this law every seven years.
4. The Lord to Moses (vv. 14–15): You are about to die. Bring Joshua before me.
5. The Lord to Moses (vv. 16–21): Israel will forsake me in Canaan.
6. The Lord to Joshua (v. 23): I will be with you, Joshua.
7. Moses to Levites (vv. 24–29): Israel will rebel, as it already has.

In three of these speeches Joshua is present (numbers 2, 4, and 6). Once he is spoken to by Moses (v. 7), and once by the Lord (v. 23); once he is spoken about (v. 14). One might expect v. 23 to follow v. 15; that is, the fourth speech leads naturally into the sixth speech. Thus we read, "'Call Joshua, and present yourselves in the tent of meeting, that I may commission him.' And Moses and Joshua went and presented themselves in the tent of meeting" (v. 14 RSV); "and the LORD appeared" (v. 15); and then, "the LORD commissioned Joshua" (v. 23). However, coming between the summoning of Joshua and his actual commissioning is a speech by the Lord to Moses.

The point of this speech is that Israel, once in the land of promise, will follow other gods and force God into hiding (his face). To this prophecy Joshua is listening, or at least eavesdropping. This speech is really more for his benefit than for Moses'. It is God's way of saying, indirectly, to Joshua, "Be prepared for the worst; your leadership will not deter Israel from disobedience." It is significant that throughout these events Joshua never speaks. He only listens. It is a chilling experience to be informed beforehand that your mission will meet only with mixed results. Even the reading of the law every seven years, designed to bring people to "fear the LORD," will not be a deterrent. For we note that the Lord speaks not of the possibility of apostasy, but of its inevitability. Apparently, Moses is in agreement with the Lord at this point (vv. 27, 29)! He at least viewed himself as a restraining influence, a shadow that his successor would not be able to cast. This may explain why Moses twice utters the phrase "Be strong and courageous," once to Israel (31:6) and once to Joshua (31:7), while the Lord says it four times to Joshua (Deut. 31:23; Josh. 1:6, 7, 9). Joshua has a double challenge on his hands, filling the big, empty shoes of Moses and shepherding a sometimes recalcitrant flock.

The Song of Moses (32)

This poetic composition is, more than anything, a graphic contrast between the nature of God and the nature of his people. He is the Rock (vv. 4, 18, 30, 31); they are on the rocks, or following the wrong rock (v. 37).

In the preceding chapter Moses seems to produce two documents. One is the law (31:9, 11, 12, 13, 24, 26), and the other is a song (31:19, 21, 22, 30). Moses "writes" both the law (31:9, 24) and the song (31:19, 22). Both the song (31:19) and the law (31:26) are said to function as a "witness" against later generations of Israelites. It is probably best to think that Moses is the author of two distinct compositions that, while different, have a common purpose. It is not impossible, however, that in ch. 31 "the law" and "the song" to which the chapter refer are one and the same. This would be more conceivable especially if we render the Hebrew word *tôrâ*, customarily translated "law," instead as "instruction, teaching," a meaning that it sometimes carries elsewhere. In such a case *tôrâ* would refer to the function of ch. 32, while "song" would refer to its form (Weitzman 1997: 44).

Throughout the poem there is a change of speakers, going back and forth from Moses to God, just as in ch. 31, where Moses and God share speaking responsibilities:

Moses: vv. 1–19
God: vv. 20–35
Moses: v. 36
God: vv. 37–42
Moses: v. 43

An extensive study by G. E. Wright (1962) laid the foundation for subsequent understandings of this poem. He suggested that the composition is a "covenant lawsuit," with a summons to witnesses (v. 1), an accusation in the form of a question (v. 6), the plaintiff's (God) benefits to the accused (vv. 7–14), a statement of breach of covenant (vv. 15–18), and subsequent sentencing and judgment on the guilty (vv. 19–29).

This analysis has been accepted more or less by most commentators. Only in a few instances has a distinctive alternative been raised. Mendenhall (1975: 70) suggests that the poem is not a covenant lawsuit, but rather a prophetic oracle. He argues, "Here Yahweh is *not* suing anyone for breach of covenant; instead the breach *had* taken place, the consequences *had* been suffered, and the issue is whether or not Yahweh would be a reliable refuge for the future."

This interpretation has the advantage of shifting the major part of the poem from a diatribe against the people to a doxology to God. In the past God may have "hid his face" (v. 20); now Moses will try to let Israel see that face again. Whether they will see it is uncertain. Moses himself is not sure of that. For that reason, in the introduction to the poem he can speak only wishfully: "May my teaching drop like the rain, my speech condense like the dew" (v. 2 NRSV). Thiessen (2004) agrees with Wright to a point. Rather than seeing the whole chapter as a covenant lawsuit, Thiessen sees the chapter as a hymn with an embedded covenant lawsuit. Deuteronomy 32 functions liturgically as a model of how future generations of worshipers are to express themselves before their God.

It would seem odd, if ch. 32 is a covenant lawsuit, that Moses would style the poem as "my teaching," an expression that seems more at home in the world of the Book of Proverbs, as does labeling the audience of this poem as "foolish and unwise" (v. 6) and "without sense" (v. 28), and God calling them to be "wise and understanding and discerning" (v. 29). Weitzman (1994; 1997) suggests that ch. 32, given the fact that Moses recites its words just before he dies, is Moses' "swan song," one that combines the legal dimensions of a covenant lawsuit and the didactic elements of the wisdom tradition. Hence, it is a poem that is both accusatory and instructional.

It is futile to attempt to identify specific historical events to which the writer is alluding, although essentially the poem is a résumé of Israel's history. Even phrases that perhaps are identifiable seem strange. For example, we are struck by the statement "He found him in a desert land" (v. 10a RSV; compare an echo of this in Hos. 9:10, "Like grapes in the wilderness, I found Israel" [NRSV]). The "desert land" can hardly be Egypt, although the equation is possible. Did God "find" Israel in the wilderness? Equally futile is the attempt to identify the enemies of

vv. 27–43. Are they Arameans, Assyrians, Babylonians, Samaritans, or perhaps others?

The timelessness of the poem is accented not only by the vagueness of language but also by the constant change of pronominal subject throughout. To illustrate, "They have acted corruptly toward him, to their shame they are no longer his children. . . . Is this the way you repay the LORD, O foolish and unwise people?" (vv. 5–6 NIV). Or, "You grew fat, bloated, and gorged! He abandoned God who made him. . . . They made him jealous" (vv. 15–16 NRSV). As Fokkelman (1998: 142–43) has observed, the timelessness of the poem "exhorts to reflection: every generation in Israel (and then, every reader willing to imagine himself in that position) is here made conscious of their elected status . . . and of the accompanying pitfalls of . . . moral laziness . . . and hence of their own responsibility in the face of God."

I noted that the prevalent metaphor in this chapter for God is "rock." Obviously, the idea that is conveyed is one of stability, permanence, refuge, and security. But Moses is concerned to go beyond God's Gibraltar-like qualities. The parental metaphors, for instance, are interesting. At one point we read, "Is he not your Father, your Creator?" (v. 6 NIV). Later the writer changes to gynomorphic language: "You deserted the Rock, who fathered you; and you forgot the God who gave you birth" (v. 18 NIV). (Jeremiah perhaps parodies this verse when he speaks to his backslidden contemporaries, those who say to a tree, "You are my father," and to a stone, "You gave me birth" [Jer. 2:27], and in Jeremiah perhaps an ironic shift of sex roles.) The Hebrew of v. 18 makes even more vivid a God who went through childbirth: "You deserted the God who gave birth to you, you forgot the God who writhed in labor (to bear) you." The first of these verbs, yālad, "give birth to," appears 208 times in the Old Testament to express giving birth, and only a little over twenty times for fathering. The second verb, ḥûl, "writhe in labor," clearly refers to the labor pains of pregnancy, as in Isa. 51:2: "Sarah writhed in labor" (NIV: "Sarah gave you birth") to bring Israel forth.

He is a God who has kept Israel as "the apple/the pupil of his eye" (v. 10b). The phrase is particularly pregnant. The Hebrew reads literally, "He kept them as the little man [ʾîšôn] of his eye." How close do you have to get to another person before you see yourself reflected, diminutively, in that person's eyes? God has gotten that close to Israel. Israel too he has known face-to-face.

Verses 23–33 are especially interesting. God is about to unleash the ultimate punishment on his people—annihilation—but after further reflection he stops. Here we have an instance of self-deliberation on the part of God. Of these verses Gerhard von Rad (1966: 198) says, "This section is therefore an interlude which takes us out of the turmoil of historical processes and allows us to overhear a soliloquy within the depths of the divine heart." God's decision is to exercise restraint, not because Israel is meritorious, but because his honor is at stake.

But if the Lord exercises restraint on Israel's behalf, Israel's neighbors cannot expect to receive the same treatment. Against them the Lord will move with a vengeance or just retribution (used four times in this section [vv. 35, 41, 43]). Before we dismiss this notion as much too primitive and at odds with Christian thought, let us recall similar sentiments that appear in the New Testament: "O Sovereign Lord . . . how long before thou wilt judge and avenge our blood on those who dwell upon the earth?" (Rev. 6:10 RSV), and "He has avenged on her the blood of his servants" (Rev. 19:2 NRSV). Both these verses from the Book of Revelation are remarkably similar to Deut. 32:43.

Moses and David are the most significant authors of Old Testament Scripture. Moses' Deuteronomy and David's Psalms give to the community of faith what is most essential for its well-being: a law book and a song book. One provides guidelines and boundaries, while the other emphasizes worship, celebration, and prayer. Yet the celebratory Psalter begins with an emphasis on law ("Blessed is the one . . . who delights in the law of the LORD" [Ps. 1:1–2]). Similarly, Deuteronomy, this preeminently legal document, ends with a song. Just as Israel must not divorce worship from law, so also Israel must not divorce law from worship. As Patrick Miller (1999: 15) compellingly puts it, "Deuteronomy 31 and 32 indicate that Israel must sing the song as regularly as it reads the law."

The Blessing of Moses (33)

This second poem also is addressed by Moses to Israel. But unlike the poem in ch. 32, this one is directed mostly to individual groups rather than to the whole. The whole community is addressed only in the preface (vv. 1–5) and in the conclusion (vv. 26–29), where the focus in these framing sections is on Israel's God rather than on Israel's destiny. In between (vv. 6–25) there is an individual word from Moses to Reuben, Judah, Levi, Benjamin, Joseph, Zebulun, Gad, Dan, Naphtali, and Asher.

This is not the first time in the Pentateuch that such oracles have been addressed to the tribes of Israel. The best parallel to this chapter is Genesis 49, the blessing of Jacob.

But in comparing the two, one notices a crucial difference. The oracles in Genesis 49 are sometimes judgmental, sometimes salvific. By contrast, the oracles of Deuteronomy 33 are consistently salvific and

promissory. They promise continued existence (v. 6); priestly prerogatives (v. 10); safety (v. 11); choice gifts (vv. 13–16); affluence (vv. 18–19);
reward of land (vv. 20–21); possessions (v. 23); prosperity and strength
(vv. 24–25).

We need only to contrast Jacob's word to Reuben with Moses' word
to Reuben. Jacob says to Reuben, "Unstable as water, you shall no
longer excel because you went up onto your father's bed; then you
defiled it" (Gen. 49:3–4 NRSV). But to the Reubenites Moses says, "May
Reuben live, and not die out, even though his numbers are few" (Deut.
33:6 NRSV).

Observing that this chapter contains no exhortations, but rather in-
vocations of future blessings, Brevard Childs (1979: 220–21) remarks,

> The canonical function of ch. 33 serves to place the law fully within
> the perspective of divine sovereignty, shifting the focus from Israel's
> behaviour to God's ultimate purpose. The Mosaic legislation is thus
> subordinated to the overriding purpose of God for his people and the
> final eschatological realization of his will is attested to in spite of the
> nation's failure.

The blessings on the tribes are framed by eulogies spoken about God.
Verses 1–5 are an introductory praise of God. The poem ends with the
same emphasis: "There is none like God, O Jeshurun" (v. 26 NRSV). Thus
the order is: the blesser (vv. 2–5), the blessings (vv. 6–25), the blesser
(vv. 26–29).

The Death of Moses (34)

Moses received orders from the Lord to walk to the top of Pisgah (32:48–
52). That was delayed by the blessing of Moses (ch. 33). Now begins
the ascent. He is given one last kaleidoscopic view of the land that his
people will inherit, and then he dies. The scene is reminiscent of Abraham seeing the land before him in Genesis 13. The expression "all the
land" or "the whole land" occurs in the Pentateuch for the first time in
Gen. 13:15 and for the last time in Deut. 34:1 (Romer and Brettler 2000:
406). Moses is buried (by God) in a grave of which only the general location was known (v. 6). Once vilified in life, Moses may become larger
in death than in life. Perhaps the reason for such privacy is to prevent
the possibility of turning Moses' burial site into a shrine to which the
faithful may travel to worship the deceased (necrolatry). More likely the
secrecy is designed to deter the common practice in the ancient world
known as necromancy, the attempt to make contact with the deceased

via a medium or directly (especially if the deceased are family or famous) for wisdom and counsel.

Moses lived to be 120 years old. Right up to the time of his death he maintained excellent vision (to "show" the land to a man who was blind would be absurd) and use of his faculties (v. 7), although old age did hamper him from continuing military activities ("I am no longer able to go out and come in" [31:2 RSV]).

Throughout Deuteronomy, and especially in the last few chapters, it is he who has been blessing Israel. Now it is time for someone to bless him (vv. 10–12).

Joshua recognizes his limitations. He is no Moses, nor is he an alter ego for Moses, for it was Moses alone whom the Lord knew face-to-face (see Exod. 33:11). To be sure, there is no attempt to apotheosize Moses. No one is allowed to say, "I am of Moses" or "I am of Joshua." Moses does not become a cult hero. Joshua is not Moses, and Moses is not God.

The emphasis that is made in these concluding verses is not on Moses' knowledge of the Lord, but on the Lord's knowledge of Moses. To Moses the Lord will never be able to say, "I never knew you; depart from me" (Matt. 7:23 RSV). Can anything less be the hope of every believer?

In one sense Deuteronomy, and indeed the entire Pentateuch, end as an incomplete story. Deuteronomy ends with neither Moses nor Israel entering the land, although Moses is allowed to see it. What God promised repeatedly to the patriarchs, and as early as Gen. 12:7, is not realized by the Pentateuch's end. Von Rad handled this easily (and artificially) enough by simply replacing the concept of a Pentateuch with that of a Hexateuch, making Joshua the climactic ending of a six-book unit rather than allowing Deuteronomy and Moses to be the climactic ending of a five-book unit.

However, the way the Pentateuch ends may be a theological affirmation rather than a theological problem. For one thing, as Sanders (1972: 44–45) has pointed out, the placement of Deuteronomy between Numbers and Joshua, between wanderings and end of wanderings, "displaced Joshua and its conquest as the climax of the canonical period of authority. . . . True authority lay with the Mosaic period only."

Additionally, the Pentateuch ends both realistically ("You are not yet where God wants you to be") and hopefully ("Soon you will be where God wants you to be"). Wilderness is where you are, but wilderness is not where you will remain. To quote Walter Brueggemann (1997: 211), "The text, moreover, is left open to all sorts of displaced human communities, for the Pentateuch, in the end, is a promise of a homecoming and a home, to be given by the God of all promise who will not finally settle for wilderness, exile, or displacement."

Deuteronomy 31–34

Bergey, R. 2003. "The Song of Moses (Deuteronomy 32.1–43) and Isaianic Prophecies: A Case of Early Intertextuality?" *JSOT* 28:33–54.

Blenkinsopp, J. 1977. *Prophecy and Canon: A Contribution to the Study of Jewish Origins.* SJCA 3. Notre Dame, Ind.: University of Notre Dame Press. Pp. 80–95.

Britt, B. 2000. "Deuteronomy 31–32 as a Textual Memorial." *BibInt* 8:358–74.

Brueggemann, W. 1997. *Theology of the Old Testament: Testimony, Dispute, Advocacy.* Minneapolis: Fortress. Pp. 209–12.

Cassuto, U. 1974a. "The Song of Moses (Deuteronomy Chapter XXXII, 1–43)." In *Biblical and Oriental Studies.* Trans. I. Abrahams. 2 vols. Jerusalem: Magnes. Vol. 1, pp. 41–46.

———. 1974b. "Deuteronomy XXXIII and the New Year in Ancient Israel." In *Biblical and Oriental Studies.* Trans. I. Abrahams. 2 vols. Jerusalem: Magnes. Vol. 1, pp. 47–70.

Childs, B. S. 1979. *Introduction to the Old Testament as Scripture.* Philadelphia: Fortress.

Christensen, D. L. 1984. "Two Stanzas of a Hymn in Deuteronomy 33." *Bib* 65:382–89.

———. 1989. "Dtn 33,11—A Curse in the 'Blessing of Moses'?" *ZAW* 101:278–82.

Coats, G. W. 1977. "Legendary Motifs in the Moses Death Story." *CBQ* 39:34–44. Repr., in *A Song of Power and the Power of Song: Essays on the Book of Deuteronomy.* Ed. D. L. Christensen. SBTS 3. Winona Lake, Ind.: Eisenbrauns, 1993. Pp. 181–91.

Cross, F. M., and D. N. Freedman. 1975. *Studies in Ancient Yahwistic Poetry.* SBLDS 21. Missoula, Mont.: Scholars Press. Pp. 97–122.

Fisch, H. 1988. *Poetry with a Purpose: Biblical Poetics and Interpretation.* Bloomington: Indiana University Press. Pp. 55–79.

Fokkelman, J. P. 1998. *Major Poems of the Hebrew Bible.* 3 vols. Assen: Van Gorcum. Vol. 1, pp. 54–149.

Freedman, D. N. 1980. "The Poetic Structure of the Framework of Deuteronomy 33." In *The Bible World: Essays in Honor of Cyrus H. Gordon.* Ed. G. Rendsburg et al. New York: Ktav. Pp. 25–46.

Frick, F. S. 1999. "'Oil from Flinty Rock' (Deuteronomy 32:13): Olive Cultivation and Olive Oil Processing in the Hebrew Bible—A Socio-Materialist Perspective." *Semeia* 86:3–17.

Geller, S. A. 1982. "The Dynamics of Parallel Verse—A Poetic Analysis of Deut. 32:6–12." *HTR* 75:35–56.

Heiser, M. S. 2001. "Deuteronomy 32:8 and the Sons of God." *BSac* 158:52–74.

Hidal, S. 1978. "Some Reflections on Deuteronomy 32." *ASTI* 11:15–21.

Knowles, M. P. 1989. "'The Rock, His Work Is Perfect': Unusual Imagery for God in Deuteronomy xxxii." *VT* 39:307–22.

Labuschagne, C. J. 1974. "The Tribes in the Blessing of Moses." *OtSt* 19:97–112.

———. 1997. "The Setting of the Song of Moses in Deuteronomy." In *Deuteronomy and Deuteronomic Literature: Festschrift C. H. W. Brekelmans.* Ed. M. Vervenne and J. Lust. BETL 133. Leuven: Leuven University Press. Pp. 111–29.

Lohfink, N. 1994. "The Deuteronomistic Picture of the Transfer of Authority from Moses to Joshua." In *Theology of the Pentateuch: Themes of the Priestly Narrative and Deuteronomy.* Trans. L. M. Maloney. Minneapolis: Fortress. Pp. 234–47.

Lundbom, J. R. 1976. "Lawbook of the Josianic Reform." *CBQ* 38:293–302.

———. 1990. "Scribal Colophons and Scribal Rhetoric in Deuteronomy 31–34." In *Haim M. I. Gevaryahu Memorial Volume.* Ed. J. J. Adler. Jerusalem: World Jewish Bible Center. Pp. 53–63.

Mann, T. W. 1979. "Theological Reflections on the Denial of Moses." *JBL* 98:481–94.

McCarthy, D. J. 1971. "Installation Genre?" *JBL* 90:31–41.

Mendenhall, G. E. 1975. "Samuel's 'Broken *Rib*': Deuteronomy 32." In *No Famine in the Land: Studies in Honor of John L. McKenzie.* Ed. J. W. Flanagan and A. W. Robinson. Missoula, Mont.: Scholars Press. Pp. 63–74. Repr., in *A Song of Power and the Power of Song: Essays on the Book of Deuteronomy.* Ed. D. L. Christensen. SBTS 3. Winona Lake, Ind.: Eisenbrauns, 1993. Pp. 169–80.

Miller, P. D., Jr. 1999. "Deuteronomy and Psalms: Evoking a Biblical Conversation." *JBL* 115:3–18.

Nigosian, S. A. 1996. "The Song of Moses (Dt32): A Structural Analysis." *ETL* 72:5–22.

———. 1997. "Linguistic Patterns of Deuteronomy 32." *Bib* 78:206–24.

Peels, H. G. L. 1994. "On the Wings of the Eagle (Dtn 32, 11)—An Old Misunderstanding." *ZAW* 106:300–303.

Polzin, R. 1980. *Moses and the Deuteronomist: A Literary Study of the Deuteronomic History.* New York: Seabury. Pp. 71–72.

Porter, J. R. 1994. "The Interpretation of Deuteronomy xxxiii 24–25." *VT* 44:267–70.

Rad, G. von. 1966. *Deuteronomy: A Commentary.* Trans. D. Barton. OTL. Philadelphia: Westminster.

Romer, D. C., and M. Z. Brettler. 2000. "Deuteronomy 34 and the Case for a Persian Hexateuch." *JBL* 119:401–19.

Sanders, J. A. 1972. *Torah and Canon.* Philadelphia: Fortress.

Sanders, P. 1996. *The Provenance of Deuteronomy 32.* OTS 37. Leiden: Brill.

Skehan, P. W. 1951. "The Structure of the Song of Moses in Deuteronomy (Deut. 32:1–43)." *CBQ* 13:153–63. Repr., in *A Song of Power and the Power of Song: Essays on the Book of Deuteronomy.* Ed. D. L. Christensen. SBTS 3. Winona Lake, Ind.: Eisenbrauns, 1993. Pp. 156–68.

———. 1971. *Studies in Israelite Poetry and Wisdom.* Washington, D.C.: Catholic Biblical Association of America. Pp. 67–77.

Steck, J. D. 1990. "A History of the Interpretation of Genesis 49 and Deuteronomy 33." *BSac* 147:16–31.

Stevens, D. E. 1997. "Does Deuteronomy 32:8 Refer to 'Sons of God' or 'Sons of Israel'?" *BSac* 154:131–41.

Stuart, D. K. 1976. *Studies in Early Hebrew Meter.* HSM 13. Missoula, Mont.: Scholars Press. Pp. 153–69.

Talstra, E. 1997. "Deuteronomy 31: Confusion or Conclusion? The Story of Moses' Threefold Succession." In *Deuteronomy and Deuteronomic Literature: Festschrift C. H. W. Brekelmans.* Ed. M. Vervenne and J. Lust. BETL 133. Leuven: Leuven University Press. Pp. 87–110.

Thiessen, M. 2004. "The Form and Function of the Song of Moses (Deuteronomy 32:1–43)." *JBL* 123:401–24.

Weitzman, S. P. 1994. "Lessons from the Dying: The Role of Deuteronomy 32 in Its Narrative Setting." *HTR* 87:377–93.

———. 1997. *Song and Story in Biblical Narrative.* Bloomington: Indiana University Press. Pp. 37–58.

Wiebe, J. M. 1989. "The Form, Setting and Meaning of the Song of Moses." *Studia Biblica et Theologica* 17:119–63.

Wittstruck, T. 1976. "So-Called Anti-Anthropomorphisms in the Greek Text of Deuteronomy." *CBQ* 38:29–34.

Wright, G. E. 1962. "The Lawsuit of God: A Form-Critical Study of Deuteronomy 32." In *Israel's Prophetic Heritage: Essays in Honor of James Muilenburg.* Ed. B. Anderson and W. Harrelson. New York: Harper & Row. Pp. 26–67.

Index